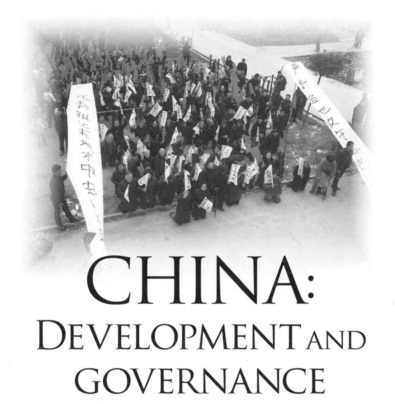

# CHINA:
## DEVELOPMENT AND
## GOVERNANCE

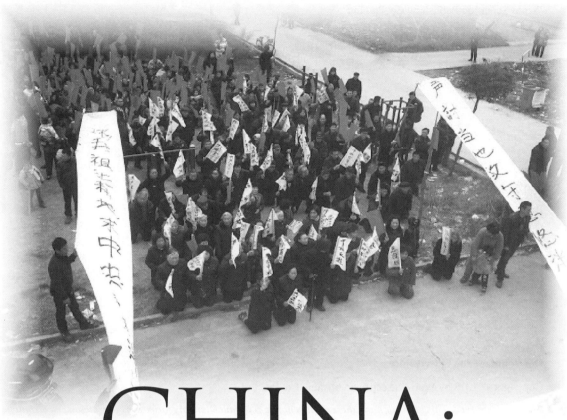

# CHINA:
## DEVELOPMENT AND GOVERNANCE

*Editors*

## WANG Gungwu • ZHENG Yongnian

East Asian Institute, National University of Singapore, Singapore

**World Scientific**

NEW JERSEY · LONDON · SINGAPORE · BEIJING · SHANGHAI · HONG KONG · TAIPEI · CHENNAI

*Published by*

World Scientific Publishing Co. Pte. Ltd.

5 Toh Tuck Link, Singapore 596224

*USA office:* 27 Warren Street, Suite 401-402, Hackensack, NJ 07601

*UK office:* 57 Shelton Street, Covent Garden, London WC2H 9HE

**British Library Cataloguing-in-Publication Data**
A catalogue record for this book is available from the British Library.

**CHINA**
**Development and Governance**

ISBN 978-981-4425-83-4
ISBN 978-981-4425-84-1 (pbk)

In-house Editors: Lee Xin Ying and Agnes Ng

Typeset by Stallion Press
Email: enquiries@stallionpress.com

Printed in Singapore by B & Jo Enterprise Pte Ltd

# Editors

**Professor Wang Gungwu**

Professor WANG Gungwu is Chairman of the East Asian Institute, University Professor at the National University of Singapore (NUS), Faculty of Arts and Social Sciences and Emeritus Professor of the Australian National University. He is also Chairman of the governing board of the Lee Kuan Yew School of Public Policy and Chairman of the Board of Trustees of the Institute of Southeast Asian Studies.

Professor Wang received his BA (Honours) and MA degrees from the University of Malaya in Singapore, and his PhD in Mediaeval History from the School of Oriental and African Studies of the University of London (1957). His teaching career took him from the University of Malaya (Singapore and Kuala Lumpur, 1957–1968, Professor of History 1963–1968) to the Australian National University (1968–1986), where he was Professor and Head of the Department of Far Eastern History and Director of the Research of Pacific Studies. From 1986 to 1995, he was Vice Chancellor of the University of Hong Kong. He was Director of the East Asian Institute of NUS from 1997 to 2007.

Professor Wang holds many appointments and awards. He has been made a Commander of the Order of the British Empire (CBE) in 1991. He was conferred the International Academic Prize of the Fukuoka Asian Cultural Prizes. He was awarded the Public Service Medal by the Singapore government in 2004 and a second medal in 2008. In Singapore, he is a member of the new Board of the Chinese Heritage Centre; and of the Board of Governors of the Institute of Defence and Strategic Studies (later renamed as S. Rajaratnam School of International Studies), both at Nanyang Technological University.

Professor Wang is a prolific author and is renowned for his scholarship on the history of the Chinese diaspora in Southeast Asia, and the history and civilisation of China and Southeast Asia. In over five decades, he has written more than 500 scholarly works of books, monographs and other edited volumes.

**Professor Zheng Yongnian**

Professor ZHENG Yongnian is Director of the East Asian Institute (EAI) at the National University of Singapore. He received his BA and MA degrees from Beijing University, and his PhD from Princeton University. He was a recipient of the Social Science Research Council-MacArthur Foundation Fellowship (1995–1997) and the John D and Catherine T MacArthur Foundation Fellowship (2003–2004). He was Professor and founding Research Director of the China Policy Institute of the University of Nottingham in the United Kingdom. Professor Zheng is the editor of the *Series on Contemporary China* (World Scientific Publishing), *China Policy Series* (Routledge), *China: An International Journal* and *East Asian Policy*. His research interests include both China's domestic transformation and its external relations. His papers have appeared in journals such as *Comparative Political Studies*, *Political Science Quarterly* and *China Quarterly*. He is also the author and editor of numerous books.

Besides his research work, Professor Zheng has also been an academic activist. He served as a consultant to the United Nations Development Programme on China's rural development and democracy. In addition, he has been a columnist for *Xin Bao* (Hong Kong Economic Journal, Hong Kong) and *LianheZaobao* (Singapore) for many years, writing numerous commentaries on China's domestic and international affairs.

# Preface

## WANG Gungwu and ZHENG Yongnian

The East Asian Institute (EAI) is celebrating its 15th Anniversary in 2012. It was first set up as a full-time autonomous research organisation in April 1997 under a statute of the National University of Singapore. Its main mission is to promote both academic and policy-oriented research on East Asian development, particularly the political, economic and social development of contemporary China (including Hong Kong and Taiwan), and China's growing ties with the region and the world at large, including Japan, Korea, India, ASEAN, the European Union and the United States.

In line with this mission, EAI has established extensive networks with universities and think-tanks particularly in China, and increasingly in Japan and Korea. Every year, EAI receives applications from numerous scholars not only from the region but also from the United States and Europe to spend some time at the institute. EAI scholars themselves also conduct numerous study missions overseas. We also hold a number of conferences and undertake several research projects every year. Through such events and interactions, there is a constant and vibrant exchange of insights and ideas which further strengthens the vibrancy of the academic and policy-oriented research foundation of EAI. Today, EAI is recognised as one of the leading institutes in the whole of Southeast Asia dedicated to the study of contemporary China.

Our achievements today did not come easy. The challenges for starting contemporary Chinese studies in a place like Singapore were daunting from the start. In the 60s and 70s, China lent moral and material support to communist insurgency movements that threatened to overthrow the post-colonial regimes in Southeast Asia including Singapore. Singapore was particularly concerned given its vulnerability following its separation from Malaysia in 1965 and the intractable challenges of economic growth and nation-building. Politically, it was taboo to have any form of contact with China, much less to conduct research on China. Information on China was based primarily on Western media accounts and research done by Western scholars. It was only in the late 1970s, after Deng Xiaoping had embarked on the open-door and reform policy, that China's relations with its neighbours including Singapore improved.

In a way, how EAI came to be what it is today mirrors this trend of taking incremental steps that is in line with the circumstances of the times. It began by initially focussing on a narrow and less sensitive area of Confucian studies to a comprehensive and in-depth look at developments in China today. Although EAI was officially established 15 years ago, its origins can be traced further back to June 1983 when the Institute of East Asian Philosophies (IEAP) was established as a privately constituted non-profit resource and research centre for the study of oriental philosophies, with a focus on the translation, interpretation and evaluation of Confucian ethics. In January 1992, IEAP was renamed Institute of East Asian Political Economy (IEAPE) with its research focus on China's economic reform and open-door policy. Building on this basis, EAI has since 1997 broadened this research focus to look at not only the political, economic and social developments in contemporary China but also China's relations with other countries as well as developments in Japan and Korea. We consciously follow an academic approach that is as far as possible "non-Western" and "non-PRC". We believe that this approach of analysing and interpreting developments in China that avoids certain ideological prisms would better meet the needs and interests of our audience that includes policy makers, academics and the public.

**Book Theme**

Five years ago, at the 10th anniversary of EAI's founding in 2007, we published a commemorative volume on various aspects of China's development within the overall context of a rising China. Five years on, China is now regarded by many observers to have risen. So to commemorate the 15th anniversary this year, we have decided to have a volume that looks beyond a rising China by focussing on the theme of governance.

For over three decades, China has succeeded in achieving an unprecedented annual growth of 10%, thereby lifting millions out of poverty. Indeed, a large majority of the population in China have benefited from the open-door and reform policy with notable improvements in their living standards. Very few Chinese today would hanker after the years of central planning with its rigidness and austerity campaigns. In its external relations, China has become a key player at various regional and international platforms. Its participation is needed to help address global and regional issues ranging from the health of the world economy, the *eurozone* debt crisis, terrorism, piracy to global warming and climate change.

Yet, the very success of China's open-door and reform policy has brought about its own set of challenges. In the economic realm, these challenges include the need to rebalance the economy (from an investment-driven, export-oriented model to a more consumption-driven model) and upgrade the economy (from low value-added to higher value-added industries). In the social realm, the challenges include the widening income gaps (between the rural and urban residents, between the coastal and inland regions, and between the state and non-state sectors), the poor integration of the migrant population in urban areas, insufficient low cost housing and medical coverage, and rampant corruption. In the political arena, there are increasing calls for political reforms to take into account the growing aspirations of the Chinese public for greater political accountability and transparency. There appears to be a growing consensus within China that political reforms have lagged far behind economic reforms. On top of these challenges, the Chinese Communist Party (CCP) and government have to grapple with a myriad of views and criticisms, and the potential for mass action with the exponential growth of Chinese Internet users, bloggers and microbloggers. In the foreign policy arena, China has also at times come under criticisms for not doing enough to deal with global and regional concerns such as working towards a denuclearised Korean Peninsula and pressing President Assad of Syria to halt atrocities on its own citizens.

With these many pressing and urgent issues to handle, we believe it is important and timely to examine the issue of governance in China. Here, governance refers generally to the process of decision-making and the process by which decisions are implemented (or not implemented). Good governance may be regarded as encompassing eight major characteristics. It is participatory, consensus-oriented, accountable, transparent, responsive, effective and efficient, equitable and inclusive, and follows the rule of law. Based on this definition, good governance would involve outcomes that benefit the majority of the population after taking into account the views from relevant parties or stakeholders that include the civil society. Ultimately, good governance, whether in practice or perception, is expected to more likely promote socio-political stability and enhance the legitimacy of any ruling party or government.

In China, both the CCP and government do recognise the importance of good governance and have even selectively embraced these characteristics of good governance and practised them to different degrees. Indeed, many of the challenges confronting China today have something to do with governance, whether it is in terms of the decision-making process or implementation process. Going even further, it may reasonably be argued that many of the challenges facing China are more likely to be ameliorated or mitigated if there is a good decision-making process or good implementation process in place.

However, and perhaps not surprisingly, the CCP and government are not enamoured with this "good governance" term. This can primarily be attributed to the fact that good governance tends to diminish or weaken the leading role of the CCP vis-à-vis other stakeholders. Instead, the CCP and government prefer the term "social management" that affirms the leading role of the CCP. On this basis, social management was raised to a level of strategic importance when President Hu Jintao addressed senior officials at the Central Party School in February 2011. In his address, Hu identified the key tasks of social management as including the strengthening of the party and government-led mechanism for the maintenance of public rights and interests; the improvement of management and services for migrant workers and other special groups; the fostering of the social management and social service system at the grassroots; the enhancement of the public security system to ensure food and drug safety, work-related safety, social order and emergency response capabilities; the bolstering of the management of non-governmental organisations (NGOs); and the heightening of control of Internet-transmitted information and management of cyberspace, and provision of better guidance to public opinion over the Internet.

Since Hu's address, the CCP and government have allocated more resources and stepped up various mechanisms and processes to tighten social management within China. To a large extent, social management is being used as a means to ensure stability in China. And stability has assumed much greater importance in 2012 in light of the Bo Xilai debacle (that has affected the delicate power balance at the top) and in view of the impending leadership transition from Hu to Xi Jinping. Even when Xi takes over, he will have to grapple with the issue of governance or social management as China calls it to prevent the many challenges that China faces from boiling over. Whether Xi succeeds in this endeavour would have implications for stability in China and the longevity of the CCP's hold on power.

## Book Structure

This commemorative volume examines China's development and governance in the political, economic, social and foreign policy dimensions. In each section, there is an introduction to provide readers with a broad perspective before delving into individual chapters that look at specific topics or issues. The chapters are contributed by present and past scholars at EAI and are intended for even non-specialists. The writing style is succinct and informal to enable readers to have a good sense of what is happening within China as well as in terms of China's relations with other countries.

Finally, but not least, we wish to mention the EAI staff who have helped to make this volume possible. In particular, Lye Liang Fook has played a key role in organising this project and Jessica Loon has done an equally good job in the copy editing and liaising with the publisher. She is assisted in her editing efforts by Chia Shuhui, Ho Wei Ling and Lily Hong Ciyuan.

# Contents

# I

# The Art of Governance: Managing Rising Expectations

## Introduction

### CHEN Gang

Although Hu Jintao and Wen Jiabao have more political room to manoeuvre in their second term following the 17th Party Congress in 2007, a spate of unexpected disasters, events and strong vested interests have prevented the Party-state from making substantial progress in their policy initiatives. The global financial tsunami triggered by the US subprime-loan crisis in 2008 has not only undermined the dominance of pro-market and small-government neoliberalism in China, but also consolidated the leadership's *paluan* (fearing instability) mentality, thus preventing the leaders from making breakthroughs in their journey towards democratisation. The Chinese leadership has sidestepped the shockwaves of the western debt crisis, curbed inflation and deftly tackled social protests in different parts of the country. Despite the quiet confidence, the Chinese leadership is keeping a close tab on the mushrooming of disgruntled social groups and an increasingly vocal and politically more conscious intelligentsia. The internet age has globalised protests from the "Arab Spring" to "Occupy Wall Street". Chinese citizens today are no longer apolitical or passive; their deft usage of social networking sites like Weibo (or Twitter-like mini-blogs) to challenge China's political establishment testifies that China has entered a new age. The global financial crisis has proven to be a double-edged sword for the Chinese government. On the one hand, the party-state has successfully minimised exposure to the western economic downturn through the massive launch of Keynesian-type stimulus measures and reinforced state sectors in the national economy; on the other hand, the enhanced state capitalism has sparked a domestic backlash on issues of *guojin mintui* (the state advances, the private sector retreats) and *guofu minqiong* (the state is rich, the people are poor).

The *paluan* (fearing instability) mentality has prevented the government from scaling back economic development plans that will create more resources for it to muddle through. When China was celebrating the 30th anniversary of Deng's economic reform in 2008, Hu assured the Chinese Community Party (CCP) that "it will not go back to the old road and will also not side-track into changing its flag".[1] In the face of a string of challenges such as runaway inflation, rampant corruption and social unrest, the CCP's major preoccupation in recent years has been to ensure political and social stability in the lead-up to the leadership transition in 2012.

Though political reform has not been showing much progress, the Hu-Wen leadership is still making insistent efforts to improve the quality of governance. It has also demonstrated to the world its strong state capacity by successfully mobilising resources to cope with natural and man-made disasters, and to pull off spectacular events like the Beijing Olympics and the Shanghai Expo. Besides, the CCP has seemingly institutionalised its crucial leadership succession first with the change of leadership from Jiang Zemin to Hu Jintao and now with the fifth generation of leaders coming on board at the coming 18th Party Congress scheduled in the later part of 2012. In an attempt to expand "intra-Party democracy" through combining the mechanisms of election and consultation, the CCP Central Organisation Department for the first time held a tentative polling in 2007 to vote for candidates to the Politburo Standing Committee among provincial/ministerial-level-and-above officials. Xi Jinping got the most votes, followed by Li Keqiang, He Guoqiang and Zhou Yongkang. This kind of internal polling, despite being opaque and lacking in supervision, is an important step towards "intra-Party democracy" proposed by the 17th Party Congress in 2007. The four generations of PRC leaders illustrate a consistent trend towards a more collective leadership, away from "strong-man" politics.[2] It is foreseeable that for the fifth generation of leaders led by Xi and Li, all the Politburo Standing Committee members will be vested with equal political authority, so more power-sharing with checks and balances, and more pluralistic decision-making processes can be expected.[3]

At the top level, Vice President Xi Jinping's and Vice Premier Li Keqiang's ascension to the respective positions of Party secretary in 2012 and premier in 2013 is a certainty. According to the unwritten rule of "seven-in and eight-out" (*qishang baxia*, an arrangement adopted by the Politburo in which the 67-year-olds and below will stay, and the 68-year-olds will exit), all the other seven existing Politburo Standing Committee (PSC) members including Hu Jintao and Wen Jiabao will retire after the next reshuffle, while eight incumbent Politburo members under the age of 68, plus potential "dark horses" like State Councillor Meng Jianzhu (64), CCP Central Secretariat Secretary Ling Jihua (55) and Wang Huning (56) are eligible to vie for the remaining seven seats.

Over the years, the CCP leadership transition has evolved from a "two-front" model to a generational-transfer model. The "two-front" model adopted by Mao and Deng had the two leaders semi-retire to the "second front" to be strategists while the successors remained at the "front-line" to run the day-to-day state affairs. However, the model failed to produce suitable successors. After the Tiananmen Incident in 1989, Deng decided to change the mode of succession from the "two-front arrangement" to a generational-transfer model whereby political leaders are divided into successive generations. According to Deng, the first mature CCP leadership started with Mao, while the second generation referred to the CCP leadership that initiated reform and opening up policies, i.e. Deng's generation. Deng's purpose of rewriting CCP history in such a way was meant to introduce a new leadership — the post-Tiananmen leadership — which would take over from his generation and move forward. Over a span of more than one decade, the baton was passed on from Jiang Zemin's third generation leadership to Hu Jintao's fourth generation leadership. Now, the baton is to be handed to the fifth generation leadership headed by Xi Jinping. It is unlikely that this new leadership would introduce major political reform measures within its first five years in office probably because the fundamental ideologies of the CCP will restrain the Party from carrying out any political reforms. The top priority of the new leadership will be social reforms rather than economic growth. Externally, instead of an "assertive" China, the new leaders are likely

---

[1] "We'll forge ahead with reforms: Hu," *China Daily*, 19 December 2008.

[2] Cheng L, "China's Leadership, Fifth Generation," *Caijing Magazine*, December 2007.

[3] Zheng Y and Chen G, "Xi Jinping's Rise and Political Implications," *China: An International Journal*, vol. 7, no. 1, 2009, p. 22.

to try their utmost to restore the image of China as a peaceful, rising major power which is willing to operate within the confines of the current international order as a stakeholder.

Social reform aside, calls for political reform, a buzzword which had been dormant for decades after 1989, have recently re-emerged among Chinese intellectuals. These calls for political reform share certain commonalities. First, most of the discussions and deliberations occur mainly within the elite circle. They are not being discussed by the public. Second, many of the discussants are retired Party-state cadres and descendants of old revolutionaries who intend to persuade and influence the forthcoming Party Congress as well as the new leadership that will come to office at the Congress. The recent discussions on political reform are basically societal responses to the Hu Jintao leadership's failure to restructure Chinese politics, citing the five "no's" from Wu Bangguo, the No. 2 ranking party leader and China's NPC Standing Committee chairman, as a typical official refusal to genuine political reforms. CCP's promotion of the "China model" is perceived by many as a kind of propaganda tactic to appease social demands for political reforms. Though Premier Wen Jiabao, CCP's No. 3 ranking leader, has displayed a sympathetic and even positive response to the growing demands for political reforms, his suggestions have not been openly endorsed by Hu Jintao or any of his colleagues. The 18th Party Congress is unlikely to adopt any kind of systematic plan for political reforms although the CCP is very likely to continue to appease the public with skilful rhetoric and slogans.

The new leadership headed by Xi Jinping is likely to promulgate some new political slogans as catchwords to increase its popularity, but genuine political reforms are not likely to be in the cards. The regime's continuous disregard for pressure to introduce political reforms will further widen the gaps between the Party-state and many of the intellectuals and the ordinary citizens; between governmental policies and social-political reality; and between the hidden crises China faces and the state capacity to cope with them. The disillusion with political reforms after the 18th Party Congress is likely to bring forth another wave of social tensions and political confrontations.

In response to the criticism that political reforms lag behind economic reforms in China, the CCP is trying to rely more on the contested intra-Party balloting system to select its high-rank cadres instead of via the opaque one-candidate-one-position appointment process. Three cities in Jiangsu province have introduced contested elections within local Party committees for their top Party positions in 2011. Jiangsu's practices are perceived as a kind of local experiment sponsored by the top leadership to promulgate the intra-Party balloting system to the municipal level. Since the balloting results in Jiangsu showed that the winners of the balloting are still the Party's favourites and that the provincial Party committee was involved throughout the entire process, competitive elections are only a means to help the Party single out capable and loyal officials. Nevertheless, Jiangsu's reform clearly evinces the Party's will to promote openness and competition, and to implement contested elections (*cha'e xuanju*) in cadre selection. Advocated by Li Yuanchao, the Jiangsu-born director of the CCP Central Organisation Department, the intra-Party balloting system may be a solution to rampant corrupt practices such as the selling and buying of government posts or the bribing of others to attain higher positions.

China's lower-level political governance, which includes township government line-up, functions, responsibilities, and exercise of power, has been riddled with incompetency and inefficiency to effectively govern vast localities. In recent years, the central government has been promoting township reform to redefine government functions and responsibilities in order to improve government services and governance of local affairs. Thanks to the nationwide township reforms since 2009, township governments are now expected to serve rather than control the people and such reforms can in the long run, reduce township administrative costs while increasing administrative efficiency. Township functions after reform will be more service-oriented rather than management- and production-oriented. Reformed township governments are supposed to shift the foci of their responsibilities from attracting business and investment, setting up commerce and production, and arranging planting and harvesting, to providing public service and guidance for economic crops production, and maintaining social harmony.

The marketisation of CCP grassroots organisations after they lost the monopoly of social resources and rewards has caused a subtle but fundamental change in the relationship between Party organisations and Party members. The increasing importance of professionalism, technical and technocratic competence and entrepreneurship — essential features of modernisation — diminishes the importance of Party membership in one's career success. Village elections have introduced new dynamics into village politics that tend to undermine the legitimacy and authority of the village Party. In the context of market economy, the Party's effort at rebuilding and maintaining an expansive network of grassroots organisations that penetrates every corner of society is costly and in many cases, impossible.

At the grassroots level, the increasing tension and friction in the Chinese society generated by income inequalities, land disputes, corruption, etc., has generated dissatisfaction and resentment among the general public, threatening regime legitimacy. The CCP's "stability maintenance" strategy in a narrow sense consists of five governmental departments or branches and one Party organisation: the Ministry of Public Security, Ministry of State Security, Ministry of Justice, the People's Court, the People's Procuratorate, as well as the Party's Politics and Law Committee. Maintaining status quo may actually lead to dissatisfaction and resentment build-up, or even threaten the stability of the regime in the long term. Top leaders therefore should consider coming up with reforms to ameliorate the lives of the people such as having a more just legal system, a more responsive government and a fairer redistribution system to prevent social unrests.

Several major riots have caught the attention of CCP leaders. The bloody ethnic clash between Muslim Uyghurs and China's dominant Han group in Xinjiang in July 2009 had prompted the Beijing government to reflect upon its ethnic policies and promote a new deal that focusses on economic growth of the region. Beijing's decade-long affirmative action policies had contributed to the growing ethnic divide, reinforced the ethnic consciousness of the minorities and discouraged the development of Chinese identity. Beijing's new policy package in response to the Xinjiang bloodshed includes resource tax reform that allows indigenous people to share the profits from oil and gas extraction, and direct government investments that ultimately help to improve local infrastructure and people's livelihood. Nonetheless, the effectiveness of the new plan in the long run is questionable because it unfortunately has largely ignored religious issues.

To improve its communication with and obtain feedback from the public, the Chinese leadership has made use of the Internet to establish closer ties with the people as well as to have a better gauge of public reactions and make improvements to official policies. The ultimate challenge for the leaders is to strike a balance between netizens' demands for greater transparency and accountability on the part of the CCP and the government over the longer term and meeting this growing aspiration, and yet maintain the dominant position of the CCP.

A bigger role has also been allocated to women in Chinese politics. The rising influence of women in Chinese politics is attributed to the open-door policy. The policy has accelerated the alignment of Chinese women's pursuit of equal opportunity and favourable gender policy with international norms. However, despite institutional initiatives that have provided a stable institutional environment for advancing women's participation, China still lags far behind many other countries in terms of increasing women's representation in powerful political bodies.

This state of affairs shows that despite China's rise as a major power, more needs to be done to improve its governance and consolidate CCP's rule in the fast-changing state. The CCP has made many policy choices in response to a range of challenges arising from a multitude of areas like leadership transition, democratisation, local governance, social management, Internet regulation, food security and women's political participation. Although the Party-state seems to have survived all major tests so far in managing the world's most populous society and second largest economy, it still faces challenges in determining how and when to begin political reforms. This is a tough issue especially for an authoritarian state. In the years to come, China will be compelled to translate its political reform rhetoric into reality when its double digits rate of economic growth comes to an end, necessitating a colossal shift from an export- and investment-led growth model to one which is more consumer-led. Without meaningful political reforms that could tilt the distribution of national income from government departments and state-owned enterprises to the households and private sectors, economic restructuring like consumption stimulation, industrial upgrade and indigenous innovation will not be attainable. The increasing pressure for political liberalisation from the increasingly urbanised, well-educated and Internet-savvy mass may impel the ruling party to introduce bolder measures in its move towards a pluralistic democracy.

# 1

# China's Fifth Generation Leadership

## Characteristics and Policies

BO Zhiyue*

*The new leadership that will emerge as a result of the 18th National Party Congress will be a mix of several cohorts with the fifth generation leaders in dominance.*

In the past 66 years, the mode of succession for the Chinese Communist Party (CCP) top leadership has evolved from a "two-front" model to a generation transfer model.[1]

When Mao Zedong, one of the founding members of the CCP, was installed as the highest authority in power and ideology at the Seventh Party Congress of the CCP in 1945, the Party was still an "opposition party" in China. After the CCP established the People's Republic of China in 1949, Mao Zedong introduced a "two-front arrangement" model for succession.

According to the model, Mao Zedong himself would semi-retire to the second front to ponder over major issues while leaving other top leaders such as Liu Shaoqi, Zhou Enlai and Deng Xiaoping to stay at the first front to run the day-to-day state affairs. However, the model failed to produce any viable successor. Two of the candidates, Liu Shaoqi and Lin Biao, lost their lives in power struggles for succession.

When he returned to power in the late 1970s, Deng Xiaoping continued Mao's model of "two-front arrangement" with significant modifications. Instead of one individual at the second front, Deng introduced a whole new institution — Central Advisory Commission (CAC) — to assist the first front, which composed of top leaders such as the general secretary of the CCP and the premier of the State Council.

Deng's variant model, unfortunately, also failed to produce viable candidates. The second front, i.e. the CAC, kept intervening in the state affairs of the first front leaders, resulting in the sacking of two top party leaders, Hu Yaobang and Zhao Ziyang, in a row.

---

*BO Zhiyue is Senior Research Fellow at the East Asian Institute, National University of Singapore.
[1] For a detailed discussion, see Bo Z, *China's Elite Politics: Political Transition and Power Balancing*, Singapore: World Scientific, 2007, pp. 42–49.

In the aftermath of the Tiananmen Incident, Deng Xiaoping decided to change the mode of succession from the "two-front arrangement" to a generational transfer model in which political leaders are divided into successive generations.

## From the First to the Fourth Generation Leadership

Until 1989, the concept of generations in the CCP leadership did not exist. The founding fathers of the People's Republic of China had been invariably referred to as the old generation revolutionaries (*lao yi dai ge ming jia*), but no further delineation was made to differentiate the veteran leaders.

The concept of the first generation leadership was posthumously reconstructed by Deng Xiaoping. According to him, the CCP's leaderships from 1921 to 1935 did not count because none of them were mature enough.[2] The first mature CCP leadership started with Mao Zedong, Liu Shaoqi, Zhou Enlai and Zhu De.[3]

Deng also dismissed Mao's successor, Hua Guofeng, as a transitional figure because he did not have his own ideology. He was simply an advocate of Maoism as he adopted a policy of "whateverism" ("We will resolutely uphold whatever policy decisions Chairman Mao made, and unswervingly follow whatever instructions Chairman Mao gave").

Thus the second generation, according to Deng, refers to the CCP leadership that initiated reform and opening policies, i.e. Deng's generation. Technically, Deng himself belonged to the first generation leadership, but he played a very important role in starting new policies of reform and opening up to the West.

Deng's point of retelling the CCP history in terms of generations was meant to introduce a new leadership, the post-Tiananmen leadership, which would take over from his generation and move forward.

At the 14th National Congress of the CCP in October 1992, Deng not only retained the services of the third generation leadership with Jiang Zemin at the helm but also selected a candidate, Hu Jintao, as the core of the fourth generation leadership.

In 10 years, at the 16th National Congress of the CCP held in November 2002, the baton was passed on from the third generation leadership to the fourth generation leadership.

## Emergence of the Fifth Generation Leadership

The first individual to be considered a candidate for the fifth generation leadership was Li Keqiang (born July 1955). At the age of 37 in 1992, he was to succeed Song Defu (born February 1946) as the first secretary of the Central Committee of the Chinese Communist Youth League (CCYL) at the forthcoming 13th National Congress of the CCYL in 1993.

Therefore he was nominated as a candidate for an alternate membership with the 14th Central Committee of the CCP in 1992 when he was still a member of the Secretariat of the Central Committee of the CCYL. However, Li failed to obtain a seat partly because deputies in the 14th National Congress of the CCP did not feel the need to elect an alternate member from the CCYL in addition to a full member (Song Defu) from the same institution.[4]

At the 15th Party Congress held in September 1997, two candidates emerged. Li Keqiang was elected a full member of the Central Committee of the CCP as the first secretary of the Central Committee of the CCYL without a glitch.

---

[2] For a complete list of CCP top leaders, see Appendix.

[3] Deng X, "We Must Form a Promising Collective Leadership that will Carry out Reform" (31 May 1989) in Deng X, *Selected Works of Deng Xiaoping,* vol. 3, Beijing: Renmin Chubanshe, 1993, pp. 296–301.

[4] For details, see Zong H, *Disidai* (China's New Leaders: The Fourth Generation), Carle Place, NY: Mirror Books, 2002, p. 398.

However, another young candidate, Xi Jinping (born June 1953), almost failed to enter the 15th Central Committee of the CCP as an alternate member. A deputy secretary of Fujian province since 1995, Xi's background as a princeling (because his father was Xi Zhongxun) was probably more of a liability at the time.

Among the candidates for alternate membership, Xi Jinping was ranked no. 151, one place short of the originally planned number of alternate members. Xi was eventually included as an alternate member of the 15th Central Committee of the CCP because he was selected as a candidate for the fifth generation leadership.[5]

The majority of the fifth generation cohort entered the 16th Central Committee of the CCP in 2002 as full members, and many entered the 17th Politburo in 2007.

## Characteristics of the Fifth Generation Leaders

Technically speaking, a fifth generation leader is someone who is able to work for another two five-year terms beyond the 18th Party Congress. In other words, this person will have to be 67 or younger in 2017 (i.e. he or she was born in 1950 or later).

More precisely, the fifth generation cohort refers to people who were born between 1950 and 1954; the 5.5th generation cohort composes of people who were born between 1955 and 1959; and the sixth generation cohort includes those who were born between 1960 and 1964.

However, the new leadership that is expected to be formed by the forthcoming 18th National Congress of the CCP would be a mix of several cohorts who were born in the late 1940s through the 1960s.

Using a combination of age 68 and age 65 rules, members of the 17th Central Committee of the CCP who would stay on in the 18th Central Committee can be identified.

Generally speaking, they are mostly young, well-educated and have extensive management experiences in the central and local governments. The average age of the remaining members of the 17th Central Committee would be about 58, with the majority in their fifties. The actual average age of the 18th Central Committee would be lower because there will be younger new entrants.

The remaining members of the 17th Central Committee are highly educated. The majority are graduates despite of the fact that the credibility of their graduate diplomas is questionable. Among them, there are 49 PhD holders (Table 1).

They have extensive experiences in their areas of specialty. The current chief provincial leaders, for instance, have managed various provincial units for 12 years on average and many have multiple provincial experiences.

**Table 1**   Education of the Remaining Members of the 17th Central Committee

| Education | Freq. | Percentage |
|---|---|---|
| High School | 1 | 0.42 |
| Three-Year College | 10 | 4.17 |
| Four-Year College | 67 | 27.92 |
| Graduate Diploma | 62 | 25.83 |
| Masters | 51 | 21.25 |
| Ph.D. | 49 | 20.42 |
| Total | 240 | 100.00 |

*Source*: Author's database.

---

[5] Ibid., pp. 398–399.

## Possible Lineup of the New Politburo Standing Committee

If the age limit is still a qualifying requirement as per the two previous Party Congresses, that is, those who are 68 or older will have to retire, out of the current 25 Politburo members, 11 would stay on, including two Politburo standing members and nine Politburo members (Table 2). Among them, seven would be able to work for another five-year term (the 4.5th generation cohort); two for another two five-year terms (the fifth generation cohort); and two for another three five-year terms (the 5.5th generation cohort).

If the Politburo Standing Committee of the 18th Central Committee membership number is to remain at nine members, there would be some competition among the remaining members of the current Politburo.

In addition to Xi Jinping and Li Keqiang, the new Politburo Standing Committee members might be selected from this group: Yu Zhengsheng, Liu Yandong (female), Liu Yunshan, Wang Qishan, and Li Yuanchao. The underdogs are Zhang Dejiang, Zhang Gaoli and Wang Yang.

A native of Shaoxing, Zhejiang, Yu Zhengsheng is a descendent of an elite family in China.[6] The history of his clan reflects the evolution of China in the past 160 years, and he is closely connected to both Mao Zedong and Jiang Jieshi, two of the most important political figures in contemporary China.

Yu's father, Yu Qiwei (alias Huang Jing), had been married to Li Yunhe (alias Jiang Qing),[7] who later became the fourth wife of Mao Zedong.

Yu's great uncle (son of the brother of his great grandfather), Yu Dawei (1897–1993), was Jiang Jieshi's confidant. A non-KMT member and non-military professional, Yu Dawei served as Jiang's Defence Minister for a decade.[8]

Yu Zhengsheng is also very close to Deng Pufang, son of Deng Xiaoping, the paramount leader of China from 1978 to 1997. Yu Zhengsheng and Deng Pufang worked together for a year in the 1980s.

A two-term Politburo member, Yu is likely to move up at the forthcoming 18th Party Congress. He is a strong candidate for the position of the National People's Congress Standing Committee chairman.

**Table 2**   The 17th Politburo Members Who Would Stay On

| Name | Year of Birth | Cohort | The 17th Politburo | Prospect |
|---|---|---|---|---|
| Yu Zhengsheng | 1945 | 4.5 | Member | Promotion |
| Liu Yandong (f.) | 1945 | 4.5 | Member | Promotion |
| Zhang Dejiang | 1946 | 4.5 | Member | Stay |
| Zhang Gaoli | 1946 | 4.5 | Member | Stay |
| Liu Yunshan | 1947 | 4.5 | Member | Promotion |
| Wang Qishan | 1948 | 4.5 | Member | Promotion |
| Li Yuanchao | 1950 | 5 | Member | Promotion |
| Xi Jinping | 1953 | 5 | Standing Member | Stay |
| Wang Yang | 1955 | 5.5 | Member | Stay |
| Li Keqiang | 1955 | 5.5 | Standing Member | Stay |

*Source*: <http://www.xinhuanet.com/politics/leaders/> (accessed 5 July 2012).

---

[6] For details, see Gao Y, *Yu Zhengsheng he Ta de Jiazu* (Yu Zhengsheng and his Clan), Carle Place, NY: Mirror Books, 2009.
[7] Ibid., pp. 55–102.
[8] Ibid., pp. 37–54.

Similarly, Liu Yunshan is also a two-term Politburo member as well as a two-term Secretariat member. He is likely to replace Li Changchun as a member of the Politburo Standing Committee in charge of propaganda.

Wang Qishan would move up as the executive vice premier and concurrent member of the Politburo Standing Committee, and Zhang Gaoli is a strong candidate for the position of the secretary of the Central Disciplinary Inspection Commission (CDIC). Wang Qishan has been a capable vice premier and Zhang Gaoli has performed well as party secretary of Tianjin.

Zhang Dejiang and Liu Yandong are both strong candidates for the position of chairmanship of the Chinese National People's Political Consultative Conference (CNPPCC). Zhang Dejiang has extensive central and local experiences. He has served as party secretary in Jilin, Zhejiang and Guangdong. He is the vice premier of the State Council, and starting in March 2012, Zhang is also concurrent party secretary of Chongqing.

However, Liu Yandong possesses unique resources as a candidate for the CNPPCC position. She is the only female member of the Politburo and has extensive connections with both Jiang Zemin and Hu Jintao; she has vast experiences in the united front affairs.

Liu Yandong's father, Liu Ruilong (1910–1988), was one of the two people who introduced Jiang Shangqing (1911–1939), Jiang Zemin's uncle, into the Chinese Communist Youth in 1927.

Liu Yandong graduated from the same university, Qinghua University, as Hu Jintao and worked with Hu Jintao in the Secretariat of the Central Committee of the Chinese Communist Youth League in the 1980s. She was deputy director of the United Front Department of the CCP Central Committee from 1991 to 2002 and its director from 2002 to 2007. She was also concurrent vice chairman of the CNPPCC from 2003 to 2008.

Li Yuanchao, currently a Politburo member, a Secretariat member and the Central Organisation Department director, is likely to replace Xi Jinping as vice president of China. He would be in a position to become president in case Xi Jinping ceases to function in that capacity for whatever reasons.

Wang Yang is likely to be transferred to Beijing after the 18th National Congress of the CCP but not very likely to be promoted to the Politburo Standing Committee. He is a strong candidate for a vice premiership but not likely to become the executive vice premier.

Nevertheless, in the event that the age limit is revised downward by one year at the 18th Party Congress, Yu Zhengsheng and Liu Yandong would have to exit and a somewhat different line-up would include some younger candidates in the Politburo Standing Committee, including Wang Yang and Hu Chunhua, party secretary of Inner Mongolia. A frontrunner of the sixth generation leadership, Hu would undergo a training period for the top job in the Party if he enters the Politburo Standing Committee in 2012.

## Policy Orientations of the New Leadership

As the fundamental orientation for the next five years has been set in the 12th Five-Year Programme, the top priority of the new leadership is not to introduce new radical policies.

Their main focus, as Xi Jinping alluded in his speech at the Central Party School on 1 March 2011, would be on implementation. "Implementation," Xi said, "is an extremely important link in exercising leadership and a fundamental requirement of the Party's ideological line and mass line."

Therefore, it is unlikely that this new leadership would introduce major political reform measures within its first five years in office. This is because the basic ideological line of the CCP is to refrain from carrying out any political reforms.[9]

---

[9] For a methodic analysis of the debate on political reforms among the current top leadership, see Bo Z, "What is Next for China's Political Reforms? Different Views at the Top," *EAI Background Brief*, no. 624, Singapore: East Asian Institute, National University of Singapore.

It is also unlikely for the new leadership to conduct any substantial economic reforms. The major concerns of the current leadership are no longer quantitative growth. They want to change the mode of growth from one that is focussed on GDP alone to one that is more balanced, more sustainable and more environment-friendly.

The top priority of the new leadership would be on social reforms. With more than 85,000 cases of mass incidents every year since 2005, China has been facing many social issues. It will be a great challenge to come up with a new social management system to handle these social issues.

Externally, the new leaders would also try to maintain good relations with the United States and Europe as well as its neighbouring countries such as Japan, the two Koreas, and members of Association of Southeast Asian Nations.

Instead of an "assertive" China, the new leaders will try their utmost to restore the image of China as a peaceful, rising major power that is still willing to operate within the confines of the current international order as a "responsible stakeholder".

## Appendix: Top Leaders of the Chinese Communist Party (1921–)

| Name | Election | Title | From | To |
|---|---|---|---|---|
| Chen Duxiu | First Congress | Secretary of the Central Bureau | 7/1921 | 7/1922 |
| Chen Duxiu | Second Congress | Chairman of the Central Executive Committee | 7/1922 | 6/1923 |
| Chen Duxiu | Third Congress | Chairman of the Central Bureau | 6/1923 | 1/1925 |
| Chen Duxiu | Fourth Congress | General Secretary of the Central Executive Committee | 1/1925 | 5/1927 |
| Chen Duxiu | Fifth Congress | General Secretary | 5/1927 | 7/1928 |
| Xiang Zhongfa | Sixth Congress | Party Chairman | 7/1928 | 1/1931 |
| Xiang Zhongfa | Fourth Plenum of the Sixth Central Committee | General Secretary | 1/1931 | 1/1934 |
| Bo Gu | Fifth Plenum of the Sixth Central Committee | General Secretary | 1/1934 | 1/1935 |
| Zhang Wentian | A Politburo meeting | General Secretary | 1/1935 | 3/1943 |
| Mao Zedong | A Politburo meeting | Chairman of the Politburo and Secretariat | 3/1943 | 4/1945 |
| Mao Zedong | Seventh Plenum of the Sixth Central Committee | Chairman of the Central Committee | 4/1945 | 6/1945 |
| Mao Zedong | Seventh Congress | Chairman of the Central Committee | 6/1945 | 9/1956 |
| Mao Zedong | Eighth Congress | Chairman of the Central Committee | 9/1956 | 4/1969 |
| Mao Zedong | Ninth Congress | Chairman of the Central Committee | 4/1969 | 8/1973 |
| Mao Zedong | 10th Congress | Chairman of the Central Committee | 8/1973 | 9/1976 |
| Hua Guofeng | Third Plenum of the 10th Central Committee | Chairman of the Central Committee | 10/1976 | 8/1977 |
| Hua Guofeng | 11th Congress | Chairman of the Central Committee | 8/1977 | 6/1981 |
| Hu Yaobang | Sixth Plenum of the 11th Central Committee | Chairman of the Central Committee | 6/1981 | 9/1982 |
| Hu Yaobang | 12th Congress | General Secretary | 9/1982 | 1/1987 |
| Zhao Ziyang | Seventh Plenum of the 12th Central Committee | Acting General Secretary | 1/1987 | 11/1987 |

*(Continued)*

*(Continued)*

| | | | | |
|---|---|---|---|---|
| Zhao Ziyang | Thirteenth Congress | General Secretary | 11/1987 | 6/1989 |
| Jiang Zemin | Fourth Plenum of the 13th Central Committee | General Secretary | 6/1989 | 10/1992 |
| Jiang Zemin | 14th Congress | General Secretary | 10/1992 | 9/1997 |
| Jiang Zemin | 15th Congress | General Secretary | 9/1997 | 11/2002 |
| Hu Jintao | 16th Congress | General Secretary | 11/2002 | 10/2007 |
| Hu Jintao | 17th Congress | General Secretary | 10/2007 | |

*Source*: <http://news.xinhuanet.com/ziliao/2003-01/21/content_698625.htm> (accessed 27 June 2012).

# 2

# Debating Political Reform

## Societal Pressures and Party-State Responses

WU Guoguang*

*Political reform has again become a hot topic in China's intellectual discussions, which amounted to various societal pressures on the regime. The Party-state, however, has so far responded passively.*

Virtually silenced for decades after 1989, "political reform" recently re-emerged on the agenda of discussions and deliberations of Chinese intellectuals about the nation's development and future. Societal pressures on the regime in this regard are mounting, especially over the new leadership that is designated to come into power at the forthcoming 18th Party Congress in late 2012. This chapter will briefly summarise these discussions and, accordingly, analyse the leadership's responses.

### Contending Approaches: Political Reform in Discussions

With the publication of his book *Remaking Our Cultural Historical Views* in 2011, Zhang Musheng is considered a pioneer in the recent wave of intellectual, political and policy discussions of China's political reform.[1] His stand is three-fold: first, he claims to transcend the division between the left and the right; second, he cautions that the current Chinese model has met with huge crises, and is not sustainable. Zhang is harshly critical of the current Chinese leadership's inaction in handling China's "crises", using the metaphor of "beating the drum and passing the flower" to

---

*WU Guoguang is Professor of Political Science and Chair in China and Asia-Pacific Relations at the University of Victoria, Canada.
[1] Zhang M, *Remaking Our Cultural Historical Views*, Hong Kong, Dafeng chubanshe, 2011. Also, see *Lianhe zaobao*'s interview with Zhang Musheng, 27 September 2011.

portray Hu Jintao's irresponsibility of not solving China's problems.[2] Thirdly, Zhang suggests the return to the CCP's old programme of so-called "new democracy", which had been advocated by the CCP in the 1945–1949 period to differentiate its envisaged political system of governing China from the Nationalist Party's "(old) democracy".

Zhang's close connections with Liu Yuan were a factor that contributed to the great curiosity about his idea of "new democracy" and its possible influence over the Chinese leaders. The youngest son of former PRC (People's Republic of China) President Liu Shaoqi, who was a major spokesman of the CCP's "new democracy" in the early 1950s, People's Liberation Army (PLA) General Liu Yuan, in his own words, "forcefully supports" Zhang as declared in his foreword to Zhang's book. Liu, who is also believed to be very close to the designated Party Chief Xi Jinping, has already begun to show his firmness in handling cases such as General Gu Junshan's corruption.[3]

Another major voice of political reform comes from Hu Deping, a son of another former CCP leader, reform-minded Party Chief Hu Yaobang, who retired as a deputy minister years ago. He chaired a series of forums in the late half of 2011, which sent out a strong message calling for democracy, rule of law and constitutionalism in China. Forum speakers condemned Mao's Cultural Revolution and recommended "further emancipation of thought" just like what the CCP did in the late 1970s when post-Mao reforms started.[4]

Qin Xiao, also a recently retired deputy ministerial level state enterprise leader, organises a different liberal circle through his Boyuan Foundation, a non-governmental organisation (NGO) registered in Hong Kong.[5] The current focus of this Foundation is on economic and financial reforms, but it also actively and critically participates in the debate on the so-called "China model" through organising forums and sponsoring the publishing of research outcomes. Qin suggests that "modernity" is a transcendence of the regime's official programmes of "modernisation" as he also praises "universal values" which in the current Chinese context are seen as the values represented by and practised in Western industrial democracies.

Debates on Mao Zedong's political legacies have formed an integral section of the discussion of political reform, which splits Chinese society between those who cite Mao's ways as exemplified by the Cultural Revolution as remedies to current socio-economic inequality and governmental corruption, and those who call for critical reassessments of Mao to move China beyond political authoritarianism. Mao Yushi, a leading economist who has no relations with the late chairman, takes the lead in criticising Mao Zedong in his web article of 26 April 2011 calling for the de-deifying of the communist leader.[6] Thereafter, he received indignant responses from Maoists. Through the well-known Maoist website *Utopia* (*Wuyou zhixiang*), numerous articles and notes went online in defence of Mao and his legacies.[7] This often-regarded Left fundamentalist school,

---

[2] The metaphor is about a traditional Chinese game: While the drum beating goes on, a spray of flowers is passed around and when the beating stops, whoever has the flower would be penalised. To Zhang, Hu is the Chinese version of King Louis XV who did not care about the country after his reign, "Après moi, le déluge" ("After me, the deluge"). Louis XV (1710–1774) was a French king, 15 years after whom the French Revolution broke out.

[3] See, for example, <http://canchinese.com/article-1379–1.html> (accessed 2 February 2012). Though there has so far been no official information available on this corruption case or Liu Yuan's role in dealing with it, Gu's name was silently removed from the official webpage of the PLA General Logistics Department where Liu is Commissar in charge of political affairs.

[4] For these forums, see, for example, <http://www.boxun.com/news/gb/china/2011/09/201109010200.shtml> (accessed 1 September 2011); <http://news.mingpao.com/20111009/caa1.htm> (accessed 9 October 2011). Also, Zhang J, "Gaige pai fandui gaige huichao, huyu xianzheng," *Yazhou zhoukan*, 11 September 2011, pp.36–37.

[5] For an overview and further details, see the website of the Boyuan Foundation, <http://www.boyuan.hk/project_intro_view.php?charset=en&id=5> (accessed 25 September 2011).

[6] Mao Y, "Ba Mao Zedong huanyuan cheng ren," at, for instance, <http://china.dwnews.com/news/2011–04–26/57658778.html> (accessed 26 April 2011). Also, see Jiang X, "Mao Zedong zai xian fengbao, yong Mao fan Mao yingxiang shibada," *Yazhou zhoukan* [Asia Weekly] (Hong Kong), 25 September 2011, pp. 26–33.

[7] See the website, <http://www.wyzxsx.com/> (accessed 25 September 2011).

however, also shares the opinion that China is crisis-ridden; it recommends the return to the pre-reform Maoist political economy as a way of overcoming the crises, while blaming today's Chinese capitalism for all the evil outcomes. Many retired Party-government officials also play a leading role in this group.

Among those who requested for a return to the original idealism of the CCP, the "Association of Yan'an Descendants" is an example which suggested some democratic measures for the reform of the existing Chinese political system. In their open letter to the forthcoming 18th Party Congress, this organisation suggested direct elections of the CCP leaders at every level, and the establishment of three parallel committees in the national leadership, namely, the Central Committee, the Central Policy Committee, and the upgraded Central Disciplinary Committee, all directly responsible to the National Party Congress (NPC) to provide a system of checks and balances within the CCP national leadership.[8]

Similarly, to keep single-party rule while democratising the ruling system, some leading Party theorists jointly recommended a book that advocates "constitutional socialism", authored by Hua Bingxiao, a young professor and Party cadre at the Northwestern University in Xi'an.[9] This book imagines a "constitutional socialist political system" under the CCP's single-party leadership. While democratic elections are introduced within the current political framework, the Party leaders are elected by the parliament-like NPC.

## Transcending Left and Right: Consensus in the Making

These discussions calling for political reform have some general features in their scopes and social affiliations. First, most of them took place mainly within the elite circles, rather than as discussions open to the public. This is partially because the regime has tightened control of the mass media and the publishing of the discussions are usually disallowed in the print media.

Second, many of the discussants are retired Party-state cadres and descendents of old revolutionaries (or "princelings", a loosely defined group with fuzzy boundaries). The political trust they enjoy from the current regime explains this phenomenon even though their discussions do cause the regime's unease and suspicion. Their self-appointed responsibilities to the nation and to the regime are among the incentives leading to the discussions, while it is obvious that they have the intention of using their discussions to influence the forthcoming Party Congress as well as the new leadership that will come to office at the Congress.

It is too early to say that different schools of thought have emerged in the ongoing Chinese discussions of political reform, but there are contending ideas on how to reform China's existing political system. The spectrum can be roughly dichotomised as Left and Right; the Left believes in the fundamental framework of the current political system and the Right in adding various elements of democratic constitutionalism to the system.

Although the confrontation between Maoist fundamentalists and liberals still exists, a new trend that seeks dialogue and understanding across the ideological spectrum has begun to emerge. In fact, many who are involved in the discussions share more consensus than they appear to. A major consensus is that the assessment of the current socio-political situations of China can be summarised in one word: crises. The Left condemns Dengist market reforms for the crises, while the Right targets political authoritarianism. What is particularly interesting is that they all blame the Hu Jintao leadership, especially Hu himself, for not taking sufficient measures to deal with the crises. Thus they constitute challenges to the current Party-state leadership.

---

[8] <http://www.xici.net/d140760264.htm> (accessed 27 September 2011).

[9] *Nanfang dushi bao* [South Metropolitan], 26 December 2010, p. GB22. For Hua's book, see Hua B, *Chaoyue ziyou zhuyi: Xianzheng shehui zhuyi de sixiang yanshuo* (Xi'an: Xibei daxue chubanshe, 2010). Also, see an interview of Ma Licheng by *Lianhe zaobao*, 24 September 2011.

The discussants seek the political restructuring of the CCP's continuous leadership, though they may have different conceptions of what constitutes future CCP leadership in state power. For some of the Right, the long-term goal may be a political system in which there is no single-party monopoly of state power.

An important consensus is their common emphasis on the promotion of "intra-party democracy", which basically means increasing democratic participation and political competition within the CCP. They may have different understandings and projections of "intra-party democracy", but as Zhang Musheng, Hu Deping, Hua Bingxiao and the Association of Yan'an Descendants have indicated, they prefer a gradual path to political reform starting with democratic experiments within the CCP.

## The Regime is Splitting? Inconsistent Responses from the Party-State

Officially, the Chinese national leadership has not commented on the re-emerging discussions on political reform. There are indirect responses, however, which come in four ways: ideological propaganda as implicit criticism of the discussions in general and, in particular, of the liberal ideas expressed in the discussions; political repression over comments made in the discussions; positive consonance with the discussions, and the suggestion of the Maoist practice as an alternative to political reform.

"Political reform" for post-Tiananmen Chinese leaderships has been purely rhetorical. The recent discussions of political reform are basically critical assessments of, and societal responses to, the Hu Jintao leadership's failure to restructure Chinese politics to remedy the problems caused or deepened by the profound socio-economic transitions. The leadership, on the other hand, has its own rhetoric of political reform, and tries to use it to defend the regime's stance and to counteract criticisms.

Wu Bangguo's five "no's" is a typical official refusal to any genuine political reform. As number two ranking party leader and China's NPC Standing Committee chairman, Wu delivered a speech at the NPC annual session on 10 March 2011, explicitly repudiating ideas like a rotation of multiple ruling parties, a diversity of ideological guidelines, a system of checks and balances among three separate power organisations and a bicameral legislative structure, a federal system and a privatisation of property right.[10] The speech represents the official stance to those issues covered by the recent intellectual discussions of political reform.

The regime has also used its "positive" propaganda to contain the social impact of the demand for political reform. One is the lauding of the "China model," especially its political aspects and the condemning of the weaknesses of Western democracy in the official media. Examples of such efforts to promote the regime's "soft power" can be found in a lengthy article, "Chinese Democracy Is Still Better," published in *The Guangming Daily*, a Party mouthpiece.[11] The author Fang Ning, a deputy director of the Institute of Political Science, the Chinese Academy of Social Sciences, is a well-known "New Leftist". Unlike Maoists and China's "Old Left", the "New Leftists" generally do not demand for political reform in China. The Party-state meanwhile has continuously tightened control over the mass media and informal meetings by elite groups, though how to effectively control new social media is still a challenge to the regime.

Amidst such official announcements, ideological propaganda and political repression, Premier Wen Jiabao, CCP's number three ranking leader, has displayed a sympathetic and even positive response to the growing demand for political reform. As early as August 2010, Wen began to call for political reform, the first time that a top Chinese leader has openly discussed this sensitive issue beyond official clichés since the 1989 Tiananmen crackdown. Since then, Wen has repeated his call

---

[10] *Renmin ribao*, 19 March 2011, p. 2. For an analysis, see Bo Z, "What Is Next for China's Political Reforms? Different Views at the Top", *EAI Background Brief*, no. 624, 12 May 2011.

[11] Fang N, "Chinese Democracy Is Still Better", *Guangming Daily*, 21 September 2011.

for political reform many times, on both domestic and international occasions, including his interview with CNN's Fareed Zakaria in New York in September 2010. At the interview, Wen expressed his determination for political reform with his statement, "I will not fall in spite of a strong wind and heavy rain and I will not yield till the last day of my life."[12]

On 14 September 2011, at the Summer Davos Forum in Dalian, Wen Jiabao again elaborated his idea of political reform in his dialogue with entrepreneurs. This time Wen emphasised five points, ranging from the separation between the Communist Party and the state to "expanding people's democracy" through elections.[13] This was the bravest, lengthiest, most systematic and most sophisticated statement from Wen (as well as from the entire leadership since 1989) on political reform. This speech, as with Wen's previous talks on political reform, immediately stirred domestic and overseas public opinions which provided different interpretations to the speech's contents and implications. Some highlighted the hint of the Zhao Ziyang concept of the party-state separation, even though Wen cited Deng Xiaoping rather than Zhao when mentioning the terms; others saw more empty talk than substantive plans of political reform in Wen's statement, while there are still others who paid major attention to Wen's differing stance towards political reform in comparison with other leaders' silence on the topic. In any case, Wen has obviously showed his sympathy for the necessity of political reform and his points are in consonance to those elite discussions analysed earlier, particularly opinions with liberal inclinations.

Wen's 14 September speech could be said to be even more liberal than many intellectual discussions, as exemplified by his emphases on judicial independence, political transparency and, especially, the objectives of political reform to promote equality, justice and tranquillity. In the last point, Wen demonstrates that he is fully aware of the growing conflicts between government officials and ordinary citizens, and that it should be a major goal of political reform to solve this through expanding citizens' participation in politics. He blames the overconcentration of power in the hands of the Communist Party and implicitly suggests the promotion of democratic elections to the levels of township and even county.

Wen's suggestions have not been openly endorsed by Hu Jintao or any other of his colleagues in the Chinese top leadership. He is not totally alone, however, in the advocating of political reform in the leadership. In Guangdong, the region known for being "a step ahead" of China in reforms,[14] the "further emancipation of thought" was once advocated by the provincial party secretary Wang Yang, the youngest member of the Politburo and a hopeful candidate for the next Politburo Standing Committee. His recent relatively "soft" and sophisticated way of managing the Wukan villagers' protest provided an alternative method to dealing with social discontent. In addition, Wang is also conducting some experiments in allowing NGOs more social spaces.

In this context, another high profile Politburo member Bo Xilai's practice in Chongqing can be viewed as an alternative response to the pressure of political reform. Unlike Wen and Wang, Bo, also a hopeful for the nine-member Politburo Standing Committee at the forthcoming Party Congress, turned to Maoist spirits and traditional "socialist" practices to cope with issues such as crimes, apathy of social morality and socio-economic inequality. Bo's campaigns to crack down mafias, the mass performance of revolutionary songs, and the socio-economic programmes that emphasise "becoming rich together," have accelerated his rise as a political star in China. Bo's "Chongqing model" has been hailed as the saver of the problematic "China model" and the sinking

---

[12] See an analysis in Bo, "What Is Next for China's Political Reforms?".

[13] See a summary at <http://www.chinaelections.org/newsinfo.asp?newsid=214508> (accessed 28 September 2011). What is curious is that official Chinese web pages like *Xinhua wang* (<http://www.xinhuanet.com/> by the state news agency Xinhua) and Renmin wang (<http://www.people.com.cn/> by the CCP Central Committee organ *Renmin ribao*, or *People's Daily*) no longer contain this speech of Wen's on the date the author accessed the website.

[14] This phrase is borrowed from Ezra Vogel, a well-known US China expert based at Harvard University. See Vogel, E, *One Step Ahead of China: Guangdong in Reform*, Cambridge, MA, Harvard University Press, 1989.

world dominated by perishing capitalism.[15] In addition, Bo's rise highlighted and accelerated *de facto* political competition among the new generation leaders, despite such competition being formally prohibited by the communist regime's political disciplines. The latest development, however, has become indeed dramatic and highly uncertain since, first, Bo's deputy Wang Lijun fled to the US Consulate General in Chengdu on 6 February 2012, and then on 15 March 2012, Bo himself was removed from his Chongqing office while retaining a seat at the Central Committee Politburo. Bo's political future seems dim and the Chongqing model's credibility is also highly problematic.

## The 18th Party Congress: Possible Impacts

It is apparent that the discussions on political reform are targeted at influencing the forthcoming 18th Party Congress in the hope that the Party Congress will initiate a new programme of political reform, or even possibly carry out some political reform measures when the Congress meets in 2012. It is highly doubtful, however, that the 18th Party Congress will adopt any kind of systematic plan for political reform, although it is very likely to continue with its rhetoric and slogans of political reform. There is no sign, at least so far, that the Party Congress per se will be conducted in a reformed way, say, with competitive elections even in a limited sense, or that it will drastically restructure the central leadership as suggested in the proposal of the three committees. What can be expected is the further repression of discussions as the Party Congress draws near.

The primary point of discussions is apparently the next leadership, which is commonly believed to be the Xi Jinping-Li Keqiang leadership. The new leadership, particularly Xi Jinping as the designated Party chief, is likely to promulgate some new political slogans as catchwords to raise its popularity. However, genuine political reform is not likely to be on the cards. In any case, the new leadership will not be able to amass enough power, at least in its first few years of office, to initiate and implement a political reform programme that will inevitably endanger the Party's embedded interests.

Suggestions for power restructuring are a reflection of power struggles among different elite groups. A case in point is Wen's reiteration of "the separation between the Party and the state". It can be postulated as his move to assist his designated successor Li Keqiang to limit the future Party chief's power. In so doing, Wen can improve his relationship with Hu Jintao, Li's political patron, while balancing the power of the princelings, the group to which Wen never shows sympathy.

A day before Wen's Dalian speech, *The Chinese Youth Gazette* published an unusual article to criticise the "dependence on the number one leader".[16] This article has caused much bewilderment as this newspaper is the mouthpiece of the Communist Youth League, a major powerbase of Hu Jintao. Wen's speech, however, has provided an answer. The article is not targeted at Hu Jintao, but his successor. The reduction in the Party's dependence on the top leader would certainly serve the interests of Hu Jintao, Li Keqiang and, perhaps to a lesser degree, Wen Jiabao.

The reemergence of the discussions is an indication of an erosion of confidence in the so-called "China model", which will, in all likelihood, negatively influence public perceptions of the legitimacy of the current regime. The regime's continuous disregard of the pressure concerning political reform, let alone the programmes of political reform, will further widen the divide between the Party-state on the one side and many of the intellectuals and the ordinary citizens on the other; between governmental policy and social-political reality, and between the hidden crises China faces and the state capacity to cope with them. The disillusion with political reform after the 18th Party Congress is likely to bring China to another high wave of social tensions and political confrontations.

---

[15] See, for example, a forum on "*Shijie weiji xia de Chongqing moshi yu Zhongguo weilai*" [The Chongqing model and China's future under the crises of the world], <http://www.wyzxsx.com/Article/Class16/201109/259722.html> (accessed 5 October 2011).

[16] *Zhongguo qingnian bao*, 13 September 2011, p. 7.

# 3

# Intra-Party Democracy in Practice

## Balloting for City Leaders in Jiangsu

ZHENG Yongnian and CHEN Gang*

*The Chinese Communist Party has introduced a contested intra-Party balloting system to select high-rank cadres. Jiangsu province introduced contested elections to select top leaders in 2011. However, the Party's long-term goal is still meritocracy rather than democracy even with the institutionalisation of cadres selection.*

While the Chinese Communist Party (CCP) is busy reshuffling thousands of Party committee secretaries and members of the Party committees at various levels before the 18th Party Congress scheduled in 2012, three municipalities in the eastern part of Jiangsu province have made changes to the non-transparent selection process through introducing contested elections to select top Party leaders. As an experimental move towards intra-Party democracy, a buzzword in Chinese politics since the 17th Party Congress in 2007, Wuxi, Nantong and Suqian cities in Jiangsu province for the first time in history nominated a total of 1,127 candidates for the three Party secretary positions. After going through two rounds of screening by two panels of provincial-rank cadres based in Jiangsu, the list was narrowed down to six candidates. Members of the Standing Committee of the Jiangsu Provincial Party Committee then balloted and the three with the highest votes became the Party secretaries of the three cities.[1]

The new selection mechanism, dubbed as "open recommendations and balloting" (*gongtuipiaojue*), has been supported by Li Yuanchao, the Jiangsu-born director of the powerful CCP Organisation Department in charge of cadre promotion and demotion. Many observers view the balloting within the Provincial Party Committee as a promising sign of internal democratisation. "The practice of selecting a city-level Party secretary from an enlarged circle of candidates is certain to pave the

---

*ZHENG Yongnian is Director of the East Asian Institute, National University of Singapore. CHEN Gang is Research Fellow at the same institute.

[1]"Jiangsu for the first time selected three municipal party secretaries through open recommendations and balloting", (*Jiangsu shouci gongtuipiaojue chansheng sanming shiweishuji*), *People's Daily*, 19 April 2011.

way for deeper reforms of the official promotion system", said Wang Shoulin, a professor at the Air Force Command Collage under the People's Liberation Army. "It will be an important stroke of the brush in the history of the CCP democratization process."[2]

China started direct village elections in 1988; now almost every village in China — homes to some 600 million farmers — is required to hold direct elections regularly for a new village committee which is vested with the power to decide on important issues such as land and property rights. However, since village committees are formally excluded from China's five-level governmental apparatus (central, provincial, municipal, county and township) and more villagers are settling down in urban areas, such grassroots elections can only play limited role in China's democratisation. Semi-competitive elections have moved to township level, with increasing experimentation especially since 1998 in places like Lingshan in Sichuan province, Caiji in Jiangsu province[3] and Dapeng in Guangdong province.[4] In late 2001 to early 2002, about 2,000 townships in Sichuan province implemented semi-competitive elections.[5]

Meanwhile, bribery and violence have marred grassroots elections of the Party's branches and the villagers' self-governing bodies. According to an investigation conducted by provincial prosecutors, the heads of more than half of the 18 villages or communities in Longquan township of Haikou city, Hainan province, were elected after buying votes or feting voters. In some cases, local hooligans and gangsters intimidated villagers to vote for particular candidate.[6]

After years of experimentation, the Chinese authorities are still reluctant to promulgate semi-competitive elections for above-township-level Party/government positions.[7] Due to the slow progress in promoting elections, Wang Yukai, a professor from the China National School of Administration, has urged the Party-state to select county leaders through intra-Party balloting.[8] In reality, political reform is losing steam in China. Recently, no substantial institutions have been introduced for further democratisation even within the Party. To bring political reforms in line with economic reform in China, the Party is trying to rely more on the contested intra-Party balloting system than the opaque one-candidate-one-position appointment process to select high-rank cadres. However, the Party has not deviated much from its traditional way of selecting cadres. Selection is still largely based on meritocracy rather than democracy. Competitive elections are means and not an end to help the Party single out capable and loyal officials for important positions, and exclusive elections are just a part of the Party's complicated system of cadre selection based on meritocratic principles and political integrity. As a result, Jiangsu's experimentation with a more

[2] "Communist Party Begins Major Reshuffling of Local Leaders", *Global Times*, 29 April 2011.

[3] "Direct Elections Move to Township Level", *China Daily*, 18 May 2004.

[4] In an early model for further experiments on direct township election, all registered voters in Dapeng Town in Shenzhen, Guangdong province, were allowed to participate in a form of sea election (*haixuan*, where any adult in the constituency can be a candidate in the election) to nominate candidates for town magistrate in 1999. Voters representing about one-fifth of the town's population and selected by the election organising committee from among local officials, Party members, village committee members, villager-small-group chiefs, town resident committee members, and representatives of enterprises and unions, then voted for one among the five qualified candidates who received more than 100 votes on the first ballot, in what was called an "opinion poll". The winning candidate's name was then submitted to the township people's congress for a confirming vote. See Horsley, JP, "Village Elections: Training Ground for Democratization", *The China Business Review*, March–April 2001.

[5] The term "semi-competitive elections" is used because these elections are far from being free and competitive elections as one sees in many countries. Lai H, "Semi-Competitive Elections at Township Level in Sichuan Province", *China Perspectives*, no. 51, 2004. See also <http://chinaperspectives.revues.org/787?&id=787#bodyftn1> (accessed 9 July 2012).

[6] "Bribery being Bred in Grassroot Elections", *China Daily*, 22 July 2010.

[7] There have been occasional reports recently about intra-Party elections for county-level party secretaries. See, for example, "CCP Tries to Push Political Elites onto Election Stage", (*zhonggong changshi tuidong zhizheng zhiguo guanliliang zoushang jingxuan wutai*), *Xinhua News*, 12 June 2011.

[8] "Wang Yukai urges direct election of county leaders", (*wangyukai: tuijin xianjizhixuan*), *People's Daily*, 19 December 2010.

transparent and more competitive process to reshuffle local leadership did not yield any surprises. The Party's favourite candidates still emerged winners in the elections and the entire process is still controlled by the provincial Party committee.

Mao Xiaoping from Wuxi, Ding Dawei from Nantong and Miao Ruilin from Suqian were all mayors in their respective cities and their challengers also hold key positions in the provincial Party committee. Going from mayor to municipal Party secretary is the norm in China's politics. Meanwhile the comprehensive process used in Jiangsu province is not mandatory and local authorities can opt not to follow it.

Nevertheless, Jiangsu's reform is a clear evidence of the Party's will to promote openness and competition, and to implement contested election (*cha'e xuanju*) in cadre selection. In 2007, CCP General Secretary Hu Jintao said in his report to the 17th Party Congress that the Party should "expand intra-Party democracy" and "reform the intra-Party electoral system and improve the system for nominating candidates and electoral methods".[9] The CCP apparently did not simply pay lip service to such a goal of "intra-Party democracy" as members of the 17th CPC Central Committee were elected with a 7.7% margin, higher than that of 5.1% at the 16th Party Congress five years ago.[10] It was reported that prior to the 17th Party Congress, the CCP Central Organisation Department held a tentative poll among provincial/ministerial level-and-above officials, asking them to vote on candidates of Political Bureau Standing Committee members. Xi Jinping got the most votes, followed by Li Keqiang, He Guoqiang and Zhou Yongkang.[11]

Besides Jiangsu, other places like Beijing city and Zhejiang province have also made similar changes to the selection process of department chiefs. Beijing, Zhejiang, Hunan, Jiangxi and Guangdong provinces have opened up high-level civil vacancies to a broad range of qualified candidates who need to go through exams, interviews and balloting before they can be appointed to respective positions.

## CCP's System of Selecting Cadres

The objective of cadre management in China is to make sure that professionally competent people are recruited and promoted, and that they remain loyal to the Party's ideologies and political views.[12] All Party and government officials are managed by the Party according to detailed regulations relating to recruitment, appointment, transfer, reward, training etc,[13] which supplement the Civil Service Law. Concerning the management of cadres above county/division level (*xianchu ji*), the most important provisions are contained in the "Regulation on Selection and Appointment of Party and Government Leading Cadres" (*dangzheng lingdao ganbu xuanba renyong gongzuo tiaoli*) issued in 2002 by the CCP Organisation Department.

All these regulations emphasise that when selecting and appointing leading cadres in Chinese civil service system, a number of basic principles including openness, equality, competition and the selection of the best must be adhered to. Although the selection and appointment are based on meritocratic principles (*ren ren wei xian*), cadres should also have both political integrity and

[9]"Hu Jintao's Report at 17th Party Congress", *China Daily*, 25 October 2007, <http://www.chinadaily.com.cn/china/2007–10/25/content_6204667.htm> (accessed 8 July 2012).

[10]During the 17th Party Congress, 204 out of the 221 candidates were elected members of the new CPC Central Committee, representing a rejection rate of 7.7%. About half of the new members were new faces.

[11]"The Election Process of New Members in the Standing Committee", Duowei yuekan 33, December 2007, p. 2.

[12]Brodsgaard, KE, "China's Cadres: Professional Revolutionaries or State Bureaucrats? (I)", *EAI Background Brief,* no. 94, 11 July 2001.

[13]See, for example, "Regulation on the Appointment, Dismissal, Promotion, and Demotion of Civil Servants (Trial)" (*Gongwuyuan zhiwu renmian yu zhiwu shengjiang guiding (shixing)*), issued by the CCP Central Organisation Department and the Ministry of Personnel, 29 February 2008.

ability (*de cai jian bei*) and are ultimately managed by the Party (*dang guan gan bu*).[14] Civil servants to be promoted to leading Party and government posts at section (village)-head level are required to have at least a college diploma (*dazhuan*) and worked at the deputy post for more than two years.[15] Candidates to be promoted to posts higher than the county (division) level must have held at least two posts at lower level organs, and candidates who are promoted from deputy post to a head post (*zhengzhi*) generally must have worked at the deputy post for more than two years.[16] Leading cadres at bureau level (*ju, si, ting*) or above should at least have a bachelor's degree (*daxue benke*).[17]

Candidates to be considered for selection and appointment to leading posts should be proposed through the so-called democratic recommendation (*minzhu tuijian*)[18] process conducted by the Party committee at the same level, or by a higher level organisation or personnel department. At the time of an official's change of term, various people and personnel are consulted, and they include Party committee members, leading members of government organs, leading members of the discipline inspection commissions and people's courts, and leading members of lower level Party committees and governments. Members of democratic parties and representatives of groups without Party affiliation will also be consulted.

A candidate who has been nominated will have to undergo evaluation (*kaocha*)[19] based on elaborate procedures, which may include interviews with a number of leading officials in his or her own department. Evaluations are held throughout the official term. Leading members of Party committees and government departments are also evaluated in the middle of their term. Any promotion or dismissal arising from the evaluations must undergo a process of deliberation (*yunniang*) and be reported to the Party committee at the higher level.

The regulations require a two-thirds quorum of members of a given committee when appointment and dismissal of cadres are involved. The regulations include details concerning job transfer. Any leading member of a local Party committee or government who has served in the same post for 10 years must be transferred to a new post. The Party has recently worked out a new plan for "deepening the cadre management system" covering the 2010-2020 period.[20] The plan further details and expands the provisions of the 2002 regulations, which are applicable to the whole cadre corps and not just leading cadres. The plan, emphasising "democratic recommendation", "public opinion polls" and "contested election (*cha'e xuanju*)", stipulates that deepening the reform of the Party and government cadre system involves:

— Improving the system of recommendation, public opinion polls and assessment in selecting and appointing cadres.
— Promoting the implementation of a public notification system among Party and government leaders before they assume office.
— Promoting openness and transparency in Party and government cadre election and implementing contested election (*cha'e xuanju*) in both the Central Committee and the National People's Congress.

---

[14] See, for example, the (2002) Regulation on Selection and Appointment of Party and Government Leading Cadres (*Dangzheng lingdao ganbu xuanba renyong gongzuotiaoli*), Article 2.
[15] See Article 19 of the "Regulation on the Appointment, Dismissal, Promotion, and Demotion of Civil Servants (Trial)" (*Gongwuyuan zhiwu renmian yu zhiwu shengjiang guiding (shixing)*), CCP Central Organisation Department and the Ministry of Personnel, 29 February 2008.
[16] "Regulation on Selection and Appointment of Party and Government Leading Cadres (2002)", Article 7.
[17] Ibid.
[18] Ibid., Articles 10–19.
[19] Ibid., Chapter 4, Articles 20–28.
[20] "2010–2020 *nian shenhua ganbu renshi zhidu gaige guihua gangyao*" (The Plan for Deepening the Cadre Management System During the 2010–2020 period) (21 December 2009), <http://www.hnredstar.gov.cn/yueyang123/gbgz/gb_gbgln/t20091221_275446.htm> (accessed 8 July 2012).

— Implementing the tenure system among Party and government cadres, which should also apply to all cadres above county level, i.e. leading cadres.
— Implementing a probation system for Party and government cadres.
— Formulating a resignation and retirement system for Party and government cadres.
— Improving policies and measures for dealing with incompetent and incapable cadres.
— Electing more women and representatives from minority groups to take on various cadre jobs.
— Amending the "Interim Regulations for the Selection and Appointment of Party and Government Cadres".
— Promoting an assessment system for Party and government cadres.
— Promoting rotation and exchange of Party and government cadres.
— Strengthening the supervision of the election and appointment of cadres.
— Improving the cadre training system.
— Devising a salary and benefit system that suits the features of Party and government organs. This involves monetising the distribution of benefits among cadres, including housing, pension, insurance systems, etc.

The plan is a reflection of China's leadership's preoccupation with selecting qualified cadres. The focus of this theme goes back to October 2004, when former Vice President Zeng Qinghong published an important article in the *People's Daily* in which he stressed the importance of strengthening the Party's governing capacity. Zeng discussed the "painful lesson of the loss of power" by the communist parties in the former Soviet Union and Eastern Europe.[21] Zeng attributed the collapse of the Soviet Communist Party to the rigidness and inflexibility of its governing system which ultimately led to the Party's diminishing capacity to govern. To Zeng, establishing clear rules and regulations, and ensuring constant cadre renewal are necessary to attract new talent.

**Elite Selection**

China had traditionally adopted the examination and recommendation system, rather than by competitive election when selecting its officials. During the Han Dynasty (206 B.C.–220 A.D.), most appointments in the imperial bureaucracy were based on recommendations by prominent aristocrats and local officials. Recommended individuals were mostly from aristocratic families. When the Sui Dynasty (581–618 A.D.) established the imperial examination system in A.D. 605, ancient China began to select most of its administrative officials from among civilians through institutionalised imperial examinations for over 1,300 years. However, even during that period, bureaucratic appointments did not fully rely on examination results but sometimes upon the recommendation of powerful people.

Such a cultural heritage still has significant impact upon today's Chinese politics, with the Party-state largely reliant on the civil service examinations for recruiting grassroots cadres and recommendations from political elites of the Party committees at various levels for the promotion of officials. In most cases, the Party secretary or the administrative chief (*yibashou,* or chief official of the organisation) in the Party committee has the arbitrary power to make promotion decisions.

The non-transparent process of promoting officials recommended by the *yibashou* has caused rampant corrupt practices such as the selling and buying of government posts or bribing for higher positions. In one of China's largest "selling official posts" scandals, Ma De, former Party secretary of the Suihua city in Heilongjiang province, was charged with taking bribes amounting to more than six million *yuan* (US$726,000) between 1992 and 2001. Most of the bribes were offered by

---

[21] *People's Daily*, 8 October 2004.

ambitious county heads and leading officials of government departments under Ma's jurisdiction. More than 260 government officials were alleged to be involved in Ma's case, including Tian Fengshan, former minister of land and resources, and Han Guizhi, former chairwoman of the Heilongjiang Provincial Committee of the Chinese People's Political Consultative Conference (CPPCC).[22]

The recent increase in corruption cases involving ministerial/provincial-level officials[23] has raised concerns over the selection criteria and procedures for senior officials. Selling-official-post scandals have undermined the Party's promotion principle that cadres should have both political integrity and ability (*de cai jian bei*). This has also put the Party's reputation and legitimacy at stake.

The Party issued its first interim regulation on the selection and appointment of officials in 1995, which included detailed procedures regarding nomination, screening, transferring, discipline and monitoring; the regulation was revised into a formal statute in 2002. Although the institutionalisation of elite management has introduced a number of mechanisms to curb arbitrary personal decisions while enhancing the institutional dominance of the Party,[24] the lack of competitive elections in the whole system has made the official selection process less fair and transparent.

China has institutionalised direct village elections in most parts of the country, but since village committees are formally excluded from China's five-level governmental apparatus (central, provincial, municipal, county and township), such grassroots elections can only play limited role in promoting democratisation and officials' accountability.

Semi-competitive elections have been practised at township level with increasing experimentation especially since 1998 in places like Lingshan in Sichuan province, Caiji in Jiangsu province and Dapeng in Guangdong province. Nevertheless, after years of experimentation, the Chinese authorities are still reluctant to hold contested elections for above-township-level Party/government positions. The new mechanism applied to the selection of Party secretaries in Jiangsu's three cities, dubbed as "open recommendations and balloting" (*gongtuipiaojue*), has the support of Li Yuanchao, the Jiangsu-born director of the powerful CCP Organisation Department in charge of cadre promotion and demotion. Many observers view the balloting within the Provincial Party Committee as a promising sign of internal democratisation that could be further moved to higher levels for the sake of anti-corruption and fairness. Li himself was a strong advocate of such intra-Party polling mechanism on cadre selection during his tenure as Jiangsu Provincial Party Secretary from 2002 to 2007.

Recent reports have revealed that the Party is encouraging polling within local Party committees for selecting county/district-level Party secretaries. In June 2011, seven candidates from different government departments competed for the Party secretary position of Yangxi county, Guangdong province, through delivering speeches in front of over 100 voters from the upper-level Party Committee of the Yangjiang city. In 2008, four counties and districts under the Guiyang city, Guizhou province, made their top positions of Party secretary open to qualified Party-member competitors, who had to go through contested polling (*cha'e xuanju*) within the municipal Party committee in Guiyang.[25]

---

[22] "Official on Trial for Selling High-level Jobs", *China Daily*, 22 March 2005.

[23] For further research on high-level corruption in China, please refer to *China's Recent Clampdown on High-Stakes Corruption*, by Chen G and Zhu J, *EAI Background Brief,* no. 490, 19 November 2009.

[24] Bo Z, "The Institutionalization of Elite Management in China", in *Holding China Together — Diversity and National Integration in the Post-Deng Era*, ed. BJ Naughton and Yang D (New York: Cambridge University Press, 2004), p. 99.

[25] "CCP Tries to Push Political Elites onto Election Stage", (*zhonggong changshi tuidong zhizheng zhiguo guganliliang zoushang jingxuan wutai*), Xinhua News, 12 June 2011.

## Will the Party Institutionalise Intra-Party Elections?

Jiangsu's reform evinces the Party's will to promote openness and competition and implement contested election (*cha'e xuanju*) in cadre selection. In 2007, CCP General Secretary Hu Jintao said in his report to the 17th Party Congress that the Party should expand intra-Party democracy, reform intra-Party electoral system and improve candidate nomination system and electoral methods. In response to the urge for intra-Party balloting of county or even city leaders from people such as Professor Wang Yukai, the Party is likely to change the one-candidate-one-position appointment process in more places to ease public anxiety over the sluggish political reform.

On the institutionalisation of cadre selection, the Party's long-term goal is still meritocracy rather than democracy. Rampant bribery and violence that have characterised grassroots elections of the Party's branches and the villagers' self-governing bodies have reminded the Party of the innate flaws pertaining to popular elections.

The Party itself is becoming more pluralistic. The passing of the strong-man era has propelled China's leadership structure towards an increasingly power-sharing direction that facilitates intra-Party consultations, bargaining or even polls behind closed doors. The weaker the incumbent leader is, the more likely he/she is to rely on "collective decision-making" (*jiti juece*) when appointing successors. Certain informal rules and institutions based on balance of power among different factions and restriction of incumbent leaders' power have emerged in China's elite politics, ensuring that candidateship of future successors is not solely the reflection of the Party Secretary's own will, but an outcome of compromises among different groups, or even one step further, the result of polls in a limited sense. This way of producing future leadership guarantees policy continuation and stability while forestalling individual dictatorship and corruption. As the Party, rather than the public, chooses future leaders, no matter who they are, they will commit to preserving the Party power and representing the extensive interest of different groups within the Party.

# 4

# Township Government Reform

## Improving Local Governance?

### TAN Qingshan*

*The ongoing township reform aims to transform township government into service-oriented and responsive administration. This chapter explores different models of township transformation as well as the pitfalls of the current reform.*

The Politburo of the Communist Party of China (CPC) adopted a document on 21 August 2010, instructing grassroots Party organisations to be more open in Party affairs. The document stresses such openness as a necessity for expanding grassroots democracy within the Party, safeguarding the democratic rights of Party members, and improving local governance.[1]

Local governance is a major issue in today's China as the central government is trying hard to establish a harmonious society. Many "mass incidents", popular protest and social unrest can be attributed to improper or ineffective local governance. The recent Wukan incident highlighted the exigency to improve local governance. Mounting social problems present a sharp contrast to the image of a rising power on the international scene.

Local governance has been in the spotlight in recent years, due to social conflict and instability caused by local state-society tension in many parts of the country. According to various sources, the Chinese government spent a huge amount of money every year on "maintaining social stability" (*weiwen*).[2] In the meantime, Beijing has delegated the primary responsibility of maintaining social order on local officials. Local government officials may still regard economic development as their priority, but now have to maintain social stability as their primary responsibility, the importance of

*TAN Qingshan is Professor of Political Science at Cleveland State University and Kuang Yamin Professor at Jilin University.

[1] *People's Daily*, August 21, 2010, p. 1.

[2] Ming Pao reported that China spent 514 billion *yuan* on internal security, which was close to or surpassed military spending in 2009, *Ming Pao*, 6 March 2010.

which far surpasses their work on social security, health care, environmental protection and education.

In the context of this discussion, local governance specifically refers to political governance of township governments to clearly distinguish it from local administrative management. Local governance includes township government make-up, functions and responsibilities, exercise of power and effective governance.

Local governance in China has taken on different countenance in recent years, particularly at the township level, largely in response to local government restructuring and reorientation. The central government has been promoting township reform that redefines government functions and responsibilities in order to improve government services and governance of local affairs.

Until township government reform, many believed that local governments created more problems than solving them. Local governance was riddled with incompetency, inefficiency and inability to effectively govern vast localities. Some described townships as predatory in their close contact with the local people.[3] Others characterised township governments as having "inadequate power, big responsibility, and low competency" (*quan xiao, ze da, neng ruo*).[4]

Another major problem that township governments (*zhuanyi zhifu*) faced was the lack of financial resources. Often, the central government delegated responsibility to local governments while retaining financial control. Local governments ended up either not doing anything due to the lack of resources or borrowing heavily to fulfill their responsibilities, resulting in shouldering heavy debt burden. According to a recent study, the total township debt in 2008 was estimated at between 600 billion *yuan* and 800 billion *yuan*, averaging 20 million *yuan* per township.[5] If the borrowing of county government was included, the total county government debt would swell to three trillion *yuan*, accounting for 30% of national GDP in 2004.[6]

## Reforming Townships

The current township transformation started in 1998 when the CPC issued an important policy regarding rural reform at the Third Plenary of the 15th Central Party Committee. The document, titled "The CPC Decision on Several Important Issues of Agriculture and Rural Work", gave directions to township governments to experiment with rural "tax and fee" reform. The central government was aiming at restructuring township governments through a scheme of "*chexiang bingzhen*" (eliminating and merging townships). Since 2001, the total number of township governments had been reduced from 41,535 to 38,553 in 2004 and further to 35,077 in 2010 (Table 1).

In 2004, the CPC issued another important document, the central document No. 1, the first such document after 18 years that stressed the importance of rural development.[7] The central edict further raised the issue of deepening reform on township governments.[8] Not only did the central

---

[3] Saich, T, "The Blind Man and the Elephant: Analysing the Local State in China", in *East Asian Capitalism: Conflicts, Growth and Crisis*, ed. L Tomba, Feltrinelli, Milan, 2002, pp. 75–100.

[4] Xu Y, "Xianzheng, xiangpai, cunzhi: xiangcun zhili de jiegou zhuanhuan" (County Government, Township Office, Village Self-government: Structuring Transformation of Rural Governance), *Jiangsu shehui kexue* (*Jiangsu Social Sciences*), no. 2, 2002.

[5] Yan J, "Cong xiangzhen fuzhai xi zhengfu caizheng yusuan fazhihua (An Analysis of Rule of Law in Government Budgets by Evaluating Township Debts), *Fazhi yu shehui* (*Legal Systems and Society*), no. 25, 2008.

[6] Zhu H, "150 yi yusuan zhichu: xianxiang zhaiwu 'dingshi zhadan' youwang jiechu" (15 Billion *Yuan* Budgetary Expenditure: Hopeful Elimination of the 'Time Bomb' of County and Township Debt), *China Economic Times*, 14 March 2005.

[7] For an analysis of the central document, see Tan Q, "China's Future Lies in Rural Development", *Lianhe zaobao*, 15 March 2004.

[8] See <http://www.gov.cn/test/2006-02/22/content_207415.htm> (accessed 13 December 2010).

**Table 1**  Number of Townships, 2001–2010

| Year | 2001 | 2002 | 2003 | 2004 | 2005 | 2006 | 2007 | 2008 | 2009 | 2010 |
|---|---|---|---|---|---|---|---|---|---|---|
| Towns and townships | 41,535 | 40,402 | 39,439 | 38,553 | 36,566 | 34,675 | 35,764 | 35,398 | 35,268 | 35,077 |

*Source: China Civil Affairs Statistical Yearbook* 2011, China Statistics Press, Beijing, 2011, p. 70.

government want to execute complete rural "tax and fee" reform by totally eliminating rural taxes and fees, it also intended to go beyond reducing the numbers of townships to experiment with changing the functions of township governments.

The new round of township reform was initially experimented in four provinces — Heilongjiang, Jilin, Anhui, and Hubei — focussing on institutional restructuring. Since 2005, township reform has been experimented in more provinces, and by 2008, more than 18,000 townships had conducted the experiment. Based on the experiments, in January 2009, the central government mandated all provinces to start the township reform and targeted 2012 as the year for completing the reform.[9]

Township reform has several important features. First, township governments are asked to change their orientation towards governance. Township governments are now expected to serve rural people rather than control them. The new governing philosophy is consistent with the "people-oriented" (*yi ren weiben*) policy by Chinese President Hu Jintao. With this new orientation, township governments have to alter the way they used to govern the countryside, namely from managing and controlling rural villages to providing services and public goods to rural population.

Second, township reform aims to reduce costs and inefficiency of township administration. Before reform, township governments were overstaffed, resulting in more government workers than the actual work required. In some townships, there were as many as seven to 12 heads and vice heads.[10] Average township employment was usually budgeted at between 30 and 50 headcount, but governments often had more than a hundred employees. The new cost-cutting experiment started with the reduction of township cadres. For example, in Anhui, township Party and government officials were reduced from between 10 and 15 to between six and eight; in Heilongjiang, from between nine and 11 to five only; and in Hubei, from 16 to about seven to nine. Township reform restricts township government staffing by controlling transfer payments to township governments (*zhuanyi zhifu*).

Third, township reform has put an emphasis on reducing and consolidating the number of agencies and institutions. The goal is to restructure township governments to better perform government functions. In many places, township Party and government institutions were integrated; township officials concurrently hold Party and government positions. After reform, township government offices were typically reduced to between five and eight integrated offices. In one township the author visited, the government was restructured into eight offices. There are 17 township Party and government officials responsible for managing the township government. There are another 70 township government employees working in the eight offices.[11]

Fourth, township service agencies are to be consolidated and transformed. Before the reform, an average township government had about 20 to 30 agencies that were supposed to provide social and agricultural services. The reform required township governments to consolidate social services and transform other service agencies by way of marketisation.

---

[9]Sheng R, "Xinyilun xiangzhen jigou gaige quanmian qidong" (A New Round of Township Reform has Started), *People's Daily*, 25 March 2009.

[10]Author's fieldwork in Jiangxi, 2005.

[11]This township is located in Lichuan county, Jiangxi, with a population of 85,000, 16 villages and one urban community. Author's field research, 14 July 2010.

According to a recent state document, three models of transformation have been promoted. The first model has township governments consolidating all the agencies into about three to five social service centres. The second model transforms non-social service agencies into market-oriented enterprises or consulting firms, and services are outsourced to these firms. The third model assigns the management of these agencies to their professional superiors in the county government.[12]

## New Features of Township Reform

What is the difference between the current round of township reform and the previous reform? According to one central Party official, this "township reform is not only an important part of local government reform, but also a key to comprehensive rural reform". Although a clear blueprint for such a comprehensive rural reform has yet to be drawn up, government officials and scholars have long advocated an approach to rural reform that would include villages, townships and county governments. Some emphasised that any township restructuring would have to align with strengthening village self-government and reforming county governments.[13]

The central government encourages township reform to make institutional innovation in light of building a new socialist countryside. Scholars argued that village self-government and rural "tax and fee" reform have made township-level government outlived its usefulness; therefore, the abolition of township governments or the introduction of self-government is recommended.[14] The central government however did not accept the argument; instead, it promoted township institutional reform to produce leaner and more efficient and effective local governments.

Township reform also redefines township functions to be more service-oriented rather than management- and production-oriented. Reformed township governments are supposed to shift their focus from attracting business and investment, setting up commerce and production, and planning cultivation and harvest to providing public services and guidance in economic crop production, and maintaining social harmony. Moreover, township reform strives to achieve the goal of developing "limited township government, more active society" (*xiao zhengfu, da shehui*).

This reform, if accomplished, will not only control the runaway costs of operating township governments, but also rationalise local government institutional set-up such that efficient and effective local governance can be achieved. More importantly, many economic and service functions will be performed by various social and economic intermediaries and non-governmental organisations that could lead to civic culture development in the countryside.[15]

Without reform, state and society in the countryside are too closely intertwined, and it requires government and society to make spaces between them for individual goals. That is one of the reasons that township governments often created more social problems than solving them, simply because township officials were managing almost every aspect of rural life, thus leaving no room for mistakes. Any mismanagement would arouse social unrest and problems.

With the concept of "limited government", township governments are relieved of the duty of micromanaging farmers' life, thus allowing commercial and societal organisations to provide

---

[12] Sheng R, op. cit.

[13] Zhan C, "Guanyu shenhua xiangzheng tizhi gaige de yanjiu baogao (Report on Deepening Reform of Township Governments), *Kaifang shidai* (*Open Times*), no. 2, 2004.

[14] For example, a former township head, Zhou Shaojin, made the argument in his study, "Xiangcun zhengfu cunzai zhiyi ji guojia jiceng zhengquan goujian shexiang (Questioning the Existence of Township Governments and Ideas for Grassroots Government Development), *Renda yanjiu* (*People's Congress Research*), no. 6, 2004; see also, Hu X, "Xiwang jinkuai chexiao xiangzhen zhengfu" (Hope to Abolish Township Governments As Soon As Possible), *Jiangsu nongchun jingji* (*Jiangsu Rural Economy*), no. 1, 2004; Yu J, "Xiangcun zizhi, genju he lujin (Township Self-Government, Basis and Path), *Strategy and Management*, no. 6, 2002.

[15] For an earlier model on outsourcing government services, see "Xianan xianggai: hou shuifei shidai de nongcun gongyi fuwu fanben" (Township Reform in Xianan: A Model for Rural Public Service in the Post-Tax and Fee Reform Era), at <http://news.xinhuanet.com/newscenter/2008-10/26/content_10254977.htm> (accessed 16 November 2010).

necessary services to villagers. With this, township governments can better concentrate on providing public goods and essential government services, and maintaining public order.

## Has Township Reform Changed Anything?

To what extent has township reform changed the role of township and improved local governance? One of the most obvious changes in the role of township governments is the curb on township governments' predatory behaviour towards villagers, thanks to the elimination of rural tax. In the past, villagers were afraid of township officials who came to villages to collect taxes and fees, or order forced abortions.

Reform, however, has brought about new issues. Without a mandate to extract resources, many township officials are at a loss over their role in rural governance. In order to reorientate and instil positive attitude in township officials to serve the villagers, various training programmes have to be initiated to update township officials on new governing philosophies, skills and knowledge to better serve the villagers.

Reining in the extractive role, township officials are now charged with a new primary responsibility of maintaining social stability. Particularly, township Party committee secretary has been tasked with the number one responsibility of keeping social order in the township. In fact, the most noticeable addition to the government structure is the Office of Maintaining Social Stability (*weiwen ban*), which deals with social governance, petition, production safety and public order issues. Furthermore, townships require every village committee to establish the *weiwen ban*, and the village Party chief is appointed to take charge of villagers' petition to higher authorities. Townships even sign contracts with villages to clearly spell out each other's responsibility. In Hubei, for example, villages set up an office that allows villagers to "speak out if you have anything to say" (*youhua jiushuo bangongshi*); on the fourth, 14th and 24th of each month, villagers can visit the office to speak out their mind to two village officials on duty in the office.[16] Through such practice, township officials hope that "grievances will be addressed within villages, big problems will be solved within townships and petitions will not bypass local authorities" (*xiaoshi buchucun, dashi buchuzheng, shangfang buyueji*).

Township reform has largely changed the predatory local state, created some space between society and state in the countryside, reoriented township governments towards social governance, and reduced a number of bureaucratic agencies. But such township transformation has not resulted in effective local governance for several reasons.

First, township governments do not have their own fiscal budget. The lack of financial power debilitates townships, which have to depend on transfer payments from county governments. More often than not, the payment falls short of covering expenditure of township. One common problem facing rural areas is irrigation, and yet, townships and villages do not have the money to carry out repair or rebuilding works. In the past, such funds could be raised by imposing fees on villagers, but not any more since the rural reform. Without financial independence, township governments could not take any initiatives; many township governments become "caretakers". As social unrest affects an official's career advancement, the uppermost concern of officials is to prevent any breakout of social unrest under their jurisdiction. Thus, effective governance leaves much to be desired for villagers.

Second, townships still bear the heavy burden of local economic growth. Conventional wisdom has it that local governments can reap benefits from local development. But at the township level, government officials prefer not to take on such a burden if given the choice, which unfortunately they do not have, since county governments assign tax quota to townships each year. The only avenue for townships to fulfil tax revenue quota is to develop local non-agricultural economy, thus putting pressure on township officials to seek investment. For townships that have difficulty

---

[16] Author's interviews with township officials in Hubei, 15 July 2010.

developing local economies and in tax revenue collection, they have to either face cuts in transfer payments (in some townships, full salaries are also contingent on tax collections) or buy state tax receipts from county governments as a channel to contribute to county revenues.

Not every township is suitable for or attractive to outside investments. Some townships tried to dangle free land rental as a bait to attract investments, which in turn created more social problems as villagers raised their objections in protest. Township officials pointed out the obvious drawbacks of this development burden—that it is a waste of time and effort, and undermines effective local governance.[17]

Third, township transformation has not reduced the symbolic and often mandatory works of township officials imposed from higher authorities, as evidenced by the countless meetings and review process. Township officials often complain that more than one-third of their work and time involved receiving officials — from county, municipal and provincial governments — who visit to review the works of township. The preparation work involved in hosting official reception and making reform adjustments based on review report had consumed substantial amount of township officials' time. According to one survey, principal township officials spent 32% of their working hours on attending meetings, 22% on hosting high-level officials, 15% on work evaluation, 9% on economic development, 17% on enforcing birth control programmes and only 2% of their working hours to serve the public.[18]

There is nothing wrong with government review of township works from higher authorities if works under review are related to villagers' welfare and needs. The chief concern is that some of the works done were just for the review, and not for the sake of truly solving villagers' problems. For example, some of the model villages were built too far away from villagers' land, while brand new townhouse-like homes did not set aside areas for villagers to raise livestock.[19]

Fourth, the overall emphasis on maintaining social stability by the central government raises an important issue about township governance, which has been discussed widely among township officials — that is, how to govern at the township level: by "rule by harmony" (*hexie zhiguo*) or rule of law (*yifa zhiguo*). Most of them argue strongly for strengthening rule of law and law enforcement.

Local governments including county governments spend large amount of money on maintaining social stability, and apportion very little money on county and township legal infrastructure building. Most of the local governments are short of court facilities, lawyers and judges. A common complaint among villagers is the small pool of legal counsels and lawyers available.

## Challenges for Township Reform

There are serious challenges confronting township reform. For one, reform is still incomplete. As of 2010, 20,673 townships have completed government restructuring, accounting for 60.3% of the total townships. The central government requires all townships to complete reform by 2012.[20] Poverty and unfavourable conditions are factors deterring townships from undergoing reform. It requires greater policy coordination and goodwill of township governments to carry out the difficult reform.

Reform calls for township governments to be service-oriented, but does not entrust township government with financial power. Township governments are at the mercy of county governments

---

[17] Author's interviews with township officials in Hubei, 15 July 2010.

[18] Chen W, "Hou nongyeshui shidai xianzhen zhengfu de zhineng dingwei yanjiu" (Study on Defining Township Government Functions in the Post-Rural Tax Era), 5 July 2010, at <http://www.zgxcfx.com/Article_Show.asp?ArticleID= 25823> (accessed 17 May 2011).

[19] The author visited a model village which was under construction in Hubei and was told that the township developed this model village in the hope to raise property values in the township.

[20] See <http://politics.people.com.cn/GB/1026/11929993.html> (accessed 9 July 2010).

to transfer payments based on the amount of tax revenue that township governments have generated in the previous year. For more affluent townships (those with industrial firms), governments usually negotiate with county governments for a percentage of return on the excess portion of their tax revenue. Poorer townships, however, have to rely on county transfer payments to pay their bills.[21] Many township officials criticised the ineffectiveness of the reform in improving the township ability to govern; on the contrary, it has weakened local government's power to fulfil township responsibilities.[22]

Institutional reduction and government restructuring have reduced the staff strength of government employees, and to an extent, simplified the government structure. However, reform in institutional reduction can become a number game and agency shuffling. On the surface, township governments have reduced the number of agencies, which in reality, are simply merged and renamed to form bigger groups. For example, many townships followed the model of establishing service centres, consolidating all the agencies into three centres, namely centres for agriculture, social services and birth control. But several years later, they found out that these centres could not function effectively because they do not have their counterparts in the county government. Normally, township agencies, such as post offices or civil affairs offices, are subordinate to similar county agencies. That explains the reversal of many township government centres to specific offices, just like the eight offices of restructured townships.

Turning government services over to market has also met with resistance from townships. Some township governments simply wanted to protect their bureaucratic turfs and thus resisted any move that will weaken their authority over these professional and technical agencies. They are reluctant to marketise the services, and instead, kept them as government-affiliated agencies.

Only in Hubei, where the model of marketisation started, townships began to terminate these agencies and outsource the services to private firms or individuals. Not all Hubei township officials agree with the outsourcing of government services. For example, a township official in Suizhou believed that some government agencies should not be privatised, such as the Office for Agricultural Technology (*nongji zhan*), which assists farmers to adopt better agricultural technology. The official further pointed out that limited market size and information inaccessibility in the countryside imply that farmers need the government to do a better job in this regard.[23]

Without government transparency, townships outsourcing services may encourage rent-seeking behaviour of township officials. The Hubei model of "doing things with money" (*yi qian yangshi*) may help alleviate overemployment in local governments, but may create corruption problems, if outsourcing is not conducted in an open, transparent process. A proper mechanism to ensure open and transparent public bidding or contracting of government services is non-existent. It is not surprising that cronyism, and the use of power and connections can outbid legal contention and contracts. It opens the door for local officials to seek rents under the table when governments purchase services from the public or private sectors. Since township governments have limited revenues after reform, this could open up a new avenue for local officials to cut corners.

## Local Governance in Transition

Since the first direct township election in Buyun, Sichuan, many experiments have been carried out to transform township governments. The latest round of township reform is the continuation of rural "tax and fee" reform that aims to restructure and reorientate township governments in order to improve rural governance. The elimination of rural tax has reduced direct conflict and

---

[21] For poorer townships that only have agriculture-based economy, the county transfer payment calculation is usually based on township agricultural tax before "tax and fee" reform.

[22] Author's interview with township officials, from 12 to 16 July 2010.

[23] Author's interview in Suizhou, Hubei, 15 July 2010.

confrontation between township governments and villagers, creating a situation in which township officials have fewer incentives to get in touch with local people.

The current township reform remains transitional as long as townships depend on county for financial support and officials remain disconnected from villagers whom they are supposed to serve. Local governance is undergoing a transformation from a predatory local state to "governance deficiency" at the township level.

Thus, the outcome of this reform largely depends on how the central government redefines the role of local government, particularly county and township governments. The central government has yet to present its blueprint for an integrated reform that restructures county and township governments. The current township reform will not enhance effective local governance insomuch as township governments remain the weakest in the Chinese administrative system. It is time to think about a fundamental revamp of local government by forgoing township-level government for township self-government. Township self-government will not only reduce administrative costs and inefficiency, but more importantly, incorporate social capital and participation for better local governance.

# 5

# Innovations in China's Local Governance

## An Assessment

XIA Ming*

*China's experimentations with innovative mechanisms at local levels to explore a politically safe pathway to democracy have so far failed to promote democratic governance in terms of both scale and scope.*

A "free and democratic China" was once a rallying cry for the Chinese communist revolution. In 1945, Chinese communist leader Mao Zedong once stated his ambition for a "free and democratic China": " 'A free and democratic China' will be a country where its governments of all levels up to the central government are produced by universal, equal, and confidential elections and the government is accountable to the people who elect it. It will follow Sun Yat-sen's 'three principles of the people', Lincoln's principle of 'government of the people, by the people and for the people', and Roosevelt's 'four freedoms'."[1] Based on the face value of his words, Mao endorsed a universalistic understanding of democracy.

In Deng Xiaoping's emphasis on "China's special characteristics" and economic development, democracy was regarded as a luxury for the Chinese within the foreseeable future. However, his successor Jiang Zemin's signature improvisation in front of a democratic audience — a recitation of Lincoln's Gettysburg speech[2] — showed that Jiang also had a universalistic understanding of democracy. Over time, the Communist Party of China (CPC) has shifted its position from a universal understanding of democracy to a class-based one (capitalist versus proletarian democracy)

---

*XIA Ming is Professor of Political Science at the City University of New York (Graduate Center and College of Staten Island).
[1] Translated from *The Collected Works of Mao Zedong,* vol. 4, People's Publishing House, Beijing, 1993, p. 27.
[2] Jiang Z, 2006, *The Collected Works of Jiang Zemin*, vol. 1, People's Publishing House, Beijing, 2006, at <http://cpc.people.com.cn/GB/64184/64185/180137/10818680.html#> (accessed 16 August 2012); Yang J, *Political Struggles during China's Reform Era*, Excellent Culture Press, Hong Kong, 2004, p. 266.

and finally to a culturally specific one (Western vs. Chinese democracy). Under Hu Jintao and Wen Jiabao (2003–), the pressure for democracy has mounted as China continues to rise economically. Furthermore, the Chinese government has formulated and promoted a discourse stating that democracy has two forms: a Western form and a Chinese socialist form. An official discourse on China's political reform comprises four arguments. First, democracy is a good thing; therefore, it is the ultimate goal for China. Second, the substantive contents of democracy and the strategy to achieve it in China differ from that of the West as China is subject to the "organic unity" of "the Party as the leadership, the people as the masters and rule of law".[3] Third, democratisation would be achieved through incremental changes, through "trials and pilot programmes" which would eventually add up to a mature democracy as like "from a concrete case to a broader application" (*congdian dao mian*).[4] Fourth, the Chinese government has the capacity for political innovation in order to lead China to a "socialist democracy with Chinese characteristics".

A good illustration comes from Yu Keping, an official-scholar and advisor to the government, who claims: "The CPC refuses to follow the path of Western-style democracy, being determined instead to follow the path of socialist democratic politics with Chinese characteristics."[5] The essential part of these characteristics is the "organic unity of the Party as the leadership, the people as the masters and the rule of law".[6] Since current economic development and Chinese democracy have complemented and nurtured each other well, as Yu has argued, China thus needs to improve its governance instead of carrying out structural changes. Under Chinese democracy with socialist characteristics, the Chinese government has actively encouraged innovation in political reform and has been working positively towards good governance. Although not without disagreement, the Chinese leaders and their advisors (Yu has been a leading mind) claim and try to convince the population that the sponsoring and initiation of innovations in local governance ("amounting to reform") will lead to the development and maturity of a specific kind of Chinese democracy. China will contribute a "vertical democracy" that has challenged the Western democracy to the world.[7]

## Local Innovations for Governance and Consequence

Numerous sizeable and hundreds of small scale experiments have been conducted in the political realm since the reforms were initiated. For example, since 2002, there have been about 115 cases identified from 1,500 proposals for innovating local governance having won the award for "innovations and excellence in local governance" (Table 1).

For a deeper analysis of local experiments and innovations, four national macro-cases have been selected: the Review and Assessment System, the Villagers' Committees and their Elections, non-governmental organisations (NGOs) and the Civil Society, and the "Small Government, Big Society" in Hainan. All of them were initiated in the 1980s, when Zhao Ziyang, as the premier and the Party secretary general, was pushing for the most far-reaching political structural reforms ever seen in Chinese communist history to date. Eight micro-cases (Table 2) were also selected for their high-profile publicity (mostly promoted by Yu Keping), which were implemented under the Jiang Zemin era (1997–2003) except for one under the Hu-Wen era (2003–).

The vicissitude of local reforms is reflected in changing political discourses. In China, all formal publications on politics/political science are from state-owned outlets and under the close scrutiny of the Party, specifically under the daily monitoring of the propaganda apparatus of all levels as what is published is highly political.

---

[3]Yu K, ed., *The Reform of Governance*, Leiden: Brill, 2010, p. 13.

[4]Ibid., p. 33.

[5]Ibid., p. 12.

[6]Ibid., p. 13.

[7]Naisbitt, J and D, *China's Megatrends: The Eight Pillars of a New Society*, Harper Business, New York, 2010.

**Table 1**   Number of Awards for "Innovations and Excellence in Local Chinese Governance" Received by Provinces and the Municipalities Under the Direct Leadership of the Central Government (2002–2011)

| Beijing | 7 | Shandong | 5 | Gansu | 0 | Hubei | 4 | Guangdong | 8 |
|---|---|---|---|---|---|---|---|---|---|
| Shanghai | 5 | Liaoning | 1 | Qinghai | 0 | Hunan | 2 | Guangxi | 6 |
| Chongqing | 3 | Jilin | 1 | Xinjiang | 3 | Sichuan | 11 | Hainan | 2 |
| Tianjin | 1 | Heilongjiang | 2 | Anhui | 2 | Xizang | 1 | | |
| Hebei | 6 | Neimenggu | 1 | Jiangsu | 10 | Guizhou | 3 | | |
| Henan | 2 | Shaanxi | 2 | Zhejiang | 18 | Yunnan | 2 | | |
| Shanxi | 0 | Ningxia | 2 | Jiangxi | 1 | Fujian | 4 | | |

*Source*: <www.Chinainnovations.org> (accessed 4 April 2011).

**Table 2**   Micro-Cases of Local Governance Innovations: Initiation and Current State

| Innovation/ Place | Current State and Remarks |
|---|---|
| Public Recommendation, Direct Election, 1998; The Central District, Suining, Sichuan | The innovation intended to make elections more democratic and participatory by allowing voters' nomination, direct election and campaigning to create the electoral connections between voters and government officials. In 2001, *Central Committee Document No. 21* clearly stated that those localities that had elected township heads by means of direct elections and direct voting by voters in the past had not acted in accordance with constitutional regulations or the organic law for local organisations. Sichuan province issued a special document to suspend the practice of electing township heads. |
| Democratic Forum, 1999, Wenling, Zhejiang | Facing the decreasing effectiveness of traditional control and paternalistic control with the masses, Chen Yimin, Section Chief of the Theory Section of the Wenling Municipal Propaganda Department, suggested trying a "democratic forum" to conduct an equal conversation-style communication with the citizens before making important decisions in 1999. In 2005, this practice was applied to the budget discussion in two township People's Congresses (PCs): either the randomly chosen citizens were invited to review the proposed government budget and to recommend their budget priorities, or, the members of the township PC were given the chance to do so. It still exists, but has only expanded to one county, Ninghai, within the province. The original Democratic Forum was narrowed down to focus only on the government budget issue. |
| Sea Election: Two-Ballot System, 1999, Dapeng Township, Shenzhen, Guangdong | It had the same intention as "Public Recommendation, Direct Election" above. Suspended after the Party Centre did not allow direct elections for township/county-level governments in 2004. The key officials who were responsible for it were transferred, which also confirms a Chinese saying: "The tea gets cold after the honourable ones are gone." |
| Appropriation based upon Democratic Selection, 2006, Huinan Township, Nanhui District, Shanghai | Starting from 2006 in Huinan township, the township government earmarked at least 15% of the total budget to the People's Deputies in the township PC to decide how to spend it and for which projects. It still exists but has failed to export to other provinces. The governments still do not want to reveal all items, especially those for maintaining stability and for the Party expenses. But in 2007, due to the budgetary crises at the township and village levels, the Chinese government introduced a new system: "the township budget being managed by the county (or urban district)," which placed the three reforms of the budgetary process in disagreement with the central policy. Scholars and practitioners involved in these reforms have shown their concern for the sustainability of local reforms of the budget at the township level. |
| Citizen's Voice Net, 2003, Wuhui, Anhu | It has survived three mayors and still exists today. It encountered many challenges: Lack of funding, bureaucratic delays and lethargy from other government departments (some refused to share information or respond to requests in an efficient manner); lack of authority to prod and to threaten; the core participants are mostly local elites, a digital gap made it less relevant to citizens at the lower order; the tight control over the Internet limits its effectiveness. The researchers who investigated this case carefully concluded: "To deepen the effort to build e-governance and to enhance the government capacity across the board for social service, |

*(Continued)*

**Table 2**   *(Continued)*

| Innovation/ Place | Current State and Remarks |
| --- | --- |
| | the entire structure of administrative management has to be reformed, the government flow chart realigned, and the information barrier among departments eliminated. We need interconnection, communication, and coordination among different jurisdictions and departments." |
| Yantian Model, 1999, Yantian Township, Shenzhen, Guangdong | To reconcile the logic of self-government for the community and bureaucratic control from the government, the Yantian district government designed a formula under which the residents committees are elected directly by the residents meetings where all residents, both with and without permanent residential registration, can cast votes; meanwhile, a community service station implements decisions from the residents committee and a community work station implements the government policies as an agency of the government. It has been continued in many other places, including Shanghai. The Party and government control of residents' councils is actually moving backwards against real autonomy at the grassroots level. |
| Eight-Step Work Procedure, 1999, Maliu Township, Kaixian County, Chongqing | Since 1999, the new leadership in Maliu Township responded to the rising tensions between the villagers and the government with regards to collecting fees and constructing public projects by creating an open budget and inviting villagers to decide how much money to raise from them and to supervise how it was spent. It had empowered people to defend their interests against predatory local governments. This was abandoned after the Party secretary was transferred out. |
| Separation of Three Administrative Powers, 2003, 2008, Shenzhen, Guangdong | Within the government (namely the executive branch), three functions are differentiated and given to decision-making, the executive and the supervisory boards respectively align with the goal of "small government, big society." Proposed in 2001 by scholars at Shenzhen University based upon the experiences in Hong Kong and Singapore, it was revealed to the public in 2003 by Shenzhen mayor Yu Youjun and a heated media debate stalled the reform. In 2008, the central government's reform of "larger ministries" and the endorsement of the principle of checks among the three administrative powers at the 17th Party Congress resuscitated the reform. Shenzhen officials brought it back but it has quickly fallen into limbo: it has not been openly tabled; neither has it been pushed for implementation. The downfall of Mayor Xu Zongheng, the supporter behind the reform, created a déjà vu: the first try failed due to the then mayor's transfer and corruption charges. The most difficult part of this reform is that Shenzhen is expected to "make an administrative breakthrough in the government without touching the political reform." |

*Source*: Prepared by the author.

Chinese social sciences have been characterised by "mobilisation publications", namely a sudden surge of writings on a specific theme in response to the Party's call. An examination of how papers in Chinese journals fared using the CNKI database (China National Knowledge) was conducted to gauge the changing outcome of political reforms.

Figure 1 shows the results of a key word search on the four macro-cases. Firstly, the 30-year political development has its high peaks and low valleys, obviously determined by booster or damper events in politics (Table 3). Based on the Four Cardinal Principles (the catch-phrase for conservatism) as a comparison, its two high peaks happened in 1986 and 1990 respectively, corresponding with the anti-bourgeois liberalisation campaign and the Tiananmen crackdown. After Deng's death in 1997 when Jiang Zemin indisputably took full charge, the conservative influence in China's political development has been on the skids and this tendency only slowed down in the post-Olympic era. The discourse on both Civil Society and Villagers' Self-Government was less significant in the 1990s. The former had a breakthrough in 2001 and reached a peak in 2002 thanks to Jiang's "Three Represents" theory and his intention to keep China's development abreast with the changing times and the rest of the world (*yu shi ju jin, yu shi ju jin*). The turning point for the Villagers' Self-Government discourse happened in 1998 after Jiang called for the development of grassroots democracy.

Secondly, the discursive gap between Civil Society/Villagers' Self-Government and the Four Cardinal Principles has been widening for decades, which indicates the strong trend of liberalisation

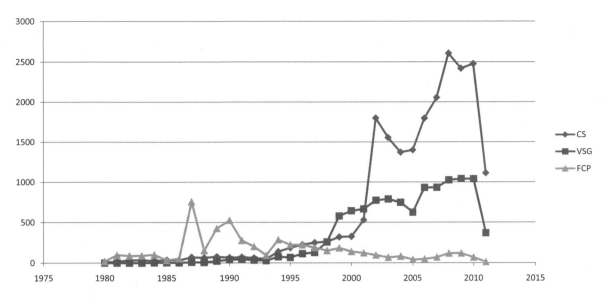

**Figure 1** Papers in Chinese Journals (Limited to the Mainland) on Civil Society, Villagers' Self-Government, and the Four Cardinal Principles (1980–2010)

*Note*: CS: Civil Society; VSG: Villagers' Self-Government; FCP: Four Cardinal Principles.

*Source*: Compiled by the author based upon CNKI search. The year 2011 has six-month data.

**Table 3** Boosters and Dampers in Chinese Political Development

| Boosters (Sluice-opening Events) | Dampers (Sluice-closing Moments) |
|---|---|
| 1979–1982 — From the "liberation of thought" to the making of the new constitution. | October 1983 — Anti-spiritual contamination |
| | 1986 — Anti-bourgeois liberalisation |
| 1987 — The Political Report of the 13th Party Congress on Political Reform | 1989 — Tiananmen crackdown and political succession |
| 1992 — Deng Xiaoping's southern tour | 1997 — Death of Deng, Jiang Zemin's political succession completed |
| 1997.09 — 15th CPC National Congress: Jiang Zemin's call for grassroots democracy | 1999 — Clampdown on the Falun Gong |
| 2000.02 — Jiang proposed the "Three Represents" theory | 2003 — Political successions |
| | 2003–2004 — "Colour Revolutions" in Georgia and Ukraine |
| 2002.11 — 16th CPC National Congress calling for inter Party democracy, continued emphasis on "three represents", allowing private entrepreneurs to join the CPC. | 2008.08 — Post-Olympic era |
| | 2008 — Reactions to the global financial crisis and the "Charter 08 Movement" |
| 2007.10 — 17th CPC National Congress calling for "systems for grassroots level autonomy". | 2010.11 — Reaction to Liu Xiaobo's award of Nobel Peace Prize |
| 2008 — Reform of "Larger Ministries" | 2011 — "Jasmine Revolutions" in the Middle East. |

*Source*: Created by the author.

in the Chinese academic world, presumably partially reflecting the political tempo of the entire society. If the trends of Chinese political discourse are taken as a good barometer, local reforms and innovations in the political realm can be argued to have been tenacious, but opportunistic by edging forward when the political climate allows, and vulnerable to sudden changes of ideological policies and personnel politics (Table 3). However, the overall trend demonstrates an encouraging "two steps forward and one step back" pattern. Thirdly, the year 2008 witnessed a conservative turn of Chinese politics: Civil Society discourse passed its highest ever point and is on the decline; the Villagers' Self-Government discourse has reached a plateau; and the Four Cardinal Principles has struggled to move ahead (Figure 2). As part of this conservative turn, in 2011, Zhou Benshun, deputy director of the CPC Central Comprehensive Management Commission and general secretary of the Central

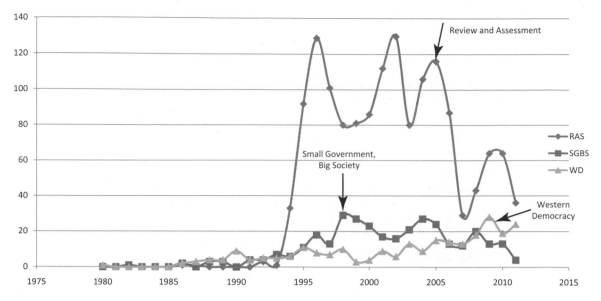

**Figure 2**    Papers in Chinese Journals (Limited to the Mainland) on "Review and Assessment", "Small Government" and "Western Democracy"

*Source*: Compiled by the author based upon CNKI search. The year 2011 has six-month data.

Political and Legal Commission, explicitly wrote in *Jiushi* (Seeking Truth, the CPC theoretical magazine) that the principle of "Small Government, Big Society" and civil society as the "third realm" are two "faux pas" (*wu qu*). He also warned about the "trap of civil society" set up by the West and the threat of "social organisations with evil intention".[8]

The Chinese political development has had a conspicuous "stop-and-go" pattern. One unique phenomenon has appeared in local innovations for good governance: "blossom and wilt, but bear no fruit," namely, local governments nationwide have experimented with many new mechanisms and practices to improve the quality of governance, but many macro-level cases wilted after several years. Micro-level cases too were suspended after several years with none having been popularised at a national level (Table 2). *The Chinese Democratisation Index Report* (2011) has made the following conclusion with regards to all local innovations recognised by the Innovations in Local Governance Award during the past 10 years: "Almost the absolute majority of awarded innovations have had difficulty surviving and many simply disappeared. The number of innovations has also decreased."[9]

### Explanations for Snag in China's Pathway to Democracy

When comparing China's parallel political and economic transitions, it was observed that the political arena has failed to replicate the successful experiences of China's economic development. Chinese political development did not result in a synergy between local and central governments. One success of China's economic development was the assured patronage of top leaders when local experiments promised new directions and breakthroughs. The top leadership thus acted as a "midwife" at opportune moments to assist in the smooth birth of new ideas and nurture their growth at the national level. Deng Xiaoping played such a role in both the "Household Responsibility system" in the countryside (the Xiaogang Village Revolution) and the "Special

---

[8]Zhou B, "Take a New Path of Social Management with Chinese Characteristics", *Qiushi*, 16 May 2011, at <http://www.qstheory.cn/zxdk/2011/2011010/201105/t20110513_80501.htm> (accessed 25 June 2012).

[9]The Research Group of the Chinese Democratisation Index Report, *The Chinese Democratisation Index Report*, World and China Institute, Beijing, 2011, p. 26.

Economic Zones" in the coastal areas (the Shenzhen Revolution). Thereafter through the 1992 Southern Tour and Zhu Rongji's reforms, Deng was instrumental in facilitating the liberalisation of price and the privatisation of ownership, two benchmarks of a market economy.[10]

The political development in China has not found either a midwife or a patron who can muster the necessary political resources and navigate through difficult factional power struggles to push forward democratic development. Although there were some efforts to form some kind of symbiosis between the top leadership and local innovations, two problems still persist. Firstly, in contrast to paramount leader Deng, the advocates for political development lack political clout to influence the decision-making apparatus, being relatively low in rank. For example, Peng Zhen clearly acted as a midwife and patron for the Villagers Committee election. As the dynamo behind People's Congress expansion and the patron for the villagers' self-government, Peng was ranked sixth in the mid-1980s when his career was at its peak. Tian Jiyun, the advocate for "Review and Assessment", had never entered the circle of top 10 power elites. Both had never joined the most powerful organ of the Party — the Standing Committee of the Politburo.

Secondly, history shows that even if a leader of certain standing advocates political reform, new initiatives will not be expanded upon if the number one leader is cautious and unlikely to throw his weight behind the reform. For example, Zhao Ziyang, a secretary general; Wen Jiabao, a premier; and Zeng Qinghong, a vice president of the state, have been reform-minded and bold in pushing for new experiments in the political realm. Unfortunately, their limited political power did not permit them to jump-start political liberalisation. Regrettably, Zhao's blueprint for political reform, Zeng's interest in social democracy and Wen's repeated calls for political reforms have produced no tangible results.

The absence of a Socratic midwife in the political front is due to multiple reasons. The primary one is the unique world view of the top leaders. The current leadership suffers a huge cognitive gap between its understanding of democracy and its urgency in Chinese development. Their formative years were traumatised by "the Great Leap Forward", "the Great Famine" and "the Great Proletarian Cultural Revolution" in an isolated totalitarian regime. To compare them to their predecessors (Deng and Jiang) and successors (Xi Jinping and Li Keqiang), they are mostly closed-minded and less ambitious. Hu Jintao has been known for his extreme cautious attitude and his reluctance to take the role of midwife to assist in the birth of political innovation. To compare him to Deng Xiaoping and even to Jiang Zemin, Hu pales in terms of political wisdom, courage and vision. It is difficult to expect any political initiative from him.

The second obstacle arises from the current decision-making mechanism. Due to vested interests, in particular from the big state-owned enterprises (energy, communication and manufacturing industries as well as financial institutions) and the control cartel (the army, public and state security apparatus), a consensus is required within the CPC Politburo Standing Committee before any major decision can be made. Since every member has veto power over major decisions, the top elite of the nine Standing Committee members has fallen into a gridlock. Inertia, instead of initiative, has been the major feature of the Hu-Wen years. The lethargic response towards local political innovations has become especially damaging when China needs visionary leadership to respond to complex social, economic and political challenges, especially after 2008.

The third is the frequent transfer of local leaders which often disrupts local innovation. Since all reforms tend to chip away the existing system or bend some old rules, their continued existence and development depend on the courage and vision of both the local reformers and their patrons. The personnel changes (transfer, promotion, demotion or retirement) often leave local innovations unattended or ignored as new leaders launch new projects to claim credit, while local innovations initiated by their predecessors tend to wither away.

The fourth is that the middle class in China, like many East Asian countries during rapid economic growth, hesitates to challenge the state for increased democratic rights. The Chinese

[10]Xia M, *The Dual Developmental State: Development Strategy and Institutional Arrangements for China's Transition*, Ashgate, Aldershot, UK, 2000, ch. 3.

state-dominated reform has created an urban middle class (government functionaries, professionals and business people) who are highly dependent on the state. So far this group of people have not demonstrated strong independent-mindedness against state control as the growth machine is able to generate prosperity at least in the coastal areas and urban regions. The conservative and inactive middle class has yet to generate the required societal push for immediate structural change.

From Deng Xiaoping to Jiang Zemin, two local innovations, the Shenzhen model and Pudong model in Shanghai, have led China's economic development. The Wenzhou (Zhejiang) model, which was developed at a later stage and has been characterised by a spontaneous market order and private entrepreneurship, stands in contrast to this state-guided strategy. During his tenures as Party secretary of both Zhejiang and Shanghai, Xi Jinping had endorsed the Wenzhou model, which is similar to Hainan's "Small Government, and Big Society", for China's future course; this augurs well for possible further liberalisation in China. Bo Xilai, former Party secretary in Chongqing, had complicated the political landscape by stirring up an unconventional populist local innovation, the Chongqing model. For its emphasis on the role of a strong individual leader and the utility of Maoism and Maoist practices for social equity, it was criticised indirectly by Wen Jiabao who indicated that the "lingering effect of Chinese feudalism" and "the poisonous residue of Cultural Revolution" are still two major threats to China's further reform.[11] To some extent, China's future direction towards either a Maoist or a liberal direction has been swayed by Bo's falling from power, which ended the competition between the two local models: Wenzhou model versus Chongqing model.

The eventual demise of many local innovations towards democracy is due to the lack of support, or the resistance and intervention from the central government or the Party centre. There are at least four obstacles to China's response to the democratic challenge: ideological conservatism, institutional gridlock at the top leadership, lack of courage and vision of Hu Jintao, and resistance of vested interests against any changes to the status quo. Together, they have made orderly, top-down democratisation elusive. Despite some attempts from the reform-minded wing of the Party (e.g. Wen Jiabao), the stability-maintainers have been able to block any substantive and qualitative moves towards democracy (see Table 2 as an illustration). In the last two decades of the 20th century, the people in Huarong county, Hunan province have already learned an important lesson with regards to political innovation: "Without reform at the top, reform at the bottom will always be reversed; reform conducted in my jurisdiction without reciprocation from others will be a waste of time; reform which does not open up opportunity for cadres is a mess-up; if the block has started reform, but the line leading to the top does not change, reform will bring in disaster."[12] The message from this local wisdom still applies today: a systemic national top-down change is needed instead of the bottom-up local piece-meal innovations.

## China's Democratisation Uncertain

Elections and votes in a democratic system are almost equivalent to price mechanism and ownership (property rights) in a market economy. As long as people have the ownership of votes in political life and the electoral mechanism to cast their votes for the people who could govern with accountability, the country is considered a democracy. However, the current discourse on Chinese democracy has rejected the core idea of democracy; namely, political accountability of the

---

[11] On 23 April 2011, Wen Jiabao said the following words in a meeting with Wu Jianmin from Hong Kong: "The obstacle to the reforms on the mainland (sic) mainly comes from two forces: one is the lingering effect of Chinese feudalism, and the other is the poisonous residue of Cultural Revolution". See "Wen Jiabao confronting Bo Xilai: The Chongqing model is forced to cool off" at <http://www.aboluowang.com/news/data/2011/0508/article_124382.html> (accessed 25 June 2012).

[12] The original Chinese version is as follows: "Xiagai shang bugai, gaile yao chonggai; wogai ni bugai, gaile ye baigai; ganbu wu chulu, gaile shi hugai; kuaigai tiao bugai, gaile fan shouhai".

ruling party must be based upon electoral connections. The lack of electoral connections between the ruling party and the people casts doubt upon the Chinese official discourse on democracy. It is obvious that there has been an unquenchable quest and ceaseless attempts for democratic practices at the grassroots level, which invalidates the official pretext for delaying democratisation by arguing that the Chinese people are not culturally ready and do not have the adequate qualities for democracy. Instead, "an understanding of the inevitability and necessity of developing democratic elections" by the leaders is needed and needs to be deepened along with economic and social developments.[13]

Yu Keping has this ideal: "The government is the state's preeminent political authority. It remains located at the centre of civil and political life and public governance. It is the locomotive driving society forward, and officials are in the political driver's seat."[14] Unfortunately under Hu Jintao, this is not the case. The stagnation or miscarriages of all aforementioned cases on national and local political innovations have been attributed by Chinese scholars to the bigger structural forces from the centre. Some Chinese scholars believe that under the CPC leadership (which includes its control over the army, the cadre and the media) and a centralising political structure, real political reform can be carried out to create an authentic democracy.[15] In reality, the communist leadership (an indisputable privilege inscribed in the constitution) in the current power matrix has often been the incompatible and impossible partner to both "the people as masters" and 'the rule of law". At both the discursive and institution levels, China's officially sanctioned democracy is full of contradictions, which will ultimately turn into a pseudo-democratic shenanigan and a killer to the genuine attempts at building democracy in China. Therefore, the "organic unity" laid down by the communist leadership has actually turned into an "impossible trinity".

Though findings have attributed the failure of local innovations in democracy to major obstacles arising from the inadequacy of national law and the Party's omnipotent and omnipresent power in political system, the Chinese top leadership is still reluctant to initiate structural reforms to nurture a democratic transition. In the National People's Congress (NPC) meeting in March 2011, Wu Bangguo, the chairman of the NPC Standing Committee, said so six times in response to questions about China's move towards Western democracy: "No rotation of power among multiple parties, no pluralism in the guiding principle of the country, no separation of three powers, no bicameralism, no federalism, and no privatisation." If the bridge to democracy has already been built by Western thinkers and practised by the majority of countries in the world, it is unwise for the Chinese leadership to insist on "crossing the river by groping for stones". As political dissent is not tolerated, "the harmonious society" has degenerated into a "harmonising society". Understandably some Chinese scholars have announced the death of reform and the beginning of political trickery (*zheng zhi hu you*).[16] Wen's lonely and fruitless voice for political reform has been misconstrued as "acting" due to the conspicuous gap between his rhetoric and delivery.

Samuel Huntington once commented: "Economic development makes democracy possible; political leadership makes it real."[17] After three decades of rapid economic growth, the ball now is in the court of Zhongnanhai. The top Chinese leaders have started talking about a "top design in the superstructure" that is needed for China's development. The question is when the top design will be ready. Most China observers do not expect too much from the current leadership. Thus any major breakthrough in meaningful top-down political reform will depend upon how the Bo Xilai and Wang Lijun case would be handled since the results of factional competition between the Wenzhou model

[13] Huang W and Chen J in Yu, 2010, p. 91.

[14] Ibid., p. 24.

[15] Zhou T et al, *The Assault of a Fortified Position: A Research Report of Political Structural Reform in China after the 17th Congress*, Shengchan Jianshe bingtuan chubanshe, Xinjiang, 2007, pp. 6–9.

[16] Wu G 2008. "Where is China heading for under two policies at all costs", 16 December 2008 at <http://www.chinesepen.org/Article/sxsy/200812/Article_20081216213352. shtml> (accessed 16 August 2012).

[17] Huntington, S, *The Third Wave: Democratization in the Late Twentieth Century*, Norman, OK: University of Oklahoma Press, 1991, p. 316.

endorsed by Xi Jinping and the Chongqing model advocated by Bo Xilai point to two different directions for China's political economy. It may have to wait for the next generation of leadership at the 18th Party Congress in 2012. However, social forces (e.g. the irreversible expansion of civil society and the emergence of oppositional forces such as the Charter 08 movement led by Nobel laureate Liu Xiaobo) have become more restive for a bottom-up change. A race between the Chinese ruling elite and social forces will determine the manner and direction of China's democratisation.

# 6

# The Impact of Market on the Grassroots Organisations of the Chinese Communist Party

Lance L P GORE*

*Chinese reforms have eroded the institutional foundation of the CCP's grassroots organisations. Marketisation is redefining the relationship between Party organisations and Party members and weakening the organisational integrity of the Leninist party.*

By any measure, the Chinese Communist Party (CCP) is the largest political party in the world. At the end of 2010, its membership reached 80.27 million, more than double the 37 million in 1978 when the post-Mao reform era began. It rivals the population of a major nation. Were it a nation, the CCP would have ranked the 17th most populous out of the 196 countries of the world. The percentage of Party members in the population had also inched up from less than 0.9% in 1949 when the CCP came to power to almost 6% in 2010.

Membership-wise, today's CCP is very much a product of the reform era. Figure 1 indicates that at the end of 2008 Party members who joined the Party in the reform era (after October 1976) took the lion's share of the total Party membership — 72.29% or 54.89 million. In comparison, the revolutionary generation (those who joined the Party before 1 October 1949, when the People's Republic of China was founded) had shrunk to less than 1% (0.97%, or roughly 733,000). The Cultural Revolution generation (those who joined the Party between 1966 and 1976) accounted for 16% and those who joined before the Cultural Revolution, 11%.

The growth of Party membership has stabilised in recent years at around 2.5% per annum. However, the growth of the CCP carries with it tremendous momentum and is set to continue in the foreseeable future. At the end of 2010, the CCP had 3.892 million grassroots organisations — 187,000 grassroots Party committees (the lowest level of Party committees), 242,000

*Lance L P GORE is Visiting Senior Research Follow at the East Asian Institute, National University of Singapore.

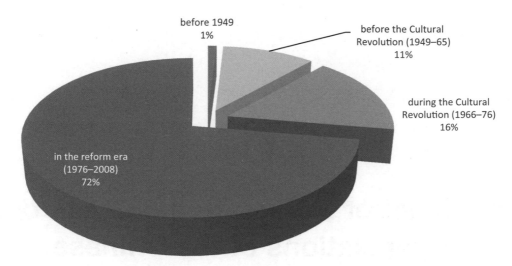

**Figure 1**    Membership Composition by Time Period of Joining The Party (2008)

*Source*: COD "Intra-party statistics communiqué, 2008". *People's Daily*, July

general branches and 3.463 million branches.[1] The Party constitution mandates that these grassroots organisations recruit new members regularly, and even if each of these grassroots organisations recruits only one new member a year, the net growth of the Party would be well over two million.

The organisations of the ruling party are like a giant fishnet that spans the entire social landscape of China, penetrating every corner of the economy and society in addition to tightly gripping state power. Table 1 indicates the extent to which various categories of organisations in China have been penetrated by the CCP at the grassroots level. On the surface, it appears the Chinese state remains very much a party-state and the CCP seems to continue to live in its past legacy in a time capsule. However, the market has fundamentally eroded this organisational structure and altered the nature of the Party's grassroots organisations; it is redefining the meaning of being a Party member. To understand the impact of the market, we need to look first at the basic characteristics of the communist rule.

## Basic Characteristics of Communist Rule

The CCP has retained the basic structure of a Leninist party. It is organised as a giant pyramid, with committees, branches, groups and other types of Party organisations both in and outside the government. Figure 2 outlines the overall organisational structure of the party. It shows that, above the grassroots level, the overall structure of the Party (the right side above the village level) closely parallels the structure of the government (the left side above the village level), with Party cells embedded in government bureaucracies. As a general rule, the Party (i.e. its committees at various levels) makes major policy decisions while the government implements those decisions. The Party groups (*dangzu*) which are embedded in the government bureaucracies ensure that the Party's policies get implemented. At the grassroots level, Party cells also penetrate virtually all organisations of significant size or importance in society.

The communism is also characterised by "micro-rule". The Party controls not only the government but also, through its grassroots organisations, almost all other organisations in society, such as a factory, a school, a hospital, a research institute, a village, an urban community, a unit of

---

[1] Press release by Wang Q, deputy director of the Central Organisation Department of the CCP on 24 June 2011, <http://cpc.people.com.cn/GB/74838/137931/225181/index.htm.> (accessed 12 July 2012).

**Table 1**   The Rate of Party Coverage at Grassroots Level

|  | Total Number of Administrative Units | Total Number of Party Organisations | Rate of Penetration % |
|---|---|---|---|
| Townships and Towns | 34,324 | 34,321 | 99.99 |
| Communities (*Shequ*) | 79,000 | 78,000 | 98.74 |
| Villages | 606,000 | 605,000 | 99.83 |
| Enterprises | 2,634,000 | 595,000 | 22.59 |
| *State-owned* | 249,000 | 216,000 | 86.75 |
| *Private* | 2,385,000 | 380,000 | 15.93 |
| Non-profit organisations[a] | 578,000 | 464,000 | 80.28 |
| *Colleges/Universities* | 1,622 | 1,622 | 100.00 |
| *Research Institutes* | 7,982 | 7,765 | 97.28 |
| NGOs [b] | 81,000 | 12,000 | 14.81 |

*Notes*: [a] *Shiye danwei.* [b] *Minban feiqiye danwei.*
*Source:* Central Organisation Department: *"Dangnei tongji gongbao"* (Communiqué of Intra-party Statistics). Xinhua News Agency, 1 July 2009.

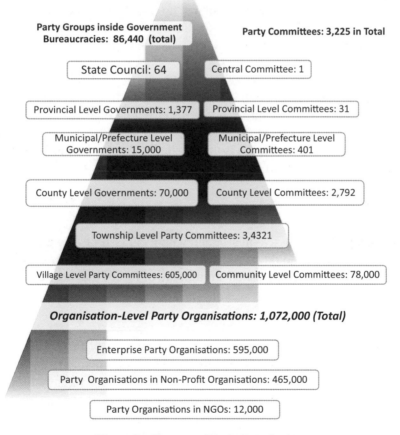

**Figure 2**   Structure of Party Organisations

*Source*: Press release by Wang Q, deputy director of the Central Organisation Department of the CCP on 24 June 2011, <http://cpc.people.com.cn/GB/74838/137931/225181/index.html> (accessed 12 July 2012).

the military, and so on. These organisations are customarily referred to as *danwei* (or "work unit"). The Party cells resident in *danwei* used to be (in many cases still are) the "centre of leadership", running *danwei* on behalf of the ruling party. The power and prestige of Party organisations are derived from their control of public, corporate and other types of administration at the national, local, as well as grassroots levels. In other words, the CCP rule consists of not only its control over state power but also the micro-level domination of *danwei* by Party cells. In the Mao era, most *danwei* were either created or incorporated by the party-state, allowing the latter unchallenged authoritative claims over them. The embedded Party cell represented the interests, objectives and policies of the party-state; they allowed the authority of the Party to reach from the top of the government to the shop floor of a factory.

The individual's dependence upon his or her work unit used to be total. Because of the Maoist suppression of the market, the Chinese work unit took on an extensive array of social functions and was responsible for key aspects of the lives of its members. It strived to provide some or all of the following services to its members: employment, schools for the children of the employees, medical care facilities, housing, grocery stores, barbershops, sports and entertainment facilities, public baths, transportation, security service, cafeteria or dining halls, and even the employment of the younger generation of *danwei* members, all being either danwei-subsidised or of member-only access. Because cross-*danwei* mobility is very limited in the Mao era, the Chinese work unit had a tendency to become a self-contained miniature society. This "organised dependency"[2] of the individuals upon their *danwei* and through *danwei* upon the entire communist system was an effective leverage with which the party exercised domination over the entire population. To a great extent, such institutional arrangement is designed to run a planned economy. *Danwei* were embedded in the structure of the party-state and functioned as the implementers of the planning directives issued by the planning apparatuses of the party-state to allocate resources in the absence of the market.

However, the flipside of the micro-rule of the CCP is the dependence of Party organisations on *danwei* for power and prestige. A Party cell is "in power" only when it runs a functional organisation (*danwei*). These organisations are in turn the "carriers" (*zaiti*) of Party organisations. It was the durability or permanency of *danwei* in the pre-reform era that undergirded the stability of Party organisations at the grassroots level. And it is the erosion of *danwei* by market forces in the reform era that throws these organisations off balance.

## The Political Impact of the Market

It is only natural that a party so massive in size and with its grassroots organisations so extensively embedded in the society that it should be profoundly affected by a market-driven socio-economic transformation. Marketisation has unleashed a multitude of forces that are pulling apart the Party's grassroots organisations.

### General Impact

What the post-Mao reform has done politically is, first and foremost, the dismantling of the organised dependency. The Party's power is premised upon its monopoly of resources and opportunities through the *danwei* system. The emergence of the market as a competing mechanism of resource allocation undermines this monopoly. Marketisation drains resources from Party control, develops new resource base and opens up new opportunities outside the organisational grip of the Party. The individual can now have a career and a life outside party-state control; he or she no longer needs to rely on the party-state for a job, a living quarter, or for vital supplies such as

---

[2]Walder, A, 1986, *Communist Neo-Traditionalism: Work and Authority in Chinese Industry*. Berkeley: University of California Press.

food, clothing, health care, education services and so on — he or she can satisfy these needs readily and without hassle from the market. Marketisation causes the unloading of many of the roles performed by *danwei* to the market and the corresponding transfer of resources from within the *danwei* system to the open market.

A state-owned enterprise (SOE) producing for the market ceases to be a *danwei* in the classic sense; it is transformed into a business that hires and fires workers on a regular basis in response to market conditions. It is detached from the supply network of the party-state and must struggle for survival in the competitive marketplace. The market has thus replaced state planning as the main mechanism of resource allocation in society and thereby changed the rules of the game. The result is either a disintegration of *danwei* or their transformation into market-based organisations, melting down the institutional foundation of the Party's micro-rule and throwing the millions of the Party's grassroots organisations off balance. Without controlling the administration and resources of the "carrier" organisations, it would be difficult for Party cells to attract new members; nor would they be able to uphold the strict organisational hierarchy and discipline that is the trademark of a Leninist party. It is especially true of the CCP today when value or ideological consensus is no longer attainable in a pluralising society. Without the rewards afforded by the administrative power and resource control of the "carrier" organisations, the Party has no leverage over its members and therefore cannot count on their loyalty to maintain the Party's organisational integrity.

Inevitably the increasing importance of professionalism, the technical and technocratic competence, and entrepreneurship — the essential ingredients of modernisation — diminish the importance of Party membership in an individual's career success. The development of the job market also undermines the CCP's control over human resources. In short, the loss of its monopoly over resources and rewards in society has caused a subtle but fundamental change in the relationship between Party organisations and Party members. The Party has to compete with multiple sources of rewards to attract a following.

### *Impact on the Party in Rural Areas*

One of the consequences of the market-driven socio-economic transformation is the massive exodus of labour from the rural areas. For 30 years the younger, better-educated and more talented villagers have been leaving in droves to pursue non-farming opportunities in cities and the coastal belt. The result is a massive bleeding of the rural human resources. In many areas of the major labour-exporting provinces (such as Jiangxi, Sichuan, Hunan, Anhui and Henan) the countryside is virtually abandoned to the old, the sick, women and children, or left idle because of labour shortage. The bleeding also dries up the candidate pool of new Party members and creates a shortage of younger Party members to staff village-level Party organisations. In addition, an "old Party secretary syndrome" was widely reported from rural China. It refers to the phenomenon of one person serving as village Party secretary for decades (such as the one in Wukan village, Guangdong, where a recent large-scale peasant protest attracted worldwide attention). These old Party secretaries attempt to block the younger and more talented people from joining the Party for fear of being disposed. This is because they usually have few marketable skills or business talent and have to guard whatever meagre benefits that are vested in their positions.

The rural Party is also facing stiff competition from revitalised kinship, religious and even criminal organisations. Many village Party branches have become subservient to these organisations and to their interests and objectives. Village elections have also introduced a new dynamic into village politics that tends to undermine the legitimacy and authority of the village Party. The combined effect is the gradual "hollowing out" of the village Party.

### *Impact on Party Organisations in Business Enterprises*

The presence of Party organisations inside SOEs is the legacy of the micro-rule of the CCP in the planned economy era. However, once becoming businesses operating in the marketplace, even SOEs are forced to play by market rules and adopt market practices and institutions. This tends to diminish Party organisations in businesses. Party organisations are often marginalised if they cannot reinvent themselves and find a role that contributes to business survival. Cutting back on Party organisations and personnel in many SOEs is widely reported.

Unlike *danwei*, businesses are inherently unstable; they are in perpetual flux and can go bust anytime. Their instability causes the unsustainability of Party organisations embedded in them. In private businesses, the capitalist owners are wary or even hostile to the organisational presence of a communist party; when forced to do so, the owners often seek to serve concurrently as Party secretary and monopolise Party positions with their families or friends. For these reasons, the rate of Party penetration is the lowest in private businesses as shown in Table 1. Furthermore, the Party secretaries and Party affairs staff seek to pursue their careers in the direction of business executives, engineers, technicians, or any other professionals that would allow them to develop marketable skills; by doing so they neglect Party work. The development of the labour market puts considerable constraints on the Party's practice of appointing enterprise cadres (managers) because market competition tends to enforce the market criteria of human resources over the Party's political and ideological standards for appointment and promotion. The existence of market opportunities has also caused many SOE cadres to bolt from the Party's control into the human resources market — a "brain drain" for the Party.

The CCP has dealt with these problems with a strategy of "mutual penetration and interlocking appointments", that is, top executives sitting on the Party committee and top Party personnel joining the management team or chair the board. Predictably, the Party secretaries and Party affairs workers will always focus on the business side of their appointments to the negligence of Party work; Party organisations are thus effectively assimilated into business management. The political meddling by the CCP in enterprises has resulted in perhaps the most complex corporate governance structure known — the so-called "three olds versus three news" (*lao san hui, xin san hui*). The governance of the SOEs is a hybrid of three old communist institutions (the Party committee, the trade union, and the conference of workers' representatives) and three new capitalist institutions (board of directors, board of supervisors and shareholders conference).

### Party Organisations in the Mobile Population

The disintegration of the *danwei* system has created a mobile society. China's mobile population consists of not only migrant peasant workers but also increasingly the professionals and white-collar workers of urban origin. There are millions of communist party members among them who have lost contact with their home Party cells. The communities where they aggregate are part of the new social spaces created by the market. The greatest challenge of party-building is the fluidity and anonymity of these communities of strangers. Local Party authorities often do not have a clue as to how many Party members live in these communities and how to reorganise and reincorporate them into the organisational hierarchy of the Party.

On their part, these Party members often do not have the incentive to be reconnected with the Party — they enjoy the freedom of living in anonymity and are glad to be rid of Party disciplines and obligations such as Party meetings and study sessions. Local Party authorities often have to use the police registries to find out who are the Party members in their community, or to lure them from their hideouts with free services such as job referrals and consultancy — Party organisations have little leverage over these mobile members who make a living on the market.

Party cells formed out of total strangers who follow different careers and divergent daily routines are but a shadow of the Party cells in a stable *danwei*. The footloose attribute of Party members in the community and their lack of organic relations to each other, as well as the absence of a solid organisational base that *danwei* used to provide, are constantly eroding whatever that has been accomplished in community party-building.

### *The Party and College Students*

One "bright spot" for the CCP is its apparent success in recruiting college students. In 2008, for example, matriculated college students accounted for only 1.6% of the national population but contributed to 38% of new Party members. In contrast, peasants constituted 55% of the population but contributed only 20% of new Party members. A college student is 67 times more likely to be recruited into the communist party than a peasant. College students are also among the most eager in the Chinese society in seeking Party membership.

In spite of the impressive recruitment results, party-building on college campuses is also deeply impacted by the market environment. College students seeking to join the Party are motivated by diverse considerations, many at odds with the Party's principles and objectives. For college students whose future is filled with many possibilities and contingencies, membership in the ruling party is one of many factors to consider when making post-graduation career plans. Party membership may give them some advantages in certain careers. And for a successful career with the party-state, which is still the most desired career choice among college graduates, it is a prerequisite.

"Job advantage" is one motive for joining the Party found in many studies conducted by Party affairs researchers in China. The rapid expansion of college enrolment following the Asian financial crisis in 1997 began to exert enormous pressure on the job market four years later. In 2010, 6.2 million fresh college graduates entered the job market; adding the graduates of previous years still on the job market, as many as 10 million college-educated young people are active on the job market currently. College graduates who are CCP members tend to be quicker in finding jobs and often better jobs too. Many employers, not only SOEs and state-owned non-profit organisations, but also private and foreign businesses, seem to have developed a preference for Party member graduates. There is a simple reason for this phenomenon: the CCP's elitist approach to party recruitment. By the time college students graduate, most of the best and brightest among them have been herded into the Party through a long process starting from the elementary school — good students win prizes and these prizes in turn attract Party recruiters. As a result, Party membership becomes a reliable indicator of quality — not necessarily ideological or political quality, but quality in terms of knowledge, skills and leadership capability. It is a strange twist in the spontaneous adjustment of the job market to the communist polity.

## The Market's Continuous Challenges to the CCP

The impact wrought on the organisations of the CCP by the market-driven social transformation is serious, pervasive and of long-term significance. The transition to a market economy is melting down not only the "iron rice bowl" concept of employment but also the micro-rule of the CCP grassroots organisations; there is no longer a stable base of "carriers" for them to continue their traditional form of existence and operation. Marketisation has created a completely new socio-economic reality to which the CCP has to adjust its rule.

In a fluid and fast-changing market environment, the CCP faces the challenge of finding new forms of existence and new ways of exercising power. While an extensive organisational infrastructure is necessary to run a planned economy, a market economy has its own mechanisms for economic transactions. Party organisations under a unified leadership and clear chains of command at least in theory can play a role to integrate the national economy and coordinate economic activities in a planned economy; in a market economy, however, such organisations serve no apparent purpose other than an ill-considered fear of losing power. The Party's effort at

**Table 2**   Size Comparison of the Ruling Communist Parties in the Mid-1980s

| Party | Size of Membership (1,000) | As Share of the Population (%) |
|---|---|---|
| Korean Workers' Party (North Korea) | 3,200 | 16.0 |
| Communist Party of Romania | 3,500 | 15.4 |
| Communist Party of Czechoslovakia | 1,670 | 15.4 |
| Socialist Unity Party of Germany (East Germany) | 3,300 | 13.8 |
| Communist Party of Bulgaria | 930 | 10.4 |
| League of Communists of Yugoslavia | 2,200 | 9.5 |
| Hungarian Socialist Workers' Party | 870 | 8.2 |
| Communist Party of the Soviet Union | 19,000 | 7.0 |
| Communist Party of Cuba | 700 | 6.4 |
| Polish Unified Workers Party | 2,120 | 5.7 |
| Albania Party of Labour | 140 | 4.7 |
| Mongolian People's Revolutionary Party | 88 | 4.6 |
| Chinese Communist Party[a] | 47,750 | 4.2 |
| Communist Party of Vietnam | 2,200 | 2.9 |
| Lao People's Revolutionary Party | 84 | 1.7 |

*Note*: [a]CCP figures are for 1987.

*Source*: *Xiandai zhijie zhengdang*, Beijing: Qiushi chubanshe, 1989, cited in Rang Y, "An Exploration on Controlling the Number of Party Members", *Hunan Shangxueyuan xuebao*, no. 3, 2002, pp. 92–93.

rebuilding and maintaining an expansive network of grassroots organisations that penetrates every corner of society is costly and in many cases, simply impossible. With the dismantling of "organised dependence" and the transformation of incentives of Party members, these organisations can no longer be expected to deliver the same service or loyalty to the Party. Instead, they increase the Party's exposure to the society at a time when the Party is widely subject to criticism of corruption.

Size is no guarantee for the perpetuation of the Party's rule. Table 2 demonstrates that many former communist regimes had much higher party-member to population ratios in the mid-1980s but collapsed just the same. Quantitative expansion cannot counterbalance the qualitative changes in Party members and the deterioration of Party organisations. Party members' views, values, identities and incentives are now shaped more by the market than by Party indoctrination, and Party organisations at the grassroots level increasingly stand on shifting sand. The CCP needs to carefully reconsider the model of its rule — to rule not only more effectively, but also more cost-effectively.

# 7

# China Struggles to Maintain Stability

## Strengthening its Public Security Apparatus

### XIE Yue and SHAN Wei*

*Faced with rising social unrests, China has taken efforts to strengthen its policing and monitoring capabilities. This system of maintaining stability has expanded rapidly and leaders of the system enjoy more opportunities for promotion.*

In 2005, three years after coming to power, Chinese President Hu Jintao announced the objective of "constructing a harmonious society". Together with the "idea of scientific development", Hu outlined his political blueprint — balanced development between economic growth and social harmony — which requires the Chinese Communist Party (CCP) and the government to pay more attention to social problems that may undermine regime stability.

Over the past decades, market-oriented economic reform in China has generated friction in the society, such as income inequalities, land disputes, corruption, etc. These problems, provoking dissatisfaction and resentment among the general public, have constituted threats to regime legitimacy. Several major incidents in the recent couple of years, including ethnic riots in Tibet and Xinjiang, as well as a series of school killings and strikes in Honda and other foreign-invested companies,[1] have made stability issues more salient.

A major strategy adopted by the Chinese leaders is to enhance its "maintenance of stability system" (*weiwen xitong*) and strengthen its policing and monitoring capabilities.

In a broad sense, the system includes the entire state apparatus that could be mobilised to maintain the stability of the regime, such as the police, the media, state-controlled mass organisations and censorship agencies. In a narrow sense, the system of maintaining stability consists of five governmental departments or branches and one Party organisation: the Ministry of

---

* XIE Yue is Professor, School of Political Science and International Relations, Tongji University, China. SHAN Wei is Research Fellow at the East Asian Institute, National University of Singapore.
[1] In the first half of 2010, there were a series of strikes in foreign invested factories in Shenzhen, Shanghai, Jiangsu, and Jiangxi. The strikers generally demanded for a raise in salary.

Public Security, the Ministry of State Security, the Ministry of Justice, the People's Court, the People's Procuratorate, as well as the Party's Politics and Law Committee.

In the past two decades, this system of maintaining stability has expanded rapidly. Expenditure growth in the policing system has been higher than that for the national GDP; total expenditure for this system will be higher than that for military spending and social welfare according to the latest budget plan. Leaders of the system also enjoy more opportunities for promotion.

The expansion of the policing system is driven by growing collective protests and the regime's incompetence in accommodating to popular demands. Chinese leaders may have to look at other options to maintain regime stability, such as a more just legal system, a more responsive government and a fairer redistribution system.

## Structure of the Policing System

For decades, China has relied on the "management of stability" system. The structure of this system has undergone many changes to develop into a very complicated bureaucratic system which consists of six departments at the central level: the Ministry of Public Security, the Ministry of State Security, the Ministry of Justice, the Supreme People's Court, the Supreme People's Procuratorate and the People's Armed Police. Each agency takes responsibility for a different part of security and has its own coercive forces. Figure 1 presents the structure of the system.

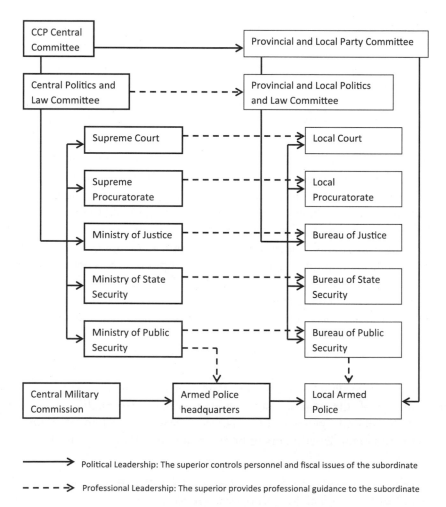

**Figure 1**   The Policing System in China

*Source*: Prepared by the authors.

Constitutionally, the Ministry of Public Security, the Ministry of State Security and the Ministry of Justice are components of the State Council. The Supreme Court and the Procuratorate are accountable to the National People's Congress. In practice, all these agencies are under the leadership of the central Party committee.

In the centre of the system are the Ministry of Public Security and its regional and local subordinates, which are the counterparts of police departments in other countries. The ministry and its sub-branches are supposed to enforce laws and reduce crime rate. With time, however, this system has played a crucial role in monitoring and suppressing social unrest. Under the ministry are the Bureaus of Public Security, the Armed Police, the Ministry of National Security and the Ministry of Justice. The Bureaus of Public Security are led by local governments at levels of provinces, prefectures and counties.

The Armed Police is a paramilitary force under both the State Council and the Central Military Commission, China's supreme authority of the armed forces. The Minister of Public Security is the first political commissar of the Armed Police. The subagencies of the Armed Police oversee all provinces, prefectures and counties. There are also branches in certain industries, such as the railway police, the transportation police, the civil aviation police and the forestry police.

Established in 1982, the Armed Police is tasked with maintaining security in localities, protecting senior leaders and handling emergencies, such as large-scale protests. Nationwide, there are 1.2 million armed police, about half the size of the military.[2]

The Ministry of National Security is China's intelligence agency, which collects information both domestically and internationally. The ministry is also monitoring non-governmental organisations and mass activities to prevent any possible collective actions against the government that threatens stability.

China's Ministry of Justice plays a marginal role in the party-state system and is in charge of administrative issues related to jails and lawyers, as well as grassroots legal meditation organisations. It contributes to the cause of maintaining stability by promoting legal meditations over civil conflicts and by monitoring lawyers who challenge the authorities for civil rights.

The People's Court is China's tribunal institution, investigating and vindicating legal cases, and sometimes mediating civil conflicts. The People's Procuratorate plays the role of a public prosecutor and assesses the fairness of rules made by the court.

All levels of these state agencies are under the leadership of the CCP, particularly, the Central Commission of Politics and Law. The committee is to direct, coordinate, supervise, and monitor the operations of the police, the state security bureau, the court, the procuratorate, etc.[3] Table 1 presents the current members of the Central Politics and Law Committee. The secretary of the committee at each administrative level is the direct boss of the heads of the aforementioned agencies. The secretary is usually one of the members of the Party's Standing Committee, the core decision-making organ at the administrative level.

## Expanding the Policing System

### *The Swelling Size*

In spite of repeated efforts to reduce the size of its bureaucracy in the past three decades, the CCP leaders have never tried to curtail expenses of the policing system. Instead, all the agencies under the system have been expanded on a large scale. In 1988, only 0.769 million served in the public

---

[2] Lü G, "Armed Forces in China and Its Police's Nationalization", *Beijing Spring*, 160, September 2006. It is reported that the size of armed force is over 1.5 million in the year of 2012. But there is no official statistics confirming this number. See <http://www.molihua.org/2012/02/pk.html> (accessed March 2012).

[3] "Politics and Law Committee", *Baidu Encyclopedia*, at <http://baike.baidu.com/view/1488137.htm> (accessed March 2012).

**Table 1**  Current Members of the Central Commission Of Politics and Law (CCPL)

| Name | Membership in the CPLC | Other Major Concurrent Post(s) |
|---|---|---|
| Zhou Yongkang | Secretary | Politburo Standing Committee member; Director of the Central Committee for Comprehensive Management of Public Security[a] |
| Meng Jianzhu | Deputy Secretary | State Councillor; Minister of Public Security |
| Wang Lequan | Deputy Secretary | Politburo member |
| Wang Shengjun | Member | Chief Justice of Supreme Court |
| Cao Jianming | Member | Chief Procurator of Supreme Procuratorate |
| Geng Huichang | Member | Minister of State Security |
| Wu Aiying | Member | Minister of Justice |
| Sun Zhongtong | Member | Deputy Secretary of the Central Commission for Discipline Inspection[b] |
| Chen Yiping | Member | Associate Director of the Central Committee for Comprehensive Management of Public Security |
| Wang Jianping | Member | Commander of the Armed Police Force |
| Zhou Benshun | Secretary General | Associate Director of the Central Committee for Comprehensive Management of Public Security |

*Notes*: [a] The Central Committee for Comprehensive Management of Public Security (*zhongyang shehui zhian zonghe zhili weiyuanhui*) is a committee led jointly by the CCP and the State Council to handle public security issues. It works in a united office (*heshu bangong*) with the Central Politics and Law Committee.
[b] The Central Commission for Discipline Inspection (*zhongyang jilü jiancha weiyuanhui*) is the CCP's disciplinary organ which monitors, supervises and inspects behaviour of party officials.
*Source*: Prepared by the authors.

security system; in 2008, the number had reached two million, nearly three times higher than it was 20 years ago.[4]

In the past two decades, the policing system has built up a number of new agencies. Right after the 1989 Tiananmen incident, a Culture and Economy Directorate was established within the provincial Bureau of Public Security to monitor intellectuals, university professors and students. In 2006, under the Politics and Law Committee, an Office of Maintaining Stability (*weiwen ban*) was set up. The office is designed to coordinate all the departments and bureaus in the policing system and expedite responses to any incidents that could threaten social stability.

Some private sectors have also been included in the system to maintain stability at the grassroots. Starting from 1985, a number of private security service companies have been established. In 2007, there were 2,300 of such companies with over one million employees.[5] Apart from providing security services to enterprises and individuals, recent news reports revealed that some of the companies were hired by local governments to detain protesters in secret prisons, known as "black jails".[6]

The expansion of the policing system has also been extended to the countryside. From 2003 to 2006, the Ministry of Public Security promoted the "three-*ji*" project (*jiceng, jichu, jibengong*),[7]

[4] *The Law Yearbook of China* (1989 and 2009), The Press of China Law Yearbook, Beijing; Xie X and Yu R, "Research over Government Model of Security in China under Good Governance", *Rule by Law and Society* (*fazhi yu shehui*), no. 9, 2008.
[5] Shu L, Wang M and Sun Y, "Security Personnel Outnumbers Polices", Overlook, 24 July 2007.
[6] "China Police Investigate 'Black Jails' for Protesters", *BBC News*, 27 September 2010, at <http://www.bbc.co.uk/news/world-asia-pacific-11420443> (accessed October 2010).
[7] The "three-*ji*" project started from late 2003, with emphasis placed on working at the grassroots level (*jiceng*), setting a good foundation for stability (*jichu*) and exercising basic skills of policing (*jibengong*). The project was involved in collecting grassroots information, building branches of public security in the countryside and improving the professional skills of the police.

which sought to reinforce the police forces in rural areas and to improve their capacity to manage civil conflicts.

### High Costs

The expansion of the policing system requires heavy financing. Expenditure growth of the policing system since 1995 has surpassed the national GDP growth rate. The majority of the expenses were spent on improving equipment, recruiting personnel and meeting administrative expenditure.[8]

Figure 2 reports China's total governmental expenditure on national defence and the policing system. Spending on domestic security and stability increased dramatically in 2006 and has since been close to military expenses. In 2010, the cost of public security was 552 billion *yuan* while the defence expense was 533 billion *yuan*. For the first time the policing expenditure surpassed the military costs. The fiscal expenditure report of 2011 has yet to be published. But according to the budget plan of the year, in 2011 the planned spending on public security would be 624 billion *yuan*, while the military expense would be 601 billion *yuan*.[9] That is to say, the spending on public security and policing system remained outstripping the defence budget.

Variance among different local governments is wide in terms of their expenditure in the policing system. Developed provinces tend to invest more on stability issues than the less developed provinces. For instance, from 1995 to 2008, Guangdong province, the richest province in China, spent over 223 billion *yuan* in policing, while one of the poorest provinces, Ningxia, spent only 8.3 billion *yuan*.[10] The five provincial units which registered the highest expenditure are Shanghai, Guangdong, Jiangsu, Zhejiang and Shandong — the five most industrialised areas in China.

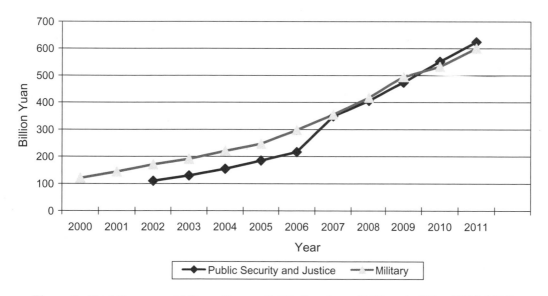

**Figure 2**  Total Governmental Expenditure on Public Security and Military in China (2000–2011)

*Note*: Before 2002, the cost of public security and justice was included and itemised as "administrative expenditure".
*Sources*: The data from 2000 to 2010 are obtained from *The China Statistics Yearbook*, China Statistics Press, Beijing, vol. 2001–2011. The data for 2011 are from the budget plan announced by the National People's Congress in March 2011.

---

[8] He Q, "Why the Increase of Security Expenditure is Unable to be Stopped", 2010, at <http://shuangzhoukan.hrichina.org/article/564> (accessed October 2010).
[9] Buckley, C, "China Internal Security Spending Jumps Past Army Budget," Reuters, 5 March 2011.
[10] *China Statistical Yearbook*, 1996 to 2009, China Statistics Press, Beijing.

### Regulating Policing Behaviours

The ever-expanding policing forces, however, have not enhanced stability. In the past two decades, the number of mass protests had grown 10 times.[11] There were a considerable number of cases of collective resistance that were caused by the improper use of policing force. These collective resistance cases have put much pressure on the CCP which views such resistance as threatening its political legitimacy. Beijing leaders in recent times have therefore tightened regulations over the policing forces.

Major leaders of different departments and bureaus have been made responsible for social unrest. Under the cadre responsibility system, in the event of a mass protest, the leaders in charge will be seriously punished in a "one-ballot veto" (*yipiao foujue*) regardless of his performance in other regards. At the grassroots level, a police department is included in the responsibility network.

For example, in June 2009, a large-scale riot took place in Shishou city, Hubei province. Tens of thousands of demonstrators protested against corruption in the local police force. The protestors burned police cars and set fire to some government buildings. The city party secretary and police chief were held responsible and dismissed. A number of policemen were also punished for their improper behaviour that led to the protests.[12]

In 2009 and 2010, the Ministry of Public Security made further efforts to regulate police behaviours. County and prefecture-level bureau directors were required to attend a special training programme in Beijing. The programme aimed to train local police chiefs on how they should behave in a protest.

### Political Promotion

A political tradition within the CCP is to assign a concurrent position to those who hold a politically important post, thus giving appointed officials greater power to enforce the Party's policies. Assigning a vice provincial ranking to a mayor of a major city in the province, or assigning a Politburo membership to a Party boss of an important province are such examples. After 1989, the CCP has begun to use this method to incrementally politicise the policing system.

In 1999, the suppression of *Falun Gong,* a mass religious organisation, became a central task of the policing system. The head of the Central Politics and Law Committee was promoted from a Politburo member to a Standing Committee member. It was then that this concurrent appointment of head of the Central Politics and Law Committee has become an institutionalised practice.

Within the policing system, the Ministry of Public Security plays the most significant role. Its chief usually has more opportunities of promotion than leaders of other agencies. For instance, Meng Jianzhu, the incumbent head of the ministry, has more power than other ministers within the system because he is concurrently the deputy secretary of the Central Politics and Law Committee as well as a state councillor. A state councillor is placed at the same level as a vice premier and is therefore much more powerful than ordinary ministers.

The same political promotion method has been adopted in the local policing system. Heads of the Politics and Law Committee in most provinces are deputy party secretaries, and directors of public security in provinces and counties are appointed as members of the standing committee of the local party branch.

---

[11] See Figure 3 in the following section.

[12] "Mass Incidents in Shishou, Hubei," *NetEase News*, at <http://news.163.com/special/00013FJU/shishou.html> (accessed October 2010).

## Dynamics of the Expansion

The expansion of the policing system is driven by growing collective protests and the incompetence of the CCP to accommodate public demands and solve civil disputes within its existing institutions.

Figure 3 shows the number of collective protests, which had increased more than tenfold, from 8,700 in 1993 to 127,000 in 2008. In 2010, it was reported that the number was over 180,000.

Among these collective resistance cases, some are ethnic conflicts, or even separatist movements, like the riots in Tibet and Xinjiang. Some involved land dispute, corruption, house demolition, wage, pollution, etc. Based on the data from news reports of overseas media from 2006 to 2010, the number of violent protests doubled that of the non-violent ones,[13] a phenomenon that requires the attention of the Beijing authorities.

The CCP was also pushed into developing the policing system as existing institutions failed to deal with public demands and dissatisfaction adequately. Although the "Visiting and Lettering System" (*xinfang zhidu*) opens a window for citizens to participate in politics and file their complaints, a research report in 2005 revealed that only 2% of complaints filed with the central government could get satisfactory resolutions.[14]

The legal system is also incompetent in solving disputes. The number of unsettled disputes in court has grown exponentially. Even for settled cases, it is still quite difficult to enforce the decisions. In 2007, 340,700 cases or 40% of the total cases ruled by the courts had not been implemented.[15]

Fundamentally, the CCP is reluctant to conduct political reform and improve its responsiveness towards the general public, the reason for the expansion of the policing system. Rather than taking the risk of losing power, the Party prefers to adopt a less risky strategy and strengthen the coercive system, that is, expand the policing system.

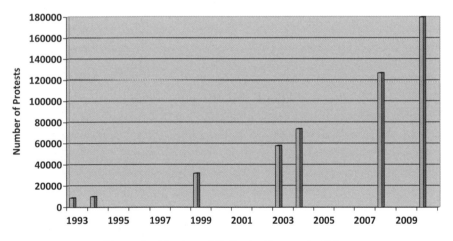

**Figure 3**  Number of Collective Protests in China

*Sources*: Shirk, SL, *China: Fragile Superpower*, Oxford University Press, London, 2007; Jacob, A, "Dragons, Dancing Ones, Set-off a Riot in China", *New York Times*, 10 February 2009. "Mass Incidents in China Increased Geometrically Each Year", International Radio of France, 21 February 2011. At <http://www.hotnewsnet.com/a/muhou/20110221/394292.html> (accessed April 2012).

---

[13] The statistics are based on Xie Yue's data collection.

[14] Yu J, "Institutional Absence of Petitioning and its Political Consequence", *Phoenix Weekly*, 32, 2004.

[15] *The Law Yearbook of China*, 1999, 2001 and 2008, The Press of China Law Yearbook, Beijing.

## Political Implications

The economic reform over the past three decades has made China prosperous, but it has also restructured interests among various social strata and hence generated many social protests, which constitute political challenges to the Chinese leaders. How to cope with these social conflicts is largely related to the direction of future reform.

In China, the established judiciary system has played only a limited role in effectively handling social unrests due to the party-state's control of the judiciary. For the CCP, the more practical measure is to strengthen the coercive machine. As a result, the policing system is gaining in importance, hence requiring additional resources.

However, maintaining stability for the short term may actually give rise to accumulated dissatisfaction and resentment, or even undermine the stability of the regime in the longer term. Therefore, top leaders in Beijing may have to rethink its options, such as a more just legal system, a more responsive government and a fairer redistribution system to prevent or deal with social unrest.

# 8

# How Secure is China's Food Security?

John WONG*

*The Chinese government has to continue with its pro-active policies of supporting agricultural development as a mere 10% of its domestic shortfall would seriously destabilise the world grain markets and drive up world inflation.*

China's population accounts for 21% of the world's total population, but the country has only about 9% of the world's available arable land. Feeding such a vast nation, with such an unfavourable man to land ratio, has always been a great challenge for China's rulers, past and present.

Historically, all Chinese emperors had to place their upmost priority on agricultural development, as serious crop failures would lead to famines, which would in turn breed peasant rebellions and eventually regime change. The rise and fall of China's dynasties in the past often happened this way. Hence the familiar old Chinese political adage: "An economy without strong agriculture is fragile, and a country without sufficient food grains will be chaotic" (*wu nong bu wen, wu liang ze luan*).

Even in modern times, with rapid technological progress in agricultural production, it remains an enormous task for the Chinese government to ensure creditable food security. Still fresh in the collective memory of the present Chinese leadership were the famines that came about after the collapse of Mao's Great Leap Forward (1959–1962). Therefore, China takes "food security" very seriously, which basically means "food self-sufficiency", with the bottom line set at 95% of domestic grain supply.

Such a stringent definition of food security naturally adds burden to the Chinese government. This is aggravated by the fact that for the past three decades, China's total population increased 72% from 960 million in 1978 to 1.3 billion in 2009 while arable land (total "sown area") increased marginally at 5.4%.

---

*John WONG is Professorial Fellow at the East Asian Institute, National University of Singapore.

Worse still, the total sown area devoted to food crops declined from 80% in 1978 to just 64% in 2009, mainly because with economic prosperity and rising incomes, farmers were growing more lucrative non-grain commercial crops. Accordingly, China has come to depend heavily on increasing productivity (i.e. output per unit of land area) to maintain its food security. This, in turn, needs further technological progress (e.g. using hybrids or other high-yielding varieties) and further intensification of cultivation with greater use of modern inputs like chemical fertilisers and pesticides.

The trouble is that barring the use of genetically modified (GM) crops, the productivity growth potential of the traditional form of technological progress based on modern seeds and modern inputs has started to slow down. Widespread use of modern inputs of industrial origins also inflicts long-term ecological damages.

Rapid economic and social changes have further worked against food production. Industrialisation and urbanisation in China as elsewhere inevitably spell agricultural decline. In China, the employment share of the primary sector (agriculture, animal husbandry and fishery) declined from 71% in 1978 to 38% in 2009, and its GDP share from 28% to just 10% for the same period. Farming is getting economically and socially unattractive to the young people. As in other densely populated East Asian economies with severe land constraints, food production in China has also become an increasingly high-cost business.

With China having achieved successful industrial take-off, economic theory suggests that it should have a stronger comparative advantage to export labour-intensive manufactured products to America in exchange for its cheaper food produced by land-extensive farming. In other words, China should scale down its existing high level of food self-sufficiency and let international trade take care of any shortfalls, much as what Japan has done.

However, with a 1.3 billion population, China (India also, for that matter) is just too big to follow the economic theory of comparative advantage by relying on international trade to achieve its food security. In 2010, China's total grain harvests amounted to a record 546 million tons, or about 24% of the whole world's total grain output. In 2010, total grain trade was 290 million tons, which works out to be just about 50% of China's total production (and consumption).

If China were to resort to the world grain markets to make up for just 10% of its domestic shortfall, such an import requirement would seriously destabilise the world grain markets and drive up world inflation. It is therefore good for China, on account of its sheer size, to rigidly adhere to its basic tenet of maintaining strong food self-sufficiency. The world at large also stands to benefit from China's efforts in maintaining creditable food security.


**Drought Threatening China's Food Security?**

On 9 February 2011, the UN's Food and Agriculture Organisation (FAO) issued a special alert that North China, the main wheat basket of the country, was suffering from a severe winter drought, the worst in 60 years; this could devastate China's wheat harvest, "putting further pressures on wheat prices, which have been rising rapidly in the last few months" it added.[1] Underlying FAO's warning is the message that should China lose its winter wheat crop, it would go to the international grain markets to make up for its shortfall. With its ample foreign exchange, China is able to buy up any amount of food that it needs. The sudden entry of such a huge buyer could certainly rock the international food markets.

FAO's routine warning was promptly picked up by the international media, with some carrying additional innuendo that a food crisis is brewing in China.[2] But this argument is vastly exaggerated

---

[1] UNFAO, "Food Global Information and Early Warning System on Food and Agriculture (GIEWS)". Special Alert 330, 8 February 2011.

[2] Bradsher, K, "U.N. Food Agency Issues Warning on China Drought", *The New York Times*, 9 February 2011. Brown, LR, "The Food Crisis Ahead", *International Herald Tribune*, 23 February 2011.

and manifestly oversimplified. To begin with, the frequent occurrence of natural calamities is a fact of life for Chinese agriculture. Every year, China suffers about 10% of crop losses as a result of bad weather and wastes.

At the same time, it is always easier for a huge and diverse country to absorb adversities and tide over natural calamities (e.g. bad weather in one region can be offset by fair weather in another). China's annual wheat output in 2009 amounted to 115 million tons, constituting only 23% of total grain output, with 42% for rice and 35% for corn. As the drought was estimated to affect one-third of the total acreage for winter wheat, the potential crop loss could possibly be offset by a reasonable bumper summer rice harvest.[3]

More significantly, China's obsession with its high level of national grain self-sufficiency is just for this kind of contingencies. Every year, the government is relentlessly pushing for higher grain production — its annual "Number One Central Document" is invariably about agricultural production — regardless of whether China has the international comparative advantage for producing such a commodity.

Accordingly, China has over the years built up a huge grain reserve amounting to over 200 million tons, or about 40% of China's annual consumption. This is government grain stock, not including individual grain reserves by individual farmers.[4] Thanks to China's substantial grain reserves, the world can count on China to balance its grain demand and supply domestically, without destabilising world grain prices.

In retrospect, the FAO in drawing international attention to China's drought had produced the positive effect of further galvanising government efforts to fight the drought with concerted financial and technical support aimed at restoring production. Both President Hu Jintao and Premier Wen Jiabao visited the drought-stricken areas. In reality, the current Chinese leadership is more wary of the drought causing inflation than any real food crisis. Accordingly, the government has allocated 98.6 billion *yuan* (US$15 billion) to farmers nationwide to boost grain production.[5]

Suffice it to say that the severe drought in the winter-wheat growing North China region is unlikely to jeopardise China's presently strong food security situation. Nor will there be any likely negative spillover to the international food markets from any perceived decline in China's wheat output this year. Figure 1 shows that every year since 2004 China has experienced serious natural disasters with a crop loss of around 6% and yet total food output has been increasing year after year.

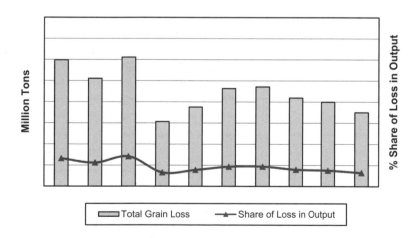

**Figure 1**   Grain Losses Due to Natural Disasters, 2001–2010

*Source: China Rural Statistics Yearbooks.*

---

[3] "Severe Drought Endangers China's Winter Wheat", *China Daily*, 9 February 2011.
[4] "Grain Reserve Hits 40% of Annual Consumption", *China Daily*, 7 March 2011.
[5] "Chinese Government Allocates 98.6 Billion *yuan* to Support Farmers", *China Daily*, 21 January 2011.

In fact, as confirmed by Agricultural Minister Han Changfu on 10 March 2011, China was still "aiming for an eighth consecutive year of increased agricultural production in 2011".[6] The expected output loss has already been built into the production structure.

## China's Road to Food Self-Sufficiency

Constantly haunted by China's historical experiences of "grain shortages leading to instability and chaos" (*wu liang ze luan*), the Chinese leadership today has set a very high standard for its food security, which almost exclusively means food self-sufficiency at over 95% of domestic supply. In 2010, China's total grain production (made up of rice, wheat, corn, pulse and other coarse grains) reached an historical record level of 546 million tons, up 2.9% from the previous record high of 530 million tons for 2009.[7] What has been China's overall performance in food security for the past six decades since the formation of the People's Republic in 1949?

China's agricultural performance for the first three decades of the People's Republic has been mixed, even though Mao Zedong started off with his development strategies strongly emphasising "[a]griculture as the foundation of the Chinese economy with grain as the key link in agricultural development" (*yi nong wei ben, yi liang wei gang*). Mao was too ideological and too obsessed with the socialist transformation of agriculture, starting from land reform to cooperatisation and then communisation. Such socialist institutional structure just did not provide the needed incentive to individual farmers, nor was it conducive to the technological transformation of agriculture.

Accordingly, growth in grain production and grain productivity for the 1952–1978 period, as shown in Figure 2, had barely out-stripped population growth. Indeed, China's overall level of food security was unstable and very precarious throughout the 1950s and the 1960s while the Great Leap Forward period of 1959–1962 was a disaster, causing a serious famine. Overall, there was little productivity growth (i.e. output per unit of sown area) for the whole period, mainly because of constant political instability. Just as agricultural production was recovering from the Great Leap Forward disaster, the country was plunged into the Cultural Revolution (1966–1976).

The state of Chinese agriculture for the second three decades starting with economic reform in 1979 experienced a complete about-turn. In fact, Deng Xiaoping's economic reform started with

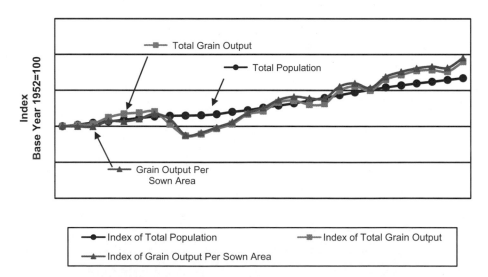

**Figure 2**    Growth of Population, Total Grain Output and Grain Productivity, 1952–1978

*Sources*: China Bureau of Statistics, United States Department of Agriculture.

---

[6] "Farmers Aim to Increase Grain Areas", *China Daily*, 18 March 2011.

[7] "China's Grain Yield to Hit Record High", *China Daily*, 28 December 2009.

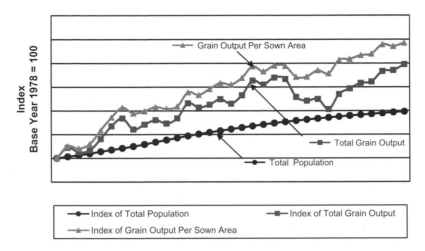

**Figure 3**   Growth of Population, Total Grain Output and Grain Productivity, 1978–2010

*Source*: China Bureau of Statistics.

agricultural reform by scrapping Mao's people's communes and providing incentives to farmers with the "household responsibility system". It was an instant success, marked by rising productivity and rising incomes. Subsequently, productivity growth was sustained by technological progress.

Thus, as can be seen from Figure 3, grain production growth for these three decades from 1979 has well outpaced population growth, indicating that China has basically achieved food self-sufficiency, especially after the early 1990s. In particular, productivity growth for these three decades has been very impressive, and the second part of the 2000s has even witnessed a new upward trend for productivity growth.

However, the self-sufficiency policy in this period suffered two setbacks, one in the early 1990s, and the other in the early 2000s. The production decline in the early 1990s had caused Lester Brown, a well-known international environmentalist and food specialist, to sound the first warning that rising incomes in China had diverted more and more food to commercial uses (e.g. making beer and feeding animals) from direct human consumption, and that China would eventually need to import more food with adverse implications for the world food markets.[8]

The upshot turned out to be a "wake-up call" to the Chinese government, which became complacent after a few years of good grain harvests. In the event, the Chinese government introduced a series of policy measures to support food production, including the "Governor Grain Bag Policy", which mandated individual provincial governors to promote food production so as to ensure their own food self-sufficiency. (Subsequently, there was also the "Vegetables Basket Policy" that required all large cities to grow enough vegetables in their suburbs.) After that, national food production was back on the rising trend.

The second downturn in production was during the 1978–2003 period, with the year 2003 being especially serious, registering a large demand-supply gap of around 7%. The government complacency aside, the production decreases in 2003 were mainly caused by the sharp decline in the sown area for food crops — food crop cultivation was at a historical low in 2003, accounting for only 65% of the total sown area.

The rapid shrinkage of sown area for food crops, mainly in the more developed coastal region, was partly caused by the loss of farmlands to other commercial crops and urban uses in the coastal region. China was set to fulfil its WTO obligations of cutting its average tariff rate for agricultural products from 22% to 15%, starting from 2004. Some grain farmers in the coastal region grew less food crops as they anticipated the influx of cheaper food imports.

---

[8] Brown, L, *Who Will Feed China? Wake Up Call for a Small Planet*, Washington, DC, 1995.

The 2003 production decline drew the attention of the FAO, which warned that China might be heading for a food crisis, with serious implications for the world food markets.[9] Again, this warning served as another "wake-up call" for the Chinese government, which promptly introduced a variety of policy measures to support food production, including more production subsidies and higher government purchase prices for grains. More importantly, the government adopted more stringent measures to arrest the continuing loss of farmlands to non-agricultural usages.

In the event, the dangerous production slide was halted in 2004 when grain production regained its upward trend for the following six consecutive years, culminating in the record harvest of 546 million tons in 2010. This works out to be about 410 kg per person in China, more than sufficient to feed its population in terms of average calorie-intake. More significantly, successive years of bumper harvests have led to the swelling of national grain reserves, which amounted to more than 40% of the yearly national consumption, a level widely recognised as well exceeding the international average of 17–18% of consumption.[10]

It may also be added that over the years, food production in China is no longer entirely for human consumption, but also for animal feed and biofuels like ethanol. In fact, China's "food security" today, broadly defined, means more than easy access to sufficient calorie-intake as it also aims to provide nutritious and diverse food items to meet people's dietary needs for their active and healthy lifestyle. China's food security in the Mao era was mainly about providing barely sufficient daily calorie-intake from grain, without adequate nutritious supplements from other sources like meat and fruits. In 1979, China's average per capita daily food consumption yielded only 2,017 calories, well below the world average of 2,500. By 2001, this had increased 47% to 2,963 calories, well above the world average of 2,800.[11]

Entering the 2000s and with growing affluence, China's food consumption structure, particularly of urban residents, has greatly diversified, with decreasing grain consumption per capita and increasing consumption of meat, eggs, aquatic products, dairy products, vegetables and fruits. In 2009, China was the world's largest producer of meat (averaging 57 kg per capita), aquatic products (38 kg per capita) and vegetables (470 kg per capita), and the world's third largest producer of milk products (26 kg per capita). China's per capita consumption of meat, eggs, fruits, vegetables and aquatic products today is well above the world average, and even higher than some developed countries.

In fact, with rising incomes and economic prosperity, China is increasingly facing the problem of "food over-consumption", with soaring obesity rates, especially in urban areas. At the national level, food security is therefore no longer an issue, though a wide gap still exists between urban and rural residents, and between the developed coastal region and the less developed interior China. Food security for many poor counties in western China and the hilly regions is still unstable and inadequate.[12]

As China has basically realised its food security at the national level, its participation in the world grain markets over the years has also become minimal, except for the two particular years of 1994 and 2003 when China's food production plunged. In recent years, soybean has been China's only major food import item. For wheat, with the exception of 2004 when China's overall production plummeted, China imports only a tiny amount mainly for urban consumption. As shown in Figure 4, for most years China's wheat imports were about 2% of its total output even when domestic wheat production had suffered from poor weather.

The 2011 drought was indeed very damaging to the winter wheat crop. As argued earlier, the actual crop losses might turn out to be considerably less than it was originally estimated, in part because of

---

[9] State of Food Insecurity Report, FAO.

[10] "Large Country Must Have Sufficient Reserve", *Global Times*, 22 March 2011.

[11] FAO. *The State of Food Insecurity in the World 2002*, Rome, 2002.

[12] See Xiao Y and Nie F, *A Report on the Status of China's Food Security*. Beijing, China Agricultural Science and Technology Press, 2008.

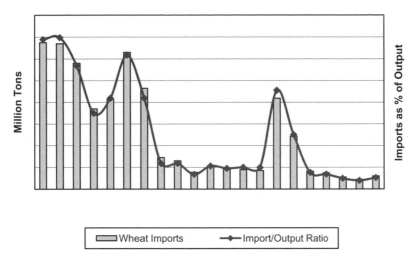

**Figure 4** China's Wheat Imports, 1990–2010

*Source*: *FAO Database.*

the government's relentless support to the wheat farmers.[13] From China's past trade behaviour as well as China's existing large food reserves, one can safely surmise that China is most unlikely to resort to large-scale imports from the world grain markets to make up for any potential wheat production shortfall in the immediate term. The FAO's alert will turn out to be just a false alarm.

## Recurrent Challenges to China's Food Security

Recently, China's Vice Premier Hui Liangyu (who oversees China's agriculture) reaffirmed that China would uphold its "policy of food self-sufficiency".[14] However, China's food security status remains vulnerable to a number of recurrent challenges. Sustaining such a high level of food self-sufficiency for a big country is not something that the Chinese government can take for granted. However, the Chinese government tends to become complacent after successive bumper harvests, as evidenced by the 2003 production decline. To ensure food security, the government needs to be on its toes all the time. However, beyond the government's proactive agricultural policy, China's food security is facing two major challenges.

First, China will continue to struggle, under very harsh conditions against the frequent occurrence of natural disasters and chronic water scarcity. Statistically in most years, about a third of China's total sown area is "covered by disaster" (i.e. causing output loss of about 10%) and about 2% of the sown area is "affected by disaster" (i.e. causing an output loss of about 30%). Furthermore, on account of climate change, natural disasters in recent years tend to increase in frequency and intensity.[15] This means that the Chinese government has to remain constantly vigilant, always standing ready to mobilise every effort to fight natural calamities.

Secondly, apart from natural disasters, China's agricultural production is also under the constant threat of losing its arable land to non-agricultural uses due to rapid industrialisation and urbanisation. As shown in Figure 5, China's total sown area for grains had been declining since 1990 to a dangerously low level in 2003. This prompted the government (Ministry of Land Resource) to undertake stringent measures to restrict the conversion of farmland for non-farming uses.[16] Only after strong government intervention has the sown area for grains moved up again.

---

[13] "Drought Impact on Grain Limited" *China Daily*, 7 March 2011.

[14] <http://news.xinhuanet.com/english2010/china/2911–03/25c_13798399.htm> (accessed 19 April 2011).

[15] *China Statistical Yearbook,* 2010.

[16] Ministry of Land Resources, "Policy on Land Reclamation Regulation", 30 March 2011.

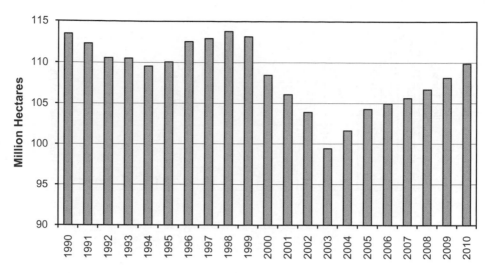

**Figure 5**   Total Sown Area for Grains, 1990–2010

*Source*: *China Statistical Yearbook,* various years.

Conserving farmlands in rural areas has been a huge undertaking on the part of the central government, whose policies and efforts are often undermined by local governments for the sake of local economic growth. Underlying the ever-increasing demand for agricultural land is the growing pressure from the rapid growth of urban population along with the rapidly declining agricultural population. This, in turn, raises the relative resource cost of farmlands used for agricultural production in terms of their higher opportunity cost due to higher returns from alternative urban uses.

Increasingly, as China's industrialisation and urbanisation continue unabated, the policy of protecting farmlands against non-agricultural usages, just for the sake of achieving food self-sufficiency, inevitably creates economic distortion leading to inefficient resource allocation. To follow the dictates of economic theory, the Chinese government either scales down its high level of food security and let international trade take care of any demand gaps, or invests even more resources on exploiting greater land productivity (i.e. higher output on a smaller piece of land). The government also needs to increase its subsidies and incentives for farmers. In this way, agriculture in China has increasingly become a high-cost business, much as in other East Asian economies.

Suffice it to say that the world is indebted to China for its effective food self-sufficiency policy and for refraining from taking options that could potentially destabilise the world's food markets. The high level of food security by itself may be politically and socially good for China, but it comes at a cost for the Chinese people.

# 9

# China's "New Deal" in Xinjiang and its Challenges

SHAN Wei and WENG Cuifen*

*About one year after the deadly ethnic conflicts in Xinjiang, the Chinese leaders unveiled a new policy package and vowed to bring lasting stability to this restive region through "leapfrog development."*

The Xinjiang Work Conference, a joint conference of the Chinese Communist Party's (CCP) central committee and the State Council, China's Cabinet, was held in Beijing from 17 to 19 May 2010 to promote a new deal in Xinjiang Uyghur Autonomous Region, the country's far west frontier. The new deal outlined a blueprint for Xinjiang's development until 2020 whereby the government will pour hundreds of billions of *yuan* to accomplish the plan.

This conference was in response to the July 2009 deadly riots in Xinjiang's capital Urumqi between mainly Muslim Uyghurs and members of China's dominant Han group. The riots resulted in about 1,700 people injured and at least 197 killed, the worst in the country in decades. The bloodshed revealed tensions between Uyghurs and Han Chinese in the region as well as the dilemmas of the CCP's ethnic policy.

China's current ethnic policy is based on the system of regional autonomy of ethnic minorities. In the autonomous areas, ethnic minorities enjoy a number of favourable policies, including a special quota system in political representation (i.e. more seats in people's congress and government), education (i.e. priority in secondary school and college admission), family planning (i.e. more than one child) and legal issues (i.e. lenient treatment in law enforcement).[1] Most of these preferential policies are guaranteed by the Regional Ethnic Autonomy Law that was promulgated in 1984.

---

* SHAN Wei is Research Fellow at the East Asian Institute, National University of Singapore. WENG Cuifen is Research Assistant at the same institute.

[1] Shan W and Chen G, "China's Flawed Policy in Xinjiang and its Dilemmas", *EAI Background Brief*, 463, 13 July 2009.

While these preferential policies are supposed to benefit ethnic minorities and win their support for the regime, the policies in Xinjiang have been beset by several problems. The first problem is economic inequality between Han Chinese and minorities. After a series of riots involving Uyghur separatist and Islamic extremist organisations in the 1980s and 1990s, the Chinese government has adopted a policy of "stability above all else" in Xinjiang. Hence, economic development is of secondary importance in the region.

Yet in the past decades, the government has continued to invest heavily in infrastructure and heavy industries in Xinjiang. The region's GDP growth since 2003 (except 2009) has been higher than that of China as a whole.[2] But this growth has failed to close income gaps across ethnicities.

Since the late 1970s, minority employees have to account for at least 60% of the workforce at local state-owned enterprises (SOEs).[3] However, many local SOEs have gone bankrupt in the recent decade, leading to a great number of laid-off minority employees. Now most enterprises are privately owned and not bound by official regulations. Private owners in Xinjiang are inclined to hire Han Chinese workers instead of local Uyghurs who are disadvantaged in language and technical skills.[4]

In the 1980s and 1990s, the Xinjiang government emphasised the development of the northern part of the region which had a better industrial foundation. As the majority of Muslim Uyghurs reside in southern Xinjiang, this geographically imbalanced development has made the Uyghur people even more disadvantaged in welfare.

To reduce this north-south economic gap, Beijing has encouraged large SOEs to invest in southern Xinjiang since the late 1990s. The introduction of large companies, most of which are energy tycoons like PetroChina and Sinopec, however, only serves to increase economic inequality between Han Chinese and Uyghurs and between Xinjiang and other provinces. These state companies prefer to hire Han workers for their technical skills. They do not need to pay income tax to the Xinjiang government as they are registered in Beijing and their oil and gas pipeline subsidiaries are registered in Shanghai.[5]

China's preferential policies in Xinjiang have also sharpened the ethnic divide, distributing benefits according to people's ethnic status. These have only heightened the ethnic consciousness of the minorities and discouraged the development of a Chinese identity. Hence, the system of regional autonomy of ethnic minorities, to a certain degree, goes against the principles of national integration.[6]

The third problem in Xinjiang is caused by the CCP's restrictive religious policy. The CCP's atheist ideology is essentially anti-religion. The perception of Party leaders that religious organisations are often involved in separatist activities has strengthened their anti-religion attitudes. Even though the government has relaxed its control in the past decade, its religious policy remains too restrictive. Such policy has offended many Muslims and has led to grievances within the Uyghur community.[7]

## Planning a Major Policy Change

From 22 to 25 August 2009, about one month after the tragic violence, Chinese President Hu Jintao visited Xinjiang and made a speech to local officials. In the speech he asserted that "the fundamental

---

[2]Please see Appendix 1.

[3]The government enforced the Three-60% ("*san ge 60%*") policy in Xinjiang, namely, ethnic minorities should constitute 60% of students in local schools, 60% of employees in local enterprises and 60% of soldiers in local enlistment.

[4]Zhou J, "Review of the Xinjiang Riot," *Zhengming*, September 2009.

[5]Hille, K, "Ethnic Groups United in Hostility towards Leaders," *Financial Time Chinese*, 8 September 2009. As SOEs send most of the natural gas explored in Xinjiang to the coastal cities, Xinjiang itself suffers from a shortage of natural gas. Every day, buses, taxis and cars form an approximately 500-metre long queue at a natural gas station between Urumqi and Kashgar. The prices of petrol and gas in this area are the highest in China. Most households in Xinjiang use wood and coal for heating due to the shortage of natural gas. The general public in Xinjiang thus feels exploited.

[6]Ma R, "A New Way to Understand Ethnic Relations: 'De-politicization' of Minority Issues." *Journal of Peking University*, vol. 41, no. 6, pp. 122–33.

[7]"Wary of Islam, China Tightens a Vise of Rules," *The New York Times*, 18 October 2008.

way to resolve the Xinjiang problem is to expedite development in Xinjiang."[8] This conveyed a clear message that Beijing was going to change the stability-first policy and sort out a development plan for Xinjiang.

In November 2009, three investigation teams were sent to Xinjiang to collect first-hand data regarding social and economic situations, religions and political stability.[9]

The teams visited every prefecture of Xinjiang and talked with local officials in numerous bureaus and local people from different ethnic groups. The final reports were compiled by the State Commission of Development and Reform and submitted to the State Council. These reports were mainly about boosting economic growth in Xinjiang and achieving lasting stability.

In late March 2010, Party and governmental leaders of 19 affluent provinces and cities were called to Beijing to attend a conference on providing assistance to Xinjiang's development.[10] Executive Vice Premier Li Keqiang addressed the meeting. Under a "pairing assistance" model arranged in this conference, the 19 provinces and cities were each required to help support the development of different areas in Xinjiang by providing human resources, technology, management and funds. Shanghai, for instance, was mainly to assist Bachu, Shache, Zepu and Yechang counties in the Kashgar prefecture.[11]

In a Politburo meeting on 23 April 2010, senior leaders decided to hold a national work conference on Xinjiang issues in May 2010 to establish strategic plans to "leapfrog development" and achieve "long-term stability". Attendees agreed that Xinjiang has an "extraordinarily important strategic status" in the Party's national development blueprint. Thus development would set the foundation for solutions to all problems in this area. As such, the Party was prepared to devote all its muscles to accelerating the pace of development.[12]

## Personnel Change: From "Stability" to "Development"

Beijing then made a personnel change to further prepare for the policy changes. Xinjiang party secretary, Wang Lequan (also a Politburo member), was replaced by Zhang Chunxian, then party chief of Hunan province.

Born in Shandong, Wang built up his portfolio in Shandong as its vice governor within the party-governmental system in 1989. In April 1991, he was sent to Xinjiang and assumed the office of vice governor. In 1995, he was appointed party secretary and became the highest-ranking figure in this troubled frontier region.

Having spent almost two decades in Xinjiang, Wang was known for his hard-liner stance. When he began his career in Xinjiang, the local people were terror-stricken by a series of bomb attacks and bloodshed.[13] He promoted the stability-first policy and enforced it with an iron hand. Wang

---

[8]Xinhua News Agency, "Hu Jintao Made an Important Speech to Cadres of Xinjiang Uyghur Autonomous Region," 25 August 2009. At <http://news.xinhuanet.com/politics/2009-08/25/content_11942627_2.htm> (accessed May 2010).

[9]Central News Agency, "The CCP Is Making New Policy on Xinjiang Development." 19 November 2009. The name list of the team leaders showed the importance the CCP attached to this investigation tour. Liu Yunshan, Politburo member and head of the Central Party Propaganda Department, leads the team surveying culture and education issues. Ma Kai, secretary general of the State Council, leads the team focussing on social and economic development. And Du Qinglin, head of the Central Party United Front Work Department, leads teams investigating ethnicity, religions, social stability, and party organisational building. Members of the teams were from almost all the central party departments and central governmental ministries.

[10]Xinhua News Agency, "The National Conference on "Pairing Assistance" in Xinjiang's Development was Held in Beijing." 30 March 2010. At <http://news.xinhuanet.com/politics/2010-03/30/c_128713.htm> (accessed May 2010).

[11]Please see Appendix 2 for a full list of the 19 provinces and cities.

[12]International News Online (*Guoji Zaixian*), "The CCP Politburo Held Meeting to Stabilize Xinjiang." At <http://gb.cri.cn/27824/2010/04/23/5005s2828148.htm> (accessed May 2010).

[13]Including 1990, riots in Baren township; 1992, bomb attacks in buses in Urumqi; 1993, series of explosion in multiple cities; 1996 to 1997, series of murder of governmental officials and pro-government religious leaders; 1997, riots in Yining; series of bomb attacks in Urumqi.

successfully frustrated a number of Islamic extremist and Uyghur separatist organisations and largely maintained social stability in this restive area until 2008. His image as a ruthless hard-liner won him the nickname of "secretary of stability" (*wending shuji*). For his achievements, in 2002, Beijing offered Wang a seat in the Politburo, which made him one of the most powerful provincial leaders in the nation.

As Beijing had decided to give priority to economic development and depart from the formula of "stability above all else," it was time for Wang to resign.[14] His successor, Zhang Chunxian, has a more diverse resume than Wang. Zhang was once a soldier, an engineer, a manager of state-owned enterprises and minister of transport, and has been party secretary of Hunan province since 2005.

It is believed that Zhang is a relative soft-liner and a moderate. His amiable and responsive style to journalists makes him popular.[15] The Hong Kong media once voted him the "most open-minded party secretary."[16] Based on his experience in state companies and economic-related ministries, people expect Zhang to promote a development-centred and soft-line policy.[17]

Three weeks after the new party secretary started his job, internet services in Xinjiang, shut down since the riots in July 2009, were finally restored. Zhang argued that unimpeded internet access was important for economic development in Xinjiang. Observers believe that he was trying to bring new thoughts to this troubled region and preparing for a new start.[18]

## The New Policies

The new policy package was finally unveiled in the Xinjiang Work Conference from 17 to 19 May 2010. The attendee list of the conference was quite impressive: the Party's General Secretary and State President Hu Jintao; Premier Wen Jiabao; Vice President Xi Jinping, who is widely believed to be the heir apparent to Hu; Executive Vice Premier Li Keqiang, the supposed successor to Wen; and the other members of the Politburo Standing Committee, all other vice premiers, Politburo members, as well as all the relevant cabinet ministers, provincial leaders, state-owned enterprises leaders, military leaders and chiefs of the armed police. In total there were 359 persons in attendance.

According to the official Xinhua Agency, the conference decided to take a balanced approach between stability and development in Xinjiang, giving more priority to development. The objective of policies was to "leapfrog development" and achieve "long-term stability." A consensus among leaders was that the "major contradiction" in Xinjiang was between the growing material and cultural demands of the people and the low level of social and economic development. Thus, to resolve this contradiction, the focus of the government in the region had to be on economic development.[19]

President Hu stipulated that by 2015, per capita GDP in Xinjiang should catch up with the country's average level and the residents' income and their access to basic public services should be on par with those of the country's western provinces. During this period, "marked" improvement must be achieved in the region's infrastructure, self-development capacity, ethnic unity and social stability.

Xinjiang should also become a "moderately prosperous society" (*xiaokang shehui*) in all aspects by 2020. It should improve people's living standards and build an eco-friendly environment, as well as ensure ethnic unity, social stability and security.

---

[14]Fairclough, G, "Xinjiang Official Removed in China", *Wall Street Journal*, 26 April 2010.

[15]Hille, K, "Beijing Displaces Head of Restive Region", *Financial Times Chinese,* 26 April 2010.

[16]Wang W, "Behind the Leadership Change in Xinjiang: A New Stage of Governance", *China News Net*, 29 April 2010.

[17]Voice of America, "Xi Jinping's Praise of Zhang Chunxian", 25 April 2010. At <http://www.tycool.com/2010/04/25/00051.html> (accessed May 2010).

[18]Baifeng, "New Secretary Zhang Chunxian Brought Internet Feast to Xinjiang", *Huasheng Online*, 17 May 2010. At <http://opinion.voc.com.cn/article/201005/201005171650567197.html> (accessed May 2010).

[19]"The Xinjiang Work Conference was Held, Hu and Wen Made Important Speeches", Xinhua News Agency, 20 May 2010.

To achieve these goals, priority would be given to improving the livelihoods of all ethnic groups. Previous government investment had mostly gone to infrastructure or heavy industries, which had not only benefited local ethnic minorities very little, but also actually widened the income gap between the Han and other groups.

In his speech, Hu required central fiscal investment and aid from other provinces to be spent on the livelihoods of various ethnic groups. Resource tax reforms and resource development should be directly linked to the welfare of the local people. More efforts were thus needed to create more job opportunities and vocational training for all ethnic groups.

The development plan also put the spotlight on the southern part of Xinjiang. Most industries and investment are concentrated in the northern part of the region, where most Han Chinese live, where as most Uyghurs live in the south, such as in Kashgar and Hotian. Regional inequality had widened income gaps across groups. Chinese leaders decided to fix the problem with fiscal and financial measures.

A three-pronged approach has been adopted to support Xinjiang. First, Beijing will dramatically increase government investment in the region. Premier Wen Jiabao told the meeting that the fixed asset investment for the region in the next Five-Year Programme beginning in 2011 would be more than double the amount in the current plan,[20] which means investments from 2011 through 2015 could run to two trillion *yuan*.[21]

The 19 provinces and cities that joined the "pairing assistance" programme were required to grant 0.3% to 0.6% of their annual budget to Xinjiang every year. This grant would amount to more than 10 billion *yuan* in 2011 and would steadily increase in the following 10 years.

In addition, joint-equity commercial banks, foreign banks and banks of various kinds are encouraged to open outlets and branches in remote areas, mostly in southern Xinjiang, and provide more loans to local people and enterprises.[22]

Second, the current tax system would be changed in favour of Xinjiang. The most striking reform was to change the way natural resources including oil and gas were taxed from a quantity-based to price-based levy. Xinjiang is the home to 15% of China's proven oil reserves and 22% of total proven reserves of natural gas.[23] As oil and gas are taxed according to the volume of output, Xinjiang has yet to benefit from the increase in prices in the international market.

With the new resource taxation, this autonomous region may receive 8 to 10 billion *yuan* of additional fiscal revenue annually.[24] An official from PetroChina, the largest oil producer in the region, said that the new tax system would result in a dramatic increase in company costs. If the tax rate is put at 5%, PetroChina would have to pay a tax of about six times more.[25]

Enterprises in less developed southern Xinjiang would enjoy a favourable "two-year exemption and three-year reduction" (*liangmian san jian ban*) tax policy, which previously only applied to foreign-invested companies. In the first two years after the enterprise begins to make a profit, it would be completely exempted from income tax; in the following three years, it would be allowed a 50% reduction.[26]

---

[20]Buckley, C, "China in Growth Push for Restive Xinjiang Region", 20 May 2010. At <http://in.reuters.com/article/worldNews/idINIndia-48662420100520?sp=true> (accessed May 2010).

[21]Wang Y, et al. "China to Double Xinjiang Spending to Boost Stability", *Bloomberg*, 21 May 2010. At <http://www.businessweek.com/news/2010-05-21/china-to-double-xinjiang-spending-to-boost-stability-update1-.html> (accessed May 2010).

[22]"Hundreds of Billion Yuan Will Be Invested in Xinjiang", *Hong Kong Wen Wui Po,* 18 May 2010.

[23]Wang et al., op. cit.

[24]"Oil and Gas Taxed on Price, Local Fiscal Revenue Increases 10 Billion," *Economic News Daily* (*meiri jingji xinwen*), 21 May 2010.

[25]"Resources Tax Reform Given the 'Go'", *Global Times*, 21 May 2010. At <http://business.globaltimes.cn/china-economy/2010-05/534302.html> (accessed May 2010).

[26]Qin F, "Over Two Trillion *Yuan* will Rush into Xinjiang in the Next Five Years", *China News Net*, 21 May 2010.

Finally, a new Special Economic Zone will be established in Kashgar, the hub in south Xinjiang where 90% of its residents are Uyghurs. In addition, Alataw Port and Korgas Port, China's important gateways to Kazakhstan, would become special zones for cross-border trade.

The Special Economic Zone usually enjoys preferential policies in industries, taxation, finance, land use and trade, which are especially conducive to doing business. In the 1980s and 1990s, Special Economic Zones such as Shenzhen, Zhuhai and Pudong were engines of China's economic miracle. Observers anticipate Kashgar and those border free trade zones to play the same role in Xinjiang's growth.[27]

Although priority was given to economic development, maintaining stability and fighting against ethnic separatism remain crucial to Xinjiang. While the conference did not sort out details about how to "firmly oppose and fight against ethnic separatist forces,"[28] there are signs indicating that Beijing is ready to use force to crack down on separatists.

Four senior military generals sat in the conference, conveying clearly the message that the People's Liberation Army (PLA) backed the Xinjiang development plan and any separatist attempts might face coercive actions. The four generals were Chen Bingde, Li Jinai, Liao Xilong and Chang Wanquan, heads of the four general headquarters/departments of the PLA, as well as members of the Central Military Commission.[29]

Three days after the conference, an anti-riot special police unit was established in Urumqi. Named as the "Flying Tiger Commando", this unit is to deal with emergencies such as terrorist attacks, hostage-taking and violent riots in cities.[30] With more and more such special units in Xinjiang, the government is now able to react quickly and effectively to street violence like the riots in July 2009.

**Internal and External Challenges**

What is clear is that Chinese leaders see the solution to the Xinjiang problem as one of "supplying creature comforts". They showed great confidence in economic development as the solution to the issue. If the region can develop fast enough, they assume Uyghurs will accept Chinese rule and their dissatisfactions will disappear.

In the short and medium term, this economic therapy may prove effective as the livelihoods of ethnic minorities and public services are being improved. Minority people may generally become less likely to support Islamic extremism or terrorist attacks.

Yet there are foreseeable challenges to the development process. Economic modernisation will bring a lot of rural residents into cities. Urban settings will put formerly isolated populations into contact with others, with migrant workers easily developing ethnic networks of information, jobs, and housing.[31] These new migrants usually come with unrealistically high expectations. They are likely to be frustrated and become particularly hostile to some cultural aspects of modernisation, and are therefore "ripe for radicalisation."[32] For instance, many rioters in the

---

[27]"Kashgar is about to Establish an Economic Special Zone", *21st Century Business Herald*, 19 May 2010. At <http://money.163.com/10/0519/01/670Q885400253B0H_2.html> (accessed May 2010).

[28]"The Xinjiang Work Conference was Held, Hu and Wen Made Important Speeches", Xinhua News Agency, 20 May 2010.

[29]Chen Bingde is chief of the General Staff Headquarters; Li Jinai is director of the General Political Department; Liao Xilong is director of the General Logistics Department; and Chang Wanquan is director of the General Armament Department. Comparing the Xinjiang conference with the Tibet Work Conference held in January, 2010, another top level meeting addressing Tibet's development plan, the lists of participants are roughly the same, except for the absence of the four senior military leaders at the Tibet Conference.

[30]"Flying Tiger Commando Established in Urumqi to Against Terrorism and Riots", *Xinjiang Daily*, 23 May 2010.

[31]Olzak, S, "Contemporary Ethnic Mobilization", *Annual Review of Sociology*, 9, 1983, p. 367.

[32]Richardson, JM and S Sen, "Ethnic Conflict and Economic Development: A Policy Oriented Analysis", *Ethnic Studies Report,* January 1997.

Urumqi violence were newly urbanised youth from rural areas in south Xinjiang. The ethnic conflict provided them with an opportunity to vent their grievances resulting from economic growth.[33]

In the long run, Chinese leaders may have to face other challenges. People who are economically better off and better educated are more likely to pay attention to their own history, culture, languages, and religions and hence are more likely to strengthen their ethnic identity.

The new plan largely ignores the issue of religion. In Hu's speech, there is only one sentence related to this issue — "fully implement the Party's ethnic policy and religion policy, fully strengthen and improve propaganda and ideological work …"[34] There is no sign that the existing religious policy will be changed.[35] In December 2011, the municipal government of Yining (a city in northern Xinjiang) launched a campaign in its residential communities to "dilute the religious consciousness and to advocate civilised and healthy life".[36] The government tried to forbid Muslim apparel and veils. This campaign was a miniature of the offensive religious policy in Xinjiang.

It would seem that the CCP leadership has yet to figure out a new way to handle religious issues. But this is a challenge they cannot evade. Heavy-handed restrictions on Islam have radicalised many Muslim Uyghurs[37] who join underground Koran study groups, where the imams teach the divine scripts as well as political blueprints for an independent East Turkestan. The CCP in turn takes it as a justification for more harsh control over religion. To achieve "lasting stability" in Xinjiang, Beijing may need to break this vicious circle and find a way to accommodate religion in its system.

It is also unclear how Beijing would establish a national Chinese identity among the Muslim Uyghurs, Buddhist Tibetans and some other groups to achieve national integration. Hu called for comprehensive education on ethnic unity in order to help local people identify with the "great motherland, the Chinese nation, Chinese culture and a socialist development path with Chinese characteristics." On the other hand, he said that the Party will stick to the existing system of regional autonomy for ethnic minorities, a system that has politically sharpened ethnic divisions and weakened the Chinese identity. Promoting integration among various ethnic groups based on the existing system remains a question.

In February 2012, Zhu Weiqun, associate head of the Central Department of United Front of CCP, published an article arguing that it may be advisable to remove ethnicities from the official identity card, to allow different ethnicities in the same school and to avoid establishing new autonomous regions for minorities.[38] This may be a sign of future policy change. The implications of such policies are still not clear.

Challenges may also come externally. Xinjiang will remain as an issue between China and the United States, although it may not be as controversial as the Tibet problem. While the Obama administration's response towards the Xinjiang riots was cautious, the United States still puts its

[33] Kato, Y, "The Next Step of China's Ethnic Policy". *Financial Times Chinese*, 24 July 2009.

[34] "The Xinjiang Work Conference was Held, Hu and Wen Made Important Speeches", *Xinhua News Agency*, 20 May 2010.

[35] In a comparative case, an official statement at the fourth Tibet Work Conference in 2001 claimed "protecting freedom of religious belief and legal religious activities … actively guiding Tibetan Buddhism to be adapted into the socialist society." (Xinhua News Agency, "The Fourth Tibet Work Conference.") In the fifth Tibet Work Conference, the "freedom of religion" was dropped. Please see Xinhua News Agency, "The Fourth Tibet Work Conference." At <http://tibet.news.cn/misc/2008-10/18/content_14671439.htm> (accessed May 2010) and Xinhua News Agency, "The CCP Center and the State Council Held the Fifth Tibet Work Conference." <http://news.xinhuanet.com/politics/2010-01/22/content_12858927.htm> (accessed May 2010).

[36] "Yining of Xinjiang Attempts to Dilute the Religious Consciousness." *BBC Chinese Web*, 15 December 2011. At <http://www.bbc.co.uk/zhongwen/simp/chinese_news/2011/12/111215_china_uighurs.shtml> (accessed May 2010).

[37] "Wary of Islam, China Tightens a Vise of Rules", *The New York Times*, 18 October 2008.

[38] Zhu W, "Reflections on Current Ethnic Issues", 15 February 2012, *People's Daily Web*. At <http://cpc.people.com.cn/GB/64093/64102/17122242.html> (accessed May 2010).

weight behind certain overseas Uyghur movements. Uyghur American Association and the World Uyghur Congress, two major Uyghur organisations in the western world, receive financial support from the National Endowment for Democracy (NED), an American organisation financed by the US Congress.[39] The United States also brought up Xinjiang as an issue of concern in its human rights talks with Chinese officials in May 2010.[40]

Turkey is another country that has vested interests in the Xinjiang issue due to its cultural and linguistic linkages with Uyghurs. In spite of this, Turkey is making efforts to strengthen its trade ties with China. In June 2009, Turkish President Abdullah Gul visited China with 120 Turkish businessmen. Till then, the total trade volume between the two countries was over US$17 billion.[41] Nevertheless, Turkey had the strongest reaction to the Xinjiang incident.[42]

Turkey by itself may not constitute a major challenge to China. But it has significant impact on the Turkic, also Islamic states in Central Asia, including Azerbaijan, Kazakhstan, Turkmenistan, Uzbekistan and Kyrgyzstan.[43] Any imprudent move in Xinjiang, if being interpreted as anti-Turkic or anti-Islamic, might spark off chained reactions in those countries and further complicate the Xinjiang issue.

## Appendix 1

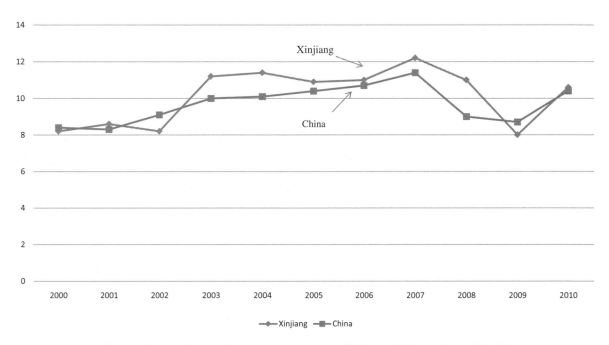

**Figure A.1**   GDP Growth Comparison between Xinjiang and China since 2000 (%)

*Sources*: Data for 2000–2009 were calculated based on statistics retrieved from China's National Bureau of Statistics. China's national annual GDP growth rate in 2010 was retrieved from the World Bank database, and Xinjiang's annual growth rate of gross regional product was cited from this website <http://www.mofcom.gov.cn/aarticle/difang/henan/201102/20110207403778.html? 2667190221=151279585> (accessed 6 July 2012).

---

[39]"Rebiya's Funding Sources: US-Based National Endowment for Democracy Proactively Offers Funds", 13 July 2009. At <http://english.peopledaily.com.cn/90001/90776/90882/6699468.html> (accessed May 2010).

[40]"China Hopes Development Solves Region's Tensions", *AP*, 20 May 2010. At <http://www.google.com/hostednews/ap/article/ALeqM5gSjMTGA_93sjHUt2y3ACaI8ak7vQD9FQJUE02> (accessed May 2010).

[41]Ayparlar, BD, "Turkish PM Erdogan: 'Incidents at Xinjiang are almost Genocide'", *Journal of Turkish Weekly*, 11 July 2009.

[42]Turkey requested to submit the Uyghur issue to the UN Security Council, in which it was a non-permanent member in 2009–2010. "Xinjiang: Erdogan Expresses Uneasiness Over Incidents", *Journal of Turkish Weekly*, 8 July 2009.

[43]"Russia Warns Turkey not to Design 'Union of Central Asian Turkic States'", *China News Net*, 2 February 2000. At <http://news.sina.com.cn/world/2000-2-2/58846.html> (accessed May 2010).

# Appendix 2

**Table A.1**  The "Pairing Assistance" Programme for Xinjiang

| Provinces/Cities Providing Support to Xinjiang | Prefectures and Counties in Xinjiang Receiving Support |
|---|---|
| Beijing | Hotan prefecture: Hotan city, Hotan county, Moyu (Karakax) county, Lop county<br>Xinjiang Production and Construction Corps (XPCC) 14th Agricultural Division |
| Shanghai | Kashgar prefecture: Bachu county, Shache (Yarkant) county, Zepu (Poskam) county, Yecheng (Kargilik) county |
| Guangdong | Kashgar prefecture: Shufu county, Jiashi county<br>Tumshuq city (XPCC Third Agricultural Division) |
| Shenzhen | Kashgar prefecture: Kashi city, Taxkorgan Tajik autonomous county |
| Tianjin | Hotan prefecture: Minfeng county, Chira county, Keriye county |
| Liaoning | Tacheng prefecture |
| Zhejiang | Aksu prefecture, Aral (XPCC First Agricultural Division) |
| Jilin | Altay prefecture: Altay city, Habahe county, Burqin county, Jeminay county |
| Jiangxi | Kizilsu Kirghiz autonomous prefecture: Akto county |
| Helongjiang | Altay prefecture: Fuhai county, Fuyun county, Qinggil county<br>XPCC 10th Agricultural Division |
| Anhui | Hotan prefecture: Pishan county |
| Hebei | Bayin'gholin Mongol autonomous prefecture, XPCC Second Agricultural Division |
| Shanxi | Wujiaqu city (XPCC Sixth Agricultural Division), Changji Hui autonomous prefecture: Fukang city |
| Henan | Hamiprefecture, XPCC 13th Agricultural Division |
| Jiangsu | Kizilsu Kirghiz autonomous prefecture: Artux city, Ulugqat county<br>Ili Kazakh autonomous prefecture: Huocheng county, 66 Regiment of XPCC Fourth Agricultural Division, Yining county, Qapqal Xibe autonomous county |
| Fujian | Changji Hui autonomous prefecture: Changji city, Manas county, Hutubi county, Qitai county, Jimsar county, Mori Kazakh autonomous county |
| Shandong | Kashgar prefecture: Shule county, Yengisar county, Makit county, Yopurga county |
| Hubei | Börtala Mongol autonomous prefecture: Bole city, Jinghe county, Wenquan county<br>XPCC Fifth Agricultural Division |
| Hunan | Turpan prefecture |

*Source*: "The List of Provinces and Cities 'Pairing' Assisting Xinjiang." *People's Daily Online*. At <http://minzu.people.com.cn/GB/166030/188109/11580975.html> (accessed May 2010).

# 10

# The Chinese Leadership and the Internet

LYE Liang Fook and Lily HONG*

*The Internet, with its ability to create a more level playing field particularly for the masses in terms of their access to information, has made the task of governing in China more challenging. Yet, the leadership in China appears to have largely been successful in using the Internet to strengthen its capacity to govern and enhance its legitimacy.*

The Internet, because of its ability to share information and ideas across space and time in a virtually instantaneous manner, has given rise to the popular view that it is an effective tool for political liberalisation in any country. Yet, there is a need to look at it from another perspective, i.e. how various ruling parties and governments are making use of the Internet. In particular, this chapter looks at how the leadership in China is tapping the Internet in an effort to improve its governance, and in the process, enhance its legitimacy.

The Internet Age has opened up new avenues and created unprecedented opportunities for China's leaders to engage the masses. Most notably, Premier Wen Jiabao participated in his first online chat in February 2009 that was hosted by the websites of the Chinese government and the official *Xinhua News Agency*.[1] He continued with this practice in 2010 and 2011. Much earlier, in June 2008, General Secretary Hu Jintao fielded questions from Chinese netizens through the *Strong China Forum* (*qiangguo luntan*), an online bulletin of the *People's Daily*. These two high-profile examples show that both the Chinese Communist Party (CCP) and the government have given their imprimatur to capitalise on the Internet's potential.

In China, the number of Internet users, also known as "netizens", has grown exponentially. This social phenomenon is a key motivation behind the leadership's efforts to tap the potential of the

---

*LYE Liang Fook is Research Fellow and Assistant Director at the East Asian Institute of the National University of Singapore while Lily HONG is Research Assistant at the same institute.

[1]"Chinese Premier Wen gives online interview at Xinhuanet", *Xinhuanet*, 27 February 2011, at <http://www.xinhuanet.com/english2010/special/wjb2011/> (accessed 10 May 2012).

Internet. With the strong growth of netizens — many of them in their formative years under the young and malleable age of 30 — the leadership wants to, through the Internet, portray a forward-looking and dynamic image to identify with them. The leadership seeks to portray itself as making an effort to better understand the people's preoccupations, especially those of the younger generation.

The Internet also provides the leadership with a channel to improve its communication with and obtain feedback from the public. The Internet, by offering a channel for the leaders to have relatively direct access to the public, minimises the chance of having their views sifted by bureaucratic interests. Having more direct access to the public is also in line with the pro-people orientation of the current Hu-Wen leadership. In fact, both leaders have consistently stressed that the power of the leadership originates from the people and therefore the leadership should be responsive to their needs. By being closer to the people, the CCP and the government can better gauge public reactions and make improvements to policies. In turn, the people will feel assured that their views are being heard, thereby reducing the possibility of pent-up frustrations. Equally important is that the Internet enables the authorities to nip grievances in the bud before they snowball.

While tapping its potential, the Chinese leadership is determined to maintain control over the development of the Internet. In fact, it plays a proactive role in managing the growth of the Internet. In 2007, General Secretary Hu Jintao set the tone when he called on government officials to "actively and creatively nurture a healthy online culture" that meets public demand. In other words, he expects officials at all levels to facilitate the development of the Internet while improving the administration of web technologies, content and network security.[2]

### Internet Development in China

Since China achieved full functional Internet accessibility in 1994, the number of netizens has grown tremendously. The numbers expanded from a mere 2.1 million in 1998 to 513 million by December 2011 (Figure 1), representing an annual growth rate of 52.6 %.

According to the China Internet Network Information Centre (CNNIC), the majority of netizens are below 30 years of age. They make up 58.2% of the total number of netizens and are well-educated. In fact, one-third of netizens is made up of students while the other two-thirds comprise the working class and retirees.

In CNNIC's latest survey published in January 2012, most Chinese netizens (80.9%) used the Internet for instant messaging in 2011, representing a spurt of 17.7% from 2010. This was followed by other key uses of the Internet such as to conduct searches (79.4%, an increase of 8.8% from 2010), for online music (75.2%, an increase of 6.5%), online videos (63.4%, an increase of 14.6%),

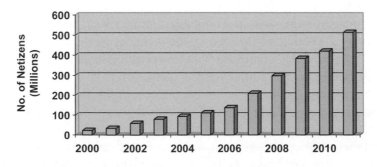

**Figure 1**  Growth of Netizens in China

*Source*: China Internet Network Information Centre.

[2]"President Hu Jintao Asks Officials to Better Cope with Internet", *Xinhuanet*, 24 January 2007 at <http://news.xinhuanet.com/english/2007–01/24/content_5648674.htm> (accessed 10 May 2012).

online gaming (63.2%, an increase of 6.6%), blogging (62.1%, an increase of 8.2%), emailing (47.9%, a decrease of 1.6%), social networking (47.6%, an increase of 3.9%), online reading (39.5%, an increase of 4%), and online shopping (37.8%, an increase of 20.8%).[3]

It is worth highlighting that among the key uses of the Internet, microblogging, known as *Weibo* in China or *Twitter* elsewhere, showed the most substantial increase. Its astonishing growth rate indicates how netizens have readily embraced the instantaneous and interactive nature of communicating on the Internet. While conventional blogging saw a slight increase of 8.2% in terms of the number of users in 2011 compared to 2010, *Weibo* users saw a surge of 296% within the same period. *Weibo* has therefore become an important means of information exchange for netizens, accounting for 48.7% of *Weibo* users in a CNNIC survey.

## Tapping the Internet's Potential

Given the explosive growth of the Internet, the Chinese government has been quick to tap its potential to try to improve governance and enhance its legitimacy. Sometime around 2005, CCP leaders started becoming more creative in influencing public opinion on the Internet.[4] Before that, a number of public relations blunders had highlighted to the CCP and the government the importance of publishing timely and accurate information. For instance, in 2003, China's public image, both domestically and externally, was battered by its initial lacklustre reaction to the outbreak of SARS in the country.[5] Subsequent major events such as the outbreak of bird flu, the Olympic torch relay and the Wenchuan earthquake further underscored the value of seizing the "right to speak" (*hua yu quan*) through various platforms including the Internet. The leadership realised that they would be in a better position to deflect criticisms of a cover-up if they release information first (even if it is incomplete). In doing so, the leadership may even be able to shape public discourse to its advantage. More significantly, this was in line with the Hu-Wen leadership's call to be more accountable to the people. This marks an important departure from previous actions where negative news was not reported.[6]

The Internet also offers the Chinese government a channel to promote a pro-people image. The *People's Daily* — the mouthpiece of CCP — has since September 2008 sanctioned an official fan club webpage for top leaders in the central government. This webpage is partly a response to a series of online informal fan clubs of key Chinese leaders that have spontaneously emerged,[7] and partly due to the Chinese leaders' desire to use the Internet as a platform to get close to the people.

Most notably, in June 2008, China's President Hu Jintao visited the headquarters of the *People's Daily* and chatted online with netizens via the *Strong China Forum*. Hu expressed his concern for the well-being of netizens at various social levels. He disclosed that he always reads domestic and foreign news online. This was the first time a top leader of China openly expressed his concern for netizens on the Internet. Just before his online debut, Hu said in a speech delivered at the *People's Daily* headquarters that the Internet has become the catalyst for promoting CCP's ideology and culture, and an amplifier of public opinion. Thus, the social influence of the new media should be fully recognised and government leaders as well as party

[3]CNNIC 29th Survey Report, January 2012, p. 33. Full report can be accessed at <http://www1.cnnic.cn/uploadfiles/pdf/2012/2/27/112543.pdf> (accessed 10 May 2012).
[4]"China's Guerrilla War for the Web", *Far East Economic Review*, July 2008.
[5]China initially left it to the local levels to deal with the outbreak. It was only when SARS spread to the other countries and these countries pressured China did Chinese leaders mount a national response to deal with the crisis.
[6]For instance, in the Tangshan earthquake of 1976, no official information about what actually happened or the number of casualties was made available at that time. This was done in the interest of protecting state secrets.
[7]Fan club of Hu-Wen, which was sanctioned by netizens, at <http://shijinbabaofan.g.ifensi.com/main/show> (accessed 15 March 2012). As of 6 July 2012, there were reportedly 9,411 members.

cadres should attach great importance to the construction, implementation and management of the Internet.[8]

Taking the cue from Hu, Premier Wen Jiabao made his online chat debut in February 2009, a week prior to the start of the annual National People's Congress and Chinese People's Political Consultative Conference sessions. Wen's dialogue with netizens lasted almost two hours. He was deluged with about 90,000 questions on various subjects ranging from the shoe-throwing incident,[9] his income level, the economic crisis, healthcare reforms to corruption.[10] Wen carried on this practice of having web chats in the early part of 2010 and 2011. He fielded questions mainly over bread and butter issues such as property prices, inflation, and the wealth gap.[11] These online dialogues thus reflected the Chinese leaders' more open and confident style of governance in the Information Age. It was a further attempt to be closer to the people by showing that the leadership was aware of their socio-economic grievances and would take measures to address them.

Chinese leaders are cognisant of the need to govern more effectively by going beyond impersonal documents and reports. As early as 2007, President Hu Jintao urged senior officials to improve their Internet literacy and use the Internet well to improve their leadership abilities.[12] Since then, Chinese leaders and officials have placed increasing attention to citizens' online views to better understand their preoccupations. Wen even stated in his online chats that the public was entitled to know the government's thoughts and actions, and to criticise government policies.

Many central government ministries and party organisations have also used the Internet to solicit opinions on issues affecting public interest. For instance, on the website of the Chinese Ministry of Civil Affairs, netizens can readily provide feedback on policies that fall within the purview of the ministry. All that is required is to email one's comments together with one's name and contact details.[13] Netizens can even email their comments directly to the Minister of Civil Affairs if they wish.[14] Likewise, the Central Commission for Discipline Inspection of the Chinese Communist Party has a website that allows netizens to report on malfeasance and corruption of party members.[15] On this website, netizens are even required to identify which province the offending party member comes from.[16] This practice of gathering feedback has also been followed by government and party organisations at lower levels. For instance, the governor of Qinghai province has even personally thanked netizens for making useful

---

[8]"*Zai renmin ribaoshe kaocha gongzuo shi de jianghua*" (Speech delivered while on a visit to the *People's Daily*), *People's Daily*, June 2009, at <http://media.people.com.cn/GB/40606/ 7409348.html> (accessed 10 May 2012).

[9]A protester threw a shoe at the Chinese premier as he was delivering a speech at Cambridge University, 2 February 2009, at <http://www.timesonline.co.uk/tol/news/uk/ article5643558.ece> (accessed 10 May 2012).

[10]"Premier Wen Talks Online with Public", *China Daily*, 20 February 2009.

[11]"Premier Wen Highlights Employment, Medical Care, Housing in Online Chat", *People's Daily Online,* 28 February 2010 at <http://english.peopledaily.com.cn/90001/90776/90785/6904249.html> (accessed 10 May 2012). See also "Wen Outlines Major Government Tasks in Annual Online Chat", *People's Daily Online,* 28 February 2011, at <http://english. people.com.cn/90001/90776/90785/7302363.html> (accessed 10 May 2012).

[12]Hu said this at the 38th regular study session of the Politburo. See "Chinese Premier to Talk Online with Public", *Xinhuanet*, 28 February 2009, at <http://news.xinhuanet.com/english/2009-02/28/content_10916529.htm> (accessed 10 May 2012).

[13]Official website of the Ministry of Civil Affairs of the People's Republic of China, at <http://www.mca.gov.cn/article/mxht/wsxf/> (accessed 10 May 2012).

[14]Ibid., at <http://www.mca.gov.cn/article/mxht/bzxx> (accessed 10 May 2012).

[15]Official website of the Central Commission for Discipline Inspection of the Chinese Communist Party, at <http://www.12388.gov.cn/xf/index.html> (accessed 10 May 2012).

[16]Ibid., at <http://www.12388.gov.cn/xf/shengji1.html> (accessed 10 May 2012).

suggestions that helped improve local governance.[17] In fact, all provinces in China have launched specific websites to promote two-way communication between the government and people. To some extent, this reaching-out-to-the-people approach is regarded by some as a practice in line with CCP's good tradition of keeping its pulse close to the people and feet firmly on the ground.

## A Channel for Social Supervision

Chinese leaders have increasingly emphasised the role of mass supervision via the Internet. In other words, netizens have now been ascribed a role, albeit within limits, to help the CCP and the government identify and report on official malfeasances. This is primarily intended to improve governance and strengthen the CCP's and the government's legitimacy.

Indeed, netizens have helped unearth a number of high-profile incidents related to official malpractices ranging from corruption to ostentatious spending, to abuses of public power. They show that Internet surveillance has become a means for China's netizens to voice their opinions, fight corruption and even stand up for their rights. Internet-related public incidents[18] such as the Lavish US Tour of Chinese Officials (in 2008), Yihuang County Residents Self Immolations in Face of Pressure by Authorities (in 2010), Xie Zhiqiang's Sex Scandal on Sina *Weibo* (in 2011), and Dalian Rises Up to Oppose Chemical Plantation P-Xylene Production (in 2011), show that the Internet has helped to draw attention to issues which have a public impact and in doing so, impelled the relevant Chinese officials to address them by taking into account the public interest.

At times, it seems that even ordinary Chinese individuals are able to stand up to abuses by local governments. In a well-known case in February 2009, Wang Shuai, who was residing in Shanghai, posted an online article criticising the city government in Lingbao city of Henan province for illegal land acquisition. In an attempt to hush Wang up, the Lingbao police reportedly travelled thousands of miles from Lingbao to Shanghai to nab and detain Wang Shuai for eight days on charges of defamation.[19] In the event, it was found that the local government had indeed acted unfairly in requisitioning land for development. The charges against Wang were dropped and his case was dismissed in April 2009. The director of Henan province's public security bureau even offered a rare public apology to Wang and his family in an online interview with the *People's Daily*, a CCP publication.[20] In this instance, it was not only the Chinese central government but also the CCP that saw the need to intervene in favour of Wang as this was a genuine case of an abuse of power by a local government. In doing so, the central government and party had attempted to portray themselves as standing up for the interests of the ordinary man-in-the-street.

In December 2010, the Information Office of the State Council published a White Paper titled "*China's Efforts to Combat Corruption and Build a Clean Government*". It stated that "China highly values the positive role played by the Internet in enhancing supervision, conscientiously strengthening the collection, research, judgment and management of information regarding combating corruption...."[21] In brief, the Chinese leadership recognises that the Internet functions as a tool in scrutinising officials and rooting out fraudulent acts within certain limits.

---

[17] "*Qinghai Shengzhang Song Xiuyan zhixin dafu wangyou renmenwang wangyou liuyan*" (Governor of Qinghai Song Xiuyan answered messages delivered by netizens), *People's Daily,* 11 February 2009.

[18] "Internet-related public incidents" refer to incidents that occur unexpectedly and which have generated intense discussions on the Internet, leading to greater supervision of how the Chinese government responds to them.

[19] "Respect Voice of the Internet", *China Daily*, 13 April 2009.

[20] "Police 'Sorry' Blogger was Detained", *China Daily*, 18 April 2009.

[21] "China's Efforts to Combat Corruption and Build a Clean Government", *Xinhuanet*, 29 December 2010, at <http://news.xinhuanet.com/english2010/china/2010–12/29/c_13669383_6.htm> (accessed 10 May 2012).

## The Internet and Prospects for Political Changes

At the governance level, it is important to grasp the role of the Internet as envisaged by the CCP and the government. Rather than regard the Internet as simply a democratising tool, China's leaders will continue to use the Internet to strengthen their communication with the people to improve governance. To them, the Internet is a tool to strengthen legitimacy and maintain a dominant hold on power.

While recognising that the Internet can help improve governance, the CCP and the government have also sought to ensure the "orderly" development of the Internet. In particular, various controls have remained in place to prevent the Internet from becoming a platform for subversive elements to challenge the authority. When necessary, the CCP and the government have shown their ability and determination to take speedy and tough action to counter threats to their dominant positions. During the height of the threat posed by the Jasmine revolution in China in early 2011, there was an anonymous call on the Internet for disgruntled Chinese to gather at designated spots in 13 cities across China to publicly air their grievances. The relevant Chinese authorities took this call for action seriously by not only tightening controls on the Internet but also physically rounding up potential "troublemakers".

Separately, the relevant Chinese authorities have also launched campaigns against pornographic or "yellow" websites to counter the spread of decadent values on the Internet that erode moral standards of officials and netizens. Several websites have been forced to close as a result. At other times, measures that are ostensibly aimed at promoting greater transparency and accountability on the Internet have been introduced. For instance, the authorities have introduced rules that require microblog users to register with their real identities. This has led *Weibo* to require users who register after 16 March 2012 to provide their real identities when they post or forward microblogs. These measures started with websites in Beijing, including *Sohu*, *NetEase* and *Sina*, with plans to extend this nationwide. According to a spokesman with the Beijing Internet Information Office, "the new rules are aimed at protecting web users' interests and improving credibility on the web".[22] Critics have however perceived this as yet another attempt by the authorities to make it easier for them to identify and even take action against those who promote unsavoury or dissenting views on the Internet.

To be sure, technology alone is unlikely to bring about political changes in China. While the Internet might facilitate some changes, it cannot determine the nature and pace of political reforms in China. A more important determinant is whether Chinese leaders see the need to introduce political reforms. Presently, some initiatives in this direction have been introduced including intra-Party democracy, local elections, legal and constitutional protection of citizens' rights, appointment of officials based on merit and greater accountability of officials. Yet, such initiatives are geared less towards achieving democracy but as a means to maintain the dominance of the CCP.

It is important not to overstate the impact of the Internet on political change in China. To some extent, cyberspace has indeed opened up a private realm for individuals to exchange information and interact with each other. Yet, this has to be set against the political realities in China such as the determination of the CCP and the government to tap the Internet for their own governing purposes and to clamp down on Internet activities when the need arises. In this regard, the Internet's much touted "liberating" effects may not be as far-reaching as it is made out to be.

What is perhaps more likely is that the mounting size of netizens will lead to more demands for greater transparency and accountability on the part of the CCP and the government over the longer term. Those with Internet access may develop a thirst for information that could only be satisfied by the CCP and the government, thus requiring the latter to open up more to meet this rising expectation. At the same time, the same group of people may also demand greater accountability of the CCP and government officials, thereby pressuring the authorities to improve and streamline the bureaucracy. How to simultaneously meet this growing aspiration and yet maintain the dominant position of the CCP could be the ultimate challenge.

---

[22]"Beijing Requires Real names in Microblog Registration", *Xinhuanet*, 16 December 2011, at <http://news.xinhuanet.com/english/china/2011–12/16/c_131310381.htm> (accessed 10 May 2012).

# 11

# Women's Political Participation in China

YANG Lijun and GUO Xiajuan*

*When China's economy was transformed from a planned one to a market-oriented one, there were changes to women's position in society. This chapter discusses the progress of women's political participation and the institutional constraints Chinese women face in improving their political status.*

In 2007, US-based *Forbes* magazine ranked then Chinese Vice Premier Wu Yi No. 2 on its annual list of the World's 100 Most Powerful Women. That was a significant indicator of the influence of women in Chinese political affairs. Wu symbolised the influence of women in Chinese political affairs and the role of Chinese women in "holding up half the sky" (*funu neng ding ban bian tian*). Indeed, women's political participation in China has gained new momentum after the country hosted the Fourth World Conference on Women in 1995. China has made substantial progress in widening women's political participation, though at a much lower level than that in many other countries, especially those in the democratic West.

The progress in the level of women's political participation can be attributed to the economic reform and open-door policy introduced in China in 1978. Women's political inclusion has greatly benefited from various gender-related institutions and policies such as the Law of the People's Republic of China on the Protection of Women's Rights and Interests, which was passed in 1992 and 2005, the Programmes for Women Development in China, namely, the 1995–2000 programme and the 2001–2010 programme and specific rules spelt out in various documents relating to

*YANG Lijun is a Research Fellow at the East Asian Institute, National University of Singapore, and GUO Xiajuan is teaching at Zhejiang University, China.

personnel appointments by the Central Organisation Department (COD) of the CCP (e.g. the Programme on Deepening the Reform of Cadre and Personnel System from 2001 to 2010).

The market-oriented reform has greatly facilitated the engagement of women in free market competition. As women's awareness of individual rights develops, the granting of political rights becomes inevitable as it serves as an extension of their material interests under the free market system. In addition, the open-door policy has accelerated the alignment of Chinese women's pursuit of equal opportunity and favourable gender policy in line with international norms.

The advancement of women's participation in politics would not have come about without the development of many institutional factors over the past decades. Since the 1990s, the CCP has put in place various policies, or affirmative action, to enhance gender equality. Female representation in different political bodies has increased significantly. To encourage women to participate, the Party-state has explored different approaches such as combining multi-candidate elections with mandatory quotas. The quota system at every level has guaranteed the presence of women in political bodies.

Since the late 1990s, the COD has enacted several decisions on training and selecting women cadres. Promoted by the All China Women's Federation (ACWF), women's participation has become an index used in evaluating officials' performances, which represents a substantial leap from the initial definition in 1982 to actual implementation. These institutional initiatives have provided a stable institutional environment for advancing women's participation.

China still lags far behind many other countries in terms of increasing women's representation in powerful political bodies. Though a few Chinese women are perceived as politically influential worldwide, the reality is that the gap between women's participation in different political power structures in China and in other countries has widened in recent decades despite China's achievement of faster economic growth compared with most other countries today.

The international ranking of female deputies of People's Congress (equivalent to Congresspersons or Parliament Members in other countries) decreased from 12th in 1994 to 42nd in 2005. The low women's representation can also be seen in the central power structure as the proportion of females in the Central Committee of the CCP declined to 7.6% in 2002 compared with a steady increase from 5% to 13% between the 1950s and the 1970s. Women face enormous challenges in terms of political participation in the largely male-dominated society of China.

## The Rise of Affirmative Action

Equal opportunity between men and women has been a principal policy of the party and government ever since the founding of the People's Republic of China. During the era of Mao Zedong, China's gender policy was to achieve Mao's ambitious goal of "women hold[ing] up half the sky." Even to this day, Mao was regarded more liberal towards women participation in politics than any other leaders, including the current leadership. In fact, Mao's wife Jiang Qing was able to preside over many male Chinese politicians.

However, most of the provisions under this policy were too general and had no substantial impact on women's rights. China's hosting of the Fourth World Conference on Women in Beijing in 1995 was a key turning point. This event served as a catalyst to boosting women's political involvement, resulting in various gender-oriented regulations. In the closing address of the 1995 World Women's Conference, then Chinese President Jiang Zemin once again emphasised that "the equality between men and women is the fundamental policy of China." Following the 1995 conference, the Chinese government has been systematically supporting women's political rights.

As a primary provision in the 1954 Constitution, gender equality is protected constitutionally in China. The Constitution states that "all citizens of the People's Republic of China have the right to vote and stand for election." Another article states that "women in the People's Republic of China have equal rights with men in all spheres of life including the political, economic, cultural, social and family spheres."[1] Women's rights are also stated in all subsequent constitutions.

Between the 1950s and 1970s, women's rights were realised and protected by China's cadre management system under which all Party cadres and government officials were appointed by the party-state. This system took gender factors into consideration when appointments were decided, leading to a great increase in the proportion of female cadres. The female proportion reached its peak in the 1970s, representing a milestone in the history of women's political inclusion in China.

The 1982 Constitution substantially advanced women's political rights. Article 48 of the 1982 Constitution states that "the state … trains and selects women cadres". In September 1982, the 12th Party Congress, which was held in Beijing, revised the Party Constitution. Article 34 of the Party Constitution states that "the Party selects women cadres according to the criteria of integrity and ability…The Party should pay great attention to cultivating and selecting women cadres as well as minority cadres." Both the State Constitution and Party Constitution facilitated the rise of affirmative action, in terms of promoting women's political participation and increasing the proportion of females in different power structures. In other words, the new emphasis on women's rights made it mandatory to realise women's inclusion.

Since 1982, a number of party documents and state policies have focussed on female cadres' training and selection. Various state personnel reforms have also emphasised women's capacity building and their sharing of power in different government departments and organisations, providing women with special protection and benefits. The party has also made efforts to recruit women to meet the target of training and selecting women cadres.[2]

In 1992, the first law on women's rights, *The PRC Law on the Protection of Women's Rights*, was enacted. It was amended in 2005. The law reiterated that "the state should actively train and select female cadres. The state organs, civil organisations, enterprises and institutions must insist on the principle of gender equality in the appointment of cadres and they are to foster and promote female cadres to (*sic*) leadership positions. The state pays attention to training and selecting minority women cadres as well."[3] These provisions have generated a positive impact on women's political participation.

According to these policy initiatives, the government should play a leading role in policy implementation and bear full responsibility for it. In 1995, China's first gender equality programme — Programme of China Women's Development (1995–2000) — was enacted. A second version (2001–2010) of the programme was developed in 2000, indicating that women's political participation has become a part of governmental actions. Various concrete objectives established in the programme have advanced the goals of women's political participation.

In April 2009, the Information Office of the State Council published the National Human Rights Action Plan of China (2009–2010). This action plan pays much heed to women's political

---

[1]The 1954 Constitution also stated that the "People's Republic of China abolishes the feudal system and constraints of women." See <http://www.npc.gov.cn/zgrdw/common/zw.jsp?label=WXZLK&id=4264> (accessed 21 March 2010).

[2]The key documents include *The Programme of Building National Leadership Bodies of the Party and Government during 1998–2003*; *The Programme on Deepening the Reform of Cadres and Personnel System during 2001–2010*; *The Interim of Reserve Cadres of the Party and Government* enacted in 2000. There were also pertinent policies and measures which were co-enacted by the ACWF and the Central Organisation Department between the late 1990s and 2002.

[3]Articles 10 and 11 of *PRC Law on the Protection of Women's Rights*, the Working Committee of Law, in the Standing Committee of the NPC (eds.), *The Current Laws and Regulations of the PRC (volume I, Laws)*, Beijing, The Intellect Property Publishing House, 2002, pp.1677–1682.

participation. In particular, people's congresses, political consultative conferences and governments at all levels should have at least one female member in their leadership. Moreover, at least half of the agencies in central government ministries, provincial governments and city governments should have a female member in their leadership, and women should make up at least 20% of the reserve cadres at provincial, city and county levels.[4] The action plan represents a new effort to guarantee women's rights to political participation.

### Benefits from the Affirmative Action

Progress in women's political participation achieved since 1949 can be divided into three stages. The first stage began in 1949 with the establishment of the People's Republic, lasting until the mid-1960s during which affirmative action and other mandatory measures enabled women to make up a relatively high proportion in political power structures. The top-down appointment system, especially its quota measures, guaranteed women's political inclusion. Consequently, women's representation in party and government organs at all levels expanded considerably.

Various indicators point to achievements in terms of women's political participation, which range from women occupying leadership positions in top offices to those in grassroots bodies. The proportion of women in the National People's Congress (NPC) and Chinese People's Political Consultant Conference (CPPCC) has increased over time. The first NPC (1954) had 147 female representatives, accounting for 12% of the total number of representatives. The second NPC (1959) had 150, accounting for 12.2%. The third NPC (1964) had 542, accounting for 17.9%. The first CPPCC (1954) had 12 female representatives, accounting for 6.6%. The second CPPCC (1959) had 83, accounting for 11.4%. The third CPPCC (1964) had 87, accounting for 8.1%.[5] At the time, there were two women in various committees of the central government, making up 3.1% of the total number of members. Out of a total of six vice presidents, there was only one female. There were 20 women in positions at or above the vice ministerial level, accounting for 4% of the total.[6] In the 1950s, local governments at all levels had female cadres. Nationwide, about 70% of townships had female directors or deputy directors.[7]

During the second stage in the 1970s, women's political participation reached its peak. Due to the implementation of affirmative action and mandatory measures, the 1970s became the most remarkable era for women's political participation in contemporary China. In 1975, at the Fourth NPC, women representatives accounted for 22.6% of the total. About one in four Standing Committee members was female, indicating that female cadres made up a high proportion of government officials at all levels since members of the Standing Committees of NPC were usually selected from key position holders in various functional departments of the government.

After a decline between the 1980s and the early 1990s, the third stage of progress in women's political participation took place in the mid-1990s. Affirmative action was re-established and effectively implemented as China responded to the international community before and after the Fourth World Conference on Women in Beijing, as well as four meetings held by the Central Organisation Department and the ACWF which discussed issues related to women's political participation. Various programmes on training and selecting women cadres followed. Since then, the compulsory quota system has played a crucial role in increasing the proportion of females in party and government bodies. Overall, women's political participation during this period was

---

[4]<http://news.xinhuanet.com/newscenter/2009-04/13/content_11177926.htm> (accessed 21 March 2012).

[5]The Green Book of Women, *Report on Women's Development in China*. At <http://www.china.com.cn/zhanti2005/node_6151922.htm> (accessed 21 March 2012).

[6]*Women in Contemporary China* (*Dangdai Zhongguo Funv*), Beijing, The *Dangdai Zhongguo chubanshe*, 1994, p. 33.

[7]Wang F, "Impacts of the Party's Leadership on Women's Political Participation," *Journal of China Women's University (Social Science Edition)*, 3, 2001. Statistics show that 70% of townships had female directors and that female cadres accounted for 7% of all county cadres.

spurred by international factors and intervention in the forms of women-oriented strategies and policies by the party-state.

In the 1990s, the quota of women cadres saw a steady increase. Statistics show there were 10 million female governmental officials across the country in 1991, accounting for 31.2% of the total. The figure rose to 12.4 million in 1994 (32.5%); 13.8 million in 1997 (34.4%); 14.9 million in 2000 (36.2%) and 15.026 million in 2005 (38.9%).[8] Women also appeared in senior official positions. In 1994, there was one female vice premier in the State Council, 16 female ministers and deputy ministers, more than 300 female mayors and deputy majors, and 21,012 women judges in the country.[9]

Meanwhile, the proportion of female party members also saw a slow but steady increase. The number of female party members reached 8.2 million by the end of 1993, contributing to 15.13% of total party membership. That increased to 8.9 million in 1994, accounting for 15.6% of the total; 11.2 million in 2000 (17.4%); 11.6 million in 2002 (17.5%)[10] and 13.6 million in the end of 2005, or 19.2% of the total.[11]

The share of women among NPC representatives also expanded. There were 626 women representatives at the Eighth NPC in 1993, accounting for 21% of the total, and 19 female Standing Committee members, making up 12.3%, 2 percentage points higher than the previous committee.[12] There were 650 female representatives at the Ninth NPC in 1998, accounting for 21.8% of the total 2,979.[13] The State Council had one female vice premier and one female state councillor.[14]

There were 193 female committee members at the Eighth CPPCC in 1993, accounting for 9.2% of the total; 341 female committee members at the Ninth CPPCC in 1998, accounting for 15.5%, and 27 female Standing Committee members, accounting for 9%, representing 12 more, or 3.1 percentage points more than at the Eighth CPPCC; and 375 female members at the 10th CPPCC in 2003, accounting for 16.8%.[15]

The key to this progress was affirmative action and its implementation on the part of the Party and the state. The state, together with the Women's Federation, explored diverse approaches, including combining multi-candidate elections with mandatory quotas to promote women's political participation. The government established regulations to guarantee women's representatives in government organisations. More importantly, the Central Organisation Department enacted a series of policies on women's political participation and initiated regular programmes to train and select women politicians. The establishment of an index of women's participation among the officials' evaluation criteria provided a strong incentive for policy implementation.

## Implementation Problems and Policy Retreats

The development of the party-state-led programme of women's participation has been to a large degree determined by general policy orientation in different eras. Despite enormous efforts to promote women's political participation by the party-state, the affirmative action policies encountered strong resistance from time to time. For example, when government policies were focussed on achieving planned targets such as economic growth and material prosperity, the goals

[8] See <www.npc.gov.cn> (accessed 21 March 2012).

[9] Ibid.

[10] Sun J, "Research on the Law of Women's Political Participation since the 4th Plenum of 13th Party Congress, *Journal of Hunan Administration Institute,* 6, 2002.

[11] See <http://www.bjd.com.cn/jryw/200608/t20060825_74807.htm> (accessed 21 March 2012).

[12] "The Development of Human Rights in China", see <http://news.xinhuanet.com/ziliao/2003-01/20/content_697637.htm> (accessed 21 March 2012).

[13] Sun, op. cit.

[14] Tang S, "The Impacts of the Third Generation of the CCP on Women Work," Sources from the Collection of Master Degree Dissertations (Year 2005), Hunan Normal University, May 2005.

[15] Sun, op. cit.

**Table 1**    Women Representatives in the NPC and its Standing Committee (%)[16]

| Year | 1954 | 1959 | 1964 | 1975 | 1978 | 1983 | 1988 | 1993 | 1998 | 2003 | 2008 |
|---|---|---|---|---|---|---|---|---|---|---|---|
| Women Representatives | 12 | 12.3 | 17.8 | 22.6 | 21.2 | 21.1 | 21.3 | 21.03 | 21.81 | 20.2 | 21.3 |
| Women in Standing Committee | 5 | 6.3 | 17.4 | 25.1 | 21 | 9 | 11.9 | 12.3 | 12.69 | 13.2 | 16.6 |

*Source*: Compiled by the authors.

**Table 2**    Male and Female Members of the Central Committees of the CCP[17]

| The Party Congress (Years) | Numbers | Percentage of Females |
|---|---|---|
| 8th Party Congress (1956) | 170 | 4.7 |
| 9th Party Congress (1959) | 279 | 8.2 |
| 10th Party Congress (1973) | 319 | 12.9 |
| 11th Party Congress (1977) | 333 | 11.4 |
| 12th Party Congress (1982) | 338 | 4.1 |
| 13th Party Congress (1987) | 285 | 7.7 |
| 14th Party Congress (1992) | 319 | 7.5 |
| 15th Party Congress (1997) | 349 | 7.3 |
| 16th Party Congress (2002) | 356 | 7.6 |
| 17th Party Congress (2007) | 371 | 10.0 |

*Source*: Compiled by the authors.

of gender equity were subordinated and thus poorly implemented. The gendered effects of economic restructuring in turn were reflected in the political sphere. As a result, the number of women representatives in party-state hierarchies at all levels declined from time to time.

The first decline occurred after the mid-1970s. The proportion of female NPC representatives decreased sharply in 1978. The lowest point was in 1983. In the 20 years from 1978 to 1998, the proportion of females in the NPC stood at about 21%, representing an increase of 0.78 percentage points in 1998 from 1993, but a drop of 0.79 percentage points after five years (2003). Table 1 shows this trend.

The low level of women's participation was also reflected in the leadership of the ruling party. Female members (including reserve members) in the Central Committee of the CCP accounted for only 7.6% in 2002, only higher than the 4.7% of the 1950s. There was actually an increase from 4.7% in the 1950s to 12.9% in the 1970s, but an apparent decline took place after 1977, reaching the lowest point of 4.1% in 1982. Since 1982, the level has increased though it still has not yet risen to the level of the 1960s, as shown in Table 2.

Women's political participation shrank not only in the CCP and NPC, but also in all other areas. The comprehensive indexes of women's participation in the party, government, legislature (NPC),

[16]For data from 1954 to 2003, see Tan L, Jiang Y and Jiang X (eds.), *Green Book of Women: Report on Gender Equality and Women Development in China (1995–2005)*, Beijing: China Academic of Social Sciences Press, 2005, p. 56. For data of 2008, see <http://www.cntheory.com/news/2008lianghcz/2008/229/0822993151ECG78AF4BKDK5IB67KG9.html> (accessed 11 September 2011) and <http://news.xinhuanet.com/misc/2008-03/15/content_7794828.htm> (accessed 11 September 2011).

[17]Department of Population, Society, Science and Technology of the State Statistical Bureau of China (ed.), *Women and Men in China: Figures and Facts*, Beijing: China Statistics Publishing House, 2004, p. 83. For 2007, see <http://news.xinhuanet.com/ziliao/2007-10/21/content_6917500.htm> (accessed 12 March 2012).

[18]Jiang, Jiang and Jia (eds.), *Report on Gender Equality and Women's Development in China*. See <http://www.studa.net/tongjixue/070521/15232668.html> (accessed 10 March 2012).

CPPCC and grassroots leaderships show the same trend. Based on data from 1995 to 2004, Table 3 shows the development of women's inclusion in the political and decision-making processes.[18]

Table 3 shows an increase of 3.13% in the integrated index between 1995 and 2004. However, that happened mainly during the first five years (1995–2000), after which the index was seen to hover around 40%. This demonstrates the trend of women's representation at different levels of the party-state's leading decision-making bodies. The low representation of women was prevalent at all levels.[19] In general, women's political participation at grassroots levels was more extensive than at higher levels, meaning that urban community committees saw a higher proportion of women. However, even at this level, a similar trend of decline occurred after 2000, as shown in Figure 1.[20]

The low level of women's representation in leading positions is also seen at the county level. A White Paper of the Chinese government (2005) proclaimed that the state has clearly defined the objective for training and selecting women cadres, and has strengthened the work of training and selecting women cadres.[21] Furthermore, a general target where there was to be at least one female cadre in each "leading group" at the county level had been set out in a 2001 document titled "Opinions on taking further measures to do well in works to train and select female cadres and to develop female Party members."[22] Apparently, the Party-state had not been able to meet its targets

**Table 3**  Assessed Results of National Gender Equality and Women's Development in Politics and Decision Making in China (1995–2004)

| Years | Integrated Index | Party-State | Legislature | CPPCC | Grassroots |
|---|---|---|---|---|---|
| 1995 | 37.53 | 24.02 | 35.30 | 22.07 | — |
| 2000 | 40.08 | 27.74 | 36.34 | 29.52 | 65.70 |
| 2001 | 40.15 | 28.14 | 36.34 | 29.52 | 65.50 |
| 2002 | 40.80 | 29.19 | 34.34 | 30.61 | 66.20 |
| 2003 | 40.69 | 29.51 | 34.84 | 32.43 | 66.10 |
| 2004 | 40.66 | 30.21 | 34.84 | 32.43 | 65.10 |

*Source*: Compiled by the authors.

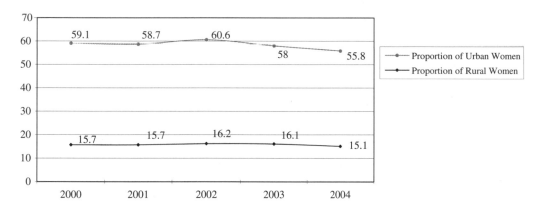

**Figure 1**  Proportion of Women in Rural and Urban Communities (2000–2004) (%)

*Source*: Compiled by the authors.

---

[19]Ibid.

[20]Department of Population, Society, Science and Technology of the State Statistical Bureau of China, ed., *Women and Men in China*. p. 83. Also see, Tan, Jiang and Jiang, op. cit.

[21]Information Office of the State Council, *Gender Equality and Women's Development in China*. See <http://news.xinhuanet.com/newscenter/2005-08/24/content_3395409.htm> (accessed 9 March 2012).

[22]The Central Organisation Department, "Notice of the CCP Organisation Department on the issuing of the 'opinions on taking further measures to do well in work to train and select female cadres and to develop female Party members'"), in the Organisation Bureau of the CCP Organisation Department (ed.), *A Selection of Commonly Used Documents in the Party's Grassroots Organisation Work*, vol. 5, Beijing, The Party Construction Readings Press, 2003, p. 788.

of promoting women to leading government and Party positions. Males accounted for an overwhelming proportion of government leaders at the local level. Data collected from 11 autonomous counties show that women leaders roughly accounted for 5%, while men accounted for 95%.[23]

## Policy Remedy and Prospects of Improvement

One of the deeper and major causes for the low level of women's participation in Party and government bodies is that the existing gender policy or affirmative action merely covers the "four leading bodies" (*si tao ban zi*) which refers to the Party, government, NPC and CPPCC. The affirmative policy only provides a general guideline for women's representation while no other quantitative index exists to measure female participation in various Party and government committees, including standing committees. Affirmative action remains, to a large extent, at a superficial level and has fallen short of bringing a substantial improvement to women's inclusion in power structures.

The policy wording on women's inclusion in power structures is often vague. The inexplicit phrase "should" has usually been used in defining women's participation. For example, Article 3 of the third amended Law of Elections for NPC and Provincial People's Congress in 1995 specifies that "the NPC and provincial People's Congress at all levels should have an appropriate [number of] women (sic), and gradually advance [the proportion of] women (sic)." Article 9 of the Organic Law of China Village Election in 1998 defines that "there should be an appropriate number of women in each village committee." In practice, "an appropriate number" has become the operating concept in China's gender policy on women's political inclusion since the 1990s. Such policy discourse has failed to substantially advance women's share in decision-making bodies in China.

This non-scientific description of women's share has made it difficult to achieve substantial progress. The current widely used definition is "at least one woman or more", instead of the quantitative index in percentage terms used internationally. Put into practice, "one woman or more" has often been translated into a figure of around 10% of a given Party and government body at the provincial level or higher, with the percentage hardly reaching 30% of the total at the township and lower levels. This regulation has thus actually restrained women's participation.

This in turn has resulted in ineffective implementation of the gender policy. The concept of "at least one woman" has gradually transformed into "only one woman" during the process of policy implementation over time, often leading to fierce competition among competent and talented women, rather than fair competition between men and women.

Furthermore, the lack of a system of policy supervision and assessment has resulted in inadequate implementation of affirmative action. Many laws and policies associated with women's participation are formalistic and largely symbolic, barely exerting any concrete policy pressure on the male-dominated Party and government organisations. The rise and fall of women's participation over the past decades demonstrates the frequently interrupted process of policy implementation at different times when policy priorities are adjusted.

---

[23] Seckington, I, "County Leadership in China: A Baseline Survey," China Discussion Paper Issue 17, China Policy Institute, University of Nottingham, 2007. Data was collected from 11 autonomous counties, 9.5% of the national total. The 11 counties include Rongshui Miao Autonomus County, Guangxi; Sanjiang Tong Autonomous County, Guangxi; Baima Yao Autonomous County, Guangxi; Jingzhou Miao Autonomous County, Hunan; Mayang Miao Autonomous County, Hunan; Tongdao Tong Autonomous County, Hunan; Zhijiang Tong Autonomous County, Hunan; Qian Guerlos Mongolian Autonomous County, Jilin; Huzhu Tu Autonomous County, Qinghai; Minhe Hui Autonomous County, Qinghai; and Shilin Yi Autonomous County, Yunnan. <http://www.nottingham.ac.uk/china-policy-institute/publications/documents/Discussion_Paper_17_County_Leadership.pdf> (accessed 10 March 2012).

In response to the decline in female representation, the ACWF has continuously made efforts to promote and re-emphasise affirmative action since the 1990s. Several specific policy documents which the ACWF helped to formulate have successfully translated mandatory indexes of women's political inclusion into practical actions, consequently ending the trend of decline after the 1994 Fourth World Conference on Women in Beijing. The affirmative action began to take effect, leading to the enactment of the Programme on China Women's Development (2001–2010) and two additional meetings on selection and cultivation of women's cadres in 2001 and 2002, which re-focussed political attention on issues concerning women's inclusion.

The decline in women's participation has also attracted the Chinese government's attention, leading to efforts to supervise and assess the process of implementing the gender policy. The Women Work Committee under the State Council organised 15 groups of national policy assessment and supervision led by 29 leaders of the provinces and ministries. The aim was to make a comprehensive evaluation of the implementation of the Programme on Women Development. Such supervision and assessment will help to continuously realise the indexes proposed in the Programme.

China's first *Green Book on Women* prepared by scholars and practitioners was published in 2006. The research team was organised by the ACWF and sponsored by the government. The Report titled "Gender Equality and Women Development in China" not only collected different policy ideas and proposals, but also provided a comprehensive evaluation of the situation of Chinese women following the programme's implementation. The report provided the public, the Party and the government with factual figures and the status of women's lives from every aspect, including political participation.

The decision on women's representation made by the NPC in March 2007 explicitly defined that the percentage of females, rather than female quotas, must reach no less than 22% of the total number of representatives of the 11th plenum of the NPC in 2008. This is a significant turning point as it is the first explicit regulation on women's participation since the reform and open door policy was introduced in 1978. This regulation clarified the previously ambiguous phrasing of women's participation by using numerical terms. Again, this regulation can be regarded as part of the party-state's efforts to boost women's participation.

Indicators show an upward trend in women's shares coinciding with these efforts. Statistics show that the number of female cadres accounts for close to 40% of the total cadres in China. A 17% increase took place at all levels, which included leadership positions taken up by women at the provincial, prefecture, county and township levels.[24] The 17th Party Congress in 2007 had 445 women representatives, 63 more than the previous session, representing a 20.1% increase. The Central Committee of the CCP had 371 members, among which 37 were women, accounting for about 10% of the total,[25] more than the 7.6% at the 16th Party Congress in 2002. With Wu Yi's retirement from the Political Bureau, Liu Yandong, head of the Party's United Front Department, was appointed a new member. One can assume that not only are the Party and government aware of the importance of women's participation, but they have also taken different approaches to improve women's political participation. Nevertheless, it is not an easy task to achieve equality for women in the male-dominated Chinese society.

---

[24] Huang Qingyi, deputy director of the State Council Women and Children Work Committee, and vice chairman of the ACWF and first secretary, addressed a press conference about the implementation of the Outline of the Development of China's Women and Children (2001–2005), reporting "China's steady growth in the number of female officials, accounting for 40% of the total number of the cadres." The press conference took place on 15 July 2007 in Beijing. See <http://news.xinhuanet.com/politics/2007-05/15/content_6101129.htm> (accessed 5 March 2012).

[25] <http://news.xmnext.com/domestic/special/zg17d/zxxx/2007/10/21/936598.html> (accessed 5 March 2012).

# II

# Enhancing and Re-Orienting Governance to Promote Sustainable Development

## Introduction

Sarah Y TONG

Despite achieving an unprecedented annual growth of 10% for over three decades, China's large continental economy is at a crossroads. While the era of high growth is drawing to an end, the investment-driven, export-oriented development model, which has served China well, requires a fundamental re-configuration. A transformation towards a domestic consumption based economy while China is still relatively poor is no doubt a demanding task. It is especially challenging when many of the Chinese leaders and much of the overall government apparatus continue to be fixated with the high growth mindset. Indeed, to safeguard growth, the state has in fact enhanced its influence on the economy, both directly through government investment and indirectly by implementing policies that favour the state and export sector. These have indeed exacerbated the structural imbalances which will hinder China's future growth. As such, if China is to sustain a healthy growth in the coming decades, the government should not only enhance its capacity to deal with emerging challenges, but more significantly re-orientate its efforts to encourage further market development and to foster a vibrant non-state sector.

## Growth and its Components

At the onset of its historical transformation in the late 1970s, China followed the successful growth path of other East Asian economies, such as Japan, Hong Kong, Singapore, South Korea and Taiwan, in pursuing growth and prosperity. This is characterised mainly by rapid industrialisation which is investment-driven and export-oriented. With three decades of double digits annual growth and even higher growth in trade, China has emerged to become the world's largest trading nation and the second largest economy. Meanwhile, this growth model is confronting increasing difficulties.

From the supply side, the initial phase of industrialisation through simply relocating unemployed or underemployed rural labour to urban industries seems to have largely run its course. On one hand, China has been suffering from a series of recurring labour shortages since the mid-2000s. Although saving rates remain high and investment abundant, productivity improvement has also stalled for years. As China's economy develops in both size and complexity, the gap with the more advanced economies narrows and there is less room for China to grow through technology catch-up.

From the demand side, China's growth is largely domestic-based, depending heavily on investment. Such has been appropriate in the past for a relatively backward developing country like China to build up production capacity and to improve its infrastructure. However, as the country develops into a middle-income economy, opportunities to invest in productive projects are no longer readily available although China still has plenty of savings to dispense. Within the existing industries however, productive investment can still be made though the returns are bound to diminish. In the medium to longer term, however, savings will inevitably decline as the population ages, forcing China to rely much less on investment.

More promising and essential is domestic consumption, especially household consumption, which is currently at a very low level by international standards. In recent years, Chinese consumers have already demonstrated their ability and growing appetite for large commodities and luxuries. Nonetheless, much more is required to develop a consumer-based society. In addition to significantly reducing the gap between the rich and the poor and expanding the middle class, a comprehensive, functioning and affordable social security system that covers unemployment, healthcare and retirement needs to be established.

Trade constitutes an essential part of China's economy, while contributing considerably to growth. From a narrow growth accounting point of view, net exports generally make up less than one tenth of annual growth. Export and export-related economic activities support growth through various other channels, such as attracting export-oriented foreign investment, generating employment, developing new industries, facilitating technology transfers and enabling Chinese industries to achieve economies of scale. However, prospects for further growth in China's exports are gloomy for three reasons. First, the world economy will likely remain depressed for years, resulting in weak external demand for China's exports. Second, production costs in China are very likely to increase as the prices for labour and other factors of production rise. Third, due in part to domestic economic difficulties, there is a growing trend of countries using protectionist policies to promote export and growth.

## The Role of the State

There is little doubt that the state has played an essential role in China's economic transformation and rapid growth over the past three decades. It is useful to examine the interactions between the state and the economy from a historical perspective to discuss this role played by the state. To a large extent, China's experience can be viewed as a successful transition from a planned economy, where the government directly runs the economy, to one that operates largely under market principles, where the government influences the economy indirectly through various regulations and policies.

There are two unique and significant features in this transition. On one hand, it is very much a state-introduced and state-led process, although bottom-up initiatives contributed tremendously to its achievement. Following other successful examples, such as Japan and the Newly Industrialised Economies (NIEs) of Hong Kong, Singapore, South Korea and Taiwan, the Chinese government considers it essential for a poor country to utilise industrial policies to achieve growth and development. At the same time, as a result of state management, the economic transformation itself often loses momentum and is thus far from complete. This may be observed from several aspects.

First, the influence of the state in the economy remains prominent, not just in absolute size but more importantly in relative significance. Within the industrial sector, for example, although state-owned and state-controlled enterprises make up only a small portion of all firms in number, their shares of assets are still substantial. Certain resource-related industries are monopolised by a handful of state-owned enterprises. Beyond industry, the state still dominates in sectors such as banking and telecommunications. In many instances, state firms remain inefficient and may have in effect crowded out more efficient non-state firms.

Second, the state no longer has a unified representative and has itself diversified into many groups with varying agenda and interests. For example, while the central leadership in Beijing is more concerned with sustaining social harmony and stability through more equitable growth, local leaders focus more on boosting growth in their localities. More specifically, while local governments build up their debt by borrowing through various financial vehicles, they jointly build up the nationwide systematic risk in the financial system. Similarly, large centrally administered state-owned enterprises may have also become significant powers in affecting China's policy-making process.

Third, the strong and diversified state power has presented growing challenges, especially as the economy is becoming increasingly integrated with the world economy and the government is promoting a "going out" strategy for the state sector. For example, while China's sovereign wealth fund (SWF), China Investment Company, is investing abroad to diversify, its efforts have been met with much suspicion regarding its intentions and motivations. Large SOEs (state-owned enterprises), in their efforts to expand their global reach, have often encountered similar doubts. Although such misgivings are not unique to Chinese SWFs or SOEs and can only weaken over time, there has been mounting evidence that the non-state sector has been increasingly squeezed out of various profitable sectors.

As such, more reforms are still needed regarding the role of the state in the economy. On one hand, the state might need to withdraw further from economic activities, except for the very few essential sectors, such as public utilities and key resources. At the same time, state capacity to monitor the governance of the state sector should be enhanced so that the state sector is better managed and the wealth generated more widely shared. More importantly, the focus of the state should be directed further towards creating and ensuring an open and fair market environment for businesses with different ownership structures.

## Enhancing Governance to Sustain Growth and Development

Thirty years of development and prosperity have fundamentally transformed China into a large, open and sophisticated modern economy. Governing such an economy and sustaining healthy growth present a great challenge. Moreover, as the country can hardly continue its rapid growth when it is heavily dependent on high savings, high investment and strong export growth, China will be compelled to move rather swiftly towards a more domestic consumption-based growth. Given the many predicaments it faces domestically and externally, such a shift will prove to be a highly difficult task.

Domestically, China suffers from a rapidly rising income gap, which is not only unjust to those left behind, but also detrimental to achieving consumption-driven growth. The income gap has several main components, including those between rural and urban residents, between coastal and inland regions, and between the state and the non-state sectors. As a large, diverse and still relatively poor country, reducing the income gap and cultivating a consumer society requires not only resources and skill, but also time.

Indeed, various policy measures will have to be introduced and implemented jointly to address the issue. For example, the taxation system will need to be further overhauled to reduce the income gap while maintaining strong incentives for high-earners. Moreover, further urbanisation is an important policy tool that can reduce the number of rural residents and improve rural income. However, this needs to be combined with a business environment that nurtures the development of small and medium enterprises (SMEs). These SMEs have been the main force in generating employment in recent years. It is also significant to expand and enhance the social security system, which itself forms an important part of the country's overall fiscal system.

To be sure, managing a large and sophisticated economy is tricky. It is therefore even more important to better define the roles and boundaries of the government. Experiences of both China and other countries have shown that, for the most part, governments are best placed to establish and maintain clear rules and a fair environment for other businesses and individuals to compete and to prosper. In addition to providing public goods, such as basic education, infrastructure investment and national defence, governments should whenever possible avoid becoming players themselves in the market place.

This by no means suggests that the government is not important. On the contrary, the government has an essential role to play in China's future economic transformation. For example, better formulated and implemented labour regulations can serve as strong tools to improve labour income and to facilitate industrial restructuring. The same is true for taxation policies, where considerable improvement could be made to facilitate the development of the tertiary sector in general and that of small and medium sized enterprises in particular. Similarly, stronger regulations and better monitoring of banks and other financial institutions are pre-requisites for the liberalisation and further development of China's financial sector.

To enhance state capacity and improve governance for sustainable growth, the issue of central-local relations will need to be tackled. This refers mainly to the fiscal arrangements between various levels of the governments. Currently, the system leaves local governments, at provincial or lower levels, highly dependent on fiscal transfers from upper-level governments for providing various public services and social welfare. As a result, local governments have strong incentives to spur local growth and extract extra-budgetary revenues, such as income from land-use transfers. A better structured fiscal system should aim to equalise the provision of public services across regions and between rural and urban regions, thus reducing the pressure on local governments to extract income from non-conventional avenues.

Externally, challenges ranging from exchange rate management to rising trade disputes also abound as China has become increasingly integrated with the world economy. As the economy expands and its regional and global influence rises, there is a growing need for the *renminbi* (RMB) to become more international. Although steps have been taken to move the RMB towards an international currency, concerns over the resilience of China's banking sector, as well as the relative underdevelopment of its financial sector, may hamper China's ambition.

On trade, the economy remains highly export-oriented although there have been some modest structural changes in recent years as a result of the current global economic crisis. However, decades of successful export promotion have led to three main consequences. Each presents its own challenges and difficulties. First, trade expanded rapidly while China was integrated into a closely linked regional production network in Asia. As such, China's trade and trade-related employment are exceedingly vulnerable to external demand and supply shocks. Moreover, as a large portion of trade-related production in China involves low-skilled processing and assembling, China is facing increasingly intensive competition from less developed economies in other parts of Asia, which depresses the wages of Chinese workers. As labour and other production costs rise, and in fact labour shortages have occurred from time to time, China is expected to lose its competitiveness in low-end labour-intensive products.

Second, a persistent trade surplus, combined with large and continuous inflows of foreign direct investment, has resulted in the rapid accumulation of foreign exchange reserves. This not only adds to rising external pressure for China to appreciate its currency, but makes the task of managing and safeguarding its value more difficult. Efforts have been made to diversify the portfolio, for example, by setting up a sovereign wealth fund and encouraging outward direct investment in other countries.

Third, as China is the final assembler before product shipment, trade imbalances between producers in Asia and consumers in the United States and the EU are shown disproportionally though bilateral trade imbalances between China and these two economies. Thus China has found itself the number one target of trade complaints and remedies and China's exports continue to face hostilities in various developed and developing markets. Managing China's economic relations, especially those with the United States and the EU, will likely remain tricky. The United States, in its own efforts to recover and revive its wavering economy, may see China as a challenger and a competitor, while the EU is still struggling with many of its internal problems.

In the longer run, China will need to significantly strengthen its capacity to innovate. Over the past decades, China has been able to benefit from a technological "catch-up" to considerably improve efficiency and productivity. This has been achieved through the large influx of foreign talents and foreign investment and associated technology, and the improvement in managerial skills. As China becomes stronger and moves closer to technological frontiers, future gains in technological advancement would need to depend more on domestic innovations. Much progress has been made, due in part to large direct input by the state. More significantly, the government should aim to create an environment that is conducive to innovation and creativity.

# 12

# China Coming to the End of its High Growth

John WONG and HUANG Yanjie*

*As the era of high growth is coming to an end, the Chinese economy is geared towards slower but steadier growth built on a structurally more balanced and environmentally more sustainable developmental model.*

Thanks to its successful economic reform and open-door policy starting in 1979, the Chinese economy has experienced spectacular performance, growing at an annual average rate of 9.9% with reasonable price stability for the period of 1979–2011. China has become the world's second largest economy with its total GDP in 2011 amounting to RMB47.2 trillion (about US$7.3 trillion), which is 110 times more than that in 1979 (Figure 1). Its per capita GDP rose 30 times from 1979 to RMB 35,000 (US$5,500) in 2011. In 1978, China produced a meagre 150,000 units of automobiles. Today, China is the world's largest automobile producer with 18.4 million units. Sustained high growth has lifted more than 500 million Chinese people out of poverty and this is far more significant than having more cars on the road. In short, China's growth performance for the past 33 years was indeed "impressive" "by any standard", as the World Bank puts it.

It is a truism to say that no economy can keep growing at such high rates without sooner or later running into various economic and social constraints such as inflation, labour shortages and environmental degradation. Not surprisingly, the talk of China coming to the end of its high growth has recently been gaining currency, not just by some foreign analysts, but even among some of China's own economists. But why now?

On 27 February 2012, the World Bank released a study titled "*China 2030: Building a Modern, Harmonious, and Creative High-Income Society*", which states that China has reached "a turning point in its development path". The report also warns that "China's growth will decline gradually in the years leading to 2030 as China reaches the limits of growth brought about by

---

*John WONG is Professorial Fellow at the East Asian Institute, National University of Singapore. HUANG Yanjie is Research Assistant at the same institute.

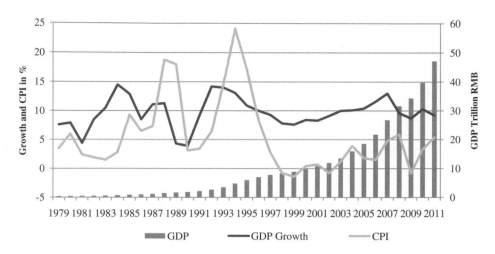

**Figure 1**   China's GDP, CPI and Economic Growth, 1979–2011

*Source*: National Bureau of Statistics.

current technologies and its current economic structure". It called for the Chinese government to step up its economic and institutional reforms in order to complete its transition to a market economy as well as to manage the successful transition from a middle-income to a high-income economy.

Back in 2007, Premier Wen Jiabao made a remark on the state of the Chinese economy as "unstable, unbalanced, uncoordinated and unsustainable". In his latest Government Work Report delivered at the National People's Congress on 5 March 2012, Wen reiterated such growth constraints and hence cut the growth target for 2012 to 7.5%, the first time since 2004 that growth target has fallen below the standard 8%.[1] In doing so, Wen has clearly signalled that China's era of double-digit rates of high growth is over.

As reflected in the agenda of various policy platforms of the Chinese leadership over the years, the Chinese government and leading intellectuals are well aware of China's many growth problems and constraints as well as their related reforms as proposed by the recent World Bank report. Specifically, many of these policy issues have already been embodied in the 12th Five-Year Programme (FYP, 2011–2015), which was formally adopted by the Fifth Party Plenum in October 2010. Much like the recent World Bank report, the major objectives of the 12th FYP are to primarily address China's existing and emerging development challenges of not only continuing with rapid economic and social progress but also rendering its economic growth more sustainable through economic restructuring and rebalancing.

The 12th FYP has thus laid down the institutional framework for China to enter the lower-growth era and is an indication of a political consensus of China's top leadership on the need for economic and social reforms in order to render future growth more sustainable. Clearly, as the economic growth pattern shifts from the single-minded pursuit of GDP increases to one that fosters more inclusive growth and emphasises "quality of GDP" and on a broader social base, this will surely herald the beginning of a lower-growth regime. In this sense, this FYP really marks the turning point in China's development. In the words of Morgan Stanley's China expert Stephen Roach, "….history will judge the 12th Five-Year Plan as watershed event in the development of modern China".[2]

---

[1]Chinese official growth forecast has always been very conservative. The official figure is usually well below what has actually been achieved. The projected 7.5% growth for 2012 is below what is widely predicted to be around 8.5% for 2012. This time is more significant because it is below 8%, a level that Wen had tried very hard to maintain during the global financial crisis.

[2]Morgan Stanley, *"China's 12th Five-Year Plan: Strategy vs Tactics"*, April 2011.

## Falling into the Middle-Income Trap?

The intellectual backdrop in China for the emerging end-of-high growth argument is much associated with the recent spate of discussions and debates on the issue of the "Middle Income Trap", which has attracted a lot of attention from academics and intellectuals from not just China but also countries that the World Bank has classified as "middle-income economies". Many developing economies, having achieved their economic take-off and grown to become middle-income economies (in terms of per capita GDP) soon found their growth plummeting and even stagnating, thereby failing to grow into high-income developed economies. They are, so to speak, "trapped" at the middle-income level because they have exhausted the technological and institutional sources of their former high growth.

The London weekly, *The Economist* (23 June 2011), in its supplement on China's growth prospects warned that "China's roaring growth cannot last indefinitely" and China should "beware of the middle-income trap". Many scholars have since raised the same question whether China will or can escape the "Middle Income Trap".[3] Just like *The Economist*, most proponents posit the likelihood of China falling into the middle income trap based on broadly similar arguments as follows: (i) China's economy cannot keep on growing at such dynamic rates; (ii) China's economic growth pattern based on over-export, over-investment and under-consumption is not sustainable; and (iii) China with its current one-child family policy and a sharply declining total fertility rate (TFR) will soon result in labour shortages and an ageing population.

The "middle-income trap" thesis originated from Latin America, which was among the first batch of post-war developing countries to launch industrialisation based on import substitution. After an initial period of high growth, most Latin American economies lost their growth momentum on account of their failure to make the successful transition from import substitution phase to export orientation, as did many East Asian economies. Of the 33 Latin American and Caribbean countries, 85% of them reached what the World Bank has classified as middle-income economies; however, they have languished in a low growth of 3–4% for more than three decades. For the developing world as a whole, of 101 middle-income economies, only 13 including Korea, Taiwan, Hong Kong and Singapore had successfully developed into high-income economies by 2008.[4] The widespread failure elsewhere further endorses the successful development experiences of the East Asian economies based on export orientation, a phenomenon the World Bank called the "East Asian miracle".[5]

The middle-income trap argument is obviously not directly relevant to China's context. Even if China's growth-inducing forces are about to weaken, China's present powerful growth engine is not about to collapse anytime soon, nor will growth be brought down to below 5% in the foreseeable future. Even more far-fetched is the demographic argument. The proportion of the Chinese population above 65 currently constitutes 9% and the median age of the population is about 35. But the immediate demographic impact on China's growth has been exaggerated. For years to come, China, instead of facing labour shortages, will have to cope with the acute problem of unemployment. China's past high economic growth has been accompanied by relatively low labour absorption rates.

Economists use the concept of support ratio, defined as the effective number of producers relative to the effective number of consumers, to measure the economic impact of an ageing population. For China, as some demographic estimates put it, the support ratio is likely to peak at

---

[3]This includes Lu Ding, a visiting scholar at the East Asian Institute. See Lu D, "Can China Escape the Middle Income Trap?" *EAI Background Brief,* no. 658, 15 September 2011. Also, "China Law Blog - China Law for Business, at <http://www.chinalawblog.com/2012/02/will_china_escape_the_middle-income-trap.html> (accessed 15 February 2012).

[4]World Bank, *China 2030: Building a Modern, Harmonious, and Creative High-Income Society,* February 2012.

[5]World Bank, *The East Asian Miracle*, New York, Oxford University Press, 1994.

near 0.9 towards 2020 and then slowly decline.[6] In other words, the ageing population will not have significant direct economic impact until after 2030 when China's population is expected to peak at 1.46 billion, though its social impact can come a little earlier. That is why the World Bank is also confident that "China has the opportunity to avoid the middle-income trap".

## What is Low Growth for China?

China could well escape the middle-income trap, but it could not avoid the coming economic slowdown. A question will then follow: What is "low growth" and how low is low for China's economy? Many foreign analysts seem to employ double standards in judging China's past economic performance. As China has been enjoying double-digit growth for two decades, foreign commentators have taken this for granted and viewed any slight decline from such super growth as "hard landing" for the Chinese economy, or at best "soft landing", as they actually did so by labelling the moderate slowdown in 2011 to 9.2% from the 10.4% of 2010 as a "soft landing"; strictly speaking, there has been "no landing" for such creditable performance![7] With China's growth for 2012 widely projected to be around 8–8.5%, any actual growth below Wen's target of 7.5% would then qualify as a "hard landing"! Suffice it to say that "hard or soft landing" is not an objective scientific term based on any established economic theory.

A more pertinent question can be posed: When will the economic slowdown set in? According to the growth projection by China's Development Research Center and accepted by the World Bank, China will still have an average growth of 8.6% for 2011–2015 and 7% for 2016–2020. This is hardly "low growth" at all, perhaps only "low" by China's past standards. These projected growth rates seem overly optimistic, particularly viewed in the present context of the adverse global economic environment. But it does indicate that China is not about to turn away from its pro-growth policies and strategies. In fact, the new Chinese leadership under Xi Jinping, who is expected to take over power later in 2012, is likely to do all it can to maintain reasonable high growth in the initial two years to facilitate smooth power transition. In the short run, there is strong political imperative for maintaining high growth. And Beijing has both the financial means and the necessary policy instruments to boost growth for years.

In the long-term perspective, the days of double-digit rates of growth are clearly gone for China. But what is "low growth" for China can still be strong growth by regional and global standards. China's future growth potential can best be analysed in the context of the past East Asian development experience.

## Sustaining High Growth the East Asian Way

China is an important component of the World Bank's "East Asian miracle", and China's post-reform (1979) development is structurally and institutionally quite akin to the general pattern of East Asia's (EA) development. EA was then defined as including Japan, China, the four newly industrialised economies (NIEs) of South Korea, Taiwan, Hong Kong and Singapore (also dubbed as the "Four Little Dragons"), and the four ASEAN economies of Indonesia, Malaysia, the Philippines and Thailand. Most EA economies, especially Japan, China and the four NIEs, were high-performance economies, having chalked up high growth at near double-digit rates for a sustained period.

Historically speaking, the EA growth process, as shown in Table 1, is marked by three waves of growth. Japan was the first non-Western country to become industrialised. Its high growth dates back to the 1950s after it had achieved rapid post-war recovery, and carried the growth momentum

---

[6]See "The Economic Consequences of Population Age", *National Transfer Accounts Bulletin*, no. 3, December 2011, East West Center.

[7]For further discussion of hard and soft landing, see Wong J, "China's Economy in Review: Moderate Slowdown in 2011, Still Weaker Growth Prospects for 2012", *EAI Background Brief*, no. 686, 5 January 2012.

**Table 1** East Asia Performance Indicators

| Countries | Population (Mn) 2009 | GDP Per Capital (US$) 2009 | Total GDP (US$ bn) 2009 | GDP Growth (%) | | | | | | |
|---|---|---|---|---|---|---|---|---|---|---|
| | | | | 1960–1970 | 1970–1980 | 1980–1990 | 1990–2000 | 2000–2008 | 2009 | 2010 |
| China | 1,335 | 3,734 | 4,984 | 5.2 | 5.5 | 10.3 | 9.7 | 10.4 | 9.2 | 10.3 |
| Japan | 128 | 39,727 | 5,068 | 10.9 | 4.3 | 4.1 | 1.3 | 1.6 | -5.3 | 3.9 |
| South Korea | 49 | 17,078 | 833 | 8.6 | 10.1 | 8.9 | 5.7 | 4.5 | 0.2 | 6.2 |
| Taiwan | 23 | 18,500 | 423 | 9.2 | 9.7 | 7.9 | 5.7 | 4.1 | -4.0 | 10.5 |
| Hong Kong | 7 | 30,065 | 210 | 10 | 9.3 | 6.9 | 3.8 | 5.2 | -3.0 | 7.5 |
| ASEAN-10 | | | | | | | | | | |
| Brunei | 0.4 | 26,486.0 | 10.8 | — | — | — | 2.1 | 1.8 | -0.5 | 1.0 |
| Cambodia | 15.0 | 692.6 | 10.4 | — | — | — | 6.4 | 9.2 | 0.1 | 5.5 |
| Indonesia | 231.4 | 2,363.6 | 546.9 | 3.9 | 7.2 | 6.1 | 3.8 | 5.2 | 4.5 | 6.1 |
| Laos | 5.9 | 910.5 | 5.6 | — | — | — | 6.1 | 6.9 | 7.6 | 8.0 |
| Malaysia | 28.3 | 6,822.0 | 193.1 | 6.5 | 7.9 | 5.3 | 6.5 | 5.5 | -1.7 | 7.2 |
| Myanmar | 59.5 | 419.5 | 25.0 | — | — | — | 6.1 | 12.6 | 4.8 | 3.3 |
| Philippines | 92.2 | 1,749.6 | 161.4 | 5.1 | 6.0 | 1.0 | 3.3 | 5.1 | 1.1 | 7.3 |
| Singapore | 5.0 | 36,631.2 | 182.7 | 8.8 | 8.3 | 6.7 | 7.4 | 5.8 | -1.3 | 14.5 |
| Thailand | 66.9 | 3,950.8 | 264.3 | 8.4 | 7.1 | 7.6 | 3.8 | 5.2 | -2.2 | 7.8 |
| Vietnam | 87.2 | 1,119.6 | 96.3 | — | — | — | 7.3 | 7.7 | 5.2 | 6.8 |

*Notes*: For GDP Growth (%), the figures for Brunei, Cambodia, Laos, Vietnam and Myanmar for the years 1990 to 2008 had been computed using the data retrieved from the Asian Development Bank website. The data for 2009 are from the ASEAN website. The data for 2010 are the authors' compilation from the Economist Intelligence Unit, *China Daily*, Singapore Statistics and *The Star*.

*Sources*: ASEAN Website <http://www.aseansec.org/19226.htm> (accessed 15 February 2012); Asian Development Bank website, <http://www.adb.org/Documents/Books/Key_Indicators/2010/ Country.asp> (accessed 15 February 2012); Economist Intelligence Unit website; *China Daily*; Singapore Statistics; *The Star*.

into the 1960s and much of the 1970s. Japan's economic growth engine was initially based on the export of labour-intensive manufactured products; it was soon forced by rising wages and increasing costs to shed its comparative advantage of labour-intensive manufacturing in favour of the four NIEs, which started their industrial take-off in the early 1960s (though Hong Kong's industrialisation started in the 1950s).

Much like China today, these four NIEs were arguably the world's most dynamic economies at that time, as they had sustained near double-digit rates of growth even longer than Japan's, from the early 1960s to the early 1990s. The rise of the NIEs thus constituted the second wave of EA's growth and integration. By the early 1980s, high costs and high wages had similarly caught up with these four NIEs, which had to restructure their economies towards more capital-intensive and higher value-added activities by passing their comparative advantage in labour-intensive products to the late-comers of China and other ASEAN economies, thereby spreading economic growth to the latter.

With near double-digit rates of high growth for over three decades since 1980, China has since been leading the third wave of EA's growth. Many Japanese scholars like to depict this pattern of development in the region as the "Flying Geese" pattern.[8] The underlying economic theory for the flying-geese growth pattern is associated with the concept of shifting comparative advantage. The "flying geese model", with all its simplicity, thus provides a highly instructive and intuitive explanation to EA's process of successful economic growth from the rise of Japan to the rise of China. Figure 2 provides a graphical expression of the flying geese model.

Most of the EA economies are open and outward-looking, with their economic growth heavily dependent on exports, particularly labour-intensive manufactured exports in their early phases of industrialisation. Exports not only provide the economies of scale for production but also facilitate the needed technological progress and productivity growth. The four NIEs had to adopt export orientation strategies because of their small markets; however, even Japan and China with large domestic market still found export-oriented strategies useful and advantageous in their early phases of industrialisation.

To achieve high growth, most of these EA economies had also devoted a high proportion of their GDP to domestic investment — over 30% of their GDP during their critical phases of industrial

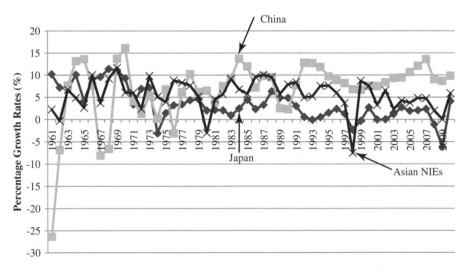

**Figure 2**   Growth Rates of China, Japan and East Asian NIEs

*Note*: East Asian NIEs include Hong Kong, Singapore, Korea and the ROC (Taiwan).

*Source*: World Bank Databank.

---

[8]The "flying geese" concept of development was coined by a Japanese economist, Kaname Akamatsu. See "A Historical Pattern of Economic Growth in Developing Countries", *Developing Economies*, vol. 1, March/August, 1962.

take-off,[9] which was generally matched by equally high levels of domestic savings. In fact, high investment and high savings provide the single most important neo-classical explanation to the high growth of the EA economies. High investment has worked on these economies much like a "virtuous circle": high rates of investment induce high export growth, and then high GDP growth, high savings and finally high investment again.

Furthermore, Japan and the four NIEs, being resource-poor and land scarce, had to overcome such physical constraints by intensifying the development of their human resources through promoting education and training. This is much in line with the modern endogenous theory of economic growth.[10] China, despite being a large country with a large resource base, has nevertheless also adopted similar development strategies that emphasise human capital formation. Investment in human capital will eventually lead to more rapid technological progress and higher productivity growth.

## China More "Dynamic" Than Other East Asian Economies

Putting China's growth in the EA perspective yields two reasonable conclusions. First, China's continuing strong economic performance is a clear signal that China is not likely to fall into the "middle-income trap" as so confirmed by the recent World Bank report. More importantly, a comparison of China's performance with the other EA economies also throws new light on the sustainability of China's long-term growth. If the four NIEs (particularly Singapore), having experienced high growth for three decades and are still full of growth potential, why not China? China should have much more internal dynamics to sustain high growth for a much longer period. Unlike Japan and the other four NIEs, China has by far a larger population, a bigger domestic market and a vast hinterland to keep growing for a longer period.

The "flying geese" theory is no longer fashionable among Japanese economists today partly because China has replaced Japan as the leading "goose" in the regional growth formation. In fact, the rise of China has much complicated this simplistic theory. The notion of shifting comparative advantage from one economy to another is clearly not so applicable to China because of its enormous size. As the Pearl River Delta region has lost its comparative advantage in labour-intensive manufacturing, it simply passes it on to other parts of China in its interior, as it is happening today. This is a scenario of one country with multiple "flying geese" formations. In this way, it will take China a longer time to exhaust its dynamic growth potential.

A similar conclusion can also be drawn by comparing Japan's high growth period (1955–1973) with China's (1990–2007). As shown in Figure 3, both countries experienced comparable growth rates of output in their periods of high growth, even though Japan had higher contribution to its growth from technological progress (total factor productivity or TFP) than that of China. However, Japan's household saving rate started to decline in 1975 when its elderly population reached 7%.[11]

China has by far higher saving rate before and even after its population has started to age. Furthermore Japan's growth potential has since been progressively weakened due to the lack of consumption demand, leading to prolonged deflation. Consequently, Japan has fallen into the "high-income trap". By comparison, China's high growth can be sustained longer because of not just its higher saving rate and relatively better demographics, but also its continuing strong demand potential for both investment and consumption. Still, China's economy must brace itself for the eventual ending of the high-growth era.

---

[9] See World Bank, *World Development Report* (various years) and Asia Development Bank, *Asian Development Outlook* (various years), which provide data on investment and savings rates of the EA economies for various years.

[10] This modern growth theory is often associated with the original idea of Paul Romer. See "Endogenous Technological Change", *Journal of Political Economy,* vol. 8, no. 5, 1990.

[11] Mirochnik, M, "High Growth: Lessons for China from the Japanese Experiences", *Journal of Economics and Philosophy,* 2 December 2010. <http://thetransatlantic.org/> (accessed 15 February 2012).

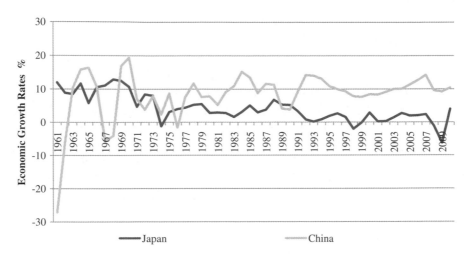

**Figure 3**    Economic Growth Rates of China and Japan, 1960–2010

*Source*: World Bank Databank.

## Continuing High Growth Not Sustainable

No economy can keep growing at such high rates forever without running into various constraints. It is not surprising that many foreign analysts and Chinese intellectuals have recently started to focus on the possibility of Chinese economy coming to the end of its high growth era.[12]

In China, policy makers and many leading economists have already come to realise that China's economy, already with a huge base, should not be growing at such breakneck rates any more. It is simply too disruptive for both China and the world. More importantly, Chinese leaders also understand that China's economy just cannot continue to grow at such rapid rates because of its many structural problems.

The eventual ending of the high growth era for China thus looks inevitable. It is only a matter of time. Other dynamic East Asian economies like Japan and the four NIEs of South Korea, Taiwan, Hong Kong and Singapore had experienced high growth for two to three decades before. As these economies matured, their growth rates had come down. The East Asian experience is instructive for China.

China's future slowdown in growth is also evident by analysing its sources of growth. Some key growth components will gradually be weakened as the economy is undergoing structural changes and macroeconomic rebalancing. The ensuing changes will offer a good picture of how China's economy will be adjusting to the coming lower growth.

## Changes in Various Growth Components

### Supply Side Analysis

A close analysis of China's existing sources of growth through the standard neo-classical economic framework of supply and demand can also shed light on its future growth pattern as well as growth potential. In simple terms, growth of an economy on the supply side is the sum total of its labour force increases and its productivity growth.

---

[12] See, for instance, "China's Boom Ends as Investment, Exports and Manufacturing Fall". *Washington Post,* 15 December 2011. Among Chinese economists who see the end of double-digit rate growth are Yu Bin, director of Macroeconomic Division, Development Research Centre; and Li Yang, vice president of the Chinese Academy of Social Sciences. Also, "Days of Double-Digit Growth 'Gone Forever'", *China Daily,* 16 December 2011.

For a large developing country like China with Lewis' condition of unlimited labour supply,[13] the main source of its growth is necessarily associated with the transfer of its surplus labour from low-productivity agriculture to high-productivity industry for development.[14] In other words, industrialisation-cum-urbanisation has been the major cause of China's strong economic growth. Thus, along with rapid industrial growth, China's urban population had increased from 19% in 1980 to 50% in 2010.

This follows that China's future growth will critically depend on its good demographics and appropriate technological progress. As stated earlier, China's population has been ageing rapidly in recent years, as people aged over 65 currently account for 9% of the population, with the mean age standing at 34. This is close to Japan's demographic profile some three decades ago. The social implications of China's ageing population in terms of rising social security burden can be more serious in the medium term. But the economic consequences of an ageing population in terms of production and employment may well come much later, possibly after 2030. This is because China's modern sectors have relatively low labour absorption rates and hence surplus labour for years to come.[15]

The growth of labour force may gradually decline starting from the late 2010s, with total labour force remaining large throughout the 2020s and facing no significant labour shortages. In fact, despite its current very high rates of economic and industrial output growth, China still has a lot of unemployment (in addition to extensive rural underemployment), simply because of technological progress and the widespread use of capital-intensive methods of production.

In 2011, despite its strong economic growth of 9.2%, only 12 million new jobs were created. For 2012, the government is planning to create another nine million new jobs. At the same time, there will be 25 million new entrants to the labour force, half of which will be university or college graduates.[16] The unemployment problem is due to not just job-mismatching, but also structural unemployment that is also affecting developed economies. Suffice it to say that the impact of a declining population on China's future growth is apt to be a long-term issue.

Future growth can also be sustained by continuing technological progress and efficiency improvement, which together bring about the rise in TFP. A large volume of studies have shown how China's post-reform rapid economic growth has benefited from significant productivity gains due to institutional reforms, market-driven resource-reallocation, better economic management as well as the import of new production technologies.[17] Several studies even show that China actually tops the world in TFP growth for the 1990–2008 period.[18]

Once China has achieved a significant breakthrough in TFP growth — at 3% a year for the past three decades — there is no question that China's future growth can again significantly depend on continuing technological progress to make up for the potential shortfalls from other physical inputs. The World Bank is therefore quite optimistic about China's capability to continue with its technological progress in future as China has already committed to continue to invest heavily in both physical and human capital formation. The World Bank has nonetheless recommended that China can do this more effectively by further improving its R&D infrastructure and creating an open innovation system linking global R&D networks.

---

[13]Lewis, AW, a Nobel Laureate in Economics assumes that the labour supply of development countries before development is perfectly inelastic, i.e. the condition of unlimited supply of labour until the turning point when wages begin to rise. See "The Dual Economy Revisited", *The Manchester School of Economics and Social Studies*, vol. 47, no. 3, 1979.

[14]This is basically Lewis's economic growth theory, which was subsequently refined by G Ranis and JC Fei, "A Theory of Economic Development", *American Economic Review*, September 1961.

[15]See, "Bolstering the Job Market", *Beijing Review*, 1 March 2012.

[16]"Growing Pressure on Job Market", *China Daily*, 8 March 2010.

[17]Lu Ding has documented a lot of these studies in the appendix to his work, "Can China Escape the Middle-Income Trap?" *EAI Background Brief,* no. 658, 15 September 2011.

[18]*The Economist,* 14 November 2009, p. 82.

## *Demand-Side Analysis*

To account for economic growth, the demand-side analysis provides an even better picture. Thus, economic growth as increases in GDP is fuelled by the rise in both domestic demand (domestic consumption and domestic investment) and external demand (exports minus imports). Except for a handful of small and highly open economies like Hong Kong and Singapore, domestic demand normally constitutes the mainstay of economic growth for most economies, particularly for such vast economies as China and the USA.

In most economies final consumption takes up around 60–70% of their GDP by the expenditure approach. China is quite exceptional in having an unusually high rate of domestic investment and concomitantly a lower level of consumption. As shown in Figure 4, China's gross investment steadily rose from about 30% of GDP in 1980 to around 48% in 2010 while gross consumption came down from 50% in 1980 to around 38% in 2010.

In terms of contribution to growth, China's economic growth since the early 1990s has been basically driven by domestic demand, with domestic investment playing a relatively more important role than domestic consumption. This necessarily follows that the contribution of external demand (or net exports) to China's GDP growth has all along been quite negligible, mostly around 5% in the 1990s and around 15% in recent years, but negative during the 2009 global financial crisis when China's exports plunged (Figure 5). It appears that the export sector does not seem to generate all that much of GDP for China, particularly since China's exports carry high import contents as around 50% of China's exports are in processing trade. A typical example is the much publicised case of a China-assembled iPad that is sold in the US market for US$499, but yielding only US$8 for the Chinese labour![19]

However, the actual economic importance of Chinese exports has been grossly understated by this simple statistical analysis as it has missed out a great deal of highly significant "indirect" economic activities that are connected with China's export industries. Most export-oriented industries create various local supporting service activities as well as investment in the upstream and downstream sectors, not to mention the multiplier effect on the economy as generated by their employees.

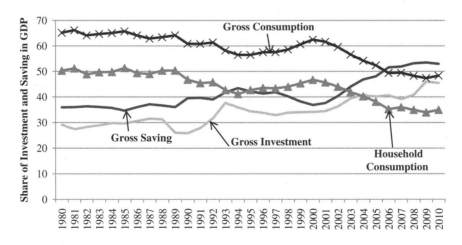

**Figure 4**   Shares of Investment and Saving in China's GDP, 1980–2010

*Source*: World Bank Databank.

---

[19]This is similar to the assembling of an iPhone in China, which sold for US$179 but created a total value-added of only US$6.5 in China. See Xing Y, "How the iPhone Widens US Trade Deficits with China: The Story of US$6.5 Value-Added to China for its Exports of US$179", *EAI Background Brief.* no. 629, 27 May 2011.

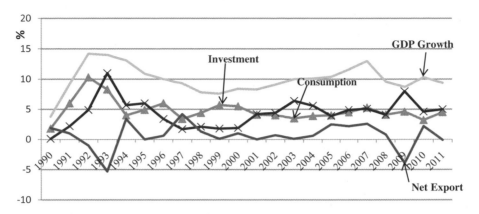

**Figure 5**   Source of China's Economic Growth, 1990–2011

*Source*: National Bureau of Statistics.

A recent study shows that about one-third of China's income growth in the years to the 2009 global financial crisis had been due to exports.[20] Multinationals in setting up export bases in China also give rise to significant technological spillovers. In other words, exports actually catalyse a lot more investment and consumption activities that are not captured in such conventional growth accounting approach. This explains why China's economy today is still highly vulnerable to external shocks.

With rising operating costs and increasing wages, China's export competitiveness for labour-intensive exports is bound to suffer.[21] As different localities in China have followed one another in raising their minimum wages in order to compete for migrant labour, average wages have gone up a lot in recent years, and minimum wages are expected to rise to 12.5% a year during the current 12th FYP.[22] This, along with the gradual appreciation of the *renminbi* (RMB), will inevitably erode China's comparative advantage in its export markets.

Since it went off the US-dollar peg in July 2005, the RMB has appreciated about 30% against the US dollar. Taking into account China's inflation and rising wages and costs, the RMB has actually appreciated over 40% in terms of real effective exchange rate (REER). All these lead to higher unit labour cost. As a result, China is facing the same problem of "shifting comparative advantage" that had once been faced by Japan and the four NIEs a few decades ago. China will soon find that the contribution of its export sector to China's GDP growth will decline, leading to a lower growth potential.

This follows that domestic investment and domestic consumption will be the principal drivers of China's future growth. Foreign analysts have often accused the Chinese economy of over-investment and under-consumption, which leads to over-production and over-export, and eventually persistent trade surplus. This constitutes the root cause of China's macroeconomic imbalance, which has also contributed to global macroeconomic imbalances. The other side of the coin for this unique situation is China's phenomenally high saving rate, which in recent years has been staying close to 50%.[23]

---

[20] Akyuz, Y, "Export Dependency and Sustainability of Growth in China", *China & World Economy,* vol. 19, 1 November 2011.

[21] See HKTDC's report, "An Update on Production Costs on the Mainland", 12 January 2012.

[22] "China Targets 13% Annual Minimum Wage Rise", *China Daily*, 15 February 2012.

[23] The basic macroeconomic identity I = S can self-explain over-investment and over-consumption. Trade surplus can also be easily explained by another simple identity: X – M = S – I, i.e. "trade surplus" as the difference between exports (X) and imports (M) just equals "saving surplus", as gross savings (S) minus gross investment (I).

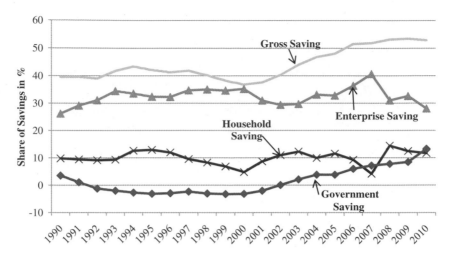

**Figure 6**   Share of Savings in China's GDP

*Source*: *China Statistical Yearbook* 2011.

As shown in Figure 6, not just Chinese households are saving a lot; the national high saving rate is basically due to the high level of enterprise savings, i.e. the retained incomes of the country's state-owned enterprises. The state simply mobilises these massive domestic savings for various capital investments from building infrastructure to the technological upgrading of key manufacturing industries. That is why China today "is home to the world's second-largest highway network, the world's third largest sea bridges, and six of the world's 10 largest container ports", as observed by the World Bank. In the process, a lot of growth has been generated.

**Rebalancing Investment and Consumption**

Heavy capital investment has been the foundation of China's pro-growth development strategy. To maximise GDP creation, the government starting from the early 1990s has mobilised its high domestic savings for all sorts of capital investment. In this way, China's economy experienced investment-driven high growth for two decades. At the same time, as many have pointed out, this strategy has resulted in unbalanced growth, with too much investment and too little consumption.

Basically, this is not a wrong development strategy for a large developing country like China in its initial phases of industrialisation to have followed the sequence of "to invest to grow first and to consume later". The other East Asian economies used the same strategy in the comparable phases of their development. China, in particular, has huge needs for investment first in basic infrastructure and the heavy industry, and then in urban facilities.

Is the Chinese economy really under-consuming? At about 40% of its GDP, China's gross consumption level is undoubtedly very low, not just by the US level of 70%, but also by India's level of around 56%. In an absolute sense, however, the Chinese people have indeed been consuming a lot, particularly in recent years when the country has started to experience emerging affluence. In 2011, China topped the world by selling more than 18 million units of automobiles, 80 million units of refrigerators and 100 million colour TV sets. In 2011, Chinese tourists made 70 million overseas trips and 2.6 billion domestic trips.[24]

Suffice it to say that China's gross domestic consumption level may be too low mainly because its gross domestic investment is too high. Such is the outcome of China's pro-growth development

---

[24]China National Bureau of Statistics, "The 2011 National Economic and Social Development Statistical Communiqué, 22 February 2011.

strategy, "grow first, distribute later". If China's regional income disparities were not so acute and its income distribution was much more equal, there would certainly have been a higher level of domestic consumption.

In the long run, China's existing pattern of investment and consumption is clearly unsustainable. As the population is getting older, domestic saving rates are bound to decline over time as is happening in Japan now. Since the economy is shifting from its pro-growth development strategies to more inclusive growth that takes into account broader social objectives ranging from satisfying *minsheng* (people's livelihood) to developing a greener society, the investment share will come down and the consumption share will correspondingly go up. The fact that consumption is presently not the main driver of China's economic growth is merely another way of saying that it will be an important untapped source of future growth.

From the World Bank report, the share of investment will decline from 42% of GDP during 2011–2015 to 34% during 2016–2030 while consumption will increase from 56% to 66%. For investment share, the proportion for basic physical infrastructure and heavy industry will decline while investment in the new social infrastructure such as education, health care, rural development and urban amenities will go up. Such a macroeconomic reshuffling of different development priorities will also accelerate structural change in the economy, with a more rapid expansion of the service sector at the expense of agriculture and manufacturing. Within manufacturing, there will also be an increase in the relative share of more skill-intensive and knowledge-based industries at the expense of labour-intensive industries.

Such macroeconomic rebalancing will lead to fundamental changes in the growth pattern, development priority and economic structure. This will, in turn, render China's economic growth more sustainable in the long run. The end result of these changes will be the gradual weakening of the basic sources of economic growth, and hence a corresponding decline in the future growth potential.

## China Adjusting to Lower but Still Strong Growth

Few would seriously question the point that China's present pattern of high economic growth is economically, socially and environmentally unsustainable in the long run. The future slowdown in growth for China looks inevitable, especially since the economy is fast maturing. But there is still a lot of uncertainties as to the exact magnitude and the rate of its slowdown. To beg the same question again: How low is low, and when will it set in to become chronic low growth for China?

The growth trajectory that was projected by China's think tank, Development Research Centre, and accepted by the World Bank, is made up of five discrete sets of average growth rates based on a series of China's FYPs: 9.9% for the 10th FYP (already achieved), 8.6% for the 11th, 7.0% for the 12th, 5.9% for the 13th, and 5.0% for the 14th.

Clearly, China's projected economic growth of 7–8% in the medium term is still strong growth by regional and global standards. It means that China's economy is able to maintain reasonably high growth during its transition to the low growth regime. This is in line with the earlier argument that China has much more internal dynamics to sustain high growth for a longer period than that of the other East Asian economies in the past.

In any case, structural transformation of the economy takes time to produce significant effects. It also takes time to implement the shift in basic development strategies. The existing pro-growth policies will operate for some time. Politically, the central government under the likely new leadership of Xi Jinping needs growth to maintain stability, while local governments all the more still want high economic growth to satisfy their various development needs. This may explain the underlining rationale for projecting a high growth rate of 8.6% for the period of 2011–2015.

As for long-term growth performance, the World Bank has assumed that China will continue with its industrial upgrading and economic restructuring efforts while also stepping up reform change in six strategic areas: (i) Redefining the role of the state and the private

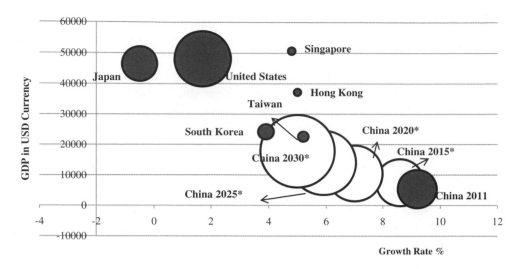

**Figure 7**   China and East Asian Economies by GDP (USD Currency) in 2011 and Beyond

*Note:* The asterisks refer to future projections of China's GDP based on estimated GOP growth rate for China between 2010 and 2030 by the World Bank.

*Source*: World Bank Databank.

sector; (ii) Enhancing innovation and adopting an open society system with links to global R&D networks; (iii) Promoting greener development; iv) Ensuring equality of opportunity and basic social needs for all; (v) Strengthening the fiscal system; and (iv) Ensuring that China continues to integrate with the global markets.[25]

Thus, by 2030, as shown in Figure 7, China's economy is expected to surpass the US economy to be the world's largest, with a total GDP of US$24.4 trillion (compared to about $15 trillion for the US economy today) at current US exchange rate. This is just a simple, nominal growth figure. In PPP (purchasing power parity) terms or taking into account the future appreciation of the RMB against the US dollar, China's GDP would of course be much larger.

Against the projected population of 1.47 billion, China's per capita GDP in 2030 will be about US$17,000 at current exchange rate ($16,000 by the World Bank) which is about the level of GDP per capita of South Korea in 2005, Singapore's in 1993 or Japan's in 1970.

China's total GDP in 2030 may look huge, but its per capita GDP (which actually measures the average standard of living of the Chinese people) will still be only a fraction that of high-income economies. In other words, China may then become a developed economy, but it is still quite a distance from being an affluent society.

Needless to say, the political and social dimensions of the development process will be even more intriguing. What is sufficiently clear is that as the economy continues to grow, the middle class will expand and the society will also change, as the development experiences of Japan and other NIEs have shown. More drastic political and social changes will follow closely on the heels of successful economic growth. Compared to the economic growth process, there are more uncertainties and complications to China's future political and social development in the years leading to 2030.

---

[25]World Bank President Zoellick's opening remarks at a high-level conference to launch this World Bank study in Beijing (27 February 2012). At <http://www.worldbank.org/en/news/2012/02/27/robert-zoellick-on-china-2030-report> (accessed 10 March 2012).

# 13

# China's Economy After Three Decades of Reforms

## A Systems Approach

Wolfgang KLENNER*

*This chapter provides an assessment of the interaction of market mechanisms and planning elements in China, and an analysis of China's stabilisation policy within the last half decade, which worked first to fight a recession and later an overheating, combining instruments from the previous planning period and newly conceived market tools.*

China's economy has evolved after three decades of reform. This chapter provides a snapshot of China's market mechanism, focussing on allocation mechanisms for commodities, labour, land and capital, property rights and the degree of openness in China. An analysis of China's stabilisation policy combining totally different tools, direct instruments from its previous economic planning period and newly conceived market economy measures will shed further light on the transformation of China's economic system in the second half of the 2000s.

## Market and Planning in China's Present Economic System

### The Status Quo

Prices and quantities for commodities, labour, land and a large segment of the capital market are generally no longer fixed by the Chinese state after the country's adoption of the market economy. In general, prices and quantities are determined by the market. But the state still regulates prices of a limited number of commodities and services such as energy and transportation. In these cases supply and demand adjust to the given prices. A labour market with regulations for minimum wages and

*Wolfgang KLENNER is Professor of East Asian Economics at the Faculty of Economics at Ruhr-University Bochum, Germany.

social insurance has been established. It is not a unified market but segmented according to the origin of the workforce which is urban, rural and temporarily urban — the segmentation of which is not much appreciated by the latter two groups. Regulations for land are still disputed. At present, all land is owned by the state or by collectives, which may sell user rights to individuals for a limited period of time, usually three to five decades. China's capital markets are strictly regulated. Interest rates for credit and savings are fixed by the state. On top of that, the central and local governments may give direct orders to banks to extend credit to specific firms or sectors, a practice which amounts to simultaneously controlling prices and quantities. As a consequence, banks are expected to fulfil two contradictory tasks: maximising profits by extending credit and attracting savings at given interest rates as well as allocating capital according "to the plan", i.e. the directives of central or local authorities since traditional planning procedures were abolished a couple of years ago. In addition to the official capital market, there are local "grey" markets that supply private firms with credit. Their interest rates are determined by the market and usually turn out to be much higher than the state's fixed rates.

Private ownership of firms, including even larger companies, and private share of state-run enterprises have been acceptable in most sectors for a long time. Nevertheless, in 2010, roughly 110,000 enterprises were state-owned,[1] which accounted for two-fifths of China's non-agricultural GDP.[2] Via forward and backward linkages to private firms, the state is able to exert influence also on the private sector. However, pivate and state firms are both expected to maximise profits and strenghten their competitiveness.

More complex are foreign economic relations. Commodities can be freely exchanged. Foreign currency required for imports is available subject to proof of commercial contracts. Import taxes are lower than those in India and Brazil. Quotas still exist, but only for a few important materials such as rare earths. International labour flows are strictly regulated, whereby leaving or entering the country is impossible without permission, which in general is very difficult to obtain. Land-use rights may be acquired by foreigners upon request. All inbound and outbound capital flows are strictly regulated — there is no capital convertibility as yet. Determined by the state, the exchange rate is basically fixed and stabilised by capital controls but has been gradually revalued during the last few years and allowed to float within narrow limits.

This system, because of the dominance of the state and the government's influence on capital allocation, does not qualify China for the status of market economy in the eyes of the EU and the United States. Nevertheless, there are more market dynamics than could be expected from this overview. Competition is extremely intense. Most markets are inundated by a large number of firms competing with each other. Local monopolies are almost abolished since the transportation network has been dramatically expanded and modernised. State firms cannot neglect markets and, at least since recently, no longer expect favourable treatment after the establishment of the National Anti-Monopoly Commission, which imposed heavy penalties on three well-known state telecommunications companies. With innovation and imitation observed everywhere, China is probably one of the few other countries where companies jostle aggressively in competition for the core market share. Competition among workers can be extremely tense too.

### Interaction and Contradictions

Crucial for the functioning of this economic system are the links between the economic sphere regulated by the state and the market sector. Simultaneous capital allocation by the market and the plan seems to work well together with less contradictions than expected from a theoretical point of view. This can be concluded from the low quota of unrepayable debts, which had been

---

[1] "China Seeks Funds from State Firms", *The Wall Street Journal*, 10 November 2010.
[2] "State Capitalism in China", *The Economist*, 13 December 2011.

reduced — from an extremely high level a decade ago to not more than 1%[3] in the beginning of 2010 — with the setting-up of asset management companies and implementation of other measures. The debt level is better than in many other market economies provided the available statistics is correct and bad loans have not been substituted by new loans. If state-allocated capital had not shown good market results, the quota should be set considerably higher. An explanation for the good performance could be that state enterprises had used credit efficiently for restructuring, modernisation, innovation and clever imitation of successful businesses to form profitable companies. Such an outcome would not be completely new in East Asia, where capital allocation within the framework of Japan's window guidance and South Korea's import substitution and export diversification strategy were proven quite effective. Cheap credit does not necessarily imply a comfortable, smooth-sailing life. As a matter of fact, Chinese state firms became quite competitive, with some of the largest firms expanding globally.

Welfare losses, however, might have resulted from the segmentation of the capital market into the official and grey segments. Many private firms excluded from official capital resources have to pay very high interest rates, and as a consequence, cannot realise less profitable, though potentially beneficial projects. But division lines might be less distinct in daily business where state firms seem to have found ways to provide funds to the private sector, thus blurring the division between the two segments.

More obvious are the contradictions of interest rates being kept, according to observers, below fictitious equilibrium rates. Low interest rates for credit are conducive to high investment, high exports and hence high economic growth, which have been the goals of China's development strategy during the last decades. Their benefits were however questioned ever since the emphasis has shifted towards sustainability of economic growth and boosting domestic consumption after China's export-led growth has lost the previous lustre in view of its increasing vulnerability to external shocks and gigantic currency reserves. The opinion is held that firms should produce more for the domestic market and that this should be strengthened by increasing the income of workers. This strategy would not require artificially low interest rates for credit.

The low, in fact negative, real interest rates for savings became a critical issue as well, contributing to speculative investment in real estate and shares. In short, the Chinese people, dissatisfied with the disproportionately low returns on their saving accounts, have been in desperate pursuit of investment and profits, thereby contributing to the destabilising effect on China's economy.

The state-set prices for energy and transportation services were said to be below equilibrium prices. The consequences can be easily recognised. Petrol stations faced problems in providing sufficient supply, at least until retail prices for gasoline were increased.[4] The day-to-day operations of China's railway system suffer as the Ministry of Railways[5] struggles with its dual role as regulator and operator to provide services at low cost and maximise profits at the same time. It is said that as a consequence, safety measures have been neglected and compromised, causing a series of fatal accidents.[6]

Land property rights and distribution are extremely sensitive, long-standing issues. One of the persistent problems is probably the fact that only user rights are on sale in the market. In Hong Kong, for instance, selling user rights and not property rights will not ostensibly hamper economic development. But, in the case of China, there is a lack of transparency in land user rights sales conducted between Chinese cadres and developers, who are the rights purchasers. Real estate has become booming business and construction companies are eager to acquire land. Cadres therefore flock to join the game. They sell large plots of urban land to developers, who uproot and displace

---

[3]Tong SY and Yao J, "China's Rising Local Government Debts Spark Concerns", *East Asian Policy*, vol. 2, no. 4, October–December 2010, p. 40.

[4]"China Seeks Funds from State Firms", *The Wall Street Journal*, 10 November 2010.

[5]Zheng Y, "The Derailment of 'Harmony' High-Speed Train and Crisis Management in China", *EAI Bulletin*, vol. 13, no. 2, October 2011, p. 2.

[6]"Chinese Train Crash Stirs Furore Online", *The Wall Street Journal*, 27 July 2011.

the residents to other areas, destroy the existing quarters, erect gigantic compounds and make lucrative profit from the sale of apartments to the public at sky-rocketing prices. Though the social and cultural issues involved are extremely delicate, the transfer of land is handled in a businesslike manner. The money for the land goes into the coffers of local governments to finance communal projects, and evidently, also quite often into the pockets of the cadres. This form of corruption is prevalent all over the world, but China's opaque land regulations offer clever cadres with an especially large spectrum of opportunities.

According to foreign capital owners, distortions result from China's exchange rate being fixed below the equilibrium rate. Expecting a revaluation, foreign capital owners found various ways of transferring capital to China. Speculative capital flows, however, common to economies with flexible exchange rate, cannot be permitted within the framework of China's present exchange rate system, which is characterised by fixed exchange rate and autonomous monetary policy. Such a system requires strict control of incoming and outgoing direct investment, portfolio investment and credit. Since speculative capital movements, though illegal, nevertheless take place, measures have to be taken to neutralise the resulting pressure on the exchange rate. An appropriate measure is to increase the domestic money supply, which however can easily result in inflation. To stabilise prices, further action is therefore necessary, such as selling bonds in order to take excess liquidity from the market. This so-called sterilisation policy, however, affects interest rates. In China, where interest rates should be kept low, sterilisation is not an easy task.

### Stabilisation Policy in a Mixed Economic System

China's economic policy makers use direct instruments for the state-controlled segments and indirect tools for the market sector. Direct instruments, the use of which has been drastically reduced during China's reforms, are basically still available. Indirect instruments had to be newly created. Their concepts could be easily taken from existing market economies. Their correct application however has to be carefully examined by trial and error processes. So far, China's economic policy, being "pioneer" in the implementation, contains considerable risks of mismatching.

Against this backdrop, China's business cycle during the past five years is examined. The risk to deal with was either an ever-increasing inflation or a hard landing of the economy. The economic tasks were quite different then. At the beginning, a drastic decline in economic growth as a result of the American subprime crisis had to be mitigated. In the ensuing years, measures had to be taken in order to calm the economy and avoid the bursting of a real estate bubble.

### Stimulating the Economy

With an extremely high foreign trade accounting for about 60% of GDP, the Chinese government was alarmed when exports declined as a consequence of the US sub-prime crisis since late 2008.[7] The previous double-digit growth was in fact considered too high and a slower growth would have been highly appreciated provided it did not fall below 8%, which is considered imperative for job creation for migrants. At that time, however, the possibility of a major recession and even perpetual stagnation similar to Japan's experience could not be completely ruled out for China. Policy makers were seriously afraid of social unrest in China's megacities caused by massive unemployment; the Chinese leadership was hence determined to implement all available policy instruments in order to keep the economy going.

Market tools such as lowering interest rates, bringing down minimum reserve ratios and increasing state expenditure were immediately applied. In addition, direct instruments aimed at

---

[7]Tong SY, "Reducing Export Dependency Essentail to China's Economic Growth", *East Asian Policy*, vol. 3, no. 4, October–December 2011, pp. 31–43.

increasing investment and consumption were used. Banks were ordered to provide credit to state-owned enterprises and local governments, and projects that were in the pipeline were simply brought forward. Thus, the usual process of time-consuming consultation and decision-making was no longer mandatory. The amount of mobilised funds was considerable, as can be judged from the drastic increase in local government debt, which might result in an increase in non-performing loans.[8] Consumption was stimulated by providing subsidies to energy-saving cars and in rural areas for electrical appliances.

The combination of direct and indirect tools yielded almost immediate results and a critical economic downturn was averted. The growth rate of China's GDP decreased only slightly, by roughly 2%. Workers in export-oriented regions were laid off, but the overall jobless rate did not increase substantially. In retrospect, however, the stimulus package administered to fight recession was far too strong. Excessive liquidiy was created and the growth rate surpassed 10% in 2010. In the summer of 2011, inflation rate soared, hitting 6.5%.[9] Price increase was especially high in the food and housing sectors. High food price had worried the urban population and rising house price discouraged those who genuinely need a flat. Real estate prices had already increased by 140% between 2007 and 2010, and even higher in large cities. By 2011, the price of an average-sized flat in Beijing, for instance, went up to USD$250,000, which is approximately 57 times the average annual income.[10] Further increase was expected, giving fewer and fewer citizens the opportunity to move into their own flat.

The expectation of rising housing prices induced individuals and firms to invest even more in real estate. This basically made sense in view of the high demand. However, such investment took place in a price segment which most citizens could not afford. As a matter of fact, most residential properties built were purchased as investment to produce a high rate of profit when price increases. It did not matter much if the newly acquired apartments remain vacant. In China, where hundreds of millions of people dream of home ownership, any investment in real estate seemed to be a safe option.

The perception changed, however, when the danger of a real estate bubble burst looms large. A price meltdown by up to 40% could not be discounted. The prospect of falling prices may bode good news for genuine apartment buyer, but not for houseowners, especially those who still need to repay their mortgages. The Chinese government is afraid of losing the confidence of the middle class if their assets depreciate in value. There is also the fear of problems sprouting in the construction sector — which accounted for about 13% of the GDP in 2010[11] according to Western estimates and employs a high proportion of low-skilled rural people — and spreading quickly to the rest of the economy, such as the iron and steel industry and transportation sector, to which it is closely interconnected.

### Calming Economic Activities

Against this backdrop, the Chinese government was determined to curb economic activities and rein in the housing prices. A broad spectrum of indirect and direct measures to calm the economy was taken. The minimum reserve ratio had been raised several times to 21% in 2010.[12] Credit was made more expensive by increasing interest rates. The direct measures taken in 2010 and 2011[13]

---

[8] Tong SY and Yao J, op. cit. pp. 38–39.

[9] "Keep the Lid on Inflation", *China Daily*, 10 November 2011.

[10] "China's Property Bubble Starts To Pop: Prices Fall In Big Cities", *The Wall Street Journal*, 9 June 2011.

[11] Ibid.

[12] Ibid.

[13] "China's Property Firms Face a Funding Squeeze", *The Wall Street Journal*, 10 August 2011; "Beijing's Gotten it Right in Financial Regulation", *Shanghai Daily*, 28 June 2011; "China's Property Bubble Starts To Pop: Prices Fall in Big Cities", *The Wall Street Journal*, 9 June 2011.

included mandatory approval to be sought by banks from higher authority prior to extending credit to construction projects; stricter mortgage rules by increasing the minimum capital requirement; restriction to state firms investing in real estate; limiting the number of properties purchased by individual households (this regulation immediately led to increasing divorce rates); restriction to construction activities in remote, scenic areas such as China's southwest, and mandatory requirement for property buyers to have paid taxes in the past five years and hold *hukou* registration from the same region; subjecting trust and securities companies that collect capital from individuals for construction companies to the same set of restrictions as banks.

Many of these measures invited severe criticism from the public — probably a novum in China's recent history — who were anxious that these measures might contribute to the burst of the bubble and hurt economic interests. Real estate owners were worried that their hope of enjoying high investment yields on their properties would dissipate. Construction companies were concerned about the lack of buyers for their newly constructed houses. Regions with steel and cement factories were worried about idle production. Local communites feared losing income if construction companies became less interested in acquiring land. Economists warned of the danger of a hard landing in China's economy and a dramatic depreciation of the value of private assets.

Depite the negative feedback, the central government and the central bank consistently introduced cooling measures in the belief that further price increase would trigger the bursting of the real estate bubble. As a result, inflation was brought down to 4.2% by the end of 2011. Escalating housing prices was arrested, and in some areas, the prices even dropped. Further decreases are expected, bringing down prices to the early-2010 level. Certainly, not all of the consequences predicted by critical voices could be avoided. Construction activities declined. Firms went bankrupt. Workers were laid off. Local governments had to abandon community projects, thereby aggravating the difficulties of construction firms. Ultimately, the central government had proven the naysayers wrong as it announced that the danger of a bubble burst was allayed, at least for the near future; a hard landing in China's economy had been avoided and the basis for sustainable economic growth had been promoted. With fewer newly built flats entering the market, rents increased. The state countered the increasing rents by building several dozens of millions of flats in the low-price segment.[14] Obviously, the Chinese government manifests adeptness in its policy mix of direct and indirect tools.

## Interventionism or Free Market?

China's experience prove that its economic system has enabled it to achieve undisputedly stellar economic performance. The following three cases reflect China's status in the global economy. First, European politicians turned to China for financial support to save the *eurozone*, which faces unprecedented financial problems; the Chinese media, surprised by the unexpected change in the attitude of the European leaders, reminded them not to come with a beggar bowl in their hands. Second, it was reported, almost in passing, that China's investment in the United States between 2003 and 2011 amounted to more than US$7 billion, and had created approximately 45,000 jobs in the United States.[15] For observers who remember how China frantically tried to attract foreign direct investment in order to modernise production and provide jobs two to three decades ago, this announcement underscores great historical significance. Third, the changes in world banking have set the world thinking. China and other East Asian countries are substantial contributors to world savings. However, East Asia's lack of expertise in finance implied that the most profitable international financial deals went to the Western banks. Now, in contrast, China's banks seem to be in a sound and stronger position as the world is facing a financial mess created by Western banks, some of which are even living on state subsidies.

---

[14] "China Push on Housing is Raising Concerns", *The Wall Street Journal*, 10 August 2011.

[15] "Investing Overseas Delivers Dividends", *China Daily*, 9 November 2011.

Economic success cannot be assessed simply by measure of growth rate and economic stability. Equitable individual and regional distribution of income and wealth, sustainability of development, workers' welfare and adequate provision of nationwide social security system are equally important issues. Most would agree that China is not very efficient as yet in achieving these goals. Nevertheless, China's success in achieving economic growth and preserving economic and social stability is more than impressive and the question remains how that was possible. The rather elusive answer that China will sooner or later have to pay the bill for not having realised a full-fledged market economy is certainly not necessarily wrong. But it has not grasped the whole picture. Closer to the point might be the explanation to Japan's and South Korea's economic success a few decades ago — both countries had a powerful administration guiding the economy at the time. Actually, there were two quite differing answers. One interpretation insisted that, as a matter of principle, governments have better insight into economic processes and business requirements and were thus able to guide Japan's and South Korea's firms towards economic success. According to the contrarian view, prudent government guidance enabled firms to achieve those results within the framework of an underdeveloped and yet to be liberalised economy which would have been brought about if markets had been fully developed. Which answer is considered correct might depend on the observer's preferences for either interventionism or free markets.

# 14

# Evolving Industrial Policies[1] in China

## A Governing Tool for Development and Restructuring

Sarah Y TONG*

*The emphasis of China's industrial policy has evolved over the decades, shifting from developing low-end consumer products, to advancing capital and technology-intensive sectors, to promoting key strategic industries such as environmentally friendly new energy and bio-tech industries.*

China's spectacular growth performance in the last three decades has been driven by rapid industrialisation, which is heavily influenced by various government policies. Between 1978 and 2011, industrial value-added in real terms grew at 11.5% a year on average, which is 1.6 percentage points higher than that for the country's gross domestic product (GDP) (Figure 1). Industrial growth was particularly important in the 1990s, contributing to over 55% of the overall economic growth.

While industry as a whole has grown consistently and significantly in size and complexity, priorities have shifted gradually to suit the country's general development goals as well as to adapt to varying domestic and external circumstances. Overall, the main objectives have moved from achieving industrialisation during the early reform era to industrial upgrading and restructuring in the most recent decade.

## Changing Priorities in China's Industrial Development

In 1978 when China was about to embark on its economic reform, industry accounted for 44% of the country's GDP. However, the sector suffered both low efficiency and a serious biasness towards heavy industry. Between the late 1970s and the mid-1980s, higher prominence was given to developing labour-intensive industries. For example, between 1979 and 1985, industrial output of

---

*Sarah Y TONG is Senior Research Fellow at the East Asian Institute, National University of Singapore.
[1] In the context of this chapter, industrial policy is broadly defined as including government policies that have significant impacts on the development of industries such as those on enterprise reforms and foreign investment.

125

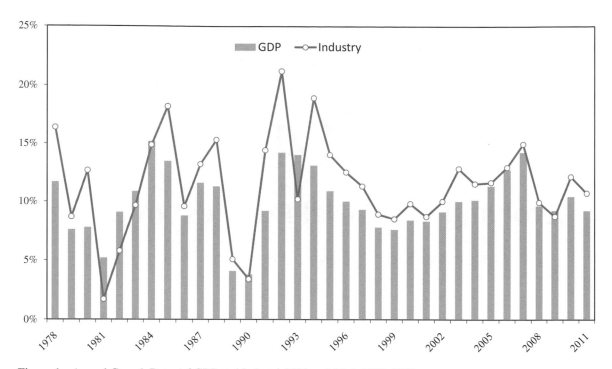

**Figure 1**   Annual Growth Rates of GDP and Industrial Value-Added, 1979–2011

*Sources*: *China Statistical Yearbook* 2011; "Statistical Communiqué on the 2011 National Economic and Social Development", National Bureau of Statistics, 22 February 2012, at <http://www.stats.gov.cn/english/newsandcomingevents/t20120222_402786587.htm> (accessed 4 July 2012).

the textile industry grew by 12.6% a year on average, compared to only 8.2% a year for the metallurgical industry. Overall, while the share of heavy industry in gross industrial output declined only modestly, from 57% in 1978 to 51% in 1990, its contribution to government budgetary revenue shrank sharply from 45% in the mid-1970s to 23% in 1990.

In the 1990s, the push for further industrialisation was closely related to achieving other government objectives such as reforming the inefficient state sector, encouraging the development of non-state industries, and promoting inward foreign direct investment and exports. Industrialisation accelerated, leading to a growth in industrial value-added from 9.6% in the 1980s to 13.9% in the 1990s, thanks to an increasingly liberalised market environment and active participation by foreign invested enterprises (FIEs).

Since the early 2000s, while sustaining industrial growth remains central to China's economy, there has been a gradual modification towards industrial consolidation and upgrading. Large state-owned enterprises (SOEs) were encouraged to merge and integrate their domestic operations, and to explore overseas markets.

More recently, under the new 12th Five-Year Programme (FYP) which covers the years 2011 to 2015, the government proposed to nurture the development of seven emerging industries to ensure the sustainability and global competitiveness of Chinese manufacturing industries. These include new generations of information technology; high-end equipment manufacturing; bio-industries; new energy; energy conservation and environmental protection; new materials, and green vehicles.

Consequently, a new wave of industry may be emerging, as did during previous FYP periods. During the Seventh FYP (1986–1990),[2] for instance, textile, chemical, tobacco, oil and gas, and

---

[2] China's five-year development planning started in 1953. Since then, 12 such development initiatives have been promulgated. For the first 10, it is called "Five-Year Plan". Since the 11th (2006–2010), the government has replaced the word *Plan* with *Programme* to highlight that the new initiatives are to be regarded as more like guiding principles rather than compulsory planning. Thus FYP stands for "Five-Year Plan" for the first to the 10th, while for the 11th and 12th, it stands for "Five-Year Programme".

food industries were among the industries that achieved the most rapid growth. During the 1990s (the Eighth and Ninth FYPs), electrical appliances and transport equipment production became leading industries of rapid growth. During the first half of the 2000s, industries like oil and gas, electronic and telecommunications equipment, information and computer technology, and transportation equipment have expanded the most rapidly.

## Government Policies are Effective in Transforming China's Industries

Over the years, the Chinese government has played a significant role in developing and transforming Chinese industries. This is achieved through both general market liberalisation and various specific policy initiatives. Moreover, as development priorities shift, strategies and policy measures vary over time and across industries.

During the early phases of reform, policy measures were primarily directed at two aspects: granting SOEs more managerial autonomy and lowering entry barriers for non-state enterprises, including township and village enterprises (TVEs) and FIEs. Since 1990s, more comprehensive reforms have been put in place to improve the overall business environment for enterprises as the country aimed to establish and strengthen a market-based economy. These include a company law, promulgated in 1993, and a taxation reform, implemented in 1994. Dual-track pricing for industrial products and exchange rate was abandoned. As part of China's efforts to join the World Trade Organization (WTO), import tariffs were gradually but considerably lowered; average nominal tariff rate declined from over 40% in the early 1990s to around 20% in the late 1990s.

Since the late 1990s, in addition to improving the regulatory environment and market institutions, the Chinese government has employed fiscal and financial measures, both directly and indirectly, to support the chosen industries and certain activities. For example, the support for certain important industries were provided through government investments as well as favourable tax rules. Favoured industries were also given easier access to bank loans. More recently, measures were also introduced to enhance indigenous technological capacity.

Due in part to strong government intervention, China's rapid industrial expansion has been accompanied by significant structural transformation. This is reflected in several aspects, including notable changing composition of ownership and the varying relative importance of different industries.

Most significantly, the strong dominant position of state-owned enterprises (SOEs) observed in the 1970s was consistently eroded as TVEs and FIEs grew more rapidly. The share of SOEs in urban employment declined from about 78% to 70% in 1985, and further to 61% in 1990 (Figure 2). By the mid-2000s, SOEs provided only less than a quarter of total urban employment. In the meantime, SOEs' share in China's gross industrial output value also decreased from nearly 80% in 1978 to less than 30% in 1996 and 1997; this was despite SOEs' share remaining relatively stable when measured by the number of enterprises (Figure 3).

The decline of SOEs in China's industries was especially drastic in the 1990s due to several factors. First, the government started to restructure the ailing state sector in the mid-1990s, through what is known as "grasp the big and let go of the small". While the state maintains control of around 2,000 large SOEs, smaller ones were privatised. Moreover, the rapid expansion of TVEs in rural China also contributed to the SOEs' shrinking share. Finally, the inflow of foreign direct investment (FDI) in industries began to gain significance in the 1990s.

Since the late 1990s, the relative importance of SOEs has continued to decline in all aspects. In 2008, state and state-controlled enterprises[3] made up about 5% of all industrial enterprises, down from 39% in 1998. These firms accounted for 28% of output, 30% of total profit, one third of

---

[3]Chinese statistical reports have only combined figures of state-owned and state-controlled enterprises since 1998. The figures are not directly comparable to those of pre-1998 years.

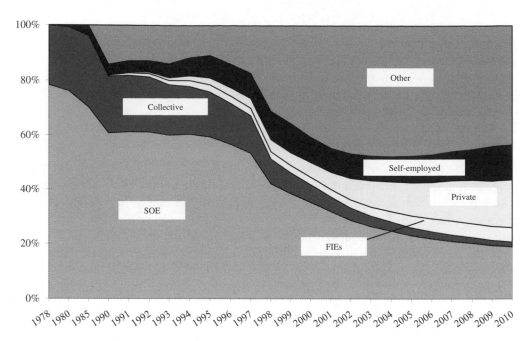

**Figure 2**   Composition of Urban Employment, 1978–2010 (% in total)

Source: *China Statistical Yearbook,* 2011, National Bureau of Statistics of China.

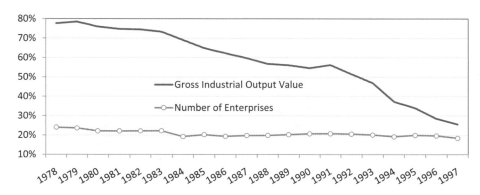

**Figure 3**   Shares of SOEs in the Overall Industry, 1978–1997

*Source*: *China Statistical Yearbook*, various years.

value-added[4] and 44% of assets in 2008, in sharp contrast to those of 50% to 70% a decade ago (Figure 4).

Within the industry, the relative importance of different sectors has changed considerably over the decades. For example, in the late 1990s, the largest industries by output were communication equipment, computer and other electronic equipment, followed by raw chemical materials and chemical products, and transport equipment (Table 1). Labour-intensive industries like textiles are also among the top industries, accounting for 6.2% of the total. More significantly, China's exports are heavily dependent on industries such as textile, apparel, leather, fur and feather related products, which jointly made up a quarter of total exports in 2001.

In 2010, the two largest industries by output were the manufacturing of transport equipment, and the manufacturing of communication equipment, computers and other electronic equipment, each accounting for about 7.9% of China's gross industrial output. The relative size of the three more labour-intensive industries, namely, textile, apparel, and leather, fur, and feather related products

---

[4]The figure for industrial value-added is that of 2007.

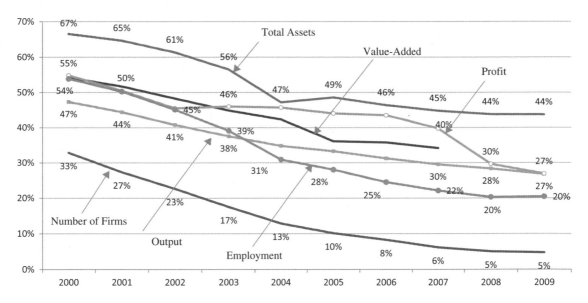

**Figure 4**   Shares of SOEs in the Overall Industry, 2000–2009

Source: *China Industry Economy Statistical Yearbook*, various years.

**Table 1**   Top Ranked Industries by Output, Value-Added, Assets and Exports, 1999 and 2010

| 1999 | Output | Assets | VA | Profit | Exports[a] |
|---|---|---|---|---|---|
| Manufacture of communication equipment, computers and other electronic equipment | 8.0% | 5.3% | 6.3% | 13.5% | 23.4% |
| Manufacture of raw chemical materials and chemical products | 6.8% | 7.0% | 5.6% | 3.4% | 3.7% |
| Manufacture of transport equipment | 6.4% | 6.4% | 5.5% | 5.5% | 3.6% |
| Manufacture of textile | 6.2% | 5.0% | 5.2% | 1.7% | 9.8% |
| Smelting and pressing of ferrous metals | 5.6% | 7.3% | 5.0% | 1.6% | 1.4% |
| Manufacture of electrical machinery and equipment | 5.5% | 4.2% | 4.7% | 6.0% | 6.8% |
| Production and supply of electricity and heat | 4.7% | 13.4% | 10.0% | 13.3% | 0.3% |
| Manufacture of non-metallic products | 4.7% | 5.2% | 4.7% | 1.8% | 2.3% |
| Extraction of petroleum and natural gas | 2.9% | 3.5% | 6.7% | 13.0% | 0.9% |
| Manufacture of textile wearing apparel, footwear and caps | 2.8% | 1.4% | 2.4% | 2.7% | 8.3% |
| Manufacture of tobacco | 1.9% | 1.6% | 4.1% | 5.6% | 0.1% |
| Manufacture of leather, fur, feather and feather related products | 1.7% | 0.8% | 1.3% | 1.1% | 5.5% |
| **2010** | **output** | **assets** | **VA[b]** | **profit** | **exports** |
| Manufacture of transport equipment | 7.9% | 8.1% | 6.0% | 9.2% | 6.5% |
| Manufacture of communication equipment, computers and other electronic equipment | 7.9% | 6.4% | 6.8% | 5.4% | 37.6% |
| Smelting and pressing of ferrous metals | 7.4% | 7.8% | 7.7% | 4.1% | 1.8% |
| Manufacture of raw chemical materials and chemical products | 6.9% | 6.5% | 6.3% | 6.9% | 3.3% |
| Manufacture of electrical machinery and equipment | 6.2% | 5.3% | 5.2% | 5.9% | 8.9% |
| Production and supply of electricity and heat | 5.8% | 12.9% | 7.5% | 3.7% | 0.1% |
| Manufacturing of general purpose machinery | 5.0% | 4.7% | 4.4% | 5.1% | 3.6% |
| Processing of food from agricultural products | 5.0% | 2.8% | 4.0% | 4.4% | 2.4% |

Source: *Statistical Yearbook of China Industries*, various years; Web CEIC Data Manager.

Notes: [a] Export figures are those of 2001; [b] Value-added figures are those of 2007.

declined, and their contributions to exports shrank by over half to about 12%. In the meantime, exports of machinery, including communication equipment, computers and other electronic equipment; transport equipment, and electrical machinery and equipment, grew rapidly to make up more than half of China's total exports of industrial products (53%).

## Managed Foreign Participation Indispensable to China's Industrial Development

While government policies have been essential to China's rapid industrialisation and industrial transformation, the country's embrace of foreign investment and trade has also been instrumental to its growth. It provided Chinese industries with easier access to more advanced production technologies, global market and managerial talent. More significantly, through export-oriented FIEs, especially those from East and Southeast Asia, China has been able to participate in and benefit from the expanding global supply chain and production networks.

China opened its doors to foreign investors when the country started economic reform in 1978. While foreign investment has since been encouraged, it became sizeable only since the early 1990s (Figure 5). The majority of inward FDI to China is in manufacturing, which took advantage of China's low labour costs and various favourable policies offered by the Chinese government at the central and local levels.

Following three decades of China's economic opening up, FIEs have become an essential part of the Chinese industry. In 2008, FIEs constituted less than 20% of China's industrial firms but provided about 30% of industrial employment. More significantly, FIEs contributed to more than two-thirds of China's industrial exports (Table 2).

As is shown, FIEs' presence was particularly dominant in the manufacture of communication equipment, computers and other electronic equipment, which contributed to not only the industry's exports, but also its value-added and employment. The industry is highly export-oriented and is characterised by extensive intra-industry trade. The active role played by FIEs was essential to this industry's rapid development in China. In 2010, over 40% of firms in the industry were FIEs,

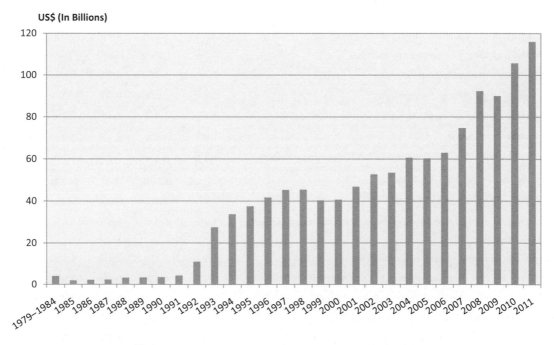

**Figure 5**   Utilised Foreign Direct Investment, 1979–2011

*Sources*: *China Statistical Yearbook* 2011; "Statistical Communiqué on the 2011 National Economic and Social Development", National Bureau of Statistics, 22 February 2012, at <http://www.stats.gov.cn/english/newsandcomingevents/t20120222_402786587. htm> (accessed 4 July 2012).

**Table 2**   Shares of FIEs in China's Top Ranked Industries, 2010

|  | # Firms | Output | Asset | VA[a] | Employment | Exports[b] |
|---|---|---|---|---|---|---|
| Overall | 16% | 27% | 25% | 27% | 28% | 70% |
| Manufacture of transport equipment | 18% | 44% | 38% | 48% | 29% | 51% |
| Manufacture of communication equipment, computers and other electronic equipment | 45% | 77% | 66% | 77% | 72% | 91% |
| Smelting and pressing of ferrous metals | 3% | 13% | 11% | 12% | 8% | 27% |
| Manufacturing of raw chemical materials and chemical products | 15% | 26% | 28% | 29% | 16% | 46% |
| Manufacture of electrical machinery and equipment | 19% | 31% | 31% | 36% | 37% | 67% |
| Manufacture of textiles | 17% | 21% | 27% | 24% | 25% | 48% |
| Manufacture of apparel, footwear and caps | 32% | 38% | 42% | 48% | 45% | 60% |

*Notes*: [a] Figures for value-added are those of 2007; [b] Figures for exports are those of 2009.
*Sources*: *China Statistical Yearbook* 2011, *Statistical Yearbook of China Industries*, various years.

which provided three quarters of the industry's employment and constituted over 90% of the industry's exports. FIEs are also strongly represented in the manufacture of apparel, footwear and caps, another highly export-oriented industry.

Past experience demonstrated that government policies which encourage foreign investment, especially that of export-oriented and technology-intensive enterprises, have served China well in developing a strong and globally competitive industry. FDI policies are likely to continue to be employed as an effective tool in promoting industrial restructuring as well as achieving other objectives such as energy conservation and environmental protection.

Table 3 compares the new guidelines for foreign investment announced in 2007 with those of 1995. Overall, relatively more sectors are now open to foreign investors, as three quarters of the sectors in the 2007 list were under the "encouraged" category, compared to only 53% in the 1995 list. The new list also indicates that there was more emphasis on quality than quantity in FDI inflow; even when the same industries were included in both lists, the 2007 guideline clearly favoured quality improvement as the bias was for larger scale and higher quality production.[5] Other changes include the promotion of foreign investment with higher technological level and resource conservation, such as the processing of environment-friendly fibre.[6]

## China's Industry in the Global Context

Following three decades of rapid growth and industrialisation, the Chinese industry has become one of the largest, highly competitive and wide-ranging industries in the world. According to the United Nations Industrial Development Organization (UNIDO), China's share in global manufacturing value-added rose from 1.4% in 1980 to 12.1% in 2007, and to a projected 15.6% in 2009 (Figure 6). Among 22 International Standard Industrial Classification (ISIC) sectors, China

---

[5]For example, in the 2007 list, the production of ethylene with an annual production capacity of 800,000 tons and above was encouraged (with the Chinese party holding majority shares), while that of 1995 was for the production of 300,000 tons and above.

[6]In the 2011 revision of the Catalogue of Industries for Foreign Investment, the tendency to promote the development of high-tech, green and resource conservation industries is even more apparent. For example, industries such as "the production of organic vegetable", "the process of special natural fibre that is in line with ecology, resource utilisation and environmental protection", "the development and production of inorganic, organic and biological membranes used for environmental protection" are added to the list of encouraged industries. At <http://www.ndrc.gov.cn/zcfb/zcfbl/2011ling/W020111229379511927834.pdf> (accessed 4 July 2012).

**Table 3**   Comparison of FDI Guidelines for 1995 and 2007

|  | Encouraged | | Restricted | |
|---|---|---|---|---|
|  | **1995** | **2007** | **1995** | **2007** |
| Sectors open (encouraged) | 53% | 74% | 35% | 18% |
| Encourage quality improvement larger scale | | | | |
| e.g. ethylene production | >300,000 tons | >800,000 tons | | |
| e.g. nuclear-power plant equipment | >600,000 KW | >1 million KW | | |
| higher technology | high-performance single-lens reflex with over six million pixels (2007); design of integrate circuit and manufacturing of large digital integrate circuit with its wire width less than 0.18 micron (2007), from 0.35 micron or smaller (1995–2004). | | | |
| Resource conservation | Manufacture of equipment for water-pollution prevention and control (2007); production of environment-friendly printing ink and environment-friendly aromatic oil (*fang jing you*) (2007). | | | |
| Promote regional development | | | | |

*Source*: "Catalogue of Industries for Foreign Investment", 1995[7]; "Catalogue of Industries for Foreign Investment 2007 Revision", National Development and Reform Commission.[8]

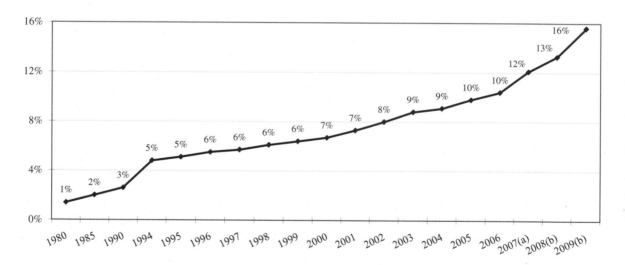

**Figure 6**   China's Share in World Manufacturing Value-Added, 1980–2009

*Notes*: 1980 to 1994 at constant 1990 prices; 1995 to 2009 at constant 2000 prices; (a) provisional; (b) estimate.
*Sources*: *International Yearbook of Industrial Statistics*, 2010, UNIDO.

was among the world's top three producers in all but one in 2008 (Table 4). Moreover, China was the largest producer among developing countries in all sectors.

However, China's competitiveness lies mainly in its low production costs, especially low labour cost. This is true in not only labour-intensive industries such as clothing and footwear, but also capital-intensive and technology-intensive industries. For example, annual wage per employee in electric motors, generators and transformers (ISIC 3110) manufacturing was about US$3,100 in China in 2007. This is not only significantly lower than those of industrialised economies like Japan (US$33,800), Korea (US$24,600) and Singapore (US$25,200), but also considerably lower

---

[7]National Planning Commission, at <http://tw.people.com.cn/GB/14866/14928/866808.html> (accessed 4 July 2012).
[8]At <http://www.ndrc.gov.cn/wzly/zcfg/wzzczjtc/W020071107540870224595.pdf> (accessed 4 July 2012).

**Table 4**    China's Rank as a Major Manufacturer, 1995, 2000 and 2008

| ISIC | | World Rank | | | China's Shares (2008)[a] | |
|---|---|---|---|---|---|---|
| | | 1995 | 2000 | 2008 | In World (Total) | In Developing Countries (Total) |
| 15 | Food and beverages | 6 | 3 | 1 | 17.4% | 41.7% |
| 16 | Tobacco products | 1 | 1 | 1 | 52.9% | 69.6% |
| 17 | Textiles | 2 | 1 | 1 | 43.2% | 62.0% |
| 18 | Apparels | 4 | 3 | 1 | 38.7% | 58.9% |
| 19 | Leather, leather products and footwear | 3 | 1 | 1 | 43.2% | 60.4% |
| 20 | Wood products (excl. furniture) | 12 | 8 | 2 | 12.4% | 49.7% |
| 21 | Paper and paper products | 10 | 4 | 2 | 15.3% | 52.9% |
| 22 | Printing and publishing | 15 | 10 | 5 | 4.4% | 30.1% |
| 23 | Coke, refined products and nuclear fuel | 4 | 3 | 2 | 18.0% | 34.7% |
| 24 | Chemicals and chemical products | 5 | 3 | 1 | 21.1% | 54.1% |
| 25 | Rubber and plastic products | 7 | 3 | 1 | 20.9% | 53.4% |
| 26 | Non-metallic mineral products | 4 | 3 | 1 | 24.1% | 51.4% |
| 27 | Basic metals | 3 | 3 | 1 | 41.6% | 76.2% |
| 28 | Fabricated metal products | 9 | 7 | 2 | 11.6% | 49.7% |
| 29 | Machinery and equipment n.e.c[b]. | 5 | 5 | 2 | 14.7% | 61.6% |
| 30 | Office, accounting and computing machinery | 7 | 4 | 2 | 8.8% | 52.2% |
| 31 | Electrical machinery and apparatus | 5 | 4 | 1 | 27.8% | 70.0% |
| 32 | Radio, TV and communication equipment | 4 | 3 | 2 | 9.9% | 63.1% |
| 33 | Medical, precision and optical instruments | 11 | 7 | 2 | 11.0% | 62.0% |
| 34 | Motor vehicles, trailers and semi-trailers | — | 4 | 3 | 13.8% | 51.6% |
| 35 | Other transport equipment | 2 | 7 | 2 | 13.6% | 40.5% |
| 36 | Furniture manufacturing n.e.c[b] | 4 | 6 | 3 | 17.2% | 60.8% |

*Notes*: [a] calculated at constant 2000 prices; [b] n.e.c: not elsewhere classified
*Source*: International Yearbook of Industrial Statistics 2010, by UNIDO.

than those in many developing countries such as Brazil (US$11,800), Chile (US$15,000), Colombia (US$8,000), Malaysia (US$8,300) and Turkey (US$12,200).

According to UNIDO, China ranked the world's number 26th in terms of industry competiveness in 2005, measured by the organisation's competitive industrial performance (CIP).[9] That was roughly the level of Hungary (#24), Thailand (#25) and Slovakia (#28). It was a considerable improvement from #31 in 2000. However, China's industries remain weak in various aspects. For example, although

---

[9]According to the UNIDO, the CIP index combines four main dimensions of industrial competitiveness: industrial capacity (manufacturing value-added (MVA) per capita), manufactured export capacity (manufactured exports per capita), industrialisation intensity (average of share of manufacturing in GDP) and share of medium- and high-technology activities in MVA, and export quality (average of share of manufactured exports in total exports and the share of medium- and high-technology products in total exports). Of note is that CIP is a relative measure that takes into account overall distribution of all countries included.

medium- to high-technology exports made up 58% of China's total in 2005, many of the products were in the category of processed exports where important parts and components were exported to China for further processing and later for re-export. Thus, the technology intensity level of the products does not necessarily reflect the technological sophistication of the production activities in China.

In recent years, the focus has shifted towards industrial restructuring and upgrading. Various measures, including government spending, policies to encourage science and technology activities and policies to encourage FDI in high-tech industries have been adopted to facilitate technological advancement. For the 11th FYP (2005–2010), the government attempted to raise the rate of total expenditure on research and development (R&D) to GDP from 1.3% to 2.0%. In 2009, total R&D expenditure reached 543 billion *yuan*, amounting to 1.7% of GDP. While China did not reach its goal, it is expected that during the current 12th FYP period (2011–2015), the ratio will climb from 1.75% in 2010 to 2.2% in 2015.

## China's 12th Five-Year Programme

In the Outline for China's 12th FYP for National Economic and Social Development, approved in March 2011, structural adjustment is one of the seven development objectives, as shown below:

1.  To sustain a stable and relatively speedy development;
2.  To achieve considerable achievement in structural adjustment;
3.  To markedly raise the level of science and technology (S&T) and education;
4.  To achieve significant outcome in resource conservation and environment protection;
5.  To achieve continuous improvement in people's livelihood;
6.  To significantly strengthen the social construct; and
7.  To further deepen economic reform and opening up.

The Outline specifies two main goals for China's industrial development, namely, to develop a modern industrial system and to enhance competitiveness of Chinese industries. These goals are expected to be achieved through both improving the current industries and nurturing the development of strategic emerging industries.

The first main task is to upgrade China's manufacturing industry through restructuring and re-organising industries across sectors and regions, and by enhancing independent innovative activities. In doing so, the government aims to focus on several key industry groups, including equipment manufacturing, ship-building, automobile, steel production, non-ferrous metals, building materials, petrochemical products, light industry and textile (Box 1).

---

**Box 1**    Key Directions for Upgrading the Manufacturing Sector for the 12th FYP

1.  Manufacture of equipment:

    - Shift from production-oriented manufacture to service-oriented manufacture
    - Apply Computer Numerical Control (CNC) technology to products, the green technology to production, and the information technology to corporate governance
    - Develop equipment essential to the strategic emerging industries and infrastructure facilities
    - Promote the level of specialisation in basic production techniques in casting, forging, welding, heat treatment and surface treatment
    - Improve the products' quality of bearings, gears, moulds, hydraulic engineering, mechanical automation and other basic components

2.  Shipbuilding
    - Build bulk carriers, oil tankers and container ships in accordance with the new international standards of ship-building

---

*(Continued)*

**Box 1** (*Continued*)

- Build large-scale liquefied natural gas (LNG) ships, large liquefied petroleum gas (LPG) vessels, offshore fishing boats, cruise ships and other high-tech high-value ships
- Promote independent design and manufacture of mobile marine drilling platforms, floating production systems, marine engineering operation ships and its key auxiliary equipment

3. Automobile
   - Achieve breakthrough in the manufacture of automotive battery, key components of driving motors and power-train control system
   - Use of high-efficient internal combustion engines, high-efficient transmission and driving equipment, light materials and structures, and ordinary hybrid technology
   - Produce energy-saving automotive products

4. Steel
   - Promote the production of steel for high-speeding railway; produce high-grade non-oriented silicon steel, high-magnetic induction-oriented silicon steel, high-strength machinery steel and other key types
   - Enhance technological development of non-blast furnace, clean steel production and comprehensive utilisation of resource
   - Develop energy management and control system, high-temperature and high-pressure Coke Dry Quenching (CDQ), waste heat utilisation, and energy saving technology of sintering flue gas desulphurisation

5. Non-ferrous metals
   - Develop production of key materials for aerospace, electronic information and other key industries
   - Develop cutting-edge technology of smelting process, in continuous technology and energy-saving technology
   - Produce renewable resources and the comprehensive utilisation of low-grade ores, associated minerals, refractory ores, tailing and waste

6. Building materials
   - Produce photovoltaic glass, ultra-thin substrate glass, special glass, special ceramics and other new materials
   - Promote municipal solid waste (MSW) incineration project using a cement kiln, sludge production line and the comprehensive utilisation of construction waste
   - Develop new materials and products suitable for green buildings

7. Petrochemical products
   - Build large-scale integrated refining base
   - Implement demonstration projects of the integration of coal and electricity, carbon dioxide use, and pollution control of mercury
   - Improve quality of petroleum products to comply with international IV standard

8. Light industry
   - Promote the use of new batteries, new agricultural plastics, energy-saving electric light sources and intelligent household appliances
   - Speed up independent manufacture of equipment for key industries
   - Promote forestry-paper integration projects
   - Support intensive processing of food, build public capacity to ensure food safety, and improve business credit of food industry

9. Textiles
   - Promote a new generation of high-tech functional and differential fibres
   - Accelerate the development of industrial textiles
   - Promote the independent manufacture of high-end textile machinery and associated components, and support the recycling of used textiles

*Source*: Outline for the 12th Five-Year Programme for the National Economic and Social Development, People's Republic of China, *Xinhua News*.

To achieve the objectives, the Outline highlighted five main approaches which may apply differently to different industry groups:

1. To promote the restructuring of key industries;
2. To optimise the geographic distribution of industrial activities of the industries;
3. To strengthen the technological transformation of enterprises;
4. To nurture industrial re-organisation through mergers and acquisitions, and
5. To promote the development of small and medium-sized enterprises.

The second main task is to nurture the development of several emerging industries considered strategic for the sustainability of China's industries. Three main approaches have been identified (Box 2):

1. To promote leapfrog development in key areas, such as energy saving, new generation of information technology, biotechnology, high-end equipment manufacturing, new energy, new materials and new energy vehicles
2. To implement key development and innovation projects in certain sectors
3. To strengthen policy support and guidance.

---

**Box 2**   Innovation and Development of Emerging Strategic Industries for the 12th FYP

1. Energy-saving and environment-protecting industry:

   - Implement pilot projects to promote energy saving and environment protection
   - Promote high-efficient, energy-saving and advanced environment protection products, and industrialisation of resource recycling

2. New generation of information technology

   - Build a new generation of mobile communication network, and develop the next generation internet and digital broadcasting networks
   - Build pilot projects of internet of logistics (*wulianwang*)
   - Implement the industrialisation of internet products
   - Develop industrial bases for integrated circuits, flat panel display, software and information service

3. Bio-industry

   - Build databases of genetic information of medicine, important animals and plants, and industrial bacteria
   - Establish R&D and industrial bases for biological engineering products, pharmaceutical and biomedical engineering products
   - Build bases for R&D, experiments, detection of bio-breeding, and seed propagation
   - Establish demonstration platform for bio-manufacturing

4. High-end equipment manufacturing

   - Establish the industrial platform for the production of new domestic dry-lease regional aircraft, general aviation aircraft and helicopters
   - Build space infrastructure of satellites for navigation, remote-sensing and communications
   - Develop intelligent control systems, high-end CNC machinery, high-speed trains and urban rail transportation equipment

5. New energy

   - Build industrial bases for a new generation of nuclear power equipment, large-scale wind turbines and components, new components of high-efficient solar power, biomass conversion technology, and smart grid equipment
   - Implement demonstration projects of large-scale use of offshore wind power, solar power and biomass energy

---

(*Continued*)

**Box 2** (*Continued*)

6. New materials
   - Promote R&D of carbon fibre, semiconductor materials, high temperature alloy materials, superconducting materials, high-performance rare earth materials, nano-materials, which are urgently needed by the industries of aerospace, energy resources, transportation and heavy equipment

7. New energy automotive industry
   - Promote R&D, large-scale commercial demonstration projects and industrialisation of plug-in hybrid vehicles and pure electric vehicles

*Source*: Outline for the 12th Five-Year Programme for National Economic and Social Development, People's Republic of China, *Xinhua News*.

To upgrade China's existing manufacturing sector and promote emerging strategic industries, as well as reduce regional gaps, the Outline has also identified goals and strategies for regional development. The main objectives are to enable regions to benefit from their comparative advantages by facilitating the flow of factors of production across regions, and deepening cross-region cooperation and healthy interaction, thus gradually reducing regional gaps. Therefore, the Outline highlights different development priorities for different regions. For western regions, the focus is on infrastructure and resources-related manufacturing industries. For old industrial bases in the northeast and elsewhere, the Outline emphasises equipment manufacturing, raw materials and automobile industries. For central China, the Outline stresses the importance of energy and raw materials, modern equipment manufacturing and high-tech manufacturing. For eastern regions, the emphasis is on the seven emerging strategic industries as well as on modern manufacturing.[10]

## Government-Led Industrial Restructuring Continues

The Chinese government will continue to place great efforts on accelerating the transformation of Chinese industries. In the latest push for high-technology and high value-added manufacturing activities, the government has reinforced the role of technology and innovation. The country aims to increase the share of emerging strategic industries' total added-value in GDP from 3% in 2010 to 8% by 2015 and to 15% by 2020.

As in the past, policies towards FDI will form part of China's overall development strategies. FDI inflow is encouraged in the seven emerging strategic industries, including high-end manufacturing, new high-tech industries, modern services, new energies, energy saving and environmental protection industries. In contrast, FDI is prohibited in industries of high pollution, and high energy and resource consumption.

There is no doubt that China welcomes foreign contribution to its efforts to upgrade its industries and develop crucial new industries. At the same time, however, it seems that significantly more emphasis has been placed on domestic R&D. First, few in China believe that foreign investors will transfer frontier technologies to China. Second, China aims to considerably strengthen its indigenous capacity in scientific research and technological advancement deemed essential for China's rise to become a major world power. Therefore, the role of foreign investors will be important, yet secondary or complementary.

China's achievement over the last three decades in transforming the economy has been most remarkable. The Chinese government has instituted economic liberalisation, decentralisation and economic opening. China's recent experience in overcoming the negative impact of the global economic crisis may have strengthened the belief that an able state and state sector are essential to

---

[10]Regional development and policies are the foci of Chapter 15 and thus will not be discussed further here.

sustaining a healthy growth. It is thus expected that the government will continue to play a vital role in China's efforts to restructure the economy.

Nonetheless, Chinese leaders also face many formidable challenges in formulating and implementing various industrial policies. As China is a large and diverse country with highly uneven development, the extent of central leaders' control will be limited and may further decline. Even within the central government, the power of economic management may have to be shared among a group of leaders, as the number of tasks and the degree of sophistication increase, while the economy grows in size and complexity.

Overall, China's central government and its ministries will continue to be essential to formulating policy agenda and approving key development initiatives. However, it is reasonable to expect that local governments, as well as powerful SOEs, will play increasingly important roles in driving China's future development.

# 15

# China's Regional Development Policies

YU Hong*

*Regional industrial development in China has been unequal since 1978. The eastern region is China's industrial powerhouse. The Chinese government intends to achieve a more balanced regional development by implementing new initiatives in the future.*

The 31 provincial-level administrative units of mainland China can be roughly grouped into three macro-regions, namely the eastern, central and western regions, for purposes of examining regional cooperation and state policy orientation.[1] Within each of the three regions, there are also many more sub-regional areas, e.g. the Pearl River Delta (PRD), Yangtze River Delta (YRD) and Beijing-Tianjin-Hebei (Jing-Jin-Ji) regions. There is huge variation across China's regions in terms of population size, geographical conditions and level of economic development. China faces serious challenges posed by unbalanced regional development and regional economic disparities have increased considerably since 1978.

Prior the early 2000s, many reform and opening-up policies implemented by the Chinese central government had favoured the eastern region, which largely contributed to the highly disparate nature of regional development. The eastern region, in close proximity to the coastline, enjoys advantageous geographic location over the inland central and western regions. The majority of China's state-approved development zones are located along the eastern region. China's five special economic zones are all located along the east coast of China. Moreover, 57% of economic and technological development zones and 52% of high-tech industry development zones are located in eastern China (Table 1). Encouraged by preferential state policies and the plentiful

*YU Hong is Research Fellow at the East Asian Institute, National University of Singapore.
[1]According to the official definition of these three macro-regions, the eastern region covers the 11 administrative provinces of Liaoning, Beijing, Tianjin, Hebei, Shandong, Jiangsu, Shanghai, Zhejiang, Fujian, Guangdong and Hainan; the central region includes the nine administrative provinces of Heilongjiang, Jilin, Inner Mongolia, Shanxi, Henan, Hubei, Hunan, Anhui and Jiangxi, while the western region covers the 11 administrative provinces of Ningxia, Shaanxi, Gansu, Qinghai, Xinjiang, Xizang, Guangxi, Sichuan, Chongqing, Yunnan and Guizhou.

**Table 1**   Location of Special Zones for Economic and Technology Development Approved by China's Central Government

| Type | Eastern Region | Central Region | Western Region | Total |
|---|---|---|---|---|
| Special Economic Zone | 5 | 0 | 0 | 5 |
| Economic and Technological Development Zone | 27 | 10 | 10 | 47 |
| High-tech Industry Development Zone | 28 | 13 | 13 | 54 |
| Bonded Zone | 15 | 0 | 0 | 15 |
| Total | 75 | 23 | 23 | 121 |

*Sources*: Peng (2003)[2]; "List of High-Tech and New-Tech Development Zones", Ministry of Science and Technology of the People's Republic of China, 2009.

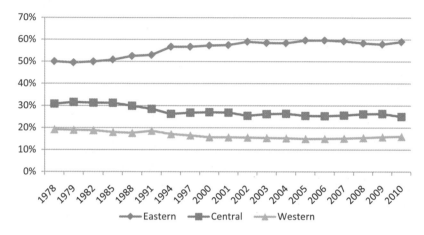

**Figure 1**   Regional Shares of China's GDP, 1978–2010

*Note*: The figures are based on the current price.

*Sources*: National Bureau of Statistics of China, *China Statistical Yearbook*, various years, China Statistics Press, Beijing.

supply of cheap labour in the eastern region, foreign investors have established a large number of export-oriented manufacturing factories in this region.

China's uneven development strategy contributed to the widening of economic disparity among its regions, especially during the 1990s and early 2000s. The eastern region's share in China's GDP increased to 58% in 2005, from 50% in 1979, while western China experienced a steady decline in its relative economic importance, from 19% in 1979 to about 16% in recent years (Figure 1). The importance of the eastern region in national industrial activities is evident. In 2003, the eastern region accounted for 64% of China's total industrial value-added, up from 57% in 1991 (Figure 2). Regional variations measured by the coefficient of variation (CV) in gross regional product (GRP) by province, have risen considerably over the past few decades. Figure 3 shows that CV rose markedly between the late 1980s and the mid-1990s, from 0.69 in 1988 to 0.79 in 2000. Since the early 2000s, the CV has again risen significantly, from around 0.80 in 2001 to 0.86 in 2007 despite efforts such as the Great Western Development Strategy initiated in the late 1990s to reduce regional disparity. Nonetheless, there are signs that regional disparity has started to decrease in recent years. The CV had declined to 0.81 by 2010.

---

[2]Peng S (ed.), *Zhongguo jingji tequ yu kaifaqu nianjian 2003* (*China Special Economic Zone & Development Area Yearbook* 2003), China Financial & Economic Publishing House, Beijing, 2003.

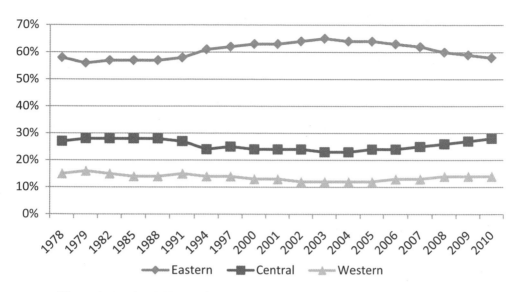

**Figure 2**  Regional Shares of China's Industrial Value-Added Output, 1978–2010

*Note*: The figures are based on the current price.

*Sources*: National Bureau of Statistics of China, *China Statistical Yearbook*, various years, China Statistics Press, Beijing.

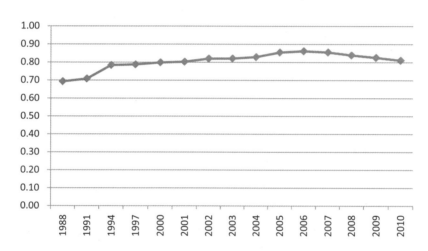

**Figure 3**  Coefficients of Regional Variation in Gross Regional Product, 1988–2010

*Note*: The coefficient of variation (CV) is calculated as standard deviation/mean.

*Sources*: Figures were calculated by the author using data of the GRPs of provinces from the *China Statistical Yearbook*, various years.

## New State Strategy to Achieve a More Balanced Regional Development

The increase in regional inequality poses a threat to China's sustainable development and Beijing has begun to actively pursue a more balanced regional development since the late 1990s. Pursuing a balanced regional development, in Beijing's perspective, serves three important purposes. First, narrowing regional disparities is essential to regain political loyalty of the western region. The Chinese leaders have found it increasingly difficult to justify the increase in regional disparities. Second, reducing disparities is essential to social stability in the underdeveloped western region, which is home to many ethnic minorities. The uprising and social unrest that occurred in Xizang (Tibet) in 2008 and Xinjiang in 2009 clearly demonstrate the political sensitivity and significance of the western region to China. Third, pursuing a more balanced regional development is crucial to boost domestic consumption and investment, and reduce the overdependence of China's economy on foreign trade and investment.

Efforts to develop inland regions started with the government's initiative, the Great Western Development Strategy, in 1999. In addition, the state effort to "revitalise traditional industrial bases in the north-east region" was presented in late 2002, while an important state initiative to develop the central region has been implemented since early 2004. The notion of "comprehensive or coordinated regional development", which has been in place since the early 2000s, is aimed at promoting coordinated regional development across provincial boundaries. In addition, the concept of development based on the formation of different functional areas[3] has been unveiled and has attracted increasing policy attention over the past few years. In theory, by implementing these state policy initiatives, the central and western provinces should have achieved relative equal footing with the eastern provinces in competing for resources and favourable policies from Beijing. Nevertheless, these government initiatives have yet to yield a significant effect in reducing regional disparities. As shown in Figures 1, 2 and 3, regional economic disparities continued to widen and have only recently started to shrink.

Government strategy has tended to focus more on the formation of urban metropolises and industrial clusters over the past few years. This policy orientation can be seen in the recent spur in metropolis and megacity-centred development plans. The Chinese central government has approved an increasing number of regional plans to forge large metropolitan areas since 2007; high-profile projects include the setting up of Comprehensive Testing Zones for National Urban-Rural Reform in Changsha-Zhuzhou-Xiangtan and Wuhan city (December 2007), Tianjin Binhai New Area (November 2009), Guangzhou-Foshan megacity (December 2009), and the development of Chengdu-Chongqing Economic Zone (May 2011).

In fact, as a result of the government's new initiatives, more FDI has flowed into China's central and western regions over the past few years. China's inland regions are becoming increasingly attractive to foreign investors. Inter-regional transportation in China's inland regions has improved dramatically in recent years. Moreover, Beijing, the central and western governments are providing various policy incentives for attracting foreign investment and foreign-owned firms to establish heavy (energy, mining and automobiles) and light manufacturing (food, textile and logging) plants in the inland regions.[4]

## China's Main Industrial Powerhouses

The state-initiated preferential policies to stimulate industrial development have dramatically improved the performance and productivity of China's industrial sector over the last three decades. Fast expansion of production capacity and the opening up of foreign markets to more industrial goods in many industrial sectors have both been impressive over the past few years. Significantly, the success of industrial upgrading and economic restructuring in China depends on the performance of the eastern region. In particular, the PRD (covering Guangdong), YRD (covering Shanghai, Jiangsu and Zhejiang) and the Jing-Jin-Ji regions (covering Beijing, Tianjin and Hebei), which are all located in eastern China and accounted for more than 43% and 47% of national GDP and industrial value-added respectively in 2010,[5] are the most prosperous regions and economic

---

[3]According to the concept of "functional areas", a region is classified into one of the four types, namely, area for optimised development, area of main development, area where development should be restricted and area where development is prohibited.

[4]The government documents are as follows: (i) *Cujin zhongbu diqu jueqi guihua* (Plan to boost the rise of central region) issued by the National Development and Reform Commission, September 2009; (ii) *Shangwubu bangongting guanyu kuodakaifang tigao xishouwaizishuiping cujin zhongbu jueqi de zhidao yijian* (Guidance on expanding openness and increasing FDI to boost the economy of the central region) issued by the Ministry of Commerce of the People's Republic of China, December 2005; (iii) *Guowuyuan guanyu zhongxibu diqu chengjie chanye zhuanyi de zhidao yijian* (Guidance from the State Council on the transfer of industries to the central and western regions) issued by the State Council of China in 2010; (iv) *Zhongguo xishou waizi zhengce* (Policies to attract foreign investment) issued by the Ministry of Commerce, February 2001; (v) *Waizi touzi chanye zhidao mulu* (Guidance on priority industries for foreign investment) issued by the Ministry of Commerce, 2007; (vi) *Zhongguo zhongxibu diqu waishang touzi youshi chanye mulu* (List of priority industries for foreign investment in the central and western regions of China) issued by the Ministry of Commerce, 2008.

[5]National Bureau of Statistics of China, *China Statistical Yearbook 2011*, China Statistics Press, Beijing, 2012.

powerhouses in China. The industrial upgrading and economic growth of the PRD, YRD and the Jing-Jin-Ji regions will determine the sustainability of China's development and its future prosperity. This chapter primarily focusses on these regions and examines their industrial development policies.

## The Pearl River Delta (PRD) Region

The PRD region has been the vanguard of China's economic reforms since 1978. It has transformed itself into a global manufacturing base for many low-end and value-added, and labour-intensive products, based on its competitiveness derived from an abundant supply of cheap labour and ample land resources.[6] The top five industries in Guangdong, measured by the value-added of output, are (i) communications equipment, computers and other electronic equipment; (ii) electrical machinery and equipment; (iii) transport equipment; (iv) metal products; and (v) manufacture of raw chemical materials and chemical products. These industries jointly accounted for nearly 50% of Guangdong's industrial output and 46% of industrial value-added in 2010.[7]

The export-oriented manufacturing factories set up by foreign investors have played a crucial role in the rapid industrialisation and economic take-off of the PRD. However, the 2008 global economic crisis exposed the weaknesses of this region. The current heavy dependence on export-oriented and labour-intensive manufactures has left the PRD vulnerable to negative external shocks. This development model is not sustainable due to escalating production costs and wages, and a shortage of industrial land. Over the recent years, this region has attempted to upgrade its economy towards more high-end and high value-added knowledge-based industries.

In January 2009, the central government released the Outline of the Plan for the Reform and Development of the PRD Region 2008–2020, which highlights long-term industrial development policies and development priorities. Industrial upgrading is the focal point of the development outline. Low-end manufacturing industries are expected to be relocated to areas on the underdeveloped periphery while the PRD will concentrate on developing high value-added manufacturing and modern service industries.[8] While simultaneously nurturing the new and high-tech industries, the PRD region also focusses on the development of advanced manufacturing industries. Examples of advanced manufacturing industries include modern equipment manufacturing (automobiles, steel, petroleum, and shipbuilding and ocean engineering equipment). The promotion of high-tech industries primarily focusses on electronics and information, biomedicine, new materials, environmental protection and new energy sectors. Traditional industries such as textile and garments, manufacture of food and beverage will be required to achieve technological upgrading and strengthen competitiveness. The Outline specified various measures to achieve the region's structural transformation. First, the government will establish special development zones to cultivate the development of various advanced industries. Second, the government will enhance the region's technological and innovative capacity by injecting more resources in R&D activities. Third, the government will also adopt favourable policies to assist in the development of high-tech industries, such as pre-tax deduction of R&D expenses and expanding government procurement on products that incorporate indigenous technology.[9]

Nonetheless, the region is facing numerous challenges in sustaining rapid growth. First, skilled labour force is in serious shortage. Second, industrial relocation and upgrading is difficult and costly. Many small and medium-sized, export-oriented businesses, having benefited from the existing

[6]Zhang J and Hou Y, *Coordinating Regional Development*, China Development Publisher, Beijing, 2008.
[7]*Guangdong Statistical Yearbook 2011*, China Statistics Press, Beijing.
[8]Yu H and Zhang Y, "New Initiatives for Industrial Upgrading in the Pearl River Delta", *EAI Background Brief*, no. 464, National University of Singapore, 2009.
[9]"China's National and Regional Industrial Development", a report prepared for the Ministry of Trade and Industry, Singapore, *East Asian Institute*, National University of Singapore, March 2011.

industrial clusters and low input costs, are reluctant to upgrading production. Third, technological capacity and human capital development are two aspects that the PRD is weak in. The ratio of R&D expenditure to GRP is considerably lower in the PRD region than in the other regions.

### Yangtze River Delta (YRD) Region

The YRD has been an important engine driving rapid economic development in China during the reform period. The YRD region contributed to about 20% of national GDP and industrial value-added in 2009. The central government approved the Development Outline for the YRD Region in May 2010. The YRD Outline highlighted development priorities for the region's industries. Overall, this region seeks to accelerate its industrial upgrading and become a key production base for advanced manufacturing and China's centre of modern services of worldwide importance. The development priorities are devoted to four key strategic sectors, namely equipment manufacturing (ocean engineering equipment, alternative-fuel engines and shipbuilding), petrochemicals, steel and electronic information. For conventional industries such as textile and clothing, the government is expected to increase R&D spending and encourage mergers and acquisitions by large enterprises to enhance production competitiveness. Further, the government will promote emerging industries, which include biomedicine, civil aerospace and aviation, renewable energy and new materials. The local governments in the YRD region, such as that of Shanghai, have implemented measures to support industrial development.[10] Nevertheless, due to their similarities in economic structure, excessive competition exists among Shanghai, Jiangsu and Zhejiang. Various local governments have even established administrative barriers which hamper inter-regional cooperation.[11]

### The Jing-Jin-Ji Region

The Jing-Jin-Ji region enjoys a comparative political advantage because Beijing is the national capital and political centre of China. Close proximity to the central government has allowed the local governments within this region to gain support from the ministries. Backed by strong support from the central government, the Jing-Jin-Ji region has experienced rapid economic growth in the last decade. In 2008, its contribution to China's GDP exceeded that of the PRD for the first time. The development of high-tech industries has been impressive in this region over the last few years. The output value of new and high-tech industry was 727.7 billion *yuan* in 2008, accounting for 30.6% of total industrial output of the Jing-Jin-Ji region. One of the main centres of development for high-tech industries is the Tianjin Binhai New Area (TBNA). A new and high-tech industry-led economy has gradually emerged in this region, with development of aircraft manufacturing at the core. The TBNA is likely to be the driving force for the economic growth of the Jing-Jin-Ji region.

Compared to other regions, the Jing-Jin-Ji region spends more on R&D and shows stronger capability in technological innovation. In 2008, total government expenditure on R&D in this region was 86.4 billion *yuan,* or 2.6% of its GRP, considerably higher than that of the PRD (1.4% of its GRP) and YRD (2% of its GRP) regions. Strong research capability and a large pool of skilled workers offer the Jing-Jin-Ji region a competitive edge. Educational advantages provide opportunities for scientific research, high technological innovation, and above all, the practical application of technology. With Beijing as the key educational centre, there are more than 230 universities and 700 research institutions and clusters of scientists and researchers

---

[10] *Guanyu cujin shanghai xinnengyuan chanye fazhan de ruogan guiding* (Several Regulations on Boosting New Energy Industries Development in Shanghai), Reform and Development Commission of Shanghai, November 2009.

[11] Zhang J and Wu F, "China's Changing Economic Governance: Administrative Annexation and the Reorganization of Local Governments in the Yangtze River Delta", *Regional Studies*, vol. 40, no. 1, 2006.

within this region. Priorities for industrial development of Beijing, Tianjin and Hebei are as follows: Hebei focusses on the development of industries, such as food, automobiles, steel and equipment manufacturing; Tianjin gives priority to the development of petrochemical, biomedicine, aerospace and ocean equipment manufacturing, while Beijing targets high-tech and modern service industries.

Nevertheless, the Jing-Jin-Ji region has to deal with water shortage, which poses immense challenge to its sustainable industrial development.[12] The annual local water output in Beijing is below 300 cubic metres per capita, which is significantly lower than the international definition of a dangerously low level of water supply of 1,000 cubic metres per capita per year. Almost all surface water sources have either dried out or become polluted in the Jing-Jin-ji region.[13] Fast industrial growth requires plentiful supply of water, particularly in the steel and automobile sectors. Although this region has abundant human resources and strong infrastructure, water shortage could become a fatal constraint on its sustainable development.

## Challenges for Regional Industrial Development

First, different regions compete to develop various industries, often resulting in excessive inter-regional and intra-regional competition. Moreover, the domestic market is largely fragmented, as local governments attempt to shield local industries from competition of non-local enterprises. Although the Chinese industries have grown rapidly in terms of total output, a large number of enterprises continue to compete at the lower end of the value-added chain. As a result, many industries, especially steel and automobiles, suffer from serious overcapacity.[14] Industrial consolidation and factories mergers across provinces remain slow and difficult. Local leaders, whose political promotion are largely determined by local GDP growth, will hinder China's attempt to achieve a more coordinated and balanced regional industrial development.

To realise the targets outlined in the national 12th Five-Year Programme (2011–2015) moving from investment- and export-led growth to one driven by domestic consumption, China's industries should focus more on qualitative improvement and indigenous technology innovation. This change in focus encompasses two key elements: firstly, accelerating the development of newly emerging industries to sustain China's long-term industrial competitiveness, and secondly, restructuring and upgrading existing traditional industries. However, the policy implementation may prove difficult to achieve.

The duplication of industrial structure is another unresolved problem. A case in point is the Jing-Jin-Ji region. Beijing, Tianjin and Hebei, three provincial level cities within the Jing-Jin-Ji region, have developed similar traditional industries: e.g. steel, petrochemical, electronic information and automobile manufacturing. They are also competing in new industries such as finance, biotechnology, medicine and aerospace.[15] The industrial linkages within the Jing-Jin-Ji region are weak. Industrial development priorities for these three regions are also quite similar. In terms of the advanced manufacturing industries, Beijing and Tianjin have been focussing on developing industries such as smelting and pressing of ferrous metals, transport equipment and electrical equipment and machinery. In the new and high-tech industries, all three regions have been promoting industrial sectors such as biomedicine, new materials, environmental protection

---

[12] Jiang et al., "Integrated Evaluation of Urban Development Suitability Based on Remote Sensing and GIS Techniques–A Case Study in Jingjinji Area, China", *Sensors*, vol. 8, 2008, pp. 5975–86.

[13] Zhai B, Jia Y and Xu Q, "A Long Way to Go: the Coordinative Development in the Capital Region of China?", 40th ISoCaRP Congress, 2004, pp. 1–11.

[14] Yang M and Yu H (eds.), *China's Industrial Development in the 21st Century*, World Scientific Publishing Company, Singapore, 2011.

[15] Deng L, "Strategic Analysis on Industrial Coordinative Development in the Jing-Jin-Ji Economic Zone", *Productivity Research*, Beijing Academy of Social Sciences, vol. 3, 2007, pp. 117–20.

**Table 2**   Industrial Development Priorities in the Jing-Jin-Ji Region

| Region | Advanced Manufacturing Industries | New and High-Tech Industries |
|---|---|---|
| Tianjin | Smelting and pressing of ferrous metals, ocean engineering equipment, petrochemicals, transport equipment, electrical equipment and machinery, aircraft manufacturing | Biomedicine, new materials, environmental protection, new energy, water, aerospace |
| Beijing | Smelting and pressing of ferrous metals, transport equipment, electrical equipment and machinery | New materials, new energy, biomedicine, water, environmental protection |
| Hebei | Petrochemicals, equipment manufacturing, automobiles, telecommunication, electrical equipment and machinery | Biotechnology, medicine, new materials, new energy, environmental protection |

*Source*: Compiled by the author.

and new energy (Table 2). This lack of industrial cooperation may result in duplicated development and "cut-throat" competition, and may also limit the development of an integrated domestic market.

Beijing, Tianjin and Hebei each seeks to thrive as an independent economy and implements different development strategies. Unlike the cities within the PRD and YRD regions, both Beijing and Tianjin are centrally administrated municipalities that will likely make it more difficult for the Jing-Jin-Ji region to forge close socio-economic ties. Although Beijing is the political and educational centre of the Jing-Jin-Ji region, Tianjin and Hebei do not regard themselves as subordinate players. There are currently no formal regional administrative mechanisms or regular government meetings to coordinate the development of this region and local governments appear to be unwilling to forge closer ties between the different cities. Policy regarding the construction of ports reflects the absence of coordination. Along the merely 640 kilometre-long coastline of this region, Tianjin Port has been facing fierce competition from the emerging Qinghuangdao, Tangshan, Huanghua and Caofeidian ports.

## Regional Economic Disparities Likely to Prevail

The eastern region, the most prosperous region and China's industrial powerhouse, has played a key role in national economic development. To pursue sustainable industrial growth and ride on the next wave of rapid economic growth in China, the eastern region is keen to accelerate the pace of industrial upgrading and economic restructuring. This applies particularly to the PRD, YRD and Jing-Jin-Ji regions where the local governments have been promoting the development of high-end and value-added emerging industries, and increasing industrial productivity as the global economic crisis exposed the vulnerability of labour-intensive and low-end manufacturing activities. These regions therefore seek to gradually evolve into a global base for advanced manufacturing and centre of modern services by moving up the production value chain and implementing new policy initiatives.

China's effort towards sustainable industrial and economic development and transformation from an export-oriented to a more domestic consumption-driven economy require concurrent rapid development of the inland central and western regions. Beijing has, since the early 2000s, recognised the need to channel greater efforts into stimulating industrial growth in the underdeveloped western and central regions. As outlined in China's 12th Five-Year Programme, the government is expected to pay more attention to pursue a more balanced regional development over the next five years. Therefore, the accelerated pace of industrial restructuring and upgrading in the eastern region post-crisis has provided the central and western regions opportunities to stimulate local industrial growth with the relocation of low-end and labour-intensive industrial sectors from the eastern region to inland regions.

Nevertheless, the State's efforts have yet to bear much fruit, as the eastern region continues to dominate China's economic development and take a lead in national industrial upgrading. The relocation of low-end and low value-added manufacturing industries to the inland regions will allow eastern China to free more land space to develop high-end and value-added service industrial sectors, thereby reinforcing its existing economic power. At the same time, a lack of regional cooperation, excessive regional competition and duplicated development structures pose serious challenges for the central government's pursuit of a balanced regional industrial development.

# 16

# The 12th Five-Year Programme

## A Turning Point in China's Socio-Economic Development

John WONG*

*China's 12th Five-Year Programme (FYP) is designed to deal with China's many "growth problems" arising from its long periods of breakneck economic growth. This is to be done by restructuring its development strategies and rebalancing its economic growth patterns. The result will render China's future growth more sustainable.*

The Fifth Plenum of the 17th Chinese Communist Party's Central Committee in mid-October 2010 adopted the proposal of the 12th Five-Year Programme (FYP, 2011–2015), which sets out broad guidelines and strategic priorities for China's economic and social development over the next five years. This Party document was formally ratified by the National People's Congress (NPC) in March 2011, and it has since become an official national policy blueprint for the country's overall economic and social development in the following five years.

The main objectives of this 12th FYP are to address China's existing and emerging development challenges, which include not just rapid economic progress but also more sustainable economic growth through economic restructuring and rebalancing while grappling with China's many burning socio-economic issues.

This calls for a radical shift in China's existing growth patterns and strategies based on an all-out pursuit of GDP increases to one that takes better growth quality into account, i.e. the question of "quality versus quantity". In this regard, future economic growth will de-emphasise external demand (or exports) as an important source of growth while expanding domestic demand, particularly domestic consumption and other social service activities that will better lead to the improvement of "people's livelihood" or *minsheng*.

Premier Wen Jiabao once said in 2007 that China's growth is "unstable, unbalanced, uncoordinated and unsustainable". The basic tenet of China's future economic growth, therefore,

---

*John WONG is Professorial Fellow at the East Asian Institute, National University of Singapore.

should be one that is more "balanced" and more inclusive. Such new development strategies will also be effective in addressing many other related important socio-economic issues like income inequality and regional disparity as well as better environmental protection. In the words of Morgan Stanley's China expert Stephen Roach, "history will judge the 12th Five-Year Plan as a watershed event in the development of modern China".[1]

## The Need for Macroeconomic Rebalancing and Structural Change

China's economy has chalked up an average annual growth rate of 9.9% for more than three decades starting from 1979 (Figure 1). With its total GDP in 2011 at 47 trillion *yuan* (or about US$7.3 trillion at market exchange rate), China has recently replaced Japan as the world's second largest economy after USA. In PPP (purchasing power parity) terms, China's economy has long been the world's second largest. In 1978, China's total GDP accounted for only 0.5% of global GDP; but by 2011, its global share of GDP increased to about 10%. China's per capita GDP in 2011, at 35,000 *yuan* or about US$5,500, was however still only a fraction of the average of high-income economies. By the World Bank classification, China today is a middle-income economy.

When an economy has reached middle-income status, it is a mark of its successful economic take-off. At the same time, this also signals the need for the economy to change gear by shifting its basic development strategies with a view to accelerating its process of economic restructuring and upgrading in order to avoid the "middle-income trap" that has plagued numerous developing economies. When the East Asian newly industrialised economies of South Korea, Taiwan and Singapore became middle-income economies, they started to expand from labour-intensive to more capital-intensive and higher value-added activities, making a successful transition to high-income economies. Viewed in this context, China's economic growth today has just reached this crucial stage of the much-needed structural change and adjustment.

In the case of China, there is also an important international dimension to its economic restructuring and rebalancing. China's dynamic economic growth owes a great deal to its successful implementation of export-oriented strategies. China's exports have been growing at 16% a year for the past three decades. Its exports in 2010 amounted to US$1.6 trillion, taking up 12% share of the

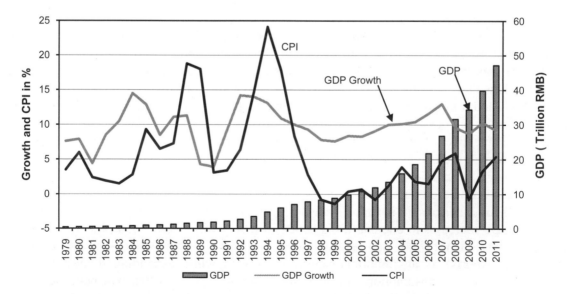

**Figure 1**   China's GDP, CPI and Economic Growth, 1979–2011

*Source*: National Bureau of Statistics.

---

[1]Morgan Stanley, "*China's 12th Five-Year Plan: Strategy vs. Tactics*", April 2011.

world market and replacing Germany as the world's leading exporting country. For many years in a row, China has been consistently enjoying a huge trade surplus (US$183 billion in 2010). As a result of its persistent trade surplus together with its large annual influx of capital (i.e. the twin surpluses on both current and capital accounts), China has built huge foreign exchange reserves (currently at US$3.2 trillion). This has in turn led to mounting pressure on the *renminbi* (RMB) to revalue as well as subjecting China to increasing trade frictions with its trade partners.

In basic macroeconomic terms, the root cause of China's trade surplus is China's high gross savings (X–M = S–I), which, in turn, is the result of China's low consumption. In other words, China's economic growth pattern is not "balanced' from the global perspective. China is under-consuming, over-saving, over-investing and over-producing, and therefore it is over-exporting. Since China is a large economy with enormous global impact, its macroeconomic imbalance will affect global macroeconomic balance. If China has incurred a huge trade surplus, other economies must take huge deficits. Hence, there has been tremendous international pressure for China's economy to readjust and rebalance itself.

In recent years, labour costs have been surging and the RMB exchange rate rising. All these plus inflation have eroded China's export competitiveness for labour-intensive products. Take the first eight months of 2011: the average price of Chinese exports went up 10.3%.[2] Apart from strong external pressures, there are also domestic imperatives for China to undertake a radical overhaul of its basic development strategies. Viewed from this angle, this timely 12th FYP is both domestically and internationally significant.

## The Salient Features of the 12th FYP

Overall, the 12th FYP is made up of 16 parts and 62 chapters. Part 1 is much like a concluding summary, starting with the macro development environment and setting out some guiding principles on how to transform the existing growth pattern and create the preconditions for "scientific development". More significantly, it also lays down some explicit hard environmental targets such as maintaining farmland at 1.8 billion mu (121 million hectares) while increasing national forest coverage to 22%, cutting water consumption per unit of value-added industrial output by 30%, increasing the efficiency of agricultural irrigation to 0.53, increasing non-fossil fuels in primary energy consumption to 11.4%, and reducing energy consumption per unit of GDP by 16% and $CO_2$ emissions by 17%. Accordingly, China will make significant stride towards the "green economy" by reducing the total emission of COD (chemical oxygen demand) and $SO_2$ by 8% and nitrogen oxide by 10%. Furthermore, all these are binding targets that are deemed achievable.

Part 2, with 4 chapters, is about how to accelerate the construction of the new socialist countryside by strengthening the agricultural sector and improving the livelihood of the farmers. Part 3, dealing with industrial upgrading and developing strategic core industries, is the most important component from the standpoint of industrial transformation. Part 4 is on how to promote the service sector while Part 5 deals with regional development and urbanisation. Following successful industrialisation, China's next phase of development is focussed on the more rapid expansion of the service sector along with the gradual urbanisation.

Part 6 is about promoting the development of the "green economy" and the environmentally friendly "green society", which are most critical for the production of the better quality GDP and better quality of life. Part 7 deals with innovation, science and education, and human resource development. This is obviously an essential precondition for industrial upgrading and the successful development of emerging strategic industries.

Part 8 is about pro-people development, emphasising the need to improve people's livelihood through expanding related public social services from education, health care and social security. China's economic development has come to a stage where it has built the material base to go into

---

[2] "Chinese Export Prices Rises", *China Daily*. 4 October 2011.

this much-needed area of social development. With the rise of the middle class, particularly in the urban areas, the demand for more social services and better social infrastructure is also on the increase. Some of the social development targets like basic pension scheme and basic medical insurance for urban residents are binding.

Part 9 deals with measures that will strengthen "social management", which is basically a form of social control with Chinese characteristics. It is also about community building and social planning. With rising social protests, the Chinese leadership is getting increasingly concerned with the problem of maintaining social order and social harmony. Admittedly, one can see certain ideological rhetoric and political undertone in this aspect of the plan.

Part 10 deals with cultural development while Part 11 is about the need for strengthening the institutional framework of the "socialist market economy", including measures to deepen the reform of the state-owned enterprises. Part 12 spells out the ways and means to further open up certain areas and regions, giving rise to a new pattern of regional development.

Parts 13, 14 and 15 are basically used to articulate the Party's rhetoric on how to promote democracy (with Chinese characteristics), how to nurture the political awareness of the people in Hong Kong and Macau on the concept of one China, and how to strengthen national defence and national unity.

Finally, Part 16 is devoted to the issues of programme implementation. This ends up surprisingly very short and brief, lacking substantive details on how various parts of the plan are to be implemented and realised. This further serves to affirm what we have observed earlier that the 12th FYP is really a far-cry from the First FYP, which is a prototype of economic planning under a command economy, complete with a lot of details on how to achieve the planned targets. In contrast, the 12th FYP is really a "toothless" plan, which is more like a kind of roadmap for Chinese policy makers to go about with China's economic and social development in the next five years.

In summary, the 12th FYP contain three major components. The first is concerning environmental protection and related measures that will facilitate the development of a "greener" economy and a "greener" society for China. In this regard, the targets are quite realistic and deemed achievable (Table 1). The second component is about China's next phase of social development aiming at

**Table 1**   Key Green Targets in the 12th Five-Year Programme

| Target | | 2010 | 2015 | Change Over Five Years (%) | Forecast or Binding |
|---|---|---|---|---|---|
| Farmland reserves (billion mu) | | 1.818 | 1.818 | 0 | binding |
| Decrease in water consumption per unit of value-added industrial output (%) | | | | 30 | binding |
| Increase of water efficiency coefficient in agricultural irrigation | | 0.5 | 0.53 | 0.03 | forecast |
| Increase of non-fossil fuel usage in primary energy consumption (%) | | 8.3 | 11.4 | 3.1 | binding |
| Decrease in energy consumption per unit of GDP (%) | | | | 16 | binding |
| Decrease in CO$_2$ emissions per unit of GDP (%) | | | | 17 | binding |
| Total decrease in emissions of major pollutants (%) | Chemical Oxygen Demand (COD) | | | 8 | binding |
| | Sulphur Dioxide (SO$_2$) | | | 8 | |
| | Ammonia Nitrogen | | | 10 | |
| | Nitrous Oxides | | | 10 | |
| Forest Increase | Forest coverage rate (%) | 20.36 | 21.66 | 1.3 | |
| | Forest stock (m$^3$) | 137 | 143 | 6 | binding |

*Source*: <http://news.xinhuanet.com/politics/2011-03/16/c_121193916.htm> (accessed 16 August 2012).

**Table 2** Key Socio-Economic Targets of China's 12th Five-Year Programme Period

| Indicators | 2010 | 2015 | Average Annual Growth Rate | |
|---|---|---|---|---|
| **Economic development** | | | | |
| — GDP (trillion *yuan*) | 39.8 | 55.8 | 7% | Expected |
| — Urbanisation rate (%) | 47.5 | 51.5 | 4%[a] | Expected |
| **People's livelihood** | | | | |
| — Per capita disposable income of urban residents (*yuan*) | 19109 | >26810 | >7% | Expected |
| — Per capita net income of rural residents (*yuan*) | 5919 | >8310 | >7% | Expected |
| — Registered urban unemployment rate (%) | 4.1 | <5 | | Expected |
| — Number of new jobs in urban areas (million) | | | 45[a] | Expected |
| — Number of urban residents enrolled in basic pension scheme (million people) | 257 | 357 | 1%[a] | Binding |
| — Rate of enrolment in basic medical insurance in urban and rural areas (%) | | | 3%[a] | Binding |
| — Number of low-income apartments built in urban areas (units) | | | 36 million[a] | Binding |
| — Total population (billion) | 1.341 | <1.39 | <7.2% | Binding |
| — Average life expectancy (years of age) | 73.5 | 74.5 | 1 year[a] | Expected |

*Note*: Target is set to increase the income of urban and rural residents at a rate no lower than GDP growth rate; [a] Accumulative figure over five years.

*Source*: <http://news.xinhuanet.com/politics/2011-03/16/c_121193916.htm> (accessed 16 August 2012).

improving people's livelihood. This involves "soft" targets and its implementation process can be a long-drawn one (Table 2).

The third component deals with the critical aspect of China's economic restructuring and industrial upgrading, which is most crucial for China's sustainable economic growth in the longer run. The projected key targets include 7% annual growth, 4% expansion of the service sector as a percentage of GDP by 2015, and increasing average urban disposable income to over 26,800 *yuan* and average disposable rural income to over 8,300 *yuan*.

## The 12th FYP in Action

Operationally, the main thrust of China's economic restructuring is articulated in five "insistences" (*jianchi*) or striving to do:

(1) Strive to achieve strategic adjustment towards greater domestic consumption, with the expansion of domestic consumption to be built into the long-term economic and social development structure. This involves, among others, appropriate policies to promote faster but orderly urbanisation of small and medium cities, better income distribution, wider coverage of the social safety net and expansion of basic public services.

(2) Strive to modernise agriculture in order to cope with the "three *nong*" problems (*nongye, nongcun* and *nongmin* or agriculture, villages and peasants). Agricultural development involves greater technological transformation of agriculture and more rural infrastructural development; the objective is to raise agricultural productivity, which is in turn needed to raise the level of national food security. The goals of other aspects of rural development involving villages and peasants are basically concerned with measures to increase the incomes of peasants and narrow the rural-urban income gap.

(3) Strive to develop a modern industrial structure. This is basically about industrial upgrading, i.e. policy measures to accelerate the transformation of manufacturing industries from labour-intensive into more technology-intensive or higher productivity activities. The process calls for increasing industrial efficiency and productivity by stepping up innovation and technological transformation as well as increasing the role of the market and encouraging more private enterprise participation. Externally, China's enterprises especially the large SOEs are encouraged to go out and interact more with the global economy. Economic restructuring is also about promoting modern service sector activities, which are essential for a balanced pattern of economic development.

Of greater significance is that the 12th FYP has specifically targeted priority development of seven strategic industries — alternative energy, new information technology, biotechnology, advanced equipment manufacturing, advanced materials, clean-energy vehicles and environment-friendly technologies. To underscore their importance, the government had already committed to spend US$1.5 trillion over the next five years to promote these industries.

(4) Strive to promote well-coordinated regional development. This is basically about more sustainable and more rational spatial transformation involving rural and urban areas, and among different regions such as Eastern China, Central China and Western China. It is also concerned about the challenges of the next-phase development of several well-defined regions such as the Pearl River Delta, the Yangtze River Delta and the Binhai Bay. Within each region, development is centred on the cities, and hence new policy measures are devised to tackle migration, land use and a variety of urban infrastructural development. In terms of the sources of economic growth, successful regional development will contribute to greater domestic consumption.

(5) Strive to promote energy conservation and upgrade environmental quality. The 12th FYP takes environmental goals such as reducing pollution and increasing energy efficiency much more seriously than before. In fact, for the first time, it has set up some "green indicators" such as new carbon emissions target for local governments and relevant agencies to follow, so that China can reduce carbon emissions per unit of GDP by 2020.

## A New Development Departure

The 12th FYP is essentially a road-map for China's economy to move towards three important destinations. The Chinese economy, having chalked up impressive growth for the past three decades, cannot keep growing at such high rates without sooner or later running into various constraints and problems. China's economic growth has to slow down, and it has to adjust its economic and social structures for this eventually.

Many foreign analysts and Chinese intellectuals have recently started to focus on the possibility of the Chinese economy coming to the end of its high growth era.[3] At the international level, the

---

[3] See, for instance, "China's Boom Ends as Investment, Exports and Manufacturing Fall", *Washington Post,* 15 December 2011. Among Chinese economists who see the end of double-digit rate of growth are Yu Bin, director of Macroeconomic Division, Development Research Centre, and Li Yang, vice president of the Chinese Academy of Social Sciences. See also "Days of Double-Digit Growth 'Gone Forever'", *China Daily*, 16 December 2011.

World Bank released a study on 27 February 2012 titled, *China 2030: Building a Modern, Harmonious, and Creative High-Income Society,* which states that China has reached "a turning point in its development path". The report also warns that "China's growth will decline gradually in the years leading to 2030 as China reaches the limits of growth brought about by current technologies and its current economic structure". The World Bank has therefore urged China to step up its unfinished economic and institutional reforms so as to make a successful transition to a high-income economy in 2030.

In actual fact, many of China's growth problems and constraints as well as their related reforms as proposed by the recent World Bank report are not new to the Chinese government since these problems and issues have already been on the agenda of various policy platforms for some time. Specifically, a lot of these policy issues have already been embodied in the 12th FYP. This marks the fundamental significance of this programme.

Suffice it to say that the 12th FYP is well-designed and well-intentioned to shape China's future economic and social development. It is more a turning point than a game changer. To succeed, it will need many more FYPs down the road.

# 17

# Shadow Banking in China

## A Call for Financial Reforms

YAO Jielu and YANG Mu*

*Concerns over China's shadow banking sector have been rising since Beijing started to tighten its monetary policy in 2010. This calls for further reforms in the country's financial sector.*

In March 2012, the Chinese authorities approved a financial reform pilot project in Wenzhou, a city with a reputation for entrepreneurship and informal lending. According to the statement issued by the State Council, this "general financial reform zone" project will legalise the city's underground lending, allowing private lenders to operate as investment companies to augment the credit to small and medium enterprises (SMEs). The move clearly demonstrates Beijing's concerns over not only China's shadow banking sector which may pose systematic risks to financial stability, but also the country's ill-structured formal banking sector which fails to lend to small borrowers.

The problem of shadow banking has been in the spotlight ever since the Chinese government started to tighten its monetary policy in 2010 to rein in credit and cool surging inflation. Limited access to bank lending has driven SMEs to seek alternative methods of financing from larger cash-rich institutions; restrictions on bank loans to the real estate sector have forced many businesses to borrow "underground". Commercial banks, meanwhile, have bypassed loan quotas through off-balance sheet credit. All of these practices have stimulated the development of China's informal financial sector.

China's shadow banking encompasses a wide range of informal financing activities including both underground lending and banks' off-balance sheet credit. While the latter are legal though under-regulated, the former's activities are wholly or partly outside of the law. The People's Bank of China (PBoC), China's central bank, put the size of underground private lending at 3.38 trillion *yuan* as of May 2011, based on a survey it carried out in June 2011. The off-balance sheet loans of

---

*YAO Jielu is Research Assistant at the East Asian Institute, National University of Singapore. YANG Mu is Senior Research Scholar at the same institute.

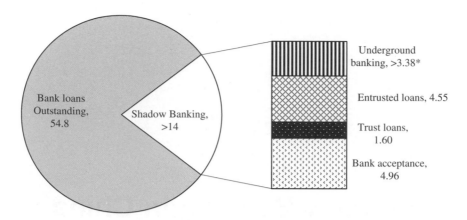

**Figure 1**    Size of China's Shadow Banking Relative to Outstanding Bank Loans (in Trillions *yuan*) by the End of 2011

*Note*: PBoC estimated that the size of underground banking stood at 3.38 trillion *yuan* as of May 2011.

*Source*: People's Bank of China and CEIC.

Chinese banks, on the other hand, stood at 11 trillion *yuan* as of December 2011, according to the breakdown of total social financing (TSF), a new indicator introduced by the central bank in 2011. Thus, the overall size of China's informal lending by the end of 2011 should exceed 14 trillion *yuan*, an amount equivalent to 26% of China's formal bank loans (Figure 1).

## The Surge of Shadow Banking

The lack of access to formal credit prompted the development of China's underground lending. Though China's banking sector served the country well during the global financial turmoil by financing the government's stimulus package, it has a strong traditional bias towards state-owned enterprises and against the private sector. On the contrary, the country's private lenders have served small businesses and rural sector borrowers very well, since their ability to charge interest rates above regulatory ceilings and their knowledge of borrowers allow them to require less collateral and take more risks.

Over the past few years, however, China's private lending has changed in character from financing small and medium businesses in the real sector to funding speculators in the property and financial markets. The shift is largely due to the fact that speculation in markets with borrowed money has proved to be more lucrative than investing in traditional businesses marred by rising costs and weak global demand.

Without regulatory supervision, risks associated with underground financing activities are inherently high. Consider the crisis in Wenzhou, Zhejiang. When China's economic growth began to moderate and housing prices started to decline in 2011, more than 80 local business owners defaulted on loans from private lenders, as disclosed by the official Xinhua News Agency. Many of them fled from their bankrupt businesses and two even committed suicide. The crisis quickly sparked social unrest as the informal financial market in the city involved almost 60% of local businesses and 90% of local households according to the central bank's investigation.

Fearing market and social instability, Beijing has taken measures to lower the risks. Government officials visited the city immediately after the outbreak of the crisis to monitor the situation and to ensure that the distress would remain local. The local and provincial governments carried out a bailout plan amounting to 100 billion *yuan* to help the insolvent entrepreneurs repay high-interest loans taken from underground lenders. Moreover, Chinese authorities are cracking down on underground banking that fuels speculation, while looking for ways to legitimise underground lending that supports the real economy.

The dynamics of Wu Ying's case demonstrate the government's cautious attitude towards private financing. Wu, an entrepreneur from Zhejiang province, was sentenced to death for borrowing as much as 770 million *yuan* from private lenders whom she promised to pay an interest rate of up to 80%. Prosecutors accused her of "squandering" funds and claimed she did not use them for "normal operational activities"; Wu's lawyer however defended that she invested most of the funds in real businesses including trading companies, hotels and property developments. The death penalty meted out for an economic crime provoked a widespread public outcry. At the news conference after the meeting of the National People's Congress, Premier Wen commented on the incident, demonstrating the government's willingness to bring informal capital into the financial arena. In a rare move prior to the final verdict, the highest court also announced that the review of the case would be handled with extreme care.

The surge in banks' off-balance sheet credit, on the other hand, has been largely due to negative real interest rates, the tightening monetary policy and the funding strains faced by the banks. As deposit rates remain clustered at their benchmark and real deposit rates are close to zero or even negative, Chinese savers are not sufficiently compensated and lose money on their deposits. As a result, the demand for credit-related investment products like wealth management products has risen sharply, since they offer higher yields and have an implicit guarantee from banks. These products are generally considered banks' off-balance liabilities. Meanwhile, banks have been motivated to take credit off-balance. This practice actually helps banks to not only satisfy customer demand without being restricted by credit quotas but also meet the regulatory requirements of loan-to-deposit ratios.

Like underground private financing, banks' off-balance sheet credit also poses challenges to Chinese policy makers, as they understate banks' leverage and make the central bank's quantitative monetary tools less effective. To deal with the problems caused by banks' off-balance sheet credit, the government has required commercial banks to bring some products back onto their balance sheets. The central bank also introduced an indicator, TSF, in 2011 to broaden its definition of financing beyond bank loans and to provide systematic data on several activities unavailable previously.

Interest rate liberalisation, however, is the radical solution to the problem of shadow banking because the development of the informal financial market is a direct result of interest rate controls. According to central bank governor Zhou Xiaochuan, conditions are "basically ripe" for liberalising China's interest rate policies. The financial health of the banking sector has improved considerably over the years since the ratio of non-performing loans decreased significantly; high profits have also increased the banking sector's capacity to deal with the financial stress caused by interest rates changes. If Chinese banks are allowed to determine the interest rates by themselves, they will allocate credit more efficiently and the size of the shadow banking sector will shrink correspondingly.

## A Breakdown of China's Shadow Banking Market

Shadow banking encompasses informal financing activities both within and outside the banking sector such as private loans, bank acceptances, entrusted loans, trust loans and credit-related wealth management products. A careful examination of the nature and scale of these activities sheds light on the risks associated with them.

### *Underground Lending*

Underground lending refers to direct, informal and usually short-term financing activities among family, friends, businesses and business associations. Major participants include individuals, credit guarantee companies, financial leasing companies, pawn shops and other new-style financial companies which often exceed their charter by absorbing deposits and making loans.

In China, underground lending is most important for export-oriented SMEs along the coast and rural sector borrowers in the western regions and in north-eastern provinces like Heilongjiang and Liaoning.[1]

In June 2011, the central bank carried out a survey to overhaul China's underground lending market. The results of the survey showed that as of May 2011, the size of underground lending stood at 3.38 trillion *yuan*, accounting for almost 7% of total loans during the period. The survey indicated that the risk of private loans turning sour remained limited, since the average interest rate on private loans was around 16% and only 1% of such loans ended in default. Moreover, most of the funds flowed to the real sector, with about 60% of the loans used as working capital, 12% for market speculation and 12% as bridge loans. Based on a sample of more than 6,000 companies, the central bank's investigation also concluded that around 30% of the private loans were pooled from their related parties and employees, 20% from other companies, and 20% from legal small credit firms or pawn shops.

However, the private financing crisis in the city of Wenzhou offered a different snapshot of China's underground lending market. The city is known for the entrepreneurial flair of its native businessmen and large underground lending market. A survey conducted by the PBoC's Wenzhou branch office showed that by June 2011, the private financing market in the city was worth up to 110 billion *yuan*. But the amount was equivalent to 20% of local bank loans, far higher than the national level of 7%. Besides, only 35% of those loans were used for general business, while 20% were tied up in property and 40% held by the underground lending market (Figure 2). Commercial banks were also exposed to the risks associated with underground financing, as they accounted for about 30% of funding sources by informal lenders (Figure 3).

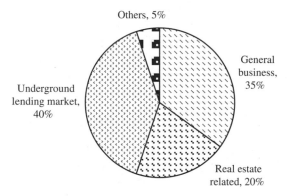

**Figure 2**   Wenzhou Underground Lending Market, by Use of Loan, as of June 2011

*Source*: The Wenzhou Branch Office of the People's Bank of China.

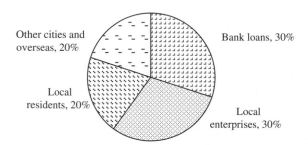

**Figure 3**   Wenzhou Underground Lending Market, by Funding Sources, as of June 2011

*Source*: The Wenzhou Branch Office of the People's Bank of China.

---

[1]OECD, "Economic Survey: China", 2010.

## Banks' Off-Balance Sheet Credit

Banks' off-balance sheet credit, on the other hand, refers to contingent liabilities of commercial banks including bank acceptances, entrusted loans, trust loans and credit-related wealth management products etc. In this context, the PBoC introduced the concept of "social financing" during the central economic working conference in December 2010. The indicator gauges all the funds raised by entities in the real sector during a certain period of time including bank loans in local and foreign currencies, entrusted loans, trust loans, bank acceptance bills, corporate bonds, equity of non-financial enterprises, insurance claims, property investment of insurance companies and others.

## Bank Acceptances

A bank acceptance is a promised future payment accepted and guaranteed by a bank. By pledging 30–50% margin deposits, a non-financial company in China can obtain an acceptance from the bank and then sell or exchange it for cash at a discount to a buyer who is willing to wait until the acceptance matures. Recorded as off-balance sheet items on the date of issue, bank acceptances are not treated as part of total loans until they are discounted and classified under discounted bills on banks' balance sheets.

Since outstanding bank acceptances and discounted bills are closely related, they usually move in line with each other. Prior to 2010, about 60% of bank acceptances were discounted and transferred to the banks' balance sheets. However, the percentage of discounted bank acceptances in total bank acceptances has dropped drastically to 20% since 2010. In other words, the percentage of undiscounted bank acceptances has been rising and they have become an increasingly important channel of off-balance sheet credit. The breakdown of TSF also showed that the outstanding undiscounted bank acceptances reached almost five trillion *yuan* by the end of 2011, equivalent to 9% of total bank loans. The new undiscounted bank acceptances amounted to 14% of new bank loans in 2011, a significant increase from 5% in 2009.

Undiscounted bank acceptances have surged for two reasons. One is that the bank acceptances sold to credit cooperatives and wealth management products remain as off-balance sheet items due to some accounting loophole. The other reason is that commercial banks have manipulated margin deposits of bank acceptances to meet the regulatory loan-to-deposit ratio. In practice, the manipulation requires close collaboration between banks and companies — after a company pays a margin deposit to get a bank acceptance, the bank will purchase (or discount) the acceptance immediately so that the company can use the proceeds as margin deposits to get another bank acceptance. Repeating such transactions lead to an increase in deposits on the bank's balance sheet in spite of a widening gap between on-balance sheet loans and off-balance sheet credit.

## Entrusted Loans

Entrusted loans are inter-company financing in China. Since direct lending and borrowing between different legal entities are prohibited under the country's regulations, banks act as agents of entrusted funds from a depositor (principal) and on-lend the funds provided solely by the depositor to a borrower designated by the principal. The breakdown of TSF showed that outstanding entrusted loans reached 4.6 trillion *yuan* by the end of 2011, equivalent to 8% of total bank loans and new entrusted loans rose from an equivalent of 5% of total bank loans in 2009 to 10% in 2011.

Though banks are not obliged to absorb losses resulting from entrusted loans, they are still exposed to the risks associated with those loans for several reasons. First, banks might be the de facto lenders when they use entrusted loans to bypass the credit limit on a specific company or to make off-balance sheet credit with the funds from wealth management products. Moreover, the overall ratio of banks' non-performing loans will rise if principals' solvency is negatively affected by borrowers' default on entrusted loans. As many of the entrusted loans have been lent to property-related business, the borrowers are likely to default on those entrusted loans if housing prices fall sharply. Given that interest rates of entrusted loans are much higher than benchmark lending rates, the borrowers may also have difficulty paying those loans if the central bank further squeezes credit. Indeed, more than 40% of borrowers in entrusted loan deals announced since January 2010 have been real estate developers facing credit curbs intended to contain inflation, according to the research by Bank of America Merrill Lynch.

### Trust Loans

Trust loans refer to a specific type of trust product created jointly by commercial banks and trust companies whose underlying assets consist solely of loans. In the late 1990s, the trust sector underwent a widespread meltdown amid strict regulation, but it began to revive in 2007 when trust companies start to collaborate with banks to informally securitise loans into investment products like wealth management products. According to the breakdown of TSF, the outstanding trust loans reached 1.6 trillion *yuan* by the end of 2011, equivalent to 3% of total bank loans.

Trust products, wealth management products in particular, are appealing to investors because they can offer a higher return than deposits and have an implicit guarantee from banks. Li Daokui, a former adviser to the central bank, even argued that a form of de facto interest rate liberalisation has already been underway through the increasing popularity of wealth management products. On the other hand, commercial banks have competed fiercely in this market to not only absorb deposits and earn fee income, but also use the proceeds from these products to purchase banks' credit assets and take them off banks' balance sheets. Some banks were also reported to use wealth management products to invest in the bonds issued by local government financing vehicles or the bonds issued by the banks themselves.[2] Though investors, rather than banks, are supposed to bear losses when the underlying investment of the products fails to perform, such losses could cause significant social and political tensions, eventually requiring intervention by the regulators or even the government. Hence, it is reasonable to consider these products as banks' off-balance sheet liabilities.

### Policies for Mitigating the Risks

Underground financing activities usually have a long debt chain. If one link is broken, the entire debt chain might collapse. Isolated cases of default could also lead to massive redemption, since individual investors have little information about the financial positions of the projects in which underground lenders invested. Chinese authorities are well aware of the contagion of a private financing crisis. After the outbreak of the Wenzhou crisis, Premier Wen Jiabao, together with PBoC Governor Zhou Xiaochuan and Finance Minister Xie Xuren, visited the city immediately to restore public confidence and to ensure that the distress would remain local. The local and provincial governments also introduced a raft of measures to contain the crisis, including the establishment of a bailout plan that amounted to about 100 billion *yuan* to help insolvent entrepreneurs repay high-interest loans taken from underground lenders.

The government is also considering legitimising underground lending that supports the real economy.[3] At the news conference marking the conclusion of the 2012 meeting of the National People's Congress, Premier Wen clearly stated that the government "should guide and permit informal capital in the financial arena, standardising it and bringing it into the open, encouraging its development and strengthening its supervision". It has also been reported that the central bank and the banking regulator will introduce trial reforms for informal lending in the city of Wenzhou. The reforms could involve giving existing underground lenders a licence to operate as small-loan companies while imposing deposit collection and capital requirements.

[2] "China Banks: Shadow Banking Conundrum", HSBC Global Research, 19 October 2011.
[3] "Beijing Looks at Legalizing Underground Lending", *The Wall Street Journal*, 15 March 2012.

Moreover, the central government has been determined to crack down on underground lending that fuels asset bubbles, given that much of underground lending has been channelled into the property market. In fact, many developers in China are unfamiliar with business cycles and reluctant to cut prices when transaction volumes fall sharply. They pay high interest rates and borrow constantly to stay afloat in the hope that Beijing will ease its tightening policy soon. If the government does not reverse its housing policy in the near future, substantial numbers of small and medium developers are expected to default. To reduce the risk, the central government has underscored the legal threshold for interest rates on private loans, making it clear that rates exceeding China's benchmark interest rate by four times are not entitled to legal protection and the borrower may decline to pay the excess interest owed as there is no default penalty. Besides, the government has insisted that property tightening policies will be followed unswervingly to bring down housing costs as well as discourage credit flows to poorly managed developers.

Like underground private financing, banks' off-balance sheet credit also poses challenges to Chinese officials. It not only leads to the understating of banks' leverage but also makes the central bank's quantitative monetary tools less effective. Some measures have been taken to mitigate the risks associated with banks' off-balance sheet credit. On one hand, the government has required banks to bring some products back onto their balance sheets. For example, the banking regulator told banks in January 2011 that they would have to re-incorporate trust and wealth management products back onto their balance sheets by the end of the year. On the other hand, the central bank introduced an indicator, TSF, in 2011to broaden its definition of financing beyond bank loans and to provide systematic data on several activities unavailable previously. This indicator takes into account key components of China's shadow banking such as entrusted loans, trust loans and bank acceptance bills.

## A Radical Solution: Interest Rate Liberalisation

Compared with interest rate liberalisation, the aforementioned policies are just short-term remedies as the informal financial market can always find a way to circumvent the government's regulations. Interest rate liberalisation, however, is the radical solution because the development of shadow banking is a direct result of interest rate controls. Though China has made substantial progress in interest rate reform since 1996 (Table 1), the problems caused by the shadow banking sector indicate that this reform needs to proceed to keep pace with the rapidly changing economy.

The central bank currently sets a ceiling for bank deposit rates and a floor for lending rates, leading to an artificially high spread between the two to safeguard the profitability of the predominantly state-owned banking sector. However, the intervention undermines the incentive for Chinese banks to price risk appropriately and stymies competition in the banking sector. It also weakens the pass-through of changes in monetary policy instruments on effective bank interest rates.[4]

On the other hand, Chinese savers are not sufficiently compensated or even lose money on their deposits, as the deposit rates have remained clustered at their benchmark and real deposit rates have been always negative (Figure 4). Research also showed that Chinese households' financial income as a total share of total income remains one of the lowest in the world.[5] In the short run, the cap on deposit rates has led to a surge in banks' off-balance sheet credit as investors have turned to wealth management products for higher returns. In the long run, it is likely to stifle government's efforts to foster domestic consumption as a driver of growth.

Moreover, the lack of market-determined interest rates creates an environment where banks tend to channel funds to large and well-connected state enterprises, away from small and medium enterprises, rural borrowers and households. Recent credit constraints imposed on banks to limit credit growth have deteriorated the situation, leading to the development of a large informal

---

[4]OECD, "Economic Survey: China", 2010.
[5]Feyziouglu, T, N Porter and E Takats (2009), "Interest Rate Liberalisation in China", *IMF Working Paper* WP/09/171.

**Table 1**   Progress on China's Interest Rate Liberalisation

| | |
|---|---|
| 1996 | Abolished the upper limit on interbank lending rates |
| 1997 | Liberalised repo rates |
| 1998–2004 | Gradually increased the upper limit on lending rates |
| 1999 | Began to gradually allow different institutions to negotiate rates on over 30 million *yuan* deposits with above five-year maturity<br>Liberalised foreign currency lending rates |
| 2000 | Liberalised foreign currency deposit rates for deposits over $3 million<br>Removed floor on foreign currency deposit rates |
| 2003 | Liberalised deposit rates in pound, franc, Swiss Franc and Canadian Dollar<br>Liberalised all foreign currency deposit rates with maturity above one year |
| 2004 | Removed ceiling on all lending rates (except for urban and rural credit cooperatives, which have a cap of 130% over reference rates)<br>Removed floor on all deposit rates |
| 2007 | Launched the Shanghai Interbank Offer Rate (SHIBOR) |

*Source*: The People's Bank of China.

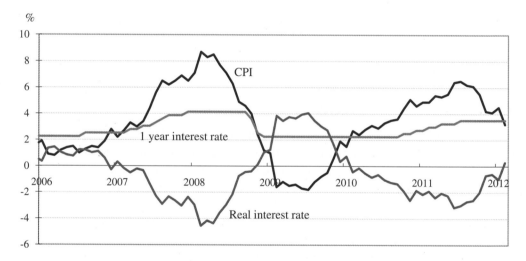

**Figure 4**   Real Interest Rate in China

*Source*: CEIC.

financial sector. Since much of the sector operates outside of the law and regulations, it is likely to threaten China's financial stability. Indeed, the latest private financing crisis in the city of Wenzhou has already sounded an alarm about the risks associated with shadow banking.

Beijing used to be hesitant to free up interest rates out of concern that the move would hurt the profitability of Chinese banks by forcing them to compete for deposits. However, the financial health of the banking sector has improved considerably over the years, with the ratio of non-performing loans significantly reduced from 17.4% at the end of 2003 to 1% at the end of 2011. High profits have also increased the banking sector's capacity to deal with the financial stress caused by interest rates changes. The official data showed that Chinese banks' profits reached a record high of 1.04 trillion *yuan* ($165 billion) in 2011, marking an increase of 16% from 2010. In short, the timing is great for China to introduce more competition into the banking sector so that credit can be allocated to its most efficient use given prevailing market interest rates.

The Chinese authorities are mulling over the plan of interest rate liberalisation as they strive to encourage a consumption-based economy and to internationalise the country's currency. In March

2012, central bank governor Zhou Xiaochuan wrote in *China Finance* magazine that conditions are "basically ripe" for liberalising China's interest rate policies.[6] He also pointed out that the concerns that have held back interest rate liberalisation are dated, with the banks now in a strong financial position. Other policy makers are also stepping up calls for the creation of a government deposit insurance scheme which protects depositors against bank insolvency. The scheme is widely perceived as a precondition for interest rate liberalisation. But it remains to be seen whether they are political rhetoric or the real reform in progress.

---

[6]"China Hints at Interest Rate Liberalisation", *The Wall Street Journal*, 20 March 2012.

# 18

# The Rise of the *Renminbi* as International Currency

YANG Mu and YAO Jielu*

*Beijing aims to develop the renminbi regionally first before going international by promoting its use in cross-border trade settlements and growing the offshore renminbi financial business gradually.*

The US dollar has been the leading international currency for more than 60 years. However, many are questioning the dollar's hegemony as the United States' economic power has been waning after two costly wars and one devastating financial crisis. Between March 2009 and July 2011, the dollar's value had fallen by 17% on a real trade-weighted basis. The US Federal Reserve's "Quantitative Easing 2" (QE2) measures in November 2010 and America's recent debt crisis have further accelerated the slide.

With the devaluation of the US dollar, the Chinese currency, the *renminbi* (RMB), is believed to be a new global currency in the making. Macroeconomic conditions favour the internationalisation of the *renminbi*. In terms of economic size, China has overtaken Japan as the world's second largest economy and surpassed Germany as the world's largest exporter. It held the world's largest foreign exchange reserves of US$3.2 trillion at the end of June 2011. Compared with the United States and the European Union, the country also achieved a relatively low inflation rate of 1.7% over the 1999–2010 period, further strengthening public confidence in the value of the *renminbi*.

More importantly, Beijing has taken steady steps to promote the international use of the *renminbi*. Since December 2008, the People's Bank of China has signed bilateral currency swap agreements (BSAs) worth RMB841 billion with 12 monetary authorities. A pilot scheme for *renminbi* cross-border trade settlement was launched in July 2009. The country is also backing Hong Kong' efforts to become an offshore *renminbi* centre.

However, Beijing has not set any goal for converting the *renminbi* into an international currency. The sheer inertia and incumbency advantage enjoyed by the US dollar suggest that any change in

---

*YANG Mu is Senior Research Scholar at the East Asian Institute, National University of Singapore. YAO Jielu is Research Assistant at the same institute.

the relative status of the currencies would take place slowly. Given the international role of the *euro* and the *yen*, the *renminbi* is in no position to eclipse the US dollar in the foreseeable future. Zhou Xiaochuan, governor of China's central bank, made this clear during an interview and said that the government could only remove domestic policy barriers to promote the *renminbi*'s international use, but the pace of its internationalisation still depends on market selection.

To date, the *renminbi* is still far from being a global currency. It lacks the essential prerequisite to become a global currency — full convertibility of capital account. Its share in international foreign exchange reserves and its role in international financial transactions remain negligible. Trade settlement in *renminbi* occurs mainly at the borders of China. By and large, if the *renminbi*'s internationalisation is considered as a process of territorial expansion, it is still at the stage of regionalisation.

## America's "Triffin Dilemma" and China's "Dollar Trap"

In theory, to achieve international stature, a currency must be in strong demand as a store of value for official foreign exchange reserves, as a medium of exchange for invoicing international trade and financial transactions, and as a unit of account for denominating international trade and financial transactions.[1] Figure 1 shows the International Monetary Fund's (IMF) Currency Composition of Official Foreign Exchange Reserves (COFER). The US dollar's share has fallen from 70% in 1999 to around 60% in 2012 In fact, the current speculation about the demise of the US dollar focusses mainly on the dollar's weakening role as a reserve currency.[2]

The problem faced by the US dollar can be characterised by the "Triffin dilemma". As the issuer of the world's predominant reserve currency, the United States has no choice but to satisfy the offshore demand for the US dollar by running a current account deficit and issuing dollar-denominated obligations to fund it. Otherwise, the shortage of liquidity would pull the world economy into a contractionary spiral. However, persistent current account deficits and accumulation of debts have also eroded public confidence in the US dollar, and there were growing concerns about the value of the dollar, the potential default of its Treasury bonds and capital losses on securitised products linked to insolvencies.[3]

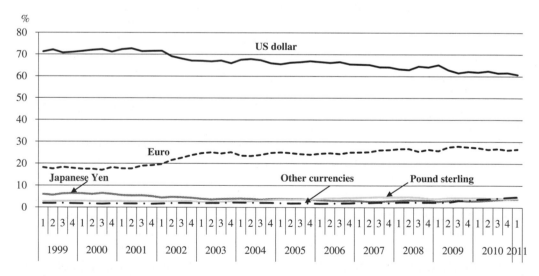

**Figure 1**   Currency Composition of Official Foreign Exchange Reserves, Q1 1999–Q1 2011

*Source*: IMF, Currency Composition of Official Foreign Exchange Reserves (COFER).

[1] Chinn, M and J Frankel (2005), "Will the Euro Eventually Surpass the Dollar as Leading International Reserve Currency?", *NBER Working Paper*, no. 11510.

[2] Huang Y (2010), "Renminbi Policy and the Global Currency System", *CCER Working Paper*, no. E2010004.

[3] Kemp, J "Global Imbalances and the Triffin Dilemma", Analysis and Opinion, *Reuters*, 13 January 2009.

While the United States has encountered the "Triffin dilemma", China has fallen into the so-called "dollar trap".[4] The country opted to peg its currency to the dollar in order to sustain export-oriented growth. However, since 2001, China has been running substantial surpluses on both the current and capital accounts. Thus, it has to purchase massive amounts of US dollars to cope with its rapid inflow, leading to a surge in the country's foreign exchange reserves.

Given that 70% of these reserves are dollar-denominated, any future fall in the dollar would mean a huge capital loss for China. China cannot sell off the large amounts of US dollars it possesses to diversify the reserves without driving the dollar down. Moreover, China's exchange rate policy partially contributes to its rising domestic prices, which leaves Beijing with few choices but to adopt a de facto quantitative squeezing policy by raising interest rates and the reserve requirement ratio.

Zhou Xiaochuan, governor of China's central bank, thus called for the establishment of a super-sovereign reserve currency based on the Special Drawing Rights (SDR) of IMF in April 2010. Since the value of the current SDR is derived from a basket of currencies including the dollar (44%), the *euro* (34%), the Japanese *yen* (11%), and the pound sterling (11%), he also proposed that the basket comprise currencies of all major economies and that GDP should be a determinant of the weights assigned to the currencies in the SDR basket. This clearly indicates China's interests in the global currency regime.

## At the Arena of International Trade

Apart from serving as a store of value, an international currency should also perform the function of a medium of exchange by invoicing and settling international trade. The US dollar is currently the primary invoice currency not only in transactions to and from the United States, but also in exports and imports by countries other than the United States, particularly emerging economies.[5] Key commodities such as oil and metals are still priced and invoiced in dollars.

However, there were concerns about the future of the US dollar as the invoicing currency for homogeneous commodities traded in organised exchanges. The economic literature also suggested that it was possible to introduce a new currency in the crude oil market, since it might be more efficient for oil producers to settle their exports in the currency they use to pay for their imports.[6]

Meanwhile, there is a mismatch between China's trade prowess and the limited role its currency is playing in international trade. As the world's largest exporter, China is now a global trading power, accounting for 10% of the world's merchandise trade in 2010. But most of its trade has been settled in US dollars. The country thus has great potential to promote its currency. China also has a strong motivation to settle international trade in the *renminbi* since invoicing in domestic currency could reduce its exposure to exchange rate volatility.

As cross-border transactions using *renminbi* settlement take off, a wind of change is blowing through foreign exchange markets. Table 1 shows that the *renminbi*'s share in the global foreign exchange market turnover had risen from 0.1% in 2004 to 0.3% in 2010. Average daily trading in the *renminbi* has also increased from almost nothing to US$1 billion in late 2011. There is no doubt that the *renminbi* makes up a sliver of the trading volumes in currency markets, dwarfed by 85% of the dollar and 39% of the *euro*. Nonetheless, it is gathering momentum each day as the markets have stepped up their demands for the *renminbi* to finance trade, investment and borrowing.

---

[4] The term was first used by Paul Krugman to describe the dilemma China faces. See Krugman, P, "China's Dollar Trap", *The New York Times*, 3 April 2009.

[5] Goldberg, LS and C Tille (2008), "Vehicle Currency Use in International Trade", *Journal of International Economics*, Vol. 76, no. 2, pp. 177–92.

[6] Mileva, E and N Siegfried (2007), "Oil Market Structure, Network Effects and the Choice of Currency for Oil invoicing", Occasional Paper Series no. 77, European Central Bank.

**Table 1**   Global Foreign Exchange Market Turnover by Currency (Percentage Shares of Average Daily Turnover in April)

| Currency | 1998 | 2001 | 2004 | 2007 | 2010 |
|---|---|---|---|---|---|
| US dollar | 86.8 | 89.9 | 88.0 | 85.6 | 84.9 |
| Euro | — | 37.9 | 37.4 | 37.0 | 39.1 |
| Japanese yen | 21.7 | 23.5 | 20.8 | 17.2 | 19.0 |
| Pound sterling | 11.0 | 13.0 | 16.5 | 14.9 | 12.9 |
| Chinese *renminbi* | 0.0 | 0.0 | 0.1 | 0.5 | 0.3 |
| Other currencies | 80.4 | 35.6 | 37.2 | 44.8 | 43.9 |
| All currencies | 200.0 | 200.0 | 200.0 | 200.0 | 200.0 |

*Notes*: As two currencies are involved in each transaction, the sum of the percentage shares of individual currencies totals 200% instead of 100%. Adjusted for local and cross-border inter-dealer double-counting (ie "net-net" basis).
*Source*: BIS Triennial Central Bank Survey of Foreign Exchange Market Activity.

## Convertibility as the Main Barrier for *Renminbi's* Internationalisation

As a unit of account, the US dollar still reigns supreme in international financial markets. The share of all outstanding debt securities denominated in the US dollar stands at approximately 46%. Despite a slight decline from 49% in 1999, its status as the prominent currency in global debt markets remains firm and deep. The dollar also plays a critical role in the foreign currency assets and liabilities of banks. Over the past decades, the dominant share of outstanding international loans and outstanding international deposits in the US dollar has maintained at more than 50% (Figures 2 to 4).

The lack of convertibility apparently precludes the *renminbi* from functioning as an international currency in financial markets. Since there are few *renminbi*-denominated investment products, suppliers to China can do little with the *renminbi* they receive other than put the currency in bank deposits. Without *renminbi* hedging tools, overseas customers are reluctant to commit to a long-term *renminbi*-denominated purchase agreement with suppliers in China, considering the probable increase in future payment obligations due to *renminbi* appreciation.

Nevertheless, removing capital controls could lead to a substantial move into foreign currency-denominated financial assets. Such a move could precipitate a domestic banking crisis, given the well-known vulnerability of China's banks. To internationalise its currency without fully opening its capital account, China decided to develop the *renminbi's* offshore markets, particularly in Hong Kong. The strategy provides not only an offshore market for *renminbi*-denominated assets but also practical experience for the gradual liberalisation of China's onshore market in terms of building market infrastructure, pricing financial assets and assessing market risks.

In short, the evolving international monetary system has provided many golden opportunities for China to internationalise its currency, and to some extent, has even forced China to pursue a larger role in the world economy with its currency. It is against this backdrop that Beijing has been taking progressive steps to develop the *renminbi* into an international currency. But policies can only lay the groundwork for the internationalisation of a currency and cannot force markets to switch to it unless there are incentives to do so. Hence, the most serious challenge facing Beijing is how to create incentives to encourage the international use of the *renminbi*.

## Promoting Trade Settlement in Renminbi

Beijing has embarked on a learning-by-doing process to develop the *renminbi* into an international currency. In the 2010 government work report, Premier Wen Jiabao made it clear that the central government would "promote pilot projects for the use of the *renminbi* in cross-border trade settlement and gradually develop offshore *renminbi* financial business". The research by Chatham

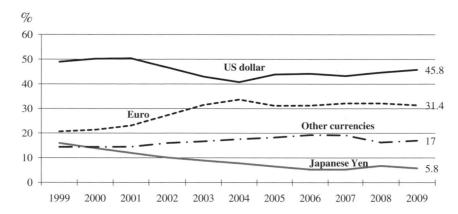

**Figure 2**   Outstanding International Debt Securities, by Currency (% of Outstanding Amounts, at Current Exchange Rates, End of Period)

*Sources*: Bank for International Settlements; European Central Bank Calculation.

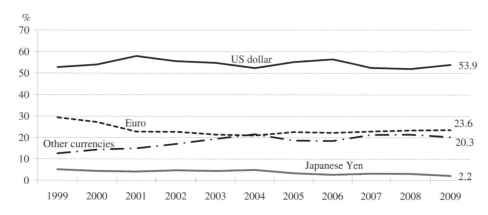

**Figure 3**   Outstanding International Loans, by Currency (% of Outstanding Amounts, at Current Exchange Rates, End of Period)

*Sources*: Bank for International Settlements; European Central Bank Calculation.

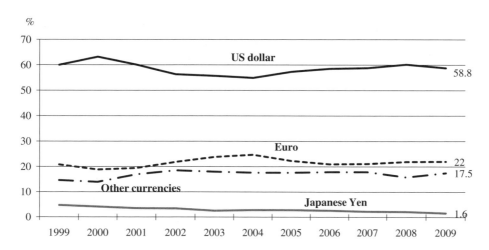

**Figure 4**   Outstanding International Deposits, by Currency (% of Outstanding Amounts, at Current Exchange Rates, End of Period)

*Sources*: Bank for International Settlements; European Central Bank Calculation.

House interprets the government's focus on these two areas as a dual-track strategy which aims to increase the regional use of the *renminbi* by taking advantage of China's trade power on the one hand and by developing the *renminbi* offshore market in Hong Kong to overcome restricted convertibility on the other.[7]

### Bilateral Currency Swaps

In the wake of the 1997–1998 Asian financial crisis, China signed a set of currency swap agreements with East Asian countries under the Chiang Mai Initiative (CMI) (Table 2). Though the main objective of the CMI was to address short-term liquidity difficulties in the region in times of financial turmoil, the network of bilateral swap arrangements encouraged financial integration in the region and thus formed a springboard for the regionalisation of the *renminbi*.

China has introduced a slew of new swap agreements outside the ambit of the CMI (Table 3) since December 2008. Like those arrangements under the CMI, the new initiatives are the

**Table 2**    Bilateral Swap Arrangements under the Chiang Mai Initiative

| BSA | One/Two Way | Currency | Size (USD Billion) | Date |
|---|---|---|---|---|
| China-Thailand | One | USD/THB | 2 | Dec-01 |
| China-Japan | Two | CNY/JPY | 3 (eq.) | Mar-02 |
|  |  | JPY/CNY | 3 (eq.) |  |
| China-Republic of Korea | Two | CNY/KRW | 4 (eq.) | Jun-02 |
|  |  | KRW/CNY | 4 (eq.) |  |
| China-Malaysia | One | USD/MYR | 1.5 | Oct-02 |
| China-Philippines | One | CNY/ARP | 2 (eq.) | Aug-03 |
| China-Indonesia | One | USD/IDR | 4 | Dec-03 |

*Note*: The sizes of the swaps have been converted to US$ (eq. stands for equivalent).

*Sources*: Bank of Japan; Gao H and Yu Y, "Internationalization of the *Renminbi*", BoK-BIS Seminar Presentation Paper.

**Table 3**    Bilateral Currency Swap Arrangements

| BSA | One/Two Way | Size | Date |
|---|---|---|---|
| China-Republic of Korea | two | RMB 180 bn | Dec-08 |
| China-Hong Kong | two | RMB 200 bn | Jan-09 |
| China-Malaysia | two | RMB 80 bn | Feb-09 |
| China-Indonesia | two | RMB 100 bn | Mar-09 |
| China-Belarus | two | RMB 20 bn | Mar-09 |
| China-Argentina | two | RMB 70 bn | Mar-09 |
| China-Iceland | two | RMB 3.5 bn | Jun-10 |
| China-Singapore | two | RMB 150 bn | Jul-10 |
| China-New Zealand | two | RMB 25 bn | Apr-11 |
| China-Uzbekistan | two | RMB 0.7 bn | Apr-11 |
| China-Mongolia | two | RMB 5 bn | May-11 |
| China-Kazakhstan | two | RMB 7 bn | Jun-11 |

*Source*: People's Bank of China.

---

[7] Subacchi, P, "One Currency, Two Systems: China's *Renminbi* Strategy", Brief Paper of Chatham House, October 2010.

government's responses to the current financial crisis. Unlike the previous ones however, the new swaps were extended to countries outside East Asia such as Argentina and Iceland, and all the deals were conducted in two-way local-currency swap arrangements. By pumping a grand total of RMB841 billion into international markets, the arrangements provided seed money for future cross-border trade transactions settled in *renminbi*. It clearly reveals China's ambition to strengthen the *renminbi*'s role in global trade settlement.

### Pilot Scheme for Settlement of Cross-Border Trade

In July 2009, Beijing launched a pilot scheme for settlement of cross-border trade in *renminbi*. Eligible companies, known as mainland designated enterprises (MDEs), in five pilot cities were allowed to invoice and settle trade (both exports and imports) in *renminbi* with selected areas outside the mainland. To qualify as MDEs, companies in the five pilot cities had to get the approval of the central authorities upon the recommendation of their respective local governments.

The *renminbi* cross-border trade settlement grew slowly in the first six months after the introduction of the pilot scheme (Figure 5). According to Li Jing from the China Academy of

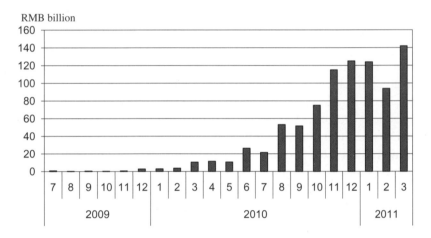

**Figure 5**   Cross-Border Trade Settlement in *Renminbi*, July 2009–March 2011

*Source*: The People's Bank of China.

Social Science, this was largely due to the difficulties Chinese companies encountered when they claimed tax rebates for exports invoiced in *renminbi*.[8] For these companies, the benefit of a switch to *renminbi* as trade settlement currency was overshadowed by the loss of tax rebates. But the volume of *renminbi* trade settlement began to pick up in the beginning of 2010 after the Chinese authorities streamlined tax rebate procedures for *renminbi* settlement and as Chinese companies gradually grew familiar with the scheme.

In July 2010, the pilot areas were broadened to include a total of 20 provinces and provincial-level municipalities in mainland China, and external trade partners were extended to all countries and regions. The scheme, originally limited to trade of goods, was also expanded to trade of services. The liberalisation of the scheme greatly boosted trade settlement in *renminbi*. According to the People's Bank of China, the number of MDEs expanded dramatically to 67,724 exporters by the end of 2010 from the original 365 firms. In 2010, the cumulative total trade transactions settled in *renminbi* amounted to RMB506 billion, constituting nearly 3% of China's total trade.

---

[8]Li J (2010), "China's Renminbi International Strategy: From Perspective of the Renminbi Cross-border Trade Settlement", Working Paper no. 2010W19, Research Center for International Finance of CASS.

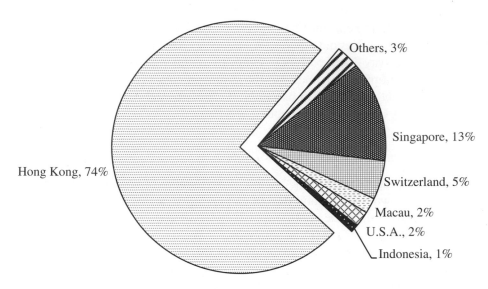

**Figure 6**    Share of the *Renminbi* Cross-Border Trade Settlement by Region, by the End of June 2010

*Source*: Li J, "China's *Renminbi* Internationalization Strategy: From Perspective of the *Renminbi* Cross-border Trade Settlement", 2010.

Two distinctive characteristics have marked the cross-border trade transactions settled in *renminbi*. First, the geographical distribution of transactions is uneven. In the mainland, Guangdong province, China's largest trade base, has taken the lion's share. By the end of June 2010, it had settled trade transactions worth RMB51 billion, accounting for 72% of the total volume conducted by all pilot areas. Outside the mainland, Hong Kong, with a well-developed financial infrastructure, has played a leading role in settling trade transactions in *renminbi*, accounting for 74% of the total volume by the end of June 2010 (Figure 6).

Second, goods imports constitute a predominant proportion of the transactions. By the end of September 2010, goods imports accounted for almost 80% of the cumulative trade transactions settled in *renminbi*; exports in goods and trade in services, by contrast, accounted for merely 9% and 11% respectively. They reflect the *renminbi's* popularity outside of the country's borders: China's trading partners are willing to receive and hold *renminbi* in the hope that the currency will appreciate and more *renminbi*-denominated investment products will appear. This also demonstrates the scarcity of the currency in international markets — since China is running substantial trade surpluses with its major trade partners such as the United States, trade settlement for imports using *renminbi* seems impossible for China.

At the microeconomic level, Chinese exporters lack the capability or incentive to change the invoicing currency from the US dollar to the *renminbi*. Positioned at the low end of the global value chain, Chinese exporters generally do not have much pricing power in international trade. Since processing exports that involve low value-added manufacturing account for more than 40% of China's trade, transactions between China and the foreign investors are more likely to be conducted in the US dollar to avoid foreign exchange risks and to facilitate cost accounting. With the lack of related *renminbi* services by commercial banks and adequate *renminbi* liquidity in international markets, Chinese companies are reluctant to use the *renminbi* as the invoicing currency.

### Developing the Renminbi's First Offshore Market in Hong Kong

The dilemma arises as China decides to promote its currency in international financial markets. On the one hand, the lack of convertibility apparently precludes the *renminbi* from becoming an attractive asset in wealth enhancement and investment portfolios of non-resident companies and individuals. On the other, given China's fledgling capital market and vulnerable banking sector, there would be embedded risks should China open its capital account prematurely. To solve the dilemma, China has been building the first *renminbi* offshore market in Hong Kong which has a well-developed financial system open to international investors, while still under Beijing's influence.

### *Renminbi Deposits*

Sanctioned by the State Council of China, designated banks in Hong Kong started to offer a range of retail banking services such as deposit-taking, currency exchange, remittance and, debit and credit cards issuance in February 2004. The *renminbi* deposits in Hong Kong leaped dramatically from RMB895 million in February 2004 to RMB549 billion in May 2011 (Figure 7) as a result of the widened scope of *renminbi* banking business in Hong Kong and expectations of the ongoing *renminbi* appreciation. In May 2011, the number of *renminbi* saving accounts and *renminbi* time deposit accounts reached 2.2 million and 465,429 respectively. The sharp rise in *renminbi* deposits has also sparked the demand for *renminbi* investment products in Hong Kong.

### *"Dim Sum" Bonds*

*Renminbi*-denominated bonds issued in Hong Kong, the so called "dim sum" bonds, have been around since 2007. The issuance of such bonds was originally restricted to mainland financial institutions which obtained relevant approval from mainland authorities. In 2009, the range of issuers was extended to mainland subsidiaries of Hong Kong banks and China's Ministry of Finance began to issue *renminbi* sovereign bonds in Hong Kong. In July 2010, Hopewell Highway Infrastructure Limited became the first foreign non-financial company to sell "*dim sum*" bonds. In August, McDonald's became the first multinational company to launch such bonds. In October, the Asian Development Bank (ADB) raised RMB1.2 billion in the "*dim sum*" bond market, the first deal of its kind by a supranational agency. Russia's VTB bank became the first emerging market issuer of "*dim sum*" bonds outside China in March 2011.

The market has seen a strong demand for *renminbi* bonds as the range of issuers has widened. The growth of the "*dim sum*" market has accelerated, totalling RMB40.7 billion in 2010 and

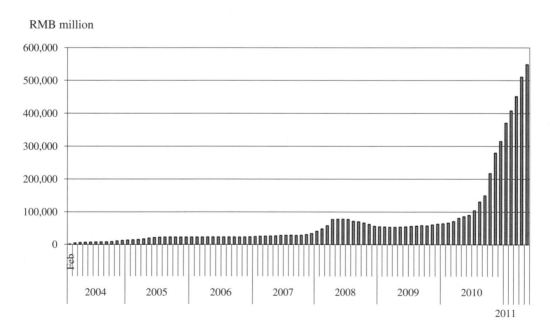

**Figure 7**   *Renminbi* Deposits, February 2004 – May 2011

*Source*: Hong Kong Monetary Authority.

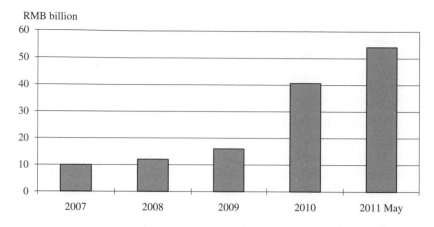

**Figure 8**   *Renminbi*-Denominated Bonds Issued In Hong Kong

*Source*: Bloomberg.

RMB54.2 billion in 2011 (Figure 8). In November 2010, the 10-year three billion *renminbi* bond offering of China Development Bank was almost 16 times oversubscribed, and the bond issuance of Caterpillar, the US-based manufacturer of earthmoving equipment, was seven times oversubscribed. Meanwhile, low yields are driving down financing cost for issuers in the "*dim sum*" market. According to Bloomberg, the market was so hot in November 2011 that the average yield investors requested to hold *renminbi*-denominated bonds in Hong Kong fell 12 basis points to 2.1%, less than half of Chinese companies' dollar-dominated bonds.

"*Dim sum*" bonds are particularly attractive to investors for three reasons. First, these bonds provide a low-risk means of gaining foreign exchange exposure to *renminbi*. Since the currency has appreciated approximately 5% during the last 12 months, the bonds are appealing to investors even though their coupon rates are relatively low. Second, "*dim sum*" bonds offer alternative investment opportunities for *renminbi* deposit holders in Hong Kong. Also, issuance of different tenors helps develop a more complete yield curve, giving investors a choice of trading strategies. Third, it has been easier and faster for non-Chinese companies to issue *renminbi* bonds in Hong Kong. An experienced issuer can expect to issue "*dim sum*" bonds in two to four weeks, while it might take several years to complete initial offerings of "panda" bonds in mainland China.

### Trade Settlement in Renminbi

The *renminbi* trade settlement experiment conducted in Hong Kong has so far been very successful. As mentioned earlier, Hong Kong was involved in 74% of the trade transactions settled in *renminbi* by the end of June 2010. Three factors had contributed to the success, and will continue to affect the development of *renminbi* trade settlement in Hong Kong.

First, *renminbi* liquidity. The bilateral currency swap agreement signed between mainland China and Hong Kong in January 2009 provided substantial liquidity for importers of Chinese goods in Hong Kong to settle trade transactions. Besides, a turning point occurred in 2009 as Hong Kong, for the first time in decades, ran a trade surplus (HK$14 billion) with mainland China; this trend continued in 2010. In the future, a self-sustaining *renminbi* liquidity environment might therefore be expected.

Second, exit routes for *renminbi*. Trade enterprises have been allowed to open *renminbi* deposit accounts with designated Hong Kong banks since July 2009. The growing "*dim sum*" bond market provided an exit for *renminbi* received by Hong Kong exporters. Given its sophisticated financial infrastructure, Hong Kong has the potential of introducing more investible *renminbi* assets in the future.

Third, other related banking services. The operation of the pilot scheme of trade settlement in *renminbi* necessitates the provision of related banking services. In addition to deposits taking, the *renminbi* services that Hong Kong banks provide include currency exchange, remittance, trade finance and cheques.[9] For example, based on actual trade transactions, trade enterprises can exchange Hong Kong dollars for *renminbi* or vice versa, conduct two-way *renminbi* remittance and utilise *renminbi* trade finance. The services are also accessible to individuals but with more restrictions.[10] If these restrictions are relaxed in the future, say by increasing the daily limit of currency exchange, there will be more *renminbi* liquidity to facilitate trade settlement and to bolster the *renminbi* clearing platform in Hong Kong.

---

[9] "Renminbi Trade Settlement Pilot Scheme", Hong Kong Monetary Authority (HKMA) Quarterly Bulletin, December 2009.
[10] For more information on the official instruction about renminbi business in Hong Kong, please refer to the website of HKMA: <http://www.info.gov.hk/hkma/eng/renminbi/index.htm> (accessed December 2011).

# 19

# China's Local Government Debts

## Thorny but Manageable

YAO Jielu*

*China's local government borrowing via Local Government Financial Vehicles has soared since late 2008. Systemic risks in the near term are limited however, given Beijing's tightening measures and strong fiscal position, among other factors.*

China sowed the seeds of a local government debt crisis in late 2008 when Beijing responded to the global financial turmoil with a stimulus package of four trillion *yuan*. Unlike the rescue programme for the Asian financial crisis in 1997, which was under the strict control of the central government, this package has been accompanied by massive local investment projects. To finance these projects, local authorities have set up thousands of Local Government Financial Vehicles (LGFVs) to borrow from state banks and bond investors.

The result was an orgy of local governments' off-balance-sheet liabilities. In June 2011, China's state audit office, the National Audit Office (NAO), delivered the first-ever official report on local government debt, estimating that local government debt had reached 10.7 trillion *yuan* (or US$1.6 trillion) by the end of 2010, half of which had been borrowed via LGFVs.[1] The market, however, saw much bigger local debt in China than what the office chalked up. It actually reached a consensus that the real size of local government debt could be around 15–20 trillion *yuan*, the equivalent of 40–50% of the country's GDP.

Local government debt, particularly borrowing via LGFVs, had been growing quickly for three reasons. First, local governments have few sources of funding for their infrastructure projects. In fact, they were prohibited from borrowing directly or issuing bonds by law until 2011 when Beijing gave permission to four local authorities to sell bonds on a trial basis. Meanwhile, infrastructure development is one of the most conspicuous indicators of the success of local leadership as it not only promotes growth but also creates jobs. While local governments are keen in pursuing rapid

---

*YAO Jielu is Research Assistant at the East Asian Institute, National University of Singapore.
[1]The National Audit Office, "The Audit Result of Local Government Debt", no. 35, 2011.

economic growth in their localities, they need not worry about economic overheating or inflation at the national level. Most importantly, the central government has been stuck in a predicament: it can neither credibly commit to ignoring the fiscal woes of troubled local governments nor cut off their access to borrow via LGFVs.

Indeed, the practice of borrowing through LGFVs is not new. According to the World Bank, its creation can be traced back to the early 1990s when the central government adopted a national strategy to marketise the infrastructure development function of local governments.[2] Since then, LGFVs have been treated as municipal corporations under the Company Law of the People's Republic of China and function as municipal-level state-owned enterprises (SOEs). Within two decades, the LGFV model has gained widespread popularity and become a major force in China's urban development. Often, the vehicles at various government levels were established to provide an essential channel to raise capital for local infrastructure projects. The China Banking Regulatory Commission (CBRC) reported that there were 8,221 LGFVs in China by the end of May 2009, of which 4,907 were established by prefecture and county-level governments.[3]

Concerns have been rising over local governments' large and growing borrowing, especially as a substantial portion of fresh lending by Chinese banks to local infrastructure projects via LGFVs. The worry is that such loans may be subject to higher credit risks. Although the rate of non-performing loans (NPLs) for major commercial banks in China stood at merely 1% by the end of 2011, this may only reflect the dilution of bad loans by a flood of new lending. Given the intrinsic risks associated with LGFVs, such as a relatively low level of transparency and the lack of effective government supervision, some of these loans are likely to turn sour eventually. In addition, local governments usually provide collateral assets, typically land, for loans by LGFVs. That is additional risks to the Chinese banks. As pointed out by central bank governor Zhou Xiaochuan, land could be overvalued during the heyday of the property market; if land prices plummet in the future, some LGFVs may default due to the difference in the assessment of the loans.[4]

On the other hand, many LGFV loans could also pose fiscal risks to some local governments. As these local governments often extend implicit guarantees on the loans borrowed by their LGFVs, infrastructure projects without sufficient cash flow may have to rely on the governments' fiscal revenue to cover interest payments and repay loans. Although China's overall fiscal position is relatively strong, local governments' capabilities in repaying the loans vary drastically. The risk of county or township governments defaulting on LGFV loans is much higher than that of provincial-level governments. With an overheated property market, even provincial-level governments might find themselves deep in debts. Indeed, land sales revenue weighs heavily on local governments' total fiscal revenue. If the property market tumbles, the proceeds from land sales to repay government debts could fall short in many localities.

The Chinese authorities are fully aware of the brewing risks. In early 2012, the state audit office identified 530 billion *yuan* worth of irregularities with local government debt. The report was conducted for the 2010 budget year. The uncovered problems included 47 billion *yuan* worth of irregular credit guarantees, 73 billion *yuan* worth of loans secured against irregular collateral, 132 billion *yuan* worth of expenditure not made by its approved deadlines, 36 billion *yuan* to the stock market, housing market and polluting plants, and 244 billion *yuan* related to fraudulent and underpayment of registered capital in LGFVs.[5] In the 2012 government report, Premier Wen Jiabao also made it clear that the government takes the issue of managing local government debt very seriously and pledged to contain the risks of LGFVs through clean-ups and regulation.[6]

---

[2]World Bank, "The Urban Development Investment Corporations in Chongqing, China", Technical Assistance Report, 2009.

[3]"The CBRC Held its 2010 Q2 Briefing on Latest Economic and Financial Conditions", <http://www.cbrc.gov.cn/> (accessed 20 April 2010).

[4]"China's Zhou Sees Bank Risks in Local-Government Financing", *Bloomberg*, 6 March 2010.

[5]The National Audit Office, "On the Executive of the 2010 Central Budget and the Correction of Problems Found in the Audit of Other Fiscal Revenue and Expenditure", no 1, 2012.

[6]Wen J, "2012 Report on the Work of the Government", 5 March 2012.

Various policies have been employed to slow down the massive borrowings by local governments since 2010.[7] To tackle the problems associated with existing loans, the Ministry of Finance (MoF) and the CBRC ordered banks to re-examine their existing LGFV projects thoroughly. To prevent problems in new loans, the central government has become more prudent in approving new local investment projects. In addition, the CBRC requires that banks rely solely on those projects' cash flow sources and collaterals to make lending decisions. In March 2012, the banking regulator also allowed banks to extend deadlines on loans issued to LGFVs to ensure the completion of their projects.[8]

With the central government's recently heightened vigilance over LGFV borrowing together with China's relatively strong fiscal position and the recent recapitalisation of major Chinese commercial banks, there seems no large systemic risks to China's banking industry or fiscal health in the near term. Nevertheless, in the longer term, there could be another surge in NPLs associated with LGFVs, especially if overall economic growth slows down considerably. If that happens, the central government might have to step in and take over the loans eventually, which would weaken China's banking sector and perhaps prove costly to the Chinese government if it has to further overhaul and restructure the banking sector.

## A Brief History of Local Government Financial Vehicles

There is neither any official definition to LGFVs nor any specific legal restrictions on the LGFVs' investment scope. The vehicles are set up by local governments to raise funds for local projects, including constructing and operating infrastructure and managing infrastructure-related commercial projects.

In practice, they are treated as municipal SOEs, subject to the "special rules governing fully state-owned companies" under Company Law. Despite many operational structures, most LGFVs are under the direct control of local governments, with the rest reporting to different branches of local governments, such as the Department of Construction, State Asset Management Department, and the Department of Development and Reform. Figure 1 demonstrates how local governments

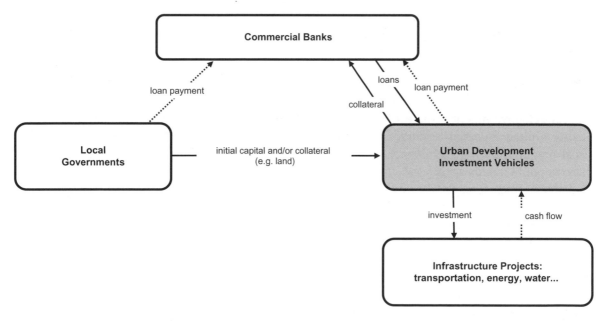

**Figure 1**    Local Government's Borrowing via LGFVs

*Source*: EAI research.

---

[7] Goldman Sachs Gao Hua, "Three Positive Ongoing Developments; Add on Attractive Risk/Reward", 5 March 2010.

[8] "China NPC: Bank Regulator Softens Line on Local Government Debt", *Fox Business*, 5 March 2012.

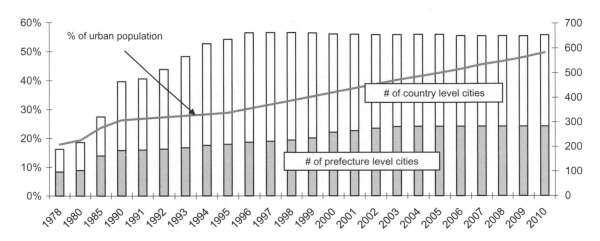

**Figure 2**   China's Urbanisation, 1978–2010

*Source*: *China Statistical Yearbook*, 2011.

borrow through LGFVs to fund local infrastructure projects. The solid lines show that local governments usually provide collateral to support LGFV borrowing, as well as the initial capital to get infrastructure projects started. Upon the completion of the projects, the LGFVs will repay loans through cash flows generated from the projects, or rely on the local governments to settle the issue.

The urban growth in China has indeed stimulated the development of LGFVs. Since the 1978 economic reform, the country's rapid growth has brought about significant urbanisation (Figure 2). By 2010, China had 653 cities and an urban population of 670 million, compared to 193 cities and 172 million urban residents in 1978. More importantly, urbanisation and urban development in China are primarily government-driven.[9] With this accelerated pace of urbanisation since the 1990s, the demand for capital investment to finance the construction and operation of urban infrastructure has been enormous, posing serious challenges to governments at various levels.

Local governments, however, have few sources of funding. According to the Budget Act and the Guarantee Law, local governments are not allowed to issue municipal bonds or to borrow directly from banks. Though the central government gave permission to four local governments to sell bonds on a trial basis in October 2011, the pilot bond project is still limited to prosperous regions. The 1994 tax reform also weakened local governments' fiscal position by significantly increasing the central government's share of tax revenue. Thus, local governments often find themselves having limited financial resources to invest in infrastructure projects. Meanwhile, facing severe fiscal pressure, local governments also have strong incentives to improve local infrastructure and provide public goods as they are widely considered as conspicuous indicators of a successful local leadership. Therefore, LGFVs of various forms have been established since the early 1990s to serve as ideal market-borrowing platforms for local governments.

The development of LGFVs can be divided into three periods.[10] The initial stage was between 1992 and 1997. The Shanghai municipal government was the first to set up a LGFV to raise funds for local infrastructure projects. In 1992, it founded the Shanghai Chengtou Corporation to invest, construct and operate the city's infrastructure facilities. Since then, the vehicles have become a way for local governments to marketise infrastructure projects. However, few existed during that period and most of them were established by provincial level governments to carry out limited functions.

---

[9]Naughton, B, "The Chinese Economy: Transitions and Growth", 2007.

[10]Wei J, "Thoughts on the Risks Associated with UDIVs and Overall Precautionary Measures", Keynote Speech on the Sixth High-level Forum of China Financial Reforms, 9 May 2010.

The period between 1998 and 2008 was pivotal for the development of LGFVs. In 1998, a LGFV was set up by a local government for the first time. Wuhu of Anhui province signed a borrowing contract with China Development Bank for a package of local infrastructure projects.[11] In 2002, the Chongqing municipal government established eight state-owned LGFVs which have sector-specific responsibilities and respective financial teams. This Chongqing LGFV model gained popularity quickly and the World Bank started a research project on it in 2006. Overall, during this period of 10 years, these vehicles had played an increasingly important role in China's urbanisation between 1998 and 2008.

LGFVs' rapid development started in 2009. The outbreak of the financial crisis in late 2008 dramatically precipitated the borrowing of local governments via LGFVs. While the central government implemented a moderately loose stance to rekindle the economy, local governments took it as a great opportunity to carry out their infrastructure projects. Take the Beijing Infrastructure Investment as an example. By the end of September 2009, its short-term and long-term loans rose by 41% from the end of 2008, totalling 43 billion *yuan*, with a credit line of 181 billion *yuan* from various banks.[12]

While LGFVs serve China's infrastructure development well, they have several inherent defects. First, those platforms are subject to a lower degree of transparency requirements. Given that they are designed mainly to raise funds for public infrastructure projects, the vehicles are not required to disclose project details, though they are commercial corporations by definition. In other words, the public do not have access to key information such as corporate governance, project management and financial statements, which intrinsically violates the principle of open and transparent operation of public projects.

Second, the vehicles lack effective supervision. Relying on bank loans, LGFVs and their projects are rarely supervised as public spending falls under the local governments' budget. For example, following the stimulus package introduced by the central government in late 2008, there was a rapid surge in LGFV borrowing to finance various ostentatious projects. It is quite likely that many of these projects would aggravate the problems of excessive expansion, overlapping investment and low efficiency, while accurate figures to confirm these are hard to come by.

Third, many LGFV loans depend on unreliable guarantees by local governments. In cases where assets, typically land, are used as collateral for the LGFV loans, there may be a huge difference in the assessment of loans when land prices plummet. In other cases where the local governments use implicit guarantees such as a "guarantee letter of local People's Congress", "supporting documents from local government" or a "commitment letter of local department of finance" to back the loans, the lending banks could face default risks by local governments.

## A Numerical Analysis of Local Government Debt

In June 2011, China's NAO delivered the first-ever comprehensive report on local government debt, estimating that local governments had run up to about 10.7 trillion *yuan* (or US$1.6 trillion) in debt by the end of 2010, the equivalent of 27% of GDP in 2010. Interestingly, the figure falls between the numbers estimated by other government departments: it is higher than the 9.1 trillion *yuan* identified by the country's banking regulatory agency, the CBRC, but lower than the 14.4 trillion *yuan* by the central bank, the People's Bank of China (PBoC) (Figure 3).

The discrepancy, however, shed light on the true scale of local government debt. Compared with the estimates by PBoC or CBRC, the NAO investigation covered a wider range of local government debts, including loans taken by subsidised public units, local government departments and organisations, and LGFVs. Thus, through the breakdown released by the NAO report, it is possible to obtain the non-LGFV borrowing. On the other hand, the NAO apparently underestimated the

[11]"The Puzzle of Local Governments Financing Risks", *China Investment*, 26 March 2010.
[12]Chen K, "A Soft Landing of LGFVs", *The 21st Century Business Herald*, 9 March 2010.

trillion yuan

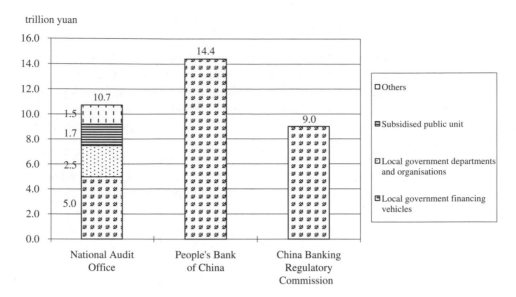

**Figure 3**    Estimates of Local Government Debt by the Chinese Government

*Sources*: National Audit Office; "People's Bank of China;" Growing Debts of China's Local Governments", Tom Orlik, *The Wall Street Journal*, 27 June 2011.

size of LGFV debt. Its figure was actually based on a sampling of 6,576 LGFVs but the PBoC reported that more than 10,000 of such vehicles had been set up nationwide by the end of 2010. Therefore, a more realistic view of the total comes from adding up non-LGFV debt in the NAO report and LGFV debt in the PBoC report or CBRC report, according to Victor Shih of Northwestern University.[13]

The following is an estimate of the size of LGFV debt. In the NAO report, the debt that went to these vehicles accounted for five trillion *yuan*, leaving non-LGFV local government debt at 5.7 trillion *yuan*. By adding up the LGFV debt in the other two reports, total local government debt at the end of 2010 could range between 15 trillion *yuan* and 20 trillion *yuan*, or 40–50% of GDP. Indeed, this figure is slightly above the estimate of Moody's Investors Service, which said China's banks may have an additional 3.5 trillion *yuan* of exposure to local government debt that did not appear in the auditor's report.[14]

Although the actual magnitude of local government indebtedness seems much worse than the auditor's report shows, local government debt is unlikely to pose systemic stress to the economy, as will be discussed in the next section. No systematic risk, however, does not mean the debt would not destabilise the economy. In the short run, it is likely to create liquidity risk for local governments and bad loans for banks. According to the official audit report, about 42% of local government debt is due before the end of 2012 (Figure 4). Hence, it came as no surprise to learn that the country's banking regulator has allowed Chinese banks to extend deadlines on loans issued to LGFVs to ensure completion of their projects.[15]

In the long run, local government debt may even stymie China's economic transformation. Since late 2008, local governments have ramped up spending, with pressure to invest in infrastructure, health, education and social security, for which they are largely responsible. But in the NAO report, the lion's share (37%) of local government debts was spent on building municipal infrastructure, followed by transportation (25%) and reserve land (11%), while social housing, together with education, science, culture and health, accounted for merely 10% of total expenditure (Figure 5). It is apparently in conflict

---

[13] Shih V, "China Needs a Credit Crunch", *The Wall Street Journal*, 29 June 2011.

[14] "China Auditor Denies Understating Debt of Local Governments", *Bloomberg*, 11 July 2011.

[15] "CHINA NPC: Bank Regulator Softens Line on Local Government Debt", *Fox Business*, 5 March 2012.

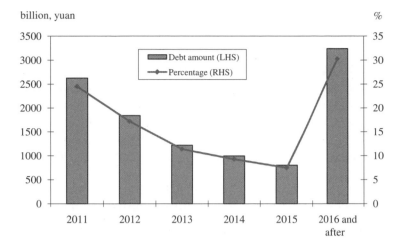

**Figure 4**　Maturity of China's Local Government Debt

*Source*: National Audit Office.

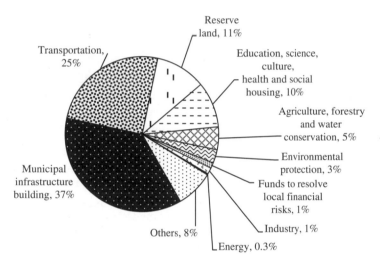

**Figure 5**　Spending of Local Government Debt

*Source*: National Audit Office.

with the central government's strategy of giving Chinese households a bigger share of the nation's wealth, thus unlocking consumption-driven growth.

## Policies for Mitigating the Risks

Chinese policy makers have acted promptly to limit problems and reduce risks. When the issue came under the spotlight for the first time in 2010, the Chinese authorities opted to reduce the risks related to LGFVs by ring-fencing the "stock problems" as well as limiting the "flow problems". For existing exposures, the banks were required to assess all LGFV borrowing and to categorise them into three groups based on their ability to repay the loans: i) loans for infrastructure projects with cash flow or sufficient collateral to cover the debts; ii) loans for social purposes but reliant on fiscal revenue for repayments; and iii) loans without either sufficient cash flow or credible guarantees from the local government.

　　Specific measures were taken to monitor existing loans in each category. The LGFVs with loans in the first category may continue to receive credit from banks, although they were required to improve the capital adequacy, introduce private investors and transform into shareholding companies. But implicit guarantees issued by local governments are no longer valid.

In terms of loans that rely on fiscal revenue or government subsidies, the Chinese banks were required to investigate the liability of local governments, especially those of county-level governments, to reduce fiscal risk. Moreover, the authorities suggested closing LGFVs relying on fiscal revenue to repay the loans if they were designed merely to raise funds. For LGFVs that not only raise funds but also construct and operate the projects, they are required to cease financing activities after completing the construction and paying back the loans. For loans in the third category, the central government underscored that the responsibility to mitigate losses and to recoup loans lies with local governments and banks.

Regarding the flow problem, or problems associated with new loans, the banking regulator has raised lending standards for LGFVs since early 2010. With rising concerns over overcapacity, inefficient spending and local governments' fiscal conditions, the central government has also been especially prudent with the approval of new local investment projects.

In November 2011, Beijing took another significant step to prevent potential defaults by provincial and city-level governments: the MoF launched a trial programme that allowed Zhejiang province, Guangdong province and the cities of Shanghai and Shenzhen to issue three- and five-year bonds on their own. These bonds are open to both Chinese investors and a limited number of qualified foreign institutions. It is also widely believed that Beijing's move would increase the transparency of local infrastructure projects and improve market supervision.

Shanghai was the first local authority among the four to sell bonds directly to investors, issuing 3.6 billion *yuan* in three-year bonds at a yield of 3.1% and 3.5 billion *yuan* in five-year bonds at 3.3% in November 2011. The demand for the bonds was so strong that the yields were significantly lower than 3.67% and 3.70% for similar bonds that the MoF auctioned on behalf of local governments in the previous month. Following Shanghai, local authorities in Guangdong, Zhejiang and Shenzhen raised 6.9 billion *yuan*, 6.7 billion *yuan*, and 2.2 billion *yuan* respectively in the bond market. Hence, the total amount raised through the pilot programme amounted to 23 billion *yuan*.

In addition, the MoF has been mulling the idea of introducing an indicator system to normalise the borrowing of local governments. The system will not only set explicit targets for indicators such as debt ratio, current ratio and debt service coverage ratio for LGFVs, but lay down rules to prevent local governments from defaulting on bank loans.

Because of the interwoven nature of the property market and LGFV loans, the Chinese authorities have also taken various measures to curb speculation in the property market. On the supply side, the Ministry of Land ensures that no less than 70% of new land supply will be used for affordable or small apartments, and it strictly forbids land supply for villas. On the demand side, the State Council increased the down payment for first-time buyers' mortgage from 20% to 30%, that for second homes from 50% to 60%, and no mortgages for third home purchases. Besides, it required higher benchmark lending rates and put credit-quota limits in more regions. In 2011, Chinese policy makers also introduced the property tax trials in Shanghai and Chongqing as part of its efforts to curb rising house prices. As a result, China's property market is gradually cooling off as the measures take effect.

## Appraising Risks Associated with Local Government Debt

Local governments' borrowing should not result in a systemic NPL crisis in the near future, not only because local governments have resources to repay their own debts, but also because the central government will step in to bail out local governments if they default on bank loans to avoid social unrest. Banks could also reduce risks associated with local government debt by rolling over those loans or through recapitalisation.

In fact, China's economic growth and fiscal position remain strong relative to the size of the potential risks. Since early 2000, the economy has maintained an average annual growth rate

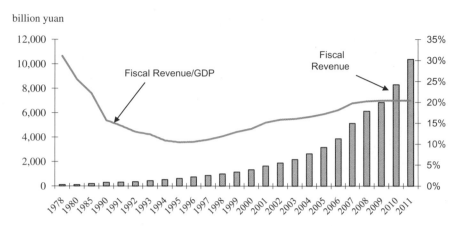

**Figure 6** China's Economy and Fiscal Position, 1978–2011

*Source*: National Bureau of Statistics, China.

of 10%, providing a favourable environment to resolve potential NPL problems in the future. According to the Economist Intelligence Unit of the *Economist*, China's total local government debt as a percentage of GDP (40–50%) is far lower than the level of public debt in developed countries such as the United States (93%), Germany (75%), France (81%) and Japan (225%).

The country's fiscal revenue has grown at an even faster pace, resulting in a rising share in total GDP, from around 12% in the mid-1990s to around 20% in recent years (Figure 6). In 2011, its national fiscal revenues rose 25% to 10 trillion *yuan* and local governments collected five trillion *yuan* at a growth rate of 27%. Since market analysts estimate that two to three trillion *yuan* of local government loans may go sour in the future, Chinese governments obviously have sufficient resources to deal with the issue.

Recapitalisation will help Chinese banks cover the capital holes created by the credit surge as well. To maintain capital adequacy ratio, many Chinese banks including the Industrial and Commercial Bank of China, China Construction Bank, China Citic Bank, and Bank of Beijing have announced aggressive recapitalisation plans since early 2012. Together with previous plans from 2011 the total scale of these plans is close to 180 billion *yuan*. Although sceptics are wondering whether these moves are efforts to get ready for a looming bad loan surge, the capital boost is a positive sign since it maintains banks' prudent buffers and gives more room for further lending.

To conclude, although there are serious concerns over the risks associated with local government debt, especially those via LGFVs, the risks are not an immediate threat to China's banking industry and fiscal health in the near future. In the coming decade, however, there could be another surge in NPLs associated with local government debt, especially if the overall economic growth slows down considerably.

# 20

# China's State-Owned Enterprises

## The Dilemma of Reform

HUANG Yanjie*

*After two decades of reform, China's state-owned enterprises have become economically and politically powerful while remaining largely inefficient and monopolistic. The prospect of reform is coloured with uncertainties as regulatory and other approaches have failed to rein in the SOEs.*

China's state-owned enterprise (SOE) reform was formally initiated in the late 1970s. SOEs were then mired in inefficiency and low profitability while burdened with having to provide basic social welfare and employment. Early reforms were focussed on granting some managerial autonomy, thus introducing incentives. Since the mid-1980s, SOE reforms were mostly characterised by the so-called *fangquan rangli* (decentralising powers and sharing profits), where central ministries have gradually transferred some decision-making powers to the managements of the SOEs and local governments while allowing them to retain larger shares of the profits for investment and employee bonuses.

More specifically, since 1984, the focus of SOE reforms has shifted from managerial adjustment to corporate restructuring. Reformers aimed to transform the SOEs into real economic entities, with the managers taking responsibility for running the enterprises. Meanwhile, large-scale experiments were carried out to reform the fiscal and financial structure of the SOEs, including the so-called *li gai shui* (from profit retention to tax) reforms. The government also experimented with stock reforms to explore different ways to improve SOE governance. However, all these reforms were not able to solve the issue of loss-making. Losses and debts thus continued to increase.[1]

A new round of SOE reforms had been carried out under former Premier Zhu Rongji since the mid-1990s, under the basic principle of *zhuada fangxiao* (grasping the large and letting go of the

---

*HUANG Yanjie is Research Assistant at the East Asian Institute, National University of Singapore.

[1] Refer to Lin Y and Cai F, *State-owned Enterprise Reform in China*, Chinese University of Hong Kong Press, 2001, ch. 1.

small). The government streamlined the SOE sector through the consolidation of the large state-owned enterprises and privatisation of state-owned small and medium sized enterprises (SMEs). Such strategy yielded large enterprises groups which were centrally managed state-owned enterprises characterised by large industrial conglomerates in upstream monopoly sectors, while the number of private and joint-stock companies mushroomed. In practice, much of the restructuring process was decentralised to local governments, which usually kept the more efficient and profitable firms and sold the inefficient and loss-making ones in a bid to protect their fiscal self-interests. As a result of the reform, there has been a dramatic reduction of SOEs and their share in the total number of enterprises (Figure 1) during a period of entrepreneurial boom in China.

The reforms in the 90s have by and large succeeded in increasing the profitability of SOEs, by downsizing the employment of the state sector and strengthening the financial positions of the remaining SOEs. The surviving SOEs are typically larger enterprises that employ more people (Figure 2) and own more assets (Figure 3) than their non-state counterparts. There have also been significant organisational changes in the industrial sector. By the late 1990s, almost all the industrial ministries (except the Railways) had been either abolished or corporatised into ministerial-ranking SOEs. Both centrally and locally managed SOEs became autonomous corporate actors without the visible hands of the multiple layers of local industrial bureaus and central ministries.

A new macro-architecture was finally established in 2003 when all remaining SOEs were placed under the supervision of either the Ministry of Finance or central or local branches of the State-owned Assets Supervision and Administration Commission (SASAC), a newly created agency under the State Council. However, as a supervisory and regulatory body, the SASAC system is a much weaker bureaucratic system compared to the former powerful industrial bureaus and ministries, which exercised direct management functions. Although it has a large nominal jurisdiction, it lacks the political authority and administrative resources to exert significant influence over large, rich and powerful SOEs. The current head of the SASAC, Wang Yong, for instance, is not even an alternate member of the Chinese Communist Party Central Committee at the time his appointment, which makes his political rank even lower than party-appointed bosses of several largest SOEs under his nominal supervision.

Moreover, bestowed as a representative of state-ownership, the SASAC has become a successful promoter when its interests in "maintaining the growth of state assets" neatly coincide with the SOEs' drive for investment and expansion. As is shown in Figure 4, centrally managed SOEs,

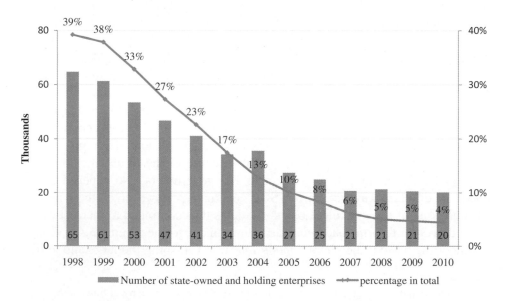

**Figure 1**   State-Owned and Holding Enterprises: Numbers and Shares in Total, 1998–2010

*Source*: National Bureau of Statistics.

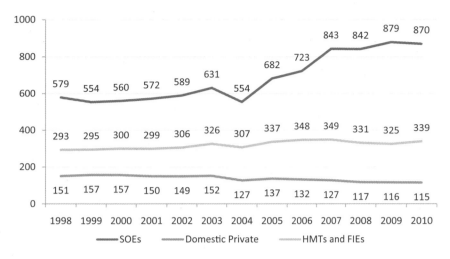

**Figure 2** Average Number of Employees per Firm, 1998–2010

*Source*: National Bureau of Statistics.

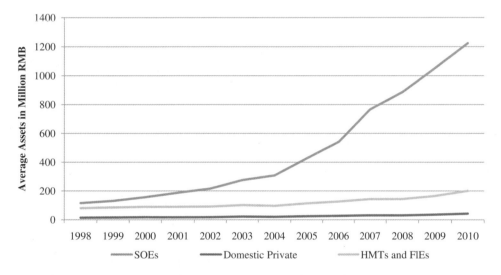

**Figure 3** Average Assets per Firm

*Source*: *China Statistics Yearbook* 2011.

which numbered less than 200, have clearly demonstrated their capacity to make huge profits relative to local SOEs.[2] Measured in net wealth, 54 of China's centrally administered SOEs were included in the most powerful *Fortune Global 500* list in 2011, pushing the number of Chinese firms listed to an unprecedented 61.[3] Most of these giant SOEs were not surprisingly in the most profitable and strategic state-dominated sectors such as banking, energy, electricity and insurance. The three largest SOEs, Sinopec, China National Petrol and State Grid, are ranked among top ten largest enterprises in the world.

---

[2] The number of centrally managed SOEs has gradually but consistently decreased over the past eight years. There were over 190 such SOEs in 2003 when the SASAC was set up. Since then the SASAC has made continuous efforts to shorten the list of centrally managed SOEs, nicknamed the *national team*. As in June 2012, there were only 120 left on the list.
[3] Of the 61 Chinese firms from mainland China and Hong Kong, there are 54 centrally managed SOEs, one locally managed SOE, two private enterprises based in mainland China and four private enterprises based in Hong Kong. For the detailed list, see <http://en.wikipedia.org/wiki/Fortune_Global_500> (accessed 17 October 2011).

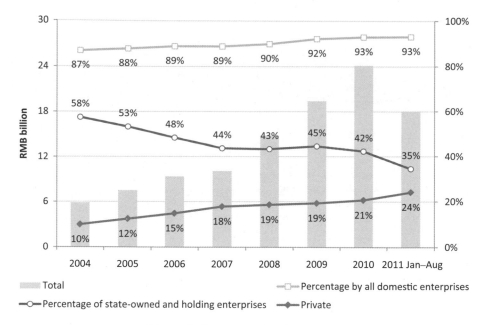

**Figure 4**  Investments in Fixed Assets

*Source*: National Bureau of Statistics.

Most recently, the SOEs have even deliberately pushed into the traditional strongholds of the private economy through a number of high-profile mergers and acquisitions.[4] In the coal mining sector, for example, the state revoked permits previously allocated to private individuals and firms operating with hundreds of small coal miners in an effort to "rationalise" the sector through re-nationalisation. Even if the SOEs had not systemically forced their way through, private capital was still being crowded out of numerous sectors from infrastructure finance to public utility and natural resource sectors according to a report by All China Federation of Industry and Commerce (ACFIC).[5]

## Current Status of the SOEs

Despite successive reforms, which have indeed improved the profitability of the SOEs, the state sector continued to perform relatively poorly vis-à-vis non-state sectors, in terms of not only job creation but also various aspects of operational efficiency. One important objective of the SOE reform in the late 1990s was to remove the government's subsidy burden with regards to the large number of loss-making SOEs. For example, in the late 1990s and early 2000s, roughly two-fifths of all SOEs were making losses, compared to only 27% of all industrial firms. Since then, despite record-making profits made by the largest SOEs, the state sector taken as a whole has remained the worst performer of the lot (Table 1). In 2009, less than 14% of all industrial firms were making losses and the share for state firms[6] was twice as high. Thus, while state-controlled firms accounted for roughly 5% of industrial firms, they made up 10% of all loss-making enterprises and nearly half of total losses in recent years.[7]

---

[4] For a review of the debate on state sector expansion, refer to *Advance of State Capitals and the Retreat of Private Capitals: the boundless Expansion of Centrally-Managed SOEs arouses the Debate on the Direction of Reform, Southern Weekly*, 20 August 2009.

[5] "China Private Sector Development Report", All China Federation of Industry and Commerce Research Center, 2009.

[6] State firms here refer to state-owned enterprises and limited liability enterprises of sole state ownership.

[7] For the first 11 months of 2008–2010, the shares of losses by state-controlled firms in total losses by firms of all industries were 66%, 44% and 45% respectively. Data for the whole year are not available. (Source: CEIC).

**Table 1**   China's Industrial Enterprises by Types of Ownership: Share of Loss-Making Firms in Total, 1999–2009

| | 1999 | | | 2001 | | | 2009 | | |
|---|---|---|---|---|---|---|---|---|---|
| | | Loss-Making | | | Loss-Making | | | Loss-Making | |
| | **Total** | **No.** | **% in total** | **Total** | **No.** | **% in total** | **Total** | **No.** | **% in total** |
| **All types of firms** | **162,033** | **44,186** | **27.3** | **171,256** | **39,344** | **23.0%** | **434,364** | **59,868** | **13.8%** |
| Domestic | 135,196 | | | 139,833 | 30,677 | 21.9% | 358,988 | 42,003 | 11.7% |
| SOEs | 50,651 | 20,812 | 41.1 | 34530 | 13,470 | 39.0% | 9,105 | 2,655 | 29.2% |
| Collectives | 42,585 | 7,362 | 17.3 | 31,018 | 4,971 | 16.0% | 10,285 | 1,481 | 14.4% |
| Cooperatives | 10,149 | | | 10,864 | 1,625 | 15.0% | 5,011 | 592 | 11.8% |
| Joint ownership | 2,771 | 602 | 21.7 | 2,234 | 478 | 21.4% | 735 | 144 | 19.6% |
| Limited liability | 9,714 | | | 18,956 | 4,234 | 22.3% | 65,926 | 10,540 | 16.0% |
| *Sole state ownership* | 1,026 | | | 1,372 | 413 | 30.1% | 1,454 | 384 | 26.4% |
| Sharing holding | 4,480 | 978 | 21.8 | 5,692 | 1,176 | 20.7% | 9,275 | 1,317 | 14.2% |
| Private | 14,601 | 1,982 | 13.6 | 36,218 | 4,655 | 12.9% | 256,031 | 25,006 | 9.8% |
| Others | 245 | | | 321 | 68 | 21.2% | 2,620 | 268 | 10.2% |
| Non-mainland | | | | | | | | | |
| Hong Kong, Macao, and Taiwan funded | 15,783 | 4,873 | 30.9 | 18,257 | 5,150 | 28.2% | 34,365 | 8,149 | 23.7% |
| Other FIEs | 11,054 | 3,362 | 30.4 | 13,166 | 3,519 | 26.7% | 41,011 | 9,716 | 23.7% |

*Sources*: *China Statistical Yearbook*, 2000, 2002 and 2010.

Another salient feature of the SOEs is their role in fixed-capital formation and land acquisition. Despite the rapid shrinking share of the SOEs in total industrial investments, they played a key role in China's investment-driven growth model, taking up on average 45% of investments nationwide during the last decade (Figure 4). Some of the larger SOEs often act irresponsibly in their investment sprees, sometimes even coming up against national and general societal interests. It was reported, for instance, that seven of the 10 most expensive land lease deeds were made between the centrally managed SOEs and local governments. The news came at a time when there was widespread concern about rising land and property bubbles, which may have caused many severe economic and social problems.[8]

Similarly worrisome was some SOEs' strong monopoly in their respective sectors. To begin with, there is huge difference between the centrally managed SOEs and locally managed SOEs in terms of profit-making capacity and degree of market control. The centrally managed SOEs, whose number has been cut down from 196 to 117 in the last decade, consistently outweighed locally managed SOEs in their total profits (Figure 5). It was observed that some of these largest centrally managed SOEs, such as the State Grid, Sinopec and Petrol China, behaved like aggressive monopolies, abusing their market power through over-pricing, providing low-quality services, making aggressive take-overs and expanding into downstream sectors.[9]

Despite their huge amount of sales revenues and profits, China's SOEs, in particular the centrally managed SOEs are often criticised as a major source of resource misallocation, hotbeds

---

[8] Zhou J, "Why the Centrally-Managed SOEs Always Play Leading Bidder?" (*Weishenme Diwang Zongshi Yangqi*), *China Youth Daily*, 15 March 2010.

[9] Reports of such pricing behaviour are frequent in various magazines, news reports and policy papers. For a good summary, please refer to *The Nature, Performance and Reform of the State-owned Enterprises*, UniRule Institute of Economics, 2011.

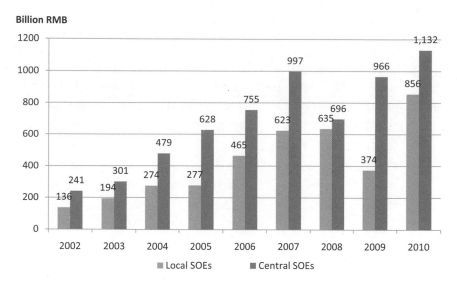

**Billion RMB**

**Figure 5**  Profits of Centrally Managed and Locally Managed SOEs

*Source*: National Bureau of Statistics.

of poor corporate governance and the main cause of the widening income gap.[10] While these criticisms could be further extended, the solutions are not straightforward, since the problems of the SOEs are inextricably linked to more profound structural problems in the Chinese political economy.

According to a recent study on China's SOEs,[11] the state sector lags far behind the non-state sectors in its overall economic performance as measured in terms of rate of return to capital. The study reckons that, while the nominal efficiency gap between SOEs and non-SOEs has generally narrowed since 2001, the gap increases to a staggering 10–15% (Figure 6), even reaching pre-2005 levels of more than 15% in 2009, if the full scale of subsidies, including subsidised interests on capital, land and energy are accounted for. Even though these measurements may understate the efficiency of the more capital-intensive state sectors vis-à-vis non-state sectors, there is little doubt that a huge efficiency gap exists between the state and the non-state sectors in their uses of capital.

Besides inefficiency, poor corporate governance and high incidence of corruption in the state sector has also long attracted much attention from both domestic and overseas analysts. High profile corruption cases are common with the top management of large SOEs. In 2009 alone, two ministerial-ranking SOEs magnates, Kang Rixin (former CEO of the China Nucleus Corporation) and Chen Tonghai (former CEO of Sinopec), were arrested for embezzling huge amount of national assets. Another recent investigation into Wu Liang Ye, a leading state-owned wine manufacturer, was carried out by China's Securities Regulatory Commission (SRC), for serious financial misconduct, which lead to heavy losses in state assets.[12] In the light of numerous cases of SOE financial fraud in the past few years, this is hardly an isolated case.

Another concern relating to SOEs is their role in China's widening income gap. Based on a 2008 income survey, the average wage rates in the state sector were 63% higher than the private sector and 17% higher than national average wage.[13] Since real income levels and welfare provisions for

---

[10] Ibid.

[11] Ibid.

[12] Wuliangye under the Investigation of SRC (*Beidiaocha de Wuliangye*), *Caijing*, issue 249, 24 September 2009.

[13] It should be noted that the "state sector" here also includes government organisations and public service providing institutions (such as public education and healthcare sectors). (Source: *The Nature, Performance and Reform of the State-owned Enterprises*, UniRule Institute of Economics, 2011.)

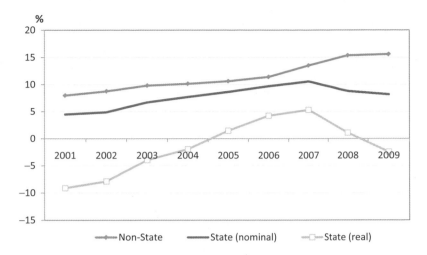

**Figure 6** Rate of Return to Equity for Private and State-Owned Enterprises

*Source*: Unirule Institute of Economics.

employees of SOEs far exceed published salaries, the actual income gap between employees of monopolistic SOEs and those in other enterprises and sectors is likely to be considerably larger.[14]

A recent study by a team of researchers led by Wang Xiaolu, a leading specialist in the study of China's income distribution, lists SOE monopoly as one of the top five factors contributing to China's dangerously high level of income inequality through a myriad of "grey" housing and other welfare benefits, most of which are financed by their exorbitant monopoly profits.[15] In 2007, analysts were alerted to the striking fact that Sinopec and Petrol China, two of the largest state-owned oil companies alone garnered and retained a total profit of US$100 billion, almost five times the amount China spent on minimum livelihood support for both rural and urban areas, which was just over US$20 billion.[16]

The State Council has long urged SOEs to turn in part of their profits as national social security contributions. In 2007, the State Council ordered the centrally managed SOEs to turn in a minimum 5% of their profits to the Ministry of Finance to contribute to China's social security fund. But in the last three out of four years, the SOEs have failed to meet even the 5% minimum requirement as a simple token of their social responsibilities. Except for the year 2009, the profits turned in on average only accounted for 2% of the total net profits of the state sector. Since even the minimum was not met, many are doubtful that the SOEs could turn in 10–15% of their profits to meet the State Council's requirements for 2012.[17]

The predominance of large SOEs in their respective industries is likely to lead to huge monopolistic profits. More specifically, the sometimes monopolist pricing behaviour of centrally administered SOEs has become a particular concern in recent years. Some, as sole suppliers of energy and transportation services, were reported to be marking-up the prices of key products. Sinopec and Petrol China, for example, reportedly decreased the supply of natural gas supplies when there was a seasonal hike in the demand for heating during the winter months from 2007 to 2010. It was regarded as a means to ask for higher fixed prices or policy support from the state, in

---

[14] Ren Z and Zhou Y, *Assessment of the Monopolistic Contribution to Intra-sector Income Inequality*, Economic Theory and Management, vol. 4, 2009.

[15] Wang X, *Grey Income and Income Inequality in China*, National Economic Research Institute of the China Reform Foundation, July 2007.

[16] Fu Z, "How to Make Centrally-Managed SOEs Truly State-Owned?" (*Ruherang Yangqi zhenzheng Chengwei Guoyou*), *Southern Daily*, 4 January 2011.

[17] See for example, *The Nature, Performance and Reform of the State-owned Enterprises*, UniRule Institute of Economics, 2011.

the form of more price subsidies, both administered by the State Council's National Development and Reform Commission (NDRC).[18]

Similarly irregular and monopolistic pricing behaviours were also widely observed across the state-owned telecommunications sector, when China Netcom and China Telecom priced internet broadband 300% over cost price.[19] Although price hikes for monopoly enterprises usually go through public hearings, most of these hearings have only been a matter of formality.

## Challenges for Future SOE Reform

Amidst many recent criticisms levelled against the SOEs, the government's response seems half-hearted. On the one hand, the government clearly recognises the critical nature of these problems and has repeatedly reaffirmed its commitment to future reforms. A recent State Council policy directive argued for more policy support for the mostly non-state privately owned small and medium enterprises (SMEs). The new policies include, among others, more equal access to bank loans and the opening of more sectors previously dominated by the SOEs to domestic private capitals.[20]

On the other hand, there has been little sign of a systemic reform, which may entail an overhaul of the overall organisation. Such reforms may involve changes in various aspects of SOE management including regulatory, legislative, as well as economic reforms. While efforts have been made in all these aspects, difficulties and obstacles abound.

From a regulatory viewpoint, the reforms will strengthen the current regulatory and supervisory systems. This will require the current supervisory body, the SASAC, to exercise tighter control and carry out necessary reforms to improve governance of the SOEs. However, the current structure of SASAC means it is unlikely to be a strong vehicle for further SOE reforms. It was observed that while the NDRC and other ministries are becoming more concerned about the problems associated with the SOEs, the governing body itself seems reluctant to lay more blame on its supervisees. Recent five-year reviews of the SASAC consistently stressed its achievements in growing the assets it administered from RMB7.3 trillion to RMB21 trillion, while hardly addressing any critical issues like income inequality and excessive SOE involvement in the real estate markets.[21]

In an all-out effort to accumulate state assets, the SASAC has established a symbiotic relationship with the most powerful SOEs. While SOEs have expanded very fast in the last decade, the SASAC has in turn, strongly defended the internal governance practices of SOEs. For instance, in response to the criticism of super-high bonuses for SOE management based on their monopolistic profits, the former head of the SASAC Li Rongrong claimed in his speech, "I would feel sorry for not awarding top management of centrally managed SOEs appropriate bonuses given such spectacular surges in SOEs profits."[22]

The incapacity of the SASAC as a regulatory body was vividly demonstrated by the failure to control the involvement of expansionary SOEs in the real estate sector. In view of real estate bubbles, the SASAC ordered 78 centrally managed SOEs whose principal business was not real estate to withdraw their investments in real estate by March 2010.[23] But this policy simply fell on

---

[18] Jiang L, *Gas Panic as the Means to Achieve Monopoly Pricing (Qihang shi Jiage Longduan Shouduan)*, *Economic Observer Daily*, 24 December 2010.

[19] "How to Reform the State Telecom Sector?" (*Ruhe Gaige Dianxing Chanye*) *People's Daily*, 21 September 2010

[20] Policy Directives on Further Promoting the Development of the Small and Medium Enterprises, At <http://www.gov.cn/zwgk/2009-09/22/content_1423510.htm> (accessed 5 January 2012).

[21] State Asset Supervision and Administration Commission, *SASAC Five-Year Review*, December 2010, p. 15

[22] Li R, "On the Role of SOEs in National Economy" (*Guoyou Qiye Zai Guomin Jingji zhong de Juese*), *Guangdong Daily*, 4 August 2009.

[23] "Timetable for the Centrally-Managed SOEs Divestment" (*Yangqi Chechu Shijianbiao*), *Daily Economic News*, 20 March 2010.

deaf ears. By early December 2010, only seven out of the 78 centrally managed SOEs had divested their subsidiary real estate business.[24]

In addition to regulatory reforms, legislative reforms have been used to prevent the abuse of monopoly power and to improve SOEs' corporate governance. However, there has been little success to date. Even before China enacted a very inclusive Anti-trust Law in June 2007, many had cast serious doubts on the applicability of the proposed anti-trust laws to China's larger SOEs.[25] Since then, there have been very few successful cases, such that few legal scholars judged it an enforceable legal tool to tame the large centrally managed SOEs.[26]

While China's Anti-trust Law was supposed to regulate monopolistic practices for both domestic and foreign firms, it has been rarely applied to the state monopolies. The first high-profile case was in May 2009 when the Ministry of Commerce (MOC) warned China Unicom and China Netcom of breaching the Anti-trust Law in their planned merger.[27] However, the SASAC promptly stepped in to exonerate the two telecom giants under its aegis, arguing that merging and restructuring state assets were not under the jurisdiction of the Anti-Trust Bureau of the MOC.[28] Since the legal system and the SOEs system are structurally parallel, both being subservient to party committees at each administrative level, it is hard to see how a politically subservient legal system is able to create a fair playground for private enterprises. Thus, anti-trust cases against SOEs are likely to be the exception rather than the rule.

Some liberal jurists in China have suggested that the SOEs should be made accountable to the National People's Congress (NPC), China's nominal legislative body, just like the government and the judicial establishment. For example, some proposed to set up a "State Asset Governance Committee" under the NPC to supervise and administer the SOEs. It is hoped that by transferring the authority on state assets from governments to the NPC, SOE management will be more accountable to the people.[29] Such reforms seem even more far-fetched and impractical as they require fundamental changes in the political system.

Most recently, the new head of SASAC, Wang Yong, reaffirmed in the New Year speech on 5 January 2012 that the new direction of reform will be more market-oriented and mean further corporatisation of SOEs. Citing the exemplary case of Xinxing Jihua Trading International, Wang suggested that all SOEs, in particular centrally owned enterprises, must further introduce incentive mechanisms in their payroll and bonus schemes and closely re-align compensations and remuneration with actual performance indicators like profits and sales.[30] This is the strongest stance for further market-oriented reform voiced by the new head of SASAC so far. However, the reform remains at a technical and managerial level.

The issue of SOE reform has been raised again in a recent comprehensive joint study of China's economic prospects carried out by the World Bank and the Development Research Centre of the State Council. Like many earlier suggestions on reform and the UniRule report, this study reaffirmed the need to further introduce market mechanisms and reduce the size of the state sector.[31] It also warned that China would risk a structural crisis if appropriate SOE reforms were not carried out in conjunction with other reforms in fiscal and financial systems.

---

[24] "No Deadline for Centrally-Managed SOEs' Real Estate Business", *Xinhua News Agency*, 6 December 2010.

[25] Owen, BM, Anti-Trust in China: The Problem of Incentive Incompatibility, *SIER Paper* No.340, Stanford Institute of Economic Research, pp. 37–38.

[26] Lin S, "Research on the Efficiency of China's Anti-trust Laws", *Asian Social Science*, 2009, vol. 5 no. 2, pp. 14–15.

[27] Officials from the Ministry of Commerce Confirmed the Illegality of the Unicom-Netcom Merger, *Economic Observer*, 1 May 2009.

[28] <http://ccnews.people.com.cn/GB/87320/7611027.html> (accessed 26 August 2011).

[29] *The Nature, Performance and Reform of the State-owned Enterprises*, UniRule Institute of Economics, 2011, pp. 97–98.

[30] <http://news.xinhuanet.com/city/2011-12/28/c_122496875.htm> (accessed 7 January 2012).

[31] *China 2030: Building a Modern, Harmonious and Creative High-Income Society*, The World Bank, pp. 42–4.

While the economic rationale of less state and more market certainly makes sense, there is a clear lack of political will within the party-state system for such policy goals. Any political moves against the vested interests of SOEs would be met with opposition from the SOE managements and associated political interests. The fact that many policy directives on SOE reforms have remained on paper has much to do with the remarkable political resilience and wide-ranging influence of the larger SOEs. It is reported that 31% of ministers and vice ministers under the State Council and various provincial positions have working experience in the SOEs.[32] In addition, CEOs of top SOEs usually hold important political offices in the CCP Central Committee as high-ranking party officials. The political capital of large SOEs thus poses a formidable hurdle for any reforms that may reduce SOEs' monopoly. Besides these political deadlocks, the central government may have other political and economic reasons to withhold any radical reforms for its concern for fiscal stability and economic control.[33] As a result, fundamental structural reforms of the SOEs are simply not an option in the Chinese government's policy menu, at least for the time being.

---

[32] Gore, LP, *China Recruits Top SOE Executives into Government: A Different Breed of Politicians? EAI Background Brief*, no. 661, East Asian Institute, pp.10–12.

[33] As a matter of fact, the central government is dependent on the centrally owned SOEs for almost one-third of its tax revenues. This is also the most stable part of all government revenues. Furthermore, the SOEs and in particular, centrally managed SOEs, serve as economic levers for the central government when it comes to boosting economic growth during economic crises.

# 21

# An Update on China's Sovereign Wealth Fund

## China Investment Corporation

Catherine CHONG Siew Keng*

*China Investment Corporation (CIC) was established to manage China's reserves, one of the largest in the world. This chapter examines the progress and lessons learnt by CIC over its five years of operation.*

A sovereign wealth fund (SWF) is a state-owned investment fund or entity that is commonly established from balance of payments surpluses, official foreign currency operations, proceeds of privatisations, governmental transfer payments, fiscal surpluses and/or receipts resulting from resource exports.[1] The concept of a SWF is not new and close to half of the top 40 SWFs in the world have been created since 2000. In an effort to manage China's foreign exchange reserves, which have risen rapidly from a mere US$1.6 billion in the year 1978 to nearly US$3.2 trillion in the year 2011, the Chinese government had set up its first SWF — China Investment Corporation (CIC) in September 2007.[2]

The establishment of CIC seems to serve two primary purposes. First, it is an initial step to diversify the portfolio of China's foreign exchange reserves. Second, and perhaps more importantly, it is a test ground to gain experience and learn from other more established SWFs. When CIC was established, there were widespread concerns internationally as to CIC's relation with the Chinese government and its various ministries, and thus the business merit of CIC's investment decisions. Unlike Temasek Holdings, of which its business decisions the Singapore government has no

---

*Catherine CHONG Siew Keng is currently a PhD student with the S. Rajaratnam School of International Studies.

[1] "What is a Sovereign Wealth Fund?" Sovereign Wealth Fund Institute, at <http://www.swfinstitute.org/what-is-a-swf/> (accessed 15 February 2012).

[2] Data from China's State Administration of Foreign Exchange, at <http://www.safe.gov.cn/model_safe/tjsj/tjsj_detail.jsp?ID=110400000000000000> (accessed 15 February 2012).

**Table 1**   World's 10 Largest Sovereign Wealth Funds (as of February 2012)

| | Country | Fund Name | Assets ($Billion) | Inception | Origin | Linaburg-Maduell Transparency Index |
|---|---|---|---|---|---|---|
| 1 | UAE-Abu Dhabi | Abu Dhabi Investment Authority | $627.00 | 1976 | Oil | 5 |
| 2 | China | SAFE Investment Company | $567.90[a] | 1997 | Non-Commodity | 4 |
| 3 | Norway | Government Pension Fund — Global | $560.00 | 1990 | Oil | 10 |
| 4 | Saudi Arabia | SAMA Foreign Holdings | $532.80 | N/A | Oil | 4 |
| 5 | China | China Investment Corporation | $439.60 | 2007 | Non-Commodity | 7 |
| 6 | Kuwait | Kuwait Investment Authority | $296.00 | 1953 | Oil | 6 |
| 7 | China-Hong Kong | Hong Kong Monetary Authority Investment Portfolio | $293.30 | 1993 | Non-Commodity | 8 |
| 8 | Singapore | Government of Singapore Investment Corporation | $247.50 | 1981 | Non-Commodity | 6 |
| 9 | Singapore | Temasek Holdings | $157.20 | 1974 | Non-Commodity | 10 |
| 10 | Russia | National Welfare Fund | $149.70[b] | 2008 | Oil | 5 |

*Note*: [a] This number is a best guess estimation. [b] This includes the oil stabilization fund of Russia.
Linaburg-Maduell Transparency Index with a scale of 1 to 10, with 1 representing the least transparent and 10 representing the most transparent.

*Source*: Sovereign Wealth Fund Institute, <http://www.swfinstitute.org/fund-rankings/> (accessed March 2012).

involvement in,[3] CIC's top management still has strong government links, thereby suggesting the possibility of government intervention in CIC's operations. Naturally, it takes time and efforts to convince the world, including foreign governments and regulators that CIC is operating largely under market disciplines without substantial government intervention.

Taking into consideration China's large overall foreign exchange reserves, an initial injection of US$200 billion from China's Ministry of Finance into CIC is considered modest. In spite of modest amount of resources and short timeframe, CIC has become one of the largest SWFs worldwide (Table 1).

CIC has made numerous cautious investments since its inception five years ago. Its investment approach and strategy are based on four underlying principles. First, it will invest on a commercial basis. The underlying investment objective is to seek long-term, sustainable and high financial returns for its shareholders within acceptable risk tolerance. Second, CIC is a financial investor. It does not seek to control any sector or company. Third, CIC is a responsible investor which abides by local laws and regulations of the countries in which it invests, and assumes its corporate social responsibility conscientiously. Fourth, CIC's investments are research-driven to provide a basis for sound and, prudent investment decisions, and allocation-driven to assure a disciplined approach to investing.[4]

---

[3] The governance framework, which defines the roles and responsibilities of the Board and management, guides the conduct of Temasek as a key institution under the Singapore Constitution and also governs the relationship with its stakeholders; neither the president of Singapore nor the Singapore government is involved in any investment, divestment or other business decisions. Also see *Temasek Holdings Annual Report 2010*, at <http://www.temasekreport.com/2010/governance/index.html> (accessed 5 July 2012).

[4] *China Investment Corporation 2010 Annual Report*, at <http://www.china-inv.cn/cicen/include/resources/CIC_2010_annualreport_en.pdf> (accessed 5 July 2012).

Three other factors also accounted for CIC's unusual vigilant approach. First, CIC was established just before the onset of the global financial crisis when the global economic outlook was highly precarious and bleak. Second, perhaps because of sheer bad luck, CIC's US$3 billion maiden investment in Blackstone Corporation in 2007 took a dive during the financial crisis. By 2009 the value of the Blackstone shares had dropped by about 64%, leaving CIC with a paper loss of US$1.9 billion.[5] This not only tarnished the image of CIC, but also caused it to be plagued by domestic criticisms. Third, to avoid possible political backlash, CIC was said to have stayed away from investing in strategic sectors overseas, such as airlines.[6] As a result, CIC keeps a portion of its capital in cash funds and equities, and a small portion in fixed income securities. As of 31 December 2009, 32% of CIC's global investment portfolio (87.4% in 2008) was in cash funds, 36% (3.2% in 2008) in equities, 26% (9% in 2008) in fixed income securities and 6% (0.4% in 2008) in other investments. A breakdown of the global portfolio shows that 77% of its holdings are diversified and 23% are direct concentrated holdings.[7]

In 2010, CIC undertook a comprehensive review of its investment objectives and approach, and gradually expanded the scope of alternative investment to include commodities as well as private equities, real estate, hedge funds and direct concentrated investments.[8] This was a shift away from traditional assets such as stocks and bonds. Thus as of 31 December 2010, CIC's global investment portfolio in alternative investments grew from 6% in 2009 to 21% in 2010, and its investments in cash funds dropped from 32% in 2009 to a mere 4% in 2010.[9] Though CIC hopes to achieve greater geographical and sectoral balance, most of its investments are still in North American, Asia-Pacific and European markets (Figure 1). CIC's investments in North America are mainly in the financial and energy sectors, while its investments in Asia-Pacific (such as Kazakhstan, Indonesia *etc.*) are largely in the energy sector. Meanwhile, sectors such as financial services, energy, materials, information technology, industrial and non-essential consumer products (including luxury goods) each accounts for 10% or more (Figure 2) of CIC's diversified equity portfolio.[10]

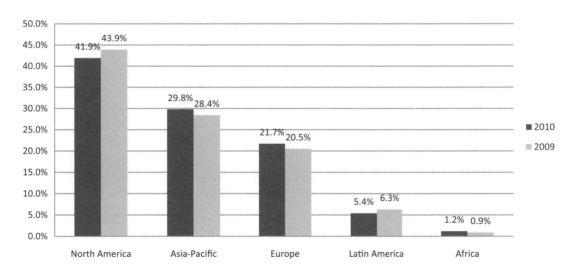

**Figure 1**   Distribution of Diversified Equities by Region

*Source*: *China Investment Corporation Annual Report 2010.*

[5] "CIC Raises Stake in Blackstone to 12.5%", China Daily website, 18 October 2008, at <http://www.chinadaily.com.cn/china/2008–10/18/content_7118069.htm> (accessed 5 July 2012).

[6] "China Investment Corporation Faces Formidable Challenges", *China Business Review*, July–Aug 2008 issue.

[7] *China Investment Corporation 2009 Annual Report.*

[8] See footnote 4.

[9] Ibid.

[10] For details of selected CIC direct investments, please refer to *China Investment Corporation 2010 Annual Report.*

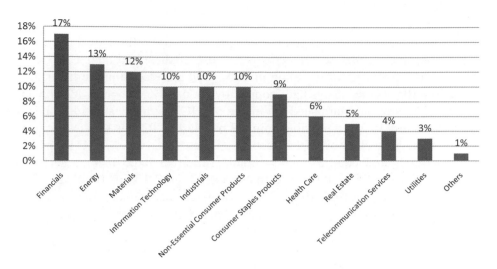

**Figure 2**   Distribution of Diversified Equities by Business Sector

*Source*: *China Investment Corporation Annual Report 2010.*

**Table 2**   Executive Committee of CIC

| Name | Designation |
| --- | --- |
| Lou Jiwei | Chairman and Chief Executive Officer |
| Gao Xiqing | Vice Chairman and President |
| Jin Liqun | Chairman of Board of Supervisors |
| Li Keping | Executive Director, Executive Vice President and Chief Investment Officer (Appointed June 2011) |
| Peng Chun | Executive Vice President |
| Fan Yifei | Executive Vice President |
| Xie Ping | Executive Vice President |
| Wang Jianxi | Executive Vice President |
| Liang Xiang | Member of the Executive Committee |
| Zhang Hongli | Executive Director and Executive Vice President (Till June 2011) |

*Sources*: Author's compilations from *China Investment Corporation Annual Report 2010* and China Vitae website, <http://www.chinavitae.com/> (accessed 15 February 2012).

## CIC's Organisation and its Management in Brief

CIC was established on 29 September 2007 in accordance with China's company law. Its fund has been managed by well-respected technocrats, several of whom with experience in managing government and private sector investments. Table 2 shows the latest composition of the current executive committee, which is responsible for the operation and international investment decisions of the fund.

CIC's leadership and direction is decided by three governing bodies, namely the Board of Directors which oversees the company's overall performance and approves the implementation of strategies and operational guidelines; the Board of Supervisors which is responsible for monitoring the behaviour of directors and executives as well as the effectiveness of supervisory procedure of the company; and the Executive Committee headed by Lou Jiwei (Figure 3).

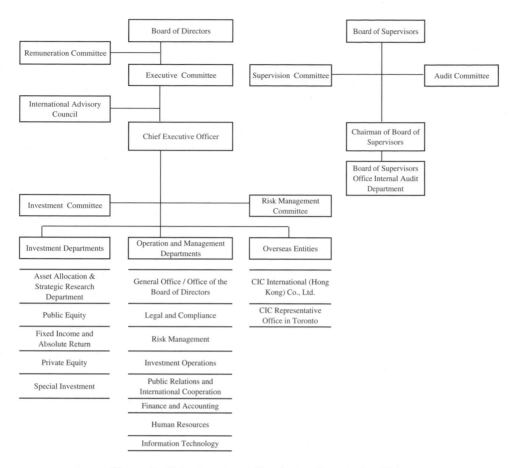

**Figure 3**   China Investment Corporation Organisation Chart

*Source*: *China Investment Corporation Annual Report 2010.*

In addition to the three governing bodies, there are several committees which are involved in the operational and investment aspects of CIC. To benefit from international experience and knowledge, CIC has also set up an International Advisory Council made up of global financial experts.

CIC has been working hard to improve its internal organisation and strengthen its knowledge base. Judging from the portfolio of CIC's key personnel, it seems that the company is likely to encounter bureaucratic turf battles during its decision-making process. This is explainable by the fact that various sections of China's bureaucracies are represented on CIC's board, including the Ministry of Commerce, National Development and Reform Commission, The People's Bank of China (PBOC) and the Ministry of Finance. More seriously, it was reported that CIC chairman, Lou, had never been a fund manager.[11]

In order to strengthen its knowledge base, CIC has been recruiting professionals with relevant overseas working experience. As of 30 June 2011, 154 out of 378 personnel in the investment management team had overseas working experience, 313 had post-graduate degrees and only 43 had foreign citizenships. CIC also places great emphasis on staff development and has in place an extensive training programme.[12]

---

[11] "Lou Suffers Blackstone's 'Fat Rabbits' in China Fund", Bloomberg.com, 27 February 2008, at <http://www.bloomberg.com/apps/news?pid=20601109&refer=home&sid=at7tCLylbz2U> (accessed 5 July 2012).

[12] Each employee will have 80 hours of training each year and an annual training plan based on a formal skills assessment and input from the performance evaluation process. Progress against the plan is monitored by the Department of Human Resources. Training is carried out at both departmental and corporate levels with programmes managed by the Department of Human Resources. In 2010, CIC implemented an on-line e-learning platform which offered many high quality courses to provide employees with a unique channel for learning and development. In 2010, CIC also launched

Although an incorporated company, CIC continues to be viewed by many as coming under heavy state influence rather than market disciplines. This is understandable since all its board members have strong links with government bodies and many of its investments have apparent national strategic significance. This is unlike Singapore's Temasek Holdings where neither the president nor the government has any involvement in any of the business decisions.

To counter such a perception and possible opposition to its investment plans, CIC has enhanced its transparency with more disclosure of its annual reports. In July 2009, CIC published its first annual report,[13] highlighting its performance for the financial year ending 31 December 2008. Internally, domestic investment — the sole responsibility of Central Huijin Investment Corporation set up to channel part of China's foreign exchange reserves to speed up banking reform — is completely separated from overseas investments which come directly under CIC management. In the 2010 annual report, CIC had selectively disclosed information such as the acquisition of the public market investment vehicles, the distribution of internally managed versus externally managed assets and highlights of direct investments. This could be seen as a positive move to enhance CIC's transparency in its business operations.

## New Found Strategies and Confidence

When CIC was established, its focus was mainly to invest in North American and European financial markets. After the initial loss in its maiden investment in the Blackstone Group in 2007, CIC has become more prudent in making investments. The loss turned out to be a blessing in disguise as it had put a halt to CIC overseas acquisitions for a while, thus preventing CIC from making more wrong investments just before the outbreak of the global financial crisis. When the global economy started to show signs of recovery, CIC stepped up its investment activities and made around US$58 billion worth of new investments.

The global financial and economic crisis which started in 2008 has presented new investment opportunities for CIC. It has since increased its equity shareholdings in certain foreign markets and diversified its portfolio. For example, despite the initial paper loss, CIC struck a deal with Blackstone, allowing it to increase its stakes to 12.5%.[14] Also in 2009, CIC took minority stakes in US firms like Morgan Stanley (resulting in an approximately 9.86% equity ownership), which was further increased to US$1.2 billion[15] in June 2009.

Since mid-2008, CIC's investments have shifted gradually from its direct equity investments to investing through third parties. In April 2008, CIC signed a deal with J.C. Flowers & Co. to launch a US$4 billion private equity fund to focus on investments in US financial assets.[16] Some of J.C. Flowers & Co.'s most notable investments include Enstar Group, Shinsei Bank, NIBC Bank N.V., Hypo Real Estate Group (Germany), HSH Nordbank (Germany) and Crump Group.

In 2009, CIC seemed to focus on raw materials and exploration in new energy and renewable energy. Geographically, CIC's investments are in North America, Southeast Asia, Central Asia and

---

an executive development programme with the Beijing University for middle and senior level managers. CIC also has a programme in place to improve the teaching abilities of staff so as to strengthen the quality of programmes taught.

[13] The annual report was prepared in accordance with requirements by the China Accounting Standards for Business Enterprises issued by the Ministry of Finance in 2006, which converges with International Financial Reporting Standards. Financial statements disclosed in the 2008 annual report included consolidated Income Statement of the year ended 31 December 2008 and consolidated Balance Sheet as of 31 December 2008 audited by its independent auditors.

[14] "China Ready to Place Bets on Hedge Funds", *Wall Street Journal*, 19 June 2009, at <http://online.wsj.com/article/SB124535652071428705.htm> (accessed 5 July 2012).

[15] "CIC Purchases $1.2 billion Morgan Stanley Common Stock", CIC's Website News Release, 2 June 2009, at <http://www.china-inv.cn/cicen/resources/news_20090828_442031.html> (accessed 5 July 2012).

[16] "China's CIC to Launch $4 billion Fund with JC Flowers", *Reuters*, 3 April 2008, at <http://www.reuters.com/article/idUSN0332446920080403 > (accessed 5 July 2012).

Russia. Its investment in Teck Resources Limited is listed in Canada; JSC KazMunaiGas Exploration Production listed in Kazakhstan; and PT Bumi Resources Tbk listed in Indonesia. These investments are principally in raw materials, mining, natural gas and oil exploration.

Since late 2009, CIC has also begun to invest in new energy and renewable energy. In November 2009, CIC invested in AES Corporation and Noble Group Limited.[17] Both companies deal with energy products. In the same month, CIC signed a binding framework agreement with GCL-Poly Energy Holdings Limited. With an investment of around HK$5.5 billion, CIC has an approximate 20% stake in GCL-Poly. CIC and GCL-Poly are in discussion to work on a joint venture to develop solar photovoltaic projects.

On 12 February 2010, CIC and Intel Capital announced their strategic collaboration on global technology innovation investments.[18] The agreement, which intended to pair the resources of CIC with the technology expertise of Intel Capital, is set to identify and support strategic investments in pioneering companies across a wide array of technology sectors including clean technology, software and services, and ultra-mobility[19] and digital homes.

In 2010, CIC even expanded the scope of its alternative investments to include commodities, as well as private equities, real estate, hedge funds and direct concentrated investments. Some of CIC's direct significant investments now include investments in AES Corporation, Chesapeake Energy, Penn West, Peace River Oil Partnership and BTG Pactual.

In January 2011, CIC's Board of Directors decided to extend CIC's investment horizon to 10 years. This change allows CIC to come up with long-term plans, invest over longer horizons, and accept a higher risk-return profile in its investment portfolio so that it can better balance short-term pressure and long-term interests.[20]

In order to better manage its portfolio, CIC established a subsidiary CIC International (Hong Kong) Co. in Hong Kong in 2010. Lawrence Lau, a prominent Hong Kong economics professor and former member of CIC's international advisory council, was appointed the chairman.[21] In January 2011, CIC opened its first representative office in Toronto, Canada. With Felix Chee as the chief representative officer, the office seeks to enhance CIC's cooperation with local companies and promote its overall investment business in Canada.[22]

## CIC Extending its Outreach

There are possibilities that CIC will expand its investment scope to include markets in the United States and Europe which it initially shunned in 2009. Although CIC has stated that it will

---

[17] Noble Group was said to have purchased the shares of an American company, USEC, on the open market between 25 May and 2 June 2010. Noble wants to become USEC's partner in marketing enriched uranium for reactors in Asia, particularly in China; for years, USEC already has American regulatory clearance to sell enriched uranium to mainland China, but has not actively pursued such sales. China could prove to be a ready buyer of USEC's products to fuel its ravenous energy needs. Also see 'Fuel Maker for Reactors Has China as Investor', *New York Times*, 18 June 2010. Available at <http://www.nytimes.com/2010/06/19/business/global/19nuke.html?_r=1&ref=china_investment_corporation> (accessed 5 July 2012).

[18] "Intel Capital and China Investment Corporation Announce Collaboration Agreement", Intel Capital Press Release, 12 February 2010, <http://www.intel.com/capital/news/releases/100211.htm> (accessed 5 July 2012).

[19] At the end of 2009, Intel® has reorganised its business to better align its major product groups around the core competencies of Intel® architecture and manufacturing operations. The Ultra-Mobility–business segment is devoted to developing the next-generation handheld device using low-power Intel architecture-based products. See Intel® website <http://www.intc.com/corpInfo.cfm> (accessed 15 February 2012).

[20] See footnote 4.

[21] "CIC Launches Hong Kong Subsidiary", FT.com, 19 October 2010, at <http://www.ft.com/intl/cms/s/0/90f5bb38-dba0–11df-a1df-00144feabdc0.html#axzz1pHSFV6nt> (accessed 5 July 2012).

[22] "CIC Opens Toronto Office", People's Daily online, 22 January 2011, at <http://english.peopledaily.com.cn/90001/90778/90859/7269319.html> (accessed 5 July 2012).

avoid investing in overseas strategic industries, Lou noted that China can help accelerate the economic growth of Western developed countries by boosting investments in infrastructure as an equity investor.[23] In January 2012, CIC acquired an approximate 8.68% stake in Thames Water, Britain's largest water and sewerage company.[24]

As for now, CIC is still very cautious with its investments and is seen as a "meaningful experiment" for China. CIC restructured its corporate operations in late 2010 with the establishment of CIC International to solely focus on overseas investments. CIC International is separated from Central Huijin and both units operate as direct subsidiaries under the control of CIC. As Central Huijin's large stakes in state-owned Chinese banks experience some regulatory obstacles regarding fund issues when investing abroad, the establishment of CIC International and subsequent reshuffling can help remove these hurdles.[25]

In late 2011, CIC received a new US$30 billion funding from an arm of the PBOC for its overseas investments, apparently for CIC International. CIC is working on a system through which the SWF will get continuous funding from the Chinese government which potentially plays a bigger role in helping to diversify the country's vast foreign exchange reserves. Access to regular funding would enable CIC to take advantage of opportunities as they arise. Talks on how to provide capital to CIC come amid a once-in-a-decade leadership transition in China slated for late 2012. Chinese Premier Wen Jiabao has singled out better management of China's foreign exchange reserves as a priority for the financial sector. Given the size of China's foreign exchange reserves, that emphasis is likely to continue after the new leadership takes over.[26]

---

[23] "China can Help West Build Economic Growth", FT.com, 27 November 2011, at <http://www.ft.com/intl/cms/s/0/e3c5aacc-18ed-11e1-92d8-00144feabdc0.html#axzz1oRWSKqkL> (accessed 5 July 2012).

[24] "China's Wealth Fund Buys Stake in British Utility", New York Times online, 20 January 2012, at <http://dealbook.nytimes.com/2012/01/20/chinas-sovereign-wealth-fund-buys-minority-stake-in-british-utility/> (accessed 5 July 2012).

[25] "Q&A: China Investment Corp.'s Wang Jianxi", *The Wall Street Journal*, 6 March 2012, <http://blogs.wsj.com/chinarealtime/2012/03/06/qa-china-investment-corp-s-wang-jianxi/> (accessed 5 July 2012).

[26] "China's CIC Works on Funding Mechanism", *The Wall Street Journal*, 6 March 2012, <http://online.wsj.com/article/SB10001424052970203458604577264754184612504.html> (accessed 5 July 2012).

# 22

# China's Economy Remains Highly Export-Oriented

Sarah Y TONG*

*A sharp decline in trade due to global economic crisis affected China's economy considerably. Measures have been taken to sustain growth, while structural imbalances continued. Rising production costs and looming protectionism will force China to re-orientate its economy towards domestic consumption.*

With an annual growth rate of 17% since 1978, trade expansion has been important to China's growth over the past three decades. Since the early 2000s, trade expansion had further accelerated, achieving an annual growth rate of 26% between 2001 and 2008. Consequently, China has become a leading trading nation, as it ranked number one in exports and number two in imports in 2009, accounting for 9.6% and 7.9% of the world's total exports and imports, respectively.[1] Trade-to-GDP ratio also went up, from around 10% in 1978 to about 30% in the early 1990s and further to over 65% in 2006.[2]

More importantly, external demand has become a significant engine for China's economic growth in recent years. Net export to GDP ratio rose from less than 3% in the early 2000s to around 8% between 2006 and 2008 (Figure 1), only to plummet to around 4% in 2009 and 2010, which was still well above the pre-2005 10-year average of 2.7%.[3] Between 2005 and 2007, net exports

---

* Sarah Y TONG is Senior Research Fellow at the East Asian Institute, National University of Singapore.

[1] In 2010, China's share in world total export and import rose further, to 10.4% and 9.1%, respectively. See *China Statistical Yearbook 2011*, China Statistics Press, Beijing.

[2] Since 2007, China's trade to GDP ratio has declined, to 63% in 2007, 57% in 2008 and more sharply to 44% in 2009, before recovering slightly to 50% in 2010. See *China Statistical Yearbook*, various issues, China Statistics Press, Beijing.

[3] The net export (trade surplus) dropped by 15% in 2011 and was estimated to amount to only 2.1% of China's GDP for the year.

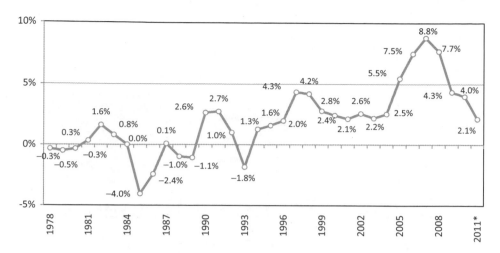

**Figure 1**    China's Net Export to GDP Ratio, 1978–2011

*Note:*estimated by the author.

*Source*: Web CEIC Data Management, Statistical Communiqué on the 2011 National Economic and Social Development, 22 February 2012.

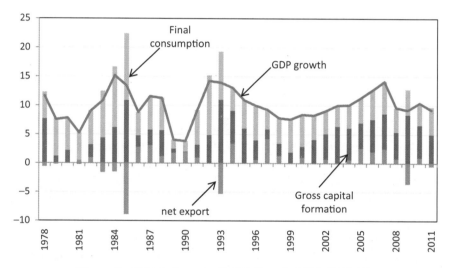

**Figure 2**    China's Sources of GDP Growth, 1978–2010 (%)

*Source*: Web CEIC Data Management.

contributed around one-fifth of China's annual economic growth (Figure 2).[4] Moreover, export is crucial for developing China's industries and generating employment. In 2009, 14% of China's industrial sales revenue came from exports. According to the Ministry of Commerce, export-related activities supported over 100 million employment in 2008.[5]

In addition, trade is an important source of productivity improvement, through realising economy of scale, intense competition, technology transfer and the inflow of export-related foreign investment. For example, export-orientation has been crucial for the expansion of industries such as the "manufacturing of communications equipment, computers and other electronic equipment", which accounted for over one-third of China's total export (38%) in 2009.

The importance of trade is also reflected in the negative drag on the overall growth by a sharp decline in trade activities since late 2008. As export demand was disappearing, growth of industrial

---

[4]The contribution of net export to GDP growth was 23% (4.4 percentage point) in 2005, 16% (5.6 percentage point) in 2006 and 18% (6.1 percentage point) in 2007.

[5]"Vice Minister Yi Xiaozhun of the Ministry of Commerce: China's Overall Economy Achieved Stable Development", 6 December 2008, at <http://finance.sina.com.cn/hy/20081206/09595599742.shtml> (accessed April 2012).

value-added declined sharply, from 15% in 2007 to less than 9.9% in 2008 and 8.7% in 2009, causing GDP growth to decelerate to below 9.6% in 2008 and 9.2% in 2009, from 14.2% in 2007.

The negative impact of the drastic export demand reduction was most serious in sectors and regions that are more export-oriented. China's most export-dependent industries are in the "manufacture of communications equipment, computers, and other electronic equipment", whose export amounted to over two-thirds of total sale (in 2009).[6] In 2009, the industry was also among the worst affected, where employment contracted by 2%, nominal output value grew by less than 2%, and real value-added grew by 5.3%.

Similarly, the global economic downturn and the resultant drop in demand for China's exports affected the coastal regions that are most export-dependent. In 2008, mainland China's top five most export-oriented regions were Guangdong, Fujian and the three Yangtze River Delta (YRD) regions of Shanghai, Zhejiang and Jiangsu, where exports amounted to 25% to 38% of industrial sales revenue.

These regions were also among the worst performers in industrial activities for 2009. For example, while industrial employment declined by 0.1% nationwide, that in Guangdong and the three Yangtze River Delta provinces declined more significantly (by 3.8% in Guangdong, 6.5% in Shanghai, 3.3% in Zhejiang and 7.1% in Jiangsu).

In contrast, regions with the best performance in industrial growth in 2009 were mostly in the inland regions, especially in central China (such as Inner Mongolia, Anhui, Sichuan, Hunan, Hubei and Jilin), that are significantly less export-oriented. Across regions, the growth rate in the number of industrial firms, industrial employment, gross industrial output and industrial value-added are found to negatively correlate with a region's export to sale ratio in industrial activities.

Due in part to concerns over such negative external shocks on the economy, the Chinese government has since the mid-2000s emphasised the need to transform the economy into one that is more consumption-driven. Some policy initiatives, such as lowering the rate of export tax rebate and enacting new labour laws, have been put in place.

Overall, however, considerable restructuring of the economy has not taken place, for mainly two reasons. First, as China's economy was badly hit by the global economic crisis, the quite modest policy initiatives were temporarily put on hold in favour of stimulating growth. Second, economic transformation is categorically a difficult and long-term process, requiring not only good policy designs but also more effective enforcement. For example, to stimulate greater domestic consumption, measures like a higher minimum wage, more effective labour regulations, more flexible exchange rate management and greater enforcement of environmental regulations are equally important.

So far, there is limited evidence showing that the growth pattern of China's economy is changing. Even with three decades of rapid economic growth, China remains a developing country with numerous development challenges, such as widening income gap and the lack of a well-functioning social safety net. As the country continues to industrialise and urbanise, exports, as well as investment, will remain a powerful engine of China's economic growth for the coming years.

## Responding to Sharp Declines in Export Demand

Between late 2008 and late 2009, China's decade-long surging trade expansion came to a grinding halt due to the sharp slowdown of the global economy. As the economies of the United States and the EU — the world's two largest consumer markets — weakened considerably, global demand for imports had also declined sharply. According to the WTO, world merchandise exports grew by a mere 2.2% in 2008, a sharp decline from 8.6% in 2006 and 6.5% in 2007. In the meantime, global GDP growth dropped from 3.5% in 2007 to 1.3% in 2008. Conditions deteriorated further in 2009,

---

[6] Calculated using data from *China Statistical Yearbook 2010* and *China Industry Economy Statistical Yearbook* 2009.

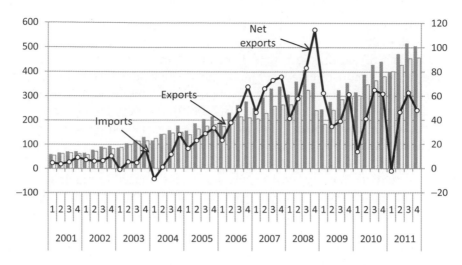

**Figure 3**   China's Quarterly Exports and Imports, 2001–2011 (US$ billion)

*Source*: Web CEIC Data Management; China Customs Statistics, Economic Information & Agency, Hong Kong, December 2011.

when world merchandise exports shrank by 12.2% and global GDP by 2.4%.[7] What is more, imports by the world's major markets, the United States, the EU, and Japan, recorded even sharper declines of 26%, 25% and 28%, respectively for the year.

In late 2008, China's exports began to experience a drastic decline, due mainly to the abrupt downturn in the global demand for import.[8] In November 2008, monthly exports contracted by 2% from that of a year ago, compared to an annual growth of 19% in October 2008. The change was even more drastic for imports, which contracted by 18% in November 2008, a sharp fall from the 15% increase in the previous month.

The downward trend continued in the following months as falls in exports rapidly caught up with sinking imports (Figure 3). The most serious monthly decline occurred in January (in imports) and February (in exports) of 2009. For the first quarter of 2009, exports contracted by 20% on a year-to-year basis, while imports declined by 31% (Figure 4).[9] China's Quarterly Export and Import, 2001–2011.

Trade statistics since February 2009 suggest a moderation in the rapid free fall, as the downward trend stabilised. Nonetheless, in each of the five months between April and August in 2009, exports were more than 20% lower than those in 2008; it was only in September that the contraction in monthly export was narrowed to 15% on a yearly basis. Meanwhile, imports recovered more steadily than exports, with a yearly contraction of around 15% between June and August and around 5% in September and October 2009. As a result, China's trade surplus in 2009 plummeted by over a third from the previous year, to less than US$200 billion.

Faced with a worsening external environment, the Chinese government quickly announced a series of measures to assist troubled exporters and to sustain trade growth. The one single measure that has been utilised most frequently is raising the rate of tax rebate for exports. Other measures implemented include relaxing restriction on process trade, reducing export tax and granting more export licences.

As early as in October 2008, the Chinese government had announced the first increase in export tax rebate rate which took effect on 1 November. Over the following 10 months, five more

---

[7] WTO, *International Trade Statistics 2010*, at <http://www.wto.org/english/res_e/statis_e/its2010_e/its10_toc_e.htm> (accessed April 2012).

[8] It should be noted that several domestic factors, such as rising labour cost and the reduction in the rate of export tax rebate, also contributed to the weakening of China's exports in 2008.

[9] Trade data used in this chapter are mostly from *China Custom Statistics* (various issues), unless otherwise specified.

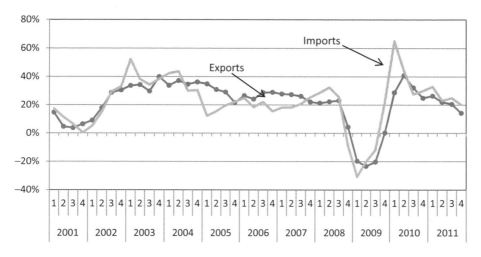

**Figure 4**  China's Quarterly Exports and Imports, Q1 2001 to Q4 2011 Year-on-Year Growth (%)

*Source*: Web CEIC Data Management; China Customs Statistics, Economic Information & Agency, Hong Kong, December 2011.

announcements on tax rebate increase for exports were promulgated by the government. Products covered by these increases are large in number, wide in variety and diverse in technological complexity.[10]

For example, the first increase announced in October 2008 covered mostly labour-intensive products, such as textiles, apparels, toys and plastic products. The second increase announced in November 2008 included many products that are highly export-dependent, such as rubber products, bags, shoes, hats, umbrellas, furniture, bedding, lamps, clocks, glassware, aquatic products, chemical products, as well as machinery and electrical products. The third round of increase announced in December 2008 covered a large number of products in machinery and electronics with relatively high technology intensity and high value-added, such as aviation navigation systems, gyroscopes, ion-ray detectors, nuclear reactors, industrial robots, as well as motorcycles, sewing machines and electric conductors.

The fourth increase announced in February 2009 again focussed on textiles and clothing, while the fifth, announced in March 2009, included products of a wide variety, including consumer electronics, textiles and clothing, chemical products, machine tools and IT products. The final increase, announced in June 2009, covered exports of TV transmission equipment, sewing machines, canned food, juices, electric gear pumps, semi-trailers, various optical components, rugs, bags, shoes, hats, umbrellas, toys, furniture, plastic products, ceramics, glassware and steel products such as steel alloy and steel structures.

Moreover, measures to stimulate process trade have been used to sustain export growth since late 2008. The first announcement came in November 2008 when the government relaxed its various restrictions on process trade initiated in 2007. Two more announcements were made in the following month. In June 2009, the number of products for which process trade was forbidden was further reduced by the government. The government also adjusted its export tax on a number of agricultural and chemical products, where export tax was either eliminated or lowered to facilitate export.

In addition to increasing tax rebate for export, other initiatives have been designed to sustain export and to transform the export structure. In October 2009, for example, a government document, "Comments on Promoting Sustainable Export Growth of China's Automobile", was announced jointly by China's National Development and Reform Commission, Ministry of Commerce, Ministry of Industry and Information Technology, Ministry of Finance, General

---

[10] For some products, the export tax rebate was raised more than once.

Administration of Customs and the National Bureau of Quality Inspection. According to the Comments, auto export is an important element of China's auto industry development and key to China's transformation of its export structure. Since the mid-2008, an increasing number of firms have been granted licences for exporting automobile and motorcycles.

In December 2009, a document, titled "Several Comments on Encouraging Technology Export", was published jointly by the Ministry of Commerce and the Ministry of Science and Technology. Shortly after, in February 2010, the Ministry of Commerce issued 10 technical guides for the export of various products, such as flowers, cosmetics, children's bicycles, household appliances and medical equipment.

In addition to merchandise export, service export was actively promoted by the government. For example, in November 2011, two documents, titled "List of Key National Cultural Exports Items (including 225 items)" and the "Directory of Key National Cultural Exports Enterprises for 2009–2010 (including 211 enterprises)", were published. These formed part of China's efforts to encourage and support exporting firms to compete in the global arena, enhance cultural export and extend the global reach of Chinese culture.

At the regional level, measures were also taken to assist exporting firms, especially in highly export-oriented localities. Take the Pearl River Delta (PRD) region, one of the worst hit in China, for example. Guangdong province has approved a monetary aid of 10 billion *yuan* for SMEs. Of which, 200 million *yuan* will be used to help export-oriented SMEs to expand exports.[11] Similarly in the Yangtze River Delta region, local governments, including those of Shanghai, Jiangsu and Zhejiang, held meetings to make concerted efforts in supporting export firms.

## Rapid Trade Recovery with Modest Structural Changes

Due in part to the various measures implemented by the Chinese government, trade has begun to recover steadily since the second quarter of 2009, with mostly positive quarter to quarter growth in both exports and imports (Figure 3), alongside improvement in global trade.[12] Entering 2010, China's trade continued to improve gradually but steadily and, by the second quarter, it had largely restored to its pre-crisis levels. Trade has since resumed strong growth, to achieve 23% increase year-on-year in 2011.

As the country's trade sector struggles to overcome the difficulties in the global market, the dynamics in the structural changes of China's trade deserve a close examination. This is because, externally, China is one of the most important contributors to global trade imbalances, and internally, adjusting trade structure is one of the government's policy objectives to facilitate sustainable growth.

To do so, the changes in aggregate trade imbalance were first examined. Total trade declined by 14% in 2009, more significantly in exports (16%) than in imports (11%). This resulted in a 34% drop in total trade surplus, from US$298 billion in 2008 to US$196 billion in 2009. In 2010, trade recovered strongly to achieve an annual growth of 35%. Again imports fared better than exports, and grew by 39% and 31%, respectively. Trade surplus hence registered a dip of a modest 6% to US$183 billion. This trend continued in 2011, when exports rose slower (20%) than imports (25%), resulting in another sharp decline (15%) in surplus. The ratio of surplus to total trade continued its downward trend, from 12% in 2007 and 2008 to 9% in 2009, 6% in 2010, and 4% in 2011 (Figure 5), a similar level to that in the early 2000s. This suggests that China is moving gradually but persistently towards a more balanced trade.

---

[11] "Guangdong SMEs to Receive 10 Bnyuan Aid", at <http://www.fibre2fashion.com/news/textile-news/newsdetails.aspx?news_id=66796> (accessed April 2012).

[12] According to the US Bureau of Economic Analysis, for example, imports of goods by the United States dropped drastically from US$556 billion in the third quarter of 2008 to US$464 billion (a 17% decline) in the last quarter of 2008 and further to US$373 billion (another 20% decline) in the first quarter of 2009. It remained at around US$362 billion in the second quarter and rose to US$395 billion in the third quarter of 2009. (Note: The statistics are census-based and seasonally adjusted).

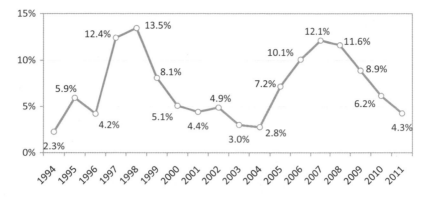

**Figure 5**  Ratio of China's Trade Surplus to Total Trade, 1994–2011

*Sources*: China Customs Statistics, various issues; Economic Information & Agency, Hong Kong.

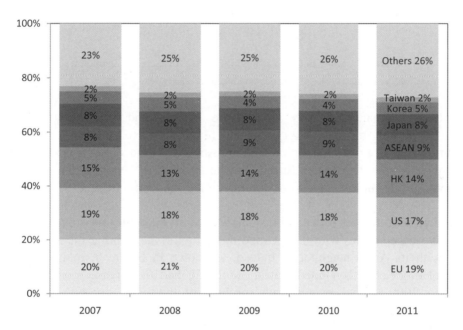

**Figure 6**  Share in China's Exports 2007–2011, Selected Economies

*Sources*: *China Customs Statistics*, various issues; Economic Information & Agency, Hong Kong.

While overall trade imbalance has narrowed both in the absolute amount and as a share to total trade, regional composition remains much skewed.[13] For example, the EU and the United States remain the most important markets for China's exports, accounting for nearly 40% of China's total exports (Figure 6). The relative importance of the two markets to China's exports would be even higher if re-exports through such places like Hong Kong and Singapore are taken into account.[14]

---

[13] Looking at the regional composition, between 2007 and 2010, the share of exports to Europe and North America, as a share of China's total exports, declined by about 1% each, while those of exports to Africa and Latin America rose by roughly 1% and 2%, respectively. On China's imports side, the share of Asia as a whole dropped by 5%, while those of imports from Africa, Europe, Latin America and Oceania all rose by 1% to 2%.

[14] For example, exports to Hong Kong amounted to around 15% of the total. A large portion of these are re-exported to other markets including the EU and the United State. Based on official statistics from Hong Kong, at least one-third of re-exports originating from mainland China were shipped to the US and the EU. Consequently, the EU and the United States may make up close to half of China's exports.

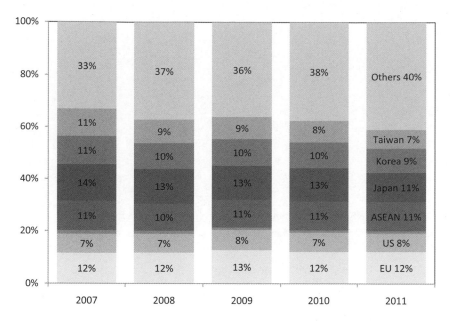

**Figure 7**   Share in China's Imports 2007–2011, Selected Economies

*Sources*: *China Customs Statistics*, various issues; Economic Information & Agency, Hong Kong.

The shares of major Asian economies, Japan, Korea, Taiwan and ASEAN have also been quite stable, jointly accounting for roughly a quarter of China's total exports.

Similar but to a lesser extent, the regional composition of China's import is also highly skewed. China's neighbours, including Japan, Korea, Taiwan and ASEAN, remain the major suppliers of China's imports, while their shares in the total declined modestly, from 47% in 2007 to 38% in 2011 (Figure 7).

The immediate consequence is that, while China's overall trade surplus is narrowing, the country continues to run large surplus with the EU and the United States, and at the same time incurring trade deficit with its Asian neighbours. Indeed, as shown in Figure 8, mainland China's trade surpluses with Hong Kong, the United States, and the EU had all increased considerably in the last two years. From 2009, China's overall trade surplus with the three economies rose from US$409 billion to US$530 billion in 2010 and US$600 billion in 2011. At the same time, China's overall trade deficit with some of its Asian neighbours, including ASEAN4, Taiwan, Korea, and Japan grew sharply from US$174 billion in 2009 to US$255 billion in 2010 and US$269 billion in 2011.

Naturally, persistent trade imbalances with China's key trading partners, especially large surpluses with major export markets, have fuelled growing concerns for increasing trade disputes and possible protectionist measures. In fact, as economic recovery remains weak and job market improvement sluggish, governments in both industrial and developing countries are under increasing pressure to resort to protectionism to safeguard the interests of their domestic industries. Although these governments have repeatedly vowed not to raise trade barriers, many have either announced or implemented measures that are deemed to obstruct trade.

Take the United States as an example. Between April and October 2009, the US Department of Commerce had initiated 12 anti-dumping (AD) or anti-dumping and countervailing duty (CVD) investigations on imports from China, compared to five during the same period in 2008. Five were initiated in October 2009 alone.[15] Between January 2009 and January 2010, a total of 18 ruling against imports from China were announced by the US Department of Commerce.[16]

---

[15] International Trade Administration, US Department of Commerce, "Press Releases 2006–2009", at <http://trade.gov/press/press_releases.asp> (accessed October 2011).

[16] These include both AD and CVD cases. There was a case of negative determination in CVD investigations on imports of certain magnesia carbon bricks from China on 17 December 2009.

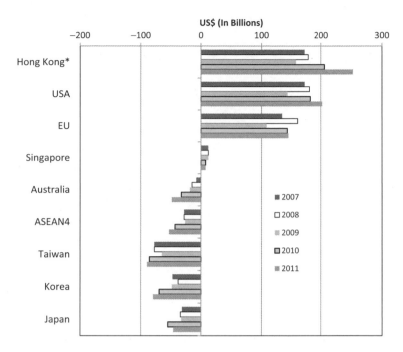

**Figure 8**   China's Trade Balances with Selected Economies, 2007–2011

*Notes*: *A large portion of mainland China's exports to Hong Kong is for re-exporting to other markets, after further processing. ASEAN4 includes Indonesia, Malaysia, the Philippines, and Thailand.

*Sources*: *China Customs Statistics*, various issues; Economic Information & Agency, Hong Kong.

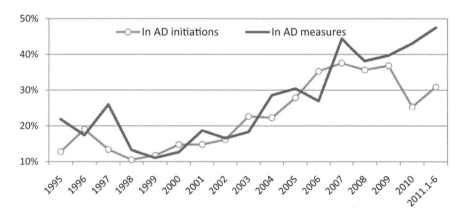

**Figure 9**   China's Share in WTO Anti-Dumping Cases, 1995–2011

*Source*: World Trade Organization, at <http://www.wto.org/english/tratop_e/adp_e/adp_e.htm> (accessed April 2012).

The US-China trade row reflects a global trend towards protectionism. According to the WTO, in 2008 and 2009, there were 213 and 209 anti-dumping initiations, a sharp rise from 165 initiations in 2007. The top three economies that initiated the most anti-dumping cases are India, the United States and the EU, jointly accounting for around 40% of all anti-dumping initiations in recent years. China has become the primary target of WTO anti-dumping cases.

As shown in Figure 9, in late 1995, China was the target of around 11% of AD initiations and measures. The shares rose to 37% for AD initiations (2009) and 48% for AD measures (January to June 2011). In addition to the United States and the EU, China was particularly targeted by India, Turkey and several Latin American countries, such as Argentina, Columbia, Mexico and Peru.

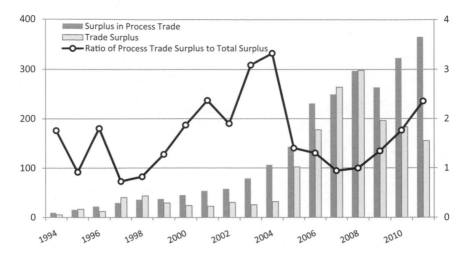

**Figure 10**   China's Trade Balance and Balance in Processing Trade, 1994–2011

*Sources*: China Customs Statistics, various issues; Economic Information & Agency, Hong Kong.

## Deeper Structural Changes to Sustain Growth

Slow economic recovery, sluggish job creation and rising protectionist sentiments in the developed world mean external demand for China's export remains tricky. To sustain healthy growth, China has to restructure its trade and economy, reduce its dependence on domestic fixed-asset investment and export, and strengthen the role of domestic demand.

Some modest changes have occurred in various aspects. In 2009 and 2010, while growth was largely supported by government-led investment boom, consumption had achieved strong growth. Domestic consumption contributed 51% to economic growth in 2011, up from 40% in 2007. Since rapid expansion in fixed-asset investment — which contributed to over 90% of the country growth in 2009 — may not continue, domestic consumption will prove to be more significant in sustaining China's future growth.

Moreover, as the relative importance of process trade has been gradually declining since the mid-2000s, the share of processing exports to total exports dropped from 57% in 2006 to 44% in 2011. Nonetheless, processing trade remains the main source of China's trade surplus, especially in the post-crisis period.

As is shown in Figure 10, the ratio of processing trade balance to total trade balance had dropped from 3.3 in 2004 to 0.9 in 2007, but had since risen to 1.3 in 2009, 1.8 in 2010 and 2.4 in 2011. This means that China's ordinary trade was actually in deficit in the last three years.[17] In recent years, China's processing trade was carried out largely by foreign-invested firms (FIEs), which accounted for around 84% of China's total investment since 2009. Overall, the downward trend of the FIEs' significance in China's trade continues, following a slight increase in 2009 (Figure 11). The relative decline in importance of both processing trade and FIEs is preferred if China is to significantly alter its structural imbalances with its main trading partners and its reliance on cheap labour for exports.

Now, as the global economy may be heading for a slowdown, China could be forced to speed up the restructuring of the economy. First, demand for Chinese products will remain weak from all major economies including the United States, the EU and Japan. Second, slow economic growth and poor employment prospect may prompt governments in the industrial world to use protectionist measures to calm domestic discontent. Third, China may be fast losing its comparative advantage in exports due to increases in domestic production cost and significant currency appreciation.

---

[17] The recent increasing importance of processing trade to balance overall trade is due in part to the Chinese government's relaxation of restrictions on processing trade to sustain trade growth.

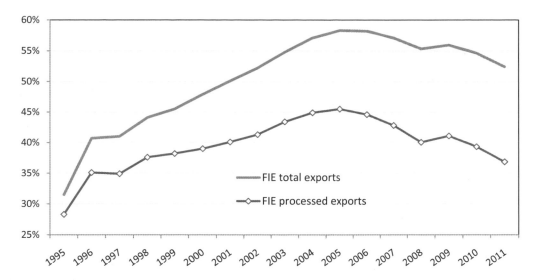

**Figure 11**   Share of FIEs and FIEs' Processing Exports to Total Exports, 1995–2011

*Sources*: *China Customs Statistics*, various issues; Economic Information & Agency, Hong Kong.

According to the Bank of International Settlements, between June 2005 and January 2012, China's trade-weighted real effective exchange rate (REER) had appreciated by nearly 30%.

To facilitate structural changes, earlier measures, such as processing trade restrictions, as well as lower export tax rebate, should be reintroduced. Both are important for industrial upgrading and trade restructuring. Other policies and reforms, such as minimum wage and labour regulations, incentives for R&D activities and tighter enforcement of environmental regulations, are also important and would help stimulate consumption and facilitate industrial restructuring.

To date, however, considerable economic restructuring has not taken place, for mainly two reasons. Economic transformation is a difficult and long-term process requiring not only good policy designs but also effective implementation. For example, to stimulate higher domestic consumption, measures like higher minimum wage, more effective labour regulations, more flexible exchange rate management and greater enforcement of environmental regulations are important.

China, with over three decades of economic growth at breakneck speed, is still a developing country with numerous development challenges, such as widening income gap and the lack of a well-functioning social safety net. As China industrialises and urbanises progressively, exports and investment will continue to be a powerful engine for its economic growth in the coming years.

# 23

# Rethinking the Success of China's High-Tech Exports

XING Yuqing*

*Trade statistics portray China as the largest exporter of high-tech products. The author argues that China's leading position in high-tech exports is a myth created by outdated trade statistics, which are inconsistent with trade based on global supply chains.*

According to a European Commission report, China surpassed the United States, EU-27 and Japan to emerge as the largest exporter of high-tech goods. In 2006, the global share of China's high-tech exports surged to 16.9%, closely followed by the United States at 16.8%, EU-27 at 15% and Japan at 8%.[1] US Census Bureau data show that since 2002, the United States has consistently run a trade deficit with China in advanced technology products. The deficit reached a record high of US$94 billion in 2010.[2] Statistics from the Chinese government present a similar story: high-tech exports reached US$492 billion in 2010, accounting for over one-third of China's total exports.

Until recently, China was not a major player in the global market of high-tech products. Resource- and labour-intensive products had dominated China's exports. In 1995, China accounted for a mere 2.1% of global high-tech exports, equivalent to only 8% of the United States'.[3] With a population of 1.3 billion, it is no surprise that China dominated the global market in labour-intensive products. What is surprising is that in just a decade, China is regarded as the number one exporter of high-tech products. This is even more shocking, given R&D expenditures account for

---

*XING Yuqing is the Director of Capacity Building and Training at the Asian Development Bank Institute and Professor of Economics at the National Graduate Institute for Policy Studies in Tokyo.
[1]Meri, T (2009), "China Passes the EU in High-Tech Exports," *Science and Technology*, Eurostat Statistics in Focus, 25/2009.
[2]US Census Bureau (2011), "U.S. Trade with China in Advanced Technology Products," at <http://www.census.gov/foreign-trade/statistics/product/atp/2010/12/ctryatp/atp5700.htm> (accessed 12 July 2012).
[3]Meri, T (2009), "China passes the EU in high-tech exports," Science and Technology, Eurostat Statistics in Focus, 25/2009.

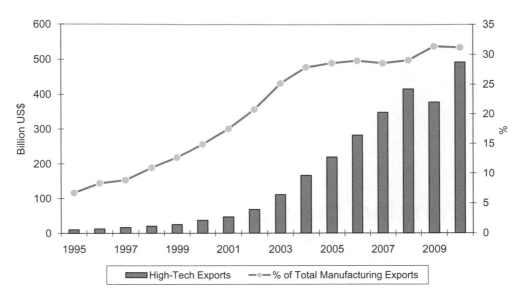

**Figure 1**   China's High-Tech Exports: 1995–2010

*Source*: *Statistics on Science and Technology*, China's Ministry of Science and Technology.

only 1.6% of GDP, and 0.7% R&D intensity.[4] So is China really a high-tech export champion, or is this just a myth?

In this chapter, I analyse the structure of China's high-tech exports and the ownership of firms that export high-tech products, and argue that i) only a fraction of the value-added in high-tech products labelled "Made in China" can be attributed to China; ii) China's real contribution to 80% of reported high-tech exports is labour not technology. This reality check suggests that China's leading position in high-tech exports is indeed a myth that has little to do with technological advancement of indigenous companies. In the next section I will present the official statistics on China's high-tech exports before analysing them in the following section to understand the true nature of China's high-tech exports. The last section will explore the role of FDI and extension of production networks of multinational enterprises (MNEs) in establishing China as the assembly hub of high-tech products.

## Reported Growth of China's High-Tech Exports

China's official statistics on high-tech trade are divided into nine product categories: computers and telecommunications, life science technologies, electronics, computer-integrated manufacturing, aerospace, optical-electronics, biotechnology, materials and others. The classification is jointly published by China's Ministry of Science and Technology and the Ministry of Commerce. The high-tech category is comparable with US trade statistics on advanced technology products.

Figure 1 shows the trend in China's high-tech exports and its share in total manufacturing exports from 1995 to 2010. In 1995, the value of high-tech exports amounted to US$10.1 billion, making up about 6.8% of total exports. From 1995 to 2010, high-tech exports grew 30% annually, much faster than the growth of overall exports. In 2010, high-tech exports totalled US$492.4 billion, accounting for 31.2% of total manufacturing exports. Before 2004, China consistently had a trade deficit in high-tech products. The rapid expansion of high-tech exports turned the trade deficit to surplus. In 2010, trade surplus in high-tech products surged to US$79.6 billion, making up 43% of China's total trade surplus.

---

[4]Tong S and Zhu J (2009), "China's Rapidly Growing Enterprise-led Innovation System, *EAI Background Brief.*, no. 461, East Asian Institute, National University of Singapore.

**Table 1**   China's High-Tech Trade by Categories, 2010

| Technologies | Exports Value (US$ billion) | Share (%) | Imports Value (US$ billion) | Share (%) | Trade Balance Value (US$ billion) |
|---|---|---|---|---|---|
| Computer and Telecommunications | 356.0 | 72.3 | 93.7 | 22.7 | 262.3 |
| Life Science technologies | 13.9 | 2.8 | 11.7 | 2.8 | 2.2 |
| Electronics | 77.5 | 15.7 | 196.2 | 47.5 | −118.7 |
| Computer-Integrated manufacturing | 7.7 | 1.6 | 34.9 | 8.5 | −27.2 |
| Aerospace | 3.5 | 0.7 | 34.9 | 8.5 | −31.4 |
| Optoelectronics | 28.6 | 5.8 | 52.3 | 12.7 | −23.7 |
| Biotechnology | 0.4 | 0.1 | 0.4 | 0.1 | 0 |
| Materials | 4.4 | 0.9 | 5.8 | 1.4 | −1.4 |
| Others | 0.4 | 0.1 | 0.9 | 0.2 | −0.5 |
| Total | 492.3 | 100 | 412.7 | 100 | 79.6 |

Sources: *Statistics on Science and Technology*; China's Ministry of Science and Technology.

Table 1 shows the structure of China's high-tech exports in 2010. Computer and telecommunications equipment and electronics comprise the majority of high-tech exports. Exports in computers and telecommunications totalled US$356 billion, about 72% of total high-tech exports; electronics ranked second with US$77.5 billion. Combined exports in the two categories accounted for almost 90% of total high-tech exports, suggesting that China's high-tech exports were concentrated on limited products.

Of note is the trade in computers and telecommunications which generated US$262 billion surplus in 2010 while the electronics category showed a deficit of US$119 billion. These figures provide some insight into China's so called high-tech trade. Many parts and components used as intermediate inputs for products in the computer and telecommunications category are classified as electronics. This is one of the reasons for the deficit in the electronics category. Global supply chains in Information and Communication Technologies (ICT) are distributed across countries and China is integrated in the low value-added portion of the supply chain. The large share and the surplus in the computer and telecommunications category is consistent with the fact that China is positioned at the last stage of the ICT production chain-assembly and current trade statistics ascribe to the entire value of an assembled high-tech product to the country shipping the product abroad. This, I argue is the reason behind the myth of China's number one status in high-tech exports. I will discuss these issues in more detail in the next section.

## High-Tech or Assembled High-Tech Products?

Chinese Customs classifies trade into two major categories: processing and ordinary trade. Processing trade involves importing parts and components as intermediate inputs, processing and assembling these intermediate inputs into finished products and re-exporting the processed products to the global market. Processed exports use both imported and domestically produced parts and components. The share of domestically made contents determines the domestic value-added towards exports. In 2010, processing trade accounted for over 40% of China's total trade.[5]

Due to the lack of technological advantages, processing trade has been the major form of high-tech exports from China since the early 1990s (Figure 2). In 1993, China exported US$4 billion

[5]China's Customs Statistics, 2010 no. 12 (December), General Administration of Customs of the PR China.

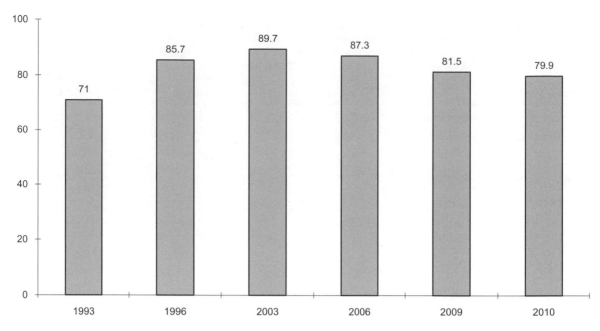

**Figure 2**    Processing Exports as a Percentage of Total High-Tech Exports

*Source*: *Statistics on Science and Technology*, China's Ministry of Science and Technology.

high-tech products, of which processing exports accounted for 71%. As more and more foreign firms have relocated labour-intensive segments of their production-chain to China and utilised China as an export platform, the share of processing exports in high-tech products grew dramatically reaching almost 90% in 2003. The share of processing exports declined slightly to 80% in 2010, but remains dominant in China's high-tech exports.

When these assembled high-tech products are shipped abroad, the Chinese Customs classifies them as high-tech exports, regardless of whether China's contribution was in labour or technology. The entire value of the assembled high-tech product is credited to China even if most of the key parts and components were imported. Therefore, the current trade statistics are misleading and they greatly inflate China's exports in high-tech products.

The series of i-products designed by Apple are a typical example. All iPods, iPhones and iPads are exclusively assembled in China. The role of Chinese workers in the global supply chain of i-products is simply to screw all parts together and make ready-to-use i-products and ship them to the world market. When these ready-to-use i-products leave Chinese ports, they are classified as high-tech exports and all value-added are fully credited to China. A false trade pattern is created by these trade statistics: China, a developing country exports high-tech products, while developed countries such as Japan and the United States import high-tech products invented by themselves.

Given the nature of current trade statistics, an interesting question is, what is the value-added by Chinese workers in high-tech exports? In other words, to what extent do current trade statistics inflate China's high-tech export value? I will use the iPhone and laptop PCs, both of which belong to the computers and information technology category, to answer these questions.

In 2009 China exported 25.7 million 3G iPhones at US$179 per unit (Table 2).[6] Total iPhone export is valued at US$4.6 billion, making up 1.2% of China's high-tech exports. The value-added by China is only US$6.5 per iPhone and the rest is attributed to imported parts and components from Germany, Japan, Korea and the United States. This implies that the total value-added iPhone exports from China were only US$167 million, or about 3.6% of the attributed US$4.6 billion.

---

[6]Xing Y and N Detert (2010), "How the iPhone Widens the US Trade Deficit with the PRC," *ADBI Working Paper* No. 257, Tokyo: Asian Development Bank Institute.

**Table 2** China's iPhone and Laptop PC Exports, 2009

|  | Volume (million) | Unit Price | Export Value (million US$) | Unit Value-Added by China* | Export by Value-Added (million US$) |
|---|---|---|---|---|---|
| iPhone | 25.7 | $179 | 4,600 | $6.5 | 167 |
| Laptop PCs | 108.5 | $484 | 52,514 | $14.5 | 1,573 |

*Note*: *Assembling costs only.

*Sources*: Xing and Detert (2010), Dedrick, Kraemer and Linden (2010), Taiwan *Information Industry Yearbook 2010*, Market Intelligence Center and the author's estimations.

In the case of a laptop PC, China is the number one laptop PC maker in the world. In 2009, it exported 108.5 million laptop PCs at an average selling price of US$484 per unit.[7] Total laptop PC exports amounted to US$52.5 billion, contributing 14% to its total high-tech exports. Dedrick, Kraemer and Linden[8] estimate that assembly represents just 3% of the entire manufacturing cost of a laptop PC. Using this estimate as a reference, the value-added per laptop PC by Chinese workers would be US$14.5 and China's total value-added exports of laptop PCs would amount to US$1.6 billion, just 3% of the total attributed to China.

As the iPhone and laptop PCs made up only 15% of China's high-tech exports, it is not appropriate to use the low valued-added in these two products to draw a general conclusion for all high-tech exports. However, given that 72% of high-tech exports belong to the category of computers and communication technology, and 80% are assembled with imported parts and components, there is no doubt that current trade statistics have greatly exaggerated the value of high-tech exports. It is also misleading to claim that China is a global leader in high-tech trade. Trade statistics fail to identify the country of origin of key technology contents and erroneously depict China as the number one high-tech exporter. To accurately describe China's position in global high-tech trade, a value-added approach should be employed with a detailed country distribution of the value-chain.

Even if the value-added approach was adopted, whether assembling high-tech products should be considered as advanced technology remains a question for debate. Assembling parts and components into finished products only requires low-skill labour and is no different from manufacturing of other labour-intensive goods. The contribution of Chinese workers to these products is not advanced technology, but labour. High-tech products made of key imported parts and components should thus be called "assembled high-tech" and excluded from the high-tech classification.

## Who Produces China's High-Tech Exports?

Another relevant question concerning China's high-tech exports is the major reasons for such a dramatic surge in high-tech exports from US$10 billion to US$492.4 billion in less than two decades. The simple answer is FDI and the extension of production networks of MNEs from Japan, Korea, Taiwan, Singapore and other economies to China.

It is well known that foreign-invested firms have been driving the rapid growth and producing more than half of China's exports. The advancement in production technology and transportation has greatly facilitated the spread of MNE production chains across borders. Conventional specialisation of products has been replaced by specialisation in parts, components and production procedures. In computers, telecommunications and electronics industries, specialisation in parts

---

[7]Market Intelligence Center (MIC), Information Industry Yearbook 2010, Taiwan: Institute for Information Industry, Taiwan.

[8]Dedrick, J, KL Kraemer and G Linden (2010) "Who Profits from Innovation in Global Value Chains? A study of the iPod and notebook PCs." *Industrial and Corporate Change*, vol. 19, no. 1, pp. 81–116.

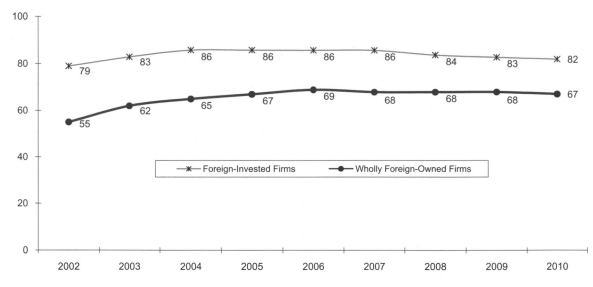

**Figure 3**  Foreign-Invested Firms' Contribution to China's High-Tech Exports (%)

*Sources*: *Statistics on Science and Technology* various issues; China's Ministry of Science and Technology.

and production procedures, and global production networks have been well developed by MNEs especially from Japan, Korea and Taiwan. China's openness to FDI and its rich endowment of labour have attracted MNEs to relocate their product capacities, outsource labour-intensive components and integrate China into their global production networks.

In high-tech products, foreign-invested firms have been playing a more crucial role, dominating China's high-tech exports. Figure 3 shows the contribution of foreign-invested firms to high-tech exports. In 2002, foreign-invested firms produced 79% of high-tech exports while wholly foreign-owned firms 55%. Since then, the dominance of foreign-invested firms has been further strengthened as more and more FDI flowed into China. In 2004, the share of foreign invested firms grew to 86%; and in 2006 the share of wholly foreign-owned increased to 69%.

High-tech exports of the Sino-foreign joint ventures may represent technological advancements of Chinese partners of these ventures. However, technology and production know-how used for producing exports of wholly foreign-owned firms belong to foreign investors and have nothing to do with Chinese indigenous firms. Technological spillover effects might lead to technological progress in local firms; however it is ambiguous to what extent they have benefited from the presence of foreign investors in the high-tech sector. The share of indigenous firms in high-tech exports had been small; furthermore in 2010 it slipped to 17%, four percentage points lower than in 1995. The relatively small share implies that the spillover effects are very limited, if any, and indigenous firms are far from being a real competitor to multinational firms in industrialised countries.

Among the foreign investors, Taiwanese IT companies made a major contribution to the rapid expansion of China's high-tech exports in the ICT sector. As indicated in Table 1, computer, telecommunications and electronics products represent the largest category in high-tech exports; close to 90% of China's high-tech exports belong to this category. Relocation of production facilities from Taiwan to China has helped China emerge as a leading IT exporter in the world. The relocation simply transplanted the success of Taiwan's semiconductors to mainland China.

Since 1980, Taiwan has developed technology and production capacities in the semiconductor and information technology industry. Taiwanese companies have become the largest original equipment manufacturers (OEM) and original design manufacturers (ODM) for leading international IT firms such as IBM, DELL, Intel, and SONY etc. OEM and ODM are the major forms of production fragmentation in information and telecommunications industries. As production technologies in IT industries gradually mature and production processes are standardised, IT

**Table 3**    Stylised Facts of Taiwanese-Owned IT Companies, 2007

| | Laptop PCs | Desktop PCs | Motherboard | LCD Monitor for PCs | Servers | Digital Camera |
|---|---|---|---|---|---|---|
| Rank in Market Share | 1 | 2 | 1 | 1 | 2 | 2 |
| Annual Output (1,000 units) | 90,165 | 46,055 | 149,097 | 117,539 | 2,950 | 49,896 |
| Global Market Share (%) | 92.8 | 32.6 | 97.2 | 70.2 | 35.2 | 42.2 |
| Exports* as percentage of output | 91.5 | 82.8 | 73.7 | 80.5 | 89.4 | 95 |

*Note*: *Exports consist of all sales outside of mainland China and Taiwan.
*Source*: *Taiwan Information Industry Yearbook 2008*, Market Intelligence Center.

**Table 4**    Shares of Major IT Products by Taiwan and Made in Mainland China (%)

| | Laptop PCs | Desktop PCs | Motherboards | Servers | LCD Monitors for PCs | Digital Cameras |
|---|---|---|---|---|---|---|
| 2003 | 54.3 | 51.7 | 73.9 | 21.3 | 79.1 | 89.2 |
| 2004 | 77.8 | 54.1 | 86.2 | 25.0 | 84.6 | 98.0 |
| 2005 | 92.8 | 57.5 | 91.6 | 42.2 | 88.7 | 98.5 |
| 2006 | 96.9 | 63.9 | 94.0 | 53.4 | 90.6 | 99.0 |
| 2007 | 97.8 | 71.7 | 96.4 | 57.5 | 91.5 | 98.0 |

*Sources*: *Taiwan's Information Industry Yearbook*, various issues.

products become commodities rather than high-tech goods. It is then easy to divide production into segments and locate them in different countries.

In terms of global market shares, in 2007, Taiwanese companies ranked number one in laptop computers with more than 90 million units, LCD monitors for PCs with 117.5 million units and motherboards with 149 million units; they also ranked number two in desktop PCs, servers and digital cameras (Table 3). Most of these IT products were sold in markets outside of Taiwan and mainland China. For instance, 95% of digital cameras, 92% of laptops and 89% of servers were exported to overseas markets.

To strengthen their competitiveness and to lower production costs, Taiwanese companies have gradually relocated their production capacities to mainland China. Relocating the production of these products to mainland China immediately increased China's output in IT products and created an ICT growth myth. Specifically, by 2007, 98% of digital cameras made by Taiwan were produced in its mainland China factories; the same could be said of 97.8% of laptop computers, 57% of servers and close to 92% of LCD monitors for PCs (Table 4). All iPhones and iPads sold in the global market are assembled by Foxconn, a Taiwanese-owned firm located in China. By 2009, Taiwanese-IT companies had relocated 95% of their assembling capacities in ICT to mainland China.[9]

Therefore, it is FDI and the outsourcing activities of MNEs that had transformed China into a global high-tech assembling factory. Taiwanese IT companies, the leading global maker in ICT products, performed the most critical role in this transition. The abundant labour resources in mainland China and the direct investment from Taiwan jointly made China a top maker of various ICT products, such as laptop PCs, digital cameras and all trendy i-products.

---

[9]Market Intelligence Center, *Taiwan Information Industry Yearbook* 2010, Taiwan: Institute for Information Industry, Taiwan.

## Myth and Reality

Trade statistics portray that in just a decade, China was transformed from an exporter of labour- and resource-intensive products to become the number one exporter of high-tech products. I argue that China as the number one exporter of high-tech products is a myth created by outdated trade statistics and incorrect product classification. The prevailing trade statistics are inconsistent with trade based on global supply chains and have mistakenly credited entire values of assembled high-tech products to China. China's real contribution to 82% of reported high-tech exports is labour not technology. High-tech products, mainly made of imported parts and components, should be called "Assembled High-Tech". To accurately measure high-tech exports, the value-added approach should be employed with detailed analysis on the value chains distributions across countries. Furthermore, if assembly is the only source of value-added by Chinese workers, in terms of technological contributions, these assembled high-tech exports are no different from labour-intensive products and should be excluded from the high-tech classification.

MNEs, in particular Taiwanese IT firms in China, have performed an important role in the rapid expansion of high-tech exports. The trend of production fragmentation and outsourcing activities of MNEs in information and communication technology has benefited China significantly because of the latter's huge labour endowment. The small share of indigenous firms in high-tech exports implies that China has yet to become a real competitor of the United States, the EU and Japan. That China is the number one high-tech exporter is thus a myth rather than a reality.

# 24

# China's Research and Development

WU Yanrui*

*This chapter presents a critical review of China's research and development (R&D). Specifically it discusses the main achievements, the role of major players and the challenges in China's R&D sector in the future.*

China has maintained high economic growth for over three decades (1978–2011). However, this growth has led to some undesirable environmental consequences which have forced policy makers to seek a new growth model in the coming decades. This model should be innovation- or knowledge-oriented and thus environment-friendly and pro-people. The purpose of this chapter is to present a critical review of China's research and development (R&D) and hence draw policy implications for China's R&D sector in the near future. The rest of the chapter begins with an overview of the trends in China's R&D sector. This is followed by an investigation of the R&D role of Chinese enterprises. Then R&D activities within the industrial sectors are examined. Subsequently, some challenges faced by China's R&D sector are discussed in the final section, concluding the chapter.

## Trends in China's Research and Development Activities

China's three decades of high growth have not only made the country the world's second largest economy but also the number one energy consumer and hence carbon emitter in the world.[1] Severe environmental damages at home and an increasing awareness of global climate changes have forced policy makers to re-chart the growth course of the Chinese economy. For this purpose, China's State Council released a major policy document in 2006 to guide the country's science and technology development in the coming decades.[2] The goal is to make China an innovation-oriented

---

*WU Yanrui is Professor of Economics at UWA Business School, University of Western Australia.
[1] IEA, *World Energy Outlook 2011*, International Energy Agency, 9 November 2011.
[2] The document is titled "*Medium-to-Long Term Program of National Science and Technology Development 2006–2020*" and is available on the Chinese government website <www.gov.cn/zwgk/2006-02/26/content_211553.htm> (accessed 24 January 2012).

society by the year 2020 and a world leading innovator in the longer term. This was echoed in the World Bank report titled *"China 2030: Building a Modern, Harmonious, and Creative High-income Society"* released on 27 February 2012.

The new development strategy was further emphasised in China's 12th Five-Year Programme (FYP, 2011–2015). According to the official policy statement, coastal China will be transformed from the "world factory" to a R&D hub, high-end manufacturing and services. The FYP designates seven strategic emerging industries (SEI) as the drivers for China's future economic development. These industries include clean energy technology, next-generation information technology (IT), biotechnology, high-end equipment manufacturing, alternative energy, new materials and clean energy vehicles. These development goals will be achieved through increased investment in R&D, education and other science and technology activities.

In fact, China's investment in R&D has maintained a steady rate of growth for decades. In recent years, this growth was boosted by the new development policies. For example, during the 2001–2011 period, the average growth rate reached 17.8% per annum which was almost twice as high as that of China's GDP. Among the world's major spenders in R&D, China was ranked number two in 2010 with a total spending of US$178 billion, only behind that of the United States (with a total spending of US$403 billion in purchasing power parity (PPP) terms). China also has the largest R&D research team with a total of about 2.6 million full time equivalent (FTE) researchers in 2010 which was almost twice as many as what the United States had.[3]

R&D expenditure as a proportion of the country's GDP (which is called the R&D intensity) has risen from 0.90% in 2000 to 1.83% in 2011 as shown in Figure 1. This puts China on par with countries such as Belgium, Canada, the Netherlands and the UK. Though China's R&D intensity is still behind those of major players such as the United States (2.79%), Germany (2.82%) and Japan (3.44%), it is well ahead of other large developing economies such as India (0.80%) and Brazil (1.10%).[4] According to China's 12th FYP and medium- to long-term development strategy,

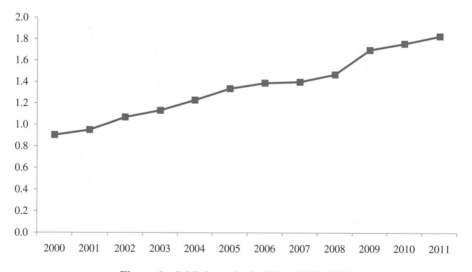

**Figure 1**   R&D Intensity in China, 2000–2011

*Note*: R&D intensity is defined as the ratio (%) of R&D expenditure over GDP.

*Sources*: *China Statistical Yearbook*, various years, China Statistics Press, Beijing; China Social and Economic Statistics Communiqué 2011, National Bureau of Statistics, 22 February 2012.

---

[3]The Chinese personnel data are drawn from *China Statistical Yearbook 2011*, China Statistics Press, Beijing. US personnel statistics are calculated using information obtained from the OECD online database, <www.oecd.org> (accessed 24 January 2011). It is noted that there may be accounting inconsistencies between the two data sources. The R&D spending figures are also drawn from the OECD online database.

[4]Data are drawn from *China Statistical Yearbook of Science and Technology 2011*, compiled by National Statistical Bureau and Ministry of Science and Technology, China Statistics Press, Beijing.

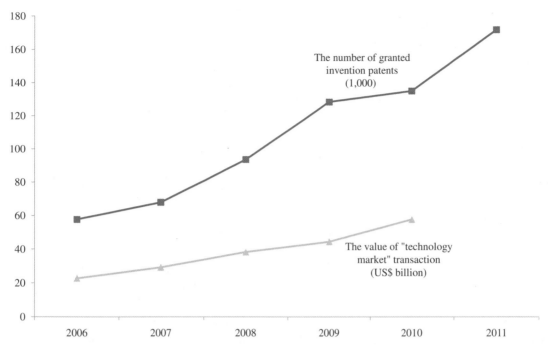

**Figure 2** Invention Patents and Technology Markets

*Note*: The transaction value was converted using the official exchange rates.

*Sources*: *China Statistical Yearbook* 2011; *China Statistical Yearbook of Science and Technology* 2011, China Statistics Press, Beijing; China Social and Economic Statistics Communiqué 2011, National Bureau of Statistics, 22 February 2012.

the country's R&D intensity is to reach 2.20% in 2015 and 2.50% in 2020. Given the current growth trend, these targets are feasible and by then, China's R&D intensity will be closer to those of the United States and Germany.

The increased effort in R&D has boosted China's innovation capacity. For example, the number of invention patents granted in China doubled during the five years from 2006 to 2010 rising from 57,786 to 135,110 items.[5] So did the value of domestic "technology market" transactions (Figure 2). Here the term "technology market" refers to commercial transfers, development, consultations and services associated with technology in China. In addition, Chinese scientists have, since 2007, been ranked number one in terms of the number of publications listed in the popular "Engineering Index".[6]

Apart from the current R&D personnel, there are also about 11.4 million undergraduate students and 0.8 million postgraduate students who are studying sciences, engineering and medicine in Chinese universities. Over 285,000 Chinese students are also studying overseas.[7] These students will potentially add to the pool of R&D researchers and hence further strengthen China's innovation capacity in the coming years.

---

[5]The cited data are drawn from *China Statistical Yearbook 2011*, China Statistics Press, Beijing. For studies of Chinese patent growth, see Hu AG and GH Jefferson, "A Great Wall of Patents: What Is behind China's Recent Patent Explosion?", *Journal of Development Economics*, vol. 90, no. 1, 2009, pp. 57–68, and Li X, "Behind the Recent Surge of Chinese Patenting: An Institutional View", *Research Policy*, vol. 41, no. 1, 2012. pp. 236–249.

[6]*China Statistical Yearbook of Science and Technology 2011*, compiled by National Statistical Bureau and Ministry of Science and Technology, China Statistics Press, Beijing.

[7]This number is reported in *China Statistical Yearbook 2011*, China Statistics Press, Beijing. It may include government-sponsored students only. In reality, there may be more than one million Chinese students studying overseas.

## The Role of the Business Sector in China's R&D

Associated with the expansion in China's R&D capacity is the important role of the business sector including private businesses. Since the mid-1990s, Chinese business enterprises have become the leading players in the country's R&D activities. In 1997, Chinese firms together accounted for 42.9% of the country's R&D spending. However, this figure rose to 60.3% in 2000, 68.4% in 2005 and 73.4% in 2010.[8] It is now in line with the likes of Japan (78.5%), South Korea (75.4%), Sweden (70.5%), Switzerland (73.5%) and the United States (72.6%).[9]

The firms' increased role in R&D is also reflected in the changing share of patents applied by and granted to the enterprise sector over the national total. For example, the share of invention patent applications by firms over the national total increased from 52.7% in 2000 to 64.7% in 2005 and further to 69.2% in 2010.[10] Among the firms, the bulk of R&D activities are conducted by the large and medium-sized enterprises (LMEs). The latter had a population of about one-tenth of the Chinese firms in 2010 while they accounted for about 77% of total R&D expenditure and 68% of the invention patent applications by all firms.[11]

In terms of ownership, domestic firms were responsible for about 74% of R&D expenditure in 2010 with the rest being undertaken by firms with funds from Hong Kong, Macau and Taiwan (9%) and other foreign-invested firms (17%). These shares are inconsistent with the market shares of the three types of firms in the country (see Table 1). For example, foreign-invested firms, particularly those owned or controlled by investors from Hong Kong, Macau and Taiwan (HMT), tend to spend proportionately less on R&D. The HMT-invested firms are highly concentrated in some areas

**Table 1**   R&D Spending Shares (%) by Ownership, 2010

| Ownership | R&D Spending | Employment | Profits |
|---|---|---|---|
| Domestic firms | | | |
| State | 19 | 16 | 14 |
| Private | 10 | 17 | 15 |
| Share-holding | 18 | 10 | 16 |
| Limited liability | 24 | 19 | 19 |
| Others | 3 | 3 | 3 |
| Offshore firms | | | |
| HMT | 9 | 16 | 11 |
| OECD | 17 | 19 | 22 |

*Sources*: Calculated using information from *China Statistical Yearbook of Science and Technology 2011*, compiled by National Statistical Bureau and Ministry of Science and Technology, China Statistics Press, Beijing.

[8]These statistics are drawn from *China Science & Technology Statistics Data Book*, online database, Ministry of Science and Technology, China <www.sts.org.cn> (accessed 24 January 2011), and *China Statistical Communiqué of Science and Technology Spending in 2010* released jointly by National Statistical Bureau, Ministry of Science and Technology and Ministry of Finance, China <www.sts.org.cn> (accessed on 24 January 2011).
[9]These are 2008 statistics reported in *China Statistical Yearbook of Science and Technology 2011*, compiled by National Statistical Bureau and Ministry of Science and Technology, China Statistics Press, Beijing.
[10]Those share figures are drawn from *China Science & Technology Statistics Data Book*, online database, Ministry of Science and Technology, China <www.sts.org.cn> (accessed on 24 January 2011). Chinese patents are officially classified into three categories, namely, invention, design and utility patents.
[11]The invention patent application share is based on the second National R&D Census conducted in 2010 and reported in *China Statistical Yearbook of Science and Technology 2010*, compiled by National Statistical Bureau and Ministry of Science and Technology, China Statistics Press, Beijing.

within the Pearl River Delta region. Thus achieving growth through innovation in those areas is very challenging. In the aftermath of the US sub-prime credit crisis, those regions have been hard hit and will probably need fundamental changes in industrial policies so that innovation efforts can be boosted.

State-owned enterprises (SOEs) were found to spend relatively more on R&D (Table 1). In contrast, domestic privately owned firms were less keen on investing in R&D activities. This situation may be the result of government policies or inherited from the pre-reform system in which SOEs were the key players. These findings were also reported in an empirical study using firm-level data by the author.[12] The same study also showed that a high level of liability or debt burden is detrimental to innovation and that firms with heavy debts are less likely to invest in R&D or be persistent innovators if they do invest in innovation. These firms' R&D intensity is also likely to be lower. This was also observed in other economies such as Japan.[13] Therefore, reducing company debt is vital for improvement in innovation.

## R&D by Sector

There are however considerable variations across the industrial sub-sectors in the Chinese economy. The top 10 sectors with the largest R&D spending in 2010 (these sectors are listed in Table 2) accounted for about 78.9% of total R&D spending within all sectors. In particular, the top four sectors have a combined share of more than 50%. In general, the R&D intensity in these sectors, defined as the ratio of R&D expenditure over total profits, is very high with the exception of the coal mining and washing sectors. On the average, these top players spend much more on R&D activities than other industrial sub-sectors. However, if the intensity is defined as the ratio of

**Table 2**   R&D Spending by the Top 10 Industrial Sectors

| Industrial Sectors | Spending Shares (%) | Spending/ Profits (%) | Spending/ Revenue (%) |
|---|---|---|---|
| Computers, communication etc. | 17.1 | 27.95 | 1.42 |
| Transport equipment | 14.5 | 14.45 | 1.31 |
| Electrical equipment | 10.6 | 19.83 | 1.59 |
| Ferrous metals | 10.0 | 24.00 | 0.88 |
| Chemicals | 6.2 | 13.84 | 1.02 |
| General purpose machinery | 5.9 | 18.24 | 1.59 |
| Special purpose machinery | 5.8 | 22.23 | 2.04 |
| Pharmaceuticals | 3.1 | 14.06 | 1.82 |
| Non-ferrous metals | 3.0 | 12.36 | 0.68 |
| Coal mining and washing | 2.7 | 4.06 | 0.63 |
| Sub-sector average | | 17.10 | 1.30 |
| Overall average | | 11.75 | 0.93 |

*Note*: The statistics refer to large and medium enterprises only. The "average" is the un-weighted mean of relevant groups.

*Source*: *China Statistical Yearbook of Science and Technology 2011*, compiled by the National Statistical Bureau and Ministry of Science and Technology, China Statistics Press, Beijing.

---

[12]Wu Y, "R&D Behaviour in Chinese Firms", Unpublished Manuscript, UWA Business School, 2012.
[13]Ogawa K, "Debt, R&D Investment and technological Progress: A Panel Study of Japanese Manufacturing Firms' Behaviour during the 1990s", *Journal of Japanese and International Economics*, vol. 21, no. 4, 2007, pp. 403–423.

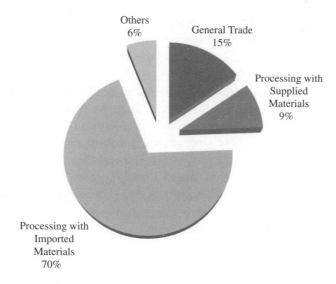

**Figure 3**   High-Tech Product Exports by Trade Mode, 2010

*Source*: The raw data are drawn from *China High-Tech Industry Data Book 2011* compiled by the Ministry of Science and Technology, Beijing <www.sts.org.cn>.

R&D spending over total revenue, three of the top spenders fall behind the industrial average. Thus there is still scope for growth in some sectors.

As expected, the top 10 sectors cover most of the so-called high technology (high-tech) industries, namely pharmaceuticals, medical equipment, computer, electronic and communication equipment and aerospace. China has done exceptionally well in the export of high-tech products. In 2006, the country became the world's largest exporter of high-tech products. In 2009, the value of China's high-tech exports amounted to US$348 billion which was greater than the combined value (US$284 billion) of high-tech exports from Germany and the United States, or the world's second and third largest exporters of high-tech products, respectively. In 2010, China's exports of high-tech products further increased to US$492 billion.[14] However, about 79% of the high-tech product exports were associated with China's processing trade which is overwhelmingly dependent upon imported materials (Figure 3).

Furthermore, China's processing trade is dominated by foreign-invested firms. As a result, solely foreign-invested firms accounted for 67% of China's high-tech exports in 2010 with an additional 16% being exported by Sino-foreign joint ventures (Figure 4). As foreign-owned firms are minor R&D players in China, China's success in high-tech product exports is not driven by indigenous innovation. Researchers have provided further evidence at the micro level to show that China has been very successful in attracting foreign high-tech enterprises and promoting exports but the country's domestic firms are still not competitive in the high-tech product market.[15] Thus it is cheap labour rather than innovation that is the key to the growth of China's high-tech product exports.

Even within the high-tech product sectors, considerable differences exist. Two sectors (electronic and communication equipment, and computers and office equipment), in particular, accounted for 71% of total R&D spending and 94% of the total value of exports in the high-tech product sectors

---

[14]The 2009 statistics are drawn from World Development Indicators 2011, the World Bank, Washington DC <www.worldbank.org> (accessed 24 January 2011). The 2010 figure was sourced from *China High-tech Industry Data Book 2011* compiled by the Ministry of Science and Technology, Beijing <www.sts.org.cn> (accessed 24 January 2011).

[15]Fu D, Wu Y and Tang Y, "Does Innovation Matter for Chinese High-tech Exports? A Firm-level Analysis", *Frontiers of Economics in China*, 2012 (in press).

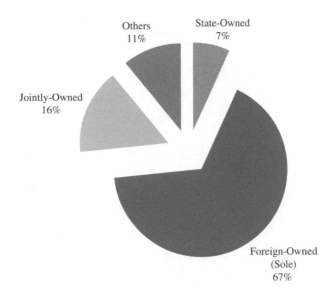

**Figure 4**   High-Tech Product Exports by Ownership, 2010

*Source*: The raw data are drawn from *China High-tech Industry Data Book 2011* compiled by the Ministry of Science and Technology, Beijing <www.sts.org.cn> (accessed 24 January 2011).

in 2010. In addition, high-tech businesses are mainly located in the coastal areas which have a 96% share of the export value and 84% of the R&D spending in the high-tech product sectors.[16]

## Outlook and Challenges

Supported by robust economic growth and government policies, China's investment in R&D as well as innovation capacity is to expand continuously. From an international perspective, it seems that China's R&D spending pattern is to follow those of Japan and South Korea (Figure 5). Given the size of the Chinese economy, it can be anticipated that the country will become a technology leader in the world. Therefore, it can be concluded that within decades, China could become a modern and creative high-income society as advocated in the China 2030 report released by the World Bank on 27 February 2012. However, several challenges will affect the sustainability of China's current growth momentum. First, there is huge disparity across the Chinese regions. Among the 31 administrative regions in China, the R&D intensity defined as the share of R&D expenditures over gross regional product varies from less than 0.5% in three regions to more than 2% in five regions in 2010 (Figure 6). The highest R&D intensity (5.82%) was recorded in Beijing while the lowest was in Tibet (0.29%). This gap adds to the broad regional inequality which is now a major social issue faced by policy makers in the country.

Second, the structure and hence quality of China's R&D has changed in recent years. The combined share of basic and applied research expenditure over total R&D spending declined from 32% in 1995 to 17% in 2010 while this figure is around 50% in major developed economies.[17] Thus, the expanded role of Chinese enterprises may have led to the rapid growth of market-driven R&D investment. The challenge ahead for policy makers is then to ensure that the market-oriented R&D activities would not grow at the expense of long-term innovation capacity building in the country.

---

[16] *China Statistical Yearbook of Science and Technology 2011*, China Statistics Press, Beijing.

[17] These statistics are drawn from "Measuring China's Innovation System: National Specificities and International Comparisons", *STI Working Paper 2009/1*, Statistical Analysis of Science, Technology and Industry, OECD, Paris, and *China Statistical Yearbook of Science and Technology* various years, China Statistics Press, Beijing.

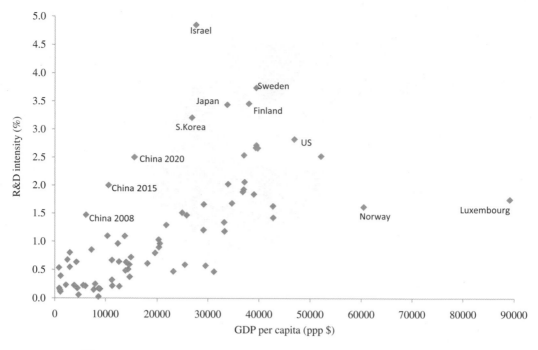

**Figure 5**    R&D Intensity and GDP per capita in Selected Economies, 2008

*Source*: The raw data are drawn from the *World Development Indicators* compiled by the World Bank <www.worldbank.org> (accessed 24 January 2011).

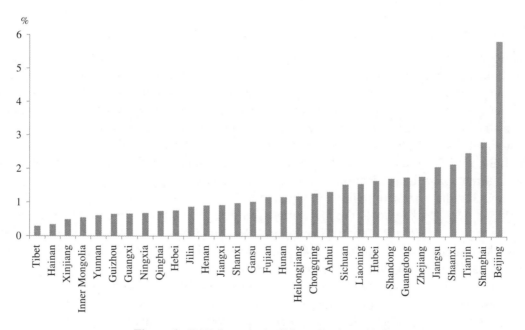

**Figure 6**    R&D Intensity in Chinese Regions, 2010

*Note*: R&D intensity is defined as the ratio (%) of R&D expenditure over gross regional product (GRD).

*Source*: Calculated using data from *China Statistical Yearbook 2011*, China Statistics Press, Beijing.

Third, while the SOEs have invested proportionately more in R&D, it seems that their investment is less efficient. Figure 7 illustrates that private firms have the largest share of invention patent applications though their investment is relatively small (see Table 1). Therefore future policies should aim to provide more incentives for private firms and encourage them to invest more in R&D and promote efficiency improvements in the SOE sectors. This view was also expressed in the

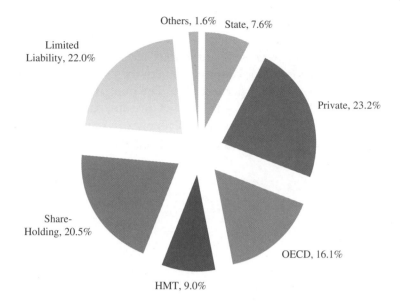

**Figure 7**   Shares of Invention Patent Applications

*Note*: The raw data are based on the second National R&D Census conducted in 2010.

*Source*: Reported in *China Statistical Yearbook of Science and Technology 2010*, compiled by National Statistical Bureau and Ministry of Science and Technology, China Statistics Press, Beijing.

World Bank's China 2030 report released on 27 February 2012. While large and medium firms are important players in China's R&D sector, small enterprises could have the advantage of being potent and flexible in some fields of innovation, and hence should be encouraged to be more active in innovation.[18]

Fourth, labour compensation as a proportion of total R&D costs in China was about 21% in 2007 and 24% in 2010.[19] It is much lower than the OECD average of about 50%.[20] Therefore China still enjoys considerable advantage in labour costs. However, low labour compensation could also make Chinese institutions less attractive in the internationally competitive labour market.

Finally, the protection of intellectual property rights (IPRs) is vital for R&D activities. Though China has made rapid progress and noteworthy achievements in IPR law reforms in the past decades, foreign investors are still concerned about China's enforcement of IPR regulations and laws.[21] The lack of protection of IPRs is detrimental to indigenous innovation too. Thus, more efforts should be made to promote IPR knowledge and awareness in the society, and enforce the related laws and regulations stringently.

## Prospects of China's R&D Sector

In summary, China has made considerable achievements in the R&D sector in terms of investment, capacity building and outcome. Growth in this sector has been particularly strong in recent years due to the support of government policies. China's economic power continues to grow and is expected to overtake the United States to become the world's largest economy in a decade. There is no doubt that China's R&D sector will expand. There are however some challenges ahead.

---

[18]Tong SY and Zhu J, "China's Rapidly Growing Enterprise-led Innovation System", *EAI Background Brief*, no. 461, East Asian Institute, National University of Singapore, 2009.

[19]*China Statistical Yearbook of Science and Technology,* 2008 and 2010, China Statistics Press, Beijing.

[20]"Measuring China's Innovation System: National Specificities and International Comparisons", *STI Working Paper 2009/1*, Statistical Analysis of Science, Technology and Industry, OECD, Paris, 2009.

[21]"Intellectual Property Rights in China: Risk Assessment, Avoidance Strategy and Problem Solving ('The China IPR Guidelines')", The UK China IPR Forum, China-Britain Business Council, 2004.

The business sector dominates China's R&D field with an investment share of over 70%. This phenomenon is reshaping the structure of China's R&D activities. The challenge to policy makers is to ensure that the quality of R&D and hence long-term capacity building would not be compromised due to the expansion of market-oriented activities. SOEs are still major investors in R&D but they suffer from poor efficiency performance. The immediate concern is how to improve efficiency in the SOEs. In the long run, the role of private businesses in R&D should be strengthened. Chinese policy makers will also face challenges in reducing regional inequality and retaining skilled R&D researchers in an internationally competitive market.

# 25

# Are Chinese Small and Medium Enterprises Victims of Institutional Pitfalls?

CHEN Shaofeng*

*China's small and medium enterprises (SMEs) have been operating at a loss in recent years. They face fierce competition from external markets and are victims of institutional pitfalls. The power-directed market economy means the prospect of SMEs is dictated by both market forces and power centres.*

Chinese small and medium enterprises (SMEs) constitute the backbone of China's vibrant economy. The data provided by the National Development and Reform Commission (NDRC) indicates that the over 11 million China's SMEs, which accounted for 99% of enterprises in China, have provided almost 80% of urban employment, contributed to 60% of China's GDP and 50% of national taxes, and created 75% of patents of invention in China.[1]

Nonetheless, this sector has been in the doldrums particularly after the eruption of the global financial tsunami. Although there are debates concerning whether the so-called *"guo jin min tui* manoeuvres (the state ownership advances, the non-state sector retreats)" holds water in China, few would deny that many SMEs are in a predicament in maintaining their operations.[2]

---

*CHEN Shaofeng is Associate Professor of International Political Economy, School of International Studies, Peking University.

[1] Data from *Zhonghua Quanguo Gongshangye lianhehui* (All-China Federation of Industry and Commerce), *Minying Jingji Lanpishu: Zhongguo Minying Jingji Fazhan Baogao,* no. 8 (2010–2011) (Bluebook of Non–State-Owned Economy: Annual Report of Non–State-Owned Economy, no. 8 (2010–2011), Beijing: Shehui kexue Wenxian Chubanshe (Social Sciences Academic Press), 2011, p. 18.
[2] For such debates, see, Wang H and Zhang W, "'*Guo Jin Min Tui' Zhenwei*" (The State Ownership Advances, the Non-state Sector Retreats: True or false), *Zhongguo Jingji Zhoukang (China Economic Weekly),* no. 11, March 2010.

In fact, a large number of SMEs have been reported to be experiencing losses or diminishing marginal profits. A survey conducted by the Research Institute of Ministry of Commerce in Wenzhou reported that more than 25% of the manufacturing enterprises were operating at a loss while only less than 30% of the firms surveyed were enjoying a comfortable profit margin of more than 5%.[3] It was predicted that nearly 20% of SMEs in Zhejiang province and 10% of textile companies in Dongguan, Guangdong province — two strongholds of SMEs in China — would close down in the next three years.[4] After years of robust growth, why are SMEs in this predicament? What are the underlying causes of SMEs' operating difficulties? This chapter aims to analyse the underlying causes from the governance perspective. It is argued that other than the unpredictable external market, Chinese SMEs are also victims of the deep-seated institutional pitfalls, which in a broader sense are in the form of power-directed market economy.[5] This chapter elaborates on these institutional pitfalls by examining government-SMEs relations, the SOEs (state-owned enterprises)–SMEs relations, as well as the influence of the state ownership-dominated financial system on the growth of SMEs.

## Government-SMEs Relations

Apparently the government has the initiative to set tones for its relations with SMEs, the role of SMEs in Chinese economy, and even the nature and scope of SMEs in China. Moreover, defining the types of SMEs is difficult and relying on some conventional indicators like assets, people and operating scale may not be sufficient. In fact, having been shaped by the vicissitudes of the Chinese political economic structure, the concept *per se* is ever changing. Hence, the connotations of SME may differ during different periods of time, much depending on the need of the power centres at different levels. We will review their ties with governments under different periods.

In the initial reform stage, township and village enterprises (TVEs) and those enterprises with collective ownership were the main forces of China's SMEs.[6] The launch of the reform and opening up in the late 1970s coincided with the Chinese eagerness to overcome poverty. Such conditions were very conducive to the growth of SMEs. On the one hand, the lack of basic consumer goods meant China had huge demand. On the other hand, local governments strongly endorsed the growth of SMEs for the sake of expanding local fiscal sources. Increased savings from income and demand, along with the availability of excess rural labour, contributed to the mushrooming of TVEs. Between 1979 and 1993, the share of non-state enterprises in China's total number of enterprises increased from 22% to 57%, most of which were local government-owned TVEs.[7] As private firms were incompatible with socialism, many SMEs had to resort to collective ownership in order to avert any likely political risks. The SMEs did not gain legal status until 1987 at the 13th National Congress of the CCP, which acknowledged that the private sector is a "necessary and helpful supplement to the public economy".

After 1994, SMEs mainly denote private enterprises and some small and medium-sized SOEs. Unlike the external environment before, the milieu where they were in had three changes. First, Deng Xiaoping's southern tour in early 1992 had removed the obstacles for the CCP's plan to

---

[3] "Ministry of Commerce Report Indicate 25% Loss-Making in Wenzhou Manufacturing SMEs", *Caixin News* (Finance News Network), 25 May 2011.

[4] Chen J, "Southern China Sees Wave of Manufacturing Bankruptcies", *Want China Times*, 20 July 2011, at <http://www.wantchinatimes.com/news-subclass-cnt.aspx?id=20110720000115&cid=1202> (accessed 2 July 2012).

[5] Wu Jinglian, a renowned Chinese economist, calls China's economic system a "government-dominated market economy", see Wu J, "'*Zhengfu zhudao xing shich jingji*' de chulu" (The Way Out for 'Government-Dominated Market Economy'), *Banyuetan*, 22 December 2011.

[6] Shi Y, "*Zhong xiao qiye chengfu 30 nian*" (Ups and downs of SMEs in the past 30 years), *Nanfengchuang*, 20 June 2011.

[7] Cheng K-T, "State-owned Enterprise Reform in People's Republic of China", *Pingdong Jiaoyu Daxue Xuebao – Renwen Shehui Lei* (Pingdong Education University Journal <Humanities and Social Sciences>), no. 27, June 2007, p. 4.

embrace a socialist market economy as the goal of China's economic reform. This move provided the necessary conditions for China to begin large-scale economic decentralisation and thus heralded a new chapter in the development of SMEs. Second, with the debut of GDP-ism[8] and the revenue-sharing system, the government became more deeply involved in economic development. Third, as China's economy gradually transformed from a deficit one into a surplus one, exports began to increase and this propelled China's economic growth. By turning their eyes to overseas markets, numerous SMEs found their niche in enhancing local GDP. This embellished local governments' performance, prompting local governments to continue to grant SMEs with land, loans and taxes privileges; the latter also gained an edge in taking advantage of China's depressed labour costs.

But the heydays of SMEs eventually come to an end with the enforcement of the "grasping the big and letting go of the small" (*zhuada fangxiao*) strategy after the mid-1990s.[9] The tenet of this policy was to pool national resources to promote the development of a handful of SOEs while pushing SMEs to the market. In order to cultivate some strong and competitive Chinese flagships, large SOEs were endowed with more privileges including monopoly rights. To achieve the goal of being "big", government officials at all levels often resorted to political and administrative means to create some giant monopolies irrespective of the economic logic and likely social consequences.[10] Figure 1 shows that the average assets of SOEs in 2009 were almost 3.5 times that of 1999. The average asset of state firms was almost 30 times that of non-state firms in 2009, whereas this ratio was merely 8.4 times that in 1999. For small and medium-sized SOEs, however, they were deregulated and pushed to the market in various manners, such as joint ventures, mergers and acquisitions, leasing, contracting, shareholding, or even sold off. By the end of 1996, over half of

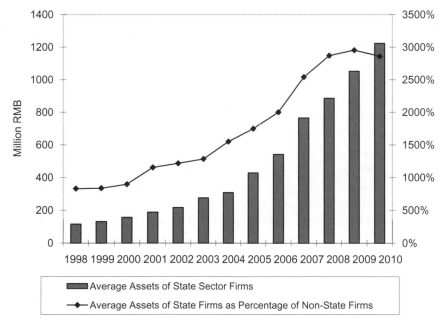

**Figure 1**   The Average Assets of SOEs

*Source*: China Statistical Yearbook 2011.

---

[8] GDP-ism means government officials at different levels pursue policies conducive to GDP growth, irrespective of the social and environmental costs they might bring about.

[9] For a detailed discussion on this strategy, see Zheng Y, *Zhu Rongji Xinzheng: Zhongguogaige de xinmoshi* (Zhu Rongji's New Deal: A New Model for China's Reform), Singapore and New Jersey: Global Publishing Co. INC, 1999, ch. 4.

[10] Zheng Y and Chen M, "China's Recent State-Owned Enterprise Reform and its Social Consequences", *China Policy Institute of the University of Nottingham*, Briefing Series – Issue 23, June 2007.

the small SOEs were privatised. Since then, big SOEs have become a new pet of governments at all levels whereas SMEs have to struggle for a survival in a business milieu that is dominated by government-backed SOEs.

Despite growing concerns and grudges about SOEs' abuses of their monopoly power, the government continued to render strong support for SOEs. In a policy issued in December 2006, the State-Owned Assets Supervision and Administration Commission of the State Council (SASAC) — an official organ representing the state to perform investor's responsibilities — emphasised the importance of consolidating the leading role of the state-owned capital in its micromanagement of the economy and of maintaining an absolute control over important industries and key economic areas.[11] Ian Bremmer has coined a term "state capitalism" to epitomise government policies that champion state-owned firms and sovereign wealth funds; provide state funding to these clients to help them lock in long-term agreements; and use the market to bolster the Chinese government's domestic political positions.[12]

Moreover, as land, water and electricity consumption, market entry and many other resources come under the control of local governments, the success or failure of a SME to a large extent hinges upon the local governments. Many local officials prefer to grant big projects to large enterprises than to small ones since they believe large enterprises would promote local GDP growth.[13] By contrast, many SMEs have to spend a lot of energy and funds to get things done.

The Chinese business environment where the SOEs and SMEs operate, has thus been primarily defined, shaped and controlled by the government in light of its own interest. The fact that the government is above market laws enables it to define the rules of the game involving operations of enterprises, industries and regions, i.e. the government decides the winner and the loser.

## SOEs-SMEs Relations

The significance of SOEs was underscored by former Vice Premier Wu Bangguo who remarked that "[o]ur nation's position in the international economic order will be to a large extent determined by the position of our nation's large enterprises and groups".[14] To that end, the Chinese government has made every effort to promote the development of large SOEs. Actions taken by Beijing are set to influence the Chinese market structure, thereby affecting the business environments of the SMEs.

First, SMEs can hardly get access to those sectors monopolised by SOEs. To ensure their high profit margins, SOEs have been granted monopoly in sectors deemed significant for national security, economic order and social life, ranging from military, telecommunications, railway, aviation and oil to banking, culture, electricity and public transportation. SMEs have thus been deprived of the right of free access to these sectors.

The central government has since recognised the importance of promoting the growth of SMEs. Since 2002, the central government has enacted several laws, regulations and policies, including the Law on the Promotion of SMEs (promulgated in June 2002), Several Opinions on Encouraging, Supporting and Guiding the Development of the Individual, Private and Other Non-Public Ownership (or called Non-Public Economy 36 Articles, promulgated in February 2005) and Several Opinions on Further Promoting the Development of SMEs (No. 36 [2009] of the State

---

[11] SASAC, "Office of the State Council Re-publish 'The Guidance Notice on Promoting the Adjustment of State-owned Assets and Restructuring SOEs' by SASAC", *Guo Ban Fa (2006 )* no. 97, at <http://www.sasac.gov.cn/2006rdzt/2006rdzt_0021/gzw/03/200701150235.htm> (accessed 2 July 2012).

[12] Bremmer, I, *The End of the Free Market: Who Wins the War Between States and Corporations?* New York & London: Penguin Group, 2010.

[13] China SMEs Association and SMEs Research Center at Nankai University, *The Blue Book of Small and Medium Enterprises in China – the Current Situation and Policies (2007–2008)*, Beijing: China Development Press, 2008, p. 253.

[14] Speech made by Vice Premier Wu Bangguo in the Inauguration of the Two Largest Corporations, 27 July 1998. CNPC, *China National Petroleum & Gas Corporation Yearbook 1999*. Beijing: Petroleum Industry Press, 2000.

Council). These documents explicitly state that private enterprises are allowed to enter some sectors monopolised by SOEs, such as banking, railroad, postal service and civil aviation, and relevant government departments are required to treat non-public economy without discrimination in investment approval, financing services, taxation, land use, and so on. However, after years of implementation, SMEs still encounter great difficulties in entering those sectors monopolised by SOEs. During the 2008/9 global financial crisis, the Chinese economy was dealt a blow and many SMEs collapsed. To save the SMEs so as not to stunt China's economic growth, the central government drew up the Several Opinions on Encouraging and Guiding the Healthy Development of Private Investment (also called the New 36 Articles, No.13 [2010] of the State Council), aiming to break industrial monopolies and enlarge non-government investment areas.

Yet, the implementation of these laws and regulations was not smooth sailing. SMEs are held back from those monopolised domains due to obstructions from vested interests — large SOEs and government departments. SOEs and government departments are concerned that SMEs' entry would intensify competition, thus affecting their monopolies on profits and undermining the relevant department's regulatory capacity.

Second, SMEs' space has been squeezed. In implementing "grasping the big" strategy, most SMEs have been taken over or forced to exit the sectors monopolised by large SOEs. As they have a smaller scale of economy, SMEs are liable to become the acquisition targets of big SOEs. When the 2008/9 global financial crisis erupted, in a bid to stimulate the economy, the Chinese government formulated a four trillion *yuan* package and Chinese banks added a seven trillion *yuan* loan, which went mostly to the pockets of SOEs. Funds to SMEs only accounted for 5% or so of the stimulus package.[15] With the new funding, large SOEs have not only consolidated their monopoly, but expanded into other areas such as coal, real estate, steel and iron, and so forth, leading to the heated debate on the so-called "state ownership advances, private ownership withdraws" phenomenon in China. Their enhanced status has generated two ramifications. One, SMEs are in an inferior position when bargaining with SOEs. The latter are price setters whereas the former are price takers. Two, the entry of SOEs into the already competitive industries is a direct menace to the survival of numerous SMEs.

Take the steel and iron industry as an example. The capital chain of many SMEs in this industry was broken as a result of the financial tsunami. Large state-owned steel and iron enterprises seized the opportunity to take over their smaller counterparts. By purchasing 56% of share rights of Ningbo Steel & Iron, Baogang Group has replaced private investors to become the largest shareholder. Taiyuan Steel & Iron Group, a leading enterprise in Shanxi province, acquired Meijin Steel & Iron Co., originally owned by the richest Yao Junliang family in Shanxi. More surprisingly, in 2009 the loss-making Shandong Steel & Iron Group — a large SOE — took over Rizhao Steel & Iron Co. — a very profitable SME. Acquisitions of Haixin Group, the largest private steel and iron company in Shanxi, by Capital Steel & Iron Group are under negotiation. Behind these deals which are in favour of SOEs is the strong support of local governments which prefer SOEs to have a bigger role in the local economy.

To worsen matters, big SOEs are not contented with what they have. They have launched a large-scale expansion into those competitive industries which used to be dominated by private enterprises. Their entry not only aggravates the over-production problem in many industries, but also reduces SMEs position in those competitive areas. In the energy field, many private enterprises like small-scale hydropower plants and coal mines have been eliminated and replaced by state-owned capitals, as evidenced by the practices in Shanxi. In the household electrical appliances market, state ownership had once shrunk, but in recent years, SOEs like Gree and Changhong are regaining their market shares.

Third, large SOEs are also one of the major culprits for pushing up production costs for SMEs. As these giant SOEs are often monopolies and control the upstream supply market of the entire

---

[15] Wu G, *Guozi Miju (The Labyrinth of State-owned Assets)*, Beijing: Renmin University Press, 2010, p. 120.

industrial chain, they raise prices of inputs necessary for SMEs' operations or to pressurise the government to do so. One typical example is the oil giants. In order to gain more initiative in oil prices, both oil giants (CNPC and Sinopec) often work out tight oil provision plans. Such quotas are susceptible to be broken by any unexpected event, resulting in refined oil shortages, thereby creating pressures to raise oil prices. As prices of refined oil are under the control of the NDRC, the latter may not give a timely response to the two giants' request for increasing prices due to other concerns such as inflation and export decline. Oil shortage may continue and spread to other regions. For instance, in September 2003, gasoline and diesel shortages occurred, an opportune time for both the CNPC and Sinopec to request the NDRC to raise oil prices. However, as they could not be perceived as not doing their part to address the oil shortage, the managements of CNPC and Sinopec made the transfer of oil resources from regions with surplus to regions suffering from oil shortage a publicly known affair even though little had been done. The situation eventually went out of hand when a crisis ensued and spread nationwide in November 2003.

One energy expert from CNPC admitted that the oil giants intentionally curbed oil supplies which subsequently contributed to the crisis.[16] It was only when the NDRC raised oil prices did the nationwide oil shortage came under control.[17] Similar phenomena were observed in the years thereafter.

As mentioned earlier, central SOEs are the major recipients of the government's stimulus package. With the funding, SOEs expanded their reach in every nook and corner. For instance, in the real estate sector, private capital used to be the major investors, but SOEs like Baoli, China Merchants Property (*zhaoshang dichan*), COFCO Property (*zhong liang dichan*), *etc* are developing rapidly today. Many SOEs acquire lands at high prices and become land kings (*di wang*). For example, Franshion Property (a branch of Sinochem) became the land king in Beijing, while Baoli Property won such an honour in Chongqing and Nanjing, and CNOOC Property became a land king in Shanghai. The emergence of land kings results in a price surge in real estate.

### China's Financial System and SMEs

The Chinese financial system is also discriminating SMEs. First, there is a systematic bias in China's state ownership-dominated banking and financial system. These institutions are more inclined to allocate funds to large state-owned institutions such as SOEs.[18] SOEs in particular are considered reputable and reliable clients. By contrast, giving loans to SMEs is much more risky. Hence, SMEs are "at a natural disadvantage in competing for loans" with big SOEs. Consequently SMEs have to rely on unofficial lending channels. As a matter of fact, the likelihood of getting loans drops with the size of an enterprise. Statistics show that of the loans given out to SMEs, over 80% are given to medium-sized enterprises with annual sales of more than RMB10 million, whereas those small and micro-sized enterprises, accounting for over 95% of total SMEs, have to seek help from private financing houses of which the interest rates are normally 30% more than official financial institutions.[19] In February 2011, Zhou Dewen, president of the Wenzhou SMEs Promotion Association, estimated that 70% of the city's SMEs could not get loans and have to rely on private sources to finance their daily operations.[20]

Second, ranked first among the economic woes that SMEs are struggling with are higher borrowing costs resulting from a tightening credit policy. Since 2008, China's monetary policy has

---

[16] Chen T and Chen J, "*Shui lai jianguan san da shiyou guatou*" ("Who Can Regulate the Three Petroleum Monopolies?"), *21 Shiji Jingji Baodao* (*21 Century Economic Report*), 30 December 2003.

[17] Ibid.

[18] Hilgers, L, "SMEs in China", *Insight*, April 2009.

[19] All-China Federation of Industry and Commerce, *Bluebook of Non-State-Owned Economy*, ibid., p. 81.

[20] "Wenzhou SME Promotion Association Estimates that 70% of its Member SMEs Running Short of Credit", *First Financial Daily*, 10 February 2011.

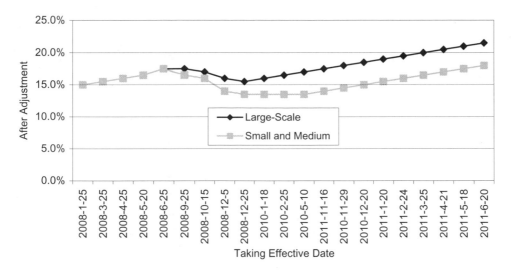

**Figure 2**   Adjustments of Deposit-Reserve Ratio

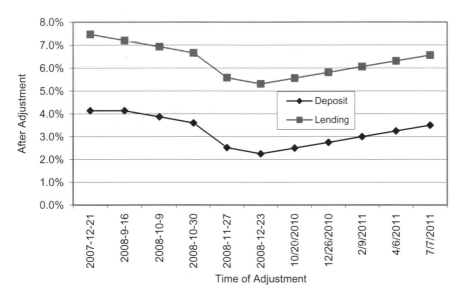

**Figure 3**   Benchmark Interest Rate

already undergone two dramatic turns. In late 2008, the government changed its anti-inflation policy to cope with the financial crisis. When it became apparent that the loose money policy fuelled extraordinary credit expansion and created another wave of inflation in late 2010, the monetary authority made a critical turn towards tightening credit controls instead.

Since January 2010, the People's Bank of China (PBC) has raised the required deposit reserve ratio from 15.5% to 21.5% for large financial institutions and from 13.5% to 18% for small and medium financial institutions (Figure 2). Meanwhile, the benchmark interest rates for one-year deposits and loans have been gradually raised from 2.25% to 3.5% and from 5.31% to 6.56% respectively since October 2010 (Figure 3). The tight credit policy has made it more difficult for SMEs to obtain loans because banks became more conservative when giving out loans to SMEs as the returns are not ensured.

By the end of 2010, the loans issued to SMEs were only 14.3% of the total loan, which was a sharp contrast with the 60% for SOEs.[21] Statistics from the Wenzhou Economic and Trade

---

[21] Hu R, "Zhejiang Private Loan Interests Rate Reaching 30%", *Daily Economic Observer*, 28 May 2011.

Commission show that between January and March 2011 the city's commercial banks made new loans worth a total of RMB23.82 billion, 33.5% lower than that in the same period in 2010. Of the local companies surveyed, 42.9% remarked that they faced financing difficulties after the central bank had further tightened credit controls in 2010.[22]

Credit crunch means bank loans are not only expensive but also not easily available. For official banking institutions, the benchmark interest rate for one-year loans was 6.31% at that time (between 6 April 2011 and 7 July 2011),[23] but the pervading actual rate climbed up to over 10%; for SMEs, the rate usually reached 20%, with the highest even hitting 70%. Moreover, many banks require SMEs to use purchase financial products, pay financial intermediary fees and so on, leading to even higher actual lending rates.[24] SMEs have only limited access to formal financial establishments and depend largely on local private loans, underground banks and self-financing. The tight credit policy drives up borrowing costs as it creates a credit squeeze on all these possible sources of finance. The squeeze is demonstrated in the exorbitant level of monthly interests for private and underground banks loans. Figure 4 shows that the interest rate of private loans in Wenzhou hovered around 24.5% in 2011. Most short-term interest rates ranged between 60% and 72%, and the highest even hit 200%.[25]

## More Measures Needed

The SMEs' plight was largely a result of institutional lapses. The SMEs are marginalised in the government's policy and financial support, and are deprived of the right of free access to sectors monopolised by SOEs, putting them at a grave disadvantage in the Chinese market. The Chinese government is aware of the challenges faced by the SMEs and has promised support, such as allowing greater access to bank loans, granting tax reduction, lowering market access threshold and optimising government procurement mechanisms. To give more support to smaller companies, the Chinese government has redefined SMEs and taken some temporary measures to help them. For instance, those SMEs whose monthly sales fall within RMB5000–20000 are allowed to enjoy value-added tax exemption.

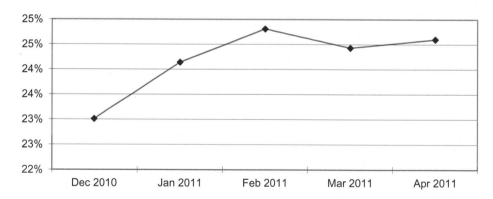

**Figure 4**    Interest Rate in Wenzhou's Private Loan Market

*Source:* Wang X and Lin C, "Financing Is the Biggest Trouble for SMEs", *China Economic Times,* 16 June 2011.

---

[22] Chen J, "Small Firms, Big Problems as Costs Rise," *China Daily*, 29 June 2011.

[23] Since 7 July 2011, the benchmark lending interest rate was further raised to 6.56%, and came back to 6.31% again since 8 June 2012.

[24] Data based on: All-China Federation of Industry and Commerce, *Bluebook of Non-State-Owned Economy*, ibid., p. 80.

[25] Wang X and Lin C, "Financing Becomes the Biggest Trouble for SMEs", *China Economic Times,* 16 June 2011.

In spite of all these measures, it is difficult for SMEs to change the *status quo*. State-owned conglomerates have reinforced their monopoly and have now become political power centres that could fend off even Beijing's efforts to rein them in.[26] Hence, as long as these institutional barriers are not removed, the government's repeated promises of promoting the growth of SMEs are just empty ones.

---

[26]Wine M, "China Fortifies State Businesses to Fuel Growth," *New York Times*, 29 August 2010.

# 26

# China as a Newly Minted Upper Middle Income Country

LU Ding*

*After China's rise to the ranks of upper middle income countries, physical capital formation will inevitably slow down due to the loss or reversal of conditions that used to favour high investment demand and high savings.*

In its *World Development Report 2012,* the World Bank ranks China as "an upper middle income country" for the first time.[1] Considering that the country had been a low income country by the World Bank definition only until a decade ago, this is a remarkable achievement for China. By international comparison, China's economic growth rate over the past three decades has been exceptionally high: It is the only country since 1960 to have ever maintained an annual GDP growth rate of over 8% for three decades. It is also one of the only two countries (with the other being Singapore) to have ever kept the economy growing at over 7% per annum for four decades in the past half a century (Table 1).

At such rates of growth, China has doubled its GDP roughly every seven years and expanded the size of its economy by more than 17 times in just 30 years. Being the world's most populous country with one-fifth of the global inhabitants, China has achieved a prolonged period of hyper economic growth at a scale unmatched by anywhere else in the world. Thirty years ago, China's economy was only one-twentieth of the United States' and it was ranked the 11th largest economy in the world. Now, China has overtaken Japan as the world's second largest economy, with its size more than one third of the United States' measured by nominal GDP or over two-thirds of the latter's as gauged by purchasing power parity. After joining the ranks of upper middle income countries, will China be able to keep its past momentum of hyper economic growth?

---

*LU Ding is Professor and Senior Associate at the University of the Fraser Valley, Canada.
[1] China's per capita Gross National Income (GNI) reached US$4,260 in 2010, which attains the level of upper middle income countries (US$3,976–US$12,275), as defined by the World Bank (World Bank, *World Development Report*, Oxford University Press, January 2012, p. 391).

**Table 1**   Number of Countries with Persistent Fast GDP Growth Performance (1960–2009)

| For at least | Number of Economies with Annual Growth Rate Over | | | | |
|---|---|---|---|---|---|
| | **5%** | **6%** | **7%** | **8%** | **9%** |
| 5 decades | 1[a] | 0 | 0 | 0 | 0 |
| 4 decades | 9 | 5 | 2[b] | 0 | 0 |
| 3 decades | 25 | 10 | 7 | 1[c] | 1[c] |
| 2 decades | 70 | 33 | 16 | 9 | 7 |
| 1 decade | 144 | 107 | 77 | 54 | 35 |

*Notes*: Growth rates are based on average annual rates of 1960–1969, 1970–1979, 1980–1989, 1990–1999 and 2000–2009 for 211 countries or economies. [a] Singapore; [b] China and Singapore; [c] China

*Sources*: World Bank, World dataBank at <http://databank.worldbank.org> (accessed 23 August 2011) and *Taiwan Statistical Data Book*.

## Main Drivers of Growth

A survey of growth accounting studies on China[2] reveals two primary drivers of China's rapid economic growth: physical capital formation and rise of total factor productivity (TFP).[3] For the post-reform years up to the end of 1990s, physical capital growth contributed to 38–63% of GDP growth. For periods since the mid-1990s, the estimates for capital's contribution range from 55% to 67%. When data are adjusted for inconsistencies, physical capital's contribution to growth is even higher. In studies that cover both periods, capital growth is found to have contributed more to aggregate growth since the mid-1990s.

The rapid physical capital formation is backed by China's persistently high and surging investment rate, which is extraordinary by international comparison. China had spent 35% to 50% of its annual income on capital formation in the past three decades (Figure 1). Since the mid-1980s, China's investment rate has been higher than the average lower middle income countries and upper middle income countries by about 10% to 20%. Since the turn of the century, the rate has exhibited a rising trend.

The second largest contributor to GDP growth identified by most growth accounting studies is TFP growth. In the pre-reform central planning period (1950s to 1970s), China's TFP growth used to be minimal or negative. For the post-reform period, significant TFP growth has been observed. A survey of 150 studies of various years and scopes obtained an average TFP growth rate of 3.62% per annum.[4] The more optimistic estimates attribute 30% to 46% of China's growth rates to gains in TFP, equivalent to 3% to 5% of annual GDP growth. The more pessimistic estimates suggest that productivity gains contribute no more than 25% of overall growth. Even in the case of more pessimistic estimates, China's TFP performance was perceived to be respectable.

A main source of TFP growth comes from application of new technologies brought in by physical capital formation. Effective use of new technology in the production process depends on the quality of the labour force, or human capital. China's achievements in literacy rates, life expectancy and primary education provision *etc.*, are remarkably higher than those of most countries at the similar level of development (Figure 2). A number of empirical studies have shown that China's economic growth has benefited from its human capital advantages.

---

[2] Lu D, "Can China Escape the Middle Income Trap?" *EAI Background Brief*, no. 658, 2011.

[3] Economists typically treat an economy's output as determined by a function of production factor inputs, such as capital and labour. Contributions made by changes in these factor inputs to output growth are estimated while the residuals of growth unaccounted for by changes of the factor inputs are interpreted as growth of TFP.

[4] Wu Y, "Total Factor Productivity Growth in China: a Review", *Journal of Chinese Economic and Business Studies*, vol. 9, no. 2, 2011, pp. 111–26.

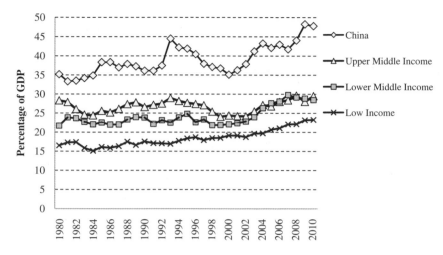

**Figure 1**  Gross Capital Formation

*Source*: World Bank, World dataBank at <http://databank.worldbank.org> (accessed 23 August 2011).

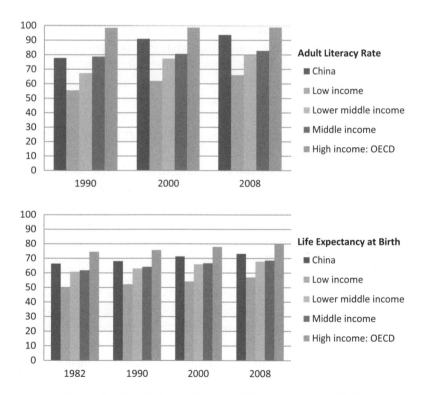

**Figure 2**  Adult Literacy Rates and Life Expectancy at Birth

*Source*: World Bank, World dataBank at <http://databank.worldbank.org> (accessed 23 August 2011).

## Rapid Physical Capital Formation

In the past three decades, both demand-side and supply-side conditions have been extremely favourable to China's rapid physical capital formation. On the supply side, China enjoys the world's highest domestic saving rates (Figure 3). The high saving rates have not only financed the extraordinarily high investment rates but also allowed China to run years of current account surplus that accumulated an immense pool of foreign reserves.

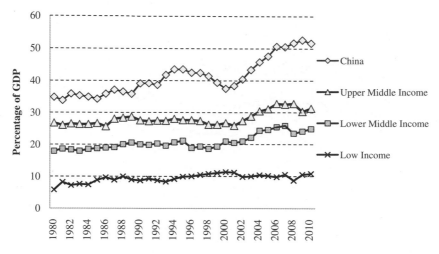

**Figure 3**    Gross Domestic Saving

*Source*: World Bank, World dataBank at <http://databank.worldbank.org> (accessed 23 August 2011).

Why has China enjoyed such persistently high and rising saving rates? Demographics have favoured household savings as the country's dependency ratio has been sharply falling since the early 1970s. Based on the life cycle theory of saving, a larger proportion of working age population with sufficient employment must result in higher saving rates.[5] On the other hand, years of draconian family planning and birth control have resulted in the shortage of marriageable girls. Expectations of fierce competition among households with boys have probably motivated many parents to save more to increase their sons' future chance of marriage.[6]

Since the 1970s, economic reforms have increased opportunities for business and housing investment. Households respond to such opportunities by saving more to overcome credit constraints. Meanwhile, China's successful economic take-off also fuels expectations of rapid future growth and raises the bar for target wealth, which raises current savings. On top of that, the former socialist welfare system was dismantled but the new social safety net has yet to become comprehensive enough to provide the necessary lifetime security. Households therefore have to save more to prepare for catastrophic illnesses and retirement. The privatisation of public housing and the reform of tertiary education in the 1990s have all increased the need to save more for housing purchases and child education.

A phenomenal change in China's saving structure has been the rise of savings by enterprises, which has contributed more to national savings than households did since the early 2000s. The rise of enterprise savings is partially due to the imperfect capital market and rigid banking practices, which make it difficult for firms, especially private firms, to obtain external financing. As a result, a major proportion of business investment has to come from retained earnings (corporate savings). Some of the business savings have also arisen from state-owned enterprises that went through corporatisation, which have not been handing over their earnings to the government since the mid-1990s, and tend to reinvest their profits.[7]

On the demand side, high returns to capital have been the prime cause of high investment. In the early stages of economic reform from 1979 to 1993, China's return on capital was exceptionally

---

[5] Modigliani, F and Cao LS, "The Chinese Saving Puzzle and the Life Cycle Hypothesis", *Journal of Economic Literature*, vol. 42, 2004, pp.145–70.

[6] It is estimated that marriage competition could potentially account for half of the increase in household savings in the 1990–2007 period (Wei S and Zhang X. The Competitive Saving Motive: Evidence from Rising Sex Ratios and Savings Rates in China, *NBER Working Paper,* no.15093, 2009).

[7] Knight, J and Ding S, Why is Investment so High in China? *Economics Series Working Papers*, no 441, University of Oxford, 2009.

high by international comparison.[8] High returns in those years largely arose from the disequilibrium in the economy. When reforms dismantled the centrally planned command system in the 1980s through the 1990s, numerous lucrative opportunities emerged for input reallocation across regions and sectors.

In later years, profitability fell but has since 1998 shown a rising trend with a persistent gap of profitability between state-owned enterprises and private firms.[9] The good returns to capital have been partially supported by the abundance of surplus labour in the rural economy and the institutional changes that have allowed hundreds of millions of rural migrant workers to be employed in urban sectors. The abundance of labour supply had kept wage rates and labour costs low until recently, resulting in high returns to capital.

High investment demand has also been driven by the optimism for sustained growth and rising earnings, prompted by the early success of economic reforms and events like China's accession to the WTO. Better investment climate in the process of market-oriented reforms boosted investors' confidence and created a virtuous cycle for a prolonged investment boom.

Meanwhile, high demand for investment, especially related to government-funded projects, has been politically motivated by the so-called "GDP-ism", the use of local GDP growth rates as a key criterion for officials' evaluation and promotion. This has provided strong incentives for government officials at all levels to push for high investment in public projects for non-business reasons.

**Prospect of Capital Formation**

Some causes of high investment and savings are transitional and not sustainable in the long term. Disequilibria that used to be associated with high returns on capital tend to be less widespread if the market becomes more efficient in reallocating capital. Reforms to improve financial market efficiency will also reduce incentives for excessive enterprise savings. Optimism and rising expectations of fast future growth are self-fulfilling and may be reversed if public perspectives of growth prospects turn negative. Events like the WTO accession and early success of reform are one-time boosts to savings and investment but their impact diminishes over time.

A fundamental change that has prolonged effects on investment and savings is China's demographic transition. Over the past three decades, China has experienced a rapid demographic transition that is highly favourable to savings, investment and human capital development. Before the early 1970s, the high birth rates and falling death rates had contributed to over two decades of fast population growth, which was only briefly interrupted by the 1959–1961 famine. After the launch of family planning programmes in the 1970s, fertility rates started to fall quickly and baby-boomers from earlier decades joined the labour force in droves. The result was a three-decade decline of the overall dependency ratio and an expanding labour force that had grown faster than the population (Figure 4). A series of historical events, including the Great Famine (1959–1962), the Cultural Revolution (1966–1976) and national family planning (since the 1970s), have contributed to a fast demographic transition. The pattern of demographic changes illustrates the concept of "demographic dividends". With falling fertility rates and entry of the earlier baby boomers into the working age, there are fewer young mouths to feed and more youthful workers in the labour force. The working-age population grows at a faster pace than the total population. If the working-age population is sufficiently employed, it will be a big boost to the growth of per capita income. Meanwhile the bulging share of the working adult population also generates higher

[8] Bai C, Hsieh C-T and Qian Y, The Return to Capital in China, *Brookings Papers on Economic Activity*, vol. 32, no. 2, 2006, pp. 61–88.

[9] Lu F, Song G, Tang J, Zhao H and Liu L, "Profitability of China's industrial firms (1978–2006)", *China Economic Journal*, vol. 1, no. 1, 2008, pp. 1–31.

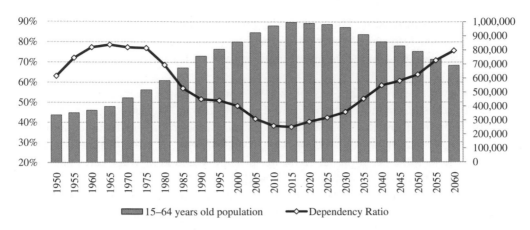

**Figure 4**   China's Working Age Population (15–64 Years Old) and Dependency Ratio

*Source*: United Nations, World Population Prospects (2010).

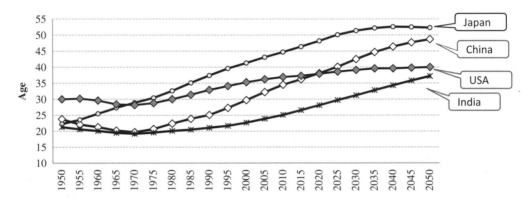

**Figure 5**   Population Median Age

*Source*: United Nations, World Population Prospects (2010).

savings that support investment growth. Such a precious "window of development opportunity" had previously happened to other developed nations, such as Japan and Korea.

In the coming years, this fast demographic transition will enter a new phase with negative impacts on savings and investment. By the mid-2010s, the dependency-ratio curve will soon reach its bottom and will embark on a steep rise while population ageing accelerates in the coming years. Based on the United Nations' projection, China's total labour force will peak around 2015 at about 998 million and will remain at a plateau through the 2020s before falling to 983 million by 2030 (Figure 4). China's population is also fast ageing. As shown in Figure 5, the median age reached its youngest bottom in 1970 at about 20 years old and has been rising ever since, having now reached 34 years old. Until 1995, China's median age had been at least 10 years younger than the United States'. Since then, the gap has been quickly closing up and soon China will have the same median age as the United States' around 2020. The steep rise of the dependency ratio will inevitably have a detrimental effect on household savings. In particular, with a falling fertility rate, the rise of the dependency ratio due to the rapid increase of the elderly population would mean a decreasing need to save for children's future education and boys' advantages in marriage.

Despite the projection that the total working age population will remain large through the 2020s, China's age structure will change drastically. Between 2010 and 2030, the youngest group aged 15–24 will fall by more than one third while the eldest group aged 60–64 will double. The sharp shrinking of the younger cohorts of working age population will cause overall labour participation rates to fall because the new labour market entrants come mainly from those aged below the mid-20s. Since older rural workers are less likely to migrate, the supply of rural labour in urban job markets will also fall with time. With the improvement of the education system, more young people will opt for further education or training before joining the labour force. The participation rates by those aged 15–24 will continue to fall over time. All these changes will result in the rapid shrinking of labour supply, causing the rise of wage rates and labour costs and subsequently, the fall in returns on investment.

The rising burden of supporting a fast growing elderly population together with the constraining effect of a shrinking labour force on the tax revenue base will work to reduce public savings in coming years. Greater public spending on social security and health care to take care of the growing elderly population also means less public money available for investment in many physical infrastructural projects.

## Prospect of TFP Growth

TFP growth may come from efficiency improvement and technological advancement. The former represents gains in output by the more efficient use of existing resources through institutional changes, resource reallocation, microeconomic management improvement etc. The latter requires the expansion of the economy's production capacity by using new technology and new ways of organising production rather than increasing inputs.

In China, efficiency improvement thanks to institutional reforms, market-driven resource reallocation and improvement in micro-economic management was the primary source of TFP growth in the first half of the past three decades. However, some efficiency improvement can be "a one-off gain or a level effect".[10] As economic reforms deepen and market institutions become more developed, the potential in efficiency improvement has gradually been exhausted or marginalised. Technological advancement thus becomes more important in later years and can have a long-lasting effect on growth.

Technological advancement has been driven by the diffusion of technology through inward foreign direct investment and powered by public and private investments in education and R&D. China's superb achievements in human capital development and persistent investment in knowledge creation and technological progress bode well for its future TFP growth. What is worth noting is that China has made significant progress in technological innovation since the turn of the century. Between 1999 and 2007, its R&D expenditure as a percentage of GDP rose from 0.76% to 1.44%, researchers in R&D per million people increased from 422.6 persons to 1,070.9 persons.[11] As a result, the number of China's resident patent applications has increased rapidly and has already overtaken that of the United States since 2009 (Figure 6).

Optimism over continuous efficiency improvement lies in China's low efficiency in many fields by international standards, especially in logistics and distribution systems and financial services.[12] Low efficiency means scope for improvement. Institutional sources of efficiency improvement are therefore far from being exhausted. The current level of urbanisation (with 51% of population residing in urban areas) is still far behind the country's level of industrialisation (with only 10% of GDP produced by the agricultural sector). Urbanisation, which reallocates labour and population from rural to urban sectors, will continue to make tremendous contributions to efficiency improvement.

Demographic trends, however, are not in favour of TFP growth. A fast ageing and shrinking labour force is likely to diminish the economy's growth vigour. As shown in Figure 5, China's median age had already reached 34 years old around 2010, which is about 10 years older than India's. This implies that the labour force median age must have already risen to the mid-40s. With

---

[10] Wu Y, Can China's High Economic Performance be Sustained by Productivity Growth? *EAI Background Brief*, no. 265, 2005.

[11] World Bank, World dataBank, at <http://databank.worldbank.org> (accessed 23 August 2011).

[12] Yu Y, Warranted Optimism on China's Medium-term Growth Prospects. *EAI Background Brief*. no. 282, 2006.

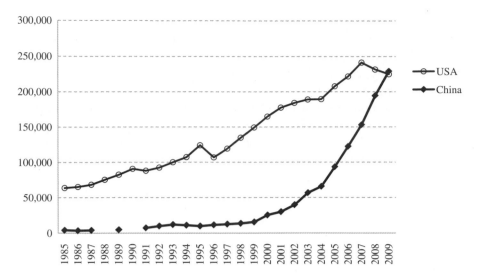

**Figure 6**    Patent Application, Resident

*Source*: World Bank, World dataBank at <http://databank.worldbank.org> (accessed 23 August 2011).

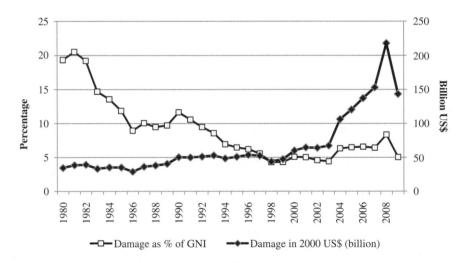

**Figure 7**    China's Environmental Damages

*Note*: Environmental damage is the sum of natural resources depletion, carbon dioxide damage and particulate emission damage.

*Source*: World Bank, World dataBank at <http://databank.worldbank.org> (accessed 23 August 2011).

further ageing of the population, the labour force gets older too. Since above middle-age employees tend to be overpaid for their declining productivity, the overall labour force productivity will inevitably be compromised. That may offset some, if not all, of the momentum of productivity growth driven by efficiency improvements and technological advancements. What is alarming is that China's median age will reach 35.6 by year 2015. That was the level of Japan's median age after 1985, when the country's golden age of fast growth came to its end.

Environmental degradation is another major drag on TFP growth. China's rapid economic growth has been heavily reliant on resource extraction. Environmental damage (the sum of natural resources depletion, carbon dioxide damage and particulate emission damage) has amounted to four to 12% of gross national income (GNI) since the mid-1980s (Figure 7). The fall of this percentage in the 1990s was only due to the fast growth of the whole economy. The magnitude of the damage has been on the rise since the mid-1980s and accelerated since the late 1990s. The drastic rise in recent years has even led to a rebound of its weight in GNI.

Since TFP growth is the residual growth rates which are not accounted for by the growth of computable inputs like capital and labour, China's heavy exploitation and overdraft of natural resources may have ironically "contributed" to its TFP growth in the past years. This pattern of growing by polluting, however, has reached its limit and cannot be sustainable in the future. By 2009, China had already overtaken the United States as the world's largest emitter of greenhouse gases and energy user while its GDP was only one-third of the US level by nominal exchange rates and two-thirds of the US level by purchasing power parity. Based on current trends, China will even surpass the United States in per capita carbon emissions by 2017, well before its projected date of overtaking the United States as the world's largest economy.[13]

Environmental damages have accumulated to a dangerous level: only 1% of the country's 560 million city dwellers breathe air considered safe by the European Union. About 700 million people drink water contaminated with animal and human waste.[14] Just water pollution and scarcity alone knock 2.3% off China's GDP annually.[15] Public protests against polluting projects and events have become more frequent and louder in recent years. In August 2001, for instance, the government in Dalian city was forced to shut down a major petrochemical plant under the pressure of massive protests.[16] With rising per capita income, public awareness of environmental values has been aroused and is increasingly influencing the policy making process. More money and effort must be diverted to natural resource conservation and cleaning up the environment. Although these endeavours will also contribute to GDP if properly counted, the days of "cheap" residual growth at the expense of environment degradation are over.

## Growing as an Upper Middle Income Economy

China's past three decades of hyper economic growth had been driven mostly by an abnormally high pace of physical capital growth and a respectable rate of TFP growth. Of these two major drivers, physical capital formation is unlikely to keep its pace. Conditions that used to favour high investment demand and high savings have either been transitional or are about to reach a point of reversal. It is inevitable that the pace of physical capital formation will slow down considerably in the coming two decades.

With slowing capital formation, economic growth has to rely more on productivity growth, which comes from efficiency improvements and technological advancements. Great potential for efficiency gains lie in fields like financial services and logistics and distribution systems. Urbanisation of hundreds of millions of rural residents will also be a rich source of reallocation efficiency. China's superb achievements in human capital development and persistent investment in knowledge creation and technological progress will continue to help future productivity growth. However, demographic trends are becoming increasingly unfavourable to productivity growth. Environmental degradation has reached a level that makes it impossible to gain further "cheap" productivity growth from an overdraft of natural resources.

Relative to the past hyper growth period, a slowdown of overall GDP growth is inevitable in the coming years. China's chance of growing beyond the middle income status depends on whether it can continue its convergence with the United States and other advanced countries in productivity growth and standard of living. That requires efforts to continuously improve efficiency, enhance human capital and promote technological progress. To achieve that, China must optimise the utilisation of its advantages in human capital and scale economy to promote technical progress and

[13] Foster, P, "China's Carbon Footprint near World's Biggest", *Daily Telegraph*, 28 September 2011.

[14] Economy, EC, "The Great Leap Backward? The Costs of China's Environmental Crisis", *Foreign Affairs*, Vol. 86 no. 5 p. 38, 2007.

[15] Grimond, J, "For Want of a Drink: A Special Report on Water". *The Economist*, 20 May 2010.

[16] Wee S-L, "Officials Bend to Massive Protest, Close Major Chemical Plant", *Reuters*, 15 August 2011.

**Table 2**   Selected Development Indicators of China, Upper Middle Income Countries and OECD High Income Countries

| | Year | China | Upper Middle Income Countries | OECD |
|---|---|---|---|---|
| GNI per capita (constant 2000 US$) | 2010 | 2,356 | 3,172 | 28,447 |
| Cost of business start-up procedures (% of GNI per capita) | 2011 | 3.50 | 13.93 | 4.67 |
| Time required to start a business (days) | 2011 | 38.00 | 40.62 | 13.61 |
| Ease of doing business index (1=most business-friendly regulations) | 2011 | 91.00 | 80.02 | 29.71 |
| Strength of legal rights index (0=weak to 10=strong) | 2011 | 6.00 | 5.60 | 7.16 |
| Logistics performance index: Overall (1=low to 5=high) | 2009 | 3.49 | 2.80 | 3.66 |
| R&D expenditure (% of GDP) | 2007 | 1.44 | 1.03 | 2.41 |
| Researchers in R&D (per million people) | 2006 | 927 | 963 | 3975 |
| Environmental damage (% of GDP) | 2008/09 | 9.83 | 15.59 | 2.30 |

*Sources*: World Bank, World dataBank at <http://databank.worldbank.org> (accessed 23 August 2011) and *Taiwan Statistical Data Book*.

efficiency improvement. That calls for further reforms to establish a business climate more conducive for innovation and entrepreneurship as well as institutional and policy changes to facilitate urbanisation and an environment-friendly development.

As shown in Table 2, although China's per capita income is still 26% lower than that of middle income countries' average, it has outperformed the latter in several indicators of business climate, R&D capacity and even in environmental quality. However, there are still glaring gaps between China and the OECD high income countries in most of the performance indicators. In the "ease of doing business index", China has yet to reach the upper middle income countries' average level.

Now having joined the ranks of the upper middle income countries, China faces an uphill task in overhauling its social safety net and other public services to ensure a smooth transition to an ageing population and a more affluent society. Social and political reforms are needed to ameliorate economic equity and social justice for the wellbeing of its citizens. The era of hyper economic growth is coming to its end but a future of quality life is beckoning.

# 27

# China's Labour Shortage and its Implications

HUANG Yanjie*

*China has been facing chronic labour shortages since its recovery from the global financial crisis. The government needs to raise wage rates and improve welfare provisions to migrant workers in order to turn the shortage into an advantage in China's socio-economic development.*

At the start of 2012 China was facing another year of tight labour market, with even more severe labour shortage and drastic wage increment expected. According to Yin Weimin, Minster for Labour and Social Security, labour shortage has become a structural issue in the Chinese economy, but, enterprises have learnt to better cope with it with the experience picked up in the last two years.[1] As usual, the situation is most serious for the export-oriented sectors in coastal industrial regions, but most inland labour-exporting provinces are also badly hit.

The recurrence of labour shortage which is fast becoming a norm illustrates vividly the emerging dynamics of a demographic shift and generation change that have become decisive factors in China's labour market. China has reaped two decades of demographic dividend and is fast approaching its end with the number of young people joining the labour sector decreasing each year.[2] The new generation of migrant workers who are increasingly becoming the most vital and mobile part of the overall labour force tend to be more assertive on wage and welfare demands.

One implication brought about by the demographic shift is the rapid erosion of competitiveness in coastal regions. As economic growth speeds up in inland regions, the differences between

---

*HUANG Yanjie is Research Assistant at the East Asian Institute, National University of Singapore.
[1] Ye W, "*Guanyu Dangqian Mingonghuang*" (On the Current Labour Shortage), *Economic Observer*, 24 February 2012.
[2] Demographic dividend is a window of socio-economic development for a society when the dependency ratio remains low (working adult population as proportion of total population) as a result of a decline in fertility rate, before it becomes an ageing society as fertility rates decline further. According to Cai Fang, China's leading demographer, China entered its demographic dividend period in the early 1980s when the dependency ratio began to drop and will soon reach the end of the period between 2010 and 2015 when the dependency ratio rises again.

wages, work conditions, job types and skill requirements between coastal and inland provinces are narrowing. However, enterprises in the coastal regions are unable to meet the challenges of offering higher wages and welfare benefits in accordance with the rising cost of living.

The shortage of migrant labour on a national scale reflects a narrowing of wage gaps and welfare standards across many different and distant provinces and economic regions. These regions are experiencing increasingly similar industrial structures. Economic development in recent years has enhanced the competitiveness of inland provinces vis-à-vis coastal ones. This phenomenon should sound the alarm for efforts to speed up industrial upgrading, particularly for labour-intensive sectors in the coastal regions.

The government and the academia believe that the ongoing labour shortage will bring about positive changes as it can exert constant pressure nationwide to bring about structural reforms. For instance, most provinces have already promised minimum wage increment and better welfare programmes. Labour shortage is regarded as a driving force which will ultimately ameliorate the living and working conditions of migrant workers.

Despite the positive changes that come along with labour shortage, there is doubt that the government has the ability to deal effectively with structural reforms — the only solution to tackling labour shortage and subsequently promoting continuous economic growth. The existing policy of minimum wage increase is becoming obsolete and losing effectiveness in the face of more rapid actual wage increments.

## The Panic-Stricken Market for Migrant Labour

In the year 2010, waves of labour shortage mainly occurred in areas with high concentration of low-cost as well as labour-intensive manufacturing and service industries. But since the year of 2011, labour shortage has occurred in almost every sector that requires large number of both skilled and unskilled migrant workers. Regions and sectors which are more badly hit include manufacturers in Shenzhen, restaurants in Shanghai, construction companies in Beijing and even companies supplying domestic helpers in Wuhan. From these examples, it is evident that labour shortage has spread across various regions and sectors.

In February 2012, the Pearl River Delta suffered a shortage of over one million migrant workers. This included an acute shortage of 200,000 workers in Shenzhen, 100,000 in Guangzhou and at least 80,000 in Dongguan — an important manufacturing centre near Guangzhou. Labour shortage is also a grave issue in the Yangtze River Delta. It is estimated that 60% of all enterprises were unable to operate at full capacity due to the lack of manpower. Though labour shortage is less severe elsewhere, inland provinces are already grappling with unexpected large gaps between demand and supply of labour such as Anhui (250,000) and Hubei (600,000).[3] Hubei Bureau of Labour and Social Security estimates that for the first time, outflow of migrant labour from Hubei will decrease by 10–15%.[4]

As inland provinces suffer from worsening labour shortage, both local and coastal enterprises begin to take drastic measures to secure workers. For example, local enterprises often resort to aggressive recruitment methods including aggressive advertisements and at-spot recruitment booths set up in railway and long-distance bus stations. As for small coastal enterprises, they often organise themselves into recruitment groups to recruit labour directly from technical schools and labour information centres in inland cities. Labour shortage is becoming so severe that Foxconn, China's labour-intensive enterprise operating in multiple assembling plants all over

---

[3] "*Zhongxibu Quegonghuang Diaocha*" (Investigating Labour Shortage in Central and Western China), *China Economic Weekly*, vol. 10, 2012, pp.15–18.

[4] "*Zhongxibu Queonghuang Zaidiaocha*" (Re-investigating Labor Shortage in Central and Western China), *China Economic Weekly*, vol. 16, 2012, pp. 17.

China, sends its recruitment teams to railway stations in Wuhan to offer jobs to migrant job-seekers.[5]

The current labour shortage weighing down China is both frictional and structural in nature. From situations observed over the past years, labour shortage can be attributed to largely the Spring Festival. During the festival and the few months after it, large numbers of migrant workers will return to their hometowns. But since the last few years, a persistent trend has been observed to indicate that structural problem is the main culprit causing a labour shortfall. In Zhenjiang and Guangdong, for instance, the shortages have persisted since China recovered from the global financial crisis in the third quarter of 2009.

Among the industrial sectors and enterprises affected, labour-intensive small and medium-sized enterprises are the most severely hit. Large state-owned enterprises and foreign investment enterprises, on the other hand, are somewhat insulated from the labour shortage since they have better capacity to adapt to changes. Furthermore, they mainly recruit labour from other segments of the market — college graduates.

Similar to previous years, there is now a shortage of both skilled and unskilled workers, though demand for the former tends to be higher. For example, the lack of qualified frontline workers, such as tool machine operators, electricians, electric welders, machine repairmen, painters, skilled technicians and workers in the manufacturing and construction sectors, is virtually a universal phenomenon in the labour market across the whole of China. Monthly wage rate for skilled workers has as a result increased drastically to RMB4,000, far outstripping the wage rates of other jobs, including even the average wage rate for fresh graduates.[6]

The current labour shortage should not be interpreted as China experiencing problems of unemployment or underemployment. What happens in reality is that the economy fails to provide suitable employment opportunities for the different groups of workers, notably college graduates. Reports also indicate that the problem of labour shortage affects mainly the younger generation and not the older generations of migrant workers.

## Structural Causes of Labour Shortage

A number of economic and social factors lead to the shortage of migrant labour, among which the most instrumental are demographic and generation changes, which probably have long-term consequences. Other important causes include low wage and low welfare standards, a mismatch between economy and China's education system, as well as the recent economic development trends in inland provinces.

After reaping 20 years of demographic dividends, China is now experiencing a rapid decrease in the proportion of the young labour force. According to Nomura Research, China's population aged between 10 and 19 has decreased from 19.9% to 13.9% over the last two decades, while the percentage of people aged between 50 and 59 has increased from 7.8% to 14%. According to Cai Feng, a leading demographer, China's labour population has been increasing at a declining rate since 2005. It will level and then decline in the year 2015.[7]

China still has years to go before its demographic dividend ends but actual labour supply has already begun to decelerate. According to Han Jun, director of the Rural Economy Research Institute under the State Council's Development Research Center, as early as 2005, national surveys in the countryside already suggested limited potential for further labour migration since able-bodied men had all moved to the cities in search of higher paid jobs.[8] Upward adjustments in wage rates are expected to occur nationwide in 2012 and this situation will probably persist into the next few years.

---

[5] <http://www.chinanews.com/sh/2012/02-03/3643609.shtml> (accessed 27 February 2012).

[6] "*Shenzhen Zaoyu Yonggonghuang*" (Shenzhen In a State of Labour Shortage), *People's Daily*, 1 February 2012.

[7] "*Cai Fang Jiaoshou Caifang*" (Interview with Prof. Cai Fang), *First Finance News*, 16 May 2011.

[8] "*Mingonghuang Kuozhandao Neidi, Jiegouxing Duanque Chengshi Changtai*" (Labour Shortage Spreads to Inland China, Structural Shortage Becomes Normality), *Observer News Weekly*, 24 May 2006.

An equally important factor behind the current shortage is the rise of second generation migrant workers who currently account for 58% of the total 242 million migrant labour force.[9] As most of this generation of migrant workers grew up in the cities and suburbs, they have developed values and work ethics that are significantly different from migrant workers of older generations. Values and ethics valued highly by the younger generation of migrant workers are self-development, comfort of life, personal rights, some degree of social justice, and the opportunity to settle in cities for the long term.[10]

Although wage rates had risen significantly in 2011, inflation has nullified any positive effects, hence making present wage offerings unsatisfactory to migrant workers. In 2011, China's consumer index rose 5.4%, the strongest growth since 2007, with prices of daily necessities like foods rising much faster than consumer durables. According to one recent survey in the Yangtze River Delta, an average migrant worker expects a minimum wage of RMB2,630, but the average wage on offer is only RMB2,200. Indeed, even if enterprises were to meet the minimum wage expectation of migrant workers, workers might still have second thoughts about taking up the job given that the minimum cost of living has risen to RMB1,930.[11]

Moreover, there is little improvement in social protection for migrant workers working in coastal cities. Without a local *hukou*, migrant workers have only limited and precarious access to basic social welfare. Migrants fare considerably worse than locals in nearly all non-income measures of welfare including housing conditions, access to education (for the children of migrant workers), social insurance and social assistance programmes. In comparison, the *hukou* control in medium-sized and small cities in central and western China are much more lax and integrative towards migrant workers coming from the neighbouring countryside. This effectively means that the cost of integrating into the local societies for migrants in these areas is lower. The trend is expected to grow as China is beginning to release *hukou* control in these small and medium-sized towns and cities.

Meanwhile, most inland provinces are now experiencing rapid economic development, and achieving higher growth rates in industrial output and GDP. Attracted by the relatively low costs of production, many large domestic and foreign enterprises have relocated their factories from the coast to inland China. Inland provinces have thus moved closer to coastal regions in terms of industrial structure, job opportunities and skill requirements. In consequence, enterprises and local governments in inland labour-exporting provinces have become active in retaining and encouraging the return of local migrant workers.

Some local and provincial governments have already taken proactive steps to attract the limited supply of migrant labour. The best example is Chongqing, a traditionally labour-exporting region where the government offers carefully designed welfare packages, including urban residences status, to retain local work forces and attract workers from outside. According to local media reports, the Chongqing model has already had some initial success in retaining migrant workers. If other inland provinces follow suit or step up their efforts, it is possible that the problem of labour shortage will worsen, particularly for coastal regions.

## Implications of Labour Shortage

### *Implications for China's Economic Development*

The presence of a panic-stricken labour market attests to the rapid changes China's labour supply is undergoing. It is also a strong indication that China's industrial restructuring has not progressed

---

[9] "*Xinshengdai Nongmingong: Shuliang, Jiegou yu Tedian*" (New Generation of Migrant Workers: Population, Structure and Characteristics), National Bureau of Statistics, November 2011.

[10] Ibid.

[11] "*Yixianqong Zuidi Qiwang Yuexin 2630 Yuan*" (Minimum Monthly Expected Wage for Frontline Workers Rise to 2630 RMB), *Suzhou Daily*, 7 February 2012.

fast enough. This persistent under-supply of migrant labour suggests that labour-intensive enterprises located in the coastal regions have largely lost their competitiveness in the labour market.

In order to survive the crisis, affected enterprises can adopt three possible courses of action, namely, implement substantial wage increases, transfer production to inland provinces and switch to capital- or technology-intensive approach for production, which is a form of self-initiated industrial upgrade. For enterprises which are unable to adapt to this new situation, the perpetuation of labour shortage may indicate a gradual end to business.

In fact, coastal enterprises and provinces are not sitting idle. Apart from special "emergency" measures to recruit labour, most enterprises have responded to the crisis with wage increment. Following the increment of about 10–20% in the year 2011, in the year 2012, the average wage rate increase of migrant workers is expected to accelerate. According to a survey conducted in the Pearl River Delta, the rate of monthly wage increment for more popular positions that require both skills and technical qualifications is expected to remain at 30% for another year. The monthly wage of experienced skilled workers could well match that of degree-holders in the professional sector. This newly emerging wage structure provides strong incentives for workers to undergo technical training.

Provincial and local governments likewise have announced another round of minimum wage increase of between 15% and 26%. The highest minimum wages are offered by Shanghai (RMB1,450), Guangzhou (RMB1,470) and Shenzhen (RMB1,500), up from about RMB1,300 in 2011.[12] In general, over the last two years, the minimum wage has been rising steadily at a remarkable rate of about 20%. As shown in Table 1, the upward pressure on minimum wage rates has spread from coastal to inland China since the year 2010. As local governments in inland regions follow the footsteps of coastal regions, minimum wage rates will rise and wage gaps will further narrow.

At the macro-level, changes in China's labour market have salutary effects on income distribution and economic structure. In 2010, for the very first time in more than a decade, the rate of increment in rural household income, made up largely by wage income of migrant workers, narrowly outstripped that of urban household income. If the rapid wage increment of migrant workers continues and at an even higher rate, this will definitely narrow China's decade-long urban-rural income inequality and align the structure of income distribution more compatible with an economy driven by domestic consumption.

**Table 1**   Minimum Wage in Representative Cities/Regions (RMB)[a]

| Years/Regions | 2008 | 2009 | 2010 | 2011 | 2012 |
|---|---|---|---|---|---|
| **Eastern/Coastal** | | | | | |
| Shenzhen | 1,000 | 1,000 | 1,100 | 1,300 | 1,500 |
| Guangzhou | 860 | 1,030 | 1,100 | 1,300 | 1,500 |
| Shanghai | 840 | 960 | 1,120 | 1,280 | 1,450[b] |
| **Central** | | | | | |
| Wuhan | 700 | 700 | 900 | 1,100 | 1,300[b] |
| **Western** | | | | | |
| Chongqing | 680 | 680 | 680 | 870 | 1,050[b] |

*Notes*: [a]Minimum wage rate here refers to minimum wage rates in operation at the end of the year for full time employees working in the metropolitan areas of these cities/regions in the list. [b]Expected minimum wage.

*Source*: China's Ministry of Labour and Social Security Database, 30 April 2012.

---

[12] *"Shenzhen Zuitigongzi Tigaozhi* 1500" (Shenzhen Raises Minimum Wage to 1500), *Southern Daily*, 15 February 2012.

## Implications for Welfare and Labour Policy

The current labour shortage may prompt some local governments to develop incentives such as social insurance programmes to expand the coverage or improve the quality of public services to migrant workers. As mentioned earlier, the problem of labour shortage has been very serious in many localities in recent times. The lack of welfare for the migrant population is one of the main reasons that has driven away the young generation of migrant workers.

Now that labour — an instrumental production factor — has become scarce, local governments which are keen to attract migrant workers will be urged to devise more attractive welfare coverage to the latter so that local firms enjoy a constant supply of workers. More attractive welfare benefits and better protection for migrant workers translate into the particular region's ability to attract more workers, resulting in economic growth in the long run.

The will to increase welfare benefits is particularly strong for governments in the western and central regions where the manufacturing sector is experiencing rapid expansion. A micro-electronics industrial park managed by Chongqing municipal government promised in February 2011 to provide comprehensive welfare packages such as health care, education and housing to migrant workers.[13] In Chengdu city, which is geographically close to Chongqing city, migrant workers have also been promised the same level of social welfare including health insurance, unemployment insurance and maternity insurance as other urban residents, beginning from 1 April 2011.[14] At Wuhan, the economic centre of the labour-exporting province of Hubei, the local government has also avowed to deliver similar public goods.

In October 2010, the National Congress approved the "Social Insurance Law" validating social insurance packages across regions.[15] In other words, various forms of social insurance such as retirement insurance,[16] health insurance[17] and unemployment insurance[18] will be provided regardless of their current residence and their place of household registration. This law complements local government's efforts to expand coverage and improve the quality of public services for migrant workers.

## Long-term Policy Concerns

As discussed in earlier sections, labour shortage will be a chronic problem for China if the economy remains at its current pace of growth, which is already showing signs of weariness. In absolute terms, China's labour supply is no doubt increasing and the transfer of labour from rural to urban sectors is still in progress. Total employment, urban employment and migrant labour force all experienced a moderate rise in 2011 (Table 2). But it can be foreseen that the growth of the labour force will eventually slow down to a point where growth becomes negative, aggravated by the underlying structural changes in the labour force, particularly in the migrant labour force.

Just as many observers have observed, labour shortage could be a blessing in disguise for the Chinese economy for the near future. First, it will serve to benefit migrant workers and alleviate the structural problem of income and consumption inequalities. The migrant labour is the social group most urgently in need of a larger share of socio-economic returns generated by 30 years of economic development. A unit increase in the income of migrant workers will result in a much more significant effect on consumption and domestic demands as compared to an increase in investment and government spending.

---

[13] <http://www.chinanews.com/cj/2011/02-12/2838666.shtml> (accessed 17 March 2011).

[14] <http://comment.scol.com.cn/html/2011/02/011013_836969.shtml> (accessed 17 March 2011).

[15] <http://news.xinhuanet.com/fortune/2010-10/29/c_12714276.htm> (accessed 17 March 2011).

[16] Article 19, social insurance law.

[17] Article 32, social insurance law.

[18] Article 52, social insurance law.

**Table 2**   Total Labour Force from 2004 to 2011

| Year | Migrant Labour Force | Urban Employment (in millions) | Total Employed Labour Force (in millions) | Total Labour Force |
|------|------|------|------|------|
| 2004 | — | 272.9 | 752.6 | 752.9 |
| 2005 | — | 283.9 | 746.5 | 761.2 |
| 2006 | — | 296.3 | 749.8 | 763.2 |
| 2007 | — | 309.5 | 753.2 | 765.3 |
| 2008 | 225.4 | 321.0 | 755.6 | 770.5 |
| 2009 | 229.8 | 333.2 | 758.3 | 775.1 |
| 2010 | 242.3 | 347.9 | 761.0 | 783.8 |
| 2011 | 252.8 | 359.1 | 764.2 | — |

*Source*: *China Statistical Yearbook* (only officially available data are listed).

Labour shortage may also accelerate the current process of industrial upgrading and labour transfer — two much needed steps in transforming China's economy structurally. This is particularly true with respect to the Pearl River Delta region. With increasing labour costs, the traditional labour-intensive export-process firms in the Pearl River Delta will have to either upgrade their production technology and increase their value, or abandon the coastal production base in search of cheap labour in inland provinces or other countries. Indeed, many migrant workers have already chosen to return to their home provinces. For instance, it is estimated that Guangdong has lost a quarter of the migrant labour force over the last two years.[19]

In addition, labour shortage could be considered a driving force for China's social policy reforms. According to Cai Fang, director of the Institute of Population and Labour Economics under the Chinese Academy of Social Sciences, China may recoup what may be termed the Second Demographic Dividends by implementing social reforms to equalise basic public goods provision for migrant workers. Like many experts on labour economics in China, he also regards the current labour shortage as a signal for a larger and more profound structural change in the future. He is also quick to point out that the existence of labour surplus will exert a soothing effect on labour shortage as labour market equilibrates with higher wages.[20]

Many observers point out that many local governments will be better motivated to provide adequate public goods to this formerly neglected social group given the economic and subsequent fiscal strains created by the continuous labour shortage. By better integrating migrant workers and letting them assimilate with urban citizens, the Chinese economy is expected to gain substantially from the increase in demand for consumption, public goods and urban infrastructure.

However, there are also heated debates regarding the nature and implications of the labour shortage. Ye Tan, a leading economic observer, casts a more pessimistic light on the issue. Without the necessary legal and institutional frameworks, she argues, labour shortage will work to promote industrial transfer rather than restructure the economy. The dynamics unleashed by labour shortage may not necessarily create orderly industrial upgrading and transfer. Rather, destabilising competitions between coastal and inland provinces might ensue as coastal regions have yet to

---

[19] Yao J, "*Guangdong ¼ Nongmingong Liushi*" (Guangdong Lost ¼ of Its Migrant Labor Force), 21st Century Economic Report, 10 March 2012.

[20] Cai F, "*Zhongguo Xuyao Kaifa Dierci Renkou Hongli*" (China Needs to Harness the Second Demographic Dividend), *First Financial News*, 16 March 2010.

mature to the extent that meets required conditions for industrial upgrading.[21] Indeed, how the mechanisms work out eventually depends on many other elements of institutional reform.

In general, reform measures that aim to facilitate labour mobility and protect migrant workers' rights as well as interests are likely to be better received and enforced by local governments if the current labour shortage continues to exert a pressure on local economies. Whatever the policy outcome might be, the current labour shortage is likely to play a facilitative role in the structural transformation of the Chinese economy.

When viewed in this light, labour shortage is actually a positive sign for both economic and social development in China. Most notably, the under-appreciated contributions of migrant workers have been recognised with the gradual increase in their wages and greater access to basic social services. The current labour shortage is likely to have an overall salutary effect on China's economic and social development.

---

[21] Ye T, *"Mingonghuang Jiasu Chanye Shengji Daxiaohua"* (Labour Shortage Leads to Industrial Upgrading: A Big Bluff), Daily Economic News, 26 February 2010.

# 28

# Can China Continue to Reap its Demographic Dividend in Economic Growth?

YAN Hao*

*Demographic dividend contributed 15% to 27% to China's GDP growth from 1980 to 2000. China can still maximise its demographic dividend by promoting employment and raising productivity while the window of opportunity stays open.*

In recent years, labour shortages have emerged as a new labour market phenomenon in China that spread gradually from the Pearl River Delta and the Yangtze River Delta regions to many inland provinces. This development is indeed puzzling as China is a country where the unlimited supply of cheap labour has been taken for granted for decades since the labour market was liberalised in the 1980s. Is China's demographic dividend drying up very soon?

Demographic dividend refers to a rise in the rate of economic growth during a period when the working age population grows more rapidly than the dependent population. With fewer mouths to feed, more resources can be freed for investment in economic development and family welfare. Other things being equal, per capita income grows more rapidly too. The demographic dividend theory emerged in the late 1990s in the study of the "economic miracles" of the East Asian tigers.[1] At times, it is just considered an empirical observation of past events with varied explanations. However, if the demographic dividend theory has certain merits in interpreting past events, it should also be useful in providing some hints of the future.

An important concept of the demographic dividend theory is the demographic window of opportunity. The demographic window is defined as the period of time when the proportion of working age population is particularly prominent. However, the exact technical boundaries

---

* YAN Hao was Visiting Senior Research Fellow at the East Asian Institute, National University of Singapore.

[1] Bloom, DE and JG Williamson, Demographic Transitions and Economic Miracles in Emerging Asia, *World Bank Economic Review*, vol. 12, 1998, pp. 419–455.

**Table 1**   Selected Population Indicators, China, 1953–2010

| Year | Total Population (million) | Aged 0–14 (%) | Aged 15–64 (%) | Aged 65 and Above (%) | Dependency Ratio (%) |
|---|---|---|---|---|---|
| 1953 | 601 | 36.3 | 59.3 | 4.4 | 68.6 |
| 1964 | 694 | 40.7 | 55.7 | 3.6 | 79.4 |
| 1982 | 1,016 | 33.6 | 61.5 | 4.9 | 62.6 |
| 1990 | 1,143 | 27.6 | 66.8 | 5.6 | 49.7 |
| 1995 | 1,211 | 26.6 | 67.2 | 6.2 | 48.8 |
| 2000 | 1,267 | 22.9 | 70.1 | 7.0 | 42.7 |
| 2005 | 1,307 | 20.3 | 72.0 | 7.7 | 38.9 |
| 2010 | 1,339 | 16.6 | 74.5 | 8.9 | 34.2 |

*Sources*: Lu Y and Zhai Z, *Sixty Years of New China Population*, China Population Press, Beijing, 2009; National Bureau of Statistics, *China Statistical Yearbook 2011*, China Statistics Press, 2011, Beijing.

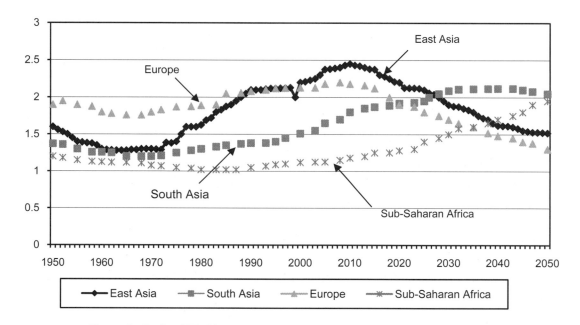

**Figure 1**   Ratio of Working Age to Dependent Population by Regions, 1950–2050

*Source*: At <http://en.wikipedia.org/wiki/File:Inverse_Dependency_Ratio_-_World_Regions_-_1950%E2%80%932050.png> (accessed 10 July 2012).

of definition may vary (Table 1). For example, the UN Population Department has defined it as a period when the proportion of children and youth under 15 years falls below 30% and the proportion of people 65 years and older is still below 15%. There are also two other definitions commonly used by economists and demographers. One (Definition A) suggests that the window of opportunity is open as long as the net producers (working age population) outnumber the net consumers (dependent population) by two times. The other (Definition B) proposes that the window of opportunity begins from the time when the total dependency ratio declines and ends at the time when it rebounds. The demographic window of opportunity typically lasts for 30 to 40 years depending on the country. As shown in Figure 1, Europe's demographic window lasted from 1950 to 2000. It began in East Asia in 1990 and is expected to last until 2015. South Asia has been projected to enter the demographic window in 2010, which may last until the middle of the present century. Much of Africa will not enter the demographic window until 2045 or later.

How does the change in age structure of a population transform into demographic dividends? It is believed that a number of mechanisms are at work. First is the rise in labour supply. As the number of people aged 15–64 increases, the total labour force expands. Particularly, more women enter the labour market as family size declines. Second is the rise in savings. People aged 15–64 are more likely to be not only working, but also saving. The growth of savings improves a country's prospects for investment and growth. Third is the rise in human capital input. As life expectancy increases, people tend to adopt healthier lifestyles, changing their attitudes and way of life. Economic growth is also stimulated with greater attention being paid to improve human capital, such as education and health. The demographic dividend does not come automatically even when the country experiences its window of opportunity. The added productivity of this large working age population produces a "demographic dividend" only if policies to take advantage of this are in place. Some of the critical conditions to capitalise on the demographic dividend include policies that promote human resource development, employment, and a free and open market environment that allows free movement of capital, labour, resources, commodities and technology.

A new concept of the second demographic dividend has been proposed lately: a population with a concentration of older working adults who have their retirement extended and a population who has a powerful incentive to accumulate assets.[2] National income rises regardless of whether these additional assets are invested domestically or abroad. The first dividend yields a transitory bonus, and the second transforms that bonus into greater assets and sustainable development.

In theory, all dividends should be computable. Two methods are usually used to calculate the contribution of the demographic dividend to economic growth: multiple regression and macro simulation. Understandably, the results of the two calculations may differ slightly from each other. By the former method, it is estimated that the demographic dividend contributed one third to the increase in per capita income in East Asia in the period 1965–1990.[3] By the latter method, it is estimated that 25% of East Asia's economic growth during its take-off period[4] can be attributed to the demographic dividend.

## How does the Demographic Dividend Work in China?

By UN definition, the demographic window of opportunity opened in China sometime between 1982 and 1990. It is plausible to take 1985 as the year when the proportion of the young population aged 0–14 dropped to below 30%. By Definition A, this opportunity came five years later in 1990 when the working age population outnumbered the dependent population by two times. By Definition B, however, it appeared much earlier in 1964 when the total dependency ratio started to fall. As the census data in Table 1 show, China's total population has kept growing over the last six decades, whereas its dependency ratio has dropped gradually after reaching a peak of 79.4% in 1964. This is primarily due to the decline in the young population aged 0–14. In fact, the younger population shrank quickly in the subsequent years, as its share dropped by 59.2% in the period 1964–2010. Despite the elderly population aged 65 and above doubling its proportion from 3.6% to 8.9%, the total dependency ratio fell by more than half in the same period. This also means a rapid increase in the working age population aged 15–64. From 1982 to 2010 alone, China's total working age population increased by 59.6% from 625 million to 997 million, or about 13 million each year on average. It came to a historical height at 74.5% in 2010.

---

[2]Lee R and A Mason, *What Is the Demographic Dividend?* At <http://www.imf.org/external/pubs/ft/fandd/2006/09/basics.htm> (accessed 10 July 2012).

[3]D Bloom and J Williamson, op. cit.

[4]Feeney, G, and A Mason. In A Mason (ed.), *Population Change and Economic Development in East Asia: Challenges Met, Opportunities Seized.* Stanford, California, Stanford University Press, 2001.

As mentioned earlier, the demographic dividend can be broken down further into three categories: the rise in labour supply, in savings and in human capital. China has been proven quite successful in reaping the dividends in all the three areas as the opportunity came.

Rise in labour force: Working age population does not necessarily equate labour force, since not all people in working ages enter the labour market. It is well documented that the labour force participation rate in China is always high and that of women is among the highest in the world. In 2008, according to the World Bank,[5] China's total labour force participation rate was 74% and that of the female labour force was 68%. A rise in working age population can easily be translated into a rise in labour force at a similar pace. Therefore, China's total labour force remains the largest in the world. More importantly, the labour cost in China is much lower than that of industrialised countries. The seemingly unlimited supply of cheap labour is considered one of China's major advantages in achieving fast economic growth.

Labour supply, no matter how abundant and cheap, contributes little to economic growth unless sufficient jobs are created simultaneously. From 1985 to 2010, as Table 2 shows, China's total employment increased by 53.1% from 498 million to 761 million. This means that as many as 264 million jobs had been created in this period. Job creation in the non-agricultural sectors has been especially impressive. While employment dropped by 10.2% in the primary industry, it increased by 112.0% in the secondary industry and by 217.2% in the tertiary industry. Service sectors are obviously the greatest contributors of job creation in China.

In the discussion of employment, the structure is as relevant a topic as the volume. It is common knowledge that the productivity of non-agricultural sectors is much higher than that of agriculture. In 1985, as shown in Table 3, the per capita GDP generated by the primary industry was only 823 *yuan* as compared to the 3,747 *yuan* and 3,108 *yuan* of the secondary and tertiary industries respectively. That means the productivity of the primary industry is 4.6 times lower than that of the

**Table 2**    Employment by Sectors, China, 1985 and 2010

| Item | Employment (million) 1985 | 2010 | Change (%) (1985–2010) |
|---|---|---|---|
| Primary industry | 311 | 279 | −10.2 |
| Secondary industry | 103 | 218 | 112.0 |
| Tertiary industry | 83 | 263 | 217.2 |
| Total | 498 | 761 | 53.1 |

*Source*: National Bureau of Statistics, *China Statistical Yearbook 2011*, China Statistics Press, 2011, Beijing.

**Table 3**    Per capita GDP by Sector, China, 1985 and 2010 (current price)

| Item | Per capita GDP (*yuan*) 1985 | 2010 |
|---|---|---|
| Primary industry | 823 | 14,512 |
| Secondary industry | 3,747 | 85,889 |
| Tertiary industry | 3,108 | 65,738 |
| All | 1,813 | 52,991 |

*Source*: Calculated by the author from *China Statistical Yearbook*, 2011.

[5]<http://data.worldbank.org/indicator/SL.TLF.CACT.ZS> (accessed 9 July 2012).

secondary industry and 3.8 times lower than that of the tertiary industry. The 2010 figures, though in current prices, indicate that the productivity of all three industries has increased remarkably in recent years. For example, the per capita GDP generated by the primary industry rose by 18 times to 14,512 *yuan*. However, it still lags behind that of the secondary industry (5.9 times lower) and the tertiary industry (4.5 times lower). It is estimated that 240 million rural migrants have so far been transferred to the non-agricultural sectors, primarily the manufacturing sector. The contribution brought by labour transfers to China's economic growth amounted to 21% of China's GDP growth in the period 1982–2000.[6]

Rise in savings: Thanks largely to the fast economic growth, people's income increases very quickly in China. From 1978 to 2007, according to a 2008 report of the Chinese Academy of Social Sciences (CASS), the average annual income of urban residents rose by 7.1 times in real terms, while that of rural residents rose by 5.3 times.[7] A sizeable share of the income usually goes into savings for a number of reasons, such as the age-old Chinese tradition of saving, unsatisfactory social security services and limited chance for private investment. No wonder, China's savings rate is high by historical experience, international standards and model predictions, and has been rising (especially in the 2000s).[8] According to the People's Bank of China, the total bank savings of Chinese urban and rural residents reached 35.2 trillion *yuan* (ca. US$4.8 trillion) by the end of 2011.[9] Similar trends have also been observed in corporate savings. High savings can be translated into high investment, a key impetus behind China's fast economic growth. Interestingly enough, China has even been blamed by 2008 economics Nobel Prize winner Paul Krugman for triggering America's recent debt crisis because of its excess savings. This accusation is of course, from a Chinese point of view, groundless.

Rise in human capital: Human capital refers usually to people's education and health status. According to the Ministry of Education, China's crude enrolment rate of post-secondary education stood at 26.5% in 2010.[10] With total enrolment reaching 30 million and total graduates reaching eight million, China now runs the largest tertiary education system in the world. Thanks to this "education dividend", Hu Angang, one of China's leading economists, believes that China has successfully emerged from a country burdened by excess population into a country endowed with enormous human resource advantages. Its human capital stock now accounts for about 27% of the world total.[11]

Demographers in China and abroad have made efforts in recent years to calculate the contribution of the demographic dividend to China's economic growth. By using mainly the multiple regression approach, Cai and Wang[12] estimated that 27% of China's GDP growth in the period 1980–2000 was attributable to the demographic dividend. A drop of 1 percentage point in the total dependency ratio can result in an increase of 0.115 percentage points in per capita GDP. By using the macro simulation approach, Feng, Wang and Mason[13] concluded that the demographic dividend contributed up to 15% of China's GDP growth in the period 1982–2000.

History proves that a suitable policy environment is necessary for capitalising on the potential of the demographic dividend. In China, nothing has been more important than the reform and

---

[6] Cai F and Wang D, *"Zhongguo jingji zengzhang de kechixuxing yu laodong gongxian"*, *Economic Research Journal* (Jingji Yanjiu) vol. 10, 1999.

[7] <http://www.stnn.cc/china/200807/t20080711_811451.html> (accessed 9 July 2012).

[8] Ma G and Wang Y, 2010, China's High Saving Rate: Myth and Reality, *BIS Working Papers*, No. 312.

[9] <http://news.sina.com.cn/c/2012-03-10/032424090300.shtml> (accessed 13 March 2012).

[10] <http://news.xinhuanet.com/edu/2011-07/06/c_121629066_4.htm> (accessed 9 July 2012).

[11] Hu A, China from a Population Power to a Talent Power. At <http://finance.sina.com.cn/hy/20100529/19428024811.shtml> (accessed 9 July 2012).

[12] Cai and Wang, op. cit.

[13] Wang F, and A Mason. 2006, The Demographic Factor in China's Transition. *Chinese Journal of Population Science.* 3, 2–18.

opening-up policies introduced by the government since the late 1970s to replace the planned economy with a free-market economy. China was liberalising its capital market, the resources market, the commodity market and the labour market exactly when it was experiencing its demographic window of opportunity. Foreign investment and technology have also played a special role in building China's production capacity and generating jobs. After its 2001 entry to the WTO, the Chinese economy has become closely integrated with the world market. The combined effect of China's competitive advantage in the supply of abundant and cheap labour has also been brought into full play. Thanks partially to the demographic dividend, China has managed to maintain near double-digit growth over the last three decades to eventually become the world's second largest economy in 2010.

## When will the Demographic Window of Opportunity Close for China?

To predict when the demographic window of opportunity closes in China, an understanding of future population growth trends is needed. A number of population projections have been made in recent years by Chinese and foreign experts. The most frequently cited sources inside China include the projection made by the State Research Taskforce for Population Development Strategy in 2007 and the projection made by the CASS Institute of Population and Labor Economics.[14] Nevertheless, the projection made by the UN Population Division in 2008[15] is used here, considering the Division's well known expertise and credibility.

The UN projection for China's population growth covers a time span of 100 years from 1950 to 2050, and the results are divided into the three categories of high, medium and low variants based on various fertility and mortality assumptions. The low variant results for the period 2010–2050 are preferred for this chapter because its fertility assumption (total fertility rate or TFR at 1.44 to 1.54 in the period 2010–2020, see Table 4) is closer to the current fertility level (TFR below 1.6) than that of the medium variant (TFR at 1.79 to 1.84). In fact, China's TFR has long been a topic of controversy among Chinese and foreign demographers. Unlike the official figure that stands at 1.8 for years, it is believed that the current fertility level has been below 1.6 since the mid-2000s.[16]

**Table 4**   Fertility and Mortality Assumptions, Low Variant, China, 2010–2050

| Period | Total Fertility | | Life Expectancy | |
|---|---|---|---|---|
| | **Rate** | **All** | **Male** | **Female** |
| 2010–2015 | 1.54 | 74 | 72 | 75 |
| 2015–2020 | 1.44 | 74 | 73 | 76 |
| 2020–2025 | 1.35 | 75 | 74 | 77 |
| 2025–2030 | 1.35 | 76 | 74 | 78 |
| 2030–2035 | 1.35 | 77 | 75 | 79 |
| 2035–2040 | 1.35 | 78 | 76 | 80 |
| 2040–2045 | 1.35 | 78 | 76 | 80 |
| 2045–2050 | 1.35 | 79 | 77 | 81 |

*Source*: UN, World Population Prospects, (2008 Revision).

---

[14]Report on China's Population and Labour Force, "*Zhongguo renkou yu laodongli wenti baogao* 2010", Social Sciences Academic Press (Shehui Kexue Wenxian Chubanshe, Beijing), 2010.

[15]<http://esa.un.org/unpp/index.asp?panel=2> (accessed 13 March 2012).

[16]Yan H, "China's One-Child Policy in Need of Change", *EAI Background Brief*, no. 300, East Asian Institute, National University of Singapore, 7 September 2006.

**Table 5**　Selected Population Indicators, Low Variant, China, 2010–2050

| Year | Total Population (million) | Aged 0–14 (%) | Aged 15–64 (%) | Aged 65 and Above (%) | Dependency Ratio (%) |
|---|---|---|---|---|---|
| 2010 | 1,354 | 19.9 | 71.9 | 8.2 | 39.1 |
| 2015 | 1,361 | 18.3 | 72.2 | 9.5 | 38.5 |
| 2020 | 1,398 | 16.9 | 71.2 | 11.9 | 40.4 |
| 2025 | 1,398 | 14.9 | 71.2 | 13.9 | 40.4 |
| 2030 | 1,387 | 13.3 | 69.9 | 16.8 | 43.1 |
| 2035 | 1,366 | 12.2 | 67.2 | 20.6 | 48.8 |
| 2040 | 1,333 | 11.7 | 64.6 | 23.7 | 54.8 |
| 2045 | 1,290 | 11.2 | 63.8 | 25.0 | 56.7 |
| 2050 | 1,237 | 10.7 | 62.6 | 26.7 | 59.7 |

*Source*: calculated by the author from UN, World Population Prospects (2008 revision).

**Table 6**　Window of Opportunity by Definition, China

| Definition | Opening Year | Closing Year | Duration (Years) | No. of Years Left |
|---|---|---|---|---|
| UN definition | ≈1985 | ≈2027 | 42 | 16 |
| Definition A | ≈1990 | ≈2037 | 47 | 26 |
| Definition B | ≈1964 | ≈2015 | 51 | 4 |

*Source*: Calculated by the author.

In its low variant, the CASS projection also uses TFR at 1.54 to 1.60 as the assumed fertility level for the period 2010–2020.

During the UN projection period, as Table 5 shows, China's total population will grow from 1,354 million in 2010[17] to its peak of 1,398 million in 2020, and then fall to 1,237 million in 2050. Of note is the population peak of the UN projection which is almost the same as the CASS projection at 1,400 million under its low variant. Nevertheless, the CASS projection predicts that the peak comes only five years later in 2025. According to the UN definition, the window of opportunity will close in China sometime between 2025 and 2030 when the proportion of the elderly population surpasses the threshold of 15%. By Definition A, the window of opportunity will close a little later in the period from 2035–2040 when the ratio of the working age population to the dependent population falls below two. Judging by Definition B, however, the closure of the window of opportunity is an imminent event that will happen a few years from now in 2015, when the total dependency ratio starts to rebound.

Table 6 shows the approximate durations of the window of opportunity in China by different definitions, which range from 42 to 51 years. Those that open early seem to close early and those that open late will close late. Worthy of note is the number of years left from now before the window of opportunity closes. Wang Feng, a demographer at Qinghua University, said very sensationally in 2010 that China has only three years left to reap the demographic dividend.[18]

---

[17]The UN projection of China's total population for 2010 is higher than the sixth National Census result of 2010 as shown in Table 1.

[18]Wang F, "*Zhongguo renkou hongli jinsheng sannian*", Caixin online, Caixin Century (Caixin Wang — "Xin Shiji"), 10 November 2010.

Obviously, what counts in his mind is Definition B. According to the other two definitions, however, China still has plenty of time, up to 26 years, to enjoy the open window of opportunity.

**Labour Supply During the Window of Opportunity**

Assuming that the window of opportunity will not close in China until around 2030, how will China's total labour force look like over the next two decades? From Table 5, China's total population will grow from 1,354 million in 2010 to 1,398 million in 2020 and then drop to 1,387 million in 2030. Table 7 shows the projected working age population by age group in 2010, 2015, 2020 and 2030.[19] In 2015, China's total working age population will reach nearly one billion, the largest ever in its history. It will fall gradually to 995 million in 2020 and then to 970 million in 2030.

It is common knowledge that the working age population is not entirely engaged in economic activities. People may withdraw from the labour force at any time or for any reason. Labour participation rate is the tool to estimate the actual size of the labour force. Table 8 shows China's labour participation rates by age group calculated by a team of Hong Kong scholars in 2010.[20] Labour participation rates among age groups 25–29 and above remain largely unchanged. In comparison, that of the two youngest age groups drops gradually year on year. The assumption is that, as China's educational system improves, more young people opt for further education or training before participating in the labour force.

As shown in Table 9, China's total labour force will grow from 747 million in 2010 to 751 million in 2015. This means that China's labour force is likely to peak by the end of the 12th Five-Year Programme period (FYP, 2011–2015) and decline after 2015, although the pace may be slow at the initial stage. For example, the total labour force of 2020 is almost the same as that of 2010. Visible decreases can only be detected later in the period 2020–2030. It is thus of

**Table 7**  Working Age Population by Age Group, China, 2010–2030 (in millions)

| Age Group | Year | | | |
|---|---|---|---|---|
| | **2010** | **2015** | **2020** | **2030** |
| 15–19 | 106 | 94 | 86 | 78 |
| 20–24 | 122 | 105 | 93 | 86 |
| 25–29 | 100 | 121 | 104 | 85 |
| 30–34 | 93 | 99 | 120 | 92 |
| 35–39 | 117 | 92 | 98 | 103 |
| 40–44 | 121 | 115 | 91 | 119 |
| 45–49 | 99 | 120 | 114 | 97 |
| 50–54 | 78 | 97 | 117 | 89 |
| 55–59 | 78 | 76 | 95 | 109 |
| 60–64 | 55 | 74 | 72 | 109 |
| All | 973 | 998 | 995 | 970 |

*Source*: Calculated by the author from UN, World Population Prospects (2008 revision).

[19]The figure of 2025 is excluded from the table due to a technical mistake in the original source. All the three variants, high, medium and low, of the projection produce identical results for 2025 in the age specific module. A letter has been sent to the UN Population Department for an early correction.
[20]Ma Z, Labor Participation Rate and Labor Force Growth: 1982–2050, *Chinese Journal of Population Science*, no. 1, 2010.

**Table 8** Labour Force Participation Rates by Age Group, China, 2010–2020 (%)

| Age Group | Year | | | |
|---|---|---|---|---|
| | 2010 | 2015 | 2020 | 2030 |
| 15–19 | 34.2 | 25.2 | 22.9 | 22.9 |
| 20–24 | 80.6 | 75.0 | 72.5 | 72.5 |
| 25–29 | 89.2 | 89.2 | 89.2 | 89.2 |
| 30–34 | 90.5 | 90.5 | 90.5 | 90.5 |
| 35–39 | 91.2 | 91.2 | 91.2 | 91.2 |
| 40–44 | 90.2 | 90.2 | 90.2 | 90.2 |
| 45–49 | 85.1 | 85.1 | 85.1 | 85.1 |
| 50–54 | 76.3 | 76.3 | 76.3 | 76.3 |
| 55–59 | 63.9 | 63.9 | 63.9 | 63.9 |
| 60–64 | 48.9 | 48.9 | 48.9 | 48.9 |

*Source*: Calculated by the author from Ma et al., *Chinese Journal of Population Science*, no. 1, 2010.

**Table 9** Total Labour Force by Age Group, China, 2010–2030

| Age Group | Year | | | | | | | |
|---|---|---|---|---|---|---|---|---|
| | 2010 | | 2015 | | 2020 | | 2030 | |
| | Million | % | Million | % | Million | % | Million | % |
| 15–19 | 36 | 4.9 | 24 | 3.2 | 19 | 2.7 | 18 | 2.5 |
| 20–24 | 98 | 13.2 | 79 | 10.5 | 68 | 9.1 | 62 | 8.8 |
| 25–29 | 89 | 12.0 | 108 | 14.4 | 93 | 12.5 | 76 | 10.7 |
| 30–34 | 84 | 11.3 | 90 | 12.0 | 109 | 14.6 | 83 | 11.7 |
| 35–39 | 106 | 14.3 | 84 | 11.2 | 90 | 12.1 | 94 | 13.2 |
| 40–44 | 109 | 14.7 | 104 | 13.9 | 82 | 11.1 | 107 | 15.0 |
| 45–49 | 85 | 11.4 | 102 | 13.6 | 97 | 13.0 | 82 | 11.5 |
| 50–54 | 60 | 8.1 | 74 | 9.9 | 89 | 12.0 | 67 | 9.5 |
| 55–59 | 50 | 6.7 | 48 | 6.5 | 60 | 8.1 | 70 | 9.8 |
| 60–64 | 26 | 3.6 | 36 | 4.9 | 35 | 4.7 | 53 | 7.5 |
| Total | 747 | 100.0 | 751 | 100.0 | 746 | 100.0 | 716 | 100.0 |

*Source*: Calculated by the author from Ma et al., *Chinese Journal of Population Science*, no. 1, 2010.

certainty that before the window of opportunity closes by 2030, China's total labour force will continue to remain the largest in the world. The 4.1% decline in 20 years from 2010 to 2030 should not have any significant impact on the economy. China is likely to have about 20 years to reap its demographic dividend.

The conventional theory of the demographic dividend concerns mainly the ratio of the working age population to the dependent population in size. However, the effect of age structure changes in the working age population cannot be underestimated. Table 10 shows that although the total labour force remains largely unchanged, its age structure alters markedly. In the period 2010–2030, for example, all younger and middle-aged cohorts under 50 will shrink to a certain extent, whereas all older age groups over 50 will see their size swell

**Table 10**   Changes in Total Labour Force by Age Group, China, 2010–2030

| Age group | Period | | | | | |
|---|---|---|---|---|---|---|
| | 2010–2015 | | 2010–2020 | | 2010–2030 | |
| | Million | % | Million | % | Million | % |
| 15–19 | −12 | −34.7 | −16 | −45.5 | −18 | −50.7 |
| 20–24 | −19 | −19.9 | −30 | −31.1 | −35 | −36.3 |
| 25–29 | 18 | 21.1 | 3 | 4.2 | −13 | −14.8 |
| 30–34 | 5 | 7.0 | 24 | 29.5 | −0.6 | −0.7 |
| 35–39 | −22 | −21.1 | −16 | −15.6 | −12 | −11.6 |
| 40–44 | −5 | −4.8 | −27 | −24.8 | −2 | −2.2 |
| 45–49 | 17 | 20 | 12 | 14.4 | −2 | −2.9 |
| 50–54 | 14 | 24.3 | 29 | 49.7 | 7 | 12.0 |
| 55–59 | −1 | −3.2 | 10 | 20.9 | 19 | 39.4 |
| 60–64 | 9 | 35.7 | 8 | 31.6 | 26 | 99.3 |
| All | 4 | 0.6 | −1 | −0.2 | −31 | −4.1 |

*Source*: Calculated by the author.

quickly. The biggest change takes place at the two ends of the age spectrum. While the youngest group aged 15–19 falls by half, the oldest group aged 60–64 almost doubles. As a consequence, China's labour force is getting old, with its mean age going up from 37.6 in 2010 to 40.7 in 2030.

People may enter the labour force at any age. However, new labour market entrants come primarily from the youngest cohort aged 15–19.[21] If the young people of this cohort in 2015 are considered as those who enter the labour force in the period 2010–2015, there will be 24 million new entrants added to the labour force, or about five million annually on average. In the period 2025–2030, the total new entrants will drop further to 18 million, or about four million annually on average. The gradual decline in the number of new entrants can partially explain why the problem of labour shortage has become increasingly acute in recent years as many labour-intensive factories prefer young recruits to older ones. It is understandable that their recruitment targets can hardly be fulfilled as new entrants become increasingly scarce.

The 25–29 cohort and the 25–34 cohort deserve special attention because they belong to the most dynamic and creative part of the population. In the period 2010–2020, there is a substantial increase in these two age groups. Therefore, efforts are needed to take full advantage of their energy and talent in the next 10 years to maximise the demographic dividend.

### What to do while the Window of Opportunity is Still Open

By the UN definition, China will continue to enjoy its demographic window of opportunity for another 20 years. In the period 2010–2030, China's working age population remains largely unchanged in size and its dominance over the dependent population stays as well. However, the population's age structure will alter noticeably. With fewer young people entering the labour market, China's labour force is getting older, as its mean age rises from 37.6 to 40.7.

---

[21]A sizeable proportion of new entrants may also come from the cohort aged 20–24. To avoid double counting in the aggregated data, however, the cohort 20–24 is not discussed in further details here.

Interpreted as part of economic growth, the demographic dividend can be achieved through a rise in labour input as well as a rise in labour productivity. In terms of labour input, the potential is still great since China is currently far from reaching the stage of full employment. The recent short supply of labour is mostly due to a mismatch of skills, wages or locations. An official source estimates, for example, that during the 12th FYP period, there will be 25 million people waiting for jobs each year in the urban areas.[22] In the rural areas, labour redundancy or underemployment is still a common phenomenon. A report for the 2011 National Congress even suggests that efforts of intensified farming can further free up 340 million rural workers in the coming years.[23] Therefore, employment creation is the top priority of economic and social development in China's 12th FYP. The target is to create a total of 45 million non-agricultural jobs in the next five years. To this end, a number of active employment policies have been announced, including the promotion of labour-intensive sectors, the service sector, small and micro-enterprises, self-employment and start-ups, and vocational education and skills training; the establishment of a unified labour market nationwide; the improvement of employment services, and the protection of workers' rights and interests through enhanced regulation and law enforcement.

Labour transfers from farming to manufacturing have been the major contributor to China's economic growth over the last 30 years. The service sector can be a promising area for generating additional dividend. Compared with the world average, the share of the service industry in China's total employment is relatively low, 34.6% in 2010. In fact, the potential of job creation is quite large as the economy becomes more modernised. A study of China's employment elasticity during the period 1980–2002[24] shows that the coefficient of the tertiary industry is the highest at 0.59, compared with 0.09 of the primary industry and 0.27 of the secondary industry. That means, other things being equal, the service sector can provide more jobs. The 12th FYP also attached special importance to the development of the modern service sector for its dual role in making better use of qualified manpower, such as university graduates, and producing higher value-added products.

Meanwhile, efforts are needed to raise labour productivity. The government hopes to achieve this by designating the transformation of growth pattern as a key task during the 12th FYP period. The old pattern that relies heavily on cheap labour, high energy and resource consumption, and the export of cheap manufactured goods is deemed as economically unsustainable. The new strategy aims at a steady, robust and balanced growth based on domestic consumption and technological innovation. At the micro level, for example, factories can improve productivity, either by technological upgrading and innovation or by intensive skills training of their employees. The latter is of particular importance as the number of new entrants into labour market will shrink gradually.

If China's market-oriented reform continues, it is reasonable to conclude that it could continue to reap its demographic dividend, as long as the window of opportunity remains open. However, given the fact that the dependency ratio will rebound eventually, Chinese leaders would do well to pay attention to the possible social implications of an ageing labour force and an ageing population that may arise. Of the options recommended, one is on relaxing the country's tight birth control policies.

It is well documented that China's tough birth control policies, the One-Child policy in particular, have played a decisive role in curtailing fertility in China. The latest census figures indicate that China's current fertility is already below replacement level. Many Chinese demographers have proposed relaxing existing birth control policies as early as possible. Boosting fertility to at least the replacement level is significant to expanding the working age population. Currently, pilot projects have been initiated in a number of cities where couples, only child or not, are allowed to have two children with certain age gap in between. It seems very likely that the One-Child policy will be abolished officially by the end of the 12th FYP period.

---

[22] <http://www.chinanews.com/gn/2011/04-19/2982475.shtml> (accessed 9 July 2012).

[23] <http:// news.qq.com/a/20120229/001717.htm 2012-2-29> (accessed 13 March 2012).

[24] "*Jiuye tanxing yu sanda chanye xina jiuye nengli*". At <http://blog.stnn.cc/oldshu/Efp_Bl_ 1002286840.aspx> (accessed 13 March 2012).

# III

# Social Transformation, Stability and Governance

## Introduction

ZHAO Litao

Terms such as "governance" and "good governance" have been popular in scholarly discussions in China. Good governance, when understood as a set of features such as being consensus oriented, participatory, rule binding, effective and efficient, accountable, transparent, responsive, equitable and inclusive, is of course desirable and inspiring. Understandably scholars have been using this concept to call for political and social reforms. Good governance, when understood as a set of operational guidelines and practices, can create frustrations and even undesirable outcomes; however, China's encounter with good governance, as will be illustrated below, has proven this point. In China's social domain, some good governance practices such as decentralisation and marketisation have produced mixed results at best.

China's official discourse has been struggling with the concept of social governance. The term formally endorsed in official documents is social management. There are fundamental differences between the two terms. Nonetheless, social management is still an unfinished project and a largely undefined concept. The competition among local governments in innovating social management has paved the way for varied local initiatives. Some may be more accommodative towards good governance than others. The most important thing for China is whether it can find ways to deal with the changing realities and challenges. This will ultimately determine how social management is defined and evaluated.

### Problems of "Good Governance" in China

China is well known for its mounting social challenges. It is the only country that has substantially improved its Human Development Index (HDI) standing since 1970 mainly through income rather than education and health achievements. From the 1990s, the contribution of economic development to social development has been declining. In this regard, China differs considerably from other East Asian developmental states. China has recognised this as a problem. As a solution, the leadership proposed "scientific outlook on development", which is a call for more balanced development between the economy, society and environment. In the social domain, innovative social management has come to the fore as the solution. The term appeared in official documents as early as 2004, but was raised to the level of strategic importance by Chinese President Hu Jintao in February 2011 at the Central Party School.

Why social management instead of social governance? To scholars advocating the concept of good governance, the lack of good governance is the root cause of what troubles China today. Embracing social management can therefore only exacerbate China's mounting social problems. When good governance is understood as a set of desirable features, China indeed has yet to work out a way to achieve good governance. China's own development experience, however, suggests that good governance as a set of operational principles is not necessarily good. This point has been raised in many critical analyses of China's social challenges.

The World Bank first linked governance to development — or lack of good governance to lack of development — in a 1989 report on Sub-Saharan Africa, which defines the crisis in the region as a "crisis of governance". Governance is understood as the process by which power is exercised in the management of a country's economic and social resources for development. While acknowledging the importance of the political dimension of governance, the World Bank tried to focus on the economic dimensions.

Post-Mao China started off as a very different country from Sub-Saharan African countries. Insofar as economic development is concerned, China's problem was less a crisis of governance. Instead, it is too much control rather than weak governance that had stifled China's economic growth. When more autonomy and incentives were given to local governments, the Chinese economy quickly took off. For arguments that China lacks good governance and that good governance is the prerequisite for economic development, China stood out as a puzzle.

Apart from all the favourable conditions that have been discussed so far, one crucial change was the injection of strong growth incentives into the Chinese economy and society. In terms of the value change, it was not so difficult to convince people that "getting rich is glorious". In fact, the shift to a moneyed lifestyle was so quick and thorough that "materialism" and "spiritual vacuum" were soon to become a social problem. At the organisational level, every government agency and public institution was given larger autonomy to make money to expand their small revenue base and diversify financial resources.

These changes, now termed as decentralisation and marketisation, occurred out of practical concerns. The Chinese government at all levels was short of funds. Severe financial constraints led to the decentralisation of public services to the point that rural education received little government support and had to rely on surcharges on farming households. Local governments were given not only larger autonomy, but also larger responsibility for funding public services. Local governments went on to delegate autonomy and responsibility to every organisation directly under their jurisdiction.

Decentralisation profoundly changed the incentives and behaviours of individuals and organisations within the public domain. Wherever possible, they established their own business or create new programmes and opportunities to charge user fees for services they provided. Marketisation therefore became a dominant strategy for public institutions to generate extra-budgetary and off-budgetary incomes to cover their operation costs (under-funded by the government) and to distribute among their own staff.

China's shift towards decentralisation and marketisation was therefore out of practical concerns and constraints. Interestingly, this occurred at a time when the World Bank was about to popularise the concept of good governance. In practical terms, good governance consists of decentralisation, marketisation and privatisation of public services and enterprises. Although China was relatively slow in privatising its state-owned enterprises, not until the mid-1990s, its embrace of decentralisation and marketisation was much earlier. Seen through the lens of decentralisation and marketisation, China's development experience seems to fit squarely with the governance discourse. In China, rapid economic growth went hand in hand with decentralisation and marketisation.

This is not the end of the story, however. "Good governance" — decentralisation and marketisation — has led to many social problems, which helps explain why the contribution of economic development to social development has been declining in China. At one level, it encouraged "entrepreneurial" and profiteering behaviours, transforming the society from one lacking growth incentives to one with extremely strong growth incentives. At another level, the strategy of decentralisation and marketisation was used to guide not only economic reforms, but also social reforms, thus blurring the boundary of economic policy and social policy.

The ability to marketise and commercialise public services of course varied widely across sectors and organisations. Nonetheless, China's public service providers were quick in adapting to the new reality. On their part, governments, particularly those at the higher levels, were able to reduce their financial burden. As a result, the state was retreating from public services, and households had to pay an increasingly larger share for access to education, health care and other security needs. Many households fell back into poverty because of various uninsured risks.

The 1994 tax reform, which changed the revenue structure in favour of the central government while leaving the expenditure structure largely intact, made it more difficult for local governments and households to fund social services, particularly for those in the poor areas. The soaring costs of education, health care and housing — China's three "new mountains" as opposed to the three "old mountains" of imperialism, feudalism and bureaucratic capitalism — became a salient source of social grievances and protests.

## Reassessing Decentralisation and Marketisation

In an exaggerated form, since 1992 China has entered an era when "nine hundred million people were doing business, with the remaining one hundred million waiting to join" (*shiyi renmin jiuyi shang, haiyou yiyi yao kaizhang*). The decentralisation and marketisation of public services have transformed public service providers into money-making organisations. Social policy was marginalised and homogenised with economic policy. The benefits of high economic growth were concentrated in individuals and organisations that were positioned to profiteer from new income opportunities. Those who were not in such a position not only benefited much less, but also paid more and more for all kinds of user fees. The gap between the rich and the poor has therefore widened, along with the large rural-urban gap and the large regional disparities.

The Chinese are now asking why more than three decades of nearly double-digit growth failed to produce a large middle class. China's middle class has been expanding, measured by objective measures such as income, education and consumption. But China's social structure is far from an oval shape. Without a large middle class to hold the society together, the rich-poor divide has resulted in widespread distrust. China's super-rich has emerged and is politically accommodated. The general public, however, has developed mixed feelings of admiration in private and resentment in public. On their part, the emerging super-rich increasingly turns to consumerism as a source of identity, or migrates to other countries to escape the hostile and insecure social environment.

The working class declined as small and medium state-owned enterprises (SOEs) were either closed or privatised. Their limited material advantages in the Mao era had been eroded in the transition to the market economy. Their pension and healthcare benefits were either unpaid and defaulted or reduced during and after the state enterprise restructuring. Urban poverty for the first time emerged on a large scale in the history of the People's Republic of China, if migrant workers are excluded as urban population. The giant SOEs that survived the restructuring are no longer the same type of SOEs. They do not generate as much employment and provide as much services to the society as before.

The private sector has expanded to create a new working class, unorganised, unprotected, working long hours under bad conditions for low wages. Mainly from the countryside, the new working class has outnumbered the traditional working class. Yet the new working class is officially classified as the "floating population". Little effort has been made to integrate this group into the city.

The undersized middle class is even smaller when measured in subjective terms. As long as the costs of education, health care and housing keep soaring, the middle class will strongly feel being squeezed. College graduates are expected to be a major source of the middle class. The reality is that many college graduates cannot find a job upon graduation. Even if they find one, very likely the salary is not higher than that of migrant workers, which cannot sustain a middle class lifestyle.

New economic and social organisations have blossomed. Non-governmental organisations (NGOs) are an integral part of good governance, and are expected to play an important role in bridging the state and the society. NGOs have been developing rapidly in China, yet they are heavily regulated to function in a rather limited space carved out by the state. Many of them are also financially dependent on the state, casting doubt on their viability. For various reasons, many NGOs operate without registration. So far NGOs have been too weak to bridge the state and the society.

The contrast of economic development and social development has led many to reassess the role of decentralisation and marketisation. No consensus has been reached. One line of thinking has been very critical of decentralisation and marketisation. China's major social problems and challenges — the large and still growing income inequality, the unaffordability of education, health care and housing, and the deteriorating environment — have a great deal to do with decentralisation and marketisation, particularly the ideology of market fundamentalism.

Another line of thinking attributes all the problems to government intervention. Marketisation as a good governance practice has been distorted by government intervention. The problem therefore lies in the government, not the market. Caught in the two opposite views, the general public was confused. Some have developed a cynical view towards the government and the market: both are not trustworthy because the government is corrupt and the market is exploitative. For a number of years, reform-minded scholars have lamented that the reform consensus is no longer there.

Still, a more balanced and nuanced view has emerged. The problem is not simply the government or the market, but that the government is doing what the market is supposed to do, and the market is doing what the government is expected to do. Worse, the government or the powerful is using the market to amass wealth in the form of crony capitalism. Decentralisation and marketisation should not be an overarching reform strategy for both the economic and social domains. Instead, marketisation should be mainly confined to the economic domain. In the social domain, such as education, health care and housing, the government should not dodge its responsibility and simply let the market take over.

The debates have not been resolved. Nonetheless, at least in the social domain, China is moving away from what one may call over-decentralisation and over-marketisation. In the case of the nine-year compulsory education, there has been some limited recentralisation in terms of financing and management. Since 2001, the responsibility has shifted from the township government to the county government. Since 2006, more efforts have been made to establish a stable and regularised mechanism for funding rural education, with the central government and the provincial government playing a larger role than before.

Similar trends can be observed for programmes of pension, health care, public housing and public assistance, and the *hukou* reform. There are still many problems in equalising the basic public services nationwide. Nonetheless, the government has recognised that the social domain is fundamentally different from the economic domain. Social development would suffer if social policy has to converge with economic policy. Decentralisation and marketisation, if used without restriction in the social domain, can do more harm than good.

## Social Management: An Unfinished Project

China's adoption of some of the operational guidelines of good governance without fully embracing the ideals of participation, transparency, rule of law, public-private partnership and so on has produced many challenges. To tackle the looming problems, China has moved to focus on social management (*shehui guanli*), the approach that the CCP has been more accustomed to and comfortable with than social governance (*shehui zhili*).

The biggest difference between social management and social governance lies in the leadership. Social governance emphasises public-private partnership, while social management stresses party leadership. According to Hu Jintao, social management is to be conducted within the framework featuring party leadership, government responsibility, social coordination and public participation. Instead of forming public-private partnership, social management connotes an unequal relationship between the party-state and the society.

Regardless of which term to use, China is facing new realities and new challenges. For one, the "floating population", a Chinese term for migrants who do not have a local *hukou*, is changing. Its size has grown over 200 million. Part of the "floating population" is getting immobile, as many were born and raised by their migrant parents in the receiving city. The new generation, seeking a permanent settlement in the city where they grew up, does not want to return to the countryside. The changing profile of the "floating population" makes integration a salient and urgent issue. The rift between locals and non-locals is looming large in many places along the coast. For another, the urban middle class, which is better educated, more vocative and more resourceful than other grieved groups, is protesting to protect their property and environmental rights. City governments cannot deal with this type of protest in the same way as they deal with the "floating population". Both the "floating population" and the urban middle class present challenges for social stability.

The changing realities call for new ways of social management. That is why Chinese leaders are talking about the need to innovate social management. In vague terms, Hu Jintao identified a number of areas for innovation. In his talk at the Central Party School in February 2011, he highlighted the need to improve mechanisms to safeguard rights and interests of the people; improve management and services for migrant workers and other special groups; improve social service capability at the grassroots level and strengthen public security mechanism to ensure food and drug safety, work-related safety, social order and emergency response capabilities; improve management of NGOs and information network; provide better guidance to public opinions on the internet; strengthen the socialist core value system, and boost social trust.

China's pragmatic approach to social management has created certain spaces for local initiatives. Many local governments are now competing in the game of innovating social management. It would not be that surprising if some local governments use the vocabulary and practices associated with good governance to market their model of innovative social management. Of course one can raise the question of whether good governance is compatible with one-party rule. As the Party's Politics and Law Committee is in charge of social management, one can reasonably cast doubt on how social management is to be different from the notorious system of stability maintenance, which is under the same committee.

It is probably meaningless at this point to ask whether social management or social governance better suits China. By introducing good governance as a new paradigm of development, the World Bank did not transform the Sub-Sahara Africa into an economy of growth and entrepreneurship. Likewise, by choosing social management over social governance, there is no guarantee that social management can address China's social problems better than social governance. Social management is still an unfinished project and a largely undefined term. The ultimate test is whether China can find ways to adapt to the changing realities. Only then can social management be precisely defined and fairly evaluated against social governance.

# 29

# Chinese Working Class and Trade Unions

Transformation and Predicament in the Reform Era

QI Dongtao*

*The Chinese working class has lost its political and economic privileges in the reform era. The Chinese trade unions have basically failed to protect workers' interests due to their institutionalised overdependence on the government.*

Politically, the Chinese working class has been named the nation's leading class in the Constitution since 1949. Under the class label system of social stratification in the Mao years, workers' political status was only inferior to revolutionary soldiers and cadres'. Therefore, workers enjoyed great advantages in joining the Chinese Communist Party (CCP), such as becoming candidates for promotion in the political hierarchy, and so on. Economically, Chinese workers enjoyed job security, stable wages, and many other benefits such as free housing and medical care. Basically, almost all aspects of their typical needs in life were taken care of by their enterprises and governments. They were the "masters" of their enterprises and permanently employed by the state without labour contracts.

In the mid-1990s, the labour contract system replaced the permanent job system nationwide. As a result, Chinese workers lost permanent job security and became free labour. In the late 1990s, Chinese state-owned enterprises (SOEs) launched a series of mass lay-offs to cut production cost and improve business efficiency. By 2005, over 85% of small and medium-sized SOEs were restructured and privatised,[1] resulting in about 30 million laid-off workers, or almost half of the SOE workers.[2] For those who were fortunate enough to keep their jobs in public-owned

---

* QI Dongtao is Research Fellow at the East Asian Institute, National University of Singapore.

[1] See <http://www.caogen.com/blog/infor_detail.aspx?ID=152&articleId=16924> (accessed 20 June 2012).

[2] Qiao J, "*Zai guojia qiye he laogong zhijian: zhongguo gonghui xiang shichangjingji zhuanxing zhong de duo chong juese*" (Among State, Enterprises and Labour: Chinese Trade Unions' Multiple Roles in the Transition to Market Economy), *Zhengda laodong xuebao* (Bulletin of Labour Research), no. 22, 2007, pp. 67–101.

enterprises, most of the previously guaranteed benefits have either been completely withdrawn or drastically reduced. Almost all the enterprises stopped providing free housing to their employees. Major benefits such as medical care and pension were outsourced to government sponsored social insurance agents and employees had to share the insurance cost with their enterprises.

### Chinese Workers' Economic Conditions: Stratification and Disadvantaged Migrant Workers

New economically privileged groups have emerged within the Chinese working class since the reform, leading to a highly heterogeneous and stratified class. In the Mao years, China had a countrywide standardised wage system for all the ordinary workers and management. Because seniority and skill mastery were the two major factors determining the level of wages then, some senior and highly skilled workers' wages in a few enterprises might be even higher than the enterprise heads'. The general wage gap between ordinary workers and management and among workers was very small. The reform has significantly increased and institutionalised the wage gap between different subgroups of the Chinese working class.

The increasing wage gap between the large SOEs' higher-level management and ordinary workers has become a hotly debated issue in recent years. In some cases, the enterprise head's annual wage is 100 times more than the workers',[3] which is quite controversial in a country with a long egalitarian tradition. Even among ordinary workers, wages vary greatly by region, industry and enterprise ownership. Not surprisingly, workers in more developed regions such as the east coast and the industries monopolised by large SOEs, such as finance, energy, telecommunications, tobacco and power industries earn much more than those in other regions and industries. In terms of wage difference by enterprise ownership, Figure 1 shows that SOE workers' average annual wages had always been lower than non-public owned enterprises workers' from 1990 through 2002. However, since 2003 SOE workers' average annual wages have been higher than non-public owned enterprises workers'. This probably shows the improved competiveness of SOEs as a result of mass lay-off restructuring and enhanced monopoly in the early 2000s. Among all

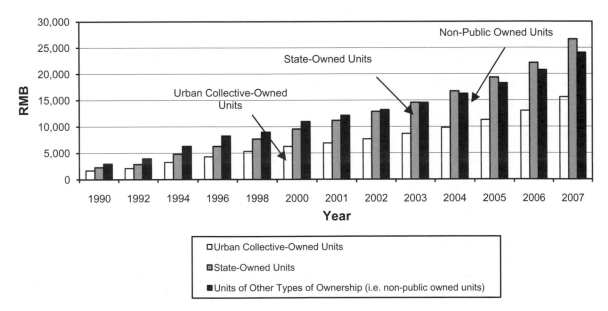

**Figure 1**   Chinese Workers' Average Annual Wages in Different Types of Enterprises, 1990–2007

*Source: Chinese Trade Unions Yearbook*, 2008, p. 501.

---

[3] For example, see <http://www.jxcn.cn/514/2005-3-21/30038@148519.htm> (accessed 20 June 2012).

the SOEs, those owned by the central government, namely central enterprises, offered the highest wages to their employees in recent years. It was reported in August 2010 that the central enterprise employees' average annual wages was about RMB54,000,[4] much higher than other SOE and private enterprise employees' average annual wages in 2009 at RMB35,000 and RMB18,000, respectively.[5] Workers in collective-owned enterprises have always received the lowest wages since 1990.

Relatively and generally speaking, SOE workers are still the most fortunate subgroup within the Chinese working class because SOEs have been regulated more strictly by the government on wages, benefits and other labour rights. In other words, SOE workers' labour rights have been violated less frequently and severely because of the government's closer supervision. There are much more violations of labour rights in non-public owned enterprises which employ over 70% of Chinese working class. Migrant workers, who constitute almost half of the whole Chinese working class, are the most disadvantaged subgroup: half of them were not employed officially (i.e. without labour contracts), 89% of them had no unemployment insurance, 83% had no pension, 70% had no medical insurance, and finally, 65% had no work accident insurance.[6]

## Chinese Workers' Political Conditions: Rising Population but Declining Political Representation

The population of the Chinese working class increased constantly from about 95 million at the beginning of the reform in 1978 to 287 million in 2008.[7] However, the representation of ordinary workers in the highest organ of state power, the National People's Congress (NPC), has declined significantly since 1978. Specifically, as shown in Table 1, the percentage of ordinary worker deputies in the NPC decreased from 26.7% in 1978 to 10.8% in 2003. Peasant representation also has a similar declining trend since the reform. Similarly, the percentage of ordinary workers in the

**Table 1**   Occupation Composition of NPC Deputies: Fifth NPC (1978) to 10th NPC (2003)

| | Total Deputies | Worker Deputies | | Peasant Deputies | | Cadre Deputies | | Intellectual Deputies | |
|---|---|---|---|---|---|---|---|---|---|
| | | No. | % | No. | % | No. | % | No. | % |
| Fifth (1978) | 3500 | 935 | 26.7% | 720 | 20.6% | 468 | 13.4% | 523 | 15% |
| Sixth (1983) | 2978 | 443 | 14.9% | 348 | 11.7% | 636 | 21.4% | 701 | 23.5% |
| Seventh (1988) | 2970 | Worker and peasant deputies were 684 (23%) in total. | | | | 733 | 24.7% | 697 | 23.4% |
| Eighth (1993) | 2978 | 332 | 11.2% | 280 | 9.4% | 842 | 28.3% | 649 | 21.8% |
| Ninth (1998) | 2981 | 323 | 10.8% | 240 | 8% | 988 | 33.2% | 628 | 21.1% |
| 10th (2003) | 2985 | 322 | 10.8% | 229 | 7.7% | 968 | 32.4% | 631 | 21.2% |

*Source*: Guo Q, "*Renda daibiao zhiye goucheng xianzhi de xianfaxue sikao*" (A Constitutional Reflection on the Composition of NPC Members), *Renda yanjiu* (People's Congress Study), Issue 6, 2009.

---

[4] See <http://acftu.people.com.cn/GB/12493256.html> (accessed 20 June 2012).

[5] See <http://www.nbd.com.cn/newshtml/20100723/20100723013629198.html> (accessed 20 June 2012).

[6] Recalculated from data in <http://www.china.com.cn/news/txt/2009-09/11/content_18507165.htm> (accessed 20 June 2012).

[7] *Zhongguo Gonghui Tongji Nianjian (Chinese Trade Union Statistics)*, 2007, p. 36, at <http://theory.people.com.cn/GB/10155027.html> (accessed 20 June 2012).

CCP has also declined. It was 18.7% in 1978, but only 9.7% in 2008.[8] Furthermore, of the newly recruited CCP members in 2008, only 7.5% were ordinary workers.[9]

### Rising Labour Disputes and Unrest

Labour disputes seem to be the unavoidable consequence of deteriorating labour conditions and workers' dissatisfaction. From 1995 when the Chinese Labour Law became effective nationwide through 2006, the number of labour dispute cases increased from 33,030 to 447,000, or by over 12 times, and the number of dispute cases per million workers increased from about 48 to 585, or by over 11 times.[10] In almost every single year, the majority of these cases were collective disputes which involved three or more workers.

Chinese workers also expressed their dissatisfaction through a variety of non-institutional channels such as protests and lodging collective complaints to the government. In 2003, 1.44 million Chinese workers participated in mass protests as the largest participating group, accounting for about 47% of total participants.[11] In recent years, more migrant workers used "suicides" to call for government's help on their payment in arrears. For instance, the fire department in Wuhan city reported in 2006 that about 80% of public suicide committers were migrant workers who wanted to get their due payment from their employers through suicides.[12]

Deteriorating labour relations have not only threatened political and social stability in China, but also become one of the major obstacles to transforming China's economy from export-driven to domestic consumption-driven. Most Chinese workers' consumption power is very low due to the low wages they receive. Wages constitute less than 10% of total cost of Chinese enterprises, while in developed countries, workers' salaries account for about 50%.[13] From 1990 through 2005, the proportion of labour remuneration in GDP declined from 53.4% to 41.4% in China. From 1993 through 2004, while Chinese GDP increased by 3.5 times, total wages increased by only 2.4 times.[14]

Improving labour conditions including wages has become the consensus among the Chinese government and scholars. Chinese trade unions have also endeavoured to protect workers' interests more effectively in recent years. Nevertheless, the trade unions have been under severe criticism by labour scholars and activists for their failure to protect Chinese workers' interests.

### Chinese Trade Unions under Criticism

Since the 1980s, union movements in most developed countries have generally declined as indicated by the constantly falling union density (i.e. percentage of employees belonging to unions) in each country (Table 2). For example, the union density in the UK and the United States decreased by 22.7% and 10.7%, respectively, from 1980 to 2007. In contrast, the union density in China has increased significantly in the last decade. Table 2 shows that the union density increased by 21.4% from 2000 to 2007. By the end of 2010, the All-China Federation of Trade Unions (ACFTU), as the sole legal trade union in China, had 239 million members,

---

[8] See <http://renshi.people.com.cn/GB/139620/9578659.html> (accessed 20 June 2012) Wang X, "*Wodang lishishang dangyuan shehui chengfen biandong qingkuang*" (Social Composition of CCP members in History), *Dang de jianshe* (*CCP's Construction*), issue 8, 2003, p. 39.

[9] Ibid.

[10] Wang K, "A Changing Arena of Industrial Relations in China: What Is Happening after 1978", *Employee Relations*, vol. 30, no. 2, 2008, pp. 190–216.

[11] Qiao J, op. cit.

[12] See <http://www.cnhubei.com/200703/ca1286244.htm> (accessed 20 June 2012).

[13] See <http://politics.people.com.cn/GB/1026/10498831.html> (accessed 20 June 2012).

[14] See <http://www.21cbh.com/HTML/2008-1-9/HTML_0DQLMP2QE4X1.html> (accessed 20 June 2012).

**Table 2**   Union Density in Developed Countries and China: 1980–2007

|  | **1980** | **1990** | **2000** | **2007** |
|---|---|---|---|---|
| The UK | 50.7% | 39.3% | 29.6% | 28% |
| Germany | 34.9% | 31.2% | 24.6% | 19.9% |
| France | 18.3% | 10.3% | 8.3% | 7.8% |
| The US | 22.3% | 15.5% | 12.8% | 11.6% |
| China | 58.1% | 59.5% | 44.5% | 65.9% |

*Notes:* Union density: union membership/total employees eligible for union membership.

*Source*: Data for the four developed countries obtained from Rampell, C, "Trade Unions' Decline around the World", 2009, at <http://economix.blogs.nytimes.com/2009/11/05/trade-unions-around-the-world/> (accessed 20 June 2012).

The 1980–2000 data for China is obtained from Metcalf, D and Li J, "Chinese Unions: Nugatory or Transforming? An Alice Analysis", 2005, at <http://eprints.lse.ac.uk/19879/1/Chinese_Unions_Nugatory_or_Transforming_An_'Alice'_Analysis.pdf> (accessed 12 March 2012). China's union density in 2007 is calculated from data in *Zhongguo gonghui tongji nianjian* (*Chinese Trade Union Statistics*), 2008.

making it the world's largest union with more members than the rest of the world's trade unions put together.[15]

However, as in many similar development cases in China's reform and opening-up era, ostensibly glorious numbers often cannot speak much about the underlying reality. Chinese and foreign labour activists and scholars have unanimously criticised the ACFTU for its inability to protect Chinese workers' rights. Chinese trade unions function differently from the Western unions. They are not autonomous labour organisations representing workers' interests, but one of the state apparatuses that serves governmental goals through mediating labour relations in China. Together with the China Communist Youth League and the All-China Women's Federation, the ACFTU is defined by the CCP as an important social pillar for its regime stability.[16]

As one of the government agencies, the ACFTU and its local branches are able to protect labour rights only to the extent that the government allows. For most local governments, labour relations are of a much lower priority than developing local GDP. If they have to develop local economy at the expense of labour rights, they usually would not hesitate to do so. Therefore, the major role of the ACFTU and its local branches is to help the governments achieve economic goals through maintaining stable labour relations.

### Chinese Trade Unions' Transformation: From "Transmission Belt" to "Society Stabiliser"

Since the establishment of the People's Republic of China (PRC) in 1949, the ACFTU has been a state apparatus that is well integrated into China's party-state structure. According to Lenin's idea, the ACFTU was defined as a two-way "transmission belt" between the Party and workers. On the one hand, it transmits the Party's ideas and orders to workers and mobilises them to work hard for the new socialist state; on the other hand, it also transmits workers' ideas and interests to the Party for its consideration in making policies. However, during Mao years, the top-down transmission of the Party's orders to workers had always suppressed the bottom-up transfer of workers' voice to

---

[15] See <http://2011lianghui.people.com.cn/GB/214385/14112143.html> (accessed 20 June 2012).
[16] See <http://news.xinhuanet.com/ziliao/2005-02/21/content_2600153.htm> (accessed 20 June 2012).

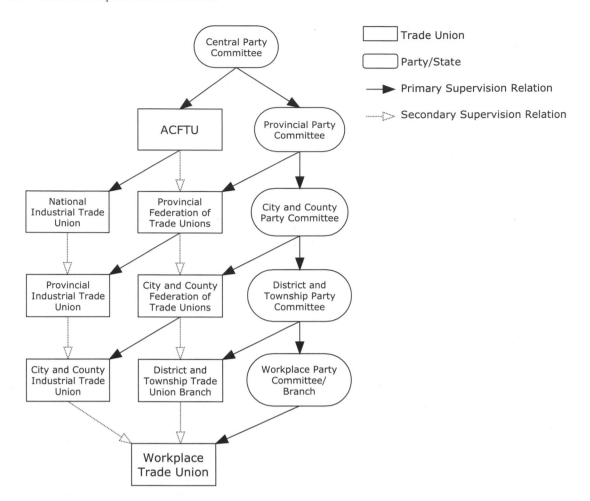

**Figure 2**   ACFTU Dual Structure of Organisation and its Relations with the Party/State

*Source*: Illustrated by the author.

the Party.[17] During the 10-year Cultural Revolution, the ACFTU completely ceased functioning. According to the socialist ideology, there were no capital-labour conflicts in China and the CCP would fully represent and protect Chinese workers' interests; therefore, having the ACFTU as the middleman for the Party and workers was unnecessary.

The ACFTU resumed its function after the Cultural Revolution and helped the Chinese government restore industrial order and promote economic reforms. As an important pillar of the CCP regime, its organisational principles and structure have been carefully maintained without profound reforms. The hierarchy of Chinese trade unions generally corresponds with the party-state hierarchy at each level (Figure 2), with the ACFTU at the top under the leadership of the Secretariat of CCP Central Committee. Under the ACFTU, in addition to 31 federations of trade unions at the provincial level, there are also 10 national industrial unions.[18] Correspondingly, the local branches of these federations of trade unions and industrial unions are established at each government level. At the grassroots level are the workplace trade unions under the nominal leadership of the upper level union and the appropriate industrial union in the same region.

Since the reform and opening up in the late 1970s, the ACFTU has gained in importance. The rise of ACFTU has actually been driven by profound changes in the Chinese working class and

[17] Chan A, "China's Trade Unions in Corporatist Transition," at <http://mondiaal.be/files/China's%20TU%20in%20Corporatist%20transition%20-%20A%20Chan_0.pdf > (accessed 20 June 2012).

[18] See <http://english.acftu.org/template/10002/file.jsp?cid=63&aid=1> (accessed 20 June 2012).

labour relations since the reform. First, as mentioned earlier, the number of urban Chinese workers increased from 95 million at the beginning of the reform in 1978 to 287 million in 2008. Labour relations have become the most important economic relation with great political implications for the Chinese government. The Chinese government has to use its trade union system to supervise workers' political activities, if any. In other words, the ACFTU must consolidate its monopoly of labour issues to stem independent labour movements. Second, the economic reforms, especially SOE restructuring and privatisation since the late 1990s, victimised many Chinese workers and created widespread grievances in China, which required the ACFTU to take actions to help the government maintain social stability. China's pro-capital and anti-labour economic regime has also generated more and more labour disputes and unrest, forcing the ACFTU to mediate in various labour issues. In a word, the Chinese government expects the ACFTU to be a stabiliser and mediator among the government, capital (employers) and workers. The ACFTU fulfils its role mainly through unionisation, legislation and labour disputes resolution.

## Growth of Chinese Trade Unions

Figure 3 shows ACFTU's unionisation efforts. In 2008, there were about 1.73 million grassroots trade unions and 212 million union members in China, both doubling the numbers in 2000. The union density also increased by 29.2% from 2000 to 2008. Foreign enterprises used to be much less unionised in China. In 2003, only 33% of them established trade unions. Since 2006, ACFTU has achieved great results in its campaign to unionise foreign enterprises. The most successful case was the establishment of a trade union for the world's leading retailer, Wal-Mart, a staunch anti-union believer; this trade union for its Chinese store was actually its first trade union in the world. By the end of 2007, 80% of foreign enterprises in China had established trade unions.[19]

To improve labour conditions, the ACFTU has also a part to play in drafting labour legislations. From 2001 to 2005, the ACFTU participated in drafting over 100 national laws and regulations, and together with other governmental agencies, it also issued more than 30 circulars on the protection of workers' rights. The three most important laws concerning labour rights are the Labour Law of 1994, the Trade Union Law of 2001 and the Labour Contract Law of 2008.

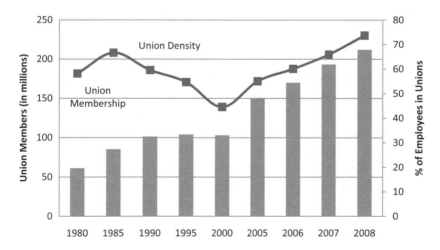

**Figure 3**   Union Membership and Union Density in China: 1980–2008

*Source*: The 1980–2000 data for China is obtained from Metcalf, D and Li J, "Chinese Unions: Nugatory or Transforming? An Alice Analysis", 2005, at <http://eprints.lse.ac.uk/19879/1/Chinese_Unions_Nugatory_or_Transforming_An_'Alice'_Analysis.pdf> (accessed 12 March 2012). China's union densities from 2005 to 2007 are calculated from data in *Zhongguo gonghui tongji nianjian* (*Chinese Trade Union Statistics*), 2006–2009.

---

[19] See <www.acftu.net> and <www.mofcom.gov.cn> (accessed 20 June 2012).

In particular, the ACFTU had contributed significantly to the drafting and promulgating of the Labour Contract Law of 2008 with its strong pro-labour position. The ACFTU's local branches have also established many legal service centres to assist workers in labour disputes. From 2000 to 2007, legal service centres increased from 2,363 with 4,960 staff to 6,178 with 18,433 staff in China.[20] Trade unions' legal consultation has contributed to a high percentage of workers succeeding in their claims in labour dispute cases.

### Chinese Trade Unions in Dilemmas

Although the ACFTU has achieved visible progress in unionisation, legislation and labour disputes resolution, it still has a long way to go in protecting workers' interests. Labour scholars and activists pointed out that the progress made by the ACFTU could not substantively improve labour conditions in China. First, a higher union density does not necessarily mean that more workers are protected; if the unions are not on the side of the workers, union membership is just a game of numbers. A study of work accidents in Pearl River Delta shows that among 582 injured workers surveyed, only 1.9% of them received care from trade unions.[21] Second, as the ACFTU does not have sufficient power, resources and capability to enforce high standards of law and regulations, promulgating new labour law and regulations is only good for the ACFTU's image-building. Finally, labour disputes resolution is a reactive way to solving labour issues. The ACFTU's more important role is to act proactively to address workers' grievances and avoid conflicts in labour relations.

The problem with the ACFTU is that although it has many grassroots unions and members, high standards of labour laws, and provision of legal aid to workers, its primary goal is not to protect workers' interests but to consolidate the CCP's regime through stabilising labour relations and maintaining industrial order. To ensure that the ACFTU does not deviate from this stabiliser role, the ACFTU and its branches have been institutionally tied to the government at the same level to do their work. Both the Labour Union Law and the ACFTU's constitution emphasise the CCP leadership in Chinese trade unions. The ACFTU has a bureaucracy that is well integrated into the Chinese government structure at each level. To ensure that the ACFTU's local branches are subordinate to the government and the Party at the same level, its chairman is usually a relatively higher-ranking official in the government and the Party of the same level. Similar institutional arrangement works for unionised workplaces. Party or management officers have been assigned to chair their workplace trade unions to ensure trade unions' subordination to workplace management. As a workplace trade union is usually on the side of capital (employer), workers cannot expect it to protect their interests in a conflict with the employer. For those government trade unions above the workplace level, their officers are government staff who have no direct and common interests with workers. These officers' job performance is evaluated by government leaders at the same level, and as a result, they are not accountable to workers but to the government. Therefore, government trade unions work to protect workers' interests to as far as the government allows.

As previously discussed, Chinese local governments have been driven by GDPism in the past decades. The performance of local government leaders is usually evaluated against the success they develop their local economy and maintain social stability. Since capital (investment) shortage has been a major concern to local governments in developing local economy, local governments tend to favour capital at the expense of labour rights. The long-term labour surplus in almost every Chinese region has exacerbated this bias towards capital. Government-business alliance is common in many Chinese regions, putting workers in a very disadvantaged position. As long as there is no serious labour unrest, government trade unions usually do not take the initiative to fight employers

---

[20] *Zhongguo gonghui tongji nianjian* (*Chinese Trade Unions Statistics Yearbook*), 2001, p. 104; *Zhongguo gonghui nianjian* (*Chinese Trade Unions Yearbook*), 2008, p. 526.

[21] See <http://www.360doc.com/content/08/0417/12/142_1195988.shtml> (accessed 20 June 2012).

for workers' interests. When labour unrest emerges, government trade unions usually play the role of a moderator to pressure both the employer and workers for a compromise.

## Failure of Chinese Trade Unions

While the historical transformation of Chinese working class in the post-Mao era may indicate how much China's economic system has changed, the dilemma of Chinese trade unions in contrast show how much China's political system has remained status quo. The great transformation from the planned economy to the market economy in China during the past three decades has been constantly generating unprecedented challenges to the CCP's authoritarian regime. To deal with these challenges and maintain regime stability, the CCP has repeatedly announced that profound reform of the political system is also necessary. Although problems and challenges from the Chinese working class have been accumulating, the major political apparatus — that is, Chinese trade unions presumably to address all these problems and challenges — has not initiated substantial reforms to break conventional institutional constraints and better fulfil its role as a society stabiliser.

# 30

# China's Middle Class

## Still in the Making

YANG Jing*

*China's middle class has been expanding and is expected to become a social stabiliser. As a heterogeneous group, however, China's middle class has yet to develop its own outlook.*

China's rising middle class has attracted the attention of both policy makers and the academia. In a mature industrial society, the middle class is the mainstream. It is not only the major source of consuming power, but also the stabiliser of the society, providing an ideal buffer zone between the upper class and the lower class.

In the Mao era, class structure remained simply as the "alliance" of workers, peasants and intellectuals. Since the 1978 economic reform, the middle class has emerged and grown in number, complexity, cultural influence and socio-political prominence amidst rapid industrialisation and urbanisation. This growth momentum is likely to continue in the 21st century. Indeed, scholars from the Chinese Academy of Social Sciences (CASS) have claimed that the 21st century will be the "golden age" for the growth of China's middle class.

Table 1 shows the changing class structure in China. From 1949 to 2006, agricultural labour decreased from 88.1% of the population (0.54 billion) to 50.4% (1.31 billion) while occupational groups expanded between 2.6 times (self-employed) and 22.4 times (sales and service workers).

Evidently, China's middle class is becoming a major component of the Chinese population. Given the persistently high heterogeneity within the group, it is not easy to define the Chinese middle class (Table 2). For example, McKinsey presents a more optimistic prediction on the

---

*YANG Jing was Visiting Research Fellow at the East Asian Institute, National University of Singapore.

**Table 1**   Changing Class Structure in China, 1949–2006 (%)

| Class Structure | 1949 | 1952 | 1978 | 1988 | 1991 | 1999 | 2001 | 2006 |
|---|---|---|---|---|---|---|---|---|
| Leading cadres and government officials | 0.5 | 0.5 | 1.0 | 1.7 | 2.0 | 2.1 | 2.1 | 2.3 |
| Managerial personnel | 0.4 | 0.1 | 0.2 | 0.5 | 0.8 | 1.5 | 1.6 | 1.3 |
| Private entrepreneurs | 0.4 | 0.2 | 0.0 | 0.0 | 0.0 | 0.6 | 1.0 | 2.6 |
| Professionals | 2.6 | 0.9 | 3.5 | 4.8 | 5.0 | 5.1 | 4.6 | 6.3 |
| Clerical workers | | 0.5 | 1.3 | 1.7 | 2.3 | 4.8 | 7.2 | 7.0 |
| Self-employed (*getihu*) | 3.7 | 4.1 | 0.0 | 3.1 | 2.2 | 4.2 | 7.1 | 9.5 |
| Sales and service workers | 0.5 | 3.1 | 2.2 | 6.4 | 9.3 | 12.0 | 11.2 | 10.1 |
| Manual workers | 2.9 | 6.4 | 19.8 | 22.4 | 22.2 | 22.6 | 17.5 | 14.7 |
| Agricultural labour | 88.1 | 84.2 | 67.4 | 55.8 | 53.0 | 44.0 | 42.9 | 50.4 |
| Semi-/Unemployed | 1.3 | — | 4.6 | 3.6 | 3.3 | 3.1 | 4.8 | 5.9 |
| Total population (N unit: billion) | 0.54 | 0.57 | 0.96 | 1.11 | 1.16 | 1.26 | 1.28 | 1.31 |

*Source*: Figures collected from *Report on Social Class Study in Contemporary China* (2002) and *Social Structure of Contemporary China* (2010), both edited by Lu X, Institute of Sociology, CASS.

growth of the middle class[1]: in 2015, upper middle class households, which have a disposable income of RMB40,001 to RMB100,000, will increase to 21.2% of urban households; and the lower middle households, which have a disposable income of RMB25,001 to RMB40,000, will reach half the number of urban households. And in 10 years' time, the proportion of upper middle class households will exceed lower middle class households and occupy around 60% of urban households in China.

Similarly, Global Market Institute of Goldman Sachs (Table 3) also anticipates that in five years' time until 2015, with rapid income growth, 60% of China's population will move up to the middle class, a big jump from 37% in 2009. And in the subsequent decade from 2015 to 2025, three-quarters of China's population should reach middle class income levels. According to the report on "The Rise of Asia's Middle Class" recently released by Asian Development Bank, the size of China's middle class based on purchasing power parity (PPP) per person per day (US$2–20) accounted for 62.68% of total population in 2005,[2] and is estimated to exceed 80% in 2030.[3]

The size of the middle class is easily exaggerated as it is not a distinct or unique group in society that can be captured by one criterion. However, various resources have projected China's middle class to rise and grow into a major component in urban China in years to come. It is believed to be a major force shaping China's economic and political future. In fact, the consuming power of the middle class has already been widely recognised.

At present, scholars usually refer to occupation, income and education as the yardsticks for classifying the middle class. The "middle class" category is then further divided into three subgroups: new middle class, old middle class and marginal middle class (Figure 1). According to the CASS study, new middle class composes Party and government officials, enterprise managers,

---

[1] They built a proprietary database of information on Chinese income, savings, and consumption patterns using primary data from the National Bureau of Statistics of China and other sources. They focussed mainly on urban Chinese consumers. For variables such as GDP growth and inflation, a base case scenario resting on a mutually consistent set of consensus estimates had been formulated. They assumed an absence of major exogenous shocks to the economy and an average growth of 6.5% in per capita GDP from 2005 to 2025, with higher annual growth initially but slowing after the year 2015.

[2] Asian Development Bank, *Key Indicators for Asia and the Pacific 2010 Special Chapter: The Rise of Asia's Middle Class*, 2010, p. 8.

[3] Ibid., p. 17.

**Table 2**   Size of the Middle Class in China from 1997 to 2030: An Estimation

| Year | Academic (s) | Measurements | Nationwide % | Urban % | Based on |
|---|---|---|---|---|---|
| Academic Estimation[a] | | | | | |
| 1997 | Zhang Jianming, Hong Dayong (1998) | Socio-Economic index (Based on education, income and occupation) | — | 48.5 (Beijing) | Survey in Beijing |
| 2001 | Zhou Xiaohong (2005) | Income, occupation, education and social attitudes | — | 11.9 (Big cities) | Survey in 5 cities |
| 2001 | Li Chunling (2005) | Occupation, income, consumption and self-identification | 4.1 | 12.0 (Big cities) | Nationwide survey |
| 2004 | Liu Yi (2005) | Income, occupation and consumption | — | 23.7 (Pearl River Delta) | Survey in Pearl River Delta |
| 2005 | Li Qiang (2005) | Occupation | 15 | — | Subjective prediction |
| 2006 | Li Peilin, Zhang Ji (2008) | Occupation, income and education | 12.1 | 25.4 | Nationwide survey |
| 2010 | CASS (2010) | Occupation, income and education | 23 | — | Nationwide survey |
| Estimation by financial sector[b] | | | | | |
| 2005 | McKinsey Quarterly (2006 special edition) | Income | — | 9.4 (upper); 12.6 (lower) | Data from National Bureau of Statistics |
| 2005 | Asian Development Bank (2010) | PPP | 62.68 | — | China Household Income Project 1995 and 2007 |
| 2009 | GMI Goldman Sachs | Income based on PPP (US$6,000–30,000) | 37 | — | World Bank |
| 2015 | (2009) | Income based on PPP (US$6,000–30,000) | 60 | — | |
| 2015 | McKinsey Quarterly | Income | — | 21.2 (upper); 49.7 (lower) | Data from National Bureau of Statistics |
| 2025 | (2006 special edition) | Income | — | 59.4 (upper); 19.8 (lower) | |
| 2030 | Asian Development Bank (2010) | Baseline income distribution ($2 and above per person per day) for consensus, real GDP growth trends | 80+ | — | Historical income distribution data and real GDP from independent sources |

*Sources:* [a][In Chinese]: Hong D and Zhang J (1998), "The Middle Class in Urban China." *Journal of Renmin University of China.* No.5, pp. 62–67. Zhou X, (ed.) (2005). *Survey of the Chinese Middle Class.* Beijing: Social Sciences Academic Press (China). Li C (2008), "The Growth and Present Situation of the Chinese Middle Classes", *Jiangsu Social Sciences*, no. 5. Liu Y (2006), "Index Definition and Empirical Study on Middle Class — Case of Pearl-River Delta", *Open Times*, no. 4. Li Q (2005), "Theories and Present Situation of Middle Class", *Society*, 1. Li P and Zhang J (2008), "Size, Identity and Attitudes of Chinese Middle Class," *Society*, 28. Lu X (ed). (2010). *Social Structure of Contemporary China*, Social Sciences Academic Press.

[b]The McKinsey Quarterly (2006), *The Value of China's Emerging Middle Class*, special edition. Global Markets Institute (GMI) of Goldman Sachs (2009), *The Power of the Purse: Gender Equality and Middle-Class Spending*; The McKinsey Quarterly (2006), *The Value of China's Emerging Middle Class*, special edition. Asian Development Bank (2010), *Key Indicators for Asia and the Pacific 2010 Special Chapter: The Rise of Asia's Middle Class.*

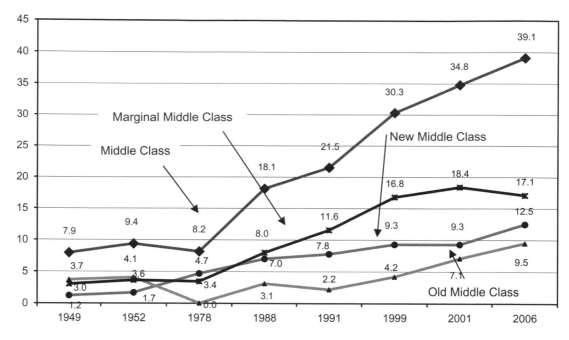

**Figure 1**    China's Middle Class, 1949–2006

*Source*: National Bureau Of Statistics and the China General Social Survey (By CASS), 2006.

**Table 3**    Components of China's Middle Class by Occupation, 2006

|  | **By Occupation** | **% Nationwide** |
| --- | --- | --- |
| New Middle Class | Leading cadres and government officials | |
| | Managerial personnel | 12.5 |
| | Private entrepreneurs | |
| | Professionals | |
| Old Middle Class | Clerical workers (senior level) | |
| Marginal Middle Class | Self-employed | 9.5 |
| | Clerical workers (middle/lower level) | 17.1 |
| | Sales and service workers | |

*Note*: The different levels of clerical workers cannot be distinguished in the China General Social Survey (CGSS), 2006. The author wants to emphasise that since the financial situation of the majority of clerical workers was similar to the marginal middle class, they were included here. Therefore, the actual proportion of new middle class should be a bit higher and correspondingly, the marginal middle class should be a few percentages lower.
*Source*: Author's own point of view.

private entrepreneurs, professionals and senior-level clerical workers; old middle class refers to the traditionally self-employed people; and marginal middle class makes up the majority of the middle class people working as lower/entry level clerical workers and employees in the sales and service sector. It is also not surprising to see more people from the new middle class obtaining quality education and higher income in comparison with the other two groups (Table 3).

The capitalist class, often referred to as comprising owners of small- or medium-sized enterprises, is usually considered a key component of the rising middle class in China. As a newly emerged class with great economic capital, those who belong to the capitalist class have been progressively recruited into the Party to participate in socio-political activities. Meanwhile, although there are indications of greater involvement of private entrepreneurs in policy-making procedures, their role remains primarily in the economic realm, thus reflecting the interdependence between them and the local governments.

Unlike its Western counterpart, the Chinese burgeoning capitalist class — mostly owners of small or medium-sized enterprises, constituting 2.6% of the total population in 2006 — is usually regarded as part of the new rising Chinese middle class. Therefore, China's middle class composes of not only the majority of white-collar workers and well-educated professionals, but also those at the top of the social hierarchy in terms of wealth.

Except for the new middle class who exhibits the most democratic mentality compared with the other two groups, China's middle class as a whole has yet to hold a distinctive socio-political ethos, be it directed at self or others. The Chinese middle class' acknowledgement of the state authority is similar to that accorded by the rest of the society. As long as the majority of the middle class are able to safeguard their current interests despite reforms in social policy, the demand for political democratisation is unlikely to become strong.

## Life Satisfaction of China's Middle Class

As the majority of the middle class are business professionals, government officials and intellectuals, most of them ranked career and professional life highly in their social life. Most, if not all, expect long-term employment and regard working life as one of their top priorities. Recent research found that they are dependent on the current economic system, generally have savings in banks and lead a comfortable life.

Figure 2 shows that about 77% of new middle class are satisfied with their current life, in comparison to 73% of old middle class and 68% of marginal middle class. Similar patterns are also found in some particular aspects of life such as family financial situation, housing and current jobs. More new middle class than old and marginal middle class claim satisfaction with their life. Therefore, in terms of happiness (Figure 3), on average, over 50% of middle class are happy with their life, compared with around 44% of working class and 42% of agricultural labour. Of the middle class, the new middle class is again found to be the happiest group.

Respondents were fairly humble when they were asked to rank their personal economic status and family socio-economic status in society, as shown in Figure 4. About 46% of new middle class and 42% of old middle class ranked their personal economic status as well as their family socio-economic status as middle or upper level of the Chinese society. Meanwhile, for the less confident marginal middle class, both figures drop to around 30%.

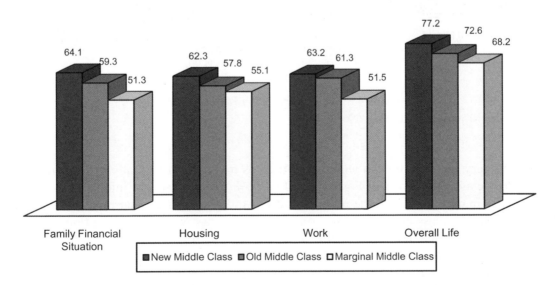

**Figure 2**   Proportions of New, Old and Marginal Middle Classes' Satisfaction with Life in 2006

*Source*: China General Social Survey (CGSS), 2006.

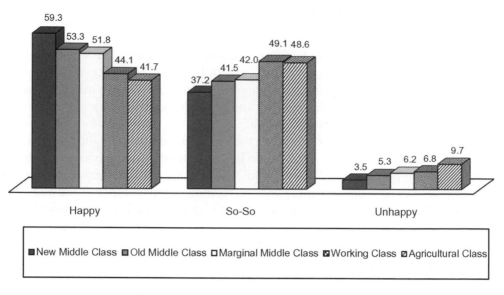

**Figure 3**   Happiness of Chinese People in 2006

*Source*: China General Social Survey (CGSS), 2006.

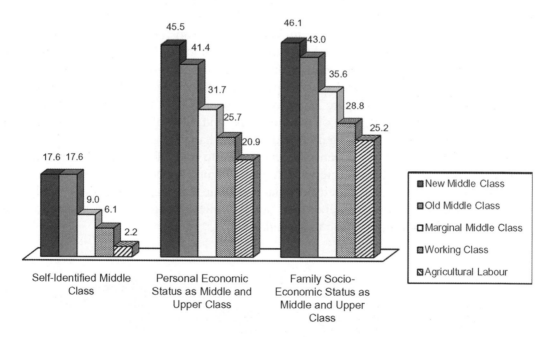

**Figure 4**   Chinese People's Self-Ranking in 2006

*Source*: China General Social Survey (CGSS), 2006.

However, very few people who were categorised as middle class actually claimed themselves to be middle class. As shown in Figure 4, only 17.6% of new and old middle class identified themselves as middle class, and the proportion drops to 9.0% for marginal middle class. In fact, 54% of new middle class claimed themselves as working class, while the proportion increased to 76% among the marginal middle class, with around 11% of both groups claiming to be agricultural labour. At the same time, for the old middle class, about 41% claimed to be working class while about 35% claimed to be agricultural labour.

There are two possible explanations to this phenomenon. One is modesty. The respondents could be too humble to label themselves as middle class. The second is the genuine feeling of inadequacy brought about by the heavy burden of housing loans and high costs of living. Some commentators have warned that if increases in housing price keep out-pacing growth of income or savings, in five to eight years' time, the majority of urban middle class in China will be gradually squeezed out of the housing market. The majority of middle class will slip to a vulnerable position as in the case of Japan. The social structure would become the shape of "工" instead of an "olive" or "onion".

The identity of China's middle class has yet to be formed, resulting in a discrepancy in the size of objective and subjective middle class groups. Soaring housing prices and costs of living strongly affect people's perception of their own class status and their socio-political preferences. It is evident that a number of China's middle class are still struggling to make ends meet. Nonetheless, some segments, particularly the financially more secured new middle class, are becoming more confident. It would benefit the Chinese government if this group continues to grow and becomes a stabilising force, and provides mainstream values to the rest of the society.

More middle class people claim satisfaction with their financial status, job, housing and overall life. Therefore, they appear to be leading a happier life than the rest of the society. The self-evaluation of these aspects of life from a high to low range of satisfaction corresponds with the order of new, old and marginal middle class groups.

## Socio-Political Attitudes of China's Middle Class

With the rapid growth of China's middle class, there has been growing interest in the socio-political attitudes of this rising group since the 1980s. Early studies of the emerging middle class described them as the most active pursuers of democracy. In the 1990s, mainstream perception had it that the middle class was politically conservative, as well as supportive of government policies and economic reform; they would therefore become a strong stabilising force of the society.

Most recent research shows that China's middle class actually hold a mix of both liberalistic and conservative views due to their divergent backgrounds and life experiences. They tend to have more positive feelings about democracy and high expectation of social justice, and show higher confidence in political participation. Most of them hope to benefit from the economic growth and safeguard their current interests; they are therefore more prepared to be subservient to an authoritarian state in exchange for economic security and socio-political stability (see Table 4).

Table 4 shows that the middle class as a whole appears to be more open-minded regarding the pursuit of democracy (S1), and has more confidence in political participation (S4) than working class and agricultural labour class. Those belonging to this class are aware of the income gap and agreeable to taxing the rich to help the poor; they also show a higher rate of acceptance on the pursuit of profit to sustain economic growth.

Within the middle class, there are differences in socio-political attitudes. The new middle class with more cultural capital shows most democratic consciousness. The old middle class tend to be more mindful of their own financial situation. They hold relatively conservative political views and are more likely to support state authoritarianism and are the least conscious about social inequality and justice. The marginal middle class are comparatively more vulnerable and therefore more sympathetic towards the lower class, exhibiting a stronger sense of social justice and democracy than the old middle class.

In China, as in elsewhere, there is a positive correlation between education and liberalism. Younger people generally display more democratic consciousness and have lower confidence in the government. Seen in this light, whether the rising middle class is a stabiliser or a challenger will depend on whether the political system can accommodate their political demands.

The rise of the bourgeois is also regarded as a potential driving force for democratisation. Some scholars speculate that continued economic growth and the increasing scale and scope of state enterprise privatisation might ultimately lead to political changes initiated by private entrepreneurs.

**Table 4**   Views on Socio-Political Issues: Middle Class (MC) Versus Working Class and Agricultural Labour Class (WC+ALC)

| | % of agreement among MC | | | | % of |
|---|---|---|---|---|---|
| | **New** | **Old** | **Marginal** | **All MC** | **WC+ALC** |
| **I. Regarding democracy and political participation** | | | | | |
| S1: Democracy is not necessary with sustainable economic growth | 33 | 40 | 37 | 36 | 44 |
| S2: The richer have more rights to speak on public issues than the poorer | 39 | 47 | 41 | 41 | 43 |
| S3: Only professionals can exercise the rights of decision-making | 50 | 54 | 50 | 51 | 54 |
| S4: Politics is too complicated to understand | 43 | 54 | 51 | 48 | 59 |
| S5: Rights to appeal regarding inadequate local policies | 85 | 83 | 84 | 84 | 81 |
| **II. Regarding current government** | | | | | |
| S6: Insufficient policies are key reasons for poverty | 72 | 70 | 75 | 73 | 73 |
| S7: Obedience to government never goes wrong | 56 | 55 | 58 | 57 | 61 |
| S8: Operation of law requires government's support and coordination | 79 | 81 | 84 | 81 | 81 |
| **III. Regarding social inequality** | | | | | |
| S9: No social development without pursuit of profits | 76 | 72 | 77 | 76 | 69 |
| S10: Enlarging rich-poor gap stimulates positivity at work | 59 | 59 | 60 | 59 | 58 |
| S11: Lack of education is a key reason for poverty | 60 | 63 | 61 | 61 | 65 |
| S12: Tax the rich to help the poor | 76 | 73 | 79 | 77 | 77 |

*Source*: China General Social Survey (CGSS), 2006.

Some scholars however believe that China's private entrepreneurs are too heterogeneous to form a cohesive identity. For the past three decades, the CCP government has been slowly whittling away the institutions that defined the planned economy to embrace market mechanisms. This has reinforced property relations between central and local governments, and further engendered cooperative relationships between local officials and businessmen. Therefore, class formation has not occurred within this group, and it is unlikely for private entrepreneurs to promote democratisation in China in the near future.

A combination of these changes and gradual privatisation was the central government's strategy for granting greater autonomy over the local economy to local governments. This transformed the relationship between local officials and private entrepreneurs from critical to an interdependent patron-client relationship.

Chinese entrepreneurs have also adopted a series of adaptive strategies and maintained close ties with local government officials, which essentially prevent them from being a force for change. According to Chen An and Dickson, Bruce J, as long as private entrepreneurs share the same interest of promoting economic growth, "many will rely heavily on government patronage for their success in making profits",[4] and "they are among the Party's most important bases of support".[5] Consequently, both sides in this debate commonly agree on the Party's embrace of the private sector and the impact of entrepreneurs as a new social group.

China's middle class has grown to become a major component in urban China. The size of the middle class indicates how sustainable economic growth has been. Modern political economists consider a large middle class, equipped with better education and understanding of democracy and politics, as well as their capability of self-justification, to be a beneficial and stabilising influence on society. And the relatively open mobility within the entire middle class provides a perfect buffer zone for the confrontation of the top and bottom, which further maintains political stability.

China's middle class is a mix of liberalists and conservatists with divergent backgrounds and life experiences. They tend to have more positive feelings about democracy and high expectation of social justice, and show more confidence in understanding and participating in politics. At the same time, the middle class as a whole appears to be less confident of its class status in society. The middle class identity has yet to be formed in China.

However, the middle class also hope for stability and to benefit from economic growth. They are prepared to be subservient to the authoritarian state in exchange for economic security and socio-political stability. As economic conditions largely affect people's perception of class status, they will also sway and shape a person's socio-political attitude. The financially more secured new middle class is the probable social stabilisers the Chinese government may count on in the future.

---

[4] Chen A, "Rising-Class Politics and Its Impact on China's Path to Democracy". *Democratization* 10, no. 2 (2003). pp. 157.

[5] Dickson, BJ, *Integrating Wealth and Power in China: The Communist Party's Embrace of the Private Sector*, 2007, pp. 827–828.

# 31

# China's New Rich Posing a Challenge to Social Stability

SHENG Sixin*

*China's economic development in the past three decades has given rise to a class of "New Rich", as well as widened the gap between the rich and the poor, thus posing a serious challenge to social cohesion and stability.*

China's dynamic economic growth since the late 1970s and its shift to a market economy have given rise to a new moneyed class, a heterogeneous group consisting of private entrepreneurs, managers of large corporations, professionals and state officials with discretionary powers. China's double-digit growth in the early 2000s resulted in a booming property market and the launching of IPOs has also provided a new method of wealth creation. Since then, China watchers have begun to talk about the coming of age of a new class of wealthy Chinese, particularly those with financial and property assets of over RMB100 million (*yiwanfuweng*). Despite the global economic downturn, McKinsey still predicts that the number of wealthy households in China will increase to more than 4.4 million by 2015, up from 1.6 million in 2008. Here, wealthy households are defined as urban households with annual income in excess of RMB 250,000.

Over the years, the Chinese Communist Party (CCP) has played an important role in legitimising the moneyed class. It officially recognised private entrepreneurs in 1988, and radically amended the Party Constitution in 2002 to allow private entrepreneurs to join the party. Through co-option and inclusion, the CCP has enhanced the political status of private entrepreneurs. The media have also played their part in legitimising wealth as a highly positive value. Discussions about social stratification were restricted in China in the 1990s for fear of social instability. Into the 2000s however, popular magazines began to report widely on the incomes and lifestyles of the wealthiest people in China. The international media and business community have also been making great efforts to legitimise consumerism and moneyed lifestyles in China. The Millionaire Fair, an annual

---

* SHENG Sixin is a PhD candidate at the Australian School of Business, the University of New South Wales, Australia. He was formerly a Research Officer at the East Asian Institute, National University of Singapore.

exhibition that was inaugurated in Europe in 2001 to showcase luxury goods and lifestyles, was held in Shanghai in April 2006. Some 10,000 VIP guests from all over China were entertained in a swirl of gala dinners, cocktail receptions and performances by international troupes.

### The Profile of China's (Super) Rich

The emergence of the super-rich is a relatively new phenomenon in China. This is evident in *Hurun China Rich List*, the earliest and the most influential annual list of China's super-rich. When the rich list was first produced in 1999, mainland China had only one US dollar billionaire (Rong Yiren). With soaring property prices, the rebounding stock market and the launch of large IPOs in the 2000s, the super-rich list has been expanding quickly. In 2007, the billionaire list swelled to 106. Indeed, China's skewed growth pattern is conducive for producing the super-rich. According to the *Hurun China Rich List*, the growth of the super-rich and the wealth they amassed by far outpaced China's GDP growth. The list is expanding quickly, even though the requirements for a listing have been raised. As Table 1 clearly shows, the average wealth of the super-rich is growing at a stunning pace.

China's super-rich share some common characteristics, which facilitate the formation of identity and group consciousness. As is often the case in emerging economies, China's super-rich are relatively young. *Hurun China Rich List* shows that in 2011, the average age of the top 1,000 Chinese super-rich was only 51. Using a different definition, a McKinsey report found that some 80% of China's wealthy is younger than 45, compared with 30% in the United States and 19% in Japan.[1]

As at the end of the 1990s, in terms of education, China's super-rich were not well educated. There was therefore a strong need for them to acquire educational credentials to enhance their social status. The rapid expansion of higher education since 1999, particularly the burgeoning number of expensive executive programmes, has provided opportunities for China's new rich to

Table 1   China's Super-Rich: Rapid Growth in Number and Wealth

| Year | Wealth of the 50th Richest (RMB in Millions) | Wealth Requirement for Listing (RMB in Millions) | Number of Super-Rich on the List |
|---|---|---|---|
| 1999 | 50 | 50 | 50 |
| 2000 | 350 | 350 | 50 |
| 2001 | 900 | 500 | 100 |
| 2002 | 1,200 | 700 | 100 |
| 2003 | 1,500 | 900 | 100 |
| 2004 | 1,900 | 1,250 | 100 |
| 2005 | 2,600 | 500 | 400 |
| 2006 | 4,200 | 800 | 500 |
| 2007 | 12,000 | 800 | 800 |
| 2008 | 10,000 | 700 | 1,000 |
| 2009 | 14,500 | 1,000 | 1,000 |
| 2010 | 15,500 | 1,000 | 1,359 |
| 2011 | 17,000 | 2,000 | 1,000 |

*Source*: *Hurun China Rich List*, 1999–2011.

[1] McKinsey & Company, *The Coming of Age: China's New Class of Wealthy Consumers*, 2009.

**Table 2**  Geographic Distribution of China's Super-Rich and their Headquarters

| Birthplace | Number (%) | Place of Headquarters | Number (%) |
|---|---|---|---|
| Zhejiang | 160 (16.0) | Guangdong | 174 (17.4) |
| Guangdong | 107 (10.7) | Zhejiang | 141 (14.1) |
| Jiangsu | 92 (9.2) | Beijing | 113 (11.3) |
| Shandong | 53 (5.3) | Jiangsu | 103 (10.3) |
| Fujian | 51 (5.1) | Shanghai | 81 (8.1) |
| Subtotal | 463 (46.3) | Subtotal | 612 (61.2) |

*Source*: *Hurun China Rich List*, 2011.

**Table 3**  Distribution of China's Super-Rich by Industry: 2009–2011

| Industry | 2011 (% of Super-Rich) | 2010 (% of Super-Rich) | 2009 (% of Super-Rich) |
|---|---|---|---|
| Real Estate | 23.5 | 20.1 | 23.7 |
| Manufacturing | 19.1 | 19.5 | 15.9 |
| Finance and Investment | 6.7 | 7.0 | 6.3–10.0 |
| Resource | 6.5 | 6.3 | 4.4 |
| IT | 5.8 | 6.7 | 4.6 |
| (New) Energy | 5.6 | 5.3 | 7.9 |
| Pharmaceutical | 5.5 | 4.6 | 6.6 |
| Clothing and Textiles | 5.1 | 4.6 | 5.0 |
| Subtotal | 77.8 | 74.1 | 77.0 |

*Source*: *Hurun China Rich List*, 2009–2011.

receive higher education and expand network ties. As a result, according to *Hurun China Rich List*, the figure jumped to 77% in 2003 from only 15% who received higher education in 1999.

As for gender composition, the rich list is as expected, male-dominated. A record number of 156 women made it to *Hurun China 1000 Rich List* in 2011, compared to 153 of super-rich women in 2010. Some of them are self-made super-rich. Examples include Zhang Yin of *Nine Dragons Paper Holdings* and Chen Ningning of the mining industry. Others inherited wealth from their husbands or fathers, like Chen Jinxia who inherited her wealth from her super-rich husband Wei Dong, and Yang Huiyan whose father transferred 70% of a Guangdong-based property development company — Country Garden — to her before its IPO in 2007.

Geographically speaking, China's super-rich are concentrated in a few developed provinces and cities. According to *Hurun China Rich List 2011*, Zhejiang, Guangdong, Jiangsu, Shandong and Fujian produced the largest number of super-rich by birthplace (Table 2). More super-rich have their business headquarters in Guangdong, followed by Zhejiang, Beijing, Jiangsu and Shanghai.

Real estate is the sector producing the largest number of super-rich, accounting for about a quarter of all super-rich. Manufacturing is the second largest sector, which reflects China's status as the world's factory. Other sectors lag far behind. Nevertheless, the number of super-rich in the resource sector has been rising in recent years (see Table 3).

## The CCP's Co-option of the New Rich

After the 1989 Tiananmen incident, the CCP sought to maintain regime stability by limiting political activism, opening up economic sectors to non-state capital and co-opting various elites into the system. The new strategy of building an extensive "elite alliance" included not only the intellectual and cultural elite, but also the economic elite in the private sector.

Unlike co-opting the intellectual and cultural elite, who enjoyed high social prestige after the Cultural Revolution, co-opting private entrepreneurs became a contentious issue. The CCP had spent decades de-legitimising capitalists. To many senior party members and officials, the CCP had always been a party against the exploitative capitalists. It was unthinkable that it would shift to embrace them. Despite much controversy in the late 1990s, Jiang Zemin decided to open up the party to private entrepreneurs. He did so by portraying the CCP as representing the broadest interests of Chinese society as well as being the most advanced productive force. Either way, he argued that private entrepreneurs should be allowed to join the party. In 2002, the Party Constitution was amended to officially endorse the radical move to embrace the "capitalists". In 2008, one-third of those on the *Hurun China Rich List* were estimated to be CCP members.

Channels of political participation for private entrepreneurs were also opened up. Becoming a delegate to the National People's Congress (NPC) or the China People's Political Consultative Congress (CPPCC) was an important way to enhance the political status of private entrepreneurs. Among the 1,000 people on *Hurun China Rich List* in 2011, 75 and 72 of which were NPC and CPPCC delegates respectively. There were also seven members of National Congress and 12 vice-chairmen of the All-China Federation of Industry and Commerce. This meant that about 15.4% of China's super-rich held national-level political status in state apparatuses, compared with 12% in 2010.

With their newly recognised political status, China's super-rich are becoming more assertive in voicing their concerns. A recent example is Zhang Yin, who topped the 2006 *Hurun China Rich List* (but fell to number two in 2007 and 15th in 2008). She made her fortune by buying scrap paper for use in China. Zhang Yin made three proposals during the annual session of CPPCC in 2008. The first was to amend the Labour Contract Law (effective as of 1 January 2008) to exempt labour-intensive companies from signing permanent contracts with their employees; the second was to cap the income tax rate at 30% instead of 45%; and the third was to lift the duty levied on imported environmental remediation facilities for five to seven years. While her proposals led to heated debate as to whether she was representing public interests or her own interests, this episode clearly shows the enhanced political status of China's super-rich and their growing willingness to voice their concerns through newly available political channels.

Many agree that property developers have become the best organised interest group in China, with the potential to reverse the central government's policy. In 2003, China's central bank released Document 121, announcing measures to control lending to the real estate sector to prevent further overheating. In response, property developers took quick action, organising conferences to shape public opinion on one hand, and working through the All-China Federation of Industry and Commerce to oppose Document 121 on the other. The State Council soon released Document 18, stressing the importance of the real estate sector and recognising its healthy development. The new document effectively overturned the central bank's decision. This episode was widely seen as the first case in which an interest group managed to mobilise support from within and without the system to reverse a major government policy.

However, the enhanced political status of China's super-rich and their increasing assertiveness does not mean that they are becoming an independent and politically active class. As the largest beneficiary of China's economic reform, they are not keen to change the existing structure that best accommodates both their economic and political interests. Ironically, the super-rich do not have much confidence in China's future, and over 50% of them have obtained permanent residence or even citizenship in other more developed countries (e.g. United States, Canada, Singapore and Australia), according to a report done by China Merchants Bank and Bain & Company in 2011.

## Public Ambivalence Towards the Rich

Surveys done in China have repeatedly shown that China's youth are increasingly success-oriented. Money and a moneyed lifestyle are becoming increasingly important in urban Chinese aspirations.

In the 1980s, Deng Xiaoping had to try hard to make people believe that "to get rich is glorious"; into the 1990s, this notion became almost universally accepted. However, the general public has mixed feelings of private admiration/aspiration and public resentment/ridicule towards China's super-rich.

History plays some part in this ambivalence towards the rich. Private entrepreneurs were de-legitimised and eliminated in the Mao era. In the early 1980s, the first ones that entered private business were most likely those who did not receive much education and could not find a job in the state or collective sector. The image of private entrepreneurs — China's richest people back then — was as bad as ever. The CCP legally recognised private enterprises in 1988. Since then, people with secure jobs in the state sector began to enter the private sector. "Jumping into the sea" (*xiahai*) became the most attractive option for many officials, academics, professionals and state workers. Those who were forced to leave their state posts after the 1989 Tiananmen incident found an alternative career path in the lucrative private business. Many of the richest in the 1990s had what it took to become a person with high social status, including a good education and good reputation brought over from their previous job. Yet their wealth was considered dirty or unjustifiable. They were believed to have amassed wealth through smuggling, bribery, tax evasion, theft of state assets and other illegal means. The biggest gainers were reportedly children of high-ranking officials or those who had cultivated good connections with them.

China's mass media not only shed positive light on the moneyed lifestyle and played an important role in legitimising money and consumerism, but also successfully focussed public attention on the "original sin" of China's richest people. For example, a Shenzhen-based lawyer collected case files of 85 influential entrepreneurs sentenced or accused of criminal offences in 2009, with 36 from state-owned enterprises and 49 from private enterprises. Among the 21 private entrepreneurs already sentenced, seven were sentenced to death. This report then attracted tremendous public attention and discussion after it was widely distributed by the state media, such as *Xinhua*, *China Daily* and so on.

By now, wealth had been fully legitimised. The problem however, is that there is now a clear distinction between wealth and the wealthy. Paradoxically, the wealthy are widely resented rather than respected in the Chinese society. Private admiration and aspiration for wealth coexists with public resentment and ridicule of the wealthy, a phenomenon rarely seen in other societies. Part of the popular resentment stems from the perception that China's super-rich made their fortune not through diligence, entrepreneurship and innovation, but through smuggling, bribery, speculation, tax evasion and theft of state assets. There is no merit to the success of the super-rich. As a result, the rich are hated as much as corrupt officials. Public resentment against the wealthy also has to do with the overriding desire for immediate economic success among the youth. Previous surveys have found that youth in all sectors and locales aspired to be high achievers, yet they were impatient and unhappy with their current conditions. This dissatisfaction has led to mixed feelings of both envy and resentment towards the wealthy, which was further aggravated by the reality of growing income inequality across regions and sectors.

## A Divided Society and its Challenge

In Chinese history, wealth does not automatically translate into social prestige. This was because the Confucian elite despised materialistic pursuits and business people. In contrast, making (clean) money is a fully legitimate pursuit today. The fact that wealth still does not translate into social acceptance and prestige reveals deep tensions between the haves and the have-nots, not between the cultural elite and the business elite. This is why some sociologists are concerned that China is heading towards a polarised society. Social cohesion is in danger today. The new rich are increasingly turning to consumerism as a source of identity and status as they are applauded by foreign investors and companies for becoming consumers in the global marketplace. Their luxurious and often exclusive lifestyle, however, has reduced their interactions with people from the lower social strata. On their part, people who are not so well-off view the rich as corrupt and lacking in social responsibility. The divide between the two groups presents a tremendous challenge to the CCP's proposals for building a harmonious society.

The growing income inequality further fuelled public resentment towards the super-rich. Another factor has to do with the cultural expectations of the rich to give back to the community as well. Traditionally, the rich were expected to have varying responsibilities towards members of their extended family, lineage, and local community. The "unkind rich" were looked down upon by other family and community members. In today's China, the super-rich are criticised for being too exploitative of their employees (usually migrant workers from poor areas) and donating too little to charity. China's super-rich will continue to be put under scrutiny. This issue was brought to the forefront during the 2008 Sichuan earthquake which heightened public awareness towards volunteering, philanthropy and corporate social responsibility. It was the first time that those on the *Hurun China Rich List* came under significant social pressure to make a donation in public.

The public hatred of the super-rich reveals deep tensions within the Chinese society. In early 2003, three leading private entrepreneurs were murdered within three weeks of each other. There were many speculations about "revenge against the rich" as the motive. The super-rich have also become consumers in the global marketplace (Box 1), making China the third largest high-end consumer of luxury goods (handbags, shoes, jewellery, perfume and the like), accounting for more than 12% of global sales today, compared with only 1% in 2000. Some even predicted that within a decade, China will likely overtake Japan and the United States to become the top luxury market.

---

**Box 1**    Consumption Behaviour of China's Super-Rich

**Preferred international holiday destinations:**

1. France,  2. US Mainland,  3. Australia,  4. Maldives,  5. Japan,  6. Switzerland,  7. Dubai, 8. Hawaii,  9. Singapore,      10. Canada,  11. Italy,      12. New Zealand

**Preferred domestic holiday destinations:**

1. Sanya,      2. Hong Kong,  3. Yunnan,   4. Tibet, 5. Macao, 6. Hangzhou, 7. Beijing, 8. Shanghai, 9. Qingdao, 10. Xinjiang,    11. Xiamen, 12. Dalian

**Preferred luxury brands:**

1. Louis Vuitton, 2. Cartier, 3. Hermes, 4. Chanel, 5. Moutai, 6. Apple, 7. Dior, 8. Prada, 9. Rolex, 10. Giorgio Armani

**Preferred educational destination for children:**

1. USA,      2. England, 3. Canada, 4. Australia, 5. Germany, 6. Hong Kong, 7. Singapore, 8. Switzerland, 9. France, 10. Japan,   11. New Zealand

*Source: Hurun* 2012 (Best of the Best Awards).

---

The rest of the Chinese society also aspires to become high achievers, yet most of them have to live with the reality that immediate economic success is not within their reach. Many of them are impatient and dissatisfied with their current conditions.[2] In the context of increasing income inequality, it is very difficult for them to accept the super-rich as respectable and their luxurious lifestyle justifiable, no matter how enviable they are.

---

[2]Rosen, S, "The Victory of Materialism: Aspirations to Join China's Urban Moneyed Classes and the Commercialisation of Education", *The China Journal*, 2004, pp. 27–51.

The division between the super-rich and the rest presents a challenge to China's social cohesion and social stability. There is no easy solution. To a large extent, it will depend on whether China's evolving market economy will produce winners based on merit, whether China's super-rich show greater social responsibility, and whether the aspirations of the younger generation are managed or accommodated in a way that the kind and degree of inequality is acceptable to them. The divide between the rich and the rest presents a tremendous challenge to the CCP's concept of harmonious society. So far it is not clear how the CCP could effectively address this problem. Moreover, the birth of the new rich has also posed uncertainties in another way as pointed out by prominent China expert Andrew Walder.[3] China's economic development in the past three decades has been creating a new elite group (i.e. corporate elite) that controls huge economic power and is yet quite independent from the government. The formation of such a group is poised to greatly impact on China, in a way which is still unknown.

---

[3]Walder AG, "From Control to Ownership: China's Managerial Revolution", *Management and Organization Review*, 2011, pp. 19–38.

# 32

# Non-Governmental Organisations in China

## Developments and Challenges

XU Ying*

*The Chinese government has cautiously welcomed the social welfare role played by NGOs; there is much to be gained if NGOs are allowed to play a larger role in social welfare delivery.*

With growing economic and social freedom since the late 1970s, non-governmental organisations (NGOs) have come to play an increasingly important role in welfare provision and environmental protection. The development of NGOs indicates profound changes in China. To enhance the understanding of the development of NGOs in China, this chapter introduces the ministries in charge of NGOs, describes the main types of NGOs and explores the relationship between NGOs and the government.

## Typology of NGOs and Ministries in Charge of NGOs

Decades of social and economic development have given rise to new forms of social organisations and the government has cautiously welcomed the social welfare role played by NGOs. Yet, while the party-state hopes to maintain political stability, the regulations on the registration and governance of NGOs remain strict.[1] This pushes many NGOs to operate without being registered, thus producing two main categories of NGOs in China: One is the formally registered NGO, and the other is the unregistered NGO.

Currently, registered NGOs are administered by three ministries and regulated according to the registration types and the nature of organisation. Specifically, the three ministries in charge of the registration and management of the NGOs are (i) the Ministry of Civil Affairs (MCA), which is

*XU Ying is Assistant Professor of The Chinese University of Hong Kong.
[1]Cooper, CM, "This is Our Way In: The Civil Society of Environmental NGOs in South-West China", *Government and Opposition,* vol. 41 no. 1, pp.109–136.

responsible for developing, drafting and monitoring regulations regarding the registration of social organisations, foundations and private non-enterprise units; (ii) the State Administration for Religious Affairs system, which is responsible for investigating the status and the theoretical issues of religion, drafting, supervising and propagandising the religious regulations and policies, and preventing illegal religious activities; and (iii) the Department of Young Volunteers of the Central Committee of the Chinese Communist Youth League (CYL), which works as a policy maker and sets up a national system governing the operation of voluntary service organisations (VSOs).[2]

### Regulations and the Registration Types of NGOs in the MCA System

China's official definitions of NGOs are mainly based on the registration typologies. According to the three official regulations issued by the State Council, all NGOs should be registered under one of the following three categories: (i) a social organisation *(shehui tuanti)*, (ii) a private non-enterprise unit *(minban qiye danwei)*[3] or (iii) a foundation, or the branches of overseas foundations.[4] In official documents, civil organisations *(minjian zuzhi)* as well as social associations *(shehui zuzhi)* are sometimes used to refer to these three categories of NGOs as a whole.

According to the *Regulations on the Registration and Administration of Social Organisations,* social organisations are officially defined as non-profit organisations which are formed voluntarily by Chinese citizens in order to realise the shared objectives of their members and to carry out activities according to their charters.

The *Regulations on the Registration and Administration of Private Non-Enterprise Units* define private non-enterprise units as non-profit social organisations which use non-state assets and are formed by enterprise course units, social organisations and other social forces or citizens.

Foundations as stipulated by the *Regulations on the Registration and Administration of Foundations* are non-profit juristic persons who utilise the assets denoted by the natural person, juristic person or other organisations to improve the commonweal.

The current regulations restrict the number, types and range of NGOs. The regulations require, for example, any social organisations or private non-enterprise units to be approved by and registered with the Civil Affairs departments at the county *(xian)* level or above, and the foundations must be approved at the provincial or central government level. Moreover, before applying for registration, social organisations, private non-enterprise units and foundations are required to find a professional management unit, a state organ above county level that must be relevant to the activities proposed by the NGO, to act as their sponsor. In addition, if the same type of NGO has already been registered in the same administrative area, the area is considered off-limits to the other NGOs.

### NGOs with Religious Backgrounds

Special attention has been given to the governance of religious organisations. Religious NGOs and their activities are regulated by the State Council's *Regulations on the Religious Affairs*. The State Administration for Religious Affairs, a vice ministerial level department under the State Council, is designed specially to supervise various religious related affairs, including the activities of religious NGOs.

Although Article 6 of the *Regulations on the Religious Affairs* stipulates that religious organisations' formation, change and cancellation should be in accordance with the *Regulations on*

---

[2]Xu Y, "Chinese Communist Youth League, Political Capital, and the Legitimizing of Volunteering in China", *International Journal of Adolescence and Youth,* (in press), 2012.

[3]There are no universally accepted English terms for *"min ban fei qi ye dan wei"* in China. For example, Qiusha Ma (2002) translated it as non-governmental non-commercial enterprises, while Yiyi Lu (2009) referred to it as private non-enterprise units.

[4]Related documents available at <http://www.mca.gov.cn/article/shfw/wmfw_mjzz.shtml> (accessed 20 May 2009).

*the Registration and Administration of Social Organisations,* there are 48 specific articles in the *Regulations on the Religious Affairs* which regulate the formulation, change, cancellation and activities of the religious organisations.

### Government-Organised Non-Governmental Organisations: Exceptions and Specified Regulations

It needs to be pointed out that though the aforementioned regulations are strict, certain organisations can dispense with the procedure of registering through the ascribed political capital, which refers to the political resources conferred to the organisation through historical inheritance, thus granting them access to the existing political system.[5] For example, Article 13 of the *Regulations on the Registration and Administration of Social Organisations* (1998) has made three exceptions to the rule: (1) civil organisations which have sent representatives to attend the National Committee of the Chinese People's Political Consultative Conference; (2) organisations authorised by the department of management for the establishment of organisations of the State Council and approved by the State Council to register for free; (3) internal organisations approved by government organs, institutions, enterprises and institutions which are active internally.

Furthermore, in 2000, MCA issued two additional official documents and further clarified the first two exceptions. They are (i) Notice from the Ministry of Civil Affairs on related problems of certain associations exempted from the registration of social associations, and (ii) Notice from the Ministry of Civil Affairs on certain social organisations exempted from the registration of social associations. The former notice allows "people's organisations" (*renmin tuanti*) and 14 "social organisations" to operate without registration.[6] The latter notice exempts the 11 sub-associations and the provincial level associations of the China Federation of Literature and Art from the registration requirement.[7]

Obviously, the aforementioned organisations which enjoy exemptions are organisations that have close relations with the Party and the government, relations which are usually built with great political capital. These organisations are called government-organised non-governmental organisations (GONGOs) and can act as the supervisory organs for NGOs most of the time. GONGOs with certain political influence may sometimes issue new regulations for monitoring certain types of NGOs as will be discussed in the next section.

### VSOs Registered in the CYL System

Unlike the MCA system covering all kinds of NGOs (e.g. VSOs, professional societies, or hobby groups), the CYL has designed a national system especially for governing the operation of VSOs, which voluntarily provide welfare services for the communities. In contrast to the MCA's regulations, the CYL system provides more space for the development of VSOs. For instance, to be registered in the MCA system, an organisation requires a professional management unit and 50

---

[5]Xu Y and Ngai N, "Moral Resources and Political Capital: Theorizing the Relationship Between Voluntary Service Organizations and the Development of Civil Society in China", *Nonprofit and Voluntary Sector Quarterly,* vol. 40, no. 2, 2011, pp. 247–269.

[6]The people's organisations include China Federation of Trade Unions, the Chinese Communist Youth League, the All-China Women's Federation, Science and Technology Association, the All-China Federation of Returned Overseas Chinese, China Federation of Taiwan Compatriots, All-China Youth Federation and the All-China Federation of Industry and Commerce.

[7]The 11 sub-associations of the China Federation of Literature and Art include Chinese Dramatists Association, the China Film Association, the Chinese Musicians Association, the Chinese Artists Association, the Chinese Association of the Artists of Quyi, the Chinese Dancers Association, the Chinese Folk Literature and Art Association, the Chinese Photographers Association, the Chinese Calligraphers Association, Association of Chinese Acrobatics and China TV Artists Association.

individual members or 30 collective members, a permanent place of residence, and a capital of no less than 30,000 *yuan*, while the CYL system only requires an organisation to have three volunteers to qualify for registration as a VSO. Hence, NGOs which aim to provide voluntary services but cannot register in the MCA system might register in the CYL system as a service unit (*fuwu zhan*).[8]

### *The Unregistered NGOs and the "Case-By-Case" Approach*

Normally, NGOs are required to find a state organ as a professional management unit prior to registration. However, not many government agencies are willing to act as a professional management unit as they have to play a supervisory role to these NGOs, thus adding to their workload. As a result, some have registered as businesses with the Industry and Commerce Bureaus instead and some grassroots NGOs cannot register and remain illegal for years. As the Chinese government is moving away from being the sole provider of social welfare, it is willing to give a larger role to the voluntary sector, registered or otherwise. Therefore, unregistered NGOs are not necessarily banned by the government. It was estimated that the number of unregistered NGOs is about 10 times that of registered NGOs.[9]

In recent years, the government tends to apply the principle of "no contact, no recognition and no ban" to associations that engage in commonweal service and refrains from intervening in their activities. Under these circumstances, some unregistered NGOs are very active. For example, a famous NGO named "*Lüjiayuan*", which successfully conducted environmental protection work all over China, was never registered.[10]

The international NGOs (INGOs) can also hardly be registered in China. According to the *Regulations on the Registration and Administration of Foundations*, the branches of INGOs or overseas foundations may register in China; however, there is still a lack of clear regulations regarding the registration of non-foundation INGOs and their activities in China. Moreover, according to the *Regulations of Branches of Social Organisations, Representative Agencies' Registration*, the registration of social organisations from Taiwan, Hong Kong, Macao and foreign countries should be "in accordance with another specific regulation". However, "another specific regulation" has not been issued yet. For instance, notable INGOs Green Peace and Rotary International have yet to be registered in China.[11]

Lacking regular regulations, the government adopts a case-by-case approach to the INGOs. INGOs will have to gain the government's trust before they can operate in China. For example, while the INGO Green Peace cannot register in China, the China Council of Lions Club was approved by the State Council on 14 June 2005 as a special case. The professional management unit of the China Council of Lions Club is the governmental organisation, "China Disabled Persons' Federation", and the president of China Council of Lions Club, Tang Xiaoquan, is also the vice chairman of the China Disabled Persons' Federation.[12]

Moreover, Chinese participation in unregistered INGOs in China has become increasingly frequent. For example, the membership density of China's INGO per million of population increased from 1.2 in 1993 to 1.9 in 2003, a 60% increase in a decade.[13] In this respect, to some extent, the development of NGOs in China facilitate the country's involvement in international cultural and social exchange activities.

---

[8]Xu Y, "Chinese Communist Youth League, Political Capital, and the Legitimizing of Volunteering in China", *International Journal of Adolescence and Youth*, (in press), 2012.

[9]Wang M and Jia X, Problems about Legislation for China's NGOs (in Chinese), *Journal of Tsinghua University*, 2003, vol.18, no. S1, pp. 100–106.

[10]Qi H, "The Freedom of Association and the System of Non–corporate Associations" (in Chinese), *Cass Journal of Foreign Law*, 2004, no. 3, p. 303.

[11]"The Set Up of China Council of Lions Club Open Door for International NGOs in China?", *Global Link Initiative*, <http://www.glinet.org/687> (accessed 20 July 2009).

[12]Ibid.

[13]Anheier, H, M Glasius and M Kaldor (eds.) Global Civil Society 2004/5, London, Sage Publications, 2005, p. 304.

**Table 1**    Registered NGOs in China (1988–2009)[14]

| Year | Social Organisations | Private Non-Enterprise Units | Foundations | Total |
|------|---------------------|------------------------------|-------------|-------|
| 1988 | — | — | — | — |
| 1989 | 4,544 | — | — | 4,544 |
| 1990 | 10,855 | — | — | 10,855 |
| 1991 | 82,814 | — | — | 82,814 |
| 1992 | 154,502 | — | — | 154,502 |
| 1993 | 167,506 | — | — | 167,506 |
| 1994 | 174,060 | — | — | 174,060 |
| 1995 | 180,583 | — | — | 180,583 |
| 1996 | 184,821 | — | — | 184,821 |
| 1997 | 181,318 | — | — | 181,318 |
| 1998 | 165,600 | — | — | 165,600 |
| 1999 | 136,764 | 5,901 | — | 142,665 |
| 2000 | 130,668 | 22,654 | — | 153,322 |
| 2001 | 128,805 | 82,134 | — | 210,939 |
| 2002 | 133,297 | 111,212 | — | 244,509 |
| 2003 | 141,167 | 124,491 | 954 | 266,612 |
| 2004 | 153,359 | 135,181 | 892 | 289,432 |
| 2005 | 171,150 | 147,637 | 975 | 319,762 |
| 2006 | 191,946 | 161,303 | 1,144 | 354,393 |
| 2007 | 211,661 | 173,915 | 1,340 | 386,916 |
| 2008 | 220,000 | 178,000 | 1,390 | 399,390 |
| 2009 | 238,747 | 190,479 | 1,843 | 431,069 |

*Source*: *Social Organisations in China*, <http://www.chinanpo.gov.cn/yjzlk/index.html> (accessed 29 February 2012) and the Ministry of Civil Affairs of the People's Republic of China, <http://www.mca.gov.cn> (accessed 29 February 2012).

## NGO Development: A Statics Inventory

China's official statistics of NGOs are only available from 1988 (Table 1). And the statistics only account for NGOs registered in the MCA system, excluding the service units in the CYL's system. The number of registered NGOs has since been increasing steadily except for the year 1999. The temporary decline of NGOs in 1999 was attributed to stricter regulations on social organisations in 1998, which meant some registered organisations no longer fit the standard of registration. Yet after a short period of adjustment, the number of registered NGOs soon began to grow gradually again.

It is worth noting that the actual number of NGOs in mainland China is much larger than those that are formally registered within the MCA system. While the number of NGOs has been growing rapidly in China, the question remains as to whether they will be given a larger space by the government, become more autonomous financially and professionally, and engage more extensively with the society.

## Challenges for NGOs

In recognition of the strengths of NGOs, the Chinese government has been promoting the socialisation of social welfare by encouraging NGOs to play a larger role in philanthropy and social welfare.

---

[14] In this statistics, "Foundations" are included in the "Social Organisations" before year 2002.

However, as China is in a period of rapid transition and social protests are on the rise, there is an apparent trust deficit between the government and the NGOs. The public also have little trust in NGOs given the legal dilemmas, political constraints, financial crises and internal problems faced by the latter. The development of NGOs in different areas has been uneven.

### *Legal Dilemma*

As mentioned earlier, in addition to the registered NGOs, there are millions of unregistered NGOs. In unregistered NGOs performing social welfare functions, the government sees a positive role and these unregistered NGOs have more autonomy than the registered NGOs. Scholars have argued that the unregistered NGOs are ironically the most promising and functional NGOs in China.[15]

However, current official rules on NGOs remain strict and government officials maintain the legal right to interfere with or control the activities of NGOs.[16] Hence, unregistered NGOs could be harassed or banned anytime when deemed necessary by the authorities. For example, on 17 July 2009, Chinese officials shut down the Open Constitution Initiative, a legal aid and research centre founded by pioneering Chinese lawyers. The authorities have also revoked the licences of more than 50 lawyers, many known for tackling human rights issues.[17]

Furthermore, few NGOs are consulted when regulations concerning NGOs are being formulated. As a result, laws and policies enacted are not conducive to building a well-functioning NGO sector and forming productive partnerships between the government and NGOs. Therefore, the legislation process is a fundamental problem restricting and marginalising the NGOs.

### Political Constraints

China has not issued a national law applicable to NGOs. Political considerations can have a significant impact on an NGO's legitimacy and development.[18] Generally speaking, religious NGOs, international NGOs and NGOs advocating human rights or having support from overseas are often viewed with scepticism and subject to much stricter control.[19]

For example, as previously mentioned, special regulations have been issued to monitor religious activities, while registered religious organisations are less autonomous than other NGOs (i.e. the academic associations or the voluntary service organisations) and unregistered religious organisations are more likely to be banned based on various regulations.[20]

### *Financial Crisis*

Another huge challenge for the NGOs is their precarious financial position as the government provides funds to NGOs according to their political ties. Most grassroots NGOs receive little financial support from the government and are struggling to survive. Only those well connected to

---

[15] Xu Y and Ngai N, op. cit.

[16] Wang M and Jia X, op. cit., pp. 100–106.

[17] Branigan, T, "China Officials Shut Legal Aid Centre", *Guardian.co.uk*, 18 July 2009, <http://www.guardian.co.uk/world/2009/jul/18/china-shuts-legal-aid-centre> (accessed 20 July 2009).

[18] Cai Y, *Collective Resistance in China: Why Popular Protests Succeed or Fail*, Stanford, California: Stanford University Press, 2010.

[19] Ibid.

[20] Anonymous, "Asia: Open Constitution Closed; China, the law and NGOs", *The Economist*, 25 July 2009, vol. 392, issue 8641, p.38.

the government are likely to get some funding from the professional management unit.[21] Sometimes, the relations between the government and some NGOs are so close that the NGOs would also offer themselves as propaganda tools to the state. On the other hand, grassroots NGOs rarely get donations from local communities because young NGOs do not have good track records to win the trust of the local people.

### *Internal Problems*

In contrast to the strict regulations on registration, the monitoring of the operation of NGOs is weak. Some NGOs' internal governance is characterised by a lack of transparency and irregularity. Some NGOs put their private interests above their mission to work for the public. Some NGO leaders even go as far as to steal and embezzle NGO funds by falsifying expenses or investing in the stock market.[22] An outstanding case is that of Guo Meimei, a 20-year-old girl who claimed that she was the general manager of the Red Cross Society of China and boasted about her luxurious lifestyle and showed off her Maserati and Lamborghini cars, expensive handbags and palatial villa. The Guo Meimei issue has damaged the reputation of the organisation and people are unwilling to donate to the Chinese NGOs.[23]

### The Role of NGOs

Though the Chinese government has cautiously welcomed the social welfare role played by NGOs, grassroots NGOs generally operate under severe political and institutional constraints. Despite the rapid growth in numbers, the NGO sector has yet to develop into a full-fledged presence that acts as a bridge between the society and the government.

With little doubt, constraining NGOs is not the best solution or policy. There is much to gain if NGOs are allowed to play a bigger role in social welfare delivery. In general, the government plays an important role in (i) formulating welfare policies and service plans; (ii) implementing laws and regulations; (iii) allocating resources; (iv) monitoring and evaluating service quality, and (v) providing services in certain areas. The role of NGOs mainly includes (i) providing welfare services; (ii) undertaking governments' welfare services projects; (iii) exploring welfare resources; (iv) providing consultation to the government in the policy-making process, and (v) pioneering new services and advocating human rights, social justice and equality.[24]

Fostering mutual trust between the government and NGOs takes time. Yet, China has to re-think its policy towards NGOs since the current situation could lead to more problems and tensions if the majority of the NGOs continue to operate without a legal status. NGOs could become a special third force apart from the government and the business world. The Chinese government will benefit much if it revamps its regulations on the registration and governance of NGOs, forms partnerships with NGOs, and allows them to perform social functions where they have an edge over the government.

---

[21] He Z, The Analysis of the Institutional Bbstacles of the Development of Civil Society Organizations in China (in Chinese), *Journal of the Party School of CPC Ningbo Municipal Committee*, 2006, no 6, pp. 23–30.
[22] More detailed examples can be found in Lu Y, "Non-Governmental Organisations in China", London and New York, Routledge, 2009, pp. 109–135.
[23] "An Online Scandal Underscores Chinese Distrust of Its Charities", 3 July 2011, *China Digital Times*, <http://chinadigitaltimes.net/2011/07/an-online-scandal-underscores-chinese-distrust-of-its-charities/> (accessed 5 March 2012).
[24] Ngai N, "Welfare Development: The Role of Government and Non-governmental Welfare Organizations," Yang Y, (ed.), *Macao's Social Welfare Development: Characteristics and Trends* Macau, Centre for Macau Studies at the University of Macau, 2006, pp. 286–96.

# 33

# *Chengzhongcun* in China

ZHONG Sheng*

*Chengzhongcun (village in the city) is a unique phenomenon of the rapid urbanisation process in China. This chapter discusses the formation and nature of chengzhongcun as well as related public policy issues.*

Since China launched its market-oriented economic reform in the late 1970s, the country has undergone tremendous urban transformation. The pace of urbanisation was relatively modest before 1995. Between 1978 and 1995, urbanisation rate in the country grew from 17.92% to 29.04%, equivalent to an average annual growth of 0.65%. Since 1995, urbanisation process has accelerated as a result of national policy adjustments on urban development.[1] From 1995 to 2009, China's urbanisation rate grew from 29.04% to 46.59%, translating into an annual growth of 1.25% (Figure 1), or an average increase of 19.29 million people in cities each year.[2]

Accompanying the unprecedented urban population growth is the fast territorial expansion of Chinese cities. In the context of urban-rural duality, urban expansion has given rise to *chengzhongcun* (village in the city). Major institutional distortions that contribute to China's urban-rural dichotomy are reflected in household registration policies, land-use systems and local governance structures.

First, all Chinese citizens have household registration, or *hukou*, that classifies them as either urban or rural residents. *Hukou* defines not only the legitimate residential place (urban versus rural) of its holder, but more importantly, a bundle of rights in social welfare, land use, family planning and so on. Although in recent years, a *hukou* document cannot stop rural-urban migration, the

*ZHONG Sheng is Lecturer at the Department of Urban Planning and Design at the Xi'an Jiaotong-Liverpool University in Suzhou Industrial Park, Suzhou, China.
[1] For example, the 10th Five-Year Plan (2000–2005) clarified China's urban development strategies, calling for an elimination of the rural-urban divide and the relaxation of the control on the growth of megacities. In addition, a series of regional policies helped expedite the urbanisation process, including the opening up of Pudong New Area (1990), the development of western China (1999), the revitalisation of north-eastern China (2003), the development of Tianjin Binhai New Area (2006), etc.
[2] See *China Statistical Yearbook* (Beijing: China Statistics Press, 2010). All data refer to mainland China.

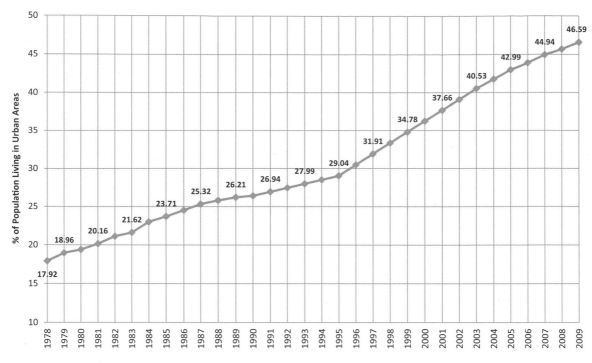

**Figure 1**   China's Urbanisation Rate, (1978–2009)

*Source:* China Statistical Yearbook 2010.

different rights attached to different types of *hukou* still constitute a constraint on the mobility of the population as migrants are usually deprived of the same rights as indigenous people (local *hukou* holders).

Second, all urban land is state-owned and the land-use right can be leased and transferred. Except for stipulated uses, people or organisations must get the land-use right from the state through the urban land market. In the rural areas, however, most land is collectively owned by farmers who have local rural *hukou*. The land-use right of rural land cannot be traded as freely as urban land although recent policy changes have opened more channels for its circulation.[3]

Third, urban communities are managed by residents' committees or street offices, which are financed by the government. In the rural areas, the grassroots governing bodies are the self-financed villagers' committees or rural collectives. Local governing bodies in the rural areas have to take care of more community issues than their peers in cities do, such as health care, education, public security and infrastructure, although funding shortages frequently prevent them from fully performing their duties.

When urban areas need more land for building new industries, infrastructure, housing, amenities, and so on, urban governments usually resort to rural-to-urban land conversion. According to the Chinese Land Administration Law, in the name of "public interest", the state (represented by urban governments) can requisition rural land and convert it into state-owned urban land provided rural land owners — rural collectives — are properly compensated. In reality, however, the term "public interest" is poorly defined. After land conveyance, the urban governments usually lease the newly acquired land to developers to build commercial projects. The formula-based compensations paid by the urban governments to rural collectives are usually much lower than what rural collectives can collect from the developers. Hence this difference constitutes a big revenue source for the cash-strapped local governments. Such land-use and public finance systems give urban governments

---

[3] For example, the "land ticket" (*dipiao*) traded in Chongqing is a new means of transferring rural land-use right in the open market in recent years. But it is still a pilot project and is restricted to Chongqing.

substantial incentives to expand their territories more than necessary because larger urban areas imply not only more space and political influence, but also more local revenues.

Collectively owned rural land comprises agricultural land and rural construction land. The former is used for cultivation and is subdivided into small land parcels and leased out to rural households under the household responsibility system for 30 years. The latter includes land for farmers' housing construction as well as rural collective industrial and commercial development. Each rural household is entitled to a piece of residential land (*zhaijidi*), which can be inherited but not transferred.

For urban governments, the cost of expropriating agricultural land is much lower than that for expropriating rural residential land because the latter involves relocation costs and other welfare payments and usually takes longer to settle. Therefore, in the rush to expand urban territories, revenue-maximising urban governments prefer to requisition agricultural land while leaving the rural residential land untouched. In these cases, the villages become enclaves surrounded by urban land. When land requisition takes place, the villages affected are usually located in the urban peripheries. These villages are called "urban fringe villages" (*chengbiancun*) or "villages outside of cities" (*chengwaicun*). But over time, urban sprawl turns the peripheries into central ones and hence *chengbiancun* or *chengwaicun* gradually become *chengzhongcun*. To some extent, *chengbiancun* and *chengwaicun* can be considered as urban villages in the making.

## Characteristics of *Chengzhongcun*

The forced and incomplete urbanisation — the urbanisation of agricultural land but not of the people — has given rise to *chengzhongcun* dotting the landscapes of many Chinese cities. Spatially, *chengzhongcun* can be seen in both developed and less-developed regions in China. But they are more common in prosperous regions, such as coastal areas and big cities, where the pace of urbanisation is faster. In places where land requisition covers both agricultural land and rural construction land, *chengzhongcun* can be avoided. Within cities, many *chengzhongcun* are in very convenient locations. Shenzhen is the most prominent case as it was built from scratch in a short period of time and almost all urban land was converted from land of rural titles.

*Chengzhongcun* communities are a rural-urban hybrid. On the one hand, indigenous residents have no land to cultivate and quite often have acquired urban *hukou*. So in occupational and household registration sense,[4] they are not farmers. On the other hand, the residential land that villagers occupy is categorised as rural land and its tenure remains unchanged. In addition, the governance structure — villagers' committees and rural collectives —remains intact. Furthermore, people in the same communities are bound by traditional kinship ties and old customs and traditions remain strong. For example, in *chengzhongcun* in Guangdong, temples play very important roles in the everyday life of indigenous villagers.

In well-developed regions, the leasing of property is usually a dominant income source for indigenous villagers. Rural land in China has not been subject to strict land-use planning. In the absence of land-use control, villagers usually build their homes individually and at the highest possible densities so that they can maximise their rental income. The large-scale in-migration to the prosperous regions provided a steady client base for the extra home spaces in *chengzhongcun*.

Another lucrative source of revenue for indigenous villagers is village collective enterprises (VCEs), which are organised in the form of shareholding cooperatives (SCs) in many places. About a decade ago, the majority of VCEs were in the manufacturing sector. In more recent years, as locational advantage has become prominent, many VCEs have gradually "deindustrialised" and increasingly turned to profitable property business. According to a study on 15 SCs in Shenzhen,

---

[4] In some places, villagers may not have been given urban *hukou*. And even if they are given urban *hukou*, the former villagers may not enjoy the same welfare benefits provided to urban residents by the urban governments.

80.2% of their business income came from property leasing.[5] As shareholders, indigenous villagers are entitled to receive dividends from SCs.

According to Chinese law, rural construction land cannot be transferred without being converted into state-owned urban land. Home rental provides an informal way for indigenous villagers to cash in on the land value over a long period of time. Because of the restrictions on land transfer, land yields (reflected in rentals) in *chengzhongcun* are lower than those in urban state land at similar locations. Poorer building and environmental quality further drags down the rental levels in urban villages. Nevertheless, the land-use right of *chengzhongcun* land was initially assigned free to individual rural households as a kind of entitlement. Therefore, for villagers whose villages happen to enjoy prime locations, the land provides a means to capture financial windfalls.

In less economically prosperous regions where the rental market is not quite active, *chengzhongcun* are not as densely built-up as in developed regions. VCEs may also be less dependent on property business and many may face financial hardship. In addition, residents are more homogenous as the proportion of migrant population can be small.

### *Chengzhongcun*: Problems or Solutions?

As *chengzhongcun* land is categorised as rural land, public investment undertaken by urban governments usually bypasses these areas. Therefore, many urban villages pose a sharp contrast to the surrounding urban areas in terms of landscapes, quality of infrastructure services and public facilities. In the absence of land-use control, buildings in *chengzhongcun* tend to be aesthetically and functionally inferior. In economically prosperous regions, *chengzhongcun* buildings are extremely congested, and safety, sanitation and health standards are not strictly adhered to. Some statistics show that in 2005, the average population density in urban villages in Futian district of Shenzhen was about 80,000 people per km$^2$ as compared to 16,000 people per km$^2$ for the whole of Futian district.[6] A common villagescape in urban villages is the so-called "kissing houses" or "handshaking houses" that are built so close to each other that residents are said to be able to touch and reach out to their neighbours. Poor ventilation, lack of natural light and poor fire access are common problems for urban village housing.

Governance is another serious issue. The inward-looking villagers' committees are primarily concerned with the affairs of local villagers. However, the number of tenants, mostly migrants from outside of the cities, may far exceed that of indigenous villagers. For example, in the 15 urban villages in Futian district of Shenzhen, there were about 17,000 local villagers; however, the total population stood at 800,000.[7] The lack of funding for grassroots organisations is likely to further aggravate the governance problem. Due to the lack of oversight, many *chengzhongcun* have become hotbeds for illegal or criminal activities, such as prostitution, drug trafficking, gambling, production of fake or defective goods, etc. Over time, the existence of underground activities stigmatises urban villages.

While urban governments have expropriated the farmers' critical productive resources — agricultural land — they have not taken much effort in helping indigenous villagers upgrade their skills so that they can be absorbed by the urban labour market. The lump-sum payment following land requisition as well as the steady rental income and dividends from SCs also reduced the villagers' incentives to work. It is quite common that indigenous villagers lay idle for a long period of time without engaging in any productive activities. A study shows that in Ruibao village in

---

[5] Tan G, "Main Characteristics of the Economy in Urban Villages", *Kaifang Daobao* (*China Opening Herald*), June 2005, pp. 51–56.

[6] Ibid.

[7] Ibid.

Guangzhou, only 22% to 27% of urban villagers of working age were working.[8] Some become addicted to gambling and endless recreation, and are a bad influence to second-generation urban villagers. In less developed regions where urban villagers do not enjoy steady rental and dividend income, the dissipation of meagre land compensation can threaten their livelihoods. In the long run, indigenous villagers' unproductive way of life can be an invitation to social instability, a major concern for the Chinese authority.

Social stratification constitutes another serious issue for urban villages. Many indigenous villagers do not work but they own properties and enjoy a steady flow of income and to some extent, welfare protection afforded by VCEs.[9] In contrast, hard-working migrant tenants usually earn much less, are not covered by the urban safety net and do not enjoy the village welfare extended to indigenous villagers. This contrasts with the differences in linguistic and cultural traditions can cause conflicts between indigenous villagers and migrant tenants, the two social strata in *chengzhongcun*. In addition, *chengzhongcun* are largely segregated spaces in big urban areas. Although many tenants work outside of urban villages, their residence and social networks are largely confined to *chengzhongcun* as affordable housing in other localities is quite limited. Both the landlords and tenants in the *chengzhongcun* are of "rural" origin[10] and their differences with urban communities outside of *chengzhongcun* in terms of attitude and way of life are quite conspicuous.

Problematic as *chengzhongcun* are, they have performed critical functions for cities. *Chengzhongcun* help enhance urban affordability by providing a large, ready supply of low-cost housing at prime locations for migrants. For example, in Shenzhen, *chengzhongcun* provided over 100 million m² of private housing space that had helped house about eight million migrant workers, including five million in the old special economic zone.[11] In Guangzhou, *chengzhongcun* provided accommodation for 80% of the 1.2 million migrant workers in the city in 2001.[12]

For the massive influx of migrants with neither economic resources nor local *hukou*, *chengzhongcun* serve as a starting point for them to gain a permanent foothold in China's booming metropolises. *Chengzhongcun* are also a buffer zone that helps cushion the overheated urban property market and hence have performed a certain degree of social function that urban governments have failed to fulfill. A survey conducted on tenants in Shenzhen *chengzhongcun* shows that they regard *chengzhongcun* as mostly providing "low-level satisfaction".[13] At the macro-economic level, high availability of low-cost housing helps reduce overall labour costs and boost competitiveness of the urban economy.

Because of the low rental at *chengzhongcun*, business people from both inside and outside of the *chengzhongcun* are attracted to the locations. The proliferation of businesses, such as grocery stores, restaurants and various kinds of service outlets, provides abundant affordable urban convenience for both *chengzhongcun* residents and people working or living in adjacent urban areas. Despite their problems and dubious image, *chengzhongcun* often attract high traffic volumes.

*Chengzhongcun* also help increase population diversity of central cities. Without these affordable spaces at convenient locations, central cities would have been turned into exclusive enclaves for

[8] Feng W, "An Analysis of Urban Villages in Rapidly Urbanising Regions", *Journal of Chongqing Industry and Commerce University,* February 2006, pp. 100–103.

[9] In southern provinces such as Guangdong, VCEs can be highly profitable and they can provide local villagers with comprehensive welfare benefits commensurate with those enjoyed by urban residents.

[10] Although tenants living in urban villages may come from other urban areas or smaller cities, the majority are of "rural" origin.

[11] See "Urban Villages Indispensable to Shenzhen?", *Lianhe Zaobao*, 30 December 2010, at <http://www.zaobao.com/wencui/2010/12/others101230nf.shtml> (accessed 29 March 2012).

[12] Tian L, "The *Chengzhongcun* Land Market in China: Boon or Bane? — A Perspective on Property Rights", *International Journal of Urban and Regional Research*, vol. 32, no. 2, 2008, pp. 282–304.

[13] Zhou L, "Seeing Urban Villages from Another Perspective", *Kaifang Daobao (China Opening Herald)*, June 2005, pp. 60–62.

the wealthy. Homogenisation of urban landscapes reduces the attractiveness of modern cities. In addition, *chengzhongcun* enable a large part of the poor population to live close to their workplace. This helps ease traffic congestion during peak hours.

In addition, in the land requisition process, urban governments have shirked their responsibility for providing social welfare and public services to the affected villagers. *Chengzhongcun* help fill this gap. VCE profits have been used to finance local villagers' health care, education, pension as well as local infrastructure. However, it should be noted that the main beneficiaries are indigenous villagers while migrant workers are excluded from the village welfare.

## The Renewal and Redevelopment of *Chengzhongcun*

To solve the perceived problems with *chengzhongcun*, since the mid-1990s, many Chinese cities have embarked on a series of initiatives to renew and redevelop *chengzhongcun*. In some places, the primary concerns are urban image and urban land supply rather than the welfare of *chengzhongcun* residents. In recent years, some cities have passed local regulations to guide *chengzhongcun* renewal and redevelopment (CRR) programmes, which greatly accelerated the pace of policy implementation.

There are several key components in the CRR programmes: (i) beautifying the landscapes (including demolishing illegal buildings and putting up new ones according to plans) and constructing new infrastructure; (ii) converting rural construction land into urban land; (iii) turning VCEs into SCs or corporatising SCs; and (iv) transforming villagers' committees into urban residents' committees and separating the administrative functions (residents' committees) from the economic functions (SCs).

As *chengzhongcun* are situated in different locations, have different economic potentials and face different types of problems, renewal strategies are usually customised for individual cases. In some places, *chengzhongcun* are fully demolished and redeveloped at higher densities, while in others, partial demolition and renovation are carried out. Some *chengzhongcun* communities (excluding the migrants) are mass relocated while others may be resettled on their original sites in newly constructed buildings but with smaller living spaces.

Although the CRR programmes have drastically improved housing conditions and infrastructure in some places, the implementation is beset by many challenges. First, physical transformation tends to be given preference over issues of "soft aspects", such as governance or villager re-employment. There is a lack of attention to human needs as physical transformation merely replaces decrepit-looking *chengzhongcun* with ostentatious-looking *chengzhongcun* without provision of assistance to villagers to fully assimilate into the urban fabric. The indifference and neglect of the impact of urbanisation on villagers had given rise to various problems of *chengzhongcun* in the past; however, the CRR programmes that are formulated to correct the problems seem to repeat earlier mistakes. In some places, although villagers' committees had been transformed into residents' committees, there is actually little change in the finance and functions of the organisations. The deficiency in public funding has forced corporatised collective enterprises to focus solely on assuming governance and social functions. As SCs control the finances, residents' committees are usually subordinated to SCs and the separation of administrative and economic functions of village collectives is difficult to materialise.

Second, as rentiers, indigenous villagers have vested interest in the land. Despite the fact that CRR programmes help improve the living conditions of indigenous villagers, there are negative impacts on villagers' income as villagers are usually relocated further away from the city centre or they have to accept a reduced housing space if they are to remain in the same locality. Villagers' enthusiasm in the CRR programmes is dampened. A survey in Xi'an shows that 60% of the villagers want to maintain the *status quo* rather than have their villages renewed or redeveloped.[14]

---

[14] Zhou X, Yang S and Li L, "The Redevelopment of Urban Villages and China's Urban-Rural Duality", *Journal of Xi'an Electronic Technology University*, January 2006, pp. 56–61.

Third, dispensing fair compensation to villagers is a crucial component of the CRR programmes. But the illegal nature of building works complicates the issue. For example, in Shenzhen, farmers were generally allowed to build houses of only two to three storeys high on their rural residential plots; however, in the absence of government supervision, most households, including those of the village cadres, have built houses of five to eight or even 10 storeys and extended the construction to encroach on public spaces. Some households overbuilt to maximise rental income, while others want to maximise compensation in anticipation of redevelopment. Completely denying the illegal spaces may threaten the villagers' livelihood as home rentals constitute their main source of income.

Fourth, the CRR programmes, like land requisitions conducted in the past, can be turned into a money-spinner to line the pockets of developers and village cadres at the expense of villagers. In affluent regions, villagers tend to be better organised (well-functioning villagers' committees and SCs) and decision-making is generally more transparent. Therefore, villagers' interests can be better safeguarded. However, in less developed regions, organisational capacity is dubious and villagers' rights in land use can be easily abused.

Fifth, true urbanisation involves villagers' full integration into the urban community. This also includes making adjustments to a change in social networks, perception and way of life on the part of villagers, which in reality cannot be forced as in the case for land requisition. For now, maintaining their rural identity still gives indigenous villagers a lot of tangible benefits as their membership in *chengzhongcun* is tied to the dividend income and in some cases, welfare benefits. This makes it difficult for villagers to completely break away from their rural tradition and to acquire a truly "urban" identity. In addition, the lack of job prospects in cities and exclusion from urban social safety net may further alienate villagers from urban communities.

Last but not least, *chengzhongcun* tenants, mostly migrant workers, suffer most from the CRR programmes. As tenants, they are not entitled to compensations. And worse, there are very few low-cost housing alternatives in cities where displaced tenants can relocate. Currently, the limited availability of urban social housing, such as *anju* housing, or low-rent housing, is generally not open to migrants (those without local *hukou*). Large-scale renewal and redevelopment of *chengzhongcun* may drastically decrease the availability of affordable housing in cities. In some places, the demolition of *chengzhongcun* has been immediately followed by rental hikes in the surrounding areas. With only limited financial resources, displaced urban village tenants may have to accept even more crowded living space elsewhere that may turn into new urban slums. Or they may leave the cities in large numbers, aggravating the labour shortages that many Chinese cities face today. Therefore, without major reforms in urban affordable housing programmes, the demolition of *chengzhongcun* also alludes to the elimination of an innovative low-cost solution to urban housing problems.

In short, China's urbanisation mainly takes two paths: rural-urban migration and in-situ urbanisation. *Chengzhongcun* are a converging point of these two paths. The CRR programmes are intended to foster China's "integrated urban-rural development". The complexity of *chengzhongcun* is suggestive of the long period of transition the country will experience in its march towards urban-rural integration. The rural-urban conversion of *hukou*, change of land ownership and establishment of new governance structures are important measures in the CRR programmes. But these external administrative efforts do not automatically turn *chengzhongcun* residents into full urban citizens. Hasty physical renewal may eventually create more problems than it solves.

# 34

# China's *Hukou* Reform

## The Guangdong and Shanghai Cases

Courtney FU Rong*

*This chapter studies the hukou reform initiated by Guangdong and Shanghai in 2010, highlighting how the new round of reform differs from previous reforms and the rationale behind the local governments' push in implementing new policies.*

The current *hukou* system was set up in 1958 as a mechanism to control China's enormous population. In some ways, it is similar to the apartheid system by which social mobility is restricted. However, as China opened up economically in the late 1970s and early 1980s, rural-urban migration was increasingly on the rise as people looked for jobs and better living conditions in the cities. This puts a strain on the *hukou* system as migrant workers, who are registered as rural residents, are not covered by the cities' social welfare network despite their contribution to city building. Social problems that arose as a result threaten the stability and sustainability of both local and national development. Hence, reform is inevitable, but its actual implementation tests the wisdom of governors at both local and national levels. With social reform being pressed and primed for formal inclusion into the 12th Five-Year Programme, a number of cities took the lead in pioneering trial reforms. Guangdong and Shanghai are two such cities. The initiatives implemented by the local governments and the rationale behind their initial hesitation in the implementation are examined.

## A New Round of *Hukou* Reform

The No. 1 document of 2010 issued by the Central Committee of Chinese Communist Party and the State Council encourages cities with adequate resources to incorporate qualified migrant workers into their social protection schemes. The document reveals particular concerns for the

---

*Courtney FU Rong is a PhD candidate at the Department of History and Religious Studies at the Pennsylvania State University.

"new generation of migrant workers", a term that made its first appearance in an official document. The central government has recognised the tension between this rising group of migrant workers, who aspire to become urbanites, and the current household registration or *hukou* system, which fails to accommodate their aspiration. There is a sense of urgency among central policy makers to accelerate the slow-paced *hukou* reforms.

At the local level, some provinces have already begun to pioneer a new round of *hukou* reform. Guangdong and Shanghai took the lead by announcing new policies in 2009. Despite minor differences in specific details, the general direction shared by both places is to institutionalise the conversion process through which a non-local *hukou* holder can become a local *hukou* holder. The new policy came into effect in 2010. The temporary residential permits (*zanzhu zheng*), which had been issued for nearly a decade, will be replaced by the new residential permits (*juzhu zheng*), which allow migrant workers to enjoy certain public services provided by the local government. Holders of residential permit, after satisfying a list of criteria set out by the government, are eligible to apply for their *hukou* in host cities which thereof make them city residents in the legal sense.

Previous *hukou* reforms have made substantial but uneven progress on two fronts. On the *hukou*-migration front, a very small number of entrepreneurs, house buyers and well-educated professionals are eligible to apply for a local *hukou*. On the non-*hukou*-migration front, a huge number of rural residents are allowed to migrate and work in other places under temporary resident permits without changing their *hukou* status.

The overwhelming majority of China's rural migrants fall under the category of non-*hukou* migration. While non-*hukou* migration has caused many problems for rural migrant workers and their families, it is still acceptable to the first generation of migrant workers, who treasure the opportunity to work off-farm more than anything else. The lack of a local *hukou* does not bother them because most of them believe that returning to their home villages permanently or resettling in nearby towns is inevitable.

Demographic changes, however, make previous *hukou* reforms inadequate. The first generation migrant workers are increasingly becoming a minority, as the new generation, or the second generation now comprises up to 60% of the 150 million migrant workers in China today.[1] Unlike the first generation who still identify themselves as peasants who will ultimately return to their home town, only about 8.7% of the second generation identify themselves as peasants. About 75% think, rightly so, that they belong to the category of workers.[2] This new generation of migrant workers, mostly born in the 1980s and 1990s, can be divided into two subgroups. In the first category, they have completed their education at least up to middle school level at their hometown or village before they migrate to cities. They have minimal experience in farming, and their emotional ties with both rural areas and rural lifestyle are weak. Most of the new generation of migrant workers belong to this category. A small minority of the new generation, who migrated to cities with their parents at a very young age or were even born in cities, fall under the second category. To them, village life is completely foreign, while city life seems more familiar to them. Growing up in the digital age of televisions, cell phones and computers, these young migrant workers are no different from city youngsters in their material needs and outlook. Many choose to work in cities not out of survival needs, but simply for the glamour of city life. However, with their *hukou* still registered under their hometown village, they are effectively excluded from the city's social protection umbrella. They face enormous discrimination in access to education, employment and public services, and yet remain a foreigner in the city, the lifestyle of which they have so naturally adopted. As an odd group of people who neither belong to the village, nor being accepted by the city, they are truly the "floating population". Obviously, the new generation can be a source of social instability if they are not properly integrated into city life. Against this new social

---

[1] *Fazhi ribao* (*Legal Daily*), 3 February 2010.
[2] Ibid.

development, a new round of *hukou* reform which makes the system easier and more regularised for migrant workers to acquire a local *hukou* seems necessary. However, the central government is somewhat powerless in this respect. It has to rely on local governments to implement the reform as social insurance plans and public services are managed and funded by local governments. For a long time, local governments are reluctant to grant local *hukou* to migrant workers because of the high cost.

It was thus a booster to the central government when Shanghai and Guangdong took the lead in pioneering a new round of *hukou* reform. The new policies discard the quota approach and adopt instead a criterion-matching method. The criteria are not particularly tailored to investors and the well-educated. Instead, they include the length of stay, contribution to social insurance plans and other requirements that are not beyond the reach of migrant workers. The new policies of Shanghai and Guangdong hence open an avenue for China's migrant workers to categorically become urbanites. As the main economic engines that spearhead China's economy, policies of Shanghai and Guangdong offer a model for other provinces to follow.

## The Guangdong Case

The new policy document, Statutes for Servicing and Managing the Mobile Population in Guangdong province (revision draft), was effective from 1 January 2010. The main thrust of this round of reform is the replacement of temporary residential permits with residential permits. Holders of the latter permits, upon meeting certain conditions, are eligible to apply for a *hukou* that is no different from that of native residents from their host city. The residential permits record the basic personal particulars of cardholders, with place of residence clearly stated as the province of Guangdong. Unlike temporary residential permits which need to be reissued whenever migrants move around to new places, new residential permits are applicable across the province. This allows migrant workers to change job and location without applying for a new permit as long as they reside in Guangdong. The procedure that migrant workers need to fulfill is to update their information at local police stations.

There are two types of residential permits — long-term and short-term. A long-term permit is valid for three years, while a short-term permit has a validity of six months. Migrants between the age of 16 and 60 who reside in Guangdong for a period of more than 30 days are required to apply for either a long-term or a short-term permit. Long-term residential permit cardholders are entitled to enjoy some of the city's public goods, an obvious difference that sets long-term residential permits apart from temporary and short-term residential permits (which are essentially official documents that establish a migrant's stay in Guangdong without entitlement to local public services). Such local public services include (i) official endorsement for business trips to Hong Kong and Macao[3]; (ii) automobile registration and driving licences[4]; (iii) equal access to urban public schools for migrant children; (iv) tuition and miscellaneous fee exemptions for education as enjoyed by children of local *hukou*; (v) long-term housing rental and public rental housing provided by the local government; (vi) urban social assistance known as the minimum livelihood guarantee scheme; (vii) vocational training; (viii) public employment service; and (ix) medical care for contagious diseases and vaccination services for children. Apparently, the new policy aims to reduce the gap between city *hukou* holders and migrant workers in their public goods entitlement.

This latest round of reform gives migrant workers an opportunity to register their *hukou* in Guangdong provided they satisfy the following conditions: (a) live in the same locality for consecutively seven years; (b) pay social insurance fees for full seven years;(c) have a fixed

---

[3]In the past, people who wish to apply for official permit to travel to Hong Kong and Macao have to return to their hometown where their *hukou* was issued and registered to process the paperwork.

[4]Similar to application to travel to Hong Kong and Macao, automobile and driving licence registration have to be done at the town where their *hukou* are registered.

residential place; (d) have lawful employment or business; (e) abide by the one-child policy; (f) pay taxes; and (g) have no criminal records.

For residential permit holders to enjoy equal treatment in education for their children in the host city, the following conditions have to be met: (a) live in the same locality for five years; (b) pay social insurance fees for five years; (c) have stable employment; and (d) abide by the one-child policy.

These requirements are generally described as "five years to gain admission into the local public school system" (*wunian ruxue*) and "seven years to be registered in the local *hukou* system" (*qinian ruhu*). By specifying the duration of stay, Guangdong's new policy gives migrant workers, who have been working and living in Guangdong province for a protracted period, a chance of settling in the city.

## The Shanghai Case

The official document for the new round of *hukou* reform in Shanghai, Trial Methods for Shanghai Residential Permit Holders to Apply for Permanent Residential *Hukou*, was issued on 23 February 2009. Like Guangdong province, the main content of the reform is to open an avenue for non-locals to become Shanghai *hukou* holders through qualifications fulfilment instead of the quota-setting mechanism in the past. The conditions laid out by the Shanghai government are similar to those in Guangdong. Applicants should (a) hold Shanghai temporary residential permit for seven years; (b) pay taxes; (c) pay social insurance fees for seven years; (d) work in jobs that require a middle level and/or above technical skill; and (e) have a criminal-free record.

Apart from the aforementioned, applicants would also be qualified by a point system. Those who score a hundred points or above in the following seven categories are eligible for Shanghai *hukou*: (a) have specified education qualifications; (b) have stable employment in Shanghai; (c) pay social insurance fees in Shanghai; (d) pay personal income tax in Shanghai; (e) employment at other provinces or overseas; (f) special employment; and (g) operate a business, make investment and pay taxes in Shanghai.

This is the fourth time that Shanghai reformed its *hukou* system. The first round was initiated in 1994. Shanghai introduced the Blueprint Resident Certificate Programme to draw talented people and investment from outside the city. Non-locals who invest in Shanghai,[5] purchase commercial housing,[6] or work in Shanghai, and meet certain standards, can obtain "blue-print resident certificates", which allow them to enjoy privileges comparable to locals who hold a "red-print resident certificates". This reform was considered a failure at drawing talents to the city because only one-tenth among migrants with blue-print resident status had special skills. The system was abolished in 2002. The second round of reform introduced the residential permit, which took effect from 15 June 2002, for migrants who hold at least a bachelor's degree as well as those who possess special talents and skills. Shanghai even announces annually a list of talent types it seeks to recruit. Building on the second round of reform, the third round of reform further specified the implementation details of the issuance of residential permits, and the entitlement of privileges. The pool of eligible applicants has also been expanded to include those with special skills and outside the city's list of talents.

---

[5]To be eligible for a "blueprint *hukou*", it requires an investment of 10 million *yuan* for mainlanders and US$200,000 for foreigners and Hong Kong, Taiwan and Macao people.

[6]The value and size of commercial housing are also specified: (i) 65 m² in Pudong new district; (ii) 320,000 *yuan* in commercial value for a house in the Pudong Lujiazui area; (iii) a commercial value of 160,000 *yuan* within the inner circle zone (*neihuanxian*); and (iv) a commercial value of 100,000 *yuan* outside of the inner circle zone.

## Just a Show or Any Real Progress?

Arguably, the growing and large-scale rural-urban migration has played a foundational role in China's growth since the late 1980s. However, problems caused by non-*hukou* migration have also surfaced over time, apart from the widely known problems such as low wages, bad working conditions, wage arrears and lack of social insurance for migrant workers. At the family level, full-family migration remains limited. Not only do the majority of migrant workers suffer from the absence of their spouse and/or children, their children are also left to their own devices, growing up without parental care during the important formative years of their development. Moreover, school-age children often have to share tasks in farming and housework. As a result, many of them do not perform well in school. This may pose a systemic disadvantage for future generations of the rural population. At the community level, many villages experience a decline in mutual help, spirit of community participation and community-building as most youths and middle-aged villagers have left their villages to make a living in cities. The elderly and school-age children lack the capacity to participate in public affairs and check the actions of village leaders, thus leading to a gradual erosion of community cohesion.

There is thus a need to push for *hukou*-migration and social integration, which the central government has been promoting in small and medium cities. The challenge is to make these cities more attractive to rural migrants who prefer to move to and work in larger cities. In fact, the Second National Agricultural Census for 2006 reveals that about half of the migration is inter-provincial, from central and western to coastal areas, and from villages and small towns to medium and large cities. Seen in this light, China's *hukou* reform is critically dependent on local governments, particularly the labour-receiving provinces and municipalities. Local governments, however, often have different interests and agenda from those of the central government — the reason that an overhaul of the *hukou* system is so difficult in China. Local governments are unwilling to grant local *hukou* to migrant workers for at least two reasons. First, it would mean substantial increase in spending on healthcare, education, public housing and other infrastructure to accommodate the migrant workers-turned-local residents. Second, protests from the local population who want to preserve their privileges will be too strong for any local government leaders to ignore.

On these two counts, Shanghai and Guangdong are looked upon with admiration for taking the lead in this round of *hukou* reform. Both are major destinations of migrants — Shanghai is a magnet for highly educated talents, while Guangdong receives primarily peasant workers. The official number of people temporarily residing in Guangdong province in 2009 was 26 million, though the actual figure could be much higher.[7] In Shanghai, more than six million (out of a total of 19 million) people did not have a permanent residency in 2009. Demographic changes offer a partial answer, particularly in the case of Shanghai. Shanghai has experienced negative population growth for more than a decade, although this has been more than compensated for by the in-migration of people. In 2008, however, the number of migrants declined by 183,000, the first time since the 1990s.[8] Therefore, Shanghai's initiative may be driven by the need to increase its population, and at the same time, leverage the population increment to optimise its population structure for future development.

Migrant workers are now also viewed as a potentially important source of social insurance fund instead of a financial burden. They can help finance current social insurance expenditures caused by the ageing population. Not many migrant workers meet the requirements as laid out by the Shanghai and Guangdong governments currently. The Shanghai authority estimated that only around 3,000 people have proof of residence for seven or more years, and only a few meet all the other requirements.[9] The same is probably true of Guangdong. As such, reforms provide no immediate solution to the problems associated with non-*hukou* migration or second generation migrants.

---

[7] *Nanfang Ribao (Southern Daily)*, 24 February 2009.
[8] See <http://news.sina.com.cn/c/2009-03-13/211517403732.shtml> (accessed 9 July 2012).
[9] See <http://www.china.org.cn/china/features/content_17468979.htm> (accessed 9 July 2012).

However, the latest round of *hukou* reform is not entirely a show. The significance of the new initiatives is twofold. Though the strict requirements imply that only a handful of migrant workers are qualified for the *hukou* conversion now, the situation is only temporary. Local governments will see the benefit of the reform as migrant workers choose to pay social insurance fees and thus contributing to the funding of current social insurance expenditures. This window period is crucial for Shanghai and Guangdong to transition into a relatively different *hukou* regime without causing instant disruption or immediate financial strain. For migrant workers, the requirements would help them establish stable expectations and serve as a guideline for them to plan their future in the next seven years or so, in terms of place of work and residence. This would have a stabilising effect insofar as population movement is concerned. For the city governments, local interests often prevail over other concerns. Unless migrant workers are perceived as an indispensable asset to the city, the city government is not likely to act in the best interest of migrant workers. Shanghai does not seem to welcome rural migrants. Its requirements for obtaining a Shanghai *hukou* are so stringent that only a small minority of the well-educated and the highly skilled could qualify. It remains to be seen whether and how Guangdong honours its commitment to *hukou* reform, a province which has benefited more from migrant workers than any other provinces in China.

# 35

# Reinventing China's Health System

QIAN Jiwei*

*Much progress, including institutional changes and infrastructure upgrading, has been made in the Chinese health system. However, issues such as addressing the incentives of providers and insurers as well as improving services and medicine quality remain.*

Health expenditure in China has grown by double digits annually for more than a decade, accounting for about 5% of GDP in 2010.[1] Out-of-pocket payment as a percentage of total health expenditure in 2010 was above 36%, implying healthcare affordability of individual patients is still a serious concern. Also, many people in China have difficulty gaining access to healthcare services, in particular primary care and public health services. Both accessibility and affordability of healthcare services are serious challenges for long-term development.

There was intense public debate in the mid-2000s among scholars about the direction of health reform: whether the future health system should steer towards the approach of "direct government intervention" or a market-oriented system. In April 2009, a guideline for health reform was released by China's State Council. The objective of health reform is to establish a comprehensive health system by 2020 in which the State will play an indispensable role whereas market mechanism serves certain useful components within the health system.

According to the guideline, the target for the first phase of reform between 2009 and 2011 is to build up a framework for China's future health system, which consists of five major components. First, social insurance schemes with universal coverage will be established to improve affordability of health services. Second, an essential medicine system will be set up for providing affordable and effective medicines. Third, networks of primary care clinics will be built to improve the accessibility of healthcare services. Fourth, equal provision of basic public health services to be provided for all citizens. Fifth, implementation of reform in public hospitals to reduce health expenditure.

The State Council gave two major reasons for the first phase of health reform. The first is to emphasise the lead role of the Chinese government in financing, managing and providing health

---

*QIAN Jiwei is Research Associate at the East Asian Institute, National University of Singapore.
[1] *China Health Statistics Yearbook*, various years, Peking Union Medical College Press, Beijing.

services. The Chinese government was planning to allocate an unprecedentedly large amount of government funds (RMB850 billion) in the health sector from 2009 to 2011. The management of social health insurance programmes, which are the major insurance schemes in China, is under the purview of local governments. In China, public hospitals and clinics still play a dominant role in health services provision, thereby enabling the Chinese government to strategically coordinate different components of health system through public service providers as well as local insurers.

The second is to launch local pilot reforms incorporating the five major components during the first phase of reform, and to identify a potential model that is applicable nationwide. For example, 17 cities are selected as pilot sites for public hospital reform to test different models. Market-based competition between service providers is adopted in two cities, while the other cities focus on hospital governance in the reform.[2]

Since 2009, much progress, including institutional changes and infrastructure upgrading, have been made in China's health system. Between 2009 and 2011, health expenditure growth was a hefty RMB1.24 trillion (up from the planned RMB850 billion),[3] while various social insurance plans now cover 95% of total urban and rural population. Expenditure to finance operations of primary care clinics and build new primary care clinics has also chalked up big increases. However, there are still some issues to be addressed, such as eradicating incentives for providers and insurers as well as improving services and medicines quality.

By 2015, the Chinese government is expected to further increase expenditure on health care and reduce the share of out-of-pocket expenditure to about 30%. Further reforms in primary care providers, public hospitals, social insurance as well as public health will continue.

The future development of health reform in China largely depends on two issues. First, how health reform can leverage market mechanism and direct government intervention. Second, how experiences from local pilot reforms can be translated into a nationwide model. This chapter first offers a discussion of the condition of health system before the 2009 reform and the various debates on health reform, followed by new initiatives for health reform since 2009, and a review of the achievement of new initiatives. Future reforms and issues are also discussed in greater depth.

## Health System before 2009 Reform

Since the early 1980s, the Chinese government, especially local governments, in shifting the policy focus of single-minded pursuit of economic growth, has relegated health care to a lower priority.[4] Health service providers, most of which are publicly owned, have difficulty funding the delivery of health services. Public hospitals, in order to generate revenue, are entitled to a 15% price markup for drug prescription and provide a range of services that are not under price regulation. Primary care and public health service providers, such as township health centres, village clinics or urban clinics, have smaller and irregular patient flow compared to hospitals, and are thus under-funded to a large extent.[5] Figure 1 shows the continual decline in the number of visits to township health centres between mid-1980s and mid-2000s.

Health insurance schemes in both urban and rural areas do not function very well. Many urban insurance schemes, funded by state-owned enterprises which have undergone restructuring since the 1980s, are not very effective. An urban social health insurance scheme (or Basic Health Insurance scheme, BHI) was initiated after the mid-1990s to replace the earlier insurance system

---

[2] Competition between public and private service providers is encouraged in Kunming and Luoyang. See Yip WC et al., "Early Appraisal of China's Huge and Complex Health-care Reforms", *Lancet*, vol. 379, no. 9818, 2012, pp. 833–42.

[3] <http://www.gov.cn/gzdt/2012-04/28/content_2125942.htm> (accessed 28 May 2012).

[4] Duckett, J, *The Chinese State's Retreat from Health: Policy and the Politics of Retrenchment*, Routledge, London and New York, 2011.

[5] Qian J, "Building Networks of Primary Care Providers in China" *East Asian Policy*, vol. 3, no. 4, October to December 2011, pp. 87–97.

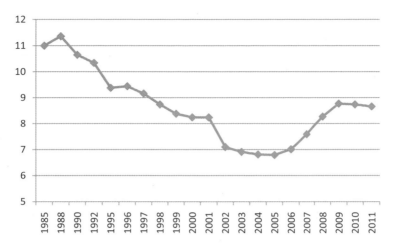

**Figure 1**   Number of Visits to Township Health Centres

*Sources*: *China Health Statistics Yearbook*, various years, Peking Union Medical College Press, Beijing; and Chinese Health Statistical Digest 2012.

funded by individual state-owned enterprises. But BHI is only valid for urban employees who work in formal sectors and the number of enrollees was about 48 million in 2000, less than one-third of the population eligible for the scheme.[6] In rural areas, health insurance schemes were supported by mutual contributions within a commune. However, after the 1980s, almost all of rural health insurance schemes were dissolved when household responsibility system replaced the commune system as the mechanism for organising production.

By 2000, the affordability issue of healthcare services became so serious that out-of-pocket payment accounted for 60% of total health expenditure. The amount of out-of-pocket payment increased from RMB26.7 billion in 1990 to RMB270 billion in 2000 (Figure 2). Government health expenditure only accounted for about 15% of total health expenditure, and a large portion of health expenditure was funded by social insurance plans and private health insurance, etc.

Accessibility of healthcare services is also a serious concern, as reflected in the drop in the number of visits to township health centres from 1.43 billion in 1981 to 0.82 billion in 2000. Many people choose to visit public hospitals instead of primary care clinics. However, supplier-induced demand in public hospitals,[7] particularly the incentives of public hospitals to generate revenue by prescribing drugs, further aggravates the affordability problem. In 2000, drug prescription accounted for over 46% of the total revenue of a public-owned general hospital on average.[8]

Since 2000, several social insurance programmes have been initiated to provide financial protection for patients. For urban residents such as retirees, students, self-employed and people working in informal sectors, an urban resident plan has been initiated in 2007 and there were 118 million people enrolled under this urban resident plan in 2008. In rural areas, a new cooperative medical scheme (CMS) was initiated in 2003 and in 2008, with total enrollees of 833 million people. In 2008, the number of people covered by all insurance programmes was over one billion (i.e. the number of enrollees under BHI was about 200 million in 2008).[9]

---

[6] See <http://www.china.com.cn/news/txt/2007-06/01/content_8328912_2.htm> (accessed 20 June 2012).

[7] Given the nature of health service, the physician is the key decision-maker during treatment. Supplier-induced demand refers to the situation in which the physician has the incentive to exploit profits from overtreatment or sale of expensive drugs.

[8] *China Health Statistics Yearbook*, various years, Peking Union Medical College Press, Beijing.

[9] Ibid.

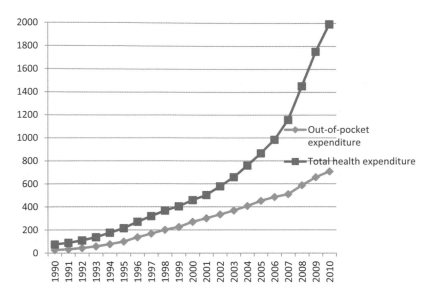

**Figure 2**    Out-of-Pocket Health Expenditure and Total Health Expenditure (Billion RMB)

*Source*: *China Health Statistics Yearbook*, various years, Peking Union Medical College Press, Beijing.

## Debates for the Direction of Health Reform Between 2005 and 2009

In the early 2000s, there was a consensus among policy makers and scholars that the role of the state should be redefined, given concerns for both affordability and accessibility of healthcare services. At least, government health expenditure should be significantly increased. However, which way the role of the state should be defined was under hot debate among scholars. There were two major camps who were arguing for totally different directions of health reform since the Development and Research Centre (DRC) under the State Council released a report on Chinese health system in 2005.

One camp consists of scholars who propose a leading role of state in the health system in provision and funding of healthcare services (a camp of "direct government intervention"). Scholars from the DRC are part of this camp.[10] They believed that the major problem of Chinese health system is due to the retreat of state in both health financing and health provision. The prescription they gave is to have a health system in which the lead role of state in providing and financing of (basic) health services, in particular for services such as primary health care, treating common diseases and provision of public health services. Tax financing is preferred compared to social insurance plans, given that it would be easier for the government to regulate health service provision in an integrated healthcare provision system. Naturally, public health and primary care services should be provided by publicly owned providers. Revenue from drug sale should be decoupled from public hospital's revenue. The government has additional two tasks: one is to equalise accessibility of health services by carefully allocating resources across regions; the other is to leave most economic treatment and medicines to service providers.

The other camp consists of scholars, who propose the lead role of social health insurance programmes. From the perspective of scholars in this camp,[11] to solve both accessibility and affordability issues, universal insurance coverage is necessary for health reform for pooling risks. Insurers, acting as a purchaser, buy services from service providers in the market. Service providers, in turn have to negotiate with insurers the reimbursement rate for healthcare services, thereby creating competition among service providers on the basis of cost-effectiveness. Scholars in this camp also proposed that the entry of more private service providers, which are more

---

[10] Ge, et al. (2007) *China Healthcare Reform*, China Development Press, Beijing.

[11] Gu, X (2008) China New Round of Healthcare reforms, *EAI Background Brief*, no. 379, East Asian Institute, National University of Singapore.

responsive to market demand, in the healthcare market will help alleviate the accessibility issues. Market mechanism, such as the choice of purchase and competition, is pivotal in the government's role as the purchaser, in which case, the majority of government health grants should be allocated as insurance funds instead of being allocated directly for provision of health services.

Views of scholars from the two camps had the support of different ministries. The Ministry of Health, representing the interests of public hospitals and health workers, supported views of the first camp, while the Ministry of Labour and Social Security, in charge of social insurance funds, supported the second camp.[12] An inter-ministry committee including 14 ministries was established in 2006 to evaluate a possible direction of health reform.[13]

## Initiatives Proposed in the 2009 Guideline for Health Reform

Eight different proposals for the health reform were presented to the inter-ministry committee in Beijing by think tanks, universities and international organisations in May 2007.[14] The health systems proposed by these eight institutions ranged in varying degree between the camps of market- oriented and "direct government intervention". After intense debate and revisions on the proposals, a guideline for health reform was eventually released in April 2009 by the State Council.

The objective of the health reform, as stipulated in the guideline, is to build a health system that is accessible and affordable to all Chinese citizens by 2020. To achieve a compromise between the two camps, the central government will play a leading role in the health system while market mechanism will be seen as complementary to the health system through competition or choice of purchase.

The guideline specifies five main tasks for the first phase of health reform between 2009 and 2011. First, to achieve universal coverage in social health insurance by 2011. Second, to establish an essential medicine system for management of essential medicines list that is most effective in medical treatment and will be sold without price markup in public-owned primary care clinics. Third, to establish networks of primary care clinics by upgrading the infrastructure of 2,000 county hospitals, over 30,000 township health centres and over 14,000 urban community health centres. The training of general practitioners for these primary care clinics will be a top priority of the reform agenda.

Fourth, to increase funding in public health services, particularly the lower-income regions by the central government. The objective is to achieve equitable access to basic public health services across regions. Fifth, to advance public hospital reform, for which reforming governance structure of public hospitals is an important component. Revenue from drug sales will be decoupled from the revenue of public hospitals in general. The central government will increase the amount of subsidies allocated to public hospitals.

Two main principles have underpinned the guideline during the first phase of the health reform: that the central government will play a lead role in reform while market mechanism will complement direct government intervention, and that local pilot programmes are encouraged in all five policy arenas and will be pivotal for future health reform.

## National and Local Progress Since 2009

A marked progress in China's health reform from 2009 to 2011 is that the Chinese government has dramatically increased expenditure on health. According to a speech made by the Minister of

---

[12] Hsiao W, "The Political Economy of Chinese Health Reform", *Health Economics, Policy and Law*, vol. 2, no. 3, 2007, pp. 241–249.

[13] See <http://finance.people.com.cn/GB/1037/4834237.html> (accessed 20 June 2012).

[14] These institutions include Peking University, Beijing Normal University, Fudan University, the DRC, World Health Organization, World Bank, McKinsey and Renmin University of China. See <http://news.xinhuanet.com/fortune/2007-11/19/content_7098474.htm>, Xinhua News Agency, (accessed 20 June 2012).

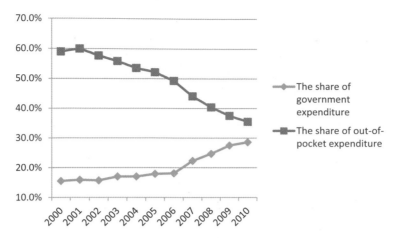

**Figure 3**   The Share of Government Expenditure/Out-of-Pocket Expenditure in Total Health Expenditure

*Source*: *China Health Statistics Yearbook*, various years, Peking Union Medical College Press, Beijing.

Finance, Xie Xuren, in April 2012, government expenditure on health increased by RMB1.24 trillion from 2009 to 2011 (up from the planned RMB850 billion).[15] The share of government expenditure in total health expenditure reached 28.6% in 2010, compared to 15.5% in 2000. Public health expenditure per capita increased from RMB15 in 2009 to RMB25 in 2011.[16] Out-of-pocket health expenditure decreased from about 60% in 2000 to 35.5% in 2010 (Figure 3).

By the end of 2011, 95% of the Chinese citizens were covered by one or more social health insurance programmes.[17] According to the government report released in February 2012, by the end of the 12th Five-Year Programme (i.e. by 2015), the reimbursement rate for inpatient service will reach at least 75% for enrollees under social health insurance.[18] In 2012, the Chinese government will subsidise RMB240 for each enrollee under the rural CMS and urban resident plan.

In September 2011, the Chinese government has declared the successful establishment of essential medicine system, in which 307 essential medicines will be procured in bulk at provincial level under a competitive bidding system and then distributed to local service providers. These essential drugs — selected based on standards such as price, quality, availability, etc. — are sold to patients without any price markup in public-owned primary care providers.

Many local pilot projects under implementation include establishing networks of primary care clinics, public hospital reform, setting up the essential medicine system and expanding social health insurance. For example, in Foshan city, Guangdong province, township health centres and county hospitals have been integrated in terms of both funding and management. In this case, primary care providers played an important part in (vertical) integrated hospitals and accounted for about 35% of total hospital revenue in 2009.[19] Similarly, since February 2008, Xiamen city has reformed the governance structure of primary care providers. All 15 community health centres in Xiamen city were merged into three public (general) hospitals. With an integrated management of hospitals and primary care providers, the referral system is expected to be improved.[20]

---

[15] See <http://www.gov.cn/gzdt/2012-04/28/content_2125942.htm> (accessed 28 May 2012).

[16] See <http://finance.chinanews.com/cj/2012/03-08/3728137.shtml>, China News Service, March 2012, (accessed 20 June 2012).

[17] See <http://news.xinhuanet.com/politics/2011-07/07/c_121633018.htm>, Xinhua News Agency, July 2011, (accessed 20 June 2012).

[18] See <http://news.xinhuanet.com/health/2012-02/23/c_122741428_2.htm>, Xinhua News Agency, February 2012, (accessed 20 June 2012).

[19] See <http://medicine.people.com.cn/GB/132552/188880/189037/11640591.html> (accessed 20 June 2012).

[20] Du L and Zhang W (eds.), *GreenBook of Health Care*, Social Sciences Academic Press, China, 2009, p. 141.

The "Anhui" model is highlighted for the essential medicine system. The procurement office in Anhui province has conducted collective procurement of all essential drugs for local health service providers since 2010, procuring the most economical and affordable drugs, which the local health service providers will sell to patients at zero markup. Drug expenditure has since been reduced by 20% in Anhui's primary care clinics in 2010.[21]

Since early 2011, the Shanghai Municipal Government has implemented public hospital reform by establishing a "health conglomerate" (*yiliao lianheti*) in each district. Each health conglomerate consists of a general hospital, several smaller hospitals and many community health centres. Patients need to go to a community health centre before they could visit higher-level hospitals with the referral from the community health centre. Currently, two such pilot health conglomerates have been established in January 2011 in two of Shanghai districts and this institutional arrangement is expected to expand to the entire city in the next three to four years.[22]

From May 2012, public hospitals in Beijing and Shenzhen city have removed 15% price markup for the sale of drugs.[23] To compensate for the financial losses after the removal, these public hospitals increased the fee for the provision of health services. For example, in Beijing, the minimum consultation fee increased from RMB3 to RMB42 per visit. For enrollees of social insurance, patients will be reimbursed RMB40 out of this RMB42 consultant fee by the insurance fund. Also, reforms to payment methods will be implemented in Beijing after May 2012.

## Further Reforms and Issues to be Addressed

In March 2012, the State Council has released a blueprint for targets of the 12th Five-Year Programme (2011–2015).[24] By 2015, the growth of government health expenditure is set to be higher than the growth rate between 2009 and 2011, and also higher than the rate of fiscal expenditure in general. The government subsidy per enrollee under social health insurance will increase to at least RMB360 in 2015. The share of out-of-pocket expenditure in total health expenditure will be reduced to less than 30%. The reimbursement rate will be raised to a level higher than 75% for inpatient services under the rural CMS and urban resident plan.[25]

By 2015, the essential medicine list would be expanded, and local governments will be responsible for financing primary care clinics. By 2015, over 150,000 general practitioners will be trained. An information network will be built to archive medical profiles and records of patients with the assistance of the information technology.

More importantly, public hospitals will undergo an overhaul in the current governance structure by 2015. Various forms of governance structure and different payment methods for public hospitals can be tested in different localities.

Although much progress has made in the past three years, affordability of healthcare service has yet to be improved. Health expenditure continues to increase by double digits, surpassing RMB2 trillion in 2011. According to a recent study, out-of-pocket expenditure per admission had increased by 18% on average for social insurance enrollees in one city between 2008 and 2010.[26] Accessibility is still a major concern given the increasing imbalance of demand of healthcare services in tertiary

---

[21] See <http://www.21cbh.com/HTML/2012-2-22/wMMDcyXzQwMzcwMw.html> (accessed 20 June 2012), *21st Century Business Herald*, 22 February 2012.

[22] See <http://www.eeo.com.cn/Politics/by_region/2011/05/04/200472.shtml> (accessed 20 June 2012), *Economic Observer*, 4 May 2011.

[23] *Caixing* Magazine, 11 June 2012.

[24] See <http://www.gov.cn/zwgk/2012-03/21/content_2096671.htm> (accessed 20 June 2012).

[25] Currently, the reimbursement rate is estimated to be less than 50%. See Meng et al., "Trends in Access to Health Services and Financial Protection in China between 2003 and 2011: A Cross-Sectional Study, *The Lancet*, vol. 379, no. 9818, 2012, pp. 805–814.

[26] Yip et al., "Early Appraisal of China's Huge and Complex Health-Care Reforms", *The Lancet*, vol. 379, no. 9818, 2012, pp. 833–842.

hospitals and primary care clinics. The number of visits to grade one hospitals (i.e. primary care providers with less than 100 hospital beds) decreased by 10 million from 2008 to 2010 while visits to grade three hospitals (large general and teaching hospitals) increased by about 140 million during the same period.

Affordability and accessibility of health care are still outstanding issues that warrant deeper discussion. First, from international experiences, social insurance could play an important role in controlling health expenditure, especially for the scenario where the local social insurer is the major buyer of health services. However, the role of social insurer to contain health expenditure is limited as out-of-pocket expenditure still increased 11.5% annually between 2007 and 2010 (Figure 3). Although some localities implemented pilot reforms for payment methods, the foremost concern of many local social insurers was merely to balance their budgets and they also lacked the incentives to explore potential payment method reforms to rein in costs of health services.[27]

Second, there are concerns about the selection of essential drugs as well as sustainability of the essential medicine system itself. Patients may be reluctant to visit primary care clinics due to the unavailability of certain medicines that are excluded in the essential medicines list in these clinics. For example, the implementation of the Anhui model in 2010 saw a significant dip in the number of visits to local township health centres. Both inpatient and outpatient visits in a township health centre in Wuhu, a major city in Anhui, had decreased by 60% in 2010.[28] Under the Anhui model, primary care clinics could only sell essential medicines procured by provincial-level procurement office at the lowest prices to patients, with no option for alternative types of medicines. Physicians are not satisfied with the essential medicine system too. According to a recent nationwide survey conducted by the Chinese Academy of Social Sciences in over 1,000 village clinics,[29] the income of village doctors has decreased by 50% on average. This is due to the fact that doctors could no longer reap additional income from drug sales after their clinics have been restricted to prescribe medicines specified in the essential medicines list only.

Third, the quality of service and incentives of physicians in the networks of primary care clinics become an important issue. Many primary care clinics are now funded by government budget and doctors are remunerated with flat monthly salary, which as a consequence, offers no incentive for them to serve more patients or improve quality of consultation.[30] Doctors in primary care clinics thus have a tendency to over-refer patients to other hospitals or render minimal medical treatment. Expecting a lower service quality in primary care clinics, patients may be more willing to visit a tertiary hospital even for mild conditions or minor diseases. It is estimated that hospital admissions had increased by 2.5 times between 2003 and 2011 — an outcome that was contrary to the health reform's objective of developing primary care networks to relieve the overload issue in hospitals.[31] Further, a recent study shows that the current scheme which allocates government health grant does not encourage primary care service providers to provide basic healthcare services to less developed regions.[32]

Fourth, the incentive structure of public hospital physicians has remained unchanged and the health expenditure in public hospitals continues to increase. For instance, a recent study has shown that over 60% of patients were prescribed antibiotics that were incompatible with their symptoms. Even for informed patients who know antibiotics are not appropriate, 39% of them were still

---

[27] For example, a recent document released by Gaoan city of Jiangsu province in 2011 highlights the importance of balance of insurance fund but sheds little light on the negotiation mechanism to reduce treatment fee in hospitals. See <http://www.jxhrss.gov.cn/rbxh/show.php?id=14829> (accessed 20 June 2012).

[28] See <http://www.eeo.com.cn/2011/1227/218813.shtml> (accessed 3 July 2012), *Economic Observer*, December 2011.

[29] 9 April 2012, *Medical and Pharmaceutical economics News (Yiyao Jinjibao)*.

[30] Ibid. For example, visits to primary care clinics had decreased in Anhui province in 2010.

[31] Meng et al., "Trends in Access to Health Services and Financial Protection in China between 2003 and 2011: A Cross-sectional Study", *The Lancet*, vol. 379, no. 9818, 2012, pp. 805–814.

[32] Qian J and Do YK, "Regional Inequality in Healthcare and Government Health Grant in China", Working paper, 2012.

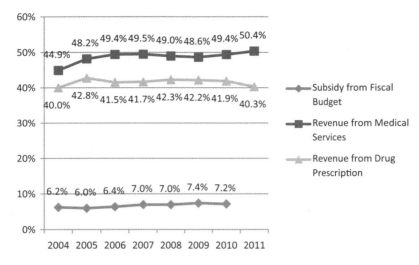

**Figure 4**   Average Share of Different Sources of Revenue in Public General Hospitals

*Source*: *China Health Statistics Yearbook*, various years, Peking Union Medical College Press, Beijing.

prescribed with antibiotics.[33] Figure 4 shows that the share of drug revenue in general hospitals was persistently constant at 40% between 2004 and 2011. Two reasons accounted for this phenomenon. On the one hand, supplier-induced demand is still expected in many hospitals given the limited role of social insurers in containing the growth of health expenditure. On the other hand, reforming hospital governance structure is still a work in progress.[34]

The aforementioned issues bear two important implications in determining the future direction of China's health reform. First, a thorough understanding of the division of labour between direct government intervention and market mechanism is pivotal for the future health system. Health reform should be included as fundamental evaluation criteria in local officials' performance assessment[35] so that local officials have strong motivation to initiate and work on health reform. Direct government intervention is more effective in producing observable results and improvement in health system such as infrastructure building (e.g. the number of hospital beds) and expansion of coverage of social health insurance.

The not so easily discernible and measurable aspects would be best dealt with by market mechanisms including purchasing and competition. For example, the purchase of services by insurers as a collective group of enrollees and the competition between service providers can induce hospitals to provide the most cost-effective treatment and to improve on the quality of healthcare services. Policy makers would do well to find an optimal mix between direct government intervention and market mechanism.

Second, many local pilot projects are implemented to solve critical problems in health care. However, finding a way to aggregate local experiences and then draw up a comprehensive health system that is applicable nationwide poses the next big challenge. Besides, it will also take massive efforts to identify whether a particular local condition or institutional arrangement contributes to the success or failure of local pilot reforms. Certainly, careful data mining and rigorous programme evaluations of local pilot reforms are necessary procedures to formulate a robust healthcare system.

---

[33] Currie et al., "Patient Knowledge and Antibiotic Abuse: Evidence from an Audit Study in China", *Journal of Health Economics,* vol. 30, no. 5, 2011, pp. 933–949.

[34] Qian J (2011), Reforming Public Hospitals in China, *East Asian Policy,* vol. 3, no. 1, pp. 75–82.

[35] Eggleston, K, "Health Care for 1.3 Billion: An Overview of China's Health System", Asia Health Policy Program Working Paper, Stanford University, 2012.

# 36

# Meeting the Ageing Challenge

## China's Social Care Policy for the Elderly

ZHANG Yanxia*

*Facing huge challenges posed by accelerated population ageing and weakening family support for the elderly, China has adopted national strategies to strengthen its social security system and establish a social care system for the elderly.*

Care for the elderly has traditionally been the responsibility of the family in China and the state mainly plays a residual role in looking after childless and disabled old people. However, a number of recent socio-economic changes have posed important challenges to the provision of elderly care, gradually making elderly care a legitimate public policy concern in China.[1] Since the 2000s, the Chinese government has formulated a social care framework that involves more sectors in care provision for the elderly. In recent years, it has established a universal social security for the elderly, putting in place a social care system for the elderly. China's national strategy proposed for the 12th Five-Year Programme (FYP, 2011–2015) is to establish a social care service system "with home-based care as the foundation, backed up by community-based services and supported by institutional care".

To assess China's capacity for meeting this ageing challenge, the driving factors leading to the social care expansion for the elderly in China would first be examined, including the accelerated population ageing, the changing family and the eroding filial piety. The Chinese government's recent policy initiatives to expand its social security system and establish a social care system for the elderly are also discussed in greater depth. The analysis will shed more light on the major challenges that China faces today in the social policy domain of elderly care.

---

*ZHANG Yanxia is Visiting Research Fellow at the East Asian Institute, National University of Singapore.
[1]Wong L, "The Third Sector and Residential Care for the Elderly in China's Transitional Welfare Economy", *Australian Journal of Public Administration,* vol. 67, no. 1, 2008, pp. 89–96.

## Emerging Ageing Challenge and Care Crisis

China's population is ageing fast. The country mainly relies on the family to provide care for the old. Family support for the elderly, however, has been weakened by dramatic demographic, economic and cultural changes. The future of the family as a key supporting pillar becomes less certain. An ageing and care crisis of potentially enormous dimensions looms large in China's future if the country fails to make adequate preparations.

### *Accelerated Population Ageing*

China is the first nation in the world to grow old before it gets rich. According to international standard, a country or region with more than 10% of its population above the age of 60 is considered an ageing society. China became an ageing country in 1999 due to rapid decline in fertility and increase in life expectancy when it registered just US$806 in per capita GDP. In contrast, most developed countries had a GDP per capita of between US$5,000 and US$10,000 when they had an ageing population. In 2010, China already had 178 million people, or 13.3% of the total population, aged 60 and above, making it the only country in the world with more than 100 million old people. Meanwhile, China's per capita GDP was still below US$4,000 in 2010, well below one-fifth of the per capita GDP of many ageing societies.[2]

China's slide to an "ageing society" will accelerate in the next two to three decades. The United Nations (UN) Population Division has projected that China will be one of the most aged countries by 2050, and with one of the heaviest old-age dependency burdens in the world. About 30% of its total population will be 60 or older by 2050, and about one in four Chinese will be 65 or older and nearly 7% of its population will be 80 or older (Figure 1). China's top legislature has recently projected that in 30 years' time (by 2042), elderly people will make up over 30% of its total population.[3]

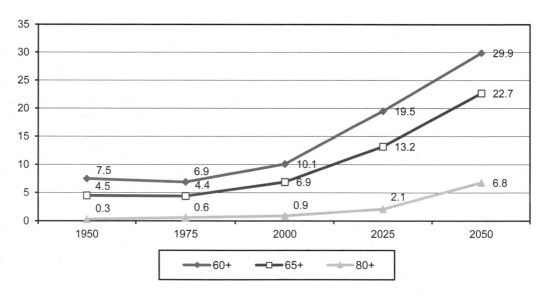

**Figure 1**   Percentage of Aged Population by Year (1950–2050)

*Source*: UN Population Division: *World Population Ageing*.

---

[2] See <http://www.gov.cn/jrzg/2011-08/24/content_1932047_2.htm> (accessed 8 June 2012).

[3] According to a recent report by the Standing Committee of the National People's Congress, China's top legislature, elderly people will account for about 17% of China's total population within five years, and over 30% by 2042. For more information, see <http://www.gov.cn/jrzg/2011-08/24/content_1932047_2.htm> (accessed 28 August 2011).

China faces enormous challenges in providing long-term care for its increasingly ageing population, especially in meeting the increased care needs of the disabled and frail elderly people. A recent national survey conducted by China National Committee on Ageing (CNCA) and China Research Centre on Ageing (CRCA) reported that there were 33 million disabled elderly[4] across the country in 2010, representing 19% of the total ageing population.[5] The recent survey also reported that there were 10.8 million elderly (6.2%) nationwide who had completely lost their ability to perform at least one basic activity in their daily life, with a higher proportion of rural elderly (6.9%) than urban elderly (5.0%) suffering from disability.

## *Weakening Family Support*

Care provision for the elderly in China follows the residual approach shaped by Confucian principles that emphasise the family's primary responsibilities and the state's residual function. The state has a responsibility to look after the urban elderly belonging to the "three-no's" — no living children or relatives, little or no income, and no physical ability to work in urban areas — and to provide "five guarantees" — basic needs of food, clothing, shelter, health care, and funeral arrangement — to childless elderly and the disabled in rural areas. In 2011, seven million childless and disabled elderly were under the state's support scheme.

The country mainly relics on the family to provide care for the elderly. The traditional value of filial piety is embedded in China's moral and social contexts. The family has always been the first line of support for the elderly people. The notion that adult children should care for their aged parents is not only based on moral values but also mandated by Chinese laws.

Although the family seems to remain the cornerstone of elderly care in China, family support for the elderly has been weakened by dramatic demographic, economic and cultural changes. Falling fertility rates — largely thanks to the one-child family policy — have led to shrinking family size and decreasing number of adult children that support the new generation of elderly. The average household size dropped from 4.4 to 3.1 between 1982 and 2010. In urban areas, the majority of the new generation of elderly people only has one child to rely on. A Chinese "4-2-1" family structure, taking the configuration of four grandparents, two parents and one child, will quickly gain prevalence. The capacities of Chinese families in extensive elderly care are thus questionable.

Declining fertility rates and massive population migration have greatly reduced the number of multigenerational families and increased the number of elderly people living alone. Nowadays, more and more elderly live separately from their adult children as their children have moved to a different dwelling or very often to a different city far away from them. CNCA recently reported that more than half of the elderly across urban and rural China lived separately from their adult children as of 2010, with the percentage hitting as high as 70% in some major cities.[6] Changes in Chinese families and living arrangements of the elderly people potentially undermine the role of the family in extensive elderly care.

Rural China faces greater challenges in providing care for its ageing population. The massive flow of young workers from rural to urban areas has led to a more aged population in rural China and the situation is projected to continue until around 2045.[7] It was reported that 40 million elderly

---

[4] In this survey, "disabled" was measured by people's ability to perform six basic activities of daily living, including bathing, dressing, using toilet, transferring from bed to chair, moving indoors and feeding oneself. "Disabled" refers to those who have partially or completely lost the ability to perform the six basic activities of daily living. The definition is different from the medical term of "disabled".

[5] See <http://www.cncaprc.gov.cn/info/13085.html> (accessed 16 June 2012).

[6] See <http://www.cncaprc.gov.cn/info/13084.html> (accessed 8 June 2012).

[7] Zhang K and Guo P, *The Blue Book of Population Aging and Status of the Elderly*, *Zhongguo shehui chubanshe*, Beijing, 2010.

(37% of rural elderly) were left behind in rural China by their adult children, who migrated to urban areas for better job opportunities. Compared with their counterparts in urban areas, rural elderly are more vulnerable because of a more severe shortage of pension, health care and other care resources.

Social norms are also changing. There is a concern of eroding the traditional value of filial piety in China. A recent study of urban elderly in Guangdong province suggests that the tradition of adult children supporting their elderly parents is slowly fading away. Elderly people reportedly provide not only domestic support, including care for grandchildren and household chores, but also financial support to their children. They, however, receive very little financial or emotional support from their adult children.[8] The traditional give-and-get contract between elderly parents and their adult children seems to be undergoing rapid changes.

Instead of blaming the young generation for valuing money more than family ties in contemporary China, some scholars argue that the ethical principles of intergenerational responsibility are not based on an equal exchange of give-and-get between the young and elderly generations. The elderly in fact do not expect equal contributions or returns from their children,[9] preferring to rely on themselves to the largest extent and relieve their children of the care burden. Many are found to have adapted to the new reality and have lowered their filial expectations. Fewer elderly people believe in "raising children in preparation of one's old age". A decreasing number of elderly people want to live with their children, while more want to live alone and depend on themselves. Nevertheless, to many elderly people, a more serious challenge they face is where to get the support if they need extensive care.

## Establishing Social Security and Social Care for the Elderly

China has been acutely aware of its ageing problem since the mid-1990s. Like Singapore, China has made great efforts to revive the tradition of filial piety. The huge challenges posed by accelerated population ageing and weakening family support imply that minimal state involvement in care provision is increasingly untenable. Since the 2000s, the Chinese government has embarked on national strategies — strengthening its social security system and establishing a social care system for the elderly — to solve the pressing ageing issues and pursue sustainable development.

### *Expanding Social Security*

China has basically established universal social security for the elderly. The country has made substantial progress in expanding health care, especially through the establishment of the New Rural Cooperative Medical System in recent years. A universal basic healthcare insurance has been established across the country. In 2011, the government provided minimum livelihood protection to nearly 22 million elderly people nationwide. It has set a specific goal to provide minimum livelihood protection by 2015 to all elderly who live below the local poverty line.

China currently strives to establish a basic social pension system for all citizens, including unemployed urban citizens and rural villagers. In urban areas, basic pension scheme has been expanded to cover the unemployed on a trial phase since July 2011. This reflects the Chinese government's resolve to establish a universal basic pension system in urban areas by 2012. In rural areas, the New Basic Rural Pension Insurance had covered 190 million rural villagers by

---

[8] The survey was conducted by Guangdong Academy of Social Sciences. Intergenerational support was rendered from elderly parents to their adult children rather than vice versa. See <http://www.chinadaily.com.cn/china/2010-10/25/content_11453473.htm> (accessed 30 May 2012).

[9] Yang S and He C, "*Zeren lunli he chengshi jumin de jiating yanglao*" (The Ethical Principles of Responsibility and the Family Support in Beijing), *Journal of Peking University (Philosophy and Social Sciences)*, January 2004, pp. 71–84.

May 2011, benefiting 51.7 million elderly people.[10] The government also plans to roll out a universal basic pension system in rural areas by 2020. The initiative towards full pension coverage is a milestone for China. Nevertheless, challenges persist, particularly the wide rural-urban income gap, and the issues of coverage rate[11] and adequacy of pension benefits.

### Establishing Social Care

The establishment of a social care service system for the elderly is not only a timely response to the ageing and care crisis, but also an effective means to increase consumption and create new employment opportunities.

During the 11th FYP (2006–2010), the focus of China's national policy for elderly care was to provide adequate affordable and convenient home-based and community-based care services to the elderly to enable them to live with minimal dependence in their own homes. The government held the view that over-development of formalised care institutions for the elderly would be harmful to China's sustainable development. Therefore, institution-based care should only play a supplementary role in the care system for the elderly.

The government has developed a home-based elderly care service system to provide daily care, rehabilitation and nursing care, and emotional care within their households. This home-based programme is mainly targeted at the elderly who are disabled, aged 80 and above, as well as those who live alone or with a spouse. Poor, frail and disabled elderly will have their service expenses borne and supported by public funding.

Community-based services have developed more rapidly in urban areas than in rural areas. Comprehensive community service centres established in urban China had increased steadily between 2001 and 2010 and doubled by 2010 (Figure 2). For instance, there were over 10,000 community service centres by the end of 2009. All community centres provide day-care services, such as meals, daily medical checks, day beds (30,000 in total number) and also various group activities such as singing, dancing and movie-watching. However, very few community service centres provide beds for boarders.

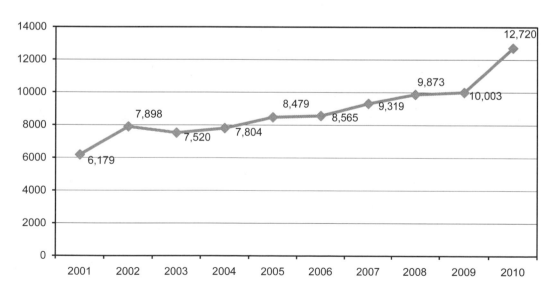

**Figure 2**  Number of Urban Community Service Centres, 2001–2010

*Source*: *China Social Statistical Yearbook 2010*, China Statistics Press, Beijing.

---

[10] See <http://www.gov.cn/jrzg/2011-08/24/content_1932047_2.htm> (accessed 8 June 2012).

[11] Coverage rate refers to the percentage of people covered by any pension programme.

During the 12th FYP, China has paid more attention to the enormous challenges of providing long-term care for its aged population and the acute shortage in care institutions for the elderly. Institutional care is considered to play a smaller role in China than in most countries. There were about 40,000 care institutions for the elderly by the end of 2010, providing 3.1 million beds to accommodate 1.8% of China's elderly population. In contrast, nursing homes in developed countries have adequate beds for about 5% to 7% of their senior citizens, and in developing countries, beds are sufficient for 2% to 3% of their senior population. The demand for institutional care is higher from the frail and disabled elderly, in comparison to other elderly groups, but more than half of the nursing homes in China could not or prefer not to admit disabled elderly who need assistance in their daily activities. Among the 33 million disabled elderly in 2010, only 300,000 (0.9%) secured a place in professional nursing homes.

The Chinese government has also attached greater importance to institutional care, which is expected to play a more prominent role instead of simply a supplementary one. By giving more emphasis to the establishment of formal care institutions and community day care centres for the elderly, the Chinese government aims to add more than three million new institution-based beds to accommodate 3% of China's elderly population by 2015. It has also planned to establish a comprehensive service network to support home-based care in all urban communities, 80% of rural townships and half of rural villages by 2015. The provision of a diversified range of community-based care services, in particular rehabilitation and nursing care, more elderly friendly communities and homes, and various cultural and educational facilities for the elderly to enrich their spiritual life, is encouraged. Currently, a comprehensive community-based service system has yet to be established to support home-based care even in urban areas. According to official statistics, less than 30% of the urban communities have established day-care centres for the elderly. Cultural and educational facilities also fall short of meeting the growing demand. The inadequacy is much more severe in rural areas.

Meanwhile, a number of provinces have been singled out for a pilot programme that provides long-term care insurance for the elderly and explores ways to enhance the economic capabilities of the elderly. To improve quality of care of various formal care institutions, minimum mandatory standards are introduced for facilities, equipment, service provisions and staff qualification.

### Discussions

It can be seen that the Chinese state has a strong political will to overcome the ageing challenge and care crisis. The government has made substantial progress since the 2000s. Nevertheless, China's social care system for the elderly is still in its infancy. It still has a long way to go to build a comprehensive and integrated service infrastructure to meet the increasing care needs of China's rapid ageing population.

The state faces at least three challenges in the elderly care domain. The first challenge is the urban-rural and regional imbalance. Social care facilities — whether home-based, community-based and institutional care — are more developed in urban areas than in rural areas. Due to the urban bias in the existing social care service system, social care facilities are still very lacking in the rural areas. The disabled rural elderly and those left behind are particularly vulnerable. There exists a wide disparity between developed and undeveloped regions largely due to differences in their local revenues. While the local governments of developed regions have ample public funding to provide direct care or purchase various care services for the elderly from the private sector or the third sector, most undeveloped regions have to wait for the central government to increase fiscal investment to be able to do so.

The second challenge is to work out a partnership framework to develop a mixed social service system in which the state, market, family and the third sector can actively and jointly assume care responsibility for the elderly. The Chinese government has played a lead role in the establishment of a social service network and providing direct care to the most disadvantaged elderly people.

However, the future development of the social care service system will also rely on non-state sectors — the family, the market and the third sector.

The government has actively encouraged non-state sectors, especially non-governmental organisations or non-profit organisations, and the private sector to provide the bulk of social care services to the elderly. Nevertheless, the private and the third sectors are seemingly disinterested in investing in care institutions mainly due to the huge long-term investment with low returns. Preferential policies in taxes and use of land that the government offers are also, in reality, not properly implemented. The existing non-state providers in care provision have merely focussed on expensive and profit-making services or low-end facilities, rather than the much needed facilities that provide basic quality care. The role of non-state sectors in easing the shortage of care provision is thus limited. In the long run, the state should effectively implement tax incentives and preferential policies in land use and grant non-state sectors with the necessary financial aid beyond tax incentives.

Last but not least, improving the quality of elderly care is a major challenge in China, due to the lack of qualified care workers, effective regulation and supervision. Low wages, low status and poor working conditions are factors why the care sector, deemed as one of the most undesirable career choices, is shunned by jobseekers. Nursing home abuse is never rare in China. Many care institutions are understaffed or employ unqualified workers. It is estimated that China needs 10 million professional caregivers to meet the needs of its ageing population. With only 300,000 caregivers in the country and less than a third of them professionally qualified, it is extremely challenging to ensure quality day-to-day care for the elderly, especially those with chronic diseases or physical disability who need intense patience and care. Devising effective methods to train a large pool of qualified care workers is a human-capital imperative for the Chinese government.

The improvement in care quality also largely depends on the effectiveness of the government's role in regulating and monitoring various service providers. China has taken important initiatives in the 12th FYP to set up the minimum standards for care facilities, equipment, service provisions and staff qualification for various formal care institutions. Nonetheless, the state is expected to play an integral role in formulating regulations and policing the implementation of the social policy domain of elderly care.

# 37

# China's Way to Good Housing Governance

ZHOU Zhihua*

*In China's transitional economy, local governments dominate housing development. The concerns for equality, effectiveness, efficiency, accountability, participation and sustainability have to be equally addressed to promote better housing governance.*

The search for good governance has become an increasingly important element of policy management and is high on the political agenda of the global leadership.[1] In China, the increasingly ferocious political contestation, large-scale urbanisation, rapid demographic changes and severe environmental pollution amidst dramatic economic progress have necessitated the quest for alternative housing governance.

China has adopted reforms that enable housing privatisation and marketisation to work together, a common strategy used in shaping the patterns of housing governance in East Asia.[2] How then is China going to change its role from one of direct control to that of guiding appropriately? What are the state's strategies in its search for effective housing governance and in defining relations between itself and the market? How has housing development shaped, and is shaped by the diverse political and socio-economic situations? This chapter aims to provide insights into China's housing trends and explore Chinese housing governance by firstly evaluating the changing roles of the state based on the norms of equality, efficiency, effectiveness, accountability, participation and sustainability, and secondly by analysing an empirical example of the recent state intervention.

---

*ZHOU Zhihua is Visiting Research Fellow at the East Asian Institute, National University of Singapore.
[1]Mok KH and R Forrest, "The Search for Good Governance in Asia", in Mok KH and R Forrest (eds.), *Changing Governance and Public Policy in East Asia*, London: Routledge, 2009.
[2]Gouri et al, Imperatives and Perspective, in *Privatisation and Public Enterprise: The Asian Pacific Experience*, eds. Gouri G, Institute Of Public Enterprise, Oxford and IBH, New Delhi, 1991.

## What is Good Urban Governance?

*Governance* in neoliberal analysis is about minimising the size of the government and transferring normal state functions to non-state mechanisms.[3] Posner (1998)[4] regards it as a new process of governing with perhaps the participation of several actors and as complex patterns of interaction among the state, private businesses and civil society. It relates to a rational use of power to achieve the expected behaviours, or outcomes that depend on the interaction between actors.[5] *Good governance* means less government: management is done through "steering", that is, setting the policy direction rather than "rowing" (delivering services).[6] International Monetary Fund (IMF) regards it as institutionalising processes for achieving an equable, effective, efficient and accountable state.[7]

*Good urban governance* "is about the responsible and sensitive management of that positive chaos of economic dynamism. The challenge is to create cities that deliver a high quality of urban life for the majority rather than the minorities".[8] It should empower people, decentralise authority and embrace participatory management.[9] It should safeguard the environmental quality of man-made and natural environments.[10] Hence, based on the norms of equality, effectiveness, efficiency and accountability proposed by the IMF, good urban governance should also focus on participation and environmental concerns. And these norms must be interdependent and mutually reinforcing.[11]

In the face of a transitional economy, there are always lengthy debates on the relations between the state and the market. On the one hand, neoliberalists claim that *governance without government* is becoming a dominant pattern of governance.[12] Markets came to be seen as the most efficient means of organising modern societies. State intervention was thought to do more harm than good.[13] On the other hand, the defects of market mechanisms and the limits to the processes of marketisation lead to alternative governance beyond those centred on the market.[14] Box (1999)[15] suggests that despite the considerable success of marketisation in increasing the efficiency of governmental bureaucracies, there is still a need for the government to intervene because of the imperfection of the market. In certain areas, the state can allocate and coordinate activities more efficiently than when the market is left alone. For good governance, the role of the state should shift from control to influence and from direct provision to steering and enabling.[16] Decentralisation is normally the channel for such a shift. However decentralisation should avoid replacing centralised state control

---

[3] Kaboolian, L, The New Public Management: Challenging the Boundaries of the Management vs. Administration Debate, *Public Administration Review*, vol. 58 no. 3, 1998, pp. 189–193.

[4] Posner, E, Fundamentals of Governance, *Choices* vol. 7 no. 1, 1998, pp. 24–29.

[5] Anderson, JL, "Techniques for Governance", *Social Science Journal*, vol. 35, no. 4, 1998, pp. 493–508.

[6] Ha S, Urbanization, Low-income Housing and Urban Governance in South Korea, in Mok and Forrest (eds.), *Changing Governance and Public Policy in East Asia*, London: Routledge, 2009.

[7] Mok KH and R Forrest, op. cit.

[8] Forrest R, Managing the Chaotic City-Social Cohesion: New Forms of Urban Governance and the Challenge for East Asia, in KH Mok and R Forrest (eds.), *Changing Governance and Public Policy in East Asia*, London: Routledge, 2009.

[9] Osborne, D and T Gaebler, *Reinventing Government*. New York: Addison-Wesley Publishing Company, Inc, 1992.

[10] Healey, P and M Barrett, Structure and Agency in Land and Property Development Processes: Some Ideas for Research, *Urban Studies*, vol. 27, no. 1, 1990, pp. 89–104.

[11] Ha S, op. cit.

[12] Peters, G and J Pierre, Governance without Government? Rethinking Public Administration, *Journal of Public Administration Research and Theory* vol. 8, no. 2, 1998, pp. 223–243.

[13] Boyer, E, "The Scholarship of Engagement", *Journal of Public Outreach*, 1(1), 1996, pp. 11–20.

[14] Turnbull, S, Governance Options — Beyond Markets and Hierarchies, 1996. <http://www.worldcitizen.org/issues/decjan96/governance.html> (accessed 15 May 2012).

[15] Box, C, "Running Government like a Business", *American Review of Public Administration*, vol. 29, no. 1, 1999, pp. 19–43.

[16] Ha S, op. cit.

entirely with market-dominated control.[17] A balanced relationship between the market and the state is the healthiest.

In short, good urban governance should enhance the norms of equality, effectiveness, efficiency, accountability, participation and environmental concerns. In transitional economies, for instance the Chinese economy, improvement in governance lies in the state's ability to come up with strategies to achieve an optimal relationship between itself and the market. The following sections will (i) briefly review Chinese housing reform, (ii) evaluate the role of the state in such norms and (iii) explore the state-market relationship by an example of the recent state intervention.

## Housing Governance in China

### Chinese Housing Reform

The last few decades have seen dramatic economic progress in China. Urbanisation is the most conspicuous change that one observes during the economic transition. The old welfare housing model is deemed to be incompatible with the transition: it created a bureaucratic system in which all housing was produced and managed by the state via local authorities and state-owned enterprises; it generated huge burden for the state, creating abominable living conditions and making it difficult to provide timely assistance to most of the needy etc. The rapid economic development, large-scale urbanisation and defects of the old welfare housing system have put pressure on the state's capacity in housing governance.

China changed its housing strategy in the late 1980s. The main aim of this strategic change is to explore alternatives to direct housing provision, enhance the choice and diversification of housing services as well as improve the competitive environment in the delivery of housing service.[18] The compendium document[19] in 1994 set out the objectives of the housing reform: the provision of economically affordable housing (*Jingji Shiyong Fang*) for lower- and middle-income families (they constitute the majority of urban citizens in China) and market housing for upper-middle income households. In 1998 the state terminated the welfare housing provision,[20] after which the public sector was scaled down dramatically and the private sector promptly came to dominate the stage. To cope with the Asian financial crisis in the late 1990s, the housing industry was positioned as a new growth engine to stimulate economic development.

The housing reform replaced the traditional socialist hierarchical approach with housing marketisation and privatisation. The role of the state has changed from providing direct housing to all urban citizens to creating an alliance between the state and the private sector.[21] The state "seek(s) every means to disengage from public housing through the promotion of homeownership".[22] "Market mechanism has become an important force in housing production, distribution and management".[23] In housing provision and most of its responsibilities, the role of the state has been taken over by the market. Table 1 shows the poor performance of economically affordable

[17] Turnbull, S, Governance Options — Beyond Markets and Hierarchies, 1996. <http://www.worldcitizen.org/issues/decjan96/governance.html> (accessed 15 May 2012).

[18] OECD, *Governance in Transition: Public Management Reforms in OECD Countries*, Paris: Organization for Economic Cooperation and Development, 1995.

[19] Notice of the State Council on Promoting the Housing Reform, [State Council/1994/043].

[20] Circular of Promoting the Continuous and Healthy Development of the Real Estate Markets, [State Council/1998/023].

[21] Huang Y and W Clark, Housing Tenure Choice in Transition Urban China: A Multilevel Analysis, *Urban Studies*, vol. 39, no. 1, 2002, pp. 7–32.

[22] Lee J, From Welfare Housing to Homeownership: The Dilemma of China's Housing Reform, *Housing Studies* vol. 15, no. 1, 2000, pp. 61–76.

[23] Zhang X, Beyond the State: New Forms of Housing Governance in China, *Asian Geographer*, vol. 21 (1–2), 2002, pp. 53–66.

**Table 1**    Investment in Real Estate Industry in 1998–2010 (billion *yuan*)

| | Investment in Real Estate Development | Investment in Residential Housing Development | Investment in Economically Affordable Housing Development |
|---|---|---|---|
| 1998 | 361.24 | 208.16 | 27.09 |
| 1999 | 410.32 | 263.85 | 43.70 |
| 2000 | 498.40 | 331.20 | 54.24 |
| 2001 | 634.41 | 421.67 | 59.97 |
| 2002 | 779.09 | 522.78 | 58.90 |
| 2003 | 1,015.38 | 677.67 | 62.20 |
| 2004 | 1,315.83 | 883.70 | 60.64 |
| 2005 | 1,590.92 | 1,086.09 | 51.92 |
| 2006 | 1,942.30 | 1,363.84 | 69.68 |
| 2007 | 2,528.88 | 1,800.54 | 82.09 |
| 2008 | 3,120.32 | 2,244.09 | 97.09 |
| 2009 | 3,624.18 | 2,561.37 | 113.41 |
| 2010 | 4,825.94 | 3,402.62 | 106.17 |

*Source*: *Bureau of Statistics 2011.*

**Table 2**    Housing Affordability in Three Major Cities, 2010 (*yuan*)

| Item/Cities | Beijing | Shanghai | Tianjin |
|---|---|---|---|
| Total amount of the housing unit | 1,543,590 | 1,286,100 | 714,600 |
| Down-payment (20%) | 308,718 | 257,220 | 142,920 |
| Monthly mortgage payment (20 years) | 9,134 | 7,610 | 4,228 |
| Monthly household income | 10,859 | 11,019 | 8,582 |
| Ratio of mortgage to household income | 84.1% | 69.0% | 49.3% |

*Notes and Sources*: i) The total amount is based on a two-bedroom flat unit of 90 m$^2$ of construction floor area and the average housing price in 2010, *Bureau of National Statistics* 2011;
ii) Mortgage calculation is based on the interest rate on 30 December 2010, <http://www.pbc.gov.cn/publish/zhengcehuobisi/631/index.html> (accessed 17 September 2012) and <http://bj.house.sina.com.cn/bxjsq/> (accessed 17 September 2012);
iii) Household income is based on the average wage in 2010 and assuming two employees per household, *Bureau of National Statistics* 2011.

housing, which was supposed to be the main housing provision resource for the majority of urban citizens.

The housing reform has successfully created a private housing market, restructured housing institutional arrangements, redefined the roles of key actors and provided more housing tenure choices for citizens. It has made huge achievements in improving living conditions and creating a new urban landscape, and contributed greatly to economic development. However, it also "has generated social fragmentations and wealth polarization, as well as revealing serious gaps in existing housing provision strategies".[24] It has produced a stratified housing structure characterised by the dominance of highly priced market housing, the lack of social housing and the prevalence of housing affordability problem (Table 2) for the majority (70% of total urban population). This has led to great social grievances in recent years.

---

[24]Ronald R and Chiu R, Changing Housing Policy Landscapes in Asia Pacific, *International Journal of Housing Policy*, vol. 10, no. 3, 2010, pp. 223–231.

## Evaluation of Chinese Housing Governance

This section reviews the changing role of the state in its search for efficient housing governance to strengthen social equality, economic efficiency, policy effectiveness, state accountability, community participation and environmental sustainability.

### Social inequality

The problem of social inequality has much to do with China's housing development. In the old housing welfare system, wide accommodation disparities existed due to the differentials in location and profit levels of enterprises. Housing conditions for workers in similar ranks or positions but working in different enterprises might differ greatly. The sale of public housing to sitting tenants created further inequalities when some were excluded from the allocation system. In the 1990s, the Housing Provision Fund (*Zhufang Gongjijin*) benefited only part of the urban population as the unemployed and retirees in the private sector or in enterprises with financial difficulties were all excluded from this scheme.

Housing inequality has worsened since the 21st century. Firstly, housing has become unaffordable to the majority. Secondly, institutional arrangements, such as social housing provision for those living in poverty, are insufficient. Thirdly, social segregation and polarisation of housing conditions between the rich and the poor have surfaced. Fourthly, despite their great contributions to China's economy, the "floating" rural-urban immigrants, as non-officially registered residents, are not entitled to certain social welfare such as accommodation. Fifthly, conflicts arose during housing demolition and urban regeneration. The upgrading of city landscapes has forced some households to move to the suburbs. In some cases, groups of thugs were called in to coerce residents into compliance. Last but not least, problems with the allocation and management of social housing have emerged. For instance, its filtering process is sometimes bureaucratic and "eligible" occupiers are disqualified from the allocation of housing.

### Economic efficiency

Like many other Asian countries, China also adopts the economic-prioritised development mode of governance: "Meeting housing needs is not the primary objective (of the state), economic development is".[25] Housing projects are normally profit-oriented and the government turns a blind eye to negative social effects even when neighbourhoods are adversely affected. In the process of demolishing buildings and constructing new ones, the government chooses to sacrifice tradition and culture for superficial architectural aesthetics. This decision sometimes leads to public protest against urban regeneration.

In Guangzhou, while all the economically affordable housing projects are located in sub-urban areas with poor transport and infrastructure facilities, many plots of land in prime locations are designated for commercial use. Commercial activities bring high revenue to the locality. Land meant for industrial developments is sometimes unnecessarily shifted to commercial developments which offer more lucrative returns to the local government. This, to some extent, depresses industrial development.

### State accountability

With the housing reform, the state tries to remove unnecessary institutional barriers and establish a private housing market. It also attempts to optimise housing resources and facilitate financial

---

[25]Lee J and Zhu Y, Urban Governance, Neoliberalism and Housing Reform in China, *The Pacific Review*, vol. 19, no. 1, 2006, pp. 39–61.

assistance. It encourages public service provisions through enabling the actors and promoting partnerships between private and public sectors. It integrates inter-sectorial professionals and encourages technological innovations in urban planning. It provides necessary infrastructure construction and undertakes numerous regeneration projects to facilitate housing development, and to create a more modern city.

The state's efforts have been met with criticisms, especially on its failure to assist disadvantaged groups in meeting their housing needs. Not until 2010, three decades after the housing reform, has the state taken note of this issue. Its efforts appear inadequate when contrasted with what East Asian and Western countries are doing for their people. Secondly, the state has not provided sufficient information and guidelines, which are particularly important in a new housing market, to facilitate housing decision-making. Fraudulences in land and housing sectors are also frequently reported by the public media. In the hierarchical government system, senior officers are vested with the authority to decide how some public resources ought to be used.

*Policy effectiveness*

Housing policies, most of which are within the context of privatisation,[26] have successfully introduced market mechanism to the housing sector and have indeed brought about great housing improvements. Policies that are favourable to localities have been effectively implemented (e.g. tax policies and land auction policies). Examples of poorly executed policies include those for economically affordable housing. Policy ineffectiveness accounts greatly for the skyrocketing price of market housing, while inadequate social housing construction has also caused housing affordability problems.

Such ineffectiveness could be attributed to several factions. Firstly, the inability of the central bureaucracy to cater to the varying economic and social needs of the vast China's territory. Effective planning to be carried out at the regional level is difficult. Secondly, terms used in policies are ambiguous. For instance, qualitative words like "better", "healthier" and "higher" are used, resulting in confusion in policy implementation. Thirdly, there is neither systematic database nor effective supervisory system to facilitate market analyses and operation.

Inefficiency in policy implementation has been largely attributed to the inconsistency between the central state and the locality. In China's planned economy, the relationship between the central and localities was straightforward: the central government organised all public resources and was accountable to all its citizens. The localities followed instructions from the central government, submitting income from regional development or making claims for deficits from the central state.

The economic reform in 1978 and the fiscal reform in 1994 changed this relation. With the economic reform, the central state has relinquished its administrative and economic power to the localities, which are now responsible for their respective regional developments; after the fiscal reform, fiscal incomes of localities are now shared between the central and local governments with the latter getting 40% share. Apparently, the role of local governments has changed from being regional agents to players backed by strong economic, financial and administrative power. However, local governments are struggling with regional development, facing heavy healthcare education and housing burdens, as well as problems created by state-owned enterprises.

Revenue from land-use right transfers and real estate taxes contribute greatly to the fiscal income. Prosperous housing development can stimulate regional GDP growth and create a modern living environment. All these are advantageous to officials climbing the career ladder. A cyclical relationship is then formed between housing development, fiscal income of the local government, regional economic growth and the city landscapes. As a result, local governments actively engaged in housing-led economic development. National revenue from land-use right transfers increased

---

[26] Wu F, China's Emerging Cities: The Market of New Urbanism, Wu F (ed.). Abingdon, Oxon: Routledge, 2007.

from 1,590 billion *yuan* in 2009 to 2,700 billion *yuan* in 2010. In 2010 the revenue from land-use right transfers accounted for 53% of the total fiscal income of Shanghai.[27]

## Community participation

Urban governance "involves individual citizens and households, of all income groups, inasmuch as they have any influence over what happens".[28] Local citizens, who know their communities well, can make suggestions to the restructuring of the environment and the neighbourhood. Through community participation, citizens are provided with a platform to explore their talents to improve the planning and delivery of social services. Cities that exclude groups in their decision-making process are often bureaucratic and exhibit unresponsive forms of governance.[29] The public has in most instances been excluded in Chinese urban governance such as decision-making and service delivery. Exclusion and marginalisation of society have caused the bureaucracy to deteriorate, resulting in inefficient planning and social discontent. Community participation is now being regarded seriously by the government. For example the slogan of "small government and big society" in the Guangdong model implies an intentional shift from authoritarian state governance to a way of governance where the public might play a larger role.

## Environmental sustainability

Rapid economic development, big population and large-scale urbanisation are threats to environmental sustainability. China constructs two billion square metres of new property every year.[30] Energy consumption by property construction accounted for 46.7% of the total in 2007.[31] In China, like many other developing countries, social and economic concerns are prioritised over environmental issues. Sustainable construction in most cases requires high initial costs resulting in lower profit returns. Despite the existence of numerous policies to reduce environmental pollution, few local governments make the effort to ensure that the policies are enforced and that innovative techniques are suitably integrated during the construction of green buildings or eco-friendly systems. Further, as some professionals have claimed, many expensive housing units are poorly constructed with life span of less than 40 years. This is not cost-effective and not environment friendly. Cities are crowded with high-density blocks without a green living environment.

Cultivated land also decreased from 1,945 million *mu* in 1998 to 1,826 million *mu* in 2008.[32] The abuse of cultivated land will bring disastrous consequences such as food shortage problem to a developing country with a huge population.

To sum up, the new mode of housing governance is still heavily influenced by socialist ideologies and institutions which are easily recognisable by their opaque public supervision, minimal community participation, monopolistic supply of key resources and services, and small decision-making body. Local governments in particular play a dominant role in Chinese housing development: (i) As the decision-maker of local housing reform, it is able to come up with housing reforms that benefit itself; (ii) It is the governor of the housing market through the issuing of policies and regulations; (iii) It controls important resources that are not available to other actors (e.g. land); (iv) It strongly affects the local banks' business. For example, many bank loans were granted under the pressure and informal instructions of officials; (v) Like an entrepreneur, it regards city planning as a business and is actively engaged in housing-led economic development.

---

[27] The Ministry of Land and Resources and the Ministry of Finance.

[28] Devas, N. Urban Governance, Voice and Poverty in the Development World, London: Earthscan, 2004.

[29] Ha S, op. cit.

[30] <http://www.prosalesmagazine.com/industry-news.asp?sectionID=0&articleID=1120287> (accessed 15 May 2012).

[31] <http://news.sina.com.cn/c/2007-10-29/001514181433.shtml> (accessed 15 May 2012).

[32] <http://baike.baidu.com/view/36275.htm> (accessed 15 May 2012).

Overall in the Chinese housing market it is the local government, and not the market players, that plays a dominating role. The institutional political and economic arrangements of the reforms have led to the dominant status of the local governments. Such an interest-involved role in an immature housing market harms market competitiveness rather than strengthens it.

## State or Market? The 2010–2011 State Intervention

This section will take the recent state intervention as an example to explore the relations between the state and the market in the housing sector. The central state realises that more efforts are required to improve the market efficiency of the private sector, the housing affordability for the majority and social housing provision for the poor. Since 2010, the central state has adopted a series of housing measures to tackle accountability of local governments, social housing construction, property tax trials, credit and purchase-limitation and so on. Amongst these measures, the two most distinctive measures are credit and purchase-limitation. Households have to make a minimum 50% down-payment of the value of the second property they are buying. In Beijing, non-officially registered households with no properties are also disqualified from buying houses if they are unable to present the five-year-minimum *Individual Income Tax Certificate* or *Social Insurance Payment Slip*, proving that they have lived in Beijing for over five years.

State intervention has caused housing transactions to decline dramatically, leading to a higher surplus of unsold units (Table 3). It was a turning point for the market when prices were observed to be decreasing in the late 2011 in some large cities with relatively faster economic growth (Figure 1). And, as JP Morgan Chase suggests, house price in 2012 will decrease by 5% to 10% at the national level and 15%–20% in certain major cities.[33] The massive aborted land auctions imply that many developers have lost confidence in the land and housing markets. Notably, the intervention reconfigures the housing structure with the construction of 36 million units of social housing in the 2011–2015 period to ease social discontent and to stimulate GDP growth.[34] The strong state intervention saw the tumbling of housing prices, as expected by the state. The setback of such intervention is in the use of absolute administrative power (purchase-limitation) to restrain the market, which will, in the long run, destroy the market mechanism. State intervention implies that there is no boundary between the state and the market in the housing sector as the state plays a controlling role with the designing of the housing governing structure.

## Towards Good Housing Governance

Chinese housing development has made remarkable improvement to housing conditions, beautifying living places and contributing greatly to economic development. However, the poor performance of social housing, the sustained high housing prices, and the housing affordability issue for the majority evince that problems still lurk in the system. Some ascribe this to market power in housing development, and yet, many attribute it to state-dominated housing governance. Questions centred on the effectiveness of housing governance and the boundary between the state and the market in the Chinese transitional economy.

To answer these questions, this chapter has evaluated the changing role of the state in the housing reforming process and takes the recent state intervention as an example to explore state-market relations. The current state of cooperation of the state and the market is ineffective in producing good housing governance so as to deliver high quality urban life to the majority. The boundary between the market and state is fuzzy: the state plays a dominating role in the housing terrain by designing the governing structure to include the role of the market. It is the locality rather

---

[33] <http://finance.people.com.cn/stock/GB/222942/16981617.html> (accessed 15 May 2012).

[34] <http://politics.people.com.cn/GB/1026/14073295.html> (accessed 15 May 2012).

**Table 3**    Transactions and Housing Stock in Some Major Cities 2011 (million m² and %)

|  | Floor Area | % Change From 2010 | Market Housing Stock | % Change From 2010 |
|---|---|---|---|---|
| Beijing | 9.6346 | −21.7 | 10,460 | 33.97 |
| Shanghai | 13.089 | −17.2 | 9,730 | 51.99 |
| Guangzhou | 8.2279 | −8.4 | 8,000 | 64.53 |
| Shenzhen | 2.717 | −15.2 | 2,650 | 30.63 |
| Hangzhou | 3.2109 | −20.6 | 3,430 | 92.50 |
| Nanjing | 4.006 | −25.2 | 6,270 | 56.01 |

*Source*: <http://fdc.soufun.com/report/4549.htm> and <http://news.xinhuanet.com/house/2012–01/11/c_122567644.htm> (accessed 15 May 2012).

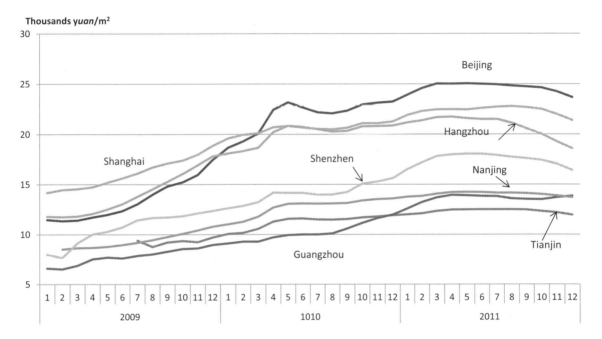

**Figure 1**    Housing Prices in Some Major Cities, 2009–2011

*Source*: <http://hangzhou.anjuke.com/market/W0QQcZ1#mode=1&hm=0&period=36> (accessed 15 May 2012).

than the market mechanism that plays a more crucial role in the housing market in Chinese transitional economy. It is the institutional political and economic arrangements that have led to the dominant status of the local government.

Experiences around the world indicate that neither the state nor the market alone can provide a satisfactory solution to the housing problem. One should not expect to see the Chinese society relying entirely on the market or the state to provide housing. Both market mechanism and state intervention are indispensable to achieving efficient housing governance, particularly in transitional regimes. The key question is, to what extent and how should the state cooperate with the market. China cannot achieve sustainable housing development and establish a harmonious society without institutional adjustments in the housing sector. The state should integrate wider political, socio-economic and cultural insights into housing governance. The norms of social inequality, economic efficiency, policy effectiveness, state accountability, community participation and environmental sustainability should be equally addressed for better housing governance.

# 38

# China Attracting Global Top Talent

## Central and Local Government Initiatives

ZHU Jinjing*

*China is accelerating its pace to attract top global talents. Local governments have joined the central government in initiating multiple schemes to bring in top science and technology researchers, technopreneurs and business professionals.*

China's ability to attract global talent is helped by the large pool of overseas Chinese students accumulated over the years. The number of overseas Chinese students had grown from 270,000 in 1996 to 2,245,000 in 2011, with the number of returnees increasing from 89,000 to 818,000. In 2011 alone, out of the 339,700 new Chinese students going overseas, 12,800 were sent by the government, 12,100 by organisations and companies, while the remaining 314,800 were self-funded students, accounting for more than 90% of the total. On the returnee side, among 186,200 returnees, 9,300 were sent by the government, 7,700 by organisations and companies, and 169,200 were self-funded students, again accounting for more than 90% of the total returnees (Table 1). This composition contrasts sharply with the 1980s and 1990s where the majority of the overseas Chinese students were sent by the government and with relatively higher qualifications. Currently, the diverse composition of overseas Chinese students influences China's returnee situation: on the one hand, the government is striving to attract top level talent back to China. On the other hand, more and more returnees who are less competitive face greater challenges in securing well-paid jobs. This chapter focusses on the former, i.e. China's policies and development in attracting high level talent from overseas, as this is considered to be highly strategic for the country's development.

China has been actively recruiting global talent since the 1990s, particularly targeting overseas Chinese. Various ministries of the central government initiated a number of very important schemes. For example, the Chinese Academy of Sciences initiated the "Hundred Talent Scheme"

---

*ZHU Jinjing is currently a PhD student at the Asian Studies Department, Cornell University.

**Table 1**   Chinese Overseas Students and Returnees

| | 1996 | 1998 | 2000 | 2002 | 2004 | 2005 | 2006 | 2007 | 2008 | 2009 | 2010 | 2011 |
|---|---|---|---|---|---|---|---|---|---|---|---|---|
| Accumulated Overseas Students (1,000) | 270 | 302 | 340 | 585 | 814 | 933 | 1,067 | 1,212 | 1,392 | 1,621 | 1,905 | 2,245 |
| Accumulated Returnees (1,000) | 89 | 99 | 130 | 153 | 198 | 233 | 275 | 320 | 389 | 497 | 632 | 818 |
| Return Ratio (%) | 32.9 | 32.7 | 38.2 | 26.2 | 24.3 | 24.9 | 25.8 | 26.4 | 28.0 | 30.7 | 33.2 | 36.5 |

*Source*: Statistics by Ministry of Education, China.

in 1994; the Ministry of Education initiated the "Yangtze River Scholar Scheme" in 1998; the Ministry of Human Resources and Social Security initiated the "Financial Assistance Scheme for High Level Returnee Talents" in 2002. Most of these schemes target high level science and technology talent. The results of these earlier programmes are significant. For example, the "Hundred Talent Scheme" and the "Yangtze River Scholar Scheme" have attracted more than 4,000 researchers in the past 15 years. Most of them are postdoctorals or associate professors.[1] (For a complete list of talent attracting schemes by central government ministries, see Table 2.)

Since the 2000s, the Chinese government has expedited its pace of attracting global talent, especially top level Chinese scholars and professionals. In 2001, for the first time, a special chapter on human resource development was included in the 10th Five-Year Plan. In 2003, China also held, for the first time, a national conference on human resource development and decided to establish a Central Group for the Coordination of Talented Personnel headed by the Central Organisation Department (COD) of the Chinese Communist Party, with recruiting global talent as one of its priorities. As a result of the state policy of sending scholars to study overseas and recruiting scholars from abroad, 77% of the presidents of Chinese universities, 84% of the academicians of the Chinese Academy of Sciences and 75% of the academicians of the Chinese Academy of Engineering have overseas study and/or work experience.[2]

One latest development of such efforts is the "Thousand Talent Scheme" initiated in December 2008, which targets top level science and technology research talent, as well as technopreneurs and business professionals. This scheme is the collective effort of the central government and local governments, in collaboration with top Chinese universities, research institutions and business organisations. By February 2012, a total of 1,871 talents had returned to China under this scheme. Complementary services and communities have been built to facilitate the scheme, though difficulties and challenges remain.

While the central government and universities are more interested in top scientists and engineers, local governments are keener in attracting entrepreneurs and high level professionals, especially those in high-tech and financial industries. So far, local governments have been very effective in promoting returnee entrepreneurship in high-tech industries such as the internet, IT, communications, media and new energy. By February 2009, China had established more than 110 overseas returnee entrepreneurship incubation centres, with more than 8,000 enterprises and 20,000 returnees.[3] Such efforts were not limited to provincial and first-tier city governments as some second-tier city governments are also very active in attracting overseas returnees. Intergovernmental efforts to create trans-local networks for returnees have also been increased. As a result, the more economic and business oriented local government initiatives have joined the more science and research oriented central government initiatives in building the national talent attracting network.

---

[1] <http://www.chinadaily.com.cn/china/2009-04/16/content_7682212.htm> (accessed 9 July 2012).

[2] <http://www.gci-online.de/modules.php?name=News&file=print&sid=1621> (accessed 9 July 2012).

[3] "China Established More than 110 Overseas Returnee Entrepreneurship Incubation Centres", 16 February 2009 at <http://www.gov.cn> (accessed 9 July 2012).

**Table 2**  Talent Attraction Schemes Initiated by Central Government Ministries

| Ministry | Talent Attraction Schemes |
|---|---|
| Ministry of Human Resources and Social Security | China's Sons Scheme |
| | Prioritising of Funding Support to Science and Technology Projects by Overseas Chinese Returnees |
| | Facilitating Scheme on Returnees' Entrepreneurship |
| | Funding Scheme for High Level Overseas Returnees |
| Ministry of Education (MOE) | MOE Yangtze River Scholars Encouragement Scheme |
| | Scheme of Bringing Wisdom to Science and Innovation in Universities |
| | MOE Spring Sunshine Scheme |
| | MOE New Century Excellent Talents Supporting Scheme |
| Chinese Academy of Sciences (CAS) | CAS Hundred Talent Scheme |
| | CAS Innovation Team's International Collaboration Partnership Scheme |
| National Natural Science Foundation of China (NSFC) | NSFC Outstanding Youth Scheme |
| China Association for Science and Technology | Overseas Wisdom Scheme |
| State Oceanic Administration | Oceanic System Overseas Returnee Talents Scheme in the 12th Five-Year Programme |

*Source*: "Thousand Talent Scheme" website: <http://www.1000plan.org/qrjh/section/3> (accessed 7 July 2012).

Most of the talent that China wants to attract are science and technology experts, and economics and business professionals. Recently, however, some new trends are emerging. In February 2012, the Chinese government, in collaboration with a Hong Kong organisation, initiated a scheme to enhance interaction with overseas talent on issues of social management, including social and legal institutions construction, social credit system construction, social stability and risk assessment, household institution management, income distribution and social emergency management.[4] Meanwhile, the Beijing city government has also begun recruiting cultural talent. It seems that both the Chinese universities and governments have begun to recognise the importance of not only science and technology talent, but also social and cultural talent.

China today is in a much better position to attract global talent than in the 1990s. Local governments have joined the central government, and state-owned enterprises (SOEs) and banks have joined universities and national laboratories, in stepping up efforts to lure global talent. Both the pull factors (globally competitive salaries, better career opportunities, and improved research and social environment) and the push factors (the global financial crisis and its consequences) work to the advantage of China.

### "Thousand Talent Scheme"

Over the last decade, the central government has been striving to implement various policies to attract top level scientists and experts. Among the various talent attracting schemes, the latest "Thousand Talent Scheme" sets the highest standard for targeted talent. Launched by the COD in December 2008 during the financial crisis, the scheme plans to recruit 2,000 talents in the next five to 10 years. Compared with earlier programmes, which continue to be in place, the new scheme not only sets the bar higher, but also casts the net wider. It aims to attract three groups of top-class candidates who (i) have an academic title equivalent to professor in internationally well-known universities and institutions, or (ii) worked as a senior managing staff within a well-known

[4] <http://www.1000plan.org/qrjh/article/19021> (accessed 9 July 2012).

international company or banking institution, or (iii) have developed technologies and patents, and established their own business abroad.[5]

The eight main categories of talent that the scheme targets to attract include life science technology and life science medicines; high-tech industry; chemistry and chemical engineering; energy, resource and environment; information science and technology; engineering and technology; mathematics and physics; as well as economics, finance and management. Moreover, according to the scheme, four types of organisations can apply to recruit global talent through the scheme. These organisations are involved in (i) national innovation projects, (ii) key scientific subjects and laboratories, (iii) central government-owned enterprises and state-owned banking institutions, and (iv) high-tech parks. As a result, the main targeted talent of the scheme are highly concentrated in science and technology research, and the business and economics professions.

Headed by the central governmental ministries, local governments, universities, research institutes and business organisations are also the main participants of the scheme. The Office for Attracting High Level Overseas Talents established by COD coordinates the evaluation and selection process. The Ministry of Science and Technology evaluates candidates for national innovation projects, and the Ministry of Education evaluates candidates for key subjects and laboratories. The State-Owned Assets Supervision and Administration Commission of the State Council and the People's Bank of China evaluate those applying for SOEs and banking institutions. Finally, the Ministry of Science and Technology and the Ministry of Human Resources and Social Security will evaluate talents with entrepreneurial skills. Organisations participating in the scheme are required to provide good career opportunities and working conditions to those who are selected.

Compared with earlier programmes, the new scheme is helped by a number of factors. First, China is able to offer a much more generous package than before, including a one-time relocation allowance of one million *yuan* and globally competitive salaries. Some provincial governments such as those in Zhejiang will even add one million *yuan* to attract talents to be stationed in the province under this scheme. Second, China's research, business and social environment has improved considerably over the years. After the 2008 Beijing Olympics, large cities such as Beijing and Shanghai have become more internationalised. Last but not least, the worst global financial crisis in decades has hit the developed countries and their universities and research institutions hard, resulting in research programmes being cut back. In contrast, China continues to increase spending on science and technology. Its SOEs and banks, some among the largest of its kind in the world, have begun to recruit talents from Wall Street and other multinational corporations.

As the original "Thousand Talent Scheme" had set the standard too high and was unable to attract relatively younger talent, in December 2010 a new "Thousand Youth Talent Scheme" was introduced, targeting at relatively younger scholars and professionals in complementarity to the existing scheme. By February 2012, the "Thousand Talent Scheme" showed considerable achievement in attracting 1,510 high level talent in six batches. Among them were 1,161 talents in the "innovation" category, or 77% of the total, while 349 talents were in the "entrepreneurship" category, 23% of the total. Moreover, the new "Thousand Youth Talent Scheme" has also attracted 361 persons. In total, the two "Thousand Talent Schemes" had recruited 1,871 members by February 2012.[6] Recently, a new scheme parallel to the aforementioned two, the "Thousand Foreign Experts Scheme" was initiated in October 2011 to complete the scheme set by targeting at high level foreign experts, as against the existing pool of returned 300,000 foreign experts to China from 2001 to 2010.[7]

Moreover, complementary services have gradually been created to facilitate the implementation of the scheme. On 29 June 2010, an official website (http://www.1000plan.org/) was launched by

[5] <http://www.sciencenet.cn/htmlnews/2009/1/215384.html> (accessed 9 July 2012).

[6] <http://journal.1000plan.org/bkgz/1.aspx> (accessed 9 July 2012).

[7] <http://www.1000plan.org/groups/viewonetopic/13675> (accessed 7 July 2012).

the COD, targeting at not only the "Thousand Talent Scheme" itself, but more generally, to provide important information and communication related to attracting high level talent, such as governmental policies at both the central and local levels, as well as community building and interaction among the high level talent, etc. (Much information in this chapter is from the website.) In addition, a nationwide "'Thousand Talent Scheme' Experts Friendship Association" was set up on 15 January 2011 in Beijing. This association is a voluntary non-governmental organisation (NGO) founded by the experts under the scheme. It aims to address the real concerns and important issues that the talents share in work and life. For example, one issue that the association tries to address is the shortage of subsequent exclusive research funding for the experts under the scheme. Another issue is the welfare of the talent and their family members. The association also serves the function of helping the government identify future candidates for the scheme.[8] Another main move of the association was to launch journals (*Thousand Talent*), e-journals, or even online blogs to encourage interaction among the talents. In addition to addressing major science and technology development issues, these media platforms have also become an open platform for talents to address more general intellectual concerns such as China's overall future development.[9]

## Local Government Initiatives

In addition to attracting science and technology talent, China has also begun to attract technopreneurs and high level business professionals. This is consistent with the national initiative of translating the potential value of science and technology into real industrial productivity and economic value. Under this re-orientation, China has been actively recruiting entrepreneurs in high-tech industries, such as the internet, IT, communications and the media, as well as professionals in the high end service industries, such as finance and accounting, consulting, law, media, publishing, public relations, advertising, tourism, meetings and exhibitions, and education.

In this regard, the central government and local governments work complementarily: While the central government has placed priority on recruiting top scientists and academicians, local governments have been more active in attracting high-tech entrepreneurs and high level professionals. Local governments work in two ways. First support the central government's initiatives in implementing central government schemes such as the "Thousand Talent Scheme"; second, initiate their own local schemes to attract talent for local needs. By January 2012 a comprehensive nationwide network had been formed: all provinces except Tibet, Xinjiang and Hainan have their local talent attracting schemes. Similar to the imbalance in the economic development, different regions of China show different paces in attracting talent. Provinces and cities in coastal regions and east China are in an advantaged position to attract overseas returnees while central and west China are relatively less active in initiating returnee schemes.

Among provinces/cities which have the most highly developed talent attracting policies, Beijing, the capital city, is at the leading position. For example, the Zhongguan Village at the Haidian District, Beijing City, alone has accumulated approximately 20,000 high-tech companies over the past 20 years, covering industries such as electronics and information, life science and medicine, energy and environment, new material, new manufacturing and aerospace etc. This village has about 40% of the academicians of the Chinese Academy of Sciences and the Chinese Academy of Engineering, working on one third of the nation's critical science and technology projects. By 2011, 418 talents within the national "Thousand Talent Scheme" were in Beijing, many of them work in the Zhongguan Village as researchers or technopreneurs. Moreover, other than the national "Thousand Talent Scheme", Beijing also started many of its own talent attraction schemes. One example is "Beijing Overseas Talent Accumulation Project". Launched in 2009, this

[8] <http://lianyihui.1000plan.org/> (accessed 7 July 2012).
[9] <http://journal.1000plan.org/> (accessed 7 July 2012).

project plans to not only bring in approximately 200 top level overseas talents, but also build more conducive institutions for the city's returnee researchers and entrepreneurs: it targets to accumulate 10 top R&D teams by leading scientists, 50 top technopreneur teams, and 10 high level overseas talent innovation and technopreneur centres. Recently, Beijing published its new "Beijing Talent Development Scheme in the 12th Five-Year Programme" in December 2011. According to this scheme, in the coming five years, Beijing is to bring in approximately 1,000 high level overseas returnees, with an overall target of 30–50,000 returnees. The plan is so specific that even the various districts of Beijing such as Haidian District and Chaoyang District also have their individual talent attraction plans. The leading position of Beijing in China's national talent attraction efforts and related institutional and infrastructural construction is indisputable.[10]

Besides Beijing and Shanghai, the two most developed cities in China, provinces in coastal areas and in east China have also shown their advantageous positions in attracting talent. For example, Jiangsu province is one of the leading provinces in attracting overseas talent. Over the last decade, Jiangsu has benefited tremendously by bringing overseas returnees in furthering R&D and restructuring its industry composition and economic development. Other than the province's eagerness to attract overseas talent, another reason for Jiangsu's leading position is the province's highly developed economy and culture (especially education). As such, it probably has a greater pool of overseas Chinese who are related geographically to it. Jiangsu started its "Innovation and Entrepreneur Talent Attraction Scheme" in 2007, giving special funding of 200 million *yuan* to attract 200 top level overseas talent annually, with each of the selected talent provided with 100 million *yuan*, comparable to the funding provided by the national "Thousand Talent Scheme". Since 2010, Jiangsu has increased its scheme funding from 200 million *yuan* to 400 million *yuan*, targeting to attract 400 high level talent annually. In addition to the initial funding support to the returnee researchers and entrepreneurs, Jiangsu will also provide R&D projects with financial support for three to five years. The results were remarkable. In 2011 alone, Jiangsu had attracted 4,631 returnees, an increase of 30.6% from 2010; among them 39 talents were within the national "Thousand Talent Scheme". The total number of high level talent accumulated from 2007 to 2011 reached more than 2,000; among them 82 talent were within the national "Thousand Talent Scheme". Jiangsu's development of talent attraction plans is so strong and systematic that not only the capital city such as Nanjing, and first-tier economically developed cities such as Suzhou and Wuxi, but many second-tier cities have also developed their local level talent attracting schemes. Almost all Jiangsu cities such as Changzhou, Yangzhou, Taizhou, Xuzhou, Nantong and Zhenjiang have several local talent attracting projects or schemes running concurrently.

Though relatively less developed, provinces in central China and west China are also gradually starting their talent attracting schemes. Provinces such as Henan, Hubei and even Qinghai all have their respective local talent attracting schemes. Again, the main focus of provincial schemes and projects are research and technopreneur talent who can facilitate their technological and industrial development and upgrading.[11]

While provincial, city and even county governments initiated their local talent attracting schemes, horizontal networks involving governments and businesses across different regions have also been forming. For example, 41 high-tech and industrial parks from Beijing, Nanjing, Shanghai, Shenzhen and some other cities formed the Association of China Returnee Entrepreneurship Parks to promote cross-regional cooperation. Moreover, local governments in different cities have played a facilitative role in cultivating trans-local networks, which allow high-tech and industrial parks with different comparative advantages to benefit each other from closer relationships. For example, Zhongguan Village in Beijing is strong in its high-tech R&D, but is relatively weak in production, while the Nanjing high-tech zone in Jiangsu province has competitive advantage in labour and

---

[10] <http://www.1000plan.org/subject/pages/7> (accessed 9 July 2012).

[11] <http://www.1000plan.org/qrjh/section/4> (accessed 7 July 2012).

infrastructure costs and production scale. There is much to be gained by cooperating through the Association of China Returnee Entrepreneurship Parks.[12]

In addition to top scientists and technopreneurs, China is also in need of high level professionals. A 2005 McKinsey Global Institute survey found that fewer than 10% of Chinese job candidates would be suitable to work in a foreign company for reasons including the lack of practical skills and the relatively low creativity of Chinese students.[13] For both foreign firms investing in China and Chinese firms going global, professionals with knowledge of international practices are always lacking. Though local governments seem to be more interested in attracting technopreneurs than high level professionals, in part because technopreneurs directly contribute to local economic growth while high level professionals do not, some provincial governments have recognised the importance of professionals in local enterprises, be they private or state-owned. For example, Zhejiang province, which has a more developed private economy than most other provinces, organised a job fair in Wenzhou in 2004 to attract overseas professionals for local private enterprises. The job fair brought international and domestic job agencies and 120 overseas returnees into contact with more than 300 private enterprises.

With Chinese banks and SOEs becoming some of the largest in the world, high level professionals were included for the first time in the central government's "Thousand Talent Scheme". Eligible candidates should have worked as senior management staff in a well-known multinational corporation or banking institution. While most overseas returnees prefer to work for multinational corporations, SOEs and banks are now able to offer attractive packages. With the growing effort by central and local governments, more high level professionals and other top talent are likely to be found in SOEs. Some private firms in high end service industries are also able to attract high level professionals. Moreover, China's SOEs and banks were previously quite closed to foreign talent. As they globalised and grew into some of the largest ones in the world, they have begun to review their human resource practices and are now keen to recruit senior managers from multinational corporations.

**Difficulties and Challenges**

Though it seems that the talent-attracting schemes by the central government and local governments are working well in attracting a large pool of high level returnee talents, they have encountered a number of difficulties. First is the institutional environment. Chinese universities and companies are bureaucratically run organisations, which may be difficult for overseas returnees to work with. For example, returnee professors and researchers usually feel that the university bureaucracy interferes excessively with academic issues, in contrast to foreign universities, where academic decisions are usually within the control of the academic committee. Returnee entrepreneurs also feel that there are too many interpersonal factors dominating business development or project application processes. The Chinese government has made some effort to address these issues, though immediate total institutional reform is unlikely. One example of such efforts is the Beijing Life Science Research Institute founded in 2005 by the Beijing city government and seven central government ministries including the National Development and Reform Commission, Ministry of Education, Chinese Academy of Sciences etc. The establishment of this institute is to not only become a scientific institute of international standards, but more importantly serve as a pilot project, which "aims to explore an operative institution for scientific research which meets the international standard as well as the Chinese indigenous situation".[14] How well the Chinese government could address these institutional challenges will greatly influence how these talent could be retained.

[12] <http://www.jdhitech.com/new/onews.asp?id=422> and <http://www.cscse.edu.cn/publish/portal6/ tab655/info7821. htm> (accessed 9 July 2012).

[13] <http://www.atimes.com/atimes/China_Business/HG06Cb05.html> (accessed 7 July 2012).

[14] <http://journal.1000plan.org/bkgz/1.aspx> (accessed 7 July 2012).

Second is the problem of resource allocation. Though the returnees in the "Thousand Talent Scheme" were provided with one million *yuan* as initial funding, with some of the provinces providing an additional one million *yuan*, there is usually no complementary funding specifically allocated for returnee research projects. In other words, besides the initial funding, returnees have to compete with their local colleagues for project funding. The situation could get more complicated given that the allocation of project funding could be influenced by interpersonal relations and bureaucratic interventions. Another problem is salary. Though the government tries to encourage participating organisations to provide returnees with high salaries, there is no guarantee they will be highly paid. In many cases, the gap in salary between returnees and local talents has created tensions between the two groups, a thorny issue that China's talent schemes have yet to address.

# 39

# China's Higher Education Reform

## The Issue of Governance

ZHAO Litao*

*China's higher education has undergone many changes since the 1990s. The state-university relationship, however, remains largely intact. The state's domination of higher education is increasingly seen as a problem within China.*

China's higher education reform took place at a time when decentralisation and marketisation were globally seen as the best strategies to reform the government and the economy. There was unprecedented emphasis on efficiency, performance and "value for money" around the globe. China's higher education was under the same pressure to reform.

Many changes have occurred along the lines of decentralisation and marketisation. Particularly, local governments became a large stakeholder in China's higher education. As of 2009, 1,538 universities and colleges (out of a total of 2,305) were administered by provincial and other local authorities, compared with only 111 by central ministries.

Decentralisation, coupled with the introduction of tuition fees, has generated additional resources for Chinese universities. As a result, the landscape of China's higher education has changed dramatically. In a matter of a few years, the number of new enrolment increased several-fold (Table 1), while universities had facelifts with many brand new buildings and facilities, and professors no longer complained about their low salaries and poor living conditions.

*ZHAO Litao is Senior Research Fellow at the East Asian Institute, National University of Singapore.

**Table 1**   Number of New Intakes, Graduates and Total Enrolment in China's Higher Education

|      | New Intake (Million) | Graduates (Million) | Total Enrolment (Million) |
|------|:--------------------:|:-------------------:|:-------------------------:|
| 1995 | 0.9 | 0.8 | 2.9 |
| 1998 | 1.1 | 0.8 | 3.4 |
| 2001 | 2.7 | 1.0 | 7.2 |
| 2004 | 4.5 | 2.4 | 13.3 |
| 2006 | 5.5 | 3.8 | 17.4 |
| 2007 | 5.7 | 4.5 | 18.8 |
| 2008 | 6.1 | 5.1 | 20.2 |
| 2009 | 6.4 | 5.3 | 21.4 |
| 2010 | 6.6 | 5.8 | 22.3 |

*Sources: China Statistical Yearbook,* various years.

Despite all these changes, China's higher education system is not converging with the American system. The state-university relationship is fundamentally different. Not protected by any legal statutes, Chinese universities are as vulnerable as before vis-à-vis the state. In fact, since the mid-1990s, the state has strengthened its control over universities through the Ministry of Education (MOE) and other central ministries. On one hand, MOE has acquired many finance-based policy instruments with the growing central budget for education; on the other hand, MOE and other central ministries introduce all kinds of national level research projects, schemes, programmes and awards. As a result, the state has consolidated its authority over the universities.

A loosely defined term — "bureaucratisation" — has been popularly used in China to analyse and criticise the close state-university relationship. For some users, "bureaucratisation" describes a phenomenon uniquely found in China: All Chinese universities, with the exception of private ones, are assigned an administrative rank which defines or certifies how important a university is. Helming China's multi-tiered system is a handful of universities with a "vice minister" rank. There were only 14 such universities before 2000 and another 17 joined this exclusive club after 2000. Below them are a much larger number of universities with a "bureau" rank. At the bottom are colleges with a "vice bureau" rank.

Others use "bureaucratisation" to describe how Chinese universities are governed. Externally, university presidents and party secretaries are managed by the Party's Organisation Department. They are socialised, promoted and evaluated as bureaucrats. Internally, in terms of institutional setup and personnel system, China's universities are no different from government departments. The term "bureaucratisation" connotes that universities behave like government agencies and university officials act like government officials.

"Bureaucratisation" has also been used to describe the cosy relationship between professors and government officials. Government officials have much to offer to universities and professors in return for a significant number of doctoral degrees acquired with little or no effort. Such a special interest link has resulted in rampant corruption in China's higher education sector, financially and morally.

For those who want to see true scholarship developing in Chinese universities, they are disappointed to see an unequal relationship between university and government, and between university staff and government officials. Many are deeply concerned that power now dominates scholarship and universities have to flatter the government.

As a result of "bureaucratisation", professionalism is lacking among Chinese universities. Essentially, China's higher education sector mirrors the larger system, in some cases even symbolises the worst of the system. In public perception, Chinese universities are no less corrupt than other sectors. To many reform-minded people in China, the higher education sector is the "last fortress of the planned economy."[1]

There is growing concern and consensus inside China that its higher education reform is less successful than expected. The dazzling enrolment expansion conceals more fundamental problems. The largest complaint is that the unprecedented investment in higher education, from government to parents, has failed to produce world-class scholars and high quality manpower.

In November 2009, China's education minister, Zhou Ji, was removed from the post two years before his retirement. Despite varied interpretations of this sudden move, there is undoubtedly widespread public dissatisfaction with China's school system in general, its higher education in particular. Zhou was the most unpopular minister, receiving more "nay" votes than 26 other ministers during the annual session of the 2008 National People's Congress when China's new cabinet was formed.

"Why do our schools always fail to nurture outstanding talents?" This was the question repeatedly asked by Qian Xuesen, the father of China's space and missile programmes and a symbol of China's scientific achievement. He told Premier Wen Jiabao that "none of our institutions of higher learning is running in the right direction of cultivating excellent talent and is innovative enough."[2] After he died at 98 in 2009, his question, now known as the Qian Xuesen Question, was used to justify the call for a complete rethinking of China's higher education reform.

## University Restructuring Since the 1990s

China's university restructuring in the 1990s aimed to reform the decades-old Soviet-style higher education system. The old system took shape in 1952 after all the higher education institutions had been nationalised, and reorganised geographically and disciplinarily. Through reorganisation, Chinese universities became over specialised when striving to cater for the manpower planning of the central planned economy.

At that time, many specialised departments were set up at the central level to not only manage specific industries, but also run and administer reorganised higher education institutions. Such realignment allowed universities/colleges to quickly produce the much-needed manpower for specific industries.

In the 1980s and 1990s, over specialisation and fragmented governance were criticised for creating problems such as functional overlapping, small scale, low efficiency, and low quality. When China was searching for an alternative, the United States provided a ready model and the prevailing neo-liberalism provided the justification. Decentralisation and marketisation became a popular strategy in China to reform the Soviet-style education system.

In 1995, the former State Education Commission (SEC) — the predecessor of the MOE — announced four major strategies to reform and restructure China's higher education system, namely, "joint development", "restructuring", "merger" and "cooperation".[3]

The idea of "joint development" first appeared in Guangdong. In 1993, the former SEC and Guangdong provincial government proposed to jointly administer Zhongshan University (Sun Yat-Sen University) and South China University of Technology. The shift to the dual-leadership did not reduce the funding from the central government. It actually generated new resources. The provincial government began to provide capital investment funds to universities under joint development to gear its curriculum and enrolment to the needs of local economic and social development. The Guangdong experience was later promoted nationwide.

---

[1] See Ngok K (2008), "Massification, Bureaucratization and Questing for 'World-Class' Status", *International Journal of Educational Management*, 2008, pp. 547–564.

[2] See <http://www.chinadaily.com.cn/opinion/2009-11/02/content_8880325.htm> (accessed 2 July 2012).

[3] See Mok KH, "Globalisation and Educational Restructuring: University Merging and Changing Governance in China", *Higher Education*, 2005, pp. 57–88.

"Joint development" initiated in the 1990s benefited universities in the economically better-off provinces. Into the 2000s, a different type of "joint development" emerged. In 2004, to help inland regions develop their higher education, the central government decided to increase investment by selecting one local university in each of the 12 provinces in the central and western regions without any centrally administered university for "joint development".

"Restructuring" as a second strategy was made necessary by China's 1998 administrative reform. Previously, the majority of China's higher education institutions were run by non-education central ministries, such as the Ministry of Coal Industry, Ministry of Light Industry, Ministry of Machine-Building Industry, Ministry of Metallurgical Industry, Ministry of Forestry and so on. With the abolition of these central ministries, the governance structure of China's higher education institutions had to change.

"Restructuring" was thus necessary to transfer most universities/colleges under non-education central ministries to the MOE, or local governments, or the joint leadership of the two. The pace of restructuring accelerated in 1998, with the number of "restructured" universities jumping from 16 in 1997 to 177 in 1998, to 226 in 1999 and to 509 in 2000.

"Merger of universities" became popular in China in the late 1990s, driven by the belief that without much new investment, the merger of universities was necessary to create stronger academic institutions, better management and more efficient use of administrative resources. In practice, the motive was to create larger, comprehensive universities and made them appear stronger, rather than to achieve real efficiency gains. Almost all top universities in China incorporated one or more smaller specialised colleges while some lower ranking universities also tried to improve their standing by merging with other less well known universities/colleges.

In comparison to the first three types of restructuring, "cooperation" involved much less structural adjustment. It took different forms, from attracting leading universities to establish local branch/campus, pooling resources from different universities to form a "university city", to creating a "teaching consortium" to provide students with the flexibility of taking courses offered by other member institutions.

University restructuring has profoundly changed the governance structure of China's higher education. MOE has consolidated its role of "guiding" and "monitoring" the whole higher education sector. In addition, it retains control of a limited number of top universities. In place of the non-education central ministries, local governments have become a large stakeholder, running and administering the majority of China's higher education institutions. Meanwhile, *min ban* (non-state) universities and colleges are steadily growing in number (see Table 2).

The new system has a clear advantage over the old one in generating additional resources, from local governments and partners, to fee-paying students. However, it did not differ in how a good university is certified or defined. As of today, the criterion remains simple and unchanged. The best universities are those under central ministries; those under provincial and city government come in second; and *min ban* universities are often viewed with scepticism.


## "Project 211" and "Project 985"

University restructuring was part of the plan to increase China's competitiveness in the global marketplace. Up to the mid-1990s, top Chinese universities were not good enough by international standards. To improve China's higher education and train high-level professionals, the Chinese government initiated Project 211 in 1995. The idea was to achieve remarkable progress in teaching, research and administration in about 100 higher education institutions and in certain key disciplinary areas in the 21st century.

During the Ninth Five-Year Plan (FYP) period (1996–2000), a total of 18.6 billion *yuan* was invested in 99 universities, with 2.8 billion *yuan* from the central government. During the 10th FYP period (2001–2005), another 18.8 billion *yuan* was spent on 107 universities, with the central government contributing six billion *yuan*. In the 11th FYP period (2006–2010), the Project's third phase, the central government pledged to spend 10 billion *yuan*.

**Table 2**   Number of China's Regular Higher Education Institutions (RHEIs) by Ownership Type

| | 2004 | | | 2006 | | | 2008 | | |
|---|---|---|---|---|---|---|---|---|---|
| | RHEIs | Offering undergraduate programmes (*benke*) | Offering short-cycle specialised courses (*zhuanke*) | RHEIs | Offering undergraduate programmes (*benke*) | Offering short-cycle specialised courses (*zhuanke*) | RHEIs | Offering undergraduate programmes (*benke*) | Offering short-cycle specialised courses (*zhuanke*) |
| **Central Ministries and Agencies** | **111** | **104** | **7** | **111** | **105** | **6** | **111** | **106** | **5** |
| Ministry of Education | 73 | 73 | 0 | 73 | 73 | 0 | 73 | 73 | 0 |
| Other ministries | 38 | 31 | 7 | 38 | 32 | 6 | 38 | 33 | 5 |
| **Local Governments** | **1,394** | **571** | **823** | **1,480** | **586** | **894** | **1,514** | **604** | **910** |
| Department of Education | 799 | 500 | 299 | 853 | 517 | 336 | 859 | 533 | 326 |
| Other departments | 595 | 71 | 524 | 627 | 69 | 558 | 655 | 71 | 584 |
| **Private/Min Ban** | **226** | **9** | **217** | **276** | **29** | **247** | **638** | **369** | **269** |
| **Total** | **1,731** | **684** | **1,047** | **1,867** | **720** | **1,147** | **2,263** | **1,079** | **1,184** |

*Sources: China Statistical Yearbook*, various years.

The total investment was not large. In fact, total government expenditure on regular higher education institutions reached 196.3 billion *yuan* and 428.6 billion *yuan* in the 1996–2000 and 2001–2005 periods, respectively. "Project 211" accounted for 9.5% of total government expenditure on higher education in the 1996–2000 period, but fell to 4.4% in the 2001–2005 period. While its financial significance has been declining, becoming a "Project 211" university matters a great deal to the status/reputation of the university.

Although "Project 211" universities make up only 6% of China's regular higher education institutions, they take on the responsibility of training four-fifths of doctoral students, two-thirds of graduate students, half of students abroad and a third of undergraduates. They account for 85% of the country's key subjects, 96% of national key laboratories, and 70% of scientific research funding.[4]

"Project 211" was soon overshadowed by another initiative known as "Project 985". Speaking at the 100th anniversary of Peking University on 4 May 1998, then Chinese President Jiang Zemin stressed that "China must have a number of world-class universities". Project 985 was launched thereafter.

Immediately, building up world-class universities became a national policy. The MOE proposed increasing the share of educational expenditure in the central budget by 1% every year for three successive years. At first, Peking University and Tsinghua University were handpicked by the central government. Each received 1.8 billion *yuan* from MOE within three years from 1999. From July to November 1999, another seven universities joined the project (Table 3). Unlike the first two, they belong to the category of "joint development", thus receiving funding from both central government and local governments.

The list was further expanded in 2001 and after to include 30 other universities. Because they entered the list later than the first nine, the 30 universities were considered relatively lower in status. In recognition of this difference, the first nine "Project 985" universities formed the C9 League in 2003 and met annually to ritualise their exclusive membership.

"Project 985" and "Project 211" provided a new way of certifying the status of a university. None of the "Project 985" universities or "Project 211" universities can afford not to declare their newly gained status on their websites as they are largely judged by their listing in these projects.

**Table 3**   Funding for China's First Nine "Project 985" Universities

| University | Funding (billion *yuan*) | Source/s of Funding |
|---|---|---|
| Peking University | 1.8 | MOE |
| Tsinghua University | 1.8 | MOE |
| University of Science and Technology of China | 0.3+0.3+0.3 | MOE + Chinese Academy of Science + Anhui |
| Nanjing University | 0.6+0.6 | MOE + Jiangsu |
| Fudan University | 0.6+0.6 | MOE + Shanghai |
| Shanghai Jiaotong University | 0.6+0.6 | MOE + Shanghai |
| Zhejiang University | 0.7+0.7 | MOE + Zhejiang |
| Xi'An Jiaotong University | 0.6+0.3 | MOE + Shaanxi |
| Harbin Institute of Technology | 0.3+0.3+0.4 | MOE + Commission for Science, Technology and Industry for National Defence + Heilongjiang |

*Source*: <http://baike.baidu.com/view/1166593.htm> (accessed 3 July 2012).

---

[4]<http://english.people.com.cn/90001/6381319.html> (accessed 4 July 2012).

While there were elements of meritocracy in the listing of the universities, the university's relationship with the state was the most important determinant. "vice ministerial" universities and centrally administered universities had a much higher chance of being listed than other universities.

For "Project 985", all the 31 "vice ministerial" universities made the list. This means that out of nearly 2,000 universities and colleges without a vice ministerial rank, only eight could become "Project 985" universities. Without exception, the eight universities that made the list are all centrally administered universities.

For "Project 211", all the 31 "vice ministerial" universities are on the list. In fact, all the 39 "Project 985" universities are also "Project 211" universities, suggesting that "Project 985" is more selective and of higher status than "Project 211". Out of the 111 centrally administered universities, 71 were funded by "Project 211" in the first phase, while only 20 local universities could benefit from the project.

A new tiered system has thus emerged with C9 League members at the top, followed by 30 other "Project 985" universities. Below them are dozens of "Project 211" universities. Further down the hierarchy are centrally administered universities that failed to make it to the two lists. At the bottom are local and *min ban* higher education institutions. Though the structure may look somewhat different from before, the underlying stratification mechanism remains the same. "Project 211" and "Project 985" served to reinforce the importance of administrative ranks of Chinese universities and consolidate the state as a status conferrer vis-à-vis the university.

## What to Do with "Bureaucratisation"?

There is a growing consensus that "bureaucratisation" is a hurdle to be removed before Chinese universities can achieve excellence, develop true scholarship and become world-class universities. On a number of occasions, Premier Wen Jiabao has acknowledged that it is better for universities not to have an administrative rank.[5]

In February 2010, China made public a government plan on education reform, known as the Outline of the National Medium and Long-Term Programme for Education Reform and Development (2010–2020). It included statements to gradually remove administrative rankings of Chinese universities and university officials.

The "bureaucratisation" issue became a hot topic during *lianghui* in 2010 (two annual sessions of 11th National People's Congress and 11th National Committee of Chinese People's Consultative Committee). There were disagreements, however, on the significance of the planned move to get rid of a university's administrative ranking.

Zhu Qingshi, former president of the University of Science and Technology of China and currently founding president of South University of Science and Technology of China (funded by the Shenzhen government), was quoted as saying that "because of administrative rankings, all operations of a university are decided by administrative power, rather than through discussions among scholars."

On the other hand, Ji Baocheng, president of the Renmin University of China, argued that in a society where people tend to gauge social status by administrative rank, taking administrative rank away from universities is to do them a disservice. He agreed that while it is the direction to go for higher education reform, all other public institutions such as publishers, media and research institutes should remove their administrative rank as well. "Who will receive you, a *kezhang* (division head), a *chuzhang* (department head), or a mayor, if you have to talk to [the] government but do not have an administrative rank?"[6]

---

[5] <http://www.chinanews.com.cn/edu/news/2010/03-11/2164649.shtml> (accessed 2 July 2012).
[6] See *"Quxiao gaoxiao xingzheng jibie shi biandi jiaoyu"* (Unilaterally Taking Administrative Rank away from Universities Will Debase Education), *Xin Jing Bao* (Beijing news), 7 March 2010.

Ji's remarks highlight challenges facing this kind of reform. As early as 1996, the State Commission Office for Public Sector Reform issued "Opinions on Several Issues regarding Public Sector Reform", proposing to separate government and public institutions and take away the latter's administrative rank step by step. As of today, nothing has been done in this regard.

The root problem is not in Chinese universities per se, but in the relationship between universities and government. If the state remains a central player in allocating resources, appointing personnel and conferring status on bases other than meritocracy, what troubles Chinese universities today will continue to trouble Chinese universities tomorrow, with or without a formal administrative rank.

# 40

# Improving Local Governance without Democratisation

## Community Building in Shanghai

SHI Fayong*

*Current community building in Shanghai has worked well in accommodating the everyday needs of local residents. It is not a mechanism for facilitating grassroots democracy but for engaging urban residents to achieve Party-state legitimacy and urban stability.*

The implementation of market-oriented reforms, including the reforms of state-owned enterprises, the fiscal system, housing and land, and the labour market, has profoundly shaped local governance in urban China and weakened the work-unit system as the main pillar of governance and control. In response, since the 1990s, the Chinese government has embarked on extensive community building programmes in cities. Neighbourhood organisations, which formerly engaged the elderly, retirees and less-educated to perform trivial and mundane tasks such as monitoring residents, collecting fees and implementing birth control measures, have been transformed into important players in local governance and community participation.

In China, "community" (*shequ*), or neighbourhood, is an administration-oriented concept. It refers to an area with hundreds of buildings and surrounded by natural boundaries such as rivers or broad roads. In Shanghai, a neighbourhood may include several lanes (*linong*), new-style urban villages (*jumin xincun*), modern condominiums (*gongyu*) and public facilities such as schools and shops. Usually, the population in a neighbourhood is around tens of thousands. To facilitate administration, local government usually divides a neighbourhood into several sub-neighbourhoods (*xiaoqu*) and establishes a Resident Committee (*juweihui,* RC hereafter) in every sub-neighbourhood to help oversee residents. Shanghai took the lead in China in revamping its neighbourhood system and promoting community building programmes.

*SHI Fayong is Associate Professor of Sociology at the Shanghai University of Political Science and Law. This research was sponsored by the Research Project of Humanities and Social Sciences for Young Scholars, State Education Ministry (10YJCZH126), 2008 Shanghai Pudong Programme, and the Research Base of Urban Public Security and Social stability, Shanghai University of Political Science and Law (2011YC2004).

## The Neighbourhood System as a Pillar of Local Governance

When the Chinese Communist Party (CCP) came to power in 1949, the neighbourhood system was established to become part of the system of local administration and control, together with the Party-government hierarchy, household registration system and the work-unit system.[1] Before the market-oriented reform, the work-unit system was the dominant body that managed the routine business of the Party-state in cities. Through state-controlled job assignments, the majority of urban citizens were allocated to state-owned or collective-owned work units such as factories, shops, schools, hospitals and government agencies at different levels. Each work unit was called a *danwei*. These work units were not only workplaces, but also main channels through which the state served and imposed control over urban citizens. Thus, work units played both political and economic roles and also became the loci of urban social control. This system resulted in citizens' "organised dependence" on their work units for housing, health care, pension, coupons for rationed goods and even permission to get married.[2]

The Party-state also utilises neighbourhood organisations as a secondary governing system to manage citizens who either did not belong to any work unit or had retired from work units. The administrative system of China's big cities generally includes two levels of government: the municipal government and the district (*qu*) governments. Every district government usually sets up several Street Offices (*jiedao banshichu*) as its local branches to administer several neighbourhoods. In many cases, Street Office normally establishes a RC in every sub-neighbourhood to help it oversee residents (Figure 1).

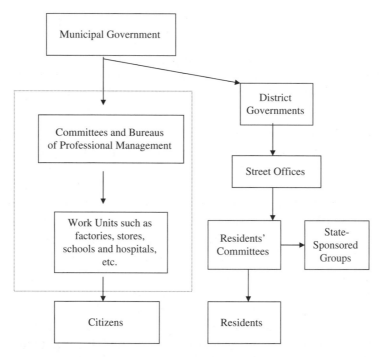

**Figure 1**   The Administrative Hierarchy in Urban China before the Market-Oriented Reform

*Source*: Prepared by the author.

---

[1] Wu F, 2002, "China's Changing Urban Governance in the Transition towards a More Market Oriented Economy", *Urban Studies,* vol. 39, no. 7, pp. 1071–1093, p. 1072.

[2] Walder, A, *Communist Neo-Traditionalism: Work and Authority in Chinese Industry*, Berkeley, University of California Press, 1986.

According to Chinese law, a RC is an autonomous grassroots level organisation that serves residents and helps promulgate state policies. Only residents in the constituency are eligible to become members and they have to be elected by the constituency. Local government has to provide operation funds and other forms of support to the RCs, but has no authority over them even though they are under its jurisdiction. However, in reality, Street Offices and police stations in neighbourhoods supervised the operation of RCs, utilising them to assist in the implementation of state policies, monitoring citizens' activities in neighbourhoods organising residents who do not belong to any work unit for regular political study and providing services to residents as well.[3] As can be seen, Street Offices have integrated RCs into the grassroots administrative system, which is called "the neighbourhood system" (*jiejuzhi*).

The Party-government hierarchy, the *hukou* system, the work-unit system and the neighbourhood system constitute a tight government control network which supervises citizens to ensure conformity with official standards of behaviour. During the era of the command economy, these administrative systems were highly effective in terms of social control. As a result, compared to other world cities, "Chinese cities after 1949 became remarkably orderly".[4]

## Challenges from Urban Reform and Development

Urban governance based on the old systems had been in a state of crisis since the 1990s. Many state-owned enterprises (SOEs) were forced to lay off workers, reduce services, go private, or shut down, thereby crippling the work-unit system which provided full employment and full social services. During this period, many cities initiated urban renewal projects. In 1992, the central government came up with plans to develop Shanghai into an international metropolis. The Shanghai government had since reconstructed the city on a massive scale. As a result, many citizens had to be moved from their former residences affiliated to their work units to newly constructed neighbourhoods. With the deepening of labour market reform and the sustained economic growth, an increasing number of citizens are now working in private and foreign firms instead of in SOEs. Shanghai has also attracted millions of migrant workers, property buyers and business owners, who are outside of the existing system of social control. These phenomena pose new challenges to the host city.

As the governing capacity of the existing system faltered, the Party-state tried to shift its emphasis of grassroots management from work units to residential neighbourhoods on the basis that neighbourhoods have "the jurisdictional capacity to regulate all activities within the area regardless of their affiliation".[5] The government required these local territorial agencies to take on more management roles to regulate new activities taking place outside work units and also to administer citizens who are beyond the control of work units. However, before the mid-1990s, local governments and RCs did not have adequate economic and political resources to fulfil such difficult tasks owing to the fact that the former neighbourhood system was a secondary administrative system. The risk of losing control was looming large. In many big cities such as Shanghai, an increasing number of citizens began to complain to all levels of government of job loss or forced resettlement, and their reactions were regarded by the central government as signs of social instability.

## Changes in Community Functions

To cope with the challenges, the Chinese government launched extensive community building projects in big cities to strengthen the neighbourhood system. The central government encouraged

---

[3] Whyte, MK, EF Vogel, WL Parish, "Social Structure of World Regions: Mainland China", *Annual Review of Sociology*, 3, 1977, pp. 179–207.

[4] Whyte, MK and WL Parish, *Urban Life in Contemporary China*, Chicago: University of Chicago Press, 1984, p. 247.

[5] Wu F, op. cit., pp. 1071–1093, p. 1080.

local governments to explore new models of neighbourhood system according to local needs. The Shanghai Municipal Government started its community building programmes in the early 1990s. The reforms focus on both the institution and the function of the neighbourhood system. The Shanghai government initiated community building programmes with the goals of strengthening social control over and providing social services to citizens, which used to be the main responsibilities of the work units. In terms of functional changes, the main projects were as follows:

### *Providing Social Services, Promoting Reemployment and Poverty Reduction*

Before economic reform was implemented, work units were responsible for providing comprehensive social services to most citizens, literally taking care of their needs "from the cradle to the grave". Street Offices and RCs only provided services such as baby-sitting, barbering and helping the aged to shop, to a small minority of citizens who did not belong to any work unit. As the services provided were much fewer than those provided by work units, Street Offices and RCs were lightly staffed. With the decline of the work-unit system and the rise of non-state sectors, social services provided by work units became even more inaccessible.

In a bid to ameliorate the situation, the government requires Street Offices and RCs to provide comprehensive social services to citizens under their jurisdiction. Since 1992, the Shanghai municipal government has regarded "developing community services" as a focus of local administration. The municipal government, the district government and Street Offices are required to provide funds for developing social services. Since then, more and more social services such as health checks, barbering, parking, simple maintenance works, consultancy and arts training have been provided. Many service facilities have also been established. For instance, in every neighbourhood, the government has established at least one comprehensive centre to provide social services to all local residents and several old folks' homes. Street Offices and RCs thus have to hire more staff members to man the new facilities and cope with the additional services provided.

Since the early 1990s, a large number of workers have been laid off every year. Most of these laid-off workers have little education and their skills become obsolete for the new economy. Unemployment has thrown many urban families into extreme poverty which threatens state legitimacy and social stability. Therefore, the state has initiated many reemployment projects. Local governments are required to organise skill training programmes for laid-off workers, and RCs are enlisted to organise these programmes, referring laid-off workers to new jobs and providing job information. The government also implements policies to alleviate poverty in the neighbourhood. Specifically, it provides relief subsidies to poor families. Schools have also reduced tuition fees for students from poor families. Affected families can apply for relief subsidies from local government agencies, and RCs, under the command of the government agencies, will investigate the financial situations of applicants and then distribute relief subsidies to those eligible.

### *Conducting "Spiritual-Civilisation Building" (Jingshen Wenming Jianshe) Projects*

During the large-scale urban renewal of the 1990s, many neighbourhoods were reconstructed and residents were forced to resettle elsewhere, breaking down the social networks that had existed amongst neighbours. As a result, residents did not know one another in new neighbourhoods. Relationships were not cordial and few had the motivation to care about public affairs. Crime rate rose, putting a tax on urban life and fuelling social dissatisfaction with local authorities.

To maintain order in the neighbourhood, the municipal government embarks on efforts to promote community cohesion and integration. After expanding social services in neighbourhoods, it has further launched the so-called "spiritual-civilisation building" projects to restore social order, improve the physical surroundings and establish social networks among residents. Specifically, the government lists five principal criteria to evaluate the performance of community building programmes: public order, clean living environment, comprehensive social services, social harmony and adequate entertainment facilities. In 2005, another criterion — high satisfaction of residents with their neighbourhoods — was added.

These criteria are further broken down into smaller measurable items. Sub-neighbourhoods which meet these criteria are to be bestowed honourable municipal-rank or district-rank titles of "Model Quarters" (*wenming xiaoqu*). The governments at various levels have also established the Committees for Spiritual-Civilisation Building, which made up of heads of all government departments, to supervise the implementation of the project. The number and the rank of "Model Quarters" are regarded as a main criterion for evaluating the performance of local governments. This induced many Street Offices to invest heavily on building "Model Quarters". Great efforts have been put into improving neighbourhood environment by planting greeneries, building service facilities, establishing walls and fences around sub-neighbourhoods to enhance security, and organising recreation activities like sports and entertainment performances as a testimonial to how peaceful and harmonious life has been under their jurisdiction.

## Institutional Capacity Building

### *Strengthening Street Offices and Resident Committees*

With more functions and services, the importance of Street Offices and RCs to enhance local governance has become more prominent. To better implement various community building projects, the Shanghai municipal government formalises the administrative system consisting of "two levels of government, three tiers of management and four levels of networks" (the municipal government, district governments, Street Offices and RCs) and grants Street Offices more power and resources.

After 1996, the municipal government has not only raised the ranks of top leaders of Street Offices, but also entrusted them with the jurisdiction of socio-political and economic developments of neighbourhoods. Most importantly, the government has enforced the policy of "refunding business tax". Under this policy, the government will refund a large portion of tax levied on enterprises registered in a certain neighbourhood to the respective Street Office so that the latter will have enough resources to promote more local developments. The more enterprises registered in a neighbourhood, the more economic resources Street Office will receive. Since then, the performance of Street Office officials and their personal income have been closely tied to local economic development. Street Offices not only set up their own businesses, but also make every effort to attract external enterprises to register in the neighbourhoods under their jurisdiction through all kinds of channels and means, including providing investors with various incentive schemes. They also welcome real estate developers to reconstruct neighbourhoods under their jurisdiction. A reconstructed and upgraded neighbourhood also generates a corresponding increase in property value. The local government therefore receives more financial resources while the need for poverty reduction is also lessened as poor families cannot afford the expensive housing and have to be resettled away. Real estate developers are thus a boon to local governments. To cope with the increasing workload from higher authorities, Street Offices have set up many branches and strengthened RCs to assist them in the management of sub-neighbourhoods. In the past, as RCs played a marginal role in urban management, they were manned by retirees or unemployed residents with little education. To improve the efficiency of RCs, Street Offices renovated RC office facilities and have also recruited middle-aged people who were former management staff of SOEs to work in RCs. In recent years, even university graduates have also been recruited as RC staff.

### *Initiating Grassroots Reforms of Civil Associations*

To improve local governance and encourage community participation, the Chinese government has been keen to develop grassroots democracy. Since the late 1990s, some large cities have initiated democratic reforms in the neighbourhoods, requiring civil associations such as the RCs and the

Homeowners' Committees (*yezhu weiyuanhui*) to elect their representatives and leaders. Higher-level governments encouraged residents to elect RC members from amongst the residents themselves. Street Offices can no longer appoint RC members. This reform was said to be an essential step towards community building by all levels of governments. Shanghai conducted elections in several RCs in 1999, a move which was expanded to all RCs in 2000. Since then, the city has been conducting RC elections triennially.

The government has also extended elections to Homeowners' Committees. Since the mid-1990s, the state has initiated a series of housing reforms. To increase the supply of commercial housing, governments at different levels have not only established many state-owned estate development companies, but also encouraged private developers to engage in estate development. Meanwhile the government has also transformed Housing Maintenance Bureaus into property management companies. Many real estate companies have also established their own property management companies to look after the housing they had sold or rented to citizens. To monitor property management companies and to manage housing maintenance funds (usually several or tens of million *yuan*), the government encourages home buyers to elect their representatives into the Homeowners' Committees. More and more Homeowners' Committees are actively involved in improving their neighbourhoods.

By initiating the elections of RCs and Homeowners' Committees, the state seeks to promote community participation and regulate grassroots communities by law. Therefore, "democracy" and "rule by law" have become popular discourses in China's urban society and have begun to influence neighbourhood politics. Although the government aims to improve local governance through grassroots elections, it is also concerned that it may lose control if grassroots democracy is fully developed. It therefore frequently intervenes in local activities, and blocks channels which the citizens could have used to voice their concerns. So far, the state only encourages "managed participation"[6] in the name of grassroots democracy.

### Strengthening Local Party Organisations

The CCP establishes its local branches in both work units and neighbourhoods — Street Working Committees (*jiedao danggongwei*) at the neighbourhood level and Party Branches at the sub-neighbourhood level — in parallel to Street Offices and the RCs, respectively. With the decline of the work-unit system, the CCP has begun to strengthen its neighbourhood branches by initiating "community party-building" programmes. Street Working Committees, made up by heads of government agencies at the neighbourhood level, is in charge of governing the neighbourhoods under its jurisdiction. As is typical of Party-government relationships, the CCP requires all government agencies at the neighbourhood level including Street Offices to be under the leadership of Street Working Committees.

To further reinforce its leadership in neighbourhoods, the CCP transfers the membership of retired party members to party branches in sub-neighbourhoods. For those who are still working and are thus affiliated with their work units, the CCP nonetheless encourages them to actively participate in the activities organised by party branches at their sub-neighbourhoods. The CCP also urges its members to join neighbourhood associations such as RCs, Homeowners' Committees, entertainment teams and exercise groups, and even to take on leadership roles so that the CCP will stay relevant to civil associations, and will have the capacity to intervene whenever the need arises (Figure 2).

### More Efficient Governance without Democratisation

To sum up, as the work-unit system as a mechanism of governance and control was weakening, the neighbourhood system began to take on a more prominent role. The functions and responsibilities

---

[6]Cai YS, 2004, "Managed Participation in China", *Political Science Quarterly*, vol. 199, no®. 3, pp. 425–451.

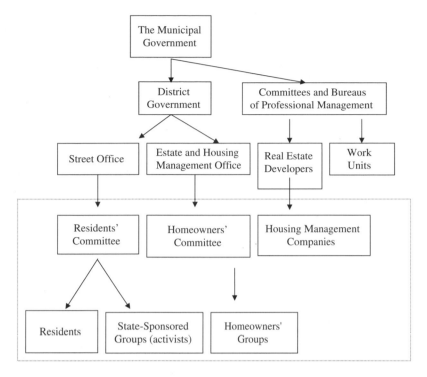

**Figure 2**    Current Administrative Hierarchy in Urban China

*Source*: Prepared by the author.

of neighbourhood organisations, together with economic and human resources, have substantially expanded. As a result, the neighbourhood system has been revitalised to helm urban grassroots governance.

By and large, Shanghai's community building has been quite successful in shifting from a work-unit based system of governance and control, to one based on community governance. Such a model of local governance has worked reasonably well thus far in Shanghai in accommodating the everyday needs of local residents. It is important to note that community building in Shanghai and elsewhere is not meant to facilitate self-determination or grassroots democracy. Instead it is a mechanism for engaging urban residents in an effort to achieve Party-state legitimacy and urban stability. The "managed participation" of residents neither fully represents their interests nor significantly promotes local democratisation. Decentralisation has also empowered local governments which often act just to satisfy self-interests and not the well-being of local residents, undermining the legitimacy of the state.

In conclusion, community building helps to provide local residents with a more vibrant community life, especially for the retirees and aged, and also seeks to improve local governance to some extent. But due to the aforementioned limitations, the democracy that China's neighbourhoods enjoy can at best be considered as oscillating between complete domination of local authorities and relatively autonomous "quasi-civic community".

# 41

# Rising Trend of Labour Strikes

## Tables Turned for Chinese Workers?

YEW Chiew Ping*

*Wage increases since 2010 have led observers to herald a "turning point" in China's industrial-labour relations and the rise of the Chinese proletariat. There are, however, reasons to doubt this sanguine outlook.*

Recent waves of labour unrest cast the spotlight on the plight of Chinese workers, who toil for long hours under poor working conditions for meagre pay but have not been able to partake of the fruits of China's wealth so far. On 16 January 2012, more than 8,000 assembly line workers at an electrical machinery plant in Guangxi Nanning staged a walkout to demand for year-end bonuses; at the close of 2011, privately owned factories in Guangdong, Shenzhen, Nanjing, Chongqing, Chengdu and Shanghai were paralysed by striking workers in protest of unfair labour practices; earlier that year, in August and October, cab drivers in Hangzhou and Xiamen went on strike to express their displeasure with escalating operating costs; from May to June 2010, Guangdong witnessed a string of suicides at Foxconn's factories and consecutive strikes at various Honda Motor plants.

In the widely reported Foxconn incident, workers scored a victory as the manufacturer of iPads for Apple, in a bid to appease aggrieved workers and alleviate public criticism, pledged to raise wages by more than 30%. Since then, the "Foxconn Effect" has rippled and pushed up wages among China's factory workers. This led some commentators and observers to herald a turning point in China's industrial-labour relations. A specialist on industrial relations at the International Labour Organisation (ILO), for instance, told the *South China Morning Post*: "The labour market in China is going through a critical turning point from unlimited to limited supply of labour and from first-to second generation migrant workers, the post-80s generation . . . This is the point when

---

*YEW Chiew Ping is Research Fellow at the East Asian Institute, National University of Singapore.

385

workers begin to take collective action to improve their wages and other working conditions, while previously they protested only when their legal rights were violated."

Do recent trends signal that tables have turned for Chinese workers? Who will command greater bargaining power against employers in asserting their rights from now on? How do the recent waves of labour unrest compare to previous instances? Multiple factors have driven the growing labour unrest in China, namely workers' increasing awareness of their rights; changing workforce demographics; paradigmatic shifts in China's labour supply; policy shifts; the institutional structure of Chinese trade unions and their role in labour conflicts.

## Collective Workers' Actions: Past and Present

Alongside the labour disputes at Foxconn and Honda in 2010, China actually witnessed a spate of labour protests in May of the same year that eluded the attention of international media, so much so that netizens labelled it, "The May Great Labour Strike." After the Foxconn and Honda incidents, labour strife has also widened to beyond southern China. Table 1 is a non-exhaustive compilation of the strikes that occurred in May 2010.

Collective labour disputes also surged from 12,784 to 21,880 instances or 71% over 2007–2008, as shown in Figure 1. According to the *China Labour Statistical Yearbook 2009*, the following

**Table 1**   Spate of Strikes in May 2010

| Date | | Incident |
|---|---|---|
| 1. | 29 April to early May | Labour strike for days following the gas poisoning of workers at Jiangsu Wuxi Nikon factory; workers refused to resume work till the source of poisoning had been identified. |
| 2. | 4 May | Strike at Jiangsu Nanjing Xinsu thermo-electricity plant to demand for higher wages. |
| 3. | 4 May | Strike at Shandong Zaozhuang Wantaier fabric factory to demand for higher wages. |
| 4. | 5 May to 11 May | Over 2,000 workers participated in a second strike at Shenzhen Baida hardware and plastic factory to protest against the relocation of the factory. |
| 5. | 12 May | Strike at Jiangsu Yizheng chemical fibre engineering plant to protest against its restructuring. |
| 6. | 14 May to 1 June | Over 5,000 workers took part in a strike and blockage of the entrance at Henan Pingdingshan Ping fabric plant to demand for higher wages and higher retrenchment compensation. |
| 7. | 17 May to 1 June | Strike at Foshan Nanhai Honda automobile parts factory to demand for higher wages. |
| 8. | 18 May to 21 May | More than 10,000 workers and their family members at state-owned Shanxi Datong Xinghuo pharmaceutical plant blocked traffic for three days to protest over insufficient retrenchment compensation. |
| 9. | 19 May to 21 May | Around 200 workers at state-owned Jiangsu Kunshan Jingang went on a three-day strike sparked by concerns over their livelihood after the sale of the state-owned enterprise. |
| 10. | 19 May | Strike at Jiangsu Suzhou Weixun for days to protest against the relocation of the factory without lay-off compensation. |
| 11. | 23 May | Over 100 workers went on strike for days following the death of an overworked worker at the Chongqing Qijiang gear factory. |
| 12. | 28 May | Over 1,000 workers went on strike at Beijing Xingyu automobile plant, a supplier for Korean Hyundai, to demand for higher wages. |
| 13. | 28 May | Over 2,000 workers went on strike at Gansu Lanzhou Weini synthetic fibre factory to demand for higher wages. |

*Sources*: "*Wu yue yilai Zhongguo bagong yilan*" ("A Look at China's Strikes since May"), *Yazhou Zhoukan*, vol. 24, no. 23, 13 June 2010, at <http://www.yzzk.com> (accessed 4 June 2010); various online sources.

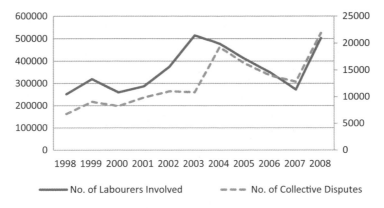

**Figure 1**  Trends in Collective Labour Disputes

*Source*: *Zhongguo Laodong Tongji Nianjian 2009*, pp. 469–470.

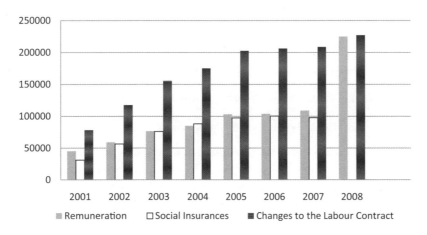

**Figure 2**  Reasons for Labour Disputes

*Source*: *Zhongguo Laodong Tongji Nianjian 2009*, pp. 469–470.

provinces recorded the highest frequency of collective disputes (in ascending order) in 2008: Yunnan (1,033 instances), Guangdong (1,897), Jilin (2,123), Shandong (2,338) and Beijing (2,656). As the effects of the financial crisis set in, the year 2009 also saw labour disputes stepping up in both scale and frequency, assuming an increasingly antagonistic and violent nature.

The cases in Table 1 may be grouped into two categories: labour strikes to demand for higher wages and other rights such as workplace safety, and strikes to protest against the restructuring or relocation of mostly state-owned factories. Comparing these labour protests with those in the past, we see continuity in collective action by laid-off workers from state-owned enterprises (SOEs) as well as a growing trend of collective action by workers demanding for better pay and work conditions. The restructuring of SOEs since 1996–1997 has sparked off sporadic protests from laid-off workers all over China.[1] In March 2002, for instance, the northeastern Chinese rustbelt cities of Liaoyang, Daqing and Fushun saw a series of large-scale protests by thousands of laid-off workers dissatisfied with their severance packages.

The two concomitant trends are supported by statistics on the causes of labour disputes as seen in Figure 2. From 2001 to 2007, disputes over remuneration constituted around half the total

---

[1] The phenomenon of laid-off workers has been widely documented and analysed by scholars. See, for example, Feng C, "Industrial Restructuring and Workers' Resistance in China", *Modern China*, vol. 29, no. 2, 2003, pp. 237–262; Cai Y, "The Resistance of Laid-off Workers in the Reform Period", *China Quarterly*, 170, June 2002, pp.327–344; Lee CK, "The 'Revenge of History': Collective Memories and Labour Protests in Northeastern China", *Ethnography*, vol. 1, no. 2, 2000, pp. 217–237.

number of disputes caused by changes to the labour contract, including termination. There was a big jump from 2007 to 2008 when the number of disputes over remuneration doubled from 108,953 to 225,061, almost on par with that over labour contract disputes. In 2009, the number of disputes over remuneration further climbed to 247,330.

In a *South China Morning Post* report, an expert at the Australian National University pointed out the differences between past and present labour conflicts: "In the past most of the strikes in China had to do with violations of the law, like unpaid wages or extremely long overtime without proper compensation . . . But this is different because it doesn't seem that any law has been violated. The workers are fighting for better wages and a better wage structure and it looks like they are well organised and know what they are doing."

And the recent labour protests were indeed well-organised. IT savvy young worker leaders adeptly used new technology to organise and mobilise fellow workers. The leaders of the Honda strike, who are in their 20s, planned and coordinated the strike through mobile phone text messages, QQ (instant messaging service), online chat rooms and word-of-mouth. Instructions were posted on internet chat rooms prior to the strike. Workers also used their mobile phones to shoot the strike in action and posted the video recordings on the Internet for greater impact.

## Shift in Workforce Demographics and Labour Shortage

Currently, 29% of China's urban workforce is under the age of 30. Those who attended senior school, college, university and graduate school constitute 45% of the workforce (see Figures 3 and 4).

A common refrain when it comes to explaining the suicides at Foxconn or China's apparent labour shortage is that the post-80s and post-90s generations of migrant workers have the characteristics of *sangao yidi* (literally "three highs and one low"), i.e. high education levels, high expectations of their career, high demands on material and spiritual enjoyment, and low tolerance at work. Their upbringing has inculcated in them a "worldview" distinct from that of their predecessors. This appears to be true to a certain extent. Whereas suicides of young workers at Foxconn appear to stem from a general disillusionment with life, radical actions such as self-ignition and jumping off buildings by individual workers in the past were motivated by specific grievances, particularly wage arrears.

China's celebrity blogger Han Han, himself of the post-80s generation, writes about how dismal prospects faced by the younger generation of workers have driven them to despair and suicide in a 28 May 2010 post titled "*Qingchun*" (Youth): "This is why so many jumped off buildings at Foxconn. Mechanical work, a bleak future, very low pay, but even lower pay and very high costs

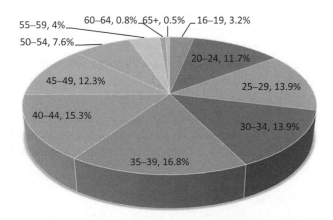

**Figure 3**　Age Composition of Urban Employees in 2009

*Source*: *Zhongguo Laodong Tongji Nianjian 2010.*

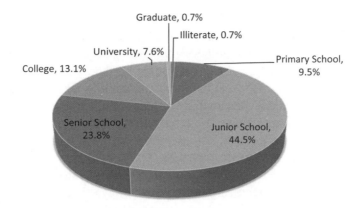

**Figure 4**  Education Attainment Composition of Urban Employees in 2009

*Source*: *Zhongguo Laodong Tongji Nianjian 2010.*

of living if you work elsewhere [away from your hometown]. The pay is only enough to feed yourself and buy you warm clothes. Other than that there is nothing else you can do."

In contrast, China Labour Bulletin, a non-governmental organisation (NGO) based in Hong Kong, claims that young workers are more mobile and have more options: "The younger generation of workers are both more aware of their rights and more self-confident and assertive. They will not accept indefinitely the appalling working conditions their parents put up with. Many will only work for a few months before moving on to another factory or a new town." This mobility is partly due to the labour shortage in the Pearl River Delta, parts of Zhejiang and Fujian since 2004 and jobs created in inland provinces. Owing to the government stimulus programme, second-tier inland cities such as Chongqing, Wuhan and Nanchang are reportedly experiencing a construction boom and rapid economic growth. Though wages may not be as high as in the delta, the more affordable cost of living and proximity to friends and family make staying closer to home an attractive option. A laid-off worker who subsequently found a job nearer her hometown in Sichuan told *TIME* magazine that although her pay was slightly lower than before, "life is much easier for me here because I'm closer to home. I much prefer this job to the old one."

Furthermore, China's one-child policy has also resulted in fewer young people entering the workforce. The US census bureau reported that the number of young people aged 15–24 entering the workforce will decrease by nearly 30% in the next decade. In spite of this, China's labour supply will still grow from 977 million in 2010 to 993 million in 2015. By these projections, it seems that the Lewisian turning point of limited labour supply and rising wages is yet to come. The recent pay hikes merely compensate for wage freezes during 2009's financial crisis.[2]

There has been much hype over wage hikes in southern China to lure back workers who were laid off when exports dipped during the financial crisis in late 2008 to early 2009. Surveys by the National Bureau of Statistics reveal that some 70 million migrant workers or half the migrant workforce returned home just before Spring Festival in 2009. From February 2010, various provinces and municipalities — Jiangsu, Zhejiang, Guangdong, Fujian, Shanghai, Shenzhen and Beijing etc. — had adjusted or would adjust the minimum wage rate upwards by more than 10%. Yet even after adjustment, the minimum wage rates still range from 600 odd *yuan* to slightly over 1,000 *yuan*. To earn decent wages, workers have to clock in excessive overtime work of more than 100 hours. Amidst the wage inflation hype, the harsh reality for many workers is still "low pay, long hours and no job security" in the words of a *China Labour Bulletin* report.

The hardship of Chinese workers is accentuated when seen in the light of the share of wages in China's Gross Domestic Product (GDP), which has been shrinking for 22 consecutive years as

---

[2] Refer to Lewis, AW, "Economic Development with Unlimited Supplies of Labour", *Manchester School of Economic and Social Studies*, 22, 1954, pp. 139–191.

reported by the *Financial Times*. From 57% in 1983, the share of wages in GDP declined to merely 37% in 2005 and thereon remained stagnant. Chinese workers cannot afford most products they produced: for every Apple iPhone selling at US$599 that Foxconn produces, Foxconn gets a mere US$11.20, and assembly line workers get next to nothing. The basic pay for an assembly line worker at Foxconn Shenzhen was 900 *yuan* before the announced increment in 2010.

In the wake of labour shortages, strikes and surging inflation since the beginning of 2011, minimum wages in some cities and provinces have been lifted again from 14% in Shanghai to 21% in Beijing. Even as wages are set to increase, the average manufacturing wage in China is only US$3.10 an hour. China's manufacturing edge is thus unlikely to be affected in the near future. A Hong Kong Trade Development Council (HKTDC) survey of 4,500 respondents, including 2,400 Hong Kong manufacturing companies, shows that 46.2% still prefer to set up factories in the Pearl River Delta, 12.7% in the Yangtze River Delta, 6.2% in Vietnam, 3.8% in Cambodia and 2.3% in Bangladesh. As Table 2 indicates, China's share of exported manufactured goods is significantly higher than that of other developing countries in 2008 although its hourly wage rate was more than double that of the rest. This led the HKTDC to suggest that China's competitiveness did not lie in price alone "but rather in an integrated bundle of factors such as quality-price ratio of the output, infrastructure support, delivery lead time as well as flexibility in meeting different specific order requirements."

In the foreseeable future, labour intensive industries may continue to relocate away from southern and coastal China to ease the problems of labour shortages and high production costs. *TIME* reported that many companies have already expanded or relocated inland in the past year in search of more plentiful and cheaper labour. Nonetheless, this is but a temporary solution. In the long run, China still has to undergo industrial restructuring and upgrade to more capital and technology intensive manufacturing. An overall pay hike will not only help to accelerate this process, but also boost demand for domestic consumption and narrow the widening income gap.

## Ineffectual Trade Unions

A *Financial Times* report has suggested that the Honda strike could hardly have taken place without official acquiescence. In particular, it is remarkable that the Guangdong provincial government did not suppress the high profile Honda strike on the pretext of "maintaining stability." On 14 June 2010, Premier Wen Jiabao addressed a group of young migrant workers in Beijing in a bid to placate the discontented. Wen acknowledged the workers' contribution to China's wealth and said that "[t]he government and the public should be treating the young migrant workers like their children." Wen's words hark back to his talk about upholding "social justice" at 2010's *lianghui*. In his annual report, he said that the government's top priority was to allow workers to share in China's economic prosperity. In this light, the wave of labour protests may serve as a timely boost to the central government's reform initiatives to resolve social conflicts, which have often been met with resistance and selective implementation at the local levels.

**Table 2**   Comparison of Manufacturing Wages and Export Share

| Country | Hourly Manufacturing Wage Rate in 2007 (US$) | Share of World Export of Manufactures in 2008 (%) | Average Annual Growth in 2000–2008 (%) |
|---|---|---|---|
| Bangladesh | 0.19 | 0.13 | 10.9 |
| India | 0.39 | 1.07 | 16.6 |
| Vietnam | 0.45 | 0.31 | 23.1 |
| China | 1.08 | 12.71 | 25.2 |

*Sources*: "Comparisons in Manufacturing Wages and Corporate Tax Rates", at <http://www.545project.com/WageComparisonandTaxRates.pdf> (accessed 9 June 2010); "The Competitive Supply Chain: China versus a Rising Asia", *HKTDC*, 3 June 2010, at <http://www.hktdc.com> (accessed 9 June 2010).

The central government's subtle acquiescence aside, clashes between government-backed union staff and workers had also been reported. Amid scuffles between unionists and workers at the Foshan Honda plant, one worker shouted, "We pay union fees every month. You should represent us, so how come you're beating us?" Another worker on strike at a Henan fabric factory told *Yazhou zhoukan* reporters, "The trade union is worse than the secret society; the latter takes your money and serves you whereas the government-controlled unions demand union fees but in turn suppress workers."

Autonomous trade unions do not exist in China. The All-China Federation of Trade Unions (ACFTU) is subordinate to the state; its workplace unions are subservient to either the management or the communist party organisations at the same level. The ACFTU's government status prevents it from organising any kind of labour mobilisation against employers. In China, collective workers' actions, facilitated by congregation at the work place, have been spontaneously organised instead of being mobilised by the unions like in the West. In fact, the role of the ACFTU and its grassroots branches has been to defuse rather than support collective workers' actions.

One of the demands voiced by workers at the Honda plant was the right to nominate their own union heads. Currently, union heads, nominated by party organisations or management in many workplaces, are often key party or management members. According to a survey of 524 union heads, more than 70% are party committee members and 35% concurrently hold managerial positions.[3] There is a conflict of interests since unions are closely tied to the institutions that prioritise profits at the expense of labour interests.

The contribution of the ACFTU lies mainly in the push for pro-labour law, such as China's Labour Contract Law that took effect from 1 January 2008. However, the implementation of the Labour Contract Law has been resisted by local governments. Some in the Pearl River Delta and Yangtze River Delta regions even came up with counter-measures to the Law. ACFTU statistics show that in 2008, 1.9 million enterprises had signed collective contracts covering 150 million workers or 89% of the workers in enterprises with unions. At the core of these collective contracts are wage demands, which have been met with strong opposition from the employers, whom the workers and unions are powerless to counter. It seems that the ACFTU is largely a toothless tiger.

## Implications

What is in store for the Chinese proletariat? Current labour shortages are concentrated in the Pearl River Delta, Zhejiang and Fujian, although there are signs that the problem is slowly spreading to less developed central and western regions. For instance, it was reported that many firms in Chongqing of southwest China have set up booths at railway and bus stations to lure job-seekers to stay at home instead of going back to the coastal region. As labour shortages become more pervasive all over China, workers will dominate the labour market and command greater bargaining power vis-à-vis employers. For the moment, however, industries still have the option of shifting to inland localities with more abundant labour supply.

One way to ease labour shortages and improve migrant workers' welfare is to reform the discriminative *hukou* system. In February 2012, the State Council announced that migrant workers who fulfil certain criteria are qualified to apply for *hukous* in small and medium cities. With this reform, businesses may find it easier to recruit and retain migrant workers from other parts of the country. Excluded from this new policy are the densely populated directly controlled municipalities and provincial-level cities.

What is certain is the shift in the demographic composition of the workforce. With the entrance of the post-80s and post-90s generations into the labour force, gradually replacing the previous generation of workers, China will probably see a rising trend of workers fighting for their rights.

---

[3] Feng C, "Union Power in China: Source, Operation, and Constraints", *Modern China*, 35, 2009, pp. 662–689.

To date, there is already an ongoing diffusion of collective workers' action to beyond coastal China as the success of some workers in securing higher wages has emboldened workers in other places.

Labour discontent is just one of many potentially explosive social problems in China. But unlike rural unrest, labour discontent is more likely to erupt into large-scale mass incidents because of the large numbers congregating at the workplace and more effective mobilisation via new communication tools. The new generation of workers' greater awareness of labour rights, however, has not been met by reforms from top-down. There is no sign that the government will grant more autonomy to trade unions anytime soon so that they can truly represent workers' interests. Furthermore, workers' right to strike was abolished in the 1982 revision of China's constitution. One of the government's challenges is hence to address the legality of labour strikes which are on the rise.

Chinese workers are in the throes of a new labour movement. They are not out to politicise it but are demanding better pay and work conditions long overdue to them. Leaving the protection of labour interests to spontaneous workers' action and suppressing them ex post is not a viable long-term solution. As China's wealth gap continues to widen, the likelihood of escalating antagonism and radicalisation of labour disputes is very high if the government continues to deprive workers of genuinely representative unions and proper, legal channels to seek redress and air their grievances.

# IV

# China's External Relations and Global Governance

## Introduction

LYE Liang Fook

After more than three decades of open door and reform policy, China has moved from being a marginal player to becoming a key actor at the centre of the world stage. This outcome did not come easy given the fact that other communist or socialist-oriented countries had earlier lost out to more successful capitalistic-oriented countries at the end of the Cold War. Furthermore, China had to fight off its "pariah" status that involved political isolation and economic sanctions imposed by other countries following the 1989 Tiananmen crackdown. Today, China has virtually shaken off the shackles of the past and is basking in the international limelight with its presence being felt in various fields.

Most significantly, in the world economy, China has overtaken Japan to become the world's second largest economy by end-2010. Some observers have surmised that China will replace the United States as the world's largest economy by 2020. Already, China is among the top partners of several countries in Europe, Asia, Africa and the Americas. China's economic interests are closely intertwined with these countries as they not only import but also export their goods (including natural resources and semi or finished products) to China. China relies a great deal on these imported goods to sustain its own growth momentum. The trade and production networks that link China with other countries have created a high level of interdependency. In addition, Chinese investments in these countries have become an ever more important driver of employment and growth, especially at a time when the economies in Europe and the United States are in difficulties. At the financial level, more and more countries are using the Chinese *renminbi* as a currency for cross-border transactions, as an alternative to the once dominant US dollar.

In global politics and diplomacy, China has developed bilateral and multilateral ties with many countries and international organisations and whose presence and participation is much sought after on various issues. At international and regional platforms, China ardently champions the interests of developing countries, itself included. It is also a key player in G-20 which has replaced the Western-dominated G-7 and G-8 as the premier forum for international economic cooperation since 2009. Furthermore, China has been called upon to do more on issues ranging from restoring confidence to the world economy, helping to alleviate the *eurozone* debt crisis and maintaining a stable and denuclearised Korean Peninsula, to fighting global warming and climate change.

In the social realm, more and more Chinese nationals are studying and working outside of China. They provide an important source of talent and labour for their host countries. Many Chinese tourists are also travelling overseas and they are known for their strong buying power. This has helped to boost the sales of luxury brand items in the United States, Europe and Asia. In addition, with China's enhanced economic clout, there has been a corresponding increase in demands by other countries to learn the Chinese language. This is driven by the desire to better grasp the opportunities China has to offer. In response, China has, since 2004, set up two key types of institutions in foreign countries to promote the learning of Chinese language and culture. By end-2010, there were reportedly 322 Confucius Institutes and 369 Confucius Classrooms established in 96 countries.

The aforementioned brief overview, not meant to be exhaustive, is intended to provide a sense of the wide-ranging impact that China has made on the rest of the world. In virtually every aspect, a Chinese presence is evident in the way we work, live or play. Such a presence would have been unimaginable more than two decades ago. Yet, this presence has resulted in a fresh set of challenges for China. On the one hand, the rest of the world has benefited from the myriad opportunities China's rise has offered. Many countries have adjusted their policies and strategies to ride on China's growth.

On the other hand, there is a concern that China's growing presence will cause it to become more assertive, or even aggressive, in the pursuit of its national interests. By extension, the greater dependence on China by other countries increases the risks to these countries should relations with China turn sour. Proponents of such a view have cited China's tough actions such as when it forced Japan to back down over the Diaoyutai Islands dispute (in September 2010) and its more recent stand-off with the Philippines over Scarborough Shoal (in April 2012) in the South China Sea as evidence of this more assertive streak. Yet others have cited China's "spoiler" role, together with Russia, in successfully preventing tougher sanctions from being imposed by the United Nations (UN) on Syria in light of the atrocities committed by the Assad regime on civilians.

## Key Themes in China's Foreign Policy

In an effort to counter negative views of its actions and intentions, China, on its part, has consistently stated that it pursues an independent foreign policy of peace, sticks to the path of peaceful development and the win-win strategy of opening up. In public statements or comments, Chinese leaders and officials have stressed the key themes or ideas of promoting a "harmonious world", advocating a "new thinking" on security related issues, living up to its "international responsibility" and promoting "regional cooperation and good-neighbourly relations".[1]

These themes or ideas were elaborated in a white paper on "China's Peaceful Development" issued by the State Council Information Office (SCIO) in September 2011. They were also included in the first version of a white paper titled "China's Peaceful Development Road" also published by the SCIO in December 2005. These two white papers on China's external relations issued so far by the SCIO indicate the importance China attaches to how it is being perceived by other countries. More specifically, they are intended to assuage the concerns of other countries of China's intentions.

To be sure, the concept of a "harmonious world" was officially put forth by President Hu Jintao when he addressed the 60th General Assembly of the United Nations in New York in September

---

[1] "China's Peaceful Development", White Paper by China's State Council Information Office, September 2011, pp. 19–24.

2005.[2] In this address which was titled "Build Towards a Harmonious World of Lasting Peace and Common Prosperity", Hu outlined four elements of a harmonious world that included (i) upholding multilateralism (as opposed to unilateralism or a bipolar world) to realise common security; (ii) upholding mutually beneficial cooperation to achieve common prosperity; (iii) upholding the spirit of inclusiveness including recognising every country's right to independently choose its development path; and, (iv) promoting UN reform actively and prudently.[3] These four elements were subsequently incorporated into China's peaceful development white papers of 2005 and 2011.

Another key theme that has been consistently stressed by Chinese leaders and officials is to promote a "new thinking on security" that is based on "mutual trust", "mutual benefit", "equality" and "coordination". Here, China regards security as broadly encompassing both traditional as well as non-traditional security matters such as terrorism, financial crises and natural disasters. In China's view, the approach to promote this new thinking is to pursue multilateral cooperation that involves coordinating or cooperation among relevant stakeholders regardless of their size or influence (that ties in with the ideas of equality and coordination mentioned earlier).

Closely related to the term of "mutual trust" is the call by Chinese leaders and officials for other countries to respect its own interests and concerns. While China has stated that it is prepared to respect other countries' interests, it also expects other countries to reciprocate this respect. China's call for "mutual respect" can be attributed to its growing interests as a result of its ever broadening and deepening ties with the rest of the world. In Beijing's eyes, this call for mutual respect is a normal outcome for a country on the rise and does not equate to greater aggression on China's part. More often than not, China's call is largely directed at the United States whom Beijing considers to have consistently ignored China's growing interests. For instance, in China's eyes, the United States has ignored its umpteen requests to wind down or cease arm sales to Taiwan in line with the three China–US joint communiqués.

On meeting its "international responsibility", China has sought to indicate through its actions that it is generally prepared to play a role to address issues of common concern to the international community. This is commonly known as global governance that involves a coordinated response by countries and/or organisations to tackle cross-border issues. Such issues would include the health of the world economy, terrorism, transnational crime, cybercrime, nuclear proliferation, maritime piracy and, global warming and climate change. While playing a role in these areas, however, China has simultaneously sought to temper expectations that it can or ought to do more on these fronts. The constant refrain from China is that it is still a developing country with many pressing domestic challenges. Hence, it is not surprising that China has asserted that getting its own house in order is the "most important fulfilment of its international responsibility". Nevertheless, as a responsible member of the international community, China has shown that it is ready to play a role at a pace that it is comfortable with and one that is in line with its capabilities.

While promoting the building of a harmonious world, Chinese leaders and officials have also not neglected their own backyard by stressing the importance of promoting "regional cooperation and good-neighbourly relations". In this regard, it has called on countries in the region to increase trade and other mutually beneficial cooperation. China has further reiterated that its prosperity, development and long-term stability provide an opportunity rather than a threat to its neighbours. Furthermore, in light of the disputed territorial claims and maritime rights in the region, China has exhorted countries in the region to settle these disputes through dialogue and friendly negotiation.

Chinese leaders and officials have further stated that China is committed to the strategy of peaceful development for the long term. In December 2011, Chinese President Hu Jintao said in

---

[2]This concept is an extension of the "peaceful rise" concept that was propounded by then Vice President of Central Party School Zheng Bijian at the Boao Forum in November 2003.

[3]Written Speech by H.E. Hu Jintao, president of the People's Republic of China at the High-Level Plenary Meeting of the United Nations' 60th Session, China's Ministry of Foreign Affairs Website, 16 September 2005 at <http://www.mfa.gov.cn/eng/wjdt/zyjh/t213091.htm> (accessed 1 June 2012).

his annual New Year's address titled "Promoting the Well Being of the World's People Together" that "peace, development and cooperation are the calls of the time and serve the common interests of all countries".[4] Separately, China's State Councillor Dai Bingguo, who oversees China's foreign policy, has stated that China's commitment to peaceful development will not change for 100 years or 1,000 years.[5]

## Peaceful Development: An Ongoing Task

China's ardent efforts, in terms of both its statements and actions, to affirm its commitment to the strategy of peaceful development have met with rather mixed results. Indeed, many countries continue to pursue ever deepening and broadening cooperation with China. At the same time, a number of these countries appear to have doubts about China's intentions or are wary of being too dependent on China.

On its part, China would require patience, resolve, diplomatic finesse and skill, and maybe even a strong sense of magnanimity in pressing on with its peaceful development strategy. This would not be easy given its several urgent domestic challenges and the strong sense of national pride among its citizens who would not take lightly to perceived slights or unfair treatment of China. Ideally, over time, through its actions rather than words, China may be able to convince some of its detractors of its commitment to this strategy as well as to even have them subscribe to this strategy.

Whether China can persist with this peaceful development strategy would also depend on the actions of other countries. The conduct of foreign relations among countries is still very much based on narrow national interests and the traditional balance of power where countries much smaller than China would instinctively want to engage other major powers to balance China's heft. Even the other major powers are also wary of China. While China's emphasis on "mutual trust", "mutual respect", "mutual benefit" and "equality" may sound good to work towards, the harsh reality is one where the interests of countries do not necessarily lend themselves to readily identify and even subscribe to these nice sounding terms.

All the chapters in this section will highlight China's enhanced presence on the world stage. More importantly, these papers reflect both the opportunities as well as challenges that China has to grapple with as a result of its present international stature. At one level, China's relations with other major powers such as the United States, the EU, the BRICS (Brazil, Russia, India, China and South Africa) and Japan will be looked at. To a large extent, how the shape of the world order will evolve will depend on China's relations with these countries.

At another level, China's ties with the smaller countries comprising the Association of Southeast Asian Nations (ASEAN) as a grouping in general and Singapore in particular will be examined. In many ways, the best demonstration of China's peaceful development will be how China conducts its relations with countries that are much smaller in size as compared to it. If China can develop ties with these countries based on equality, mutual trust, mutual respect and mutual benefit, this will lend substance to its peaceful intentions.

Going beyond China's bilateral or regional ties, other chapters will analyse issues that have an impact on China's peaceful development strategy such as its stance on global governance, its efforts to enhance its energy security and its relatively nascent initiatives at projecting its soft power. Closer to home, China will likely pay close attention to managing two potential regional flashpoints. One is the prospects for stability on the Korean Peninsula with a young leader at the helm in North Korea. The other is the disputed claims in the South China Sea that involve not only China, Taiwan and the ASEAN claimant states but also third parties such as the United States and

---

[4]"President Hu Jintao Delivers New Year Speech", *China Daily*, 31 December 2011.

[5]"We Must Stick to the Path of Peaceful Development", Speech by Dai Bingguo, 13 December 2010 at <http://www.fmprc.gov.cn/eng/topics/cpop/t777704.htm> (accessed 1 June 2012).

India. On Taiwan, the ever strengthening cross-strait exchanges especially economic linkages and what this means for Taiwan itself and for future of US-China relations will be further examined.

Many of the chapters underscore the dynamic and complex external environment that Chinese leaders and officials have to navigate and yet at the same time persist on the path of peaceful development. They do not necessarily provide solutions for China in the future and in any case this topic is beyond the scope of these chapters. What they do show, in an unambiguous manner, is that China's strategy of peaceful development is still very much a work in progress.

# 42

# China-US Relations

## Coping with a US Pivot to the Asia-Pacific Region

LYE Liang Fook*

*The US pivot to the Asia-Pacific region is seen by some in China as a move to contain its rise. China has not over-reacted so far. It has instead stressed the message of continued cooperation with the United States.*

China-US relations have entered a more challenging phase with the United States stepping up its presence in the Asia-Pacific region on several fronts. At the political level, the United States made its presence felt at the East Asia Summit in November 2011 as a full member and raised the sensitive issue of the South China Sea (SCS) disputes despite China's objections. The United States also ended its diplomatic isolation of Myanmar (that borders China) with Hillary Clinton's visit to Naypyidaw in December 2011, the first by a US Secretary of State in more than 50 years. The United States also further eased sanctions on Myanmar and appointed an ambassador to Naypyidaw.

On the economic front, the United States is pushing for a Trans Pacific Partnership (TPP) Agreement that goes beyond the usual trade and investment items to encompass broader issues like labour standards, intellectual property rights and environmental protection. China regards this as an attempt to change the rules of the game by raising the development bar for China. In a seeming initial rebuff of the TPP platform, President Hu Jintao reportedly said at the Asia-Pacific Economic Cooperation Summit in November 2011 that China prefers to work through existing global trade architecture like the World Trade Organization (WTO).[1]

At the governmental level, however, China appears less dismissive of the TPP platform by stating that China holds an "open attitude" towards all cooperative initiatives that are conducive to economic integration and common prosperity in the Asia-Pacific.[2] Reading between the lines, this

---

*LYE Liang Fook is Assistant Director and Research Fellow at the East Asian Institute, National University of Singapore.

[1]"Obama, Hu Airs Economic Disputes at APEC Summit", *Reuters*, 13 November 2011.

[2]"China Holds an Open Attitude to Trans-Pacific Partnership Pact: Official", *Xinhuanet*, 15 November 2011 at <http://news.xinhuanet.com/english2010/china/2011-11/15/c_131248604.htm> (accessed 12 April 2012).

so called "open attitude" contains an implicit message that China would be opposed to any initiative that is exclusive in nature or, more specifically, one that is aimed at keeping China out. At the same time, China is not foreclosing the option of it being part of the TPP platform at some future point if it is in its interest to do so.

On the security front, the United States has enhanced its military alliance with Australia with an agreement in November 2011 to station up to 2,500 marines in Darwin and for the US Air Force to have greater access to Australian Air Force facilities. More recently, in January 2012, Washington and Manila reportedly agreed to hold more joint exercises between the two countries and to let more US troops rotate through the Philippines. The United States and Vietnam have also signed a Statement of Intent on Military Medical Cooperation in August 2011, marking the first formal military cooperation between the two sides since ties were normalised in 1995.

The US pivot to the Asia-Pacific has aroused mixed feelings from China. At one extreme, there are those who regard US actions as containment of China that warrants an aggressive response. *Global Times*, an English language newspaper run by the Chinese Communist Party (CCP), has accused the United States of building an "anti-China alliance".[3] On the enhanced military cooperation between the United States and Philippines, *Global Times* separately advocated China to impose economic sanctions on the Philippines for raising "military tensions by playing a balancing strategy".[4] Yet, there are other publications which have espoused a more nuanced view by arguing that as Asia has become the "engine for the world economy", the US pivot to the Asia-Pacific was "not merely for security purposes but mainly for the need to sustain its economic hegemony".[5]

At the official level, however, reactions have generally been milder. They have either painted the United States as being still caught up in the old Cold War mentality of setting up military alliances or cast the United States as unnecessarily raising tensions, both of which do not conform to the needs of the region. In an earlier response, China's foreign ministry spokesman Liu Weimin reportedly questioned the appropriateness of the US strategy of broadening military alliances at a time of sluggish world economic growth.[6] *Xinhua*, China's state-run news agency, stated that the United States is welcomed to make "more contributions to peace and stability" in the Asia-Pacific region, but its "possible militarism will cause a lot of ill-will" and will be met with "strong opposition in the world's most dynamic region".[7] Echoing the same thrust, Xi Jinping, the heir apparent to Hu Jintao, has also commented that the United States' deliberate move to give prominence to the "military security agenda" such as the scaling up of "military deployment" and the strengthening of "military alliances" does not conform to the desire of most countries in the region to focus on their own economic well-being.[8]

## Bilateral Cooperation and Mutual Respect

A decade ago, the strategic context of China-US relations was more favourable. In 2002, when Chinese Vice President Hu Jintao visited the United States, the United States was still reeling from the 11 September 2001 terrorist attacks. While there were differences between China and the United States, they were subsumed under the overriding US concern to wage a worldwide war on terror. China, at that time, was perceived by the United States as a key partner in this endeavour. China was also less prominent on the international stage then as it is now. Today, China's

---

[3] "US Asia-Pacific Strategy Brings Steep Price", *Global Times*, 18 November 2011.

[4] "Make Philippines Pay for Balancing Act", *Global Times*, 29 January 2012.

[5] "Economic Consideration Behind the US Pivot to the Asia-Pacific Region", *Beijing Review*, no. 6, 9 February 2012.

[6] "China Cool on US Troop's Aussie Deployment", *Herald Sun*, 16 November 2011.

[7] "Commentary: Constructive US Role in Asia-Pacific Welcome, but not War Mongering", *Xinhuanet*, 6 January 2012 at <http://news.xinhuanet.com/english/indepth/2012-01/06/c_131346348.htm> (accessed 12 April 2012).

[8] "Full Text of Xi's Interview with *Washington Post*", *China Daily*, 13 February 2012.

spectacular growth stands in contrast to the relative decline of the United States and Europe. There is also no longer an overriding concern to bring China and the United States closer.

Notwithstanding the more challenging times, China still seeks stable relations with the United States. The United States is China's most important bilateral partner. Having stable relations with the United States would enable China to continue to benefit from the current world order and grow unimpeded. Ultimately, a conducive external environment will also allow China to continue to focus on addressing many of its pressing domestic challenges. China does not intend nor is prepared to set itself up against the United States.

To be sure, Chinese leaders from Mao Zedong, Deng Xiaoping, Jiang Zemin to Hu Jintao have attached great importance to developing ties with the United States. Mao recognised the United States' strategic importance as a counterweight to the former Soviet Union. This led to the normalisation of China-US ties in 1972. In 1979, Deng Xiaoping visited the United States to secure America's acquiescence before China embarked on its limited war with Vietnam. Hu Jintao, like Jiang Zemin before him, has also proactively engaged the United States. Hu had, in particular, visited the United States as vice president in April 2002 before he became general secretary of the CCP in November of the same year.

Likewise, Xi Jinping's visit to the United States in February 2012 as vice president mirrored Hu Jintao's earlier practice. Xi is expected to become the CCP's next general secretary in the fall of 2012. The visit has burnished Xi's credentials as a capable and confident leader who is able to strike a balance between articulating China's interest and reaching out to his American audience. More importantly, Xi's visit has reaffirmed the message that China values stable ties with the United States.

Echoing the line of other Chinese leaders like President Hu Jintao and Premier Wen Jiabao, Xi urged the United States to view its relations with China from the big picture perspective. In an interview which he gave to the *Washington Post* before his US visit, Xi said that a "sound and stable China-US relationship" is crucial for both countries and for the "peace, stability and prosperity of the Asia-Pacific region and the world at large". Xi also emphasised the importance of a "cooperative partnership" based on "mutual respect" and "mutual benefit".[9]

To further underscore how interdependent and mutually beneficial China-US relations have become, Xi's itinerary in the United States included a tour of a family-run soybean and corn farm in Maxwell (Iowa) where plans were reportedly announced for China to purchase more than US$4 billion in US soybeans in 2012. This announcement is significant as China is the biggest soybean market of the United States.[10] Xi also visited the Los Angeles port where nearly 60% of the imports that move through the port originate from China.[11]

Xi's visit reflects China's pro-activeness in setting relations with the United States on an even keel, an objective similar to Hu's visit to the United States in 2011. By being proactive, China seeks to avoid a repeat of 2010 when a series of incidents threw China-US relations off-tangent by generating their own negative momentum. These included the Google episode, US President Barack Obama's meeting with the Dalai Lama, US arms sales to Taiwan, and the strengthening of the US-Japan-South Korea nexus over China's response to Japan's detention of a Chinese ship captain and the Cheonan and Yeonpyeong incidents. On its part, US President Obama and Vice President Joe Biden had also visited China in 2009 and 2011 respectively to sustain the momentum of bilateral ties.

Besides exchanges of high-level visits, China and the United States have attempted to build a cooperative and comprehensive relationship through an institutionalised framework known as the

---

[9] *China Daily,* op. cit., 13 February 2012.

[10] In 2011, China purchased 20.6 million metric tons of soybeans from the United States, or 60% of the total shipped overseas. See "China Signs $4.3 billion of Soybean-Buying Deals with US", *Bloomberg Businessweek*, 15 February 2012.

[11] "Chinese Leader Xi, Biden Promote Trade in LA", *Associated Press*, 18 February 2012.

Strategic and Economic Dialogue (S&ED). The S&ED, represented by Secretary of State Hillary Clinton and Secretary of Treasury Timothy Geithner on the US side and Vice Premier Wang Qishan and State Councillor Dai Bingguo on the Chinese side, has met annually since 2009 to deliberate bilateral, regional and global issues. Going even further, at their third S&ED in May 2011, both sides inaugurated their first Strategic Security Dialogue, thus opening up an additional platform for civilian and military leaders from both sides to engage each other.

While simultaneously broadening and deepening ties with the United States, Beijing has urged the United States to be more sensitive to China's growing interests (commensurate with its rising economic and political presence) in the Asia-Pacific region as well as the world. In Beijing's eyes, this is a normal development for a country on the rise and does not equate to greater aggression on China's part. In particular, on long-standing issues, China would like the United States to honour its commitments and carefully and properly handle Taiwan and Tibet related issues that fall under China's "core interests". More specifically, China wants the United States to stop arms sales to Taiwan in accordance with its "One China" policy as stated in the three China-US joint communiqués and not accord any legitimacy to the Tibetan spiritual leader, the Dalai Lama, whom Beijing regards as trying to split the country.

Beijing has also increasingly objected to US naval ships conducting surveillance missions off China's coast, i.e. within China's Exclusive Economic Zone (EEZ). It is believed that China did not take too kindly to the United States sending its aircraft carrier USS George Washington into the Yellow Sea in November 2010 for military drills with South Korea after North Korea's artillery bombardment of Yeonpyeong, a South Korean island. Even though Beijing's reactions were deliberately measured in order not to worsen tensions on the Korean Peninsula, it would not have been lost on Beijing that the close proximity of a foreign aircraft carrier off its coast (i.e. within China's EEZ) posed a direct threat to China's national security. This is one vivid instance that showed US military pre-eminence and its ability to operate with relative impunity, right under Beijing's nose. Without the military means at the moment to make the United States think twice about its military manoeuvres, Beijing's constant refrain is therefore to urge the United States to abide by the principle of mutual respect.

## Uncertainties Ahead

Whether relations between China and the United States would remain on an even keel will depend on how both countries manage their differences when they arise. Preferably, both countries can bear their common interests in mind, avoid politicising issues and try to minimise their differences. However, this is easier said than done. There are a number of developments that could adversely affect China-US relations down the road.

For one, in the run-up to the US presidential and congressional elections in the fall of 2012, China has already become a convenient whipping boy for the economic ills in the United States. In particular, US Republican presidential hopeful Mitt Romney has accused President Barack Obama for being soft on China. He has vowed that if he is elected the next president, he will designate China a "currency manipulator" and take "appropriate action".[12]

Not to be outdone, President Obama has also pressed China on a broad range of issues ranging from an unbalanced trade, unfair trade practices, undervalued *yuan*, poor intellectual property rights protection, forced technology transfers and unresolved human rights concerns. Each of the above issues, if not properly managed, could negatively affect China-US relations if they are blown out of proportion or become too politicised. Already, President Obama is mulling over the creation of a trade enforcement unit to investigate unfair trading practices in countries such as China. Furthermore, the US Congress, with strong bipartisan backing, approved a measure in March 2012

---

[12]"How I will Respond to China's Growing Power", *The Wall Street Journal*, 16 February 2012.

to allow the United States to continue to impose countervailing duties on Chinese products deemed to be sold at below cost in the United States.

In an effort to calm anti-China sentiments, various Chinese leaders have cautioned the United States not to go to the hilt. Chinese Premier Wen Jiabao reportedly told visiting US Treasury Secretary Timothy Geithner in Beijing in January 2012 that both China and the United States should take care of the "core interests and concerns of each other, and resolve frictions appropriately". Wen added that both countries should take "concrete measures and promote cooperation in trade, investment, infrastructure and high-tech areas" in a "wider, closer and more balanced way".[13] Xi, during his US visit, also cautioned the United States not to allow "regrettable after-effects" arising from the jostling among potential election candidates to affect the development of ties between the two countries. Yet, given the seemingly growing anti-China sentiments in the United States, one should not discount the possibility that the US administration that comes into office after the 2012 presidential elections, will be more prepared to take a hard-line position against China because it is the politically correct thing to do.

Another development that bears watching is the potential for regional flashpoints to flare up with either the implicit or tacit role of third parties such as the United States. In 2011, Vietnam and the Philippines appeared bolder in asserting their claims in the SCS alongside US reiteration of its interest in the freedom of navigation in the area. More significantly, the United States has also shown interest to increase its military engagement of Vietnam and the Philippines in 2012.

In a move that could portend rising tensions, the Philippine Energy Undersecretary James Layug announced in February 2012 that it would issue exploration licences for oil and gas in 15 blocks, three of which were in the SCS. Although the Philippines has claimed that these three blocks are in its EEZ, China has asserted that at least two of the three blocks are in waters under Chinese jurisdiction. In April 2012, Chinese and Philippine naval vessels were involved in a stand-off at Scarborough Shoal claimed by both countries in the SCS. There does not appear to be an easy resolution over these disputed claims. With the United States declaring an interest in the freedom of navigation in the SCS and its enhanced military ties with the Association of Southeast Asian Nations (ASEAN) claimant states, the situation has become more complex. China will most probably not want to be seen as weak in staking its own claims in the SCS. Eschewing a role for the United States in the SCS disputes, Chinese Foreign Minister Yang Jiechi reportedly said in March 2012 that China and the relevant countries have the "wisdom and the ability to deal with the SCS issue properly".[14] Similarly, China also does not wish to see the United States intervene in Beijing's and Tokyo's disputes in the East China Sea based on its commitments under the Japan-US security treaty.

A more fundamental issue affecting the entire dynamics of China-US ties is a China that is on the rise and a United States that is in relative decline. During this period of adjustment, the United States is likely to be more sensitive to perceived moves on the part of the rising power, in this case China, to challenge or even supplant it. Fortunately, China has been cautious on this front. It still recognises the United States' leading role on the world stage on a host of issues and its military prowess. This awareness on China's part is important as it provides some assurance and time for the United States to find its niche in a reinvigorated role.

At the same time, however, there is a certain quiet confidence on China's part that the increased US presence in the region will not be able to thwart China's rise. There are a number of factors for this. First, China is aware that its ever-growing economic might vis-à-vis the United States' declining economic influence provide China with the capability and ability to eventually out-compete the United States. Even though at the moment there is still a wide gap between China's military strength and that of the United States, Beijing believes that it will eventually be able to close the gap with its economic heft. In the long term therefore, the prospects for China do look promising.

[13]"Premier Wen Looks at the Big Picture", *China Daily*, 12 January 2012.
[14]"China Welcomes US in Asia, but. …", *The Straits Times*, 7 March 2012.

Second, the greater interdependence among China and the regional countries especially on the economic front provides Beijing with the leverage to shape the regional landscape to its advantage. Countries that Beijing regards as "friendly" could continue to ride on China's growth. Conversely, countries that Beijing regards as "hostile" may find themselves having difficulties doing business with China. On their part, the countries in the region, largely made up of smaller countries, also would not wish to be seen as standing alongside the United States to contain China. Third, there are still doubts over the extent of US commitment to the Asia-Pacific. There is likely to be a change of personnel in the US State Department led by Hillary Clinton following US presidential elections in end-2012. Whether a revamped State Department will be as equally committed to the region remains to be seen. More fundamentally, the United States will need to demonstrate to the countries in the region what it can additionally offer on the economic front rather than merely focussing on the military or political dimensions which it has done so far. A more balanced and multi-faceted approach on the part of the United States will also be welcomed by China.

# 43

# Sino-Japanese Relations

## Dark and Bright Spots in an Ambivalent Relationship

LAM Peng Er*

*The Sino-Japanese relationship has waxed and waned given geo-strategic shifts in the post-Cold War era and the resurgence of the historical controversies over Imperial Japan's invasion of China. There are, however, some bright spots in this chequered relationship.*

The year 2012 marks the 40th anniversary of the establishment of official Sino-Japanese relations.[1] In 1972, then Prime Minister Tanaka Kakuei visited Beijing and normalised bilateral relations.[2] The years between Tanaka's Beijing visit and the 1989 Tiananmen Incident marked the "golden age" of bilateral relations.[3] At the geo-strategic level, China and Japan were aligned with the United States against the Soviet Union in the context of the Cold War.[4] Historical controversies over imperial Japan's invasion of China were swept under the carpet for the sake of better bilateral ties amidst the backdrop of a perceived Soviet "threat".

In that epoch, people-to-people relationships were also friendly because many Japanese people of the older generation were apparently guilt-ridden about their country's invasion of China. They were generally ignorant of the excesses of the Cultural Revolution and the deadly power struggles

*LAM Peng Er is Senior Research Fellow at the East Asian Institute, National University of Singapore.

[1] Ministry of Foreign Affairs of Japan, "The 40th Anniversary of the Normalization of Diplomatic Relations between Japan and China, and the Opening Ceremony of 2012 'Friendship Year for Japan-China People-To-People Exchanges', I February 2012. <http://www.mofa.go.jp/announce/announce/2012/2/0201_02.html> (accessed 3 July 2012).

[2] Japan normalise relations with the People's Republic of China only after US President Richard Nixon visited China in 1971 in a major breakthrough in Sino-American relations. This was a permissive condition for Japan, a junior US ally, to do likewise. However, the United States only established diplomatic relations with China in 1979. Japan also broke its official diplomatic ties with Taiwan to secure official ties with China.

[3] See Vogel, EF, Yuan M and A Tanaka (eds.), *The Golden Age of the U.S.-China-Japan Triangle: 1972–1989* (Cambridge: Harvard University Asia Center, 2002).

[4] On systemic or geopolitical explanations of Sino-Japanese relations, see Ming W, *Sino-Japanese Relations: Interaction, Logic and Transformation* (Stanford: Stanford University Press, 2006), pp. 201–32.

of the Maoist political system. By the 1980s, China was adopting various political and economic reforms. The Japanese model of state-led economic development was a useful reference point for the NIEs (Newly Industrialising Economies) and China, and Japanese investments and ODA (Official Developmental Assistance) contributed to Beijing's economic development.[5] Then reformist Secretary General of the Chinese Communist Party Hu Yaobang adopted a foreign policy which was friendly towards Japan and was committed to bringing thousands of Japanese youths to visit China to nurture better people-to-people relationships even though his country was relatively poor then.

This chapter argues that the halcyon days of good bilateral relations (1972–1989) are over and that the relationship, though mutually beneficial in the economic area, has become much more complicated if not problematic in the 21st century. Indeed, this multi-faceted relationship has waxed and waned given geo-strategic shifts in the post-Cold War era and the resurgence of the historical controversies over Imperial Japan's invasion of China. Moreover, the superseding of Japan as the second largest economy in the world by China by end 2010 also created unease among some Japanese. There is this fear in Japan that China's new economic power will be translated into greater military capabilities and regional ambitions.

There are, however, some bright spots in this chequered relationship. Besides becoming each other's key trading partners, many local governments have established cordial relations between "sister cities". People-to-people relationships have also intensified. Japanese non-governmental organisations (NGOs) addressing environmental protection in the Chinese mainland have proliferated, tourism has risen significantly and exchange students studying on both sides of the East China Sea have also increased remarkably.

Both countries are engaged in multilateralism and an incipient East Asian regionalism by participating in the Association of Southeast Asian Nations (ASEAN) Plus Three (APT), ASEAN Regional Forum (ARF) and the East Asian Summit (EAS). China, Japan and South Korea also initiated annual trilateral summits for its top leaders outside the ASEAN-centred multilateral frameworks and held their first meeting in Fukuoka, Japan in December 2008. Beijing and Tokyo also participate in United Nations Peacekeeping Operations (UNPKO) in Southern Sudan. Given the rising interdependency between the Chinese and Japanese economies, both countries also agreed to promote the use of the *yen* and *renminbi* in settling mutual trade transactions instead of relying on the US dollar.

This chapter analyses contemporary Sino-Japanese relations from three angles: geopolitics, economics and the lack of a common identity between the two sides. While top leaders, national governments and the media can set the tone for bilateral relations, this chapter does not ignore the roles of local governments and the lack of shared values among the Chinese and Japanese people despite their geographical, historical and cultural proximity.

## Geopolitics: the US Factor, China's Rise and Japan as a "Normal State"

The collapse of the Soviet Union and the end of the Cold War in 1991 meant that Beijing and Tokyo no longer shared a common enemy. That Japan remains a junior partner to the US superpower means that any tension between Washington and Beijing can spill over to Beijing-Tokyo relations. However, good relations between Washington and Beijing will not automatically lead to good Beijing-Tokyo relations. This is because factors intrinsic to Sino-Japanese relations especially historical controversies and territorial disputes in the East China Sea and Senkaku (*Diaoyutai*) islands can be "intervening variables" in that bilateral relationship regardless of the state of China-US relations.

The demise of the Soviet superpower does not mean that the United States, China and Japan no longer share any common strategic interests. All three powers do not wish to see the outbreak of

---

[5] It can be interpreted that Japanese ODA to China is in lieu of war reparations for Imperial Japan's invasion of China.

any military conflict on the Korean peninsula and are supportive of the Chinese-led six party talks to deal with the issue of North Korea's nuclear weapons. However, the United States is a status-quo superpower. Historically, all status-quo great powers were wary of rising powers deemed to be potential challengers to their hegemony.[6] Indeed, in the post-Cold War era, only China has the heft to become a peer competitor to the United States.

There were at least two strategic initiatives by the United States in the post-Cold War era which had implications for Sino-Japanese relations. In 1997, Washington and Tokyo tightened their alliance by adopting the US-Japan Defense Guidelines which obliged the junior ally to provide logistical support to US forces in the event of a regional crisis in "situations in areas surrounding Japan" — commonly interpreted as a crisis in either the Korean peninsula or the Taiwan Strait — to the chagrin of Beijing. Presumably, joint US-Japanese support for South Korea against North Korea (a Chinese ally) in the event of an armed conflict would not be welcomed by China. Likewise, Japanese support to the United States if the latter chooses to intervene in a cross-Taiwan Strait crisis would be alarming to China.

In July 2010, at the 17th ARF in Hanoi, Secretary of State Hillary Clinton affirmed US interest in seeing the territorial disputes in the South China Sea resolved through peaceful means, multilateral forums and appropriate channels of international law. Clinton declared that the United States was an interested party in the freedom of navigation in the South China Sea. The disputed jurisdiction over parts of the South China Sea by the six claimant parties (China, Taiwan, Vietnam, Malaysia, the Philippines and Brunei) is a potential flashpoint in East Asia. Although China prefers the dispute to be settled diplomatically on a bilateral basis, Japan (not a claimant state) supported its US ally on this issue at the ARF meeting in Hanoi. Chinese Foreign Minister Yang Jiechi then reacted angrily to the "internationalisation" of the South China Sea dispute at the Hanoi meeting by Japan and other US supporters.

In September 2010, a Chinese fishing boat rammed two Japanese coast guard ships in the vicinity of the disputed Senkaku (*Diaoyutai*) islands (administered by Japan) leading to the detention of the captain of that Chinese vessel. Instead of briefly detaining and then releasing the captain, the DPJ (Democratic Party of Japan) government initially wanted to press charges against the captain under Japanese law. However, it was impossible for the Chinese government to accept the threat of legal action because it would be tantamount to accepting Japanese sovereignty over the Senkaku (Diayutai) islands. To avoid an escalation of the crisis and jeopardise bilateral ties, the DPJ government backed down humiliatingly and released the captain without pressing charges under Japanese law.

But the whole episode was not necessarily to the advantage of China. Aurelia George Mulgan writes: "[The crisis] has energized the Japan-US alliance …. First, the United States has offered reassurance to Japan that the Senkaku Islands fall within the scope of the Japan-US Security Treaty, which obligates the United States to defend Japan. The Japanese press reported an explicit commitment from Secretary of State Hillary Clinton in talks with Foreign Minister Maehara Seiji in New York in September. Chairman of the Joint Chiefs of Staff Mike Mullen and Secretary of Defense Robert Gates have also expressed strong support for Japan, offering assurance that the US will fulfil its alliance responsibilities. These statements underline the deterrence function of the alliance, which is the chief rationale for US bases in Okinawa".[7]

In March 2011, Japan was struck by a nine-magnitude earthquake which triggered a devastating tsunami and seriously damaged the Fukushima Daiichi nuclear power plant. The United States quickly mobilised its troops and launched *Operation Tomodachi* (friend) to assist its ally in the tsunami-struck northeastern region of Japan. Despite the earlier intentions of the new DPJ government under then Prime Minister Hatoyama Yukio to seek an East Asian Community, a more equal partnership with the United States and a greater equidistance between the United States and

---

[6] Kennedy, P, *The Rise and Fall of the Great Powers* (New York: Random House, 1987).

[7] Mulgan, AG "US-Japan Alliance the Big Winner from the Senkaku Islands Dispute", East Asia Forum, 26 October 2011.

China, the alliance between Washington and Tokyo has been strengthened as evidenced by American support to Japan in the aftermath of the 2010 Chinese fishing boat collision incident and *Operation Tomodachi*. Even though Chinese Gross Domestic Product (GDP) surpassed Japanese GDP by end 2010 and may overtake US GDP by 2019,[8] the combined economic, political and military weight of the US-Japanese alliance will still be more considerable than China's in the next few decades.

The template of China's foreign policy in the 21st century is "peaceful rise" or "peaceful development".[9] Unlike Washington, Beijing does not have any military bases abroad. It has accepted the major institutions of the international system like the United Nations, the International Monetary Fund, the World Bank and the World Trade Organization. China is also supportive of ASEAN-centric regionalism in East Asia. Despite Beijing's declaratory policy of a "peaceful rise", the Japanese media, some politicians and opinion shapers are suspicious that China may flex its political and military muscles once it has risen.

While Tokyo has capped its military spending at 1% GDP since 1976 as a symbol of its pacifism, Beijing has been chalking an almost double-digit rise in its military spending for most of the past two decades. In March 2012, Beijing announced that its defence budget will rise 11.2% to RMB670.27 billion (US$106.41 billion).[10] While China reiterated that its defence budget is still relatively low (just 1.28% of GDP)[11] and it has a large territory and a long coastline to defend, many Japanese are worried about China's future intentions given the inexorable rise of its defence budget. Regardless of China's intentions, if it continues to boost its defence budget by double-digit rises in the next decade, the fear this puts in Japan will drive the latter into the embrace of its US ally.

In December 2010, Tokyo adopted the new National Defense Program Guidelines (NDPG) — a blueprint for beefing up the country's security arrangements over the next decade from fiscal 2011.[12] The Guidelines call the military emergence of China as a "matter of concern both for the region and the international community".[13] Along with the new NDPG, Japan also adopted a new Mid-Term Defense Program (MDP) which focusses more on how to cope with China's maritime activity in the East China Sea. This includes strengthening the protection of Japan's offshore islands in its southwestern region.[14] The *2011 Japanese Diplomatic Bluebook* noted: "While China, which is realizing rapid economic growth, is stressing peaceful development and coming to play an important role in the world and the region, the increase in its military strength which lacks

---

[8] The *Economist* magazine writes: "Our best guess is that annual real GDP growth over the next decade averages 7.75% in China and 2.5% in America, inflation rates average 4% and 1.5%, and the *yuan* appreciates by 3% a year. If so, then China would overtake America in 2019". See "When will China Overtake America?", *The Economist*, 16 December 2010.

[9] The Chinese media writes: "The Chinese government has released the white paper titled 'China's Peaceful Development' at the beginning of the second decade of the 21st century in which it firmly declared to the world that China will unswervingly follow the path of peaceful development." As Chinese State Councillor Dai Bingguo said, "China's path of peaceful development has become a strong commitment of the Communist Party of China, the government and the Chinese people. Despite the great unrest, adjustments and transformations in the world since the beginning of 2011, China has shown a clear and sincere attitude and determination to firmly practice the idea of peaceful development and has persistently explored a path of peaceful rise as a major power". See "China Adheres to Peaceful Development", *People's Daily*, 29 September 2011.

[10] See "Double-digit Rise for China's Defense Spending", *Channel News Asia*, 4 March 2012 and "China to Raise Military Spending by 11.2%", *The Straits Times* (Singapore), 5 March 2012.

[11] The US has a defence budget about six times that of China and it accounted for 4.8% of its GDP in 2010. Ibid.

[12] "Dynamic Defense Capability Aimed at China", *Yomiuri Shimbun*, 19 December 2010.

[13] "Defense Strategy Says China's Rise is a 'Concern'", *Asahi Shimbun*, 18 December 2010.

[14] Shoji T "Japan's Security Outlook: Security Challenges and the New National Defense Program Guidelines" in National Institute for Defense Studies, *Security Outlook of the Asia-Pacific Countries and its Implications for the Defense Sector*, NIDS Joint Research Series no.6 (Tokyo: NIDS, 2011), pp. 155–158.

transparency, and its more active maritime activities are of concern to the region and the international community".[15]

While China's rise has instilled fear in some Japanese elites, Japan's quest to become a "normal" nation is a source of concern for some Chinese opinion shapers.[16] To many Japanese, a "normal" nation is one which is no longer shackled and hamstrung by constitutional restrictions and domestic pacifism and can play a more active peacekeeping and political role in international affairs.[17] Not surprisingly, many Chinese analysts are critical of Japan's NDPG.

According to Wang Ping, "Japan's new defense guidelines ... marked the country's quickening pace toward[s] becoming a military country. ... It is understandable that Japan wishes to be a 'normal' country, but it is unacceptable that it holds back its neighbours' development and emergence by borrowing external force. ... The guidelines played up China's military threat, saying China's rise and increasing naval activities in waters surrounding Japan are a 'matter of concern'. They also stressed Japan's need to strengthen defense cooperation with countries with which it shares 'democratic values', such as the Republic of Korea (ROK), Australia and India, in addition to its key ally, the United States".[18]

The Japanese and Chinese have a different understanding of what constitutes a "normal country" for Japan. As stated earlier, the mainstream Japanese notion of a "normal country" is one which is not crippled by the past but able to exercise political initiatives in international affairs. However, some Chinese analysts suspect that Japan as a "normal" country will become a great military power and a potential threat to China. Despite the fact that Japan's population is projected to shrink from 127 million in 2012 to 87 million by 2060[19] and is ageing rapidly (not the most propitious conditions for a resurging military power),[20] many Chinese view their country's rise as peaceful

---

[15] "Pursuit of Japan's National Interests and Development of Proactive Diplomacy" in Ministry of Foreign Affairs of Japan, *Diplomatic Bluebook 2011* (Tokyo: Ministry of Foreign Affairs, 2011).

[16] The Chinese media noted: "After the Cold War, to realize the ambition of becoming a normal state, namely a political and military power in line with its status as an economic giant, Japan expedited the transformation of the SDF. However, any assertive change in the role of the SDF is illegal under Japan's pacifist constitution. To rationalize its constitutionally problematic overseas mission of the SDF in Iraq, without radical revision of its constitution, the Japanese Government has taken a series of measures, including contingency legislation". See "Japan Flexing Military Muscles", *People's Daily*, 30 July 2004.

The *People's Daily* also wrote: "A package of seven security-related bills proposed by the Japanese Government was recently passed in parliament becoming law. The passage of the bills shows that the overall frame of contingency legislation, which the Japanese Government has sought to establish, has taken shape largely after unremitting efforts over 40 years. With its legal backing, the Japanese Government may resort to force and provide support for US military action during emergencies or when supposed contingency is imminent. The contingency legislation provides complete legal procedures for revising Japan's postwar pacifist constitution and striding toward amassing military might. The change from "defeated state" to "normal state" is the long-cherished wish of [the] Japanese, and the contingency legislation is vital for the transition". See "Japan Edges Toward Armed Might", *People's Daily*, 5 July 2004.

[17] For a detailed discussion of the concept of "normal state", see Soeya Y, M Tadokoro and DA Welch, *Japan as a "Normal Country"?: A Nation in Search of its Place in the World* (Toronto: University of Toronto, 2011).

[18] Wang P, "Challenged Sino-Japanese Ties: Japan's New Defense Guidelines Lead the Country in the Wrong Direction", *Beijing Review*, 6 January 2011.

Cai Chengping wrote: "Former Finance Minister Yoshihiko Noda became the leader of the Democratic Party of Japan ... What will Noda bring to the DPJ, Japan and even the world? ... Noda is about to pick his cabinet, and is expected to include more of the younger generation of politicians. Most of these young politicians, full of vigor and ambitions, are pushing for Japan to become a 'normal' country militarily". See "Hard Stance Possible for Reckless Noda Cabinet", *Global Times*, 1 September 2011.

[19] Japan's Ministry of Health and Welfare estimates that 40% of the country's population will be of retirement age by 2060. See "Japan Population to Shrink by One-Third by 2060", *BBC News*, 30 January 2012.

[20] The main agenda in Japanese politics is the reconstruction of the northeastern coast of Japan after the March 2011 triple disasters, and a hike in its consumption tax to pay for welfare and pension cost due to an ageing society, and not military adventures abroad. Arguably, the country is hunkering down to deal with its social problems amidst two "lost decades"

and Japan's quest for "normality" as militaristic. Ironically, many Japanese view the "normality" of Japan's role as a peaceful contribution to international society (such as United Nations peacekeeping operations) while China's rise is viewed as threatening. Given the stark and conflicting mirror images of "self" and "the other" in Sino-Japanese relations, one wonders whether economic interdependency can mitigate considerably the tensions between the neighbours.

## Economic Interdependency: The Ties that do *not* Bind?

The Chinese mainland is Japan's most important trading partner. In 2010, 19.4% of Japanese exports went to China while 22.1% of its imports were from China.[21] In that year, Sino-Japanese trade was valued at US$301.9 billion, a new record.[22] Japan is also a key trading partner for China. The Chinese media noted: "The European Union remained China's largest trade partner in 2010, with EU-China trade up 31.8% year on year to US$479.71 billion. China's trade with the United States rose 29.2% year on year to US$385.34 billion while China-Japan trade jumped 30.2% year on year to US$297.77 billion".[23]

In 2011, bilateral trade rose 14.3% from the previous year to another new record of US$344.99 billion.[24] In December 2011, both countries agreed to explore the forging of a Free Trade Agreement (FTA).[25] If they succeed in establishing a bilateral FTA and a trilateral one also incorporating South Korea, then economic interdependency will be enhanced in Northeast Asia. Coupled with another agreement in December 2011 to increasingly use their currencies instead of the US dollar when settling bilateral trade, Sino-Japanese economic partnership is set to expand.[26]

While solid economic ties are presumably an important incentive for good bilateral relations, history has shown that mutual economic interests are no guarantee that diplomatic relations would not sour. Taking a leaf from history will illustrate this point. By 1931, China had accounted for 25% of Japan's external trade and 81.9% of its investments overseas.[27] Akira Iriye remarked that there was the outlook in the 1920s that "the joining of Japanese capital and technology with Chinese labor was viewed in both countries as a better way to define their relations than an emphasis on Japanese military presence on Chinese soil".[28] Unfortunately, Imperial Japan invaded China. This sorry episode in Sino-Japanese history shows that a solid economic relationship does not necessarily bind countries in friendship. In the next decade of the 21st century, Sino-Japanese trade and investments are likely to grow steadily. But the citizens of both countries do not appear to share a common vision, identity and community.

## Lacking a Common Identity in Northeast Asia

In 2007, the Southeast Asian states adopted an ASEAN Charter which gave ASEAN a legal personality. The ASEAN states pledged to promote "one vision, one identity and one community". There is this Southeast Asian aspiration that ASEAN states sharing a common identity and destiny do not expect to go to war with each other in future. In contrast, the Northeast Asian states

of economic stagnation. Simply put, Japan does not appear to have the means and intention to become a great military power again.

[21] *Nihon Kokusei Zuei* [Japan Statistical Yearbook]: 2011/2012 (Tokyo: Yanotsuneta-kinenkai, 2011), p. 316.
[22] "Japan-China Trade in 2010 Exceeds US$300 billion to Set New Record", *Asia Today*, 1 March 2011.
[23] "China's 2010 Trade Surplus Down 6.4%", *Xinhua*, 10 January 2011.
[24] "Japan-China Trade Hits a Record High in 2011", *Mainichi Daily News*, 17 February 2012.
[25] "Japan-China Looks to FTA, Debt Buys", *Reuters*, 25 December 2011.
[26] "Japan to Start Purchasing Chinese Government Bonds", *Japan Times*, 26 December 2011.
[27] See Teow H, *Japanese Cultural Policy toward China: 1918–1931: A Comparative Perspective* (Cambridge: Harvard University Asian Center, 1999), p. 88.
[28] Iriye A quoted in Teow H, op. cit., pp. 88–89.

of China, Japan and the two Koreas neither have a regional organisation nor share similar aspirations. There are many plausible reasons why the Chinese and Japanese do not share a common identity even though their histories have intersected in the past millennia with trading ties and cultural exchanges including Confucianism, Buddhism and a common writing script. These reasons include:

- different and competing national narratives about the past which include Imperial Japan's colonisation of Korea and invasion of China;
- different educational emphasis with Japanese education neglecting to adequately teach their children about Imperial Japan's occupation and atrocities in China and Southeast Asia and Chinese education instilling patriotism and nationalism (often anti-Japanese) to bolster the legitimacy of the Chinese Communist Party and failing to teach the children that post-war democratic Japan is fundamentally different from militaristic imperial Japan;
- Chinese perceptions that the Japanese have neither sincerely apologised nor are truly contrite about past Japanese invasions of China;
- Japanese beliefs that they are tired of apologising to China so many times and that the children should not be held responsible for the sins of the fathers. After all, many Japanese today are born after the end of World War II;
- different regime types: many Japanese perceive that China is ruled by a brutal and dictatorial communist party which forcibly clamped down on unarmed demonstrators during the 1989 Tiananmen Incident and Tibetans today. In contrast, Japan today is an electoral democracy and its post-war political system is totally different from the Emperor worship, militaristic system of Imperial Japan;
- post-war Japanese perception of itself as a member of Western democracies, G8 and an ally of the United States. In contrast, China perceives itself as an independent power underpinned by a great and ancient civilisation tied neither militarily nor ideologically to the West; and
- geopolitics and the system of alliances (US hub-and-spokes) in Northeast Asia that put China and Japan into different camps.

To be sure, relations between local governments of China and Japan are generally cordial based on trade, investments and cultural exchanges. Local governments do not have to deal with intractable problems like territorial disputes (the job of national governments). But missteps can also happen between local governments. Nanjing and Nagoya established sister-city ties in 1978. However, in February 2012, Kawamura Takashi, mayor of Nagoya, tactlessly and senselessly said that the Nanjing Massacre "probably never happened" while meeting with a delegation from Nanjing, capital of China's Jiangsu province. The Chinese media reported: "The Nanjing municipal government announced Tuesday night that it would suspend official exchanges with Nagoya. A spokesman from the municipal foreign affairs office said Takashi Kawamura's remarks distorted historical facts and 'seriously hurt the feelings of Nanjing's people' ".[29]

To many infuriated Chinese, the attitude of mayor Kawamura is evidence that the Japanese are unrepentant of past atrocities and therefore guilty of grave moral failure. However, mayor Kawamura of Nagoya is merely one of the 1,743 elected executives (governors and mayors) of local governments in Japan.[30] His views are therefore not representative of the national government, other local governments and mainstream Japanese society. Indeed, Omura Hideaki, the governor of Aichi (the prefecture in which Nagoya is located), chided Kawamura for rupturing ties between the cities of Nanjing and Nagoya and urged him to restore relations again. The Japanese media reported: "Aichi Governor Omura Hideaki urged Nagoya Mayor Kawamura Takashi on Monday to quickly address the issue of deteriorating ties between the city and its sister city Nanjing over

---

[29] "Central government backs Nanjing's Nagoya protest", *China Daily*, 22 February 2012.

[30] As of October 2011, there were 1,743 local governments in Japan.

the mayor's controversial remarks about the 1937 Nanjing Massacre. 'I am very concerned', said Omura, referring to the downturn in the cities' relationship sparked by Kawamura's remarks last Monday that he believes only 'conventional acts of combat', not mass murder and rape of civilians, occurred in Nanjing in 1937 during the Sino-Japanese war".[31]

While China and Japan continue to carry their burden of history (a key reason for the failure to forge a common identity), people-to-people relations have actually made progress in their daily interactions. Japanese NGOs have become more active in China especially in environmental protection.[32] Such Japanese NGOs are guided by idealism and the spirit of cooperation which transcends national boundaries. The number of students, residents and tourists between China and Japan has also increased substantially over the past decade. According to the Japan National Tourism Organization, 1.4 million Chinese tourists visited Japan in 2010.[33] Although numbers dipped due to the March 2011 triple disasters, Chinese tourists rose again by end 2011.[34] According to the Japan Foundation, there were 827,171 students in China, comprising 22.7% of the world's foreign students learning the language in 2009, learning the Japanese language.[35] In the same year, there were 79,082 students from China, comprising 59.6% of total foreign student population, studying in Japan.[36] In 2009, 680,518 Chinese citizens lived in Japan.[37]

In 2011, 3,658,300 Japanese tourists visited China.[38] Increasing numbers of Japanese students are also heading towards Chinese universities while the flow of Japanese students to US colleges is declining. The *Christian Science Monitor* notes: "As the number of Japanese students in US universities drops year by year, the numbers coming to Beijing and other cities are growing by leaps and bounds. … In 1994, 78% of Japanese choosing a foreign school went to a US college. By 2007, that percentage has dropped to 46%, according to Japanese government figures. The proportion of those heading for Chinese universities, meanwhile, climbed from 9% to 24% — more than 18,000".[39] According to the Japanese Ministry of Foreign Affairs, there were 127,282 Japanese residing in mainland China in 2009, second only to the United States (384,411 Japanese) as a place of domicile abroad.[40]

The fact remains: historical controversies and territorial disputes in the East China Sea between China and Japan have not disrupted substantial people-to-people interactions in the areas of tourism, education, work and migration. Harder to answer is whether rising numbers of students, tourists and workers between China and Japan will necessarily lead to a common identity in the long run. Notwithstanding that these are very impressive numbers of people across borders, they still comprise a small percentage of the population of both countries. Indeed, public opinion towards each other is still chilly.

The 2011 Japan Cabinet Office's public opinion survey on diplomacy reveals the emotional gap at the mass level among the Japanese towards China. Although the public outlook towards China may fluctuate from year to year, the trend is that the Japanese public is less friendly

---

[31] "Aichi Governor Urges Nagoya Mayor Kawamura to Restore Ties with Nanjing", *Mainichi Daily News*, 6 March 2012.

[32] See Takahara A, "Japanese NGOs in China" in Lam PE (ed.), *Japan's Relations with China: Facing a Rising Power* (London and New York: Routledge, 2006), U Vyas, "Japan's International NGOs: A Small but Growing Presence in Japan-China Relations", Japan Forum, vol. 22, Issue 3–4, 2010, and R Efird, "Japanese Environmental NGOs in China", *China Development Brief*, 25 January 2007.

[33] "Chinese Tourists to Japan Rises 40% in 2010", *China Daily*, 27 January 2011.

[34] "Chinese Tourists Returning to Japan in Record Numbers", *Jing Daily*, 31 January 2012.

[35] Kezai Koho Center, *Japan 2011: An International Comparison* (Tokyo: Hikari shashin, 2011), p. 98.

[36] Kezai Koho Center, *Japan 2011*, p. 9.

[37] Kezai Koho Center, *Japan 2011*, p. 7.

[38] Japan Tourism Marketing Company, "Statistics of Japanese Tourists Travelling Abroad", 6 March 2012. <http://www.tourism.jp/english/statistics/outbound.php> (accessed 3 July 2012).

[39] "For Study Abroad, More Japanese Prefer Chinese University over US One", *Christian Science Monitor*, 19 May 2010.

[40] Japanese Ministry of Foreign Affairs, *Annual Report of Statistics on Japanese Nationals Overseas* (Tokyo: Ministry of Foreign Affairs, 2010).

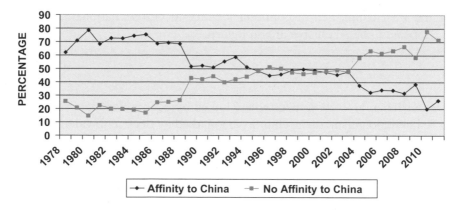

**Figure 1**   Japanese Public Opinion towards China

*Source*: Cabinet Office of Japan, *Public Opinion Survey on Diplomacy*, October 2011.

towards China.[41] Indeed, it is difficult to share a common identity when the public on both sides of the East China Sea do not like their neighbouring country. According to the 2011 Chief Cabinet survey, only 18.8% of the Japanese public had an affinity with China (Figure 1). Conversely, 76.3% felt no affinity with China. The survey also revealed those who did not feel close to China was only 14.1% in 1986 but it shot up to 37.9% in 1989 due to People Liberation Army's (PLA) violent crackdown on unarmed demonstrators in the Tiananmen Incident. Negativity towards China increased to 51.0% in 1996, in part, due to Beijing's missile tests in the Taiwan Strait in 1995 and 1996.

This unfriendly outlook towards China rose during the tenure of Prime Minister Koizumi Junichiro who stubbornly insisted on his annual visits to Yasukuni Shrine, the symbol of Japanese militarism to the Chinese and Koreans. Sino-Japanese relations hit rock bottom during the Koizumi era when there was a vicious cycle of antagonism over historical matters even though both countries enjoyed greater economic interdependency. Unhappy feelings peaked at 71.2% in 2005 and 70.7% in 2006. In September 2009, the DPJ won a historical Lower House Election and displaced the conservative LDP (Liberal Democratic Party) from power at the national level. Then DPJ Prime Minister Hatoyama Yukio sought to anchor Sino-Japanese relations in an East Asian Community (EAC) and maintain equidistance between Washington and Beijing. Bad feelings towards China dipped to 55.2% in 2009. But negative sentiments towards the Chinese mainland skyrocketed to 88.6% in 2010 due to the Chinese fishing boat collision incident near the Senkaku (*Diaoyutai*) islands the same year.

In 2011, Genron NPO and *China Daily* conducted a joint public opinion poll on bilateral sentiments. According this poll, "the ratio of the Chinese general public who had a favorable opinion toward Japan plummeted 9.7 percentage points from 38.3% in the previous poll to 28.6%. … Conversely, the ratio of those who had an unfavorable opinion of Japan surged a large 10 percentage points in the same comparison to 65.9%. … Asked to cite up to three elements that they think are major impediments to a further development of bilateral relations, the largest 63.2% of Japanese and the largest 58.4% of Chinese cite 'the bilateral territorial disputes', indicating that the confrontation off the Senkaku Islands in fall last year had made the general public of both countries more concerned with the territorial issues".[42] Given the negativity of public opinion on

[41] Cabinet Office of Japan, *Public Opinion Survey on Diplomacy*, October 2011. <http://www8.cao.go.jp/survey/h23/h23-gaiko/index.html> (accessed 3 July 2012).

[42] Genron NPO, "On the Results of the Joint Japan-China Joint Opinion Survey", 19 August 2011. < http://www.genron-npo.net/english/index.php?option=com_content&view=article&id=24:on-the-results-of-the-7th-japan-china-joint-opinion-survey&catid=1:advocacy&Itemid=3> (accessed 3 July 2012).

both sides of the East China Sea, a common identity to defuse nationalism and underpin an incipient EAC appears to be an elusive dream indeed.

## Epilogue

Though China and Japan are "conjoined twins" linked by economics, geography, culture and an incipient East Asian regionalism, their relations are marked by deep ambivalence. There are indeed bright spots in this vital relationship: intensifying economic interdependency, ongoing negotiations on bilateral and trilateral FTAs (with South Korea) and joint development in the disputed East China Sea, and an increasing exchange of people at the grassroots in the areas of education, tourism, business and NGO activities. But the relationship is also darkened by conflicting national narratives and historical "mythmaking",[43] intractable territorial disputes, and competing geopolitics (with the deepening of the US-Japan alliance). Simply put, the Chinese and Japanese do not seem to share a common identity or destiny.

Despite the fact that such differences cannot be resolved easily, both countries can still search for areas of cooperation with a spirit of pragmatism, patience and mutual accommodation of each other's core interests. Notwithstanding prickly relations, there is thus far no expectation or desire to go to war with each other. But the absence of war does not necessarily mean genuine peace, historical reconciliation or true friendship. China, as a rising power must be cognisant of the fact that smaller countries, be they Japan or the ASEAN states, are sensitive and protective of their sovereignty and will resent a Middle Kingdom model of international relations not predicated on formal equality. Japan must also reconcile itself to the fact that China will continue to rise in the foreseeable future. The two countries can also seek cooperation within the framework of the ASEAN Plus Three and UNPKO such as cooperation in Southern Sudan. Conceivably, the PLA and Japan's Self Defense Force can build confidence by working alongside future UNPKO wearing the same blue berets for a common mission to build peace. Whether East Asia will enjoy an Asian Renaissance or be rocked by turbulent geo-strategic struggles will, in part, depend on how well and wise the top leaders of China and Japan can manage their critical relationship without a zero-sum mentality.

---

[43] He Y, "National Mythmaking and the Problems of History in Sino-Japanese Relations" in Lam PE (ed.), *Japan's Relations with China: Facing a Rising Power* (London and New York: Routledge, 2006).

# 44

# China and India

## The World is Big Enough for Both

ZHAO Hong*

*China and India are still in trust deficit, which together with a lack of understanding, pose major obstacle to Sino-Indian relations. There is consequently a critical need for grassroots Sino-Indian interaction to promote mutual understanding.*

China and India are emerging economies, and their role in the world economy has been rising. In 2010, the Asia-Pacific region accounted for one-third of global GDP, while over half of the region's GDP came from China and India. Currently, China is the world's largest exporter and second largest importer behind the United States. India's share of global exports had also increased from 0.5% in 1983 to 1.4% in 2010. The share of outward FDI of China and India in total East, South and Southeast Asia FDI outflows rose from 23% in 2007 to 37% in 2008. The 21st century belongs to Asia, and the future of Asia belongs to China and India. Thus how these two powers cooperate with each other will have great impact not only on regional stability but also on the world economy.

However, these two countries are still in trust deficit. It is believed that while India may exaggerate the threat posed by China, China may underestimate Indian concerns and worries. Trust deficit and deficient understanding form the major obstacle to China-India relations. The distrust and tensions have become even more explicit in recent years. For example, on India side, a growing number of Indians now see China as a competitor, if not a rival. The *Pew Global Attitudes Survey* suggested that in 2010, only 34% of Indians held a favourable view of China, and this percentage even decreased to 25% in 2011; in 2010, 40% of Indians viewed their neighbour as a "very serious threat", and this percentage remained at 35% in 2011.[1] More damaging is the perception which is gaining ground in India that China is the only major power

*ZHAO Hong is Visiting Senior Research Fellow at the East Asian Institute, National University of Singapore.
[1]"Key Indicators Database: Opinion of China, Percent Responding Favorable, All Years Measured", *Pew Global Attitudes Project*, at <http://pewglobal.org/database/?indicator=24&survey=128&response=Faborable&mode=table> (accessed 26 June 2012).

that does not accept India as a rising global player that must be accommodated.[2] Due to the lack of sufficient understanding and in-depth exchanges between India and China, misunderstanding and suspicion will inevitably proliferate.[3]

## Different Perspectives

Trust deficit between India and China arises from different perspectives. As both countries emerge, some Indian media coverage of Chinese moves has tended to lead to zero-sum discussions of who might eat the other's lunch. Meanwhile, India's rise and growing role in Asia, especially in East Asia, have also brought forth different perceptions of its rise and impact.

Yet, Chinese public perceptions of India are generally benign. Although China's suspicion of India remains and Chinese elites certainly recognise a competitive dimension in the bilateral relationship, India is always described as a partner or "friendly competitor" rather than as an adversary or rival.[4] According to Chinese scholars, India's rise benefits China by facilitating China's own economic growth and Asian regionalism more generally. Enhanced Sino-Indian economic ties are seen to foster Asian integration, which will help further China's development.[5] Deepened economic ties are also seen to reduce China's and India's dependence on developed countries, as both countries can learn from each other in areas where they lack experience.[6]

Chinese experts analyse that India, like China, needs a peaceful, stable and secure environment for its continued development, as "both China and India face the task of developing the economy and raising people's living standard, thus both countries need a peaceful and stable international environment and a good-neighbourly and friendly peripheral environment".[7] China hopes that closer economic relations and regional integration could mitigate conflicts between these two countries.

In contrast to the Chinese benign attitude, a larger stream of Indian opinion tends to be cautious about China's rise. Some elites within India (particularly in the defence and foreign policy establishments as well as among the political parties) remain suspicious of China and regard China as a potential if not immediate threat, particularly in the context of its relationship with Pakistan, India's long-term rival in South Asia. This response arises whenever India needs to justify its high-profile military expenditure and mainly in the form of reinforcing threat perception in relation to Pakistan and China. The perspective perpetuates because of the 1962 war over the border dispute between China and India that remains seared in India's painful memories. Moreover, intense media attention had generated negative coverage on political-military issues.

Indian decision-makers also acknowledge that India's relationship with China is becoming increasingly contentious. Indian Prime Minister Manmohan Singh had suggested that "China would like to have a foothold in South Asia and we have to reflect on this reality. It's important

---

[2] Harsh, VP, "India Comes to Terms with a Rising China", in *Asia Responds to Its Rising Powers: China and India*, *Strategic Asia 2011–12*, (eds.) AJ Tellis, T Tanner, and J Keough, The National Bureau of Asian Research, Washington, DC, 2011.

[3] In 2008, the number of Indian tourist arrivals to China was only 436,600, accounting for only 3% of total Asian arrivals (14.56 million), while the number of Chinese tourists to India is around 90,000 each year. See National Tourism Administration of PRC, *The Yearbook of China Tourism Statistics*, 2009.

[4] Zhang G, "*Zhong-Yin guanxi de quedingxing he buquedingxing*" (Certainty and Uncertainty in China-India Relations), *Nanya yanjiu (South Asian Studies)*, no. 1, 2010, p. 38.

[5] Cheng R, "*Lun Zhong-Yin zhanglue hezuo huoban guanxi*" (On the China-India Strategic and Cooperative Relationship), *Guoji wenti yanjiu (Journal of International Studies)*, no. 1, 2007, p. 15.

[6] Ma J, "*Zhong-Yin guanxi de fazhan qianjing*" (Prospects for the Development of China-India Relations), *Heping yu fazhan (Peace and Development)*, no. 2, 2007.

[7] Lan J, "*Zhong-Yin dui wai zhanlue yiton yu shuangbian guanxi*" (Similarities and Differences in Chinese and Indian Diplomatic Strategies and their Bilateral Relations), *Waijiao pinglun (Foreign Affairs Review)*, no. 3, 2008.

to be prepared".[8] The Indian defence minister has argued that China's increasing assertiveness is a "serious threat".[9] And a former national security adviser and special envoy to China, M K Narayanan, had openly accused Chinese hackers of attacking his website as well as those of other government departments.[10] The distrust of China escalates at an alarming rate.

On bilateral trade and investment relations, India complains about the trade imbalance that is skewed in favour of China as well as the Chinese government subsidies for Chinese exporters. China, on the other hand, complains about India's proposal to raise tariff and non-tariff barriers on the import of Chinese goods. New Delhi is not only wary of the idea of a free trade agreement (FTA) with Beijing but also Chinese dumping of goods and investments in strategic sectors in India. What India concerns most is the Chinese government's wielding of state power — using such tools as manipulation of exchange, access to credit, and other forms of direct or indirect subsidy to exporting firms — to support Chinese trading firms, many of which are state-owned.

New Delhi is also constantly on high alert over China's investment in some strategic sectors, such as telecommunications, energy and even infrastructure sectors, and has excluded some Chinese firms that are tied to the Chinese Communist Party. There is a general belief in India that Chinese companies engage in economic and military espionage through bribery and political linkages. The Indian government has acknowledged these concerns and issued guidelines for import of military equipment, and foreign direct investments including joint ventures, particularly in infrastructure projects. For example, in May 2009, Bharat Sanchar Nigam Limited (BSNI), the public sector telecommunications giant of India, was advised by the Ministry of Defense "not to award equipment contracts to Huawei and Zhong Xing Telecommunication Equipment Company Limited" in the interest of national security.[11] The Intelligence Bureau, the premier Indian internal intelligence agency, had warned about Huawei and cautioned BSNI should not award contracts to Chinese companies, as these companies are known to have links with the Chinese state and security apparatus, and therefore, their presence in this critical sector has national security implications in a variety ways.[12]

The Chinese's attempts to participate in Indian maritime infrastructure projects, such as ports, have also attracted security concerns. Hutchison Whampoa Limited, a Hong Kong-based conglomerate with close ties to Beijing and operations in port development, container terminal management and infrastructure, was invited to submit a plan to build a container terminal in Mumbai, but the project was held in abeyance. Apparently, security concerns had prevailed and since then the company had decided to stay out of India.[13]

Unlike India, China is more receptive to India's strength in information technology (IT) and Indian companies' participation in the software industry. For instance, Tata Consulting Services Ltd (TCS), India's top IT services provider, has plans to enter the Chinese energy and utility outsourcing industries and increase its staff strength from 1,100 to 5,000 personnel by 2014.[14] TCS began its operation in China in 2002 and by 2006, it had a 66% stake in TCS China.

## Competing for Regional Influence

### Competition in South Asia

Indian Primer Minister Manmohan Singh once said that India's strategic footprint, as "a super regional power", "covers the region bounded by the Horn of Africa, West Asia, Central Asia,

---

[8] "PM Warns on China's South Asia Foothold," *Indian Express*, 7 September 2010.

[9] Rajat P, "Assertive China a Worry, says Antony", *Times of India*, 14 September 2010.

[10] "Chinese Hacked PMO Computers, says Narayanan", *Indian Express*, 19 January 2010.

[11] Vijay S, "Chinese Infrastructure Projects Trouble in India", *China Brief*, vol. X, no. 2, 21 January 2010.

[12] Vijay S, "India Confronts China at Sea", *South Asia Defence and Strategic Review*, 13 November 2011.

[13] Vijay S, op. cit.

[14] Ibid.

Southeast Asia and beyond, to the far reaches of the Indian Ocean".[15] In India's strategic consideration, its rise will firstly further consolidate its status as the leading country in South Asia that has an advantageous edge and influence over the smaller countries in the region. India is therefore conscious of China's intentions and growing influence in South Asia, as well as its ambitions to project its power into the Indian Ocean.

In South Asia, India competes with China in wooing strategically important nations, such as Myanmar, Bangladesh and Sri Lanka which are politically closer to China. India has sought to mend its fences with its neighbours and taken manifold steps to strengthen its economic and political ties with these countries. India has taken significant steps to engage with the government of Bangladesh on a number of issues, including bilateral trade, financial aid and assistance, and cooperation on terrorism among others. The two countries are also developing land and sea transport links including the use of Mongla seaports, and the construction of the Akhuara-Agartala railway line. Similarly, India has acceded to Nepal's long-standing demand for review of the 1950 Indo-Nepal Treaty of Peace and Friendship, which is seen by Nepal as compromising its autonomy in foreign and defence matters.

China's approach is to develop economic and strategic ties with South Asian nations, ensuring that India is surrounded by countries friendly towards China. For example, from 1999 to 2008, China's trade with SAARC (South Asian Association for Regional Cooperation) rose from US$4.2 billion to US$65.6 billion, greatly surpassing India's trade with SAARC members.

With individual countries, China has, over the years, developed extensive links with Bangladesh and has emerged as its largest military supplier. It signed a defence cooperation agreement with Bangladesh in 2002 and has also assisted in developing a missile launching pad near Chittagong port.[16] During the visit of Bangladesh Prime Minister Sheikh Hasina to China in March 2010, China agreed to assist Bangladesh with the US$8.8 billion construction of a deep seaport in Chittagong which New Delhi has long sought but to no avail. The port could give China access to harbours in Chittagong as well as refuelling facilities for China's aircraft. China also envisages Chittagong as a passage for its southern Yunnan province and it is for the same reason that China pushes for the construction of a road link between Chittagong and Kunming.[17]

In March 2007, the Sri Lanka Ports Authority and a Chinese consortium signed an agreement to develop a port at Hambantota which overlooks the access to the Straits of Malacca.[18] Although China has clarified that its backing for the Sri Lankan Hambantota port project is solely commercial and not a strategic plan to project its power in the Indian Ocean region, it is still considered as part of China's so-called "string of pearls" strategy to gain political influence. According to the Indian media, the Hambantota Development Zone agreement between China and Sri Lanka is "significant as China is keen to enhance its influence in the Indian Ocean".[19]

Chinese scholars hold that China's interests and goals in South Asia and Indian Ocean are mainly focussed on economy, aiming at establishing more trade partnerships and ensuring oil shipment security. As economic interests need to be protected and maintained by friendly political relationships and stable security environment, "China's military relationships with

---

[15] Rajat P, "India to 'Arm' itself for Strategic Interests", *The Times of India*, 27 October 2004.

[16] Anand K, "Chinese Puzzle in India-Bangladesh Relations", IDSA Comment, 19 April 2010, at <http://www.idsa.in/idsacomments/ChinesePuzzleinIndia-BangladeshRelations_akumar_190410> (accessed 26 June 2012).

[17] Kriti S, "Hasina's Visit to PRC: In Quest of a Comprehensive Partnership", Institute of Peace and Conflict Studies, 26 March 2010, at <http://www.ipcs.org/article/china/hasinas-visit-to-prc-in-quest-of-a-comprehensive-partnership-3074.html> (accessed 26 June 2012).

[18] "China Funds Sri Lanka Hambantota Port Development Project", at < http://www.marinebuzz.com/2007/11/02/china-funds-sri-lanka-hambantota-port-development-project/ > (accessed 26 June 2012).

[19] "China, Sri Lanka Ink deal to Develop Hambantota", The Hindu, 5 March 2007, at <http://hindu.com/2007/03/05/stories/2007030509100100.htm> (accessed 26 June 2012).

South Asian countries are developed for economic interests, and should not be understood as targeted at India".[20]

Far from moderating Indian fears, Beijing's deepening ties with India's neighbouring states have made New Delhi increasingly concerned over China's activities and intentions. There is a growing recognition in New Delhi that China's rising power has become the single biggest cause of qualitative change in the geopolitical landscape. "India's greatest concern regarding China's rapid expansion in this region is not that Beijing would carry out another 1962-style military invasion, but rather that China would employ the threat of such a military invasion to shift the overall regional balance of power in China's favour."[21] New Delhi wishes to forestall this strategic shift because of the likely adverse implications for India's security and well-being. Thus "the reality of the simultaneous rise of China and India cannot provide support to eliminate conflict of geopolitical interest between the two, instead they may highlight the potential for this conflict".[22]

### India's "Look-East" Strategy

New Delhi's "look-east" policy has several objectives: to build extensive ties and create greater diplomatic space as India extends its naval power in the Indian Ocean; to tap into Southeast Asia's dynamic economic growth; and to secure energy supplies. From American perspective, India develops its relationships with Southeast Asian countries "at the least to avoid Southeast Asia from becoming China's exclusive influential area; at the best to make Southeast Asia become a force containing China, just like China makes Pakistan a force containing India".[23] Although it would be wrong to exaggerate the debate about India's rivalry with China, as India's former foreign secretary Sudhir Devare once stated, "India does not and should not seek closer military ties with Southeast Asia as a bulwark against China or Pakistan and that such an approach would be flawed conceptually as well as disastrous politically",[24] "New Delhi is actually conscious of its limitations in Southeast Asia and therefore wishes to expand its strategic weight in the region while avoiding the creation of overt rivalry with China".[25]

Southeast Asia, geographically situated at the junction of South Asia and East Asia, is traditionally seen by India and China as their respective spheres of influence. China has been a keen player in this region for historical reasons in view of the existence of a large diaspora, trade and investment linkages and protection of its maritime interests. Thus China has worked hard to maintain a peaceful and stable environment on its periphery for its domestic economic construction and it has placed special value on having good neighbourly relations with Southeast Asia. But China is also viewed with a certain degree of fear by some Southeast Asian countries in terms of territorial claims on disputed islands in the South China Sea.

While the rising power of China represents a source of concern, India is seen as another external power for an overall balance of power in the region. For example, Singapore sees India as an essentially benign security partner which, unlike Japan or China, carries no adverse

---

[20] Zhang G, "*Jingzhen yu hezuo: diqu shijiao xia de Zhong-yin guan xi*" (Competition and Cooperation: Sino-India's Relations in Regional Perspectives), Dangdai Yatai (*Contemporary Asia-Pacific*), December 2006, Beijing.

[21] Brahma C, "Assessing India's Reaction to China's Peaceful Development Doctrine", *NBR (National Bureau of Asian Research) Analysis*, Seattle, Washington, vol. 18, no. 5, April 2008.

[22] Zhang L, "*Yindu de zhanlie jueqi yu Zhongyin guanxi: wenti qushi yu yingdui*" (India's Rise and China-India Relations), *Nanya yanjiu jikan (South Asian Studies Quarterly)*, no. 1, 2010.

[23] Frankel, FR and H Harding, *The India-China Relationship: Rivalry and Engagement*, Oxford University Press, New Delhi, 2004, p. 341.

[24] Devare S, *India and Southeast Asia: Toward Security Convergence,* Institute of Southeast Asian Studies, Singapore, 2006.

[25] Mohan CR, "India's Geopolitics and Southeast Asian Security", in *Southeast Asian Affairs 2008*, eds. S Daljit and Tin MM, Institute of Southeast Asian Studies, Singapore.

historical baggage in the region.[26] With Singapore's political support, India began to participate in the ASEAN Post-Ministerial Conferences and ASEAN Regional Forum (ARF) in 1996. After intensive efforts to achieve parity with China, Japan, and South Korea in the ASEAN scheme of partnerships, India became a summit-level partner in 2002. In April 2005, with the strong advocacy of Singapore, Indonesia, and Thailand for India's inclusion in the East Asia Summit (EAS), and endorsement from the ASEAN foreign ministers for India's participation in the EAS, India also got involved in ADMM Plus (ASEAN Defence Ministers Meeting Plus).[27] All of these indicate that India's look-east strategy had reached an important milestone.

Although the Chinese attitude towards India's "eastward expansion" has changed from apprehension to relatively comfortable, China still keeps its guard. India has now secured membership of the ARF, EAS and Asia-Europe Meeting. The FTA India signed with ASEAN in August 2009 was described as the crowning glory of New Delhi's "look-east" policy. Beyond economics, India has extended defence collaboration with Singapore, Australia and Japan, and built emerging strategic relationships with Malaysia, Indonesia and Vietnam. Moreover, India and Japan are deemed to be natural allies. China's accumulation of power has driven India and Japan closer together as "China poses the biggest strategic challenge to both Japan and India, while neither of which is a potential security threat to the other in the near or distant future".[28] The strengthening of strategic relations between India and Japan will have long-term geopolitical consequences, thus increasing strategic uncertainty for China.[29] It is not surprising therefore that China harbours some concern and has tended to view the warming of India-Japan relations as potentially threatening its position in the region.

## From Competition to Cooperation

Despite the military tension, economic relations constitute the most dynamic aspect of bilateral ties between India and China. Bilateral trade between the two countries has grown remarkably over the last decade. The bilateral trade has expanded at a 50% rate during the last six years and is expected to increase by a further 54% in the coming years. China has overtaken the United States as India's largest trading partner. There is little doubt that the overriding framework of economic cooperation, based on expansion of trade, commercial and investment linkages is to remain the most positive factor in Sino-Indian engagement and evolving partnership in the foreseeable future.

In fact, China and India have many reasons and incentives to cooperate with each other. They share the view that the global system has to change to reflect the new distribution of economic and political power, and to give a greater say in global institutions to the developing world. This similarity of outlook has manifested itself at the World Trade Organization, climate change negotiations, international financial institutions and the G20. At the Copenhagen summit on climate change, India and China joined ranks with Brazil and South Africa to negotiate the

---

[26] Brewster, D, "India's Security Partnership with Singapore", *The Pacific Review*, vol. 22, no. 5, December 2009, pp. 597–618.

[27] The inaugural ADMM Plus held in Hanoi on 12 October 2010 was a milestone in ASEAN's history. For the first time, the defence ministers of the 10 ASEAN countries gathered together with their counterparts from the eight dialogue partners, namely Australia, China, India, Japan, Korea, New Zealand, Russia, and the US.

[28] Rajeev S, "India-Japan Ties Poised for Advance as Both Nations Eye China", *The Asia-Pacific Journal*, 6 September 2010.

[29] In May 2006, India and Japan put in place a structured framework of dialogue for defence cooperation and exchanges during the Indian defence minister's visit to Japan. In December 2006, a new chapter opened in India-Japan relations with the establishment of the Japan-India Strategic and Global Partnership. In August 2007, Japanese Prime Minister Abe Shinzo and his Indian counterpart Manmohan Singh unveiled a Roadmap for New Dimensions to the Strategic and Global Partnership. Since then there has been incremental progress in India-Japan bilateral ties and the two nations are engaged in a number of official dialogue mechanisms, covering a range of subjects. See Rajeev S, op. cit.

Copenhagen Accord together with the US, and the four countries have since become known as the BASIC group.

From China's perspective, politically, history is not a big troublesome factor in Sino-Indian relations and border conflicts are being resolved slowly. Top leaders of both countries have achieved consensus on many international issues, like climate change and energy efficiency. Mutual understanding has been improving due to increasing exchanges and interaction at people-to-people level. Both countries can provide useful political leverage to the other. For example, China could use its good relations with Pakistan to help India in its pursuit of energy in Central Asia, while India might use its closer relationship with the United States and Japan to help China on issues, such as the South China Sea disputes.

Economically, both countries share common interests as they are at similar levels of development and face similar challenges, such as poverty, unbalanced development, energy shortage and low energy efficiency. Economic relations constitute the most dynamic aspect of bilateral ties between India and China. Currently, China is India's largest trading partner. Common interests and challenges could increase competition between India and China. However, if both countries could adjust the focus to reinforce cooperation and strengthen economic ties, they will find much more consensus and greater synergism for further partnership.

# 45

# China-South Korea Relations and Implications for China in Global Governance

## Some Notes after 20 Years of Relations

CHOO Jaewoo*

*China-South Korea relations recorded unprecedented development in the history of diplomacy. The interest-driven way China has handled these challenges makes the prospect of China playing a bigger role in global governance questionable.*

More often than not, we tend to see China as a "normal" society for its striking economic achievements, a society not much different from ours by appearance — capitalistic, free and non-communist. The projected images we receive from Chinese cosmopolitan lifestyle, skyscrapers, dynamic stock market, bustling traffic and alike certainly perpetuate illusion. We are therefore led to expect China to behave in a "normative" way on the diplomatic front. We also expect China to be more active in global governance, let alone regional governance. In the post-Cold War period, we have been convincing ourselves that China would show a similar resilience in the world of diplomacy and governance that it has in adapting to globalisation and interdependence. To our dismay, however, China has yet to show such resilience. From political perspectives, many have attributed China's failure to meet our expectation to the extant differences in Chinese political system, ideology and others alike. Admittedly, we, especially those from (neo-) liberalism school of thought, once had an illusion that the consequences of China's opening-up and subsequent embracement of international order and institutions, combined with globalisation effects, would marginalise the effect of political differences to the extent that it would be a non-factor to China's participation in global governance.

*CHOO Jaewoo is Associate Professor of Chinese foreign policy at Kyung Hee University, Korea, and is currently a Visiting Associate Professor in the Sam Nunn School of International Affairs, Georgia Tech, Atlanta, GA, USA.

However, we are often proved wrong. It is largely because politics does matter! Politics matters because it functions as the foundation on which a state's external behaviour is rooted and extended. Such a foundation, embedded with shared values and behaviour, is expected to facilitate China to be more compliant with international norms and rules that were set, notwithstanding diplomatic protocols. And it looks increasingly lacking in the Chinese world of diplomacy. China's external behaviour often fails to comply in part because its foreign policy is interest-driven, if not ideology-driven, and in part because it is principle-oriented. In other words, China has been expected to accrue more of the shared values from its embracement of international order and institutions. Nevertheless, China does not seem to have fully embraced, if not presenting its own existing values underlying international norms, rules, order and institutions, which are built to respect and protect such values as freedom, democracy and human rights.

## Strong Economic Ties but Bumpy Political Relations

When the study of China's external relations and its role in global governance is touched upon, what this section of the book themed external relations and global governance focusses on, there is no greater storytelling than that of China's relations with South Korea. Despite the short history in their bilateral relations since normalisation in 1992, China-South Korea relations have over the years played out to be China's own testing ground for its prospective global governance challenges. The bilateral relationship has achieved unprecedented developments in both scope and range of every aspect that no other bilateral ties come close in comparison. More than 830 weekly flights, for instance, are shuttling more than six million visitors per annum between the two countries. As of 2011, South Korea was China's fourth largest export market and second largest import market, only second to Japan. Excluding Hong Kong, China is also the third largest trading nation, only lagging behind the United States and Japan. The total trade volume is expected to surpass US$40 billion in 2015 from US$25 billion in 2011. More than 62,450 Korean students are currently studying in China and there are also about 86,000 Chinese students in Korea. One better way to understand the significance of the figures is reflected in America's pursuit of a similar endeavour. In 2009, the Obama administration concluded an agreement with the Chinese counterpart to send 100,000 American students to China in the subsequent five years. South Korean President Lee Myong-bak has had the most frequent meetings with his Chinese counterpart, Hu Jintao, every year since his inauguration in 2008. In 2008 alone, for instance, he met President Hu on eight different occasions.

The aforementioned developments were unforeseen after normalisation. Instead, the world had a high and immediate expectation: a greater window of opportunities for Korean reunification with China's dual recognition of both Koreas. Such expectation arose with the achievement of half-fulfilled "cross-recognition". The so-called "cross-recognition" was one of the ideas that were very much contemplated by the two Koreas and the surrounding powers during the Cold War period as one of the most viable, conducive ways to unification. The gist of the idea is, if the surrounding powers were to recognise both Koreas, the efficacy would be twofold. Not only would antagonistic relationship be expected to improve substantially, withering the extant tension therein, it was also thought to be one of the shortcuts to reunification. By improving relations between former adversaries, cross-recognition was expected to heighten the prospect and raise the chance of a peace treaty to replace the existing armistice, a long-standing logic behind enhanced peace and stability of the Korean peninsula. By realising the transition from armistice to peace treaty, a peace system is expected to come into existence to guarantee the implementation of the treaty, thereby paving the path to reunification. Boosted confidence and trust through the peace system based on peace accord and mutual recognition was the most passionate and romanticised scenario, just like a "love-at-first-sight" story, for those that have longed for a reunification. To the dismay of many in South Korea, China apparently has yet to rise to the occasion as a unification force. Likewise, its value as a unification force is not as highly appreciated as it once was. China is now perceived by many South Koreans as the greatest impedance to the unification cause. South Korea's disappointment and disillusionment came much sooner starting with the first North Korean nuclear crisis in 1993.

During the entire crisis, China adopted and persisted with a crisis-averse attitude, and deferred the duty of resolving conflicts to those directly involved parties. Since then, South Korea began to experience and witness security challenges and political anxieties in manoeuvring the bilateral relationship, a stark contrast despite the aforementioned quantum-leap achievements that had boosted confidence and trust between South Korea and China. Political challenges and anxieties have burgeoned in terms of not only intensity but also all spectrums of non-economic and non-civilian sectors. The trend continues into the 21st century. It started in 2002 with China's undertaking of the "Northeast Rejuvenating Project" (*Dongbeifuxinggongcheng*) or "Northeast Project" (*Dongbeigongcheng*). From China's perspectives, one of the objectives of the project was to resurrect the ancient history of the north-eastern region of China. It was however done in a "money laundering" fashion that re-possessed and re-processed the history of the peripheral states and incorporated it into its own history to legitimatise the traditional existence and development of its north-eastern region. South Koreans can instead only perceive the project to be an effort to distort their ancient history, instigating emotional debates and provoking nationalism of both countrymen. China simply shunned South Korea's protests, alas, on of the basis of non-interference of domestic affairs principle because the history at stake is defined as China's own history. Thereafter, the bilateral relationship has been bumpy at the governmental level.

## Rise of Nationalistic Sentiments

While challenges continued to arise during the Chinese project from 2002 till its completion in 2006, new strain emerged during the 2008 Beijing Olympics torch relay held in downtown Seoul where overzealous Chinese supporters and Korean spectators ended up in physical confrontation. China blamed South Korea's authority for not providing sufficient security and the South Korean spectators for being the instigators. It was however later learnt that the Chinese embassy in Korea transported most of the Chinese students studying in Korea to the relay sites and provided them with Chinese flags and poles, and other rallying gears but no Korean flags. According to normative diplomatic protocol practices, Korean flags should have been provided by the Chinese embassy. Aggravated in part by the embassy's diplomatic slip, the hyper-patriotic behaviour of Chinese students was not well received by the South Korean public.

In 2009, China's defensive negotiating posture on the resolution against North Korea for its second nuclear test undermined South Korea's confidence in its nuclear-free peninsula campaign. Although China, in the end, agreed to adopt a new resolution on the North, its endeavour in the negotiation discourse prompted South Korea to appreciate its alliance with the United States more. In 2010, China's belated expression of condolence to South Korea for the loss of lives in the sinking of the *Cheonan* vessel in March and the shelling of *Yeonpyeong* Island in November totally shattered the confidence South Koreans had in China. In 2011, the failure of the Chinese government to recognise the seriousness of illegal fishing activities by Chinese fishermen in South Korean waters angered the South Koreans. The arrest of Chinese fishermen by the South Korean coastguard unfortunately resulted in the fatal stabbing of a coastguard officer. In March 2012, China's claim of the right to patrol near the waters of a rock outcropping known as "Ieodo" (*Suyazhao*) prompted South Korea, which also stakes a claim of sovereignty, to cast serious doubts on the true intentions behind China's blue water naval scheme. China's move to snub the South Korean government's quest for clarification on the Chinese remarks and negotiation on overlapping exclusive economic zone (EEZ) reinforced South Korea's scepticism on Chinese maritime ambition. These events and incidents led to a common consequence — that is, triggering the nationalistic sentiments of both Chinese and South Koreans, and undermining South Korea's confidence in China.

## The North Korean Factor

Out of these incidents, China's response to the sinking of the *Cheonan* has raised many eyebrows to date. Some observers are sympathetic to China's stance from the perspective of alliance politics dilemma because of the North Korea factor. China as a patron state had no other choice but to keep its stance as neutral as possible, thereby reducing the risk of losing its North Korean ally. It does not want to be seen as taking the side of the North's adversaries or been trapped in something it does not desire for the sake of alliance. However, neither would be the case for China because North Korea has nowhere to defect to, unless the North's relations with others including the United States and Japan normalise, or that the costs of entrapment simply outweigh the potential gains China can garner. Hence, alliance politics dilemma does not fit into this scenario. Others attribute it to China's traditional preferences in dealing with crises, either taking a crisis-averse attitude like it did in the first North Korean nuclear crisis in 1993 and partially in the early phase of the second one in 2002, deferring the responsibility of solving a crisis to involved parties only and opposing foreign intervention even for mediation purposes.

Nevertheless, China's action still perplexes many. The perplexity arises not because outsiders fail to comprehend China's alliance politics dilemma or China's conservativeness in dealing crises. It is more of a question germane to China whether it manifests due humanity to tragedies and misfortunes of other countries. Supposedly, China and South Korea are strategic partner countries as declared in 2008. When the sinking of *Cheonan* occurred on 26 March 2010, it was natural for South Koreans to expect an immediate announcement of condolences from Beijing. Beijing, however, took almost a month to express concern and regrets for the loss incurred by an unfortunate incident to its "strategic partner". When the first message came on 20 April, it sounded more apologetic on the occurrence of the incident per se, conveying mere expression of "deep regrets".[1] It failed to deliver its condolences on the 46 lives lost aboard in defence of their nation or showed any empathy for the grief experienced by its strategic partner South Korea. China instead remained firm on its demand that the investigation process be "scientific and objective", and the related parties keep their poise and show restraint. Simultaneously, China repeatedly insisted on the resumption of the Six-Party talks, the prevention of further escalation in tension in the region and the upholding of the non-proliferation principle on the Korean peninsula.[2] It was only on 20 May that China finally expressed "condolences for the victims of the *Cheonan* incident".

In his defining article of China's status as a regional power instead of global power, Wang Jisi, regarded as an authority in the Chinese school of international relations, defended Chinese external behaviour as being defined by geographical proximity. Wang argues that China is not, and does not act as, a global power yet because it does not proactively accommodate many of the global interests that are too distant in geographical terms for them to evoke Chinese conscientiousness. Rather, China adopts a seemingly indifferent attitude when addressing global issues that are neither in direct conflict with its national interests nor in its geographical peripheries. Instead, Wang claims that China is more attentive and caring to regional affairs because Chinese national interests are more directly affected by the consequences of regional developments. Wang, therefore, defines China as a regional power and not a global actor.[3] However, China's behaviour as observed earlier proves contrary to his claim. What China has shown over the years, associated with its behaviour on regional conflicts whereby its national interests are directly affected, is not fulfilling Wang's claims.

To Beijing, China's interests may not always be directly challenged and affected by these situations, even if they fall within geographical proximity. It is perhaps because the interest that

[1] Chinese Foreign Ministry Spokesperson's Press Briefing, 20 April 2010, at <http://www.fmprc.gov.cn/chn/pds/wjdt/fyrbt/t683586.htm> (accessed 23 April 2010).

[2] Chinese Foreign Ministry Spokesperson's Press Briefing, 20 May 2010, at <http://www.fmprc.gov.cn/chn/pds/wjdt/fyrbt/t695931.htm> (accessed 22 May 2010).

[3] Wang J, "China's Changing Role in Asia," The Atlantic Council of the United States, January 2004.

China is most concerned with is closely related to preserving the status quo of power. As long as the status quo is maintained, China may well be contented. In the same vein, those interests outside the periphery may not and cannot affect the status quo in its periphery. It is, therefore, safe to argue that China's national interests are structural, structure-based and very well guided by one of the most salient foreign policy principles that China has long upheld — the Five Principles of Peaceful Coexistence. These principles were founded on the objective of creating a peaceful world of countries with different political system and ideologies. The goal can be achieved if states fully implement and practise these principles — mutual respect for each other's sovereignty and territorial integrity; mutual non-aggression; mutual non-interference in domestic affairs; equality and mutual benefit; and peaceful coexistence — in their external relationship. Although China advocates how relations between states should be governed, it fails to offer a guiding value. Rather, China prescribes a foregone conclusion, i.e. peaceful coexistence, precluding such endeavours as challenging others' independence and autonomy.

China's attitude towards South Korea is often affected and constrained by such a prescription. There is a striking pattern of behaviour on the rise on the two fronts: sovereign rights on territorial integrity and non-interference, which have become the almighty and potent weapon that can fend off all external calls for negotiation and snub the outside world. On territorial disputes between China and South Korea, for instance on the issue of negotiation venue, China often would not facilitate it if it is a South Korean initiative. More often than not, China refuses requests for clarification and verification of issues outside of the negotiation venue. Also, in cases where Seoul picks up certain remarks presumably from Beijing and would like further clarification, China will simply reject any form of information exchange. Furthermore, China often ignores issues associated with North Korea and its people on the grounds of non-interference. South Korea and other countries in the world feel indignant whenever China does not want to be explicit about its position on North Korea. The most recent example is China's response to international demands not to repatriate North Korean refugees if they are arrested in China. China persistently refuses to respond to any external enquiries and reiterates its statement that it handles the matter based on domestic law, international law and humanitarian law. Members at the meeting of United Nations High Commissioner for Refugees (UNHCR) from 12 to 13 March 2012 condemned the repatriation of 31 arrested refugees earlier in the month.

## China's Role in Global Governance

The Chinese handling of the aforementioned series of incidents indeed raises the question of the suitability of China's participation in global governance. That is, notwithstanding its assertiveness, how will China's seemingly irresponsible and uncooperative behaviour be translated into global governance? Before answering this question, it becomes more imperative to ask why China behaves in such fashion. If China continues to behave in this manner, especially in its dealings with smaller neighbouring states, one will have to question China's eligibility and capability to be a partner in global governance. Is China ready yet?

Perhaps the answer can be inferred from China's behaviour in its relations with South Korea, which may well be pessimistic. The Sino-South Korean relationship is a microcosm of global affairs. There is no better showcase that fully reflects the state of world affairs today, from traditional security issues (e.g. military confrontation against ally and nuclear proliferation problems) to non-traditional security issues (e.g. environment and North Korean refugees), from economic conflicts to territorial disputes, from nationalism to potential ethnic-related problems (e.g. the Korean Chinese minority), from issues of distortion of history to public goods problems, from humanitarian to human rights to legal issues, and from incidents of misfortunate to military provocations. From South Korean perspectives, China's behaviour in dealing with these conflicting issues is at best perceived as non-compliance with international norms and rules. China has been acting, to a large degree, irresponsibly in some cases and indifferently in others, while also condescending on many different occasions. If China's attitude is bred from arrogance because of its newly acquired status as a regional power, its long-held "affirmative action" on international relations is self-refuting. That is, all states are considered equal regardless of their size, ideology and system. The way China has shut out South Korea's call for peaceful resolution contradicts the diplomatic principles it has always advocated. Conversely, these principles are often manipulated as diplomatic tools to fend off outcries from smaller neighbouring states.

If there is a way to explain Chinese behaviour, it has to be the absence of "value" in its conduct of external relations or diplomacy. Instead, China places emphasis on the importance of principles, ideologies, strategies and interests in external relations. Furthermore, Beijing has become more assertive in relating its national interest to "common interest" (*gongtongliyi*) of the world after making a shift from ideology to national interest in its foreign policy objectives. Regardless of how China defines its national interests in any tangible terms, Chinese foreign policy and relations are clearly interest-driven. In anarchy, interest-driven external behaviour is subject to structural constraint of the international system. One of the best viable ways for China to overcome structural constraint is to reorientate its behaviour from interest-driven to value-oriented. China must emancipate from the dictation of its own interests as manifested in its behaviour, and adopt and apply values that are recognised and accepted by the world in foreign relations.

With China's rising international profile, it is expected to assume a leading role in global governance; however, without embracing the basis of governance — the "value" — it simply would not be able to fulfil its role. The principles, ideologies, strategies and interests that China upholds may have some intrinsic values, but they are not value-based or value-driven. They are rather a condominium of survival strategies. The underlying premise of global governance is built on values that are mutually respected, accepted and strived for by all members of the international community. China's overemphasis on interests and principles, if not ideology and strategy as in the past, is a self-proclaimed denial to accommodate rules and norms embedded in the foundation of today's global governance. China's external behaviour towards South Korea thus far is not motivated by values. Instead, it relied on principles and interests which lack universal values — the core objective and foundation that should be embedded in the entire notion of governance. China's continued compliance with a set of principles and preference for national interests over values will only hinder and have a detrimental effect on its aspiration for greater participation in global governance in the future.

# 46

# Comrades No More

## Beijing's Evolving North Korea Policy

YUAN Jingdong*

*Beijing's strategic objectives of maintaining stability on the Korean Peninsula and advancing its security interests in Northeast Asia are the keys to understanding Chinese policy towards North Korea and the nuclear issue.*

China has strengthened its relationship with North Korea over the past few years, especially after the late Kim Jong-il's debilitating stroke in 2008 and the dramatic events that took place in 2010. It refused to openly condemn the North regarding the sinking of the *Cheonan* and the Yeonpyeong shelling, and strongly protested US-South Korean joint military exercises in the Yellow Sea, significantly estranging its relationship with Seoul. Beijing marked the 60th anniversary of entry into the Korean War, with major ceremonial events and high-ranking military delegation despatched to Pyongyang. China has become North Korea's key food and energy supplier, and its largest trading partner. Meanwhile, Beijing claims it has limited influence over Pyongyang; indeed North Korea's provocative behaviour and brinkmanship have often embarrassed and proven deeply frustrating to its Chinese patron, and drawn Seoul, Tokyo and Washington ever closer.

China's North Korea policy must be placed in the broader contexts of its interest in a denuclearised Korean Peninsula, in particular in that it averts a possible nuclear domino effect in Northeast Asia; a stable China-Democratic People's Republic of Korea (DPRK) relationship, not from an ideological perspective but more from one of securing a strategic buffer; the growing ties between Beijing and Seoul, and China's views of the longer term prospects of a unified Korea and the consequences for China's security; and the complexity of Sino-American relations with both regional and global implications.

This chapter aims to provide a brief overview of both the complexity of the North Korean-Chinese relations since the end of the Cold War and the nuclear issue as it has deeply impacted US

*YUAN Jingdong is Associate Professor and Acting Director, Centre for International Security Studies, University of Sydney.

non-proliferation policy and regional stability, and China's perspectives and policy debates on this issue as a rising power. It outlines and analyses Chinese foreign, security and economic policies towards North Korea, and how these policies advance and influence China's strategic interests and regional security posture. Key to these analyses will be an understanding of the dynamics of cooperation and competition between Beijing and Washington on the North Korean nuclear crisis and its impact on the wider bilateral relationship and regional power relations.

## China's Changing North Korea Policy

China has maintained a close relationship with North Korea for over six decades. When the Korean War broke out in 1950, Chairman Mao overruled most of his close advisers and top generals, and dispatched the Chinese People's Volunteers across the Yalu River in support of Kim Il-sung, even losing his own son in the three-year war.[1] The subsequent close ties between the two communist countries were bound in ideologies, personal friendships, common security interests and threats they both faced. In 1961, China and North Korea signed the Treaty of Friendship, Cooperation and Mutual Assistance, committing both sides to the assistance of each in case of military attacks by a third country.[2]

With rapprochement between China and the United States in the early 1970s, the Northeast Asian strategic landscape began to change. Towards the late 1980s, with over more than a decade of economic reforms and opening up, Beijing began to subtly modify its past rigid attitudes towards South Korea, from refusal to recognition of the country, to acquiescence and encouraging bilateral commercial interactions, and to endorsement of both Koreas' admission to the United Nations in 1991. The early 1990s began a period of Beijing-Pyongyang estrangement. The two countries' fundamental strategic interests began to drift further apart. For China, economic developments and prosperity required deepening reform and further integration into the global economy; acceptance of and compliance with existing international norms and rules; and maintenance of stable relationships with major powers, as well as a stable and peaceful regional security environment. Pyongyang, however, continues to stick to its rigid feudal-socialist ideologies, especially its *juche* principle, regime survival, and increasing paranoia and sense of isolation and desertion.[3] In August 1992, against Pyongyang's entreaty and protests, Beijing formally established diplomatic relations with Seoul. The old "lip-and-teeth" relationship based on shared strategic interests has since evolved to one of ad hoc, utilitarian patron-client relationship, with growing asymmetry in responsibilities and interdependence.[4]

Beijing's new adventure into a "two-Korea" policy has always had to confront three major challenges. The first has to do with Pyongyang's provocation and brinkmanship that undermine Chinese security interests. North Korea's nuclear and missile could induce Japan and South Korea to rethink their nuclear options; US-led missile defences in the region in turn threaten China's limited strategic nuclear deterrence. Second, Pyongyang's refusal to undertake economic reforms despite Chinese entreaties and its continued pursuit of the *songun* and *juche* policies, in conjunction with the failed central planning and natural disasters, have turned North Korea into an economic basket case and led to growing illicit migration to China. Third, how to balance between short-term

---

[1] Sergei, G, JW Lewis and Xue L, *Uncertain Partners: Stalin, Mao, and the Korean War*, Stanford: Stanford University Press, 1993; and Chen J, *China's Road to the Korean War*, New York: Columbia University Press, 1994.

[2] Lee CJ, *China and Korea: Dynamic Relations*, Stanford: Hoover Institute, 1996.

[3] Snyder, S, *China's Rise and the Two Koreas*, Boulder, CO: L Rienner, 2009; Hundt D, "China's 'Two Koreas' Policy: Achievements and Contradictions", *Political Science*, vol. 62, no. 2, December 2010, pp. 132–145.

[4] Qian Q, *Waijiao shiji* (*Ten Stories of* a Diplomat), Beijing: *Shijie zhishi chubanshe*, 2003; Andrew Scobell, *China and North Korea: From Comrades-in-Arms to Allies at Arm's Length*, Carlisle, PA: Strategic Studies Institute, U.S. Army War College, March 2004.

policy imperatives and long-term strategic considerations remains the most daunting challenge for Beijing in an environment of multiple and even competing interests at home and equally complex geopolitical landscape involving other major powers in the region.

Beijing's ultimate policy objective is to ensure peninsular stability, including regime survival in the North, driven largely by its long-standing appreciation of the importance of North Korea as a strategic buffer.[5] This has led China to strengthen political ties with and offered more economic assistance to North Korea in recent years, in anticipation of a major leadership transition given Kim Jong-il's deteriorating health. The top Chinese leadership swiftly endorsed Kim Jong-un as the successor after Kim Jong-il passed away.[6] However, North Korea's strategic importance to China also provides Pyongyang with a trump card in its dealings with Beijing — China is averse to seeing the North's deteriorating situation since this would in turn affect Chinese interests, hence giving it a source of asymmetrical power.[7] In fact, while North Korea's economic reliance on China over the past decade has grown significantly, and indeed Chinese food and energy assistance has been crucial to Pyongyang, Beijing's influence remains limited, let alone its ability to coerce the North.[8]

One case in point is Beijing's effort to encourage and push for limited economic reforms from the DPRK. This would help alleviate the hardship endured by the North Koreans, which is a potential trigger for social and political instabilities; change the international perception of the North Korean regime, making the country attractive to foreign investment; reduce China's burden of economic and financial assistance, and move China-DPRK economic relations from one based on Chinese grants-in-aid to new formats of investment and development of mutual benefits. So far, there has been little indication that Pyongyang has taken Beijing's advice. The regime has continued to depend on highly authoritarian and illicit methods to keep control and for survival. All told, Chinese efforts to induce North Korea to embark on a reform path have so far failed. And it is not clear if the new Kim Jong-un regime will, if ever, contemplate tackling the country's economic woes any time soon.[9]

## Beijing's Role in Dealing with the Nuclear Issue

North Korea's nuclear programme dates back to the 1960s with assistance from the Soviet Union.[10] In 1985 Pyongyang signed the Non-Proliferation Treaty (NPT) but it was not until 1992 that it accepted the International Atomic Energy Agency (IAEA) safeguards provisions. At that time the IAEA inspections raised suspicions about a covert North Korean nuclear weapons programme. A crisis ensued, with the North threatening to withdraw from the NPT and the Clinton administration preparing for military actions. The October 1994 US-DPRK Agreed Framework, which froze North Korea's plutonium-based nuclear programme, temporarily headed off further escalation and brought the crisis under control. The implementation of the Agreed Framework, which included the provision of two light-water reactors to North Korea, encountered various political, financial

[5] Horowitz, S and Ye M, "Keeping Instability at Bay: China's Post-Deng Leaders and the Korean Crisis", *Korea Observer*, vol. 39, no. 4, Winter 2008, pp. 603–629.

[6] Chiao H, "Amid N. Korea Succession, China Makes Push for Stability", *Washington Post*, 5 January 2012.

[7] Kim SS and Lee TH, "Chinese-North Korean Relations: Managing Asymmetrical Interdependence", in *North Korea and Northeast Asia*, eds. SS Kim and Lee TH, Lanham, Rowman & Littlefield Publishers, Inc., 2002, pp. 111–112.

[8] Lee JJ, "To Fuel or Not to Fuel: China's Energy Assistance to North Korea", *Asian Security,* vol. 5, no. 1, January 2009, pp. 45–72; JM Kim, "North Korea's Reliance on China and China's Influence on North Korea", *Korean Journal of Defense Analysis, vol.* 23, no. 2, June 2011, pp. 257–271.

[9] Glaser, B, S Snyder and J Park, "Keeping an Eye on an Unruly Neighbor: Chinese Views of Economic Reform and Stability in North Korea", Washington, D.C., United States Institute of Peace, 2008; Chestnut, S, "Illicit Activity and Proliferation: North Korean Smuggling Networks", *International Security* 32:1, Summer 2007, pp. 80–111.

[10] Walter, CC (Jr.), "North Korea's Quest for Nuclear Weapons: New Historical Evidence", *Journal of East Asian Studies,* vol. 10, no. 1, February 2010, pp. 127–154.

and technical obstacles. By the time President George W Bush came into office in 2001, the agreement was in limbo and the administration was determined to take a very different approach to dealings with North Korea from that adopted by the Clinton administration. In October 2002, the Bush administration confronted North Korea, charging that it had been engaged in a covert uranium enrichment programme. After admitting to the programme (this admission was later withdrawn), Pyongyang kicked out the IAEA inspectors, withdrew from the NPT, reactivated the Yongbyon reactor and began reprocessing plutonium. The Agreed Framework collapsed and the second nuclear crisis began.[11]

While the international community was by and large in consensus that the Korean Peninsula should remain free of nuclear weapons, there was no agreement on how to get there. They were confronted with a most serious challenge — never had a member state withdrawn from the NPT.[12] The Bush administration was adamant that Pyongyang should not be rewarded for its bad behaviour; if anything, it should suffer the consequences of violating the norms and rules of the international nuclear nonproliferation regime. For these reasons, Washington steadfastly refused to engage in any bilateral negotiation with the North and demanded that Pyongyang give up its nuclear programme first. Vice President Cheney reportedly remarked that "we don't negotiate with evil, we defeat it".[13] China, however, stated its positions on the issue as the following: (i) peace and stability on the Korean Peninsula should be preserved; (ii) the peninsula should remain nuclear-free; and (iii) the dispute should be resolved through direct diplomatic dialogue between the United States and the DPRK.[14]

The Bush administration's hawkish position, including the threat of preemptive strikes, did not deter Pyongyang from adopting equally hard-line positions. Indeed, the US invasion of Iraq in April 2003 only made North Korea more determined to acquire nuclear weapons capabilities, concerned that it would be the next target of regime change.[15] To prevent further escalation, Beijing shifted its position from that of a detached on-looker to that of a more engaged party. The Chinese began to exert pressure on North Korea as well as to seek to persuade Washington to show flexibility and greater realism about the situation. Chinese frustration with the North Koreans came to a boiling point when, in a rare movement, Beijing cut off oil supplies to North Korea for three days consecutively in late March 2003, claiming technical problems.[16] Beijing also indicated to Pyongyang that it would only guarantee its security if Pyongyang met three conditions: no nukes, no threats to South Korea and Japan, and have direct dialogue with the United States.[17] The first trilateral meeting between China, North Korea and the United States was subsequently held in Beijing in April 2003.

The Six-Party Talks were initiated by the Chinese in August 2003. The Bush administration continued to refuse engaging in bilateral negotiation with North Korea and insisted that the nuclear issue was a multilateral one and therefore required all the affected parties to be involved. Whatever

[11] Wit, J, D Poneman and R Galluci, *Going Critical: The First North Korean Nuclear Crisis*, Washington, DC, Brookings Institution Press, 2004; Funabashi Y, *The Peninsula Question: A Chronicle of the Second Korean Nuclear Crisis*, Washington, DC, Brookings Institution Press, 2007.

[12] Bunn, G and J Rhinelander, "The Right to Withdraw from the NPT: Article X is Not Unconditional", *Disarmament Diplomacy* No. 79, April/May 2005.

[13] Strobel, WP, "Vice President's Objections Blocked Planned North Korean Nuclear Talks", Knight Ridder Washington Bureau, 20 December 2003.

[14] Snyder, S, "The Second North Korean Nuclear Crisis: Assessing U.S. and DPRK Negotiation Strategies", *Pacific Focus,* vol. 22, no. 1, Spring 2007, pp. 49–52; Bates, G and A Thompson, "A Test for Beijing: China and the North Korean Nuclear Quandary", *Arms Control Today,* vol. 33, no. 4, 2003, pp. 12–14.

[15] Litwak, RS, "Living with Ambiguity: Nuclear Deals with Iran and North Korea", *Survival*, 50:1, February-March 2008, pp. 91–118.

[16] Epstein, GA, "From Beijing, Stern Words for an Uneasy Ally", *Baltimore Sun*, 28 March 2003; Watts, J, "China Cuts Oil Supply to North Korea", *The Guardian*, 1 April 2003.

[17] Cheong C, "China Offers North Korea Security from Any US Attack", *The Straits Times*, 3 May 2003.

negotiated outcome emerged from the talks would then make Pyongyang accountable to not just Washington but all the parties participating in the process.[18] As the host of the talks, Beijing laid out its positions as follows: (i) denuclearisation; (ii) peninsular peace and stability; (iii) dialogue and peaceful resolution of dispute; and (iv) concerns of all parties should be fairly addressed.[19]

Beijing's more active diplomacy in the second nuclear crisis has been driven by its calculation of the larger strategic implications as well as the imminent security threats. First and foremost is to seek a non-nuclear Korean Peninsula. The implications of a nuclear peninsula are obvious. It would result in more resolute US responses, including the military options, and hence have very negative effect on regional peace and stability.[20] In addition, the domino effect will also be severe and threaten China's security interests. Second is to maintain peace and stability on the peninsula, specifically, to promote conditions that would be conducive to the resolution of the crisis and to prevent elements that could cause further escalation to would-be China's long-term interests. These in turn would require patient diplomacy, consideration of legitimate concerns of all parties involved, and the Six-Party Talks to arrive at mutually acceptable solutions step by step. Third is to seek the opportunities provided by the crisis and enhance consultation with the United States and other parties; China should also oppose using the military option to achieve denuclearisation of the peninsula and foil US efforts for strategic expansion in the region. Finally, China should exercise its influence to affect the direction of developments on the peninsula, including eventual unification and to shape them in ways that enhance, rather than undermine, China's security.[21]

However, while the process for engaging North Korea was put in place and both China and the United States found common grounds for continued cooperation and consultation, significant differences remain between the two countries over specific approaches and long-term objectives, which could in future strain bilateral relations.[22] Meanwhile, China's influence over Kim Jong-il may be limited. Neither is Beijing willing to use that limited influence—threatening to cut down or even withdraw food and energy supplies — to force Pyongyang on the nuclear issue. What other countries may consider as a viable lever — the cut-off of economic aid — could well threaten Beijing's core security interests: the preservation of the North Korean regime. Indeed, the immediate security concerns aside, China's attitude towards the Korean issue must also be seen in a broader strategic context. One consideration is the survival of the North Korean regime and the maintenance of a strategic buffer zone. China is wary of North Korea's reckless behaviour and certainly does not want the nuclear crisis to get out of control lest it leads to serious consequences. At the same time, Beijing believes that Pyongyang's nuclear gamble stems from its acute sense of insecurity and vulnerability, and hence any resolution must address this issue. This may explain why China has continued to provide economic assistance to North Korea. In this context, continuing to support North Korea is no longer driven by the need to prod up an ideological bedfellow but rather by China's long-term strategic interests. China therefore will be opposed to, or at least not support, any measures that could precipitate the collapse of the North.[23]

Whether or not such a policy stance has really served Chinese interests and can be sustained remain debatable. Indeed, North Korea's second nuclear test in 2009 touched off heated debates

---

[18] Rozman, G, "The North Korean Nuclear Crisis and U.S. Strategy in Northeast Asia", *Asian Survey,* vol. 47, no. 4, July/August 2007, pp. 601–621.

[19] Cody, E and A Faiola, "North Korean Ends 'Candid' China Visits", *Washington Post,* 22 April 2004.

[20] Song J, "Understanding China's Response to North Korea's Provocations", *Asian Survey,* vol. 51, no. 6, November/December 2011, pp. 1134–1155.

[21] Lee DR, "China's Policy and Influence on the North Korea Nuclear Issue: Denuclearization and/or Stability of the Korean Peninsula"? *Korean Journal of Defense Analysis,* vol. 22, no. 2, June 2010, pp. 163–181.

[22] Glaser, BS and Wang L, "North Korea: the Beginning of a China-U.S. Partnership"? *The Washington Quarterly,* vol. 31, no. 3, Summer 2008, pp. 165-80; Roy, D, "The North Korea Crisis in Sino-US Relations", *The Journal of Comparative Asian Development,* vol. 10, no. 2, December 2011, pp. 281–304.

[23] Gill, *China's North Korea Policy*; Lee S, "China's North Korean Foreign Policy Decoded", YaleGlobal Online, 28 July 2011.

within the Chinese security analyst community. Some argue that Beijing should no longer protect Pyongyang; others maintain that for strategic reasons, China has to remain cool-headed and not be distracted or frustrated with North Korea's bad behaviour. From an official standpoint, as far as this can be inferred from the Chinese government's responses to the sinking of *Cheonan* and the shelling of Yeonpyeong Island by North Korea, which by and large have been carefully managed but not so skilfully executed diplomatically. For one thing, Beijing has alienated Seoul and pushed South Korea closer to Washington; at the same time, Pyongyang's reckless provocation has also caused Tokyo to adopt stronger sanction measures against North Korea and provided more reason for Japan to enhance its military capabilities. The crises have provided the opportunities for the Obama administration to be more actively involved in Northeast Asian security issues, including heightened and more frequent joint military presence and exercises with its allies, and at China's doorstep. None of these developments serves Chinese interests.[24]

## A Wayward Neighbour

For China, maintaining stability on the Korean Peninsula serves its fundamental security interests. This has several elements. First, however abhorrent it may feel towards the Kim Jong-il regime, Beijing never loses sight of the bigger, strategic picture: it is critical that North Korea as a viable state, a buffer, must be sustained. A North Korea that either implodes or embroils itself in a military confrontation with the United States would seriously threaten Chinese interests and should be avoided. China therefore would not support, and even oppose if need be, any measures that threaten the very survival of the DPRK, especially as it is now in the hands of an untested leader, Kim Jong-un.

However, Beijing's concern with regional stability is not merely confined to sustaining the North Korean regime at all costs. Beijing pays equal attention to the potential fallout of continued provocation from Pyongyang. The Chinese leadership is deeply worried about the potential domino effect of an ever-escalating North Korean nuclear crisis, specifically Japan's reactions and possible policy direction. A nuclear chain reaction or domino effect would be the worst possible development for China. To the extent that North Korea's provocations could result in negative developments affecting regional balance of power, Beijing will be forced to impose some disciplines over its wayward neighbour.

China's security is possible only within the broader context of a peaceful and stable Northeast Asia. In this regard, Chinese interests in resolving the North Korean nuclear issue are driven by its own security interests as well as its concern over the implications for regional security and the international nuclear nonproliferation regime should the crisis be allowed to continue and escalate. The Korean Peninsula could never achieve long-term peace and stability with a nuclear North Korea, which in turn could lead to a nuclear-armed Japan and South Korea, gravely complicating China's security environment in the region. What Beijing seeks is both denuclearisation and peninsular peace and stability; the two are inseparable and must go hand-in-hand. This is the essence of China's North Korea policy and how it manages an increasingly frustrating problem.

---

[24] Schreer, B and B Taylor, "The Korean Crises and Sino-American Rivalry", *Survival,* vol. 53, no. 1, February-March 2011, pp. 13–19; Hiatt, F, "China's Troubling Friendship with N. Korea", *Washington Post,* 10 May 2010; B Lee, "China's Insult to South Korea", *Asia Sentinel,* 10 May 2010.

# 47

# China-ASEAN Relationship

## An "Offer-Response" Analysis

WANG Yuzhu*

*This chapter introduces an "offer-response" model whereby the first offer usually plays an important role towards an agreement. China-ASEAN economic cooperation will maintain status quo in the near future as both sides lack impetus to make an offer to improve bilateral cooperation.*

The fulfilment of the China-ASEAN Free Trade Agreement (CAFTA) in the beginning of 2010 was a new starting point for China-ASEAN cooperation. However, while some Chinese scholars, especially those believed that economic interdependence would influence bilateral relationships, argued that ASEAN (Association of Southeast Asian Nations) countries would recalibrate their "balance of power" policy towards China after the CAFTA became effective,[1] international observers were more pessimistic. Some even argued that China-ASEAN relation would stagnate early in 2007.[2] Which prediction depicts the future reality of China-ASEAN relationship? For China, economic cooperation was used as a reassure policy to maintain good relations with ASEAN countries,[3] but as Dent correctly argued, one should not underestimate the impact of ASEAN's strategic thinking on the bilateral relationship.[4]

---

*WANG Yuzhu is Research Fellow at the National Institute of International Strategy, Chinese Academy of Social Sciences.
[1] Luo W and Huang Z (2010), "On ASEAN's Acknowledgement and Response towards China's Rise — Taking ASEAN's Adjustment of Foreign Policy of Balancing among Great Powers as Case" (*dongmeng dui zhongguo jueqi de renzhi he fanying*), *Southeast Asian Studies* (*dongnanya yanjiu*), Issue no.3, pp. 61–66.
[2] Ba A (2007), "ASEAN-China Economic Relations", *Pacific Affairs*, vol. 81, no. 4, pp. 662–664.
[3] Sun X (2009), "Why does China Reassure South-East Asia?" *Pacific Focus*, vol. XXIV, no. 3, pp. 298–316.
[4] Dent, C (2010), "Free Trade Agreements in the Asia-Pacific a Decade on: Evaluating the Past, Looking to the Future", *International Relations of the Asia-Pacific*, vol.10, no. 2, pp. 201–245.

This chapter will try to provide more balanced perspectives on the future of the China-ASEAN relationship. An "offer-response" model will be set up based on the political economy and applied to case studies. The case analysis showed that the process of China-ASEAN cooperation was determined by the dynamism of the "offer-response", while this simple game was based on the interest calculation from both sides. The bilateral relationship between China and ASEAN will thus depend on this "offer-response" mechanism.

## The "Offer-Response" Model for Regional Cooperation

Usually, international cooperation aims to set up some kind of institutional arrangement. Due to the inherent bias of institutions, all game players will naturally try to maximise their own interests, which means that cooperation arrangements can only be reached with the compromise of each side. To explain the evolution of international cooperation is a challenging task which has attracted many leading scholars. For example, Axelrod believed that international cooperation started from multi-layer games.[5] This chapter will try to explain the start of cooperation from a technical or operational level. The role of the first game will be highlighted because it is the starting point of most international arrangements.

The "offer-response" model defined in this chapter is based on the model of contract making, which focussed on the reciprocity of the players and the multidirection of interest concerns. Simply put, the "offer-response" model is about the process in international cooperation, during which one player makes an initiative with its own concern (offer) and the other player responds to it after a comprehensive interest calculation. This is only the beginning, and it is still far from the arrangement can be agreed with, but as shown in Table 1, the first offer is vital to the whole reaction chain. Although the first initiative will not necessarily lead to a contract, without this first offer, there will be no cooperation.

## The Conditions for Offer-Making

As mentioned earlier, cooperation starts from an offer but there are two conditions that must be fulfilled before the player does that. Firstly, the benefits from cooperation have to be large enough to be shared, and secondly, at least one player must be in dire need of cooperation. But these are only pre-conditions for offer-making because the offer maker also faces several restrictions. That means the offer is usually made based on the anticipation of a "win-win" cooperation. However, there are other considerations in this decision making, such as whether the player has alternative measures to achieve its interests, the political relations between the two sides and the estimation of a positive response. Generally speaking, the possibility for player A to make an offer will be lower

**Table 1**   The Game of "Offer-Response"

|  |  | Player B | |
|---|---|---|---|
|  |  | **Positive Response** | **Negative Response** |
| Player A | Offer | Cooperate | Don't cooperate |
|  | Don't offer | No cooperation | No cooperation |

*Note*:
1. Player A and Player B may change their positions.
2. The status of "No Cooperation" is different from "Don't Cooperate", because in "No Cooperation", the player's attitudes are not clear. It means that if Player A chooses to offer, Player B may choose a positive or negative response.

*Source*: Prepared by the author.

[5]Axelrod, R (1984), *The Evolution of Cooperation*, Basic Books.

if he believes that player B will respond negatively. But by the same estimate, player A is more likely to make an offer if he has fewer resources to fulfil his aim even though he knows he faces a higher risk of being rejected. Furthermore, the political atmosphere is also vital for offer-making as political tension will ruin potential cooperation, as Sino-Japanese relations have demonstrated. Harmonious bilateral relationships thus make offer-making easier.

## The Significance of Making an Offer

To make an offer is the first step towards cooperation, and is thus encouraged. Firstly, offer-making is also preference-revealing. For player B, the offer from player A is a positive signal because it shows that player A holds positive views to the initiated cooperation. Therefore, offer-making can help to avoid asymmetrical information between the two sides. Secondly, offer-making is usually understood as a promise to compromise during negotiations towards a mutually beneficial arrangement.[6] As such, these may contribute to cooperation by increasing the confidence of the receiver to make a positive response. Therefore, offer-making can be treated as the major propelling force of international cooperation, which serves as the original point of a game process leading to the establishment of an agreement.

As a simple model, the "offer-response" analysis may have some shortcomings, but it can help to highlight the reciprocity of international cooperation. Here, reciprocity means that institutional arrangements must be based on the mutual recognition of a "win-win" situation. At the same time, this model can cover all the relevant elements that players may consider when deciding to make or take an offer. As the "two-level game" theory implies, the process of decision making is also related to the interaction of internal games and international games.[7] This has proved to be an important aspect in practice as far as the cooperation game among nations is concerned; especially when the binding effects of economic interdependence to international relations were over-estimated. The following case studies will show that this multidirection interest analysis is important to understanding the essence of international relations.

## The Breakthrough of China-ASEAN Relations in 1991

Although China had been a major trading partner of most Southeast Asian countries centuries ago, cooperation between China and ASEAN only started in 1991.[8] During the Cold War, ASEAN countries which were concerned about the communist domino effect were hostile to China,[9] while the isolated China believed that ASEAN was an anti-China bloc.[10] This unfriendly relationship lasted for more than two decades until a turning point was reached in 1991. A breakthrough was achieved when China's foreign minister Qian Qichen indicated in a letter to the secretary-general of ASEAN that China was keen in reviving relations with ASEAN through dialogue. This dialogue could cover cooperation in the fields of politics, economy, trade and even security. The response from ASEAN was positive and Qian was invited to attend the opening ceremony of the 24th ASEAN Ministerial Meeting (AMM) held in Kuala Lumpur, heralding the beginning of the China-ASEAN dialogue relationship.

---

[6] This valuable point was inspired by Dr Zhou Fangyin's comments on this chapter.

[7] About the "two-level" game, see Putnam (1986), "Diplomacy and Domestic Politics: The Logic of Two-level Games." *International Organization,* vol. 42, no. 3 (Summer), pp. 427–460.

[8] Prof Wang Gungwu touched upon this issue in his early studies. See Wang (1998) Wang G, *The Nanhai Trade: The Early History of Chinese Trade in the South China Sea,* Singapore: Times Academic Press.

[9] Severino, R (2006), *Southeast Asia in Search of an ASEAN Community,* Singapore: ISEAS p.3.

[10] Peking Review, 18 August 1967, vol. 10, no. 34, p. 40, cited from Zhang Y (2010), *The Logic of the Weak in International Politics: ASEAN's External Relations with Major Powers in the Asia-Pacific Region (Guoji Zhengzhi zhong Ruozhe de Luoji: Dongmeng yu yatai diqu daguo guanxi),* Beijing: Social Sciences Academic Press (China), p. 55.

## The Interest Analysis of China's Offer-Making

Viewed in the context of "offer-response" analysis framework, I found that China made the first offer. This brings us to the first question: Why did China try to break the deadlock at that time?

Generally speaking, the end of the Cold War and the following power transition in East Asia provided the foundation of new China-ASEAN relations. For China, it eliminated the root of ASEAN's anti-China fear and opened the door for both sides to work for mutual benefits. Another plausible reason for this goodwill towards ASEAN was attributed to China "being the only major socialist power left after the collapse of Eastern European and Soviet communist regimes, Beijing found itself in a position of being seriously challenged by western powers".[11] The emergence of multilateralism in China's foreign policy also contributed to this change; it helped to explain why China worked simultaneously with both ASEAN and its individual members.[12] While the need to end the post-Tiananmen diplomatic isolation was viewed as an internal impetus to engage ASEAN,[13] ASEAN's growing economic importance to China was another important factor, suggesting China's offer was the result of multidirectional interests.

China's offer was thus motivated by economic interests aimed at developing the ASEAN market. Since its reform and opening up in 1978, China had experienced a successful export-oriented development; as a result, its high growth rates were highly dependent on Western markets. Figure 1 shows that up to 1990, China's major export markets were Hong Kong, Japan, United States, Germany and Singapore, while the rest of the world accounted for 27.7% of its total exports with none of them exceeding US$100 million.[14] Furthermore, this over-dependence on Western markets had proved to be fragile in the face of Tiananmen as it was used as leverage to interfere with China's internal issues. From China's perspective, the economic sanctions after the 1989 incident were the practice of containment, to which China responded to by diversifying its export markets. Chinese leaders were also fully aware that ASEAN, a large potential market with 500 million people and numerous natural resources, could play a crucial role in China's long-term growth. Therefore, the offer-making should be understood as something more than mere diplomacy.

Having been cornered, China had taken steps to break out of its diplomatic and economic isolation. But why had the offer gone to ASEAN instead of other developing countries, for example India? China's actions were related to the conditions required for offer-making. China had worked with ASEAN on ensuring the peaceful settlement of the Cambodia issue during the last days of the Cold War, and this working relationship had given China the confidence to make the offer. This was bolstered by ASEAN's attitude towards the Tiananmen incident. Some ASEAN members, such as Malaysia and Thailand, believed that ASEAN should be open to instead of isolating China

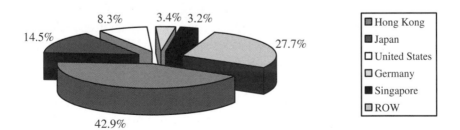

**Figure 1**    China's Export Markets in 1990

[11] Hu W (1996), "China and Asian Regionalism: Challenge and Policy Choice", *Journal of Contemporary China*, vol. 5, no. 11, p. 45.

[12] Kuik CC (2005), "Multilateralism in China's ASEAN Policy: Its Evolution, Characteristics, and Aspiration", *Contemporary Southeast Asia* 27, no. 1: 102–122.

[13] Hu W (1996), op. cit., p. 45.

[14] Du Y (2010), "Study of the Export Destinations: 1990–2007" (*zhongguo chukou maoyi guobie geju yanjiu*: 1990–2007), *China's Foreign Trade* (*zhongguo duiwai maoyi*), issue no.4, pp. 84–88.

in accordance with ASEAN's principle of non-interference. This was an important signal to China because it indicated to leaders in Beijing that ASEAN preferred cooperation to isolation.[15]

## ASEAN: Interests Concern and Positive Response

Regardless of China's motivation, without the positive response from ASEAN, bilateral relations between China and ASEAN would not have changed. Hence the next question one has to ask is why ASEAN took China's offer when some ASEAN members still have territorial disputes with China in the South China Sea.

One Chinese observer argued that when working with ASEAN to tackle the Cambodian issue, China had respected ASEAN's concerns and supported ASEAN's initiatives, which to a certain extent explained ASEAN's acceptance of China.[16] This element must have contributed to ASEAN's decision making. However, other deep-seated concerns may have been more important.

Firstly, cooperating with China was part of ASEAN's "omni-enmeshment" strategy. According to,[17] the enmeshment strategy is a process to maintain regional security, during which the targeted country was contacted and eventually enmeshed into sustainable communication aimed at regional integration. Goh argued that ASEAN countries which were concerned about the unstable multi-polarisation order of the post-Cold War region chose this omni-enmeshment strategy to avoid being negatively affected. In practice, ASEAN refused to side with any power and tried to bring more powers into the regional security architecture. From this point of view, China's offer had met ASEAN's demand and a positive response was thus natural. While some argued otherwise, this strategy can be explained by ASEAN's need to protect itself. In the light of past antagonism, ASEAN did not trust China to resolve the South China Sea issue peacefully. Cooperation was thus viewed by ASEAN elites as a way of socialising its powerful, formerly closed neighbour. They hoped that the process would prove helpful in predicting China's thoughts and behavioural patterns. In retrospect, this has proved successful.[18]

Secondly, ASEAN's choice to ameliorate its relationship with the neighbouring powerhouse can be viewed as part of its transition into the "balance of power" strategy. During the Cold War, ASEAN's guiding principle of dealing with great powers was to remain neutral. That was why ASEAN hesitated in its decision on whether to invite China to balance Vietnam when dealing with the latter's invasion in Cambodia because it might increase China's influence in Southeast Asia.[19] However, recent events indicate that ASEAN has now adopted the more practical "balance of power" policy.[20] As such, China was valued because its national interests were different from other major powers, enabling ASEAN to balance powers against each other.

Thirdly, there were underlying economic considerations in addition to existing security concerns. Table 2 shows that export-oriented ASEAN members depended on the EU, the United States and Japan for their exports. With the end of the Cold War, Western countries began to talk about fair trade and protection of intellectual property rights, and ASEAN countries found that their export environment was changing. In reality, ASEAN was aware of the need for export market

[15] Shambough, D (2004), "China Engages Asia: Reshaping the Regional Order", *International Security*, vol. 29, no. 3 Winter 2004/05, p. 68.

[16] Zhang Y (2010), op. cit., pp. 57–59.

[17] Goh E (2007), "Great Powers and Hierarchical Order in Southeast Asia: Analyzing Regional Security Strategies", *International Security*, vol. 32, no. 3, pp.113–157.

[18] Zhang Y (2010), op. cit.

[19] Leifer, M (1983), "ASEAN and the Problem of Common Response", *International Journal*, vol. 38, no. 2, pp. 318–329.

[20] Cao Y (2003), "Intercourse with Big Countries — A Commentary of the Equilibrium Strategy among Big Countries of the ASEAN" (*Zai daguo jian zhouxuan — ping dongmeng de daguo pingheng zhanlue*), *Journal Of Jinan University* (*jinan xuebao*), issue no. 3, pp. 11–21.

**Table 2**　Export Destinations of ASEAN-6 (1975–2000)

| | USA | Japan | EU | ASEAN | China | USA | Japan | EU | ASEAN | China |
|---|---|---|---|---|---|---|---|---|---|---|
| | % | % | % | % | % | % | % | % | % | % |
| 1975 | 15.4 | 23.8 | 17.7 | 12.7 | 3.0 | 19.8 | 27.0 | 14.2 | 17.3 | 0.6 |
| 1980 | 15.4 | 21.8 | 14.8 | 17.6 | 2.7 | 16.9 | 26.8 | 13.9 | 18.1 | 1.0 |
| 1985 | 15.7 | 20.7 | 15.6 | 19.7 | 5.1 | 19.7 | 25.4 | 11.3 | 19.4 | 1.3 |
| 1989 | 15.5 | 23.7 | 16.1 | 16.3 | 3.1 | 21.3 | 18.9 | 15.5 | 18.7 | 2.3 |
| 1993 | 15.1 | 24.9 | 14.3 | 17.4 | 1.9 | 20.3 | 15.0 | 15.2 | 21.1 | 2.2 |
| 1996 | 15.1 | 20.9 | 16.4 | 18.3 | 2.6 | 18.4 | 13.3 | 14.5 | 25.0 | 2.3 |
| 1999 | 16.5 | 18.4 | 12.4 | 20.3 | 4.4 | 20.5 | 11.0 | 16.3 | 21.9 | 2.8 |
| 2000 | 14.2 | 19.2 | 11.4 | 21.0 | 5.3 | 18.1 | 12.4 | 15.4 | 22.8 | 3.5 |

*Note*: The data for EU is EU-15.
*Source*: Cited from Herschede (1991), p. 182, Table 1. The data for 1993–2000 was calculated from *ASEAN Statistical Yearbook 2005*.

adjustment since the end of the Cold War.[21] That partly explained the motivation behind building the ASEAN free trade area in 1992. Thus, the concern for market adjustment, possibly last in the priority list of ASEAN members, could also be an influential factor in the decision to cooperate with China. Besides, China is a growing export market.

The aforementioned analysis shows that international political changes in the post-Cold War era provided a conducive environment for China to make the cooperation offer. This, combined with China's desperate need to end its diplomatic isolation, helped China to fulfil the offer-making conditions.

Hence, both sides were able to begin their engagement in fruitful cooperation as this offer met ASEAN's strategic and economic demands. Although strategic thinking was dominant in the beginning, economic concerns rose in prominence after the 1997 crisis.[22]

### The Establishment of China-ASEAN FTA

After the 1991 contact, China cooperated with ASEAN as a dialogue partner. New challenges to China-ASEAN relations emerged when the Asian financial crisis broke out in 1997. Both China and ASEAN countries were negatively impacted as contagion spread. However, the impact on regional economies varied due to different financial regimes, among which some ASEAN members experienced sharp currency devaluations and foreign direct investment (FDI) outflows. China's relatively better performance reminded ASEAN countries of the western promulgated "China threat". However, compared to their western counterparts who were more concerned with politics, ASEAN members were more concerned about economic competition from China.[23] Therefore, when China's attempt to re-enter WTO progressed smoothly, the concerned ASEAN leaders urged that a research study with workable recommendations be conducted to tackle the challenge of a rising China as they believed that the WTO accession would increase China's economic

---

[21] The joint statement of the 25th ASEAN economic ministers meeting showed that ASEAN leaders were aware that their exports to major Western markets would face more challenges in the post-Cold War era.

[22] Strengthening economic cooperation became the leaders' main concern after the 1997 crisis. See "Joint Statement of the Meeting of Heads of State/Government of the Member States of ASEAN and the President of the People's Republic of China", Kuala Lumpur, Malaysia, 16 December 1997. <http://www.aseansec.org/5225.htm> (accessed 8 March 2012).

[23] For the competition between China and ASEAN, see Ahearne, AG, JG Fernald, L Prakash and JW Schindler (2003), "China and Emerging Asia: Comrades or Competitors?" *International Finance Discussion Papers*, no. 789, December 2003.

competitiveness.[24] Responding to ASEAN countries' concern over the possible adverse impacts, then Chinese Premier Zhu Rongji proposed a China-ASEAN FTA (free trade agreement) during the fourth "10 + 3" informal summit held in 2000, which was accepted by his ASEAN counterparts. The subsequent feasibility studies with supportive results led to the agreement to set up a CAFTA within 10 years.

## Economics-Centred Offer

The China-ASEAN FTA was viewed as the most important event in bilateral relations as it brought China-ASEAN bilateral cooperation to an institutional level. In retrospect, the offer from China was thought to be a political deal as it was obviously aimed at dispelling growing concerns among ASEAN countries of a "China threat". As a regional power, China's rapid rise naturally caused uneasiness among its neighbouring countries. So it was natural for Chinese leaders to try to alleviate such anxiety through a free trade arrangement with ASEAN.

Even though the CAFTA offer was obviously a political decision, economic interests were also important from the very beginning as the long-term challenge for China was to maintain stable growth until it had industrialised. Although China survived the 1997 crisis, the damage suffered by ASEAN countries showed that China also needed to diversify its export markets. Chinese leaders were fully aware that ASEAN could play a crucial role in China's long-term growth. This concern was evident in former Premier Zhu Rongji's statement that China should abide by the principles of *duoyu shaoqu* (give more and take less) and x*ianyu houqu* (give first and take later) in the CAFTA. With the rapid development of its manufacturing sector,[25] it came as a rational choice for China to establish a bilateral FTA to provide institutional insurance for its exports. Following CAFTA initiation, bilateral trade increased rapidly (Table 3). Between 2001 and 2010, bilateral trade between China and ASEAN grew by about 25% a year in nominal terms, faster than that of China's total trade and far outpacing some estimates.[26]

Besides market diversification, it was argued that strategic thinking provided additional motivation to push the agreement through. For example, Chung Chien-peng believed that China expected the bilateral FTA to provide sound bases for political, security and other institutional cooperation between China and ASEAN.[27] While from the viewpoint of regional cooperation, the CAFTA was thought to be a propelling force for East Asian integration, which would pave the way for China's stable growth and prosperity in the long run. The development of regional cooperation suggested that the China-ASEAN FTA did contribute to regional integration. Japan, afraid of losing its influential position in Southeast Asia, chose to initiate a Japan-ASEAN Economic Partnership Agreement, which generated the "10+1" domino effect.[28] Seeking "soft power" through this arrangement was also argued to be an element. Though the soft power element may not be a concern in the beginning, it does play a part when asymmetrical interdependence between the two sides developed later.[29]

---

[24] Their concern was supported by the study conducted by Mckibbin, WJ and Woo WT (2004), "A Quantitative Analysis on the Effect of China's WTO Accession to World Economy" (*zhongguo rushi dui guoji jingji yingxiang de lianghuafenxi*), *Economic Research Journal* (*jingji yanjiu*), issue no. 4, pp. 16–25.

[25] According to World Bank statistics, in 2006, the proportion of manufactured products in China's exports reached 92%. World Bank, *World Development Indicators* 2008, p. 211.

[26] Joint research on the possible effects of a China-ASEAN FTA showed that the FTA would increase bilateral trade by about US$10 billion, which proved to be a very cautious estimate.

[27] Chung C (2010), *China's Multilateral Cooperation in Asia and Pacific*, Routledge.

[28] Zhang T (2008), "The Influence of Bilateral and Multilateral FTA on Promoting the Economic Cooperation between China and ASEAN" (*shuangbian yu duobian FTA dui tuijin zhongguo dongmeng jingji hezuo de yingxiang*), *World Economy Study* (*shijiejingji yanjiu*), issue no. 9, pp. 78–82.

[29] With the development of the bilateral FTA, China began to encourage more imports from ASEAN countries; this was thought to be a practical way to increase China's influence in Southeast Asia.

**Table 3**   China-ASEAN Trade, 2001–2010 (US$billion and %)

| | China's Exports to ASEAN | | China's Imports from ASEAN | | China's Trade with ASEAN | China's Trade Balance with ASEAN |
|---|---|---|---|---|---|---|
| | Amount | Share in China's Total Exports | Amount | Share in China's Total Imports | | |
| 2001 | 18.4 | 6.9 | 23.2 | 9.5 | 41.6 | −4.8 |
| 2002 | 23.6 | 7.2 | 31.2 | 10.6 | 54.8 | −7.6 |
| 2003 | 30.9 | 7.1 | 47.3 | 11.5 | 78.3 | −16.4 |
| 2004 | 42.9 | 7.2 | 62.9 | 11.2 | 105.9 | −20.1 |
| 2005 | 55.4 | 7.3 | 75.1 | 11.4 | 130.4 | −19.6 |
| 2006 | 71.3 | 7.4 | 89.5 | 11.3 | 160.8 | −18.2 |
| 2007 | 94.2 | 7.7 | 108.4 | 11.3 | 202.6 | −14.2 |
| 2008 | 114.1 | 8.0 | 116.9 | 10.3 | 231.1 | −2.8 |
| 2009 | 106.3 | 8.8 | 106.7 | 10.6 | 213.0 | −0.4 |
| 2010 | 138.2 | 8.8 | 154.6 | 11.1 | 292.8 | −16.3 |

*Source*: The Ministry of Commerce, PRC.

Although it seemed that China had enough incentives to cooperate with ASEAN, the offer was made in view of other impending challenges. The first was the resurgence of the "China threat" theory which was partly solved during the 1997 crisis when China refused to depreciate the *renminbi*. The second came from Chinese domestic demand. It was used as a tool to reinforce domestic support for China's WTO accession. In fact, China's bid to re-enter the WTO was not free from internal resistance. Thus, forming a FTA with ASEAN offered a suitable alternative to alleviate domestic pressure.

## The Strategic Thinking of ASEAN

The deepening of regional integration and closer economic relations between China and ASEAN served as the general background for the smooth progress of the CAFTA. Each step however was also assumed to be based on a rational calculation of costs and benefits by various leaders.[30] This assumption has proven valid because a recent study found that some ASEAN members were worried about the establishment of a CAFTA from an early stage.[31]

ASEAN's acceptance of China's offer was the result of strategic thinking. Theoretically, it should have fulfilled the three conditions that Lorenz argued are usually considered when regionalisation was promoted. These are, enhancing regional competitiveness, stabilising the heterogeneous challenges through cooperation and insuring sufficient entry into regional markets.[32]

Firstly, it was obvious that ASEAN intended to increase its bargaining power as a group in East Asia. Studies on small countries' cooperation strategy show that by forming a "hub-spoke" structure with regional powers, the small country (country group) will gain some functional interests as the hub.[33] However, it was not easy for ASEAN to obtain that potential position in East Asia. Soesastro

---

[30] Cai KG (2003), "The ASEAN-China Free Trade Agreement and East Asian Regional Grouping", *Contemporary Southeast Asia* 25, no. 3, 2003, pp. 387–404.

[31] Chen Q, Zhou Z and T Tang (2010), "ASEAN's Concern on China-ASEAN FTA"(*dongmeng dui zhongguo dongmeng zimaoqu de gulv*), *Quarterly Journal Of International Politics* (*guoji zhengzhi kexue*), issue no. 4, pp. 51–81.

[32] Lorenz, D (1992), "Economic Geography and Political Economy of Regionalization: The Example of Western Europe", *The American Economic Review*, vol. 82, no. 2, pp. 84–87.

[33] Li X (2008), "Small States Strategy in Regional Economic Cooperation" (*quyu hezuo zhong de xiaoguo zhanlue*), *Journal of Contemporary Asia-Pacific Studies* (*dangdai yatai*), issue no. 3, pp. 36–49.

believed that ASEAN signing the FTA with China could serve this purpose because the CAFTA was the new spoke that had ASEAN as its centre.[34]

Secondly, ASEAN had released the Declaration on the Conduct of parties in the South China Sea with China in 1996, though various parties have yet to obtain real settlement on territorial disputes in that region. As a result, ASEAN intended to institutionalise its relations with China, which was argued to be a "hedging-plus" strategy that other Asian countries (for example Japan) used to keep security.[35] According to the "hedging-plus" strategy, ASEAN, with a rising China and a declining United States, would try to foster new favourable external relations while keeping the old external relations unaffected in order to maximise self-interests. This kind of hedging can be taken as an effort to stabilise the heterogeneous challenges, or an economic measure to insure market entry. As Whalley found, small countries tend to make agreements with its major export partners;[36] thus when these countries adopt protection measures, bilateral trade remains unaffected. Some observers noted that ASEAN was interested in obtaining free access to China's vast internal market and with attracting FDI being a secondary, though important, concern.[37]

When concerns of both sides were compared, it was found that during the process of offer and response, the CAFTA was based on multidirectional interest calculations by both China and ASEAN. While it could be called a political deal, it was also an economic success.

## Towards Greater Institutionalisation?

The aforementioned case studies have shown the progress China and ASEAN have made during the last two decades based on the "offer-response" analysis. What then is the future of China-ASEAN cooperation? Will it move towards greater institutionalisation, for instance, a bilateral economic community? If we go back to the "offer-response" analysis, the answer will be NO. At least it is impossible before 2015. Although deepening bilateral cooperation will be mutually beneficial, both sides will still hesitate to make the offer to upgrade the level of China-ASEAN institutional arrangements. And we know through the case studies, the first offer is the starting point of the cooperation.

For now, bilateral cooperation under the current China-ASEAN FTA will continue and both sides will gain from it. China's assistant foreign minister Hu Zhengyue said in January 2011 that China will work closely with ASEAN to push forward China-ASEAN strategic partnership up to a new level. This comment showed that China and ASEAN are both interested in cooperating at a higher institutional level. Thus, will ASEAN try to make a first offer? Or will China make the first offer?

ASEAN is not likely to make the offer, and may even face difficulties accepting an offer aimed at upgrading the institutional level of bilateral cooperation. Currently, ASEAN is busy with internal building and faces formidable challenges in fulfilling the ASEAN Community in 2015. The ASEAN Charter was published in 2009 to establish the legal and institutional framework for ASEAN,[38] which will help ASEAN realise integration through community building. However, the progress of community building has not been optimistic even though the Score Card released in

[34] Soesastro, H (2003), ASEAN: Regional Economic Cooperation and Its Institutionalization, *CSIS Working Paper Series*, WPE 071, August 2003.

[35] Cheng T and Hsu S (2005), "Between Power Balancing and Bandwagoning: Rethinking the Post-Cold War East Asia", In I Yuan (ed.), *Rethinking New International order in East Asia: US, China and Taiwan*, (Taipei: Institute of International Relations and Center for China studies, National Chengchi University, 2005, pp. 425–460.

[36] Whalley, J (1993), "Regional Trade Arrangements in North America: CUSTA and NAFTA", in J de Melo and A Panagariya (eds.), *New Dimensions in Regional Integration*, Cambridge: Centre for Economic Policy Research, pp. 352–87. Whalley, J (1993), "Regional Trade Arrangements in North America: CUSTA and NAFTA", in J de Melo and A Panagariya (eds), *New Dimensions in Regional Integration*, Cambridge: Centre for Economic Policy Research, pp. 352–338.

[37] Chung C (2010), op. cit., p. 81.

[38] ASEAN Charter, p. 2. See also <http://www.aseansec.org> (accessed 8 March 2012).

**Table 4**   Per capita GDP changes of ASEAN members (US$)

|             | 2001  | 2009  |
|-------------|-------|-------|
| Singapore   | 20735 | 36631 |
| Brunei      | 12121 | 26486 |
| Malaysia    | 3689  | 6822  |
| Thailand    | 1837  | 3951  |
| Indonesia   | 688   | 2364  |
| Philippines | 924   | 1750  |
| Vietnam     | 415   | 1120  |
| Laos        | 328   | 911   |
| Cambodia    | 282   | 693   |
| Myanmar     | 161   | 420   |

*Sources*: Data for 2001 cited from *ASEAN Statistic Yearbook 2004*, data for 2009 cited from <http://www.aseansec.org/stat/table7.xls> (accessed 26 July 2011).

2010 showed that it is progressing smoothly. For example, narrowing the development gap is one field of economic community building, but as Table 4 shows, the absolute gap of per capita GDP between Singapore and Myanmar has widened. At the same, ASEAN's international reputation was undermined by escalating territorial disputes between Cambodia and Thailand. Under such circumstances, ASEAN lacks the necessary pre-requisites to make the offer.

More importantly, with the rapid rise of China, ASEAN countries have become increasingly uneasy. This has led to their strategic alienation from China. In practice, ASEAN choose to keep a proper distance from China. This was a rational choice for its "hub-spoke" framework, which needed to avoid the emergence of any overwhelming power that might upset the structural balance and hurt ASEAN's central position in East Asia. Logically, ASEAN will be reluctant to strengthen its relations with China unless its bilateral relations with other powers, for example Japan and India, have been or will be equally strengthened.

It seems that China is willing to promote cooperation with ASEAN, especially in the light of China's new East Asian strategy. Its basic framework was to build harmonious neighbouring relations and to actively promote the East Asian economic integration process.[39] The CAFTA, as an important component of China's FTA strategy, will naturally be promoted to serve the process of East Asian integration. However, when the restricting conditions of offer-making are involved, it is my opinion that China will not make a new offer. Instead, China will use the CAFTA as the main framework to deepen bilateral interdependence. Table 5 shows that China-ASEAN trade is growing smoothly. In 2010, ASEAN was the fourth biggest trading partner of China, but bilateral trade earnings were comparable to that of Sino-Japanese trade. Other statistics showed that bilateral investment between China and ASEAN countries also increased quickly. This means that China has no urgent need to upgrade its bilateral economic cooperation.

At the same time, some ASEAN members complained that they are not ready for tariff elimination when CAFTA is about to fulfil its zero tariff promise, and this reminded China leaders that more challenges are to be expected in the following stages towards a fully constructed CAFTA. Instead of making a new offer and risk losing face, China is more likely to work with ASEAN countries to carry out existing trade and investment arrangements.

---

[39] Sun D (2010), "Changing Economic Structure in East Asia and the Strategy of China-ASEAN FTA" (*biandong zhong de dongy jingji geju yu zhongguo dongmeng zimaoqu zhanlue*), *Journal of University of International Relations* (*guojiguanxi xueyuan xuebao*), issue no.3, pp. 55–60.

**Table 5**  China's Major Trade Partners in 2010 (US$100 million)

| | Total Trade | | Exports | | Imports | |
|---|---|---|---|---|---|---|
| | Amount | Rank | Amount | Rank | Amount | Rank |
| EU | 4,797.0 | 1 | 3,112.4 | 1 | 1,684.8 | 2 |
| US | 3,853.4 | 2 | 2,833.0 | 2 | 1,020.4 | 6 |
| Japan | 2,977.7 | 3 | 1,210.6 | 5 | 1,767.1 | 1 |
| ASEAN | 2,927.8 | 4 | 1,382.1 | 4 | 1,545.7 | 3 |
| Hong Kong | 2,305.8 | 5 | 2,183.2 | 3 | 122.6 | |
| Korea | 2,071.7 | 6 | 687.7 | 6 | 1,384.0 | 4 |
| Taiwan, POC | 1,453.7 | 7 | 296.8 | | 1,156.9 | 5 |

*Source*: Editing Unit, General Administration of Customs of China, *China Custom Statistics, 2011*.

Being a neighbour of ASEAN and a co-player of regional integration, China fully understands ASEAN's changing attitude towards its relations with China. As such, this may discourage China from making a new offer. These concerns were further aggravated by the re-emergence of South China Sea disputes. China currently may not be ready to make an offer of greater institutional arrangement.

Under such circumstances, it will be impossible for both sides to make future offers towards greater institutions. According to the "offer-response" model, China and ASEAN will have to use CAFTA as the cooperation framework till changes to the internal and/or external situations from both sides make a new offer possible. But even with no new offer, China and ASEAN can still work together for mutual benefits. In addition, the bilateral interdependence will deepen when the signed agreements have been fully carried out. Whether this relationship can be considered stagnant will depend on how it is defined.

## Economic Interdependence and Long-term Good Neighbourly Relations

The "offer-response" analysis is an economic model set up to offer a technical explanation for the beginnings of cooperation, and what is highlighted is the crucial contribution of the first offer. The case studies in this chapter show that international arrangements start with an offer. This is especially true in East Asia, where nations care a lot about their "face" (reputation).

Another important aspect of the "offer-response" model is related to the interest calculations from both sides during the decision making process. I found that even for an economic arrangement, political and security concerns are also an important element. While this element is not usually a core interest of the offeror, it must be the result of an impending pressure. This suggests that the final decision may not have been made based on an equal consideration of all the factors. Figuring out the core elements is important, not only for academic analysis, but also for diplomatic practice and requires further study.

But it is always difficult to find out player preferences, because they change with international political and security situations. For example, the progress of China-ASEAN relations was possible only when the main focus of both sides shifted from security to economic growth. This pattern has also proved to be common in East Asia.[40] The implication of this finding to both China and ASEAN should be the following: economic interdependence will never be enough for good long-term neighbourly relations.

---

[40] Breslin, S (2010), "Comparative theory, China, and the future of East Asian regionalism(s)", *Review of International Studies*, 36, pp. 709–729.

# 48

# China and Singapore

## An Asymmetrical but Substantive Relationship

LYE Liang Fook*

*Despite their asymmetry, China and Singapore enjoy a substantive relationship. With China's growing clout, it is even more important for it to have ties with Singapore based on mutual respect and mutual benefit.*

In many ways, China is an extremely big giant when compared to a very tiny Singapore. Whether it is in terms of geographical size, population strength or economic mass, Singapore pales in comparison to China. Given their asymmetrical proportions, there is a view that China does not need to pay too much attention to Singapore. With China's growing prominence on the world stage, such a view seems to have gained increased currency. By logical extension, China only needs to focus on engaging the major powers such as the United States, the European Union (EU), Japan and India and leave its relations with Singapore to adjust accordingly to big power dynamics.

Yet, this chapter highlights the fact that despite their vast asymmetry, the two countries enjoy a strong and substantive relationship. To a large extent, the current state of relations has much to do with the foundation laid by then Chinese paramount leader Deng Xiaoping and former Singapore Prime Minister Lee Kuan Yew before formal ties were established in October 1990. Both leaders saw value in enhancing their respective countries' interests based on a pragmatic or non-ideological approach.

Today, the two countries interact and cooperate in many fields ranging from politics, economics, business, the arts, culture and education to the environment. Their relationship is also manifested at various levels ranging from government-to-government ties involving the top leaders to people-to-people exchanges of tourists and students. Over the years, ties have not only deepened but also broadened into new areas. There is also a high-level institutional mechanism to regularly review and drive the bilateral relationship.

*LYE Liang Fook is Assistant Director and Research Fellow at the East Asian Institute of the National University of Singapore.

More importantly, this chapter argues that precisely due to Singapore's extremely small size compared to China's, it is in the latter's interest to pay even more attention to Singapore. By developing the bilateral relationship according to the principles of "mutual respect" and "mutual benefit" regardless of size, China can particularly demonstrate to the region and also to the rest of the world that its rise is a peaceful one which will bring about numerous opportunities for growth. This message is even more important in the midst of growing concerns over China's perceived growing assertiveness in the region.

## Turning Point in China-Singapore Relations

China-Singapore relations were very tense in the 1950s and 1960s due to China's moral and material support of communist insurgency movements in Southeast Asia that threatened to overthrow the post-colonial governments in these countries, Singapore included. However, since the mid-1970s, Beijing has started to improve its relations with Southeast Asia.

A turning point in China-Singapore relations came about in November 1978 during Deng Xiaoping's visit to Singapore. Deng was apparently impressed with the socio-economic progress that Singapore had achieved since independence in 1965. During his meeting with then Prime Minister Lee Kuan Yew in 1978, Deng reportedly told Lee that he was "glad he had come and seen Singapore again after 58 years".[1] He remarked that Singapore had undergone a "dramatic transformation" and congratulated Lee. He even said that "[i]f I had only Shanghai, I too might be able to change Shanghai as quickly. But I have the whole of China!"[2] This visit had left an indelible impression on Deng.

At the end of his 1978 visit, after Deng Xiaoping had boarded the plane to depart from Singapore, Lee had said to his colleagues that Deng's staff was going to get a "shellacking" as Deng had witnessed a Singapore that "his brief had not prepared him for". Sure enough, after Deng's visit, articles in the main Chinese Communist Party newspaper, the *People's Daily*, took a different line and portrayed Singapore in a positive light. No longer seen simply as "running dogs of the American imperialists", Singapore was described as a "garden city worth studying for its greening, public housing and tourism".[3] Another indication of the positive impression of Singapore was Deng's speech in October 1979 when he mentioned how Singapore had utilised foreign capital to generate revenue for the state, income for the workers and promoted growth of the service sectors.[4] Singapore had become a point of reference for China.

Just before his visit to Singapore in November 1978, Deng had also visited Japan (in October 1978), Thailand and Malaysia (in November 1978). Before his Singapore trip, Deng seemed to have had the impression that Southeast Asia was a backward region as in the minds of many Chinese leaders in those days. Yet what he saw in Singapore apparently strengthened his will to speed up economic reforms for China. He had seen that it was possible for Singapore to have a high level of economic development under a strong political leadership. In other words, a market economy was compatible with an authoritarian regime or more specifically, one-party dominance.

China-Singapore ties received a further boost when Deng mentioned Singapore during his Southern Tour or *Nanxun* in 1992. Thereafter, numerous official "observation groups" came to Singapore to study its development experiences. In 1992 alone, Singapore received over 400 delegations from China which were keen to study various aspects of Singapore's development

---

[1] Deng's first visit to Singapore was in 1920 when he was on his way to Marseilles in France after the end of the First World War to work and study. At that time, Singapore was still a British colony.
[2] Lee KY, *From Third World to First* (Singapore: Singapore Press Holdings, 2000), pp. 667–668.
[3] Ibid., p. 668.
[4] Ibid., p. 669.

experience.[5] This culminated in the two countries' first flagship project, the Singapore-Suzhou Industrial Park (SIP) in Suzhou in 1994, which eventually took off after overcoming initial hurdles. It is worthwhile to state here that since its inception, Singapore had conceived of the SIP as more than a commercial project. More importantly, it was intended to offer a platform for Singapore leaders, officials and businessmen to get to know their Chinese counterparts better by working jointly on the project, thereby building the basis for a longer-term relationship.

## A Broad-Based and Substantive Relationship

Today, China and Singapore enjoy multi-faceted ties on many fronts. One of the important anchors is their ever-expanding and deepening trade and investment ties. In 2011, China was Singapore's third largest trading partner with total trade amounting to S$101.4 billion, a jump of 6.4% from 2010.[6] Since 1997, China has overtaken Malaysia as the most important destination for Singapore's foreign direct investment in cumulative terms. In 2011, Singapore's cumulative direct investment in China was nearly S$62 billion, an increase of more than 6.7% from S$58.1 billion in 2010. Singapore's investments in China are predominantly in manufacturing and real estate, rental and leasing. Conversely, Singapore ranks among China's top 10 largest trading partners and investors, no mean feat for a small country.

On its part, the dynamism and resilience of the Chinese economy is making a significant positive impact on the region and the rest of the world. This is especially evident after the 2008 financial contagion that engulfed the major economies of the world. Bucking the trend, China achieved a stellar Gross Domestic Product (GDP) growth of 9.2%, 10.3% and 9.1% in 2011, 2010 and 2009 respectively, becoming an ever more important economic pillar of the world economy. In the first half of 2011, China-ASEAN trade totalled US$171.12 billion, up by 25% year-on-year. China is now the largest trading partner of Association of Southeast Asian Nations (ASEAN), while ASEAN is the third largest trading partner of China.[7]

In fact, China has continued to run substantial trade deficits with its neighbours from Japan, Korea, Taiwan, Australia and a number of ASEAN countries. By opening up its vast market to their exports, China has become a critical engine for these countries. More significantly, by importing raw materials, intermediate products, machinery and equipment, and utilising services from different Asian economies, Singapore included, and then re-exporting the finished products to different markets in the region and beyond, China operates as an important integrator of regional and global manufacturing activities (Figure 1).

At the financial level, China and Singapore have sought ways to strengthen their economic resilience and financial stability. In July 2010, the People's Bank of China and the Monetary Authority of Singapore announced the setting up of a bilateral currency swap arrangement that will provide Chinese *renminbi* (RMB) liquidity of up to RMB150 billion and Singapore dollar liquidity of up to S$30 billion. Even more significant, the two countries are reportedly keen for Singapore to become a second offshore RMB trading hub after Hong Kong. Already, there is increasing use of the RMB as the currency for trade between Singapore and China. Both sides are reportedly in talks to set up a RMB-clearing bank in Singapore. At the same time, there is growing interest in RMB-denominated products in Singapore.

On tourism, or people-to-people relations, China is Singapore's second largest visitor-generating market with 1.57 million Chinese tourist arrivals after Indonesia at 2.59 million in 2011 (Figure 2). Over the years, the number of Chinese tourists gradually crept upwards from seventh position in

---

[5] Speech by then Senior Minister Lee Kuan Yew at the International Conference on National Boundaries and Cultural Configurations", at the 10th Anniversary Celebration of the Centre for Chinese Language and Culture, Nanyang Technological University, 23 June 2004.

[6] "Singapore, China Witness Strong Bilateral Trade Growth", *China Daily*, 5 February 2011.

[7] "China-ASEAN Cooperation: 1991–2011", *China Daily*, 16 November 2011.

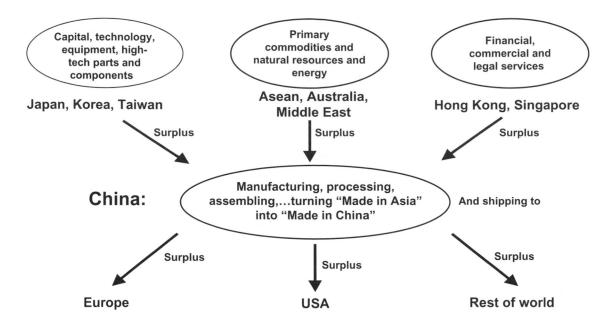

**Figure 1**   China at the Centre of Global and Regional Production Networks

*Source*: Chart provided by Prof John Wong, Professorial Fellow, EAI.

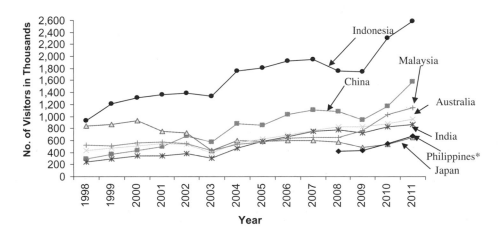

**Figure 2**   Top Six Visitor Generating Markets for Singapore (1998–2011)

*Note*: Philippines became Singapore's top six visitor generating market when it overtook Japan in 2010.

*Source*: Singapore Tourism Board Statistics and Yearbook of Statistics Singapore (2011).

1998, to third position in 2002 (overtaking Malaysia and Australia) and finally to second position in 2003 (overtaking Japan). In 2009, visitors from China contributed almost 11% of Singapore's total tourism receipts, second after Indonesian tourists at 16.7%.[8] Besides tourism, China and Singapore also have frequent exchanges in the fields of education (such as student exchanges and collaborations among educational institutions), culture (such as cultural troupe performances and exhibitions) and the media (such as airing of each other's TV programmes and collaborations in film and animation productions). The arrival of two Chinese pandas in Singapore in 2012 is yet another indication of how far relations have come. Singapore is reportedly the eighth country in the world to have received pandas from China.

---

[8] *Yearbook of Statistics* Singapore, 2011 at <http://www.singstat.gov.sg/pubn/reference/yos11/statsT-tourism.pdf> (accessed 29 March 2012).

At the political level, the two countries have kept up the momentum of high-level exchanges. In 2010, the year marking the 20th anniversary of the establishment of diplomatic relations, Singapore leaders like Prime Minister Lee Hsien Loong, President S R Nathan, Deputy Prime Minister Wong Kan Seng, Deputy Prime Minister and Minister for Defence Teo Chee Hean, Minister Mentor Lee Kuan Yew, Senior Minister Goh Chok Tong and Foreign Minister George Yeo visited China. In the same year, Vice President Xi Jinping visited Singapore where he co-officiated the groundbreaking of the China Cultural Centre with Senior Minister Goh and unveiled the Deng Xiaoping Commemorative Marker with Minister Mentor Lee. In 2011, Chinese Vice Premier Wang Qishan came to Singapore to co-chair the Joint Council for Bilateral Cooperation with his Singapore counterpart Deputy Prime Minister Teo Chee Hean. In February 2012, Singapore Foreign Minister Shanmugam embarked on his maiden visit to China since becoming foreign minister in May 2011. The visit to China was supposed to be his first introductory visit outside of ASEAN but this was not to be due to scheduling problems.

## High-Level Institutional Mechanism

Complementing the various exchanges highlighted earlier is a high-level institutional mechanism known as the Joint Council for Bilateral Cooperation (JCBC) that convenes once a year to review the state of bilateral cooperation and proactively suggests ways to improve such cooperation. The JCBC also provides a useful platform for political leaders and officials as well as businessmen from both sides to get to know each other better by collaborating on joint projects. This network of interactions has helped to lay the groundwork for stronger political and economic ties. The JCBC was launched by Prime Minister Goh Chok Tong and Premier Wen Jiabao in Beijing in November 2003. It held its eighth meeting in Singapore in July 2011 co-chaired by Chinese Vice Premier Wang Qishan and Singapore Deputy Prime Minister Teo Chee Hean. The ninth meeting was similarly co-chaired by these two leaders in July 2012 in Suzhou.

Under the JCBC are two Joint Steering Councils (JSCs), also headed by Vice Premier Wang and DPM Teo, that oversee policy-related issues on the SIP and the newly embarked on Sino-Singapore Tianjin Eco-city, the two flagship projects that involve two governments. The collaboration on the industrial park and now the eco-city are concrete examples of how the two countries are constantly finding ways to stay relevant to and benefit from each other's growth. It is important to ensure the continued success of the SIP as well as the success of the eco-city as the reputation of both governments are closely linked to these projects. If both projects do well, this will add further substance to bilateral ties.

Under the JCBC framework are seven other provincial-level cooperation councils that Singapore has with Shandong (1993), Sichuan (1996), Liaoning (2003), Zhejiang (2003), Tianjin (2007), Jiangsu (2007) and Guangdong (2009) (Table 1). They provide additional avenues for Singapore to pursue meaningful collaboration with selective Chinese provinces and underscore Singapore's cooperation with China in its regional development. Each of these councils meets on an annual basis to review and further push cooperation projects within the relevant provinces. Some of these projects include the Sino-Singapore Guangzhou Knowledge City (that held its groundbreaking ceremony in June 2010) and the Sino-Singapore Nanjing Eco High-Tech Island (officially launched in May 2009).

During Singapore Foreign Minister Shanmugam's visit to China in February 2012, it was agreed that officials from the foreign ministries of both countries will hold regular consultations to step up their contacts and cooperation. Such a platform is useful as it will allow both sides to deal with or discuss issues of common interest directly.

## Looking Forward

The strong and substantive ties between Singapore and China did not come easy. It was primarily due to the committed and visionary leadership of both sides, and depends on officials at various

**Table 1**  List of Bilateral Cooperation Councils (in Chronological Order Based on Year Established)

---

(1) Singapore-Shandong Business Council (1993)

(2) Singapore-Sichuan Trade and Investment Committee (1996)

(3) Singapore-Liaoning Economic and Trade Council (2003)

(4) Singapore-Zhejiang Economic and Trade Council (2003)

(5) Singapore-Tianjin Economic and Trade Council (2007)

(6) Singapore-Jiangsu Cooperation Council (2007)

(7) Singapore-Guangdong Collaboration Council (2009)

---

*Source*: Author's own compilation.

levels to constantly add value to the relationship. Such strong leadership, complemented by the various bilateral institutional mechanisms, will remain crucial in sustaining the momentum of bilateral ties.

From time to time, there will inevitably be hiccups in bilateral relations such as China's strong reactions to a visit by then Singapore Deputy Prime Minister Lee Hsien Loong to Taiwan in July 2004 just before he became Prime Minister. Even more recently, Singapore Minister Mentor Lee Kuan Yew's remarks in 2009 that called on the United States to balance China had caused an uproar especially among Chinese netizens. What is important is how both sides manage these hiccups when they arise. The key to better management is to demonstrate greater appreciation and mutual respect for each other's interests. On Beijing's part, it would like other countries to regard China as a "normal" country with legitimate interests as it increases its international presence. For Singapore, it would like to continue to have the room to manoeuvre among the major powers though many in China would perceive Singapore to be pro-US.

Yet, Singapore has consistently stressed that while it is close to the United States it is not its treaty ally. This distinction is crucial and does not necessarily go against China's interests. In fact, it is in China's interest to recognise this distinction and work with Singapore to build a stable, peaceful and prosperous Asia-Pacific region. The fact that Singapore is small and non-threatening is a plus point as it is in a better position to urge big players (be it the United States or China) to be more sensitive to the concerns of countries, especially the smaller ones, in the region.

For instance, Singapore Foreign Minister Shanmugam, during his visit to the United States in February 2012 (just before his China trip), reportedly urged the United States not to underestimate the extent to which the anti-China rhetoric (being whipped up in the run-up to the US presidential and congressional elections by end-2012) can spark reactions that create a new and unintended reality for the region. On the US pivot to the Asia-Pacific which is portrayed in some quarters as an attempt to contain China, Shanmugam reportedly said that any attempt by the United States to do so "will not work". Also, such efforts "will not be supported by most countries in the region". Singapore, he said, did not view the relationship between the United States and China as a "zero-sum game". He added that the "world and Asia are big enough to accommodate a rising China and a reinvigorated US".[9] The remarks that Shanmugam made were apparently appreciated by all the leaders whom he met during his trip to China. In particular, Chinese Foreign Minister Yang Jiechi reportedly told Shanmugam during talks in Beijing that having strong ties with Singapore is important in today's complex international environment.[10]

Separately, there is a view among some countries in the region that Beijing is becoming more assertive in pressing its territorial claims in the East Sea (vis-à-vis Japan) and in the South China Sea (vis-à-vis the ASEAN claimant states). Given such a perception, it is even more important for

---

[9]"Anti-China Rhetoric in US "a Mistake", *The Straits Times*, Singapore, 9 February 2012.

[10]"China Stresses Importance of Strong Ties with Singapore", *Channelnewsasia*, 10 February 2012.

China to build its existing ties with Singapore on the basis of mutual respect and mutual benefit. This will help underscore China's pledge to peaceful development. With its rising international clout, it is even more important for China to be cognisant of this. China can make a more lasting impression regionally and on the rest of the world if it can eschew the conventional practice of "might is right" and stress more on cooperation, fairness and win-win outcomes. It is also possible for China and Singapore (a non-claimant state to the South China Sea disputes) to explore how they can work together and possibly bring on board other like-minded countries such as Indonesia (another non-claimant state) to reduce the saliency of the South China Sea issue by eventually seeking an amicable and satisfactory resolution to the disputes.

# 49

# China and the EU

## Will China Come to the Rescue of Troubled Economies?

Kjeld Erik BRØDSGAARD*

*Issues of investment barriers, IPR infringements, lack of EU access to the Chinese government's procurement market, the EU's reluctance to grant China the market economy status, etc., have strained the China-EU relationship and decreased China's willingness to act as the white knight to bail out the troubled European economies.*

Relations between the United States and China are often charged with tensions. This is especially the case during election years when presidential candidates in opposition parties will usually criticise the incumbent president for being too soft on China and for allowing the Chinese to "steal American jobs". Consequently, US-China relations usually arouse more debates than other bilateral economic and political relationships China has with the outside world. However, in spite of political rhetoric and public debates, in the economic field, EU-China relations have surpassed US-China relations in importance in terms of value and volume.

## EU-China Trade

It is interesting to note that Western Europe was China's most important trading partner during the 1960s, accounting for about one-third of China's trade with the outside world.[1] During the 1980s, Japan and Hong Kong were the more important trading partners for China, and in the 1990s, US-China trade also grew rapidly. However from 2002, EU-China trade has experienced a new surge and in 2006, China's trade with the EU surpassed US-China trade, currently accounting for about 19.3% of China's trade with the outside world.[2] By 2010, the value of trade between China and the EU had quadrupled compared to 2000, reaching 395.75 billion *euro*

* Kjeld Erik BRØDSGAARD is Professor and Director at the Asia Research Centre, Copenhagen Business School.

[1] See Brødsgaard, KE and M Kirkebæk, *China and Denmark: Relations Since 1674*. Copenhagen: NIAS Press, 2000.
[2] *Zhongguo tongji nianjian 2011*. Beijing: *Zhongguo tongji chubanshe*, 2011.

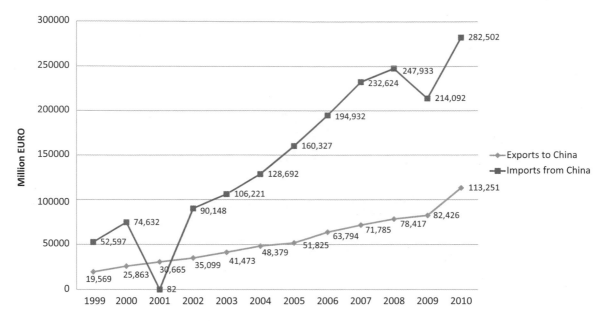

**Figure 1**    Trade with China, 1999–2010

*Source*: *Eurostat* (online data code: tet00040) (accessed 3 April 2012).

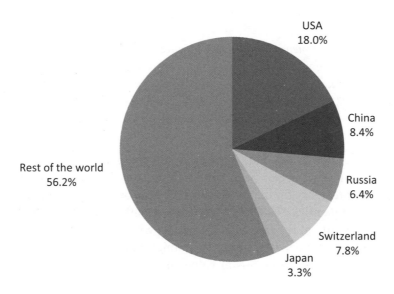

**Figure 2**    Export Share of EU's Total World Trade, 2010

*Source*: *Eurostat* (online data code: tet00040) (accessed 3 April 2012).

(Figure 1). China is now the EU's second most import trading partner after the United States, accounting for 8.4% of the EU's exports and 18.7% of the EU's imports (Figures 2 and 3). If this trend continues, China may very well become the EU's most important trading partner within the next few years.

Until the 1990s, the EU experienced a surplus in its trade with China. This has changed dramatically since 2000. According to EU sources, China now enjoys a surplus of 169 billion *euro* in its trade with the EU, almost quadrupling its trade surplus in relation to the EU (Figure 1). Currently all EU members states, except Finland, are registering trade deficits with China. The largest deficits

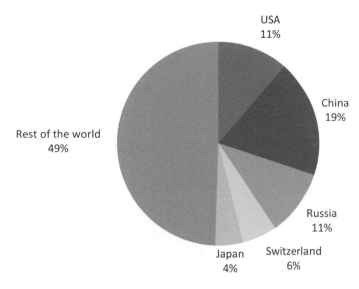

**Figure 3**    Import share of EU's Total World Trade, 2010

*Source*: *Eurostat* (online data code: tet00040). (accessed 3 April 2012).

during the first 10 months of 2011 were observed in the Netherlands (−36 billion *euro*), the United Kingdom (−24 billion *euro*) and Italy (−17 billion *euro*).[3]

Germany is by far the dominant economic power in the EU. This is also clearly the case when EU trade with China is analysed in terms of the performance of individual EU member state. Thus Germany accounts for almost half of EU exports to China. This is followed by France which accounts for 10% of EU exports to China, while United Kingdom and Italy account for about 7% (Figure 4). In terms of import, Germany is also the largest importer (22% of EU imports), followed by the Netherlands (17%), the United Kingdom (13%) and Italy (10%) (Figure 5).

According to *Eurostat*, the majority of EU exports to China are "machinery and vehicles" (60% of total exports) (Figure 6). A great part of the export in this category consists of high value-added and high technology goods and it is here that Germany continues to show its great industrial strength exporting machinery, cars and equipment of high technology content to China. "Other manufactured articles" accounts for the second most important category of EU exports to China (16%), followed by "chemicals" (11%). The EU mainly imports "machinery and vehicles" from China (48% of total imports from China) (Figure 7). This category includes power generating and industrial machinery, road vehicles and parts, ships, airplanes, railway equipment and — as increasingly important items — computers as well as electronic parts and equipment. "Other manufactured articles" is the second major import category from China (44%). Items in this category include building fixtures and fittings, furniture, watches and cameras, textiles, clothes as well as shoes and accessories. This is the category where the EU suffers the biggest deficit in its trade with China (66% of total deficit).

According to *Eurostat*, the total trade in services amounted to 38.9 billion *euro* in 2010. In this area the EU enjoys a substantial surplus of six billion *euro*. The surplus was largely drawn from "other business services" (such as trade related services, operational leasing services and

---

[3] It should be noted that Dutch imports are overestimated due to the "Rotterdam effect". Rotterdam is Europe's biggest harbour and a great number of goods destined for the rest of the EU arrive here and are recorded in harmonised EU external trade statistics in Dutch ports. For EU countries with goods that are re-exported, their shipments are recorded as intra-EU trade with the Netherlands rather than that of extra-EU trade with China. This in turn has a positive effect on their external trade balances with China.

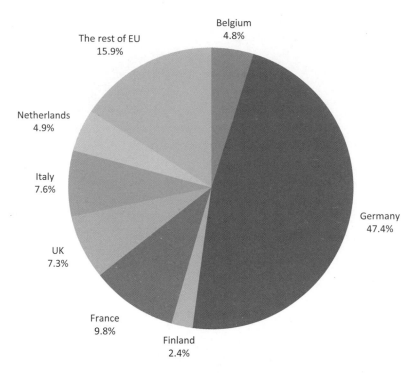

**Figure 4**    Exports to China

*Source*: *Eurostat* (online data code: DS-032655) (accessed 4 April 2012).

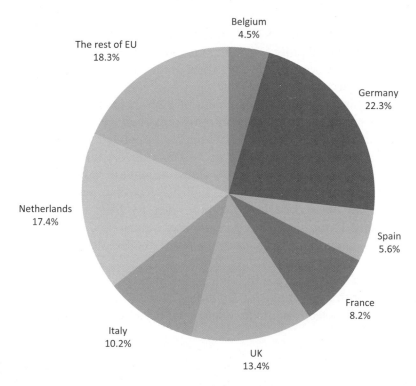

**Figure 5**    Imports from China, 2010

*Source*: *Eurostat* (online data code: DS-032655). (accessed 4 April 2012).

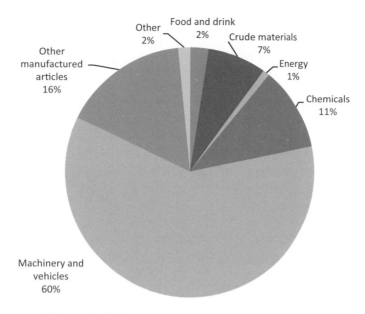

**Figure 6**   EU Exports to China, January–October 2011

*Source*: *Eurostat 2012*. 'EU-China Summit'.

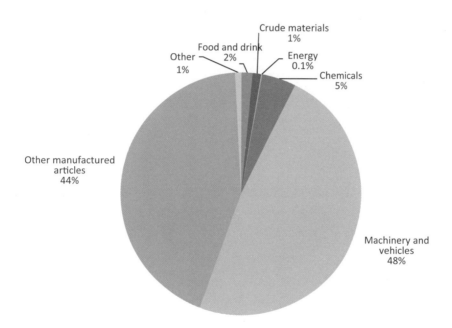

**Figure 7**   EU Imports from China, January–October 2011

*Source*: *Eurostat 2012*. 'EU-China Summit'.

miscellaneous business, professional and technical services) and from royalties and licence fees. The surplus in these categories was partly offset by a deficit in transportation.[4]

## Foreign Direct Investment

EU Foreign Direct Investment (FDI) flows into China amounted to 7.1 billion *euro* in 2010 (Figure 8). It translated into a FDI flow increase of 607 million *euro* or 9% compared to that of 2009. China's

---

[4]*Eurostat Newsrelease*, 13 February 2012.

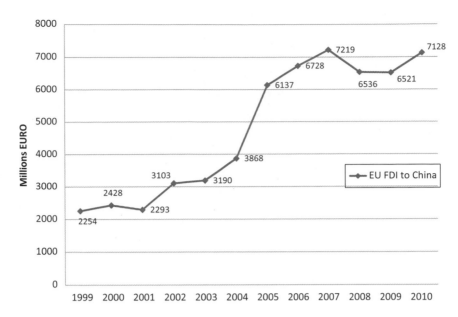

**Figure 8**    EU FDI to China, 1999–2010

*Souce*: *Eurostat* (online data code: tec00050) (accessed 3 April 2012).

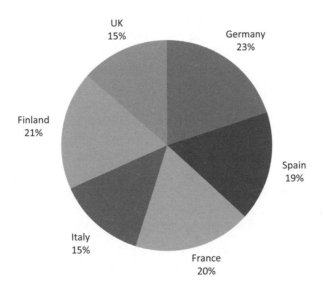

**Figure 9**    Six Largest Investors' Share of Total EU FDI to China, 2010

*Source*: *Eurostat* (online data code: tec00053) (accessed 4 April 2012).

major EU FDI partners are Germany, Finland, France, Spain, Italy and the UK (Figure 9). That Finland is able to be in the company of major European powers in terms of investment flows to China is explainable by the presence of Finnish high-tech companies — particularly Nokia — in China. This represents a major share of outward foreign direct investment for Finland but not for the EU as such, since investment in China only accounts for 5% of total EU outward FDI.[5] Since

---

[5] See Brødsgaard, KE and Hong WM, "EU-China Relations: Economics Still in Command?", *EAI Background Brief,* no. 484, 15 October 2009.

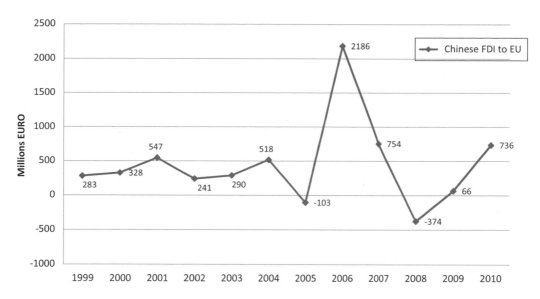

**Figure 10**   Chinese FDI to EU, 1999–2010

*Source*: *Eurostat* (online data code: tec00048) (accesed 3 April 2012).

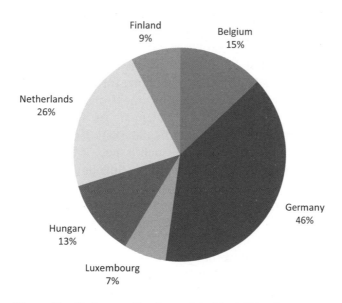

**Figure 11**   Six Largest Receivers of the Total China FDI to EU, 2010

*Source*: *Eurostat* (online data code: tec00049) (accessed 4 April 2012).

2007, the volume of EU FDI in China has stagnated, reflecting problems EU companies are experiencing concerning greenfield and brownfield investments in China.[6]

Chinese FDI in Europe also paints a rather bleak picture. In 2007, according to Chinese sources, it accounted for 3.1% of China's outflow to the world, but in 2010, this share decreased to 1.7% (Figure 10).[7] In 2010, Chinese investments mainly flowed to Germany (46% of total Chinese investments in Europe), the Netherlands (26%) and Belgium (15%) (Figure 11). From an EU perspective, Chinese FDI in Europe is rather negligible, representing less than 1% of total FDI

---

[6] See *Business Europe*, "Rising to the China Challenge", October 2011. At <http://www.europolitics.info/pdf/gratuit_ en/301573-en.pdf> (accessed 21 March 2012).

[7] *China Daily*, 3 February 2010.

inflow into Europe,[8] while US investments make up 29% of the FDI. Chinese outward investments have increased considerably in recent years, but they are directed towards Asia, Latin America and Africa rather than Europe.

## Points of Contention

There are a number of issues which prevent the EU-China trade and economic relationship from developing further. They include investment barriers, IPR infringements, anti-dumping measures and the lack of progress in granting China the market economy status (MES). China's continued refusal to accept international rules for government procurement is also an increasing point of contention.

EU companies only enjoy conditional market access in China. In industries which the Chinese authorities regard as strategic or key ones, it is almost impossible for foreign companies to establish an independent presence. These sectors are entirely dominated by Chinese state-owned enterprises (SOEs). They include power generation and distribution, telecommunications, oil and petrochemical, coal and civil aviation. Rather than relinquishing control, the Chinese state is actually increasing state-owned assets in these industries. The Chinese state also maintains strong ownership control in so-called basic and pillar industries dealing with machineries, automobiles, IT, construction, steel, base metals and chemicals. In these industries, foreign companies are required to establish joint ventures with Chinese companies and often, EU companies ended up transferring technological skills and knowledge to their Chinese partner. In sum, Chinese authorities influence almost all sectors through implementing restrictions on foreign investments.[9]

Another challenging issue regarding EU-China relations concerns the access and ownership of technology. Although China has made progress in adopting intellectual property legislation (IPR) and implementing WTO/TRIPS rules, effective enforcement of IPR laws and regulations varies significantly within China and remains highly problematic at local levels. In spite of regular government crackdowns, counterfeits still flood the market. Even when compared to other emerging markets, the Chinese still fare poorly in such issues. It comes not as a surprise when *Business Europe* reports that 85% of goods and articles infringing IPR seized at EU borders originate from China.[10]

As mentioned, a special characteristic of China's business environment is the preferential treatment given to Chinese SOEs. In particular, central SOEs under the State-Owned Assets Supervision and Administration Committee (SASAC) — the so-called "national champions" — benefit disproportionately from the government's economic policies. Examples of continued industrial policies favouring SOEs can be found in China's recent indigenous innovation policies, protection of strategic sectors, economic stimulus packages, and provisions related to public procurement. The new 12th Five-Year Programme (FYP) also emphasises traditional industries related to petrochemicals, steel and non-ferrous metals. There is also a focus on new strategic industries in green technology and energy conservation, in which SOEs will play a dominant role.[11]

Chinese central SOEs are an integrated part of the power system in China. The CEOs and board chairmen of the most powerful SOEs are on the central nomenklatura and are thus appointed by the Central Organisation Department of the Chinese Communist Party. The vice presidents are appointed by SASAC which was established in 2003 to manage central SOEs. The top managers of these companies are often rotated to hold important Party and state positions in Beijing or in the provinces. Sinopec President Su Shulin is an example. He has recently been rotated to take up the

---

[8] Brødsgaard, KE and Hong WM, "EU-China Relations: Economics Still in Command?", p. 8.

[9] *Business Europe*, "Rising to the China Challenge", p. 20.

[10] Ibid., p. 25.

[11] Brødsgaard, KE, "A Note on China's 12th Five-Year Plan", *The Copenhagen Journal of Asian Studies*, vol. 29, no. 2, 2011, pp. 143–153.

position of governor of Fujian province. Another example is Zhang Qingwei, the chairman of COMAC, who has been transferred from the company to become the governor of Hebei province. Thus in addition to clear preferential treatment in terms of industrial policies favouring SOEs, these companies also enjoy substantial political support which is often not transparent to western companies and competitors.

Discriminatory Chinese procurement practices are becoming an issue of concern among EU companies. The Chinese public procurement market is estimated to be worth several trillion *renminbi*, so naturally, western companies are eager to have access to it. Globally, European companies are highly competitive in procurement markets, but in China they are met with restricted access. In June 2009, the Chinese government issued an edict stipulating that government investment projects should primarily rely on domestically made products, which thence indirectly reinforces a policy of "buying Chinese" as the foundation of public procurement. The wind industry provides a good example of the impact this policy has had on foreign companies' ability to compete. Some European turbine manufacturers, including the Danish company Vestas, had already established factories which complied with the requirement that turbines should contain 70% locally produced content. But following the implementation of the "buy Chinese" edict, these companies were prevented from winning any of the 25 large contracts that were put up for bidding.[12] These contracts were won by seven domestic companies in the end. As a combined result of these policies, foreign suppliers' share of the Chinese wind energy market has been drastically reduced from 75% in 2004 to 12% in 2010. This has caused great concern in the global wind industry.

China has yet to accede to the plurilateral Government Procurement Agreement (GPA). In 2010, the Chinese government made an offer which was unacceptable to other GPA members. The Chinese offer for open tenders contained a threshold which is significantly higher than that set by other GPA members. Moreover, government entities, SOEs and important parts of the construction sector would not be covered. China also proposed very long transitional periods for entering into the GPA agreement.[13] In sum, 10 years after China accession to the WTO, the country still operates with government procurement practices that discriminate against foreign companies.

## Market Economy Status

To the Chinese government, the major factor impeding further progress in commercial and economic relations between the EU and China is the EU's unwillingness to grant China the MES. According to WTO rules, WTO members can use price comparisons with third countries to assess whether imports from China are unfairly priced which therefore may be subject to anti-dumping duties. If China were to be granted MES, EU authorities would no longer be able to use such comparisons. MES is important to China since it will reflect a more equal and fair treatment in cases of anti-dumping investigations as China would be placed on an equal footing with other major trading partners of the EU. MES also has political implications since it would remove the possibility of using anti-dumping measures as a weapon in trade disputes with China as was most prominently the case during the "textile war" of 2005.[14]

Although the EU Commission tends to treat its refusal to grant China MES as a technical issue, this refusal has in fact strong political connotations for China. Chinese ministers have on several occasions stated that it is completely unacceptable that China, despite being the EU's second largest trading partner, has not been recognised as having already developed a market economy. Along with the weapons embargo issue, MES remains the strongest point of contention between the EU and China. Premier Wen Jiabao appeared to associate lack of Chinese assistance to Europe

---

[12] *Business Europe*, "Rising to the China Challenge", p. 16.

[13] Ibid., p. 17.

[14] Brødsgaard, KE and Hong WM, "EU-China Relations: Economics Still in Command?".

during the current financial crisis to the EU's reluctance to grant China MES.[15] Although this was denied in the press, it undoubtedly has contributed to China's hesitance to assist the debt-ridden south European EU member states.

## EU Disunity on China

The EU is divided over how to deal with China. A 2009 report based on a comprehensive survey of European scholars, policy makers and diplomats attempts to categorise the countries in the EU into four groups based on their different views:[16] Assertive Industrialists, Ideological Free-Traders, Accommodating Mercantilists and European Followers. The group of "Assertive Industrialists" composes of the Czech Republic, Germany and Poland. They are the only EU countries which are willing to pressure China on both economic and political issues.[17]

The "Ideological Free Traders" are against trade restrictions and barriers. They are in favour of letting the market regulate their economic relationship with China as they see that the globalisation process will bring about immense advantages for their economies and industries, even though adopting this policy may mean moving jobs to China and India. However, they are ready to pressure China on political issues, in particular on issues relating to human rights. This group composes of north European countries such as Denmark, the Netherlands, Sweden and the UK.

The third group — Accommodating Mercantilists — is the largest group. These countries have not been able to phase out their labour intensive industries in due time and they fear competition from Chinese low-cost products. Given such a situation, they are therefore in favour of introducing trade restrictions and opposed to granting China MES. However, they are reluctant to confront China on political issues. Members of this group include Bulgaria, Cyprus, Greece, Hungary, Italy, Malta, Portugal, Romania, Slovakia, Slovenia and Spain, i.e. most of the EU member states in eastern and southern Europe.

The final group of EU member states prefer to let the EU Commission decide their relationship with China. They are known as the "European Followers" and consist of countries such as Austria, Belgium, Estonia, Latvia, Lithuania and Luxembourg. The governments of these countries do not see establishing economic links with China as a key priority and are happy to let others take the lead.

The authors of the report argue that these divisions are not in Europe's interest. They reinforce a negative impression that the EU is disunited and member states cannot agree with one another on important global issues. The divisions also make it possible for China to play countries or groups of countries against each other. The authors conclude that in order to deal with the EU-China challenge, the EU and its members states must find a common ground and speak with one voice. To achieve such unanimity, clear priorities have to be established and negotiating tactics formalised, so that obtaining concessions from the Chinese government becomes possible.

## Europe Changes its View on China

The European debt crisis has changed the European debate on China. For many years, the overall EU approach was to treat China as a developing country. EU strategy and position papers on China were concentrating on how to support the continued reform and transition processes in China, while little attention was given to China's growing role on the world stage. Even as late as 2006, an EU policy paper on China was still emphasising that an important part of the strategy towards

---

[15] <http://www.france24.com/en/20110914-china-still-willing-invest-europe-prime-minister-wen-jiabao-euro-debt-crisis> (accessed 8 April 2012).

[16] Fox, J and F Godement, "A Power Audit of EU-China Relations", Policy Report for the European Council on Foreign Relations, London, 2009.

[17] This section draws on Brødsgaard, KE and Hong WM, op. cit., pp. 11–12.

China was to provide assistance and aid.[18] The paper focussed on "capacity building" and "support in areas where the EU has strong experiences". The various programmes and sectoral dialogues established by the EU all aimed to help China transform itself into a modern society with capable institutions and observing human rights. It was thought that by engaging China, it would be more possible to encourage China to become a "responsible stakeholder" in international affairs.

Only with the onset of the global financial crisis in 2008 and especially under the impact of the unfolding European debt crisis from 2011 did European perceptions change. The main goal now is no longer to support China in its development process, but rather to jointly establish a level playing field where China plays by the rules of global institutions. Moreover, China's financial and economic strength, in addition to the fact that the country commands the largest foreign exchange reserves in the world, has prompted Europeans to call for Chinese assistance in seeing the EU safely through the current crisis. However, some ambivalence can be detected. On the one hand, a group of policy makers, scholars and journalists warn against a perceived Chinese attempt to take advantage of the current crisis by buying up ailing European industries; on the other hand, another group argues that more Chinese investments are needed to reinvigorate the European economy and bring debt-ridden south European countries out of the crisis.

A recent report by the European Council on Foreign Relations titled "The Scramble for Europe" belongs to the first group.[19] The report claims that China "is buying up Europe". The report states that Chinese automobile manufacturers have bought MG-Rover and Volvo and that Chinese transportation firms are acquiring and managing harbours, airports as well as logistical bases all over Europe. China's Development Bank is actively financing projects in Europe's peripheries, similar to what it is doing in Africa and Latin America. Chinese companies are exploiting Europe's open market for public procurement. Chinese purchases of public debt are eagerly sought after by debt-stricken EU member states and the Chinese government and its sovereign wealth fund are using the prospect of such bond purchases as part of their public diplomacy. They argue that China *used* to be a distant trade partner; *now* it is a powerful actor within Europe itself. China has also devised a new "European strategy". Due to recriminations on human rights, the continuation of the arms embargo and the refusal to grant MES, China has lowered its political expectations of Europe and no longer wants a "strategic partnership" with Europe. Instead it focusses on bilateral relations with EU countries while paying lip service to regional institutions. In fact, what China is doing is to apply to Europe a strategy which is paying off elsewhere in the developing world.[20]

The report also maintains that as a result of China's growing presence in Europe, the nature of the debate on China has changed. Evaluating the classification of the four distinct groups identified in the 2009 report by the European Council on Foreign Relations, the more recent report claims that the "European Followers" are on the verge of extinction. The financial aid that China is able to provide now constitutes a part of every country's strategy to try to get out of the crisis. The "Accommodating Mercantilists" are increasingly desperate for Chinese investments. South European members of this group are now more interested in getting monetary advantages from China than in protecting their labour intensive industries. The "Ideological Free Traders" in northern Europe have been frustrated by the continued barriers and restrictions to access the Chinese market. They are now split between the need to delegate more authority to Brussels to enable the Commission to put more pressure on China and a wish to seek contracts and business opportunities for themselves. The "Assertive Industrialists" have also differing policies. While

---

[18] EU Commission, "Closer Partners, Growing Responsibilities", Commission Working Document (2006). At <http://trade.ec.europa.eu/doclib/docs/2006/october/tradoc_130791.pdf.> (accessed 3 April 2012). See also EU Commission, "EU-China: Closer Partners, Growing Responsibilities," Communication from the Commission to the Council and the European Parliament. At <http://trade.ec.europa.eu/doclib/docs/2006/october/tradoc_130875.pdf> (accessed 5 April 2012).
[19] Godement, F and J Parello-Plesner with A Richard, "The Scramble for Europe", Policy Brief, European Council on Foreign Relations, July 2011.
[20] Ibid., p. 2.

Germany and German companies are increasingly faced with competition from Chinese companies moving up the value chain, the Czech Republic and Poland have become less assertive in order to attract Chinese investments.

As a result of these shifts, new groupings and fault lines have emerged. Europe is now increasingly divided between "frustrated market-openers" and "cash-strapped deal-seekers". The former "Ideological Free Traders" still believe in open Chinese access to the European market, but they also seek ways to use free trade as a negotiating tool with China. Germany has also started to focus on reciprocity in the relationship, especially in terms of public procurement. In fact both former "Ideological Free Traders" and Germany are drawn towards supporting the position of France, which is to advocate a strong common European bargaining position against China. However this emerging unity among major EU countries is undermined by the "cash-strapped deal-seekers" who see China's aid as an alternative to European or IMF loans. These new divisions weaken the EU's approach to China. The report cites a prominent Chinese academic observer who states, "There is a race to the bottom: everyone is offering us incentives for investment from China."[21]

There have been reports about China stepping in to buy assets in Italy and other south European countries.[22] However, although Chinese companies have established hundreds of representative and sales offices in Europe, available statistics and media reports do not seem to substantiate a major Chinese commercial and economic inroad into Europe. Many of the deals mentioned in "Scramble for Europe" have not been substantiated. Some of such unverified deals include the rumour that China would buy one billion *euro* Spanish bonds and that Chinese firms and banks have committed to inject $64 billion to trade and cooperation agreements in Europe from October 2010 to March 2011.[23] Instead it appears that Chinese investments in Europe are still rather modest, thus prompting scholars and policy makers to argue for a concerted European attempt to generate more Chinese investments. It is interesting to note that while market expansion appears to be the most important purpose of Chinese investments globally, in the case of Europe, the most important purpose for China is to acquire well-known brands.[24] Examples include Nanjing Auto's US$500 million acquisition of MG-Rover in 2005 and Geely's purchase of Volvo in 2010 for the sum of US$1.8 billion.[25] In 2011, two smaller Chinese car companies, Pangda and Zhejiang Youngman, also attempted to acquire Swedish Saab, but the deal fell through, as General Motors (GM), the former owner of Saab, was nervous about having its technology transferred to Chinese companies. Failure to reach a consensus over the issue pertaining to access to intellectual property also stymied a proposal by Beijing Auto to take a stake in GM's Opel unit in 2009.[26] As shown in Table 1 Chinese SOEs have recently also developed interest in investing in the European energy and utilities sectors. In January 2012, China's sovereign wealth fund, China Investment Corporation (CIC), bought an 8.7% stake in Thames Water, a utility group in the UK; and in December 2011, Three Gorges Corporation purchased the Portuguese government's stake in the utility Energias de Portugal (EDP) for 2.7 billion *euro*. It has also been announced that State Grid, China largest electricity network, is in the final bidding round for REN which operates Portugal's power transmission networks.[27] However, as in many other cases where Chinese investments have been reported, this deal has yet to be materialised.

---

[21] Ibid., p. 9.

[22] See *Financial Times*, 13 September 2011.

[23] Godement, F and J Parello-Plesner, "The Scramble for Europe", p. 4.

[24] Clegg, J and H Voss, "Chinese Direct Investment in the European Union", Leeds University Business School, Leeds University, 1 September 2011.

[25] Thøgersen, CB, "More Chinese Investment to Europe", *Berlingske Tidende*, 1 February 2012.

[26] *Financial Times*, 4 November 2011.

[27] *Financial Times*, 21–22 January 2012.

**Table 1**   Recent Chinese Investments in Europe

| Chinese Investor | European Acquisition | Amount (in US$ million) | Year |
| --- | --- | --- | --- |
| Geely | Volvo | 1,800 | 2010 |
| COSCO | Piraeus Harbour | 2,800 | 2010 |
| Shandong Heavy Industry Group | Ferretti | 178 | 2012 |
| Three Gorges Group | Energias de Portugal | 3,750 | 2012 |
| CIC | Thames Water | 9% stake | 2012 |
| Sany Heavy Industry | Putzmeister | 475 | 2012 |
| LDK Solar Co. | Sunways AG | 31 | 2012 |

*Sources*: Thøgersen, CB, "More Chinese Investment to Europe," *Berlingske Tidende*, 1 February 2012; "China's New Silk Road to Europe," <http://www.telegraph.co.uk/news/worldnews/europe/greece/7869999/Chinas-new-Silk-Road-into-Europe.html> (accessed 5 April 2012); *Business Week*, 29 March 2010; *International Herald Tribune*, 11 January 2012; *Financial Times* 21 January 2012; *China Daily*, 21 January 2012; "China's Sany to Acquire Putzmeister," <http://www.ft.com/intl/cms/s/0/7aecad0a-4a5e-11e1-a11e-00144feabdc0.html#axzz1rYYeCaUf> (accessed 2 April, 2012); "LDK Solar Makes Bid for Sunways to Secure Distribution", <http://www.businessweek.com/news/2012-01-04/ldk-solar-makes-bid-for-sunways-to-secure-distribution.html> (accessed 2 April 2012).

## Will China Rescue Europe?

During the *eurozone* crisis, there has been much talk about China assisting the EU to contain the crisis. European leaders have been looking for foreign capital to buy up government bonds in the ailing south European economies. In September 2011, for example, it was reported that China already held 4% of Italy's treasures.[28] Italian foreign minister Franco Frattini also declared that 14% of Italy's public debt was in Chinese hands. If what has been reported is true, this will make China the most important holder of Italy's treasures. European leaders have also sought Chinese investments in the European Financial Stability Facility (EFSF) which was set up in 2010 to address the European sovereign debt crisis. It was reported that after one important summit on the crisis, former French President Sarkozy called on Chinese President Hu Jintao to provide capital.[29] Given the fact that the EU is China largest export market, European leaders believe that it has to be in China's interest to help solve the south European debt crisis and prevent the *euro* from collapsing. In addition, 20% to 25% of China's foreign exchange reserves are thought to be in *euro*, which provides another important reason for China to support the *eurozone* economies.

However, China is hesitant to act as the white knight to rescue the crisis-ridden *eurozone* countries. There are several reasons for this. One reason is that Chinese leaders deem the *eurozone* crisis as more of a problem related to politics. This is clearly reflected in Wen Jiabao's statement at the Davos summer meeting where he commented that the most pressing problem was for the European leaders to bring their own house in order. When German Chancellor Angela Merkel in a visit to China in February 2012 asked Chinese investors to buy Italian and Spanish debt, Lou Jiwei, chairman of CIC, responded that more reforms in both countries were needed before China would make the move.[30] Another reason is associated with sheer commercial concerns. It is simply not seen as a wise move to invest heavily in south European bonds. Thirdly, many common Chinese folks oppose to the idea of a major rescue mission. This is reflected in Chinese microblogs as well as in official publications such as the *People's Daily*. It is voiced that per capita income in China is still much lower than that of Greece or Portugal and therefore China should focus on developing its economy instead. Finally, European opposition to accommodate Chinese wishes concerning

---

[28] *Financial Times*, 12 September 2012.

[29] <http://www.bloomberg.com/news/2011-11-01/fortress-favors-hu-over-sarkozy-in-swaps.html> (accessed 2 April 2012).

[30] AFP, 13 February 2012.

MES and the continued European weapons embargo are both not conducive to create an environment in which China will benefit from acting as a benefactor.

## Looking into the Future

EU-China commercial and economic relations have developed rapidly over the last decade and the EU is now China's most important trading partner as well as export destination. However the trade relationship is not in balance and the EU is suffering from a trade deficit which by 2011 had grown to 169 billion *euro*. In terms of mutual foreign direct investments, the picture is even less rosy. EU investments in China have stagnated since 2007 and only account for 5% of total EU outward investment currently. Chinese investments in Europe, although increasing, account for less than 1% of total FDI inflow into Europe.

There are a number of issues which prevent the economic relationship from achieving its full potential. They include Chinese investment barriers and IPR infringements, as well as Chinese reluctance to open the huge Chinese government procurement market to European companies. On the part of the EU, anti-dumping measures and lack of progress in granting China MES also strain the relationship. Moreover, EU countries often prioritise their own national interests before everything else. This is clearly detrimental to achieving a common EU cause.

Of late, there has been much talk about China coming to the rescue of the crisis-stricken *eurozone* countries in southern Europe. Although reliable information is scarce, from various incidents and reports, it seems highly probable that China is hesitant to commit major investments in Europe. Recent events indicate the need for a serious discussion among EU leaders as to what role China should or can play in the current crisis. These events highlight that perhaps it is time for European leaders to strike a grand bargain with China concerning the common future economic and political relationship. This would have to include European proposals for China to contribute financially to solve the current debt crisis. An appropriate first step might be to grant China MES so long as such a move still leaves the EU some bargaining power. The EU will have to hasten their action as according to WTO rules, China will automatically acquire MES in 2016.

# 50

# China's Diplomacy in the Middle East

CHEN Gang and Ryan CLARKE*

*As an emerging global power, China's growing involvement in the energy-rich Middle East has the potential of gradually eroding traditional US dominance in the region.*

The Middle East, a focal point of great power rivalry in the past century, has assumed heightened strategic importance for China, a rising power that once lacked interest and involvement in the region due to distance and limited historical ties. Its strengthened position in the consciousness of Chinese leaders is directly related to the trajectory of China's massive industrial expansion that has increased its dependence on reliable overseas energy supplies as well as export markets for its wide range of goods, some of which trade on low profit margins.

## China's Intensified Energy and Economic Engagement in the Middle East

China has surpassed the United States to become the world's biggest energy consumer according to the International Energy Agency.[1] It increased crude oil purchases by 14% year-on-year to a record of 203.8 million metric tons in 2009, or 4.1 million barrels a day, accounting for more than half of China's total oil consumption.[2] China is now more dependent on oil from the Middle East than the United States, with over half of its imported oil coming from the region. Among the six leading oil exporters to China, four (Saudi Arabia, Iran, Oman, Sudan) are located in the Middle

---

*CHEN Gang is Research Fellow at the East Asian Institute, National University of Singapore. Ryan CLARKE was a Research Fellow at the East Asian Institute, National University of Singapore. He is now working in the private sector.

[1] "China Tops U.S. in Energy Use", *The Wall Street Journal*, 18 July 2010.

[2] "China's 2009 Crude Oil Imports Advance to Record (Update1)", *Bloomberg News*, 10 January 2010. "China's Crude Oil Imports to Grow 12–15% in 2010 (2010 *nian zhongguo yuanyou jingkou yuji zengzhang* 12%–15%)", *Hexun News*, 22 January 2010.

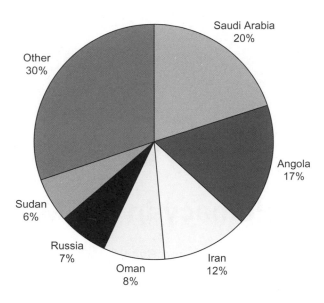

**Figure 1**   Major Oil Exporting Nations to China (2008)

*Source*: The figure is based on data from *China Customs Statistical Yearbook* (2008), p. 218.

East with Angola and Russia being the exceptions (Figure 1). Saudi Arabia is now exporting the most crude oil to China, accounting for about 20% of China's total oil imports.

In early 2009, China overtook the United States as the world's largest exporter to the Middle East and this was the first time in over 60 years that the number one ranking had changed.[3] China is very likely to be the Middle East's largest trade partner (including export and import) in the future, with the country's total trade with the Middle East exceeding US$53 billion for the first four months of 2010.[4] Besides the surging trade between China and Middle Eastern countries that has exceeded US$100 billion (in 2004 it was only 36.4 billion),[5] China's investment and contracted projects in the region are increasing rapidly thanks to its comparative advantages in constructing infrastructure like airports, roads, railways and telecommunication facilities.

The Gulf is also becoming an important destination for investment for China's own energy industry as it actively seeks business overseas and the oil economy is the key link to the growing trade between the two regions. Furthermore, the Gulf is a potential market for Chinese commodities as well as an entry point for exports to the greater Middle East and East Africa. Although resistance from the United States is likely, a platform of common interests will likely emerge between a China that seeks to maintain strong economic growth and a Gulf that is pursuing economic diversification regarding its energy exports.[6]

A common perception exists in the Middle East that Chinese economic involvement does not come with any strings attached and that Beijing will ignore criticisms from Western nations as well as some regional neighbours pressuring China to abandon this practice. This pragmatic, amoral method of diplomacy is arguably China's key advantage vis-à-vis Western powers in advancing and consolidating its interests in this region and as such, Beijing will likely be very keen to retain this tool.

---

[3] China's exports to the region had soared to US$60 billion from just US$4 billion a decade ago. For example, see Simpfendorfer, B "China is the World's Largest Exporter to the Middle East", *The Daily Reckoning*, 30 July 2009.

[4] "China, Middle East Trade Soars as Economies Rebound", *Dow Jones News*, 14 July 2010.

[5] "Chinese Premier Urges Upgrading China-Arab Cooperation", *Xinhua News*, 13 May 2010.

[6] Zha D, "Energy Interdependence", *China Security*, Summer 2006.

### *China's Middle East Diplomacy: From Passive to Cautiously Active*

Beijing has begun to realise the increasing geopolitical and geo-economic importance of the Middle East since China became a net oil importer in 1993. Gradually departing from its passive diplomacy, China began to engage the region in a more coordinated manner and adjust its policy actively in the service of growing commercial and energy interests. Chinese diplomacy has succeeded in institutionalising China-Middle East relations through mechanisms like the China-Arab Cooperation Forum and the China-GCC (Gulf Cooperation Council) Framework Agreement on economic, trade, investment and technological cooperation. China and GCC countries launched negotiations on the free trade area (FTA) in 2004 but due to divergences and obstacles, the negotiations are still in process. In spite of the slow progress, the two-way trade between the two sides in 2008 totalled nearly US$70 billion, comprising around US$42 billion worth of exports by the GCC and US$28 billion in Chinese exports to the region.[7]

The first China-Arab Forum was held in January 2004 when Chinese President Hu Jintao visited the headquarters of the Arab League in Cairo. Since then, such forums have been held every two years. In May 2010, the Fourth Ministerial Meeting of China-Arab Cooperation Forum issued the Tianjin Declaration, in which both sides agreed to forge the China-Arab "strategic cooperative relationship" featuring comprehensive cooperation and common development.[8] Also, considering the existing tensions between GCC countries and Iran, Beijing has been playing balanced diplomacy by pulling Tehran into the Shanghai Cooperation Organisation (SCO) as an observer.

In an attempt to enhance its energy security, China is using diplomacy to help its state-owned enterprises (SOEs) secure equity stakes in oil and gas fields in the Middle East. The China Petroleum and Chemical Corporation (Sinopec) has scored big successes in Iran and Saudi Arabia such as a US$100 billion contract with Iran to buy 10 million tons of liquefied natural gas (LNG) per year over 25 years, a 50% stake in Iran's Yadavaran oilfield, and a contract to explore and produce natural gas in the Rub al-Khali Basin in Saudi Arabia.[9] The China National Petroleum Corporation (CNPC), another state-owned oil giant, has invested heavily in the energy sector of Sudan and Algeria.

### *China and Iraq: A New Chapter in Beijing's Oil Diplomacy?*

CNOOC Ltd, the listed unit of China National Offshore Oil Corp, and Turkish Petroleum Corp (TPAO), clinched a deal in May 2010 to develop the Missan oil fields in southern Iraq. The two companies have obtained a 20-year technical services contract to increase the output of the Missan oil fields, located 350 kilometres southeast of Baghdad, to 450,000 barrels per day (bpd) over the next six years. The Chinese company will act as the operator and hold a 63.75% stake in the project while the Turkish state-owned company will hold an 11.25% stake and the Iraqi Drilling Company will have the remaining 25% stake in the project. However, the deal is still subject to approval from the Iraqi government.[10]

In June 2009, a partnership between British Petroleum and the China National Petroleum Corporation won the first contract awarded in Iraq, a country that has until recently seemed to be firmly in the American sphere of influence.[11] Together, they are developing the Rumaila oilfield, Iraq's largest.[12] That same month, Sinopec purchased Addax, a Swiss-based and London- and Toronto-listed energy company with substantial oil assets in the Middle East, namely Iraq's

---

[7] "GCC Projected to Become Major Global Trade Hub", *Emirates Business*, 17 May 2010.

[8] "China, Arab States Agree to Establish Strategic Cooperation Relations", *CRI News*, 16 May 2010.

[9] Calabrese, J "The Risks and Rewards of China's Deepening Ties with the Middle East", *China Brief* (Jamestown Foundation), vol. 5, issue 12, 24 May 2005.

[10] Wan Z, "CNOOC Bags Oilfield Deal in Iraq", *China Daily*, 18 May 2010.

[11] Bradsher, K, "As Iraq Stabilizes, China Bids on Its Oilfields", *New York Times*, 30 June 2009.

[12] "China Cancels 80% of Iraqi Debt", *Associated Press*, 2 February 2010.

Kurdistan region, for C$8 billion.[13] Sinopec's rival, the CNPC, started drilling in the spring of 2009 in the Ahdab oil field in south-eastern Iraq.[14]

The Iraqi government originally tried in 2008 to award oil fields to Western companies through a no-bid process. That prompted objections from a group of US Senators who wanted greater transparency and the plan was replaced with an auction, which had the effect of letting Chinese companies play a much larger role.[15] China has also made forays into the Iraqi cement industry and has started building a billion-dollar power plant in the south while the Chinese and the United Arab Emirates are in advanced talks to build residential complexes.[16] China and Iraq entered into trade deals valued at US$3.8 billion in 2009 and in early 2010, China forgave 80% of Iraqi debt as a sign of Beijing's commitment to the country.[17]

There is a perception amongst some in the West, and the United States in particular, that China is a "free rider" in Iraq as it did not participate in the invasion yet it has benefited economically. Similar complaints have been voiced regarding Chinese involvement in Afghanistan and as such, Washington is likely to actively pressure the Iraqi government to place limits on the scale and scope of energy cooperation with China. However, American leverage on this issue is likely to be limited as China was the first country to re-open its embassy in Iraq following the American offensive and has actively engaged successive Iraqi governments. Furthermore, like all other major supplier nations, it is in Iraq's long-term interests to diversify its export markets in order to maintain a degree of diplomatic space to manoeuvre in Baghdad's dealings with the West. It is this basic need for flexibility and options that American diplomacy is unlikely to be able to negate.

If current trends continue, it can be claimed that China's initial high-risk strategy of early engagement with Iraq and the deployment of substantial diplomatic personnel to what was essentially still an active war zone, will mature into an asymmetric victory for China's energy security strategy. China will have gained long-term access to one of the most energy-rich countries in the world without having to do any "heavy lifting" regarding security provision while also simultaneously avoiding any suspicion or hostility associated with that provision which could harm China's future energy and other economic prospects in the region.

### China's Increasing Regional Diplomatic Profile

Besides China's economic penetration, the emerging power is exerting more influence on such core diplomatic issues in the Middle East as nuclear proliferation, the Israeli-Palestinian conflict, terrorism, reconstruction of war-torn Iraq and arms sales in the Middle East. While the two prolonged wars in Iraq and Afghanistan as well as the financial crisis have challenged American influence in the region, China's Middle East policy, while remaining focussed on securing its long-term access to regional energy supplies, is slowly shedding its low-profile posture and moving towards playing a more active role in mediating regional disputes.

In 2002, at the request of several Arab states, China for the first time in its history appointed a special envoy for Middle Eastern affairs. The establishment of the post, which was first filled by veteran diplomat Wang Shijie and later by Sun Bigan and Wu Sike, has signalled that China is ready to play a larger mediation role in the Middle East peace process that has long been dominated by the Quartet. Chinese envoys have visited Israel and all of its neighbours, and supported the concept of "land for peace" forwarded by other major actors. However, Beijing's new involvement

[13] Mason, R, "China buys Addax for £4.4bn to Tap Iraqi Oil", *Telegraph*, 24 June 2009.
[14] Bradsher, K, op. cit.
[15] Bradsher, K, op. cit.
[16] Fadel, L and E Londono, "Risk-tolerant China Investing Heavily in Iraq as U.S. companies Hold Back", *Washington Post*, 2 July 2010.
[17] "China Cancels 80% of Iraqi Debt", *Associated Press*, 2 February 2010.

reflects very practical concerns: peace can bring the stability needed to ensure a steady flow of oil.[18]

Beijing has become more assertive on the Iraq issue although its space for manoeuvring is limited. In contrast to the previous low-profile policy that actively discouraged the raising of Chinese proposals on the Middle East, China's mission to the United Nations (UN) in 2004 issued a proposal to set a date for a US military withdrawal. Russia, France and Germany supported China's proposal, which was reflected in the final text of the UN Security Council Resolution 1546. This was an unprecedented move by China in the Middle East and the fact that it received some Western backing is noteworthy. However, its significance should not be overestimated as the United States ignored it.

### Beijing and Tehran: Oil Diplomacy becomes More Complicated

By 2009, China had become Iran's primary trading partner, with bilateral commercial sales worth nearly US$30 billion, rising from an extremely low base of US$400 million in 1994.[19] Besides trade, Beijing has also invested heavily in a wide variety of energy-related and non-energy projects[20] in Iran. Although American pressure has prevented Beijing from selling provocative weapons such as ballistic and cruise missiles to Iran, Iran was still China's second largest export market for arms sales next to Pakistan between 2005 and 2009. Such sales included anti-ship missiles and portable surface-to-air missiles.[21]

In its policies towards Iran and related nuclear issues, the Chinese leadership is walking a diplomatic tightrope to avoid direct confrontation with the United States while not harming its growing energy and diplomatic ties with Iran. Beijing's intense interest in Iran is driven by both broad geostrategic factors and more narrow economic and energy considerations. While China has joined the US-led international efforts to pressure Iran to reveal the details of its growing nuclear programme, China's stance towards Iran's nuclear activities is by no means entirely in line with that of the West because Beijing only supports limited sanctions on the condition that they are conducive to the peaceful resolution of the nuclear imbroglio. China had sought to avoid a sanctions vote, saying earlier in 2010 that it was wrong to even discuss such measures as long as a negotiated settlement remained possible. After intense lobbying by the United States and its allies, however, China surprisingly voted in favour of the UN resolution targeting Iran in June 2010 in a bid to compel Tehran to cooperate with international inspectors.

As an observer to the China-led SCO, a regional security organisation, Iran is seeking full membership in the organisation, which would make Iran feel more secure when confronting the United States on the nuclear issue. China remains cautious about Iran's petition, but the endorsement from Beijing is not totally impossible. Given its existing policies, Iran stands as a potential counterweight to excessive US influence in the Middle East, a check on US unilateralism on various issues relevant to the region, and a possible source of leverage in support of Chinese

---

[18] Jin L, "Energy First: China and the Middle East", *Middle East Quarterly*, Spring 2005.

[19] Swaine, MD, "Beijing's Tightrope Walk on Iran", *China Leadership Monitor*, no. 33, 2010.

[20] China's major upstream and downstream investment projects in Iran include Sinopec's anticipation of developing Iran's large Yadavaran oil field (with estimated reserves of three billion barrels); China National Petroleum Corporation (CNPC)'s development of the North and South Azadegan oil fields; the upgrading of Iranian oil refineries and enhancement of oil recovery capabilities; the development of the North and South Pars gas fields; the construction of a liquefied natural gas (LNG) plant; and the construction of oil and gas pipelines. It is reported that China would invest US$48 to 50 billion in oil and gas ventures as a result of such arrangements. China is also involved in Tehran's metro system, shipping and railway projects.

[21] SIPRI Arms Transfers Database, "SIPRI Trend Indicator Values of Arms Exports from China, 2005–2009." At <http://www.sipri.org/contents/armstrad/output_types_TIV.html> (accessed January 2011). See also SIPRI Arms Transfers Database, "Transfers of Major Conventional Weapons: China to Iran, 2005–2009." At <http://www.sipri.org/contents/armstrad/at_data.html> (accessed 9 July 2012).

interests vis-à-vis other regional powers such as Saudi Arabia and Israel.[22] However, there is likely to be a limit to the extent of sustained multidimensional cooperation between China and Iran given the latter's long-term strategic goals. Unlike China, Iran's leadership openly voices its disdain for the current regional and greater international system and both the actions and statements of the Ahmadinejad regime strongly suggest that Iran seeks to fundamentally alter the diplomatic framework in which issues are handled in the Middle East.

### China and the Israeli-Palestinian Dispute: Beyond Oil?

Chinese leaders conduct official diplomatic visits to the "State of Palestine" as opposed to the "Palestinian Territories" or the "West Bank/Gaza", labels typically used by the United States and other countries, and Chinese leaders treat bilateral exchanges with their Palestinian counterparts as major diplomatic events on par with other high-level state-to-state visits.[23] However, a systematic analysis of China's Palestine policy reveals that it is in fact driven by pragmatic concerns that are very much in line with the international consensus on the Israeli-Palestinian conflict led by the United States. For instance, China supports the principles outlined in the various peace initiatives that have governed the Israeli-Palestinian peace process over the years, such as the 1991 Madrid Conference, 1993 Oslo Accords, 2002 "Road Map," and the 2007 Annapolis Conference, among others.[24] Despite its revolutionary history, China is unlikely to break from the US-led international mainstream and pursue its own policy. Such an action is unlikely to bring about objective positive changes in the situation while also bringing China into direct confrontation with the United States. All of this would occur without meaningfully enhancing China's energy security or consolidating its interests in the region.

### Interaction with the US: Divergence and Convergence

As an emerging global power, China's growing involvement in the highly strategic, energy-rich Middle East has the potential of gaining offensive influence,[25] something which would gradually erode traditional US dominance in the region. While the Chinese leadership may not intend to overtly challenge American influence in the Middle East, regional desires and China's growing economic presence may necessitate a revisiting of this policy although any shifts will likely be cautious and non-dramatic.

The two countries share many common concerns in the region. Both the United States and China generally accept the current set of diplomatic "rules" and norms in the Middle East, support a two-state solution to the Israeli-Palestinian dispute, seek energy security, and oppose terrorism and nuclear proliferation. In certain aspects, it is fair to say that China has benefited from costly American actions that have maintained relative stability in the Middle East in recent years without having to make any sacrifices itself.

Despite becoming more assertive towards issues regarding Iran, Sudan and Iraq, China has so far respected the American pre-eminence in the region and has refused to openly confront the United States in areas Washington regards as being of critical strategic importance. China's new activism in the region consists of engaging those whom the United States has sought to isolate and penetrating traditional US allies. This does increase the risk of diplomatic collisions with the only superpower as it has the potential to limit American strategic space for unilateralism.

---

[22] Swaine, MD, op. cit.

[23] Zambelis, C, "China's Palestinian Policy", *China Brief*, vol. 9, issue 5, 4 March 2009.

[24] Ibid.

[25] For the purposes of this chapter, "offensive influence" refers to the ability of Beijing to attenuate the US alliance structure or otherwise marginalise American influence. For a more in-depth discussion, see Mederios et al., "Pacific Currents: The Responses of U.S. Allies and Security Partners in East Asia to China's Rise", RAND Corporation, 2008.

When formulating its Middle East policies, Beijing attempts to balance two sets of competing interests. On the one hand, it seeks to expand cooperation and influence in the region to secure overseas energy supplies and bolster its rising international status. On the other hand, it does not want its emerging role in the Middle East to antagonise the United States.[26] This balance will be increasingly difficult to maintain as some Middle Eastern countries want to see a rising China act in a Soviet Union-like role in counter-balancing US predominance. However China, viewing friendly and stable Sino-American relations as paramount preconditions for its further economic development, would rather choose to maintain a lower diplomatic profile and shy away from independent policy formation so as to avoid direct confrontation with the United States.

### Still in the Experimental Stage

Despite having received substantial attention within policy circles, the media and academia, China's approach towards the Middle East is still forming. China does not yet possess a crystallised grand strategy which guides its actions in the region and as such, Chinese actions in energy, trade and diplomacy should be viewed as components of an ambitious but fluid process that does not yet have a clearly articulated end-game. Given this reality, Chinese policy is likely to remain conservative, especially on the diplomatic front, and it is unlikely to seek to chart its own path and confront the American-led regional order in the near to mid-term. While it is tempting to attribute this stance to a present lack of capability, *this approach is also likely to hold even if/when China's offensive influence increases and it can fathom a different approach.* Challenging American hegemony in the Middle East would prove arduous and costly. The end result of any successful attempt would likely be either a multipolar yet unstable or even a China-led regional order that is still characterised by a strong latent American presence, neither of which is a desirable foreign policy outcome for Beijing.

---

[26] Alterman, J and J Garver, *The Vital Triangle: China, the United States and the Middle East*, Center for Strategic and International Studies (CSIS) Press, Washington, 2008.

# 51

# Will the United States Desert Taiwan?

John F COPPER*

*Evidence of Obama adopting a policy of ditching Taiwan is seen in frequent articles in the media and academic journals. However, whether this policy comes to fruition is less than certain because of US Congress' support for Taiwan and China's preference for Taiwan to return willingly.*

For the past three-plus years, whether the United States would remain, as it has been in the past, Taiwan's close friend and protector, has come into question. In fact, there has been considerable speculation that Washington wants to, and will, abandon Taiwan. To some this may sound like history repeating itself. This is indeed not the first time.

In 1949, when Chiang Kai-shek, his military and party fled to Taiwan after his army was defeated by Mao's communist forces, President Truman declared that the United States would no longer defend Chiang. However, with the onset of the Korean War in June 1950, Truman reversed that policy and dispatched the Seventh Fleet to the Taiwan Strait to block an invasion of Taiwan by Mao's People's Liberation Army.

An apparent attempt to abandon Taiwan occurred again in 1972 when President Richard Nixon, seeking a way out of the Vietnam War and needing an ally against the Soviet Union, met with Chinese leaders in Beijing to arrange a rapprochement between Mao's People's Republic of China (PRC) and the United States. To accomplish this mission, Nixon had to change if not end the relationship the United States had with Taiwan. He thus stated, indirectly at least, that Taiwan was a part of China and pledged to withdraw American forces from Taiwan. There was speculation that he intended to establish formal diplomatic relations with China soon and terminate relations with Taiwan. However, Taiwan's supporters objected, Watergate paralysed the Nixon White House and Nixon's apparent intention did not come to fruition.

In 1978, President Jimmy Carter concluded an agreement normalising relations with the PRC and established formal diplomatic relations with Beijing. The agreement did not make provisions to continue military or other relations with Taiwan. Carter in essence abandoned Taiwan. But the

---

*John F COPPER is the Stanley J Buckman Professor of International Studies at Rhodes College in Memphis, Tennessee. He is the author of a number of books on Taiwan, including the fifth edition of *Taiwan: Nation-State or Province?* published in 2009 and *Taiwan's Democracy on Trial* published in 2010.

US Congress, backed by public opinion, came to Taiwan's rescue and within months enacted the Taiwan Relations Act (TRA). The TRA returned Taiwan its "sovereignty" (in the US eyes), made provision for continued economic ties and more importantly, pledged US weapons sales and the presence of American forces in the region to uphold the Act.

The Obama administration has also adopted a policy of abandonment. It is different, however, insofar as it is not the product of one policy move. Rather it is a gradual or incremental policy. It has the support of the media and the academic community in the United States. It reflects the "reality" of China's rise, America's debts to China, and the view that America can no longer protect Taiwan considering America's economic overstretch and its population's tiring of war.

The Obama policy of forsaking Taiwan seems more serious in many ways than the previous ones. Yet there are obstacles to it succeeding.

## China's Rise and America's Decline

Both the impetus for and the reasoning behind America's current policy of abandoning Taiwan, many say, come from the reality that China is an economic juggernaut and that the United States is falling behind China and will never catch up. Since 1978 when China launched vast economic reforms under Deng Xiaoping, it has experienced "miracle" economic growth, weathered the "Asian financial crisis" in 1997 and sustained high growth rates through the recent global recession. Further, China continues to experience rapid economic expansion. The United States meanwhile has fallen into recession followed by a period of slow growth recovery that appears to be long-lasting.[1]

In any event, only a few observers do not believe that China will pass the United States soon to become the world's largest economic power. The International Monetary Fund predicts that it will happen in four years.[2] This will, if history is instructive, have far reaching consequences.

China's dynamic economy made it possible for it to vastly increase its military spending. Since 1991, its military budget has grown at double-digit rates annually while its navy and air force, which are relevant to China projecting military power (its army is not) and challenging US military in Asia, have grown even faster.[3]

China's most recent military budget announced in 2011 was larger than 10%. If measured in purchasing power parity (PPP) terms, it is around two-thirds of the US defence budget. Taking into consideration that the United States has global obligations, China, whose military is for the most part a regional one, is eclipsing the United States in terms of its military spending in Asia. Moreover, China's military spending is forecast to increase even faster over the next few years; in fact, by 2015, it is projected to grow by almost 20% and to double what China is spending currently. In three years China will spend four times Japan's military budget and more than the anticipated total military spending of countries in the region.[4]

---

[1] See Overholt, WH, *The Rise of China: How Economic Reform is Creating a New Superpower*, New York: W.W. Norton, 1993 for an analysis of how China's economic boom began. For an assessment of China passing the United States economically, see Subramanian, A, *Eclipse: Living in the Shadow of China's Economic Dominance*, Washington, DC, Peterson Institute, 2011, ch. 1.

[2] Gardner, D, "The Age of America Ends in 2016: IMF Predicts Chinese Economy will Surpass U.S.", in *Daily Mail*, 25 April 2011, <http://www.dailymail.co.uk/news/article-1380486/The-Age-America-ends-2016-IMF-predicts-year-Chinas-economy-surpass-US.html> (accessed May 2012).

[3] For an assessment of China's military power as it has resulted from China's economic growth, see Lampton, DM, *The Three Faces of Chinese Power: Might, Money and Minds,* Berkeley, University of California Press, Santa Monica, CA: Rand Corporation, 2008.

[4] "China's Military Spending to Double by 2015 — Report", *Wall Street Journal*, 14 February 2012, <http://blogs.wsj.com/chinarealtime/2012/02/14/chinas-military-spending-to-double-by-2015-report/> (accessed May 2012). The article cites *IHS Janes* as its source.

Some experts say China can easily afford this kind of bigger military budgets; the United States cannot compete and trying so will only make the United States further dependent upon China financially. Or it may even cause America's economy to collapse.[5]

Meanwhile China's increased spending has made it possible to develop new and very sophisticated weapons: an aircraft carrier, a stealth fighter plane, satellite killer missiles, advanced cyberweapons and more. The result has been that the survival of US bases in Okinawa and Guam cannot be assured and the US Navy must operate in seas further and further away from China.[6]

While China has bolstered its military expenditures by record amounts, the United States has reduced its military spending dramatically. Over the last two to three years, America has pared the Pentagon's budget by US$400 billion and is expected to cut a similar amount by midway into the next decade. It is projected that the United States will soon spend only 3% of its gross national product on defence, the lowest since World War II.[7]

As a result of its costly engagement in wars in the Middle East and its budget cutting, the United States has no new manned aircraft under development for the first time in its aviation history, no surface ships or attack submarines in the design phase and is losing critical skills it needs to sustain a strong military.[8] During a two-year period up to 2011, Washington has cancelled or terminated 30 defence programmes. Top military officials have been discussing new programmes to deal with the growing threat of China, but many oppose making financial and other commitments that are necessary for this.[9]

Even before the recent evidence of the United States falling behind China in military power grabbed the attention of American scholars and the US media, in 2008, one of America's premier military-linked think tanks, the Rand Corporation, published a study saying that the United States will not be able to defend Taiwan soon.[10]

## The Campaign for Dumping Taiwan

During the 2008 US presidential election campaign, Barack Obama announced some basic tenets of American foreign policy that he would adopt if he became president. He would discard the worldview held by the Bush administration (especially those of the neocons), follow the guidance of international organisations, transform America into a more likeable and respected country, and realise US interests abroad by negotiations rather than using military force. His policy ideals did not give much attention to Asia and unlike his opponent, John McCain, and many other top American leaders, he did not confirm that the United States had an obligation towards Taiwan.[11]

When a US candidate for the presidency wins, it often generates a wave of support among the media and the academic community, and of course, Washington officialdom, for his or her new policies. This election of 2008 was no exception. In fact, this phenomenon was more obvious than usual.

A change in US Taiwan policy soon became apparent. It was seen first by US military brass making the case that the United States was overcommitted and could not continue to defend Taiwan. This was followed by a "wave" of US scholars and pundits writing to justify a new American policy that cast off Taiwan.

---

[5]See Glosserman, B, "China Policy: Avoiding a Cold War Redux", PacNet #31 (Pacific Forum CSIS), 2 June 2011.

[6]Boot, M, "Slashing America's Defense: A Suicidal Trajectory", *Commentary*, January 2012, p. 18.

[7]"Ten Questions on the Future of U.S. Defense Spending Priorities for Secretary of Defense Nominee Leon Panetta", *Articles and Commentary,* American Enterprise Institute, 7 June 2011.

[8]Mackenzie, E and B McGrath, "A Day Without U.S. Sea Power", *Weekly Standard*, 6 June 2011, p. 22.

[9]Gertz, B, "Gates Warns of 'Hollowing Effect'; Sees Obama Cuts as Blow to Military," *Washington Times*, 25 May 2011 <http://www.washingtontimes.com/news/2011/may/24/gates-warns-of-hollowing-effect/?page=all> (accessed May 2012).

[10]Stiltton, J and S Perdue, *Air Combat Past, Present and Future,* (Santa Monica, CA: Rand Corporation, 2008).

[11]See Obama, B, "Renewing American Leadership", *Foreign Affairs*, July/August 2007 and John McCain, "An Enduring Peace Built on Freedom", *Foreign Affairs*, November/December 2007.

President Obama supplied hints for what he wanted in terms of a US Taiwan policy shortly after his inauguration when his administration broke from the long adhered to practice (sometimes said to be a basic tenet of US Taiwan policy) of not discussing America's military support of Taiwan with China.[12] Obama officials offered to host talks between high-ranking military officers from both China and Taiwan.[13]

The Obama policy shift of dumping Taiwan was first suggested overtly by his administration just after Senator Obama was elected president. Bill Owen, vice chairman of the joint chiefs of staff, gave an interview to the *Financial Times* in which he said the TRA is "outdated" and the US relationship with China should not be based on hedging and the idea of competition, but rather on cooperation and trust.[14] This was followed by comments from Admiral Joseph Prueher, a former ambassador to China and once commander of the US Pacific Fleet. Prueher declared that Taiwan was a serious "point of contention" between the United States and China and that US arms sales to Taiwan was a major sticking point and should be reconsidered.[15]

Supporting these opinions, the Rand Corporation published another report on the Taiwan "situation". This study warned that China's growing arsenal of short-range missiles and fighter planes would destroy Taiwan's defences in an initial strike after which China would have air superiority over Taiwan and the Taiwan Strait. The United States would be unable to deploy sufficient weapons in a timely manner to deal with the situation. It concluded that the military trends regarding America's relationship with Taiwan were in China's favour.[16]

In 2010, the Council on Foreign Relations (CFR) took the lead publishing articles in the prestigious journal *Foreign Affairs* advocating a new relationship with Taiwan that ended America's protectorate role. (CFR members are considered close to policy makers and this organisation is the most influential non-governmental organisation in the United States in the realm of foreign affairs.)

The first article of this genre posited the argument that Taiwan's more cordial stance towards China engineered by President Ma Ying-jeou after he won the presidency in 2008 should prompt the United States. The United States should expect Taiwan to logically adopt a relationship towards China like that of Finland towards the Soviet Union during the Cold War. In other words Taiwan should be "Finlandised".[17]

A second *Foreign Affairs* article appeared the following year wherein the author argued that the United States should end its guardianship role vis-à-vis Taiwan because that policy is based upon "pessimistic realism" — which will likely lead to war with China. It is also a wrong policy, stated the author, since China's main objective is economic development and that being so the United States can accommodate China's rise. The writer concluded that the United States should back away from its commitments to Taiwan so as to remove a flashpoint between the United States and China.[18]

A few months later a *New York Times* piece suggested that the United States could cope with its US$1.4 trillion debt to China, which was a drag on the US economy, by writing off the debt in exchange for terminating its arms sales to Taiwan. The author is one of the most unabashed advocates for dumping Taiwan.[19]

---

[12] President Reagan had promised this in his "Six Assurances" delivered to Taiwan.

[13] Ho C, "Offer of Talks May Boost Military Ties", *Taiwan Journal*, 29 February 2009, cited in D Hickey, "Rapprochement between Taiwan and the Chinese Mainland: Implications for American Foreign Policy", *Journal of Contemporary China*, March 2011, p. 235. Hickey, based on interviews with Chinese academics, believes the story is correct even though various officials have denied it.

[14] Owen, B, "America must Start Treating China as a Friend", *Financial Times*, 17 November 2009.

[15] "A Way Ahead," Miller Center for Public Affairs, University of Virginia, 2011.

[16] Shlapak, DA, DT Orletsky, TI Reid, MS Tanner and B Wilson, *A Question of Balance: Political Context and Military Aspects of the China-Taiwan Dispute*, Santa Monica, CA, The Rand Corporation, 2009.

[17] Gilley, B, "Not So Dire Straits: How the Finlandization of Taiwan Benefits U.S. Security", *Foreign Affairs*, January/February 2010.

[18] Glaser, C, "Will China's Rise Lead to War? Why Realism Does Not Mean Pessimism", *Foreign Affairs*, March/April 2011.

[19] Kane, PV, "To Save Our Economy, Ditch Taiwan," *New York Times*, 10 November 2011.

There have since been numerous other articles published in the media and academic journals suggesting a "new" relationship with Taiwan, one that essentially follows President Obama's lead in demoting and ultimately abandoning Taiwan. The most recent one by former National Security Adviser Zbigniew Brzezinski calls Taiwan an "endangered species" because of America's decline, Taiwan's "vulnerability to China's pressure" and the "attractiveness of an economically successful China".[20]

### President Obama's Actions to Dump Taiwan

President Obama's desire to jilt Taiwan was evident during his first trip to China in late 2009. In talks with Chinese leaders, Obama concurred, in a written statement, that Taiwan is one of China's "core interests". Core interest is understood by the United States as an issue China (or another country) would be willing to go to war over. Two of China's other core interests are Tibet and Xinjiang — both territories of the PRC.

The significance of this was such that the Chinese media gave it serious attention and interpreted it to mean the Obama administration agrees with China's position that Taiwan is part of China.[21] Taiwan reached the same conclusion as the Chinese media. A former legislator in Taiwan describes Obama's statement as leaning towards "giving Beijing what it has sought for decades ... to accept China's claim to sovereignty over Taiwan".[22]

During the visit, President Obama referred to the Three Communiqués that constitute the basis for US China/Taiwan policy. He did not mention the TRA passed by the Congress, which has superior legal status to the communiqués that are only executive agreements. (As official documents, the communiqués all favour China; the TRA favours Taiwan.)

During the first two-plus years of the Obama administration, no cabinet-level or subcabinet-level official visited Taiwan. During that time frame, Taiwan was never mentioned in any official speech by any Obama administration official and noting that the chairwoman of the House Foreign Relations Committee spoke of "appeasement in the air".[23]

President Obama's appointments to a number of high-level government positions and the reassignments of others show an attitude of neglect if not dislike for Taiwan. Robert Gates, who is known to be sensitive to China's concern about arms sales to Taiwan, is kept as the Secretary of Defence. Kurt Campbell, the Assistant Secretary of State, known for his expertise on and sympathy towards Taiwan, is tasked with dealing with Central Asian and not Taiwan issues. Evan Medieros, known for his strong support for China and dislike for Taiwan, is made China adviser in the National Security Council. A number of China experts left and were replaced by Japan experts or specialists in other areas or Asian countries.[24]

The fate of US arms sales to Taiwan further evidenced that the Obama administration wished to ditch Taiwan. The sales were delayed many months, held up by bureaucratic requirements. When sales of the planes Taiwan requested were finally granted, the F-16C/Ds (which are General Dynamics F-16 Fighting Falcon multirole jet fighter aircraft) were not approved. Instead the Obama administration allowed an upgrade of Taiwan's less capable F-16s and made no provision

---

[20] Brzezinski, Z, "8 Geopolitically Endangered Species", *Foreign Policy*, January/February 2012.

[21] "There is Room Enough for Both of Us", *China Daily*, 17 November 2009, <http://www.chinadaily.com.cn/cndy/2009-11/17/content_8982308.htm> (accessed May 2012)..

[22] Chang, P, "Is President Obama Abandoning Taiwan?" *Wall Street Journal*, 30 November 2009 <http://online.wsj.com/article/SB10001424052748703939404574566921385329470.html> (accessed May 2012).

[23] Representative Ileana Ros-Lehtinen, chairwoman of the House Foreign Affairs committee made this statement. She also referred to a "new spirit of appeasement in the air". See Lowther, W, "US Lawmaker warns China on Taiwan, *Taipei Times*, 13 June 2011; "Never Fear, Taiwan — Congress is Here", *Wall Street Journal*, 17 June 2011.

[24] "Obama's Failing Taiwan Policy," The Taiwan Link, 2 August 2011.

for Taiwan to get submarines that the latter also wanted and needed. The kicker, according to some observers, was the media report that this would be the last US sale of arms to Taiwan.[25]

During the campaign that preceded the January 2012 election in Taiwan, the Obama administration made decisions and took actions that were seen in Taiwan as trying to sway voters to vote for President Ma and the Nationalist Party. Some called the White House decisions to send high officials to Taiwan, grant visa-free status to Taiwan, arrange a national security briefing and send a former official in charge of US-Taiwan relations (who was interviewed on television just before the voting and cited "concerns" if the opposition candidate were elected). All these were seen as US interference in Taiwan's election, which Washington had frequently vowed not to do.[26] There were various interpretations to US actions. One was that the Obama administration wanted to control Taiwan's relations with China so that it could do what it wants with Taiwan.

Shortly after this, President Obama met with China's expected new leader Xi Jinping in Washington, DC and stated that he "rejects" any call for Taiwan's independence; the usual term was "not support." Obama again made reference to Washington's one-China policy "based on the three communiqués (not mentioning the TRA).[27]

## Taiwan: Still a Contentious Issue

Whether President Obama and his administration will succeed in abandoning Taiwan is uncertain. There are two sets of difficulties involved with implementing this policy. One is the US Congress and the other, China.

Obama's treatment of Taiwan has raised the hackles of many members of Congress. The Congress wants to guard its prerogatives in making US Taiwan policy. In 1979, it passed a bill legalising that relationship (the only one ever) in the form of the TRA.

The Congress thus exerted strong pressure on the administration to grant Taiwan more arms sales than the Obama administration wanted and generated support in the United States for this based on the issue of creating jobs. The Republican Party was very strong in condemning the administration for its interference in the recent election and for otherwise abandoning Taiwan.[28] The Congress can be expected to continue to support Taiwan in the future.

It is obvious that China wants to bring Taiwan back into the fatherland or incorporate Taiwan; it regards Taiwan as Chinese territory. Yet no one could be sure whether this is an immediate objective or that Beijing wants to accomplish it by any means possible. Recovering Taiwan through coercion does not seem desirable as it would undermine China's "peaceful rise" campaign. It would hurt its relations with many countries in Asia and beyond, and it would favour the military over the civilian leadership at a sensitive time.

Chinese leaders perceive time is on their side and do not see the situation as a crisis (a declaration of independence by Taiwan or an increase of Japanese influence on the island is its biggest worries and the likelihood of both have diminished in recent months). Chinese leaders would prefer Taiwan to willingly join China and they calculate that that will happen because of the economic advantages Taiwan will enjoy in doing so. In conclusion, the Obama administration may be pursuing a policy that it is unable to implement and whose timing is not appropriate. Other presidents have had this experience.

[25] "Dim Sum for China", *Economist*, 24 September 2011, p. 18.

[26] Copper, JF, *Taiwan's 2012 Presidential/Vice Presidential and Legislative Elections: Assessing Current Politics and Charting the Future*, Baltimore: University of Maryland School of Law, 2012.

[27] Shih H, "Concerns over Possible US Policy Changes Dismissed", *Taipei Times*, 15 February 2012.

[28] Lowther, W, "U.S. Republican Party focusing on Taiwan", *Taipei Times*, 13 January 2012, <http://www.taipeitimes.com/News/taiwan/archives/2012/01/13/2003523135> (accessed May 2012).

# 52

# Managing Cross-Strait Economic Relations

CHIANG Min-Hua*

*The recently signed Economic Cooperation Framework Agreement between Taiwan and China is not only a result of the intensifying economic relationship but also serves to further reinforce the economic connection between the two sides.*

Trade and investment relationships between Taiwan and China have been thriving since the 1990s even though there is no economic cooperation mechanism across the strait to support its development. The enactment of Taiwan's mainland investment policy since the 1990s has been a response to its uncontrollable upsurge in investment volume into China. The establishment of a more formal, legalised economic relationship with China became urgent with the escalation of economic interaction across the strait. Taiwan's willingness to sign the Economic Cooperation Framework Agreement (ECFA) with China in 2010 is therefore not to be seen as a move to further encourage cross-strait economic relationship, but rather, a passive reaction of the Taiwanese government towards its inevitable strengthening relationship with the mainland.

Indeed, China's preferential policies to attract foreign direct investment (FDI) since its economic opening up in 1979, cheap Chinese labour force, geographic proximity, cultural and language similarities, taken altogether, made China very attractive to Taiwanese investors. China soon became the top destination of Taiwan's outward investment, serving as a low-cost production and main export platform. In 2011, Taiwan's investment in China totalled US$14 billion, accounting for 80% of Taiwan's total outward investment. As a result of Taiwan's growing investments in China, exports of capital equipment and semi-industrial goods from Taiwan to China have increased rapidly. Since 2000, China and Hong Kong combined have surpassed the US to become Taiwan's largest export destination, accounting for 40% of Taiwan's total exports in 2011.

---

* CHIANG Min-Hua is Visiting Research Fellow at the East Asian Institute, National University of Singapore.

Meanwhile, Taiwan's imports from China increased to 16% in the same year, making China the second largest import source for Taiwan.

While China has generally opened its doors to Taiwan, the Taiwanese government is hesitant to forge closer economic relations with China. Nonetheless, the growing economic ties with China have forced Taiwan to make some changes. The more economic opening up towards China is unavoidable. In the meantime, the more institutionalised relations will further reinforce Taiwan's economic dependence on China in the foreseeable future. This chapter provides a retrospective of the policy transformation in cross-strait economic exchanges over the past three decades.

## Overview of Taiwan's Growing Investments in China: Push and Pull Factors

Due to the prohibition of direct investment in China before the 1990s, the Kuomintang (KMT) government did not record any Taiwanese outward investment in the mainland. The Chinese official figures showed that, before 1988, the cumulative realised Taiwanese investment in China already reached US$22 million. It then shot up sharply within a year to US$1,600 million in 1989.[1] By the end of 1992, Taiwan's investment amounted to US$9 billion, making it the second largest investor in China, after Hong Kong.[2] In order to deal with growing private contact between Taiwan and China, regulations on cross-strait business were enacted by the KMT government progressively. In 1990, Taiwan's Ministry of Economic Affairs (MOEA) issued the "Methods of Control over Investment and Technological Cooperation", which allowed a list of products produced on the mainland by Taiwan's manufacturers.[3] According to the "Regulations Governing Investment and Technical Cooperation with Mainland China" in 1993, Taiwan's direct investment in China was still prohibited by the Taiwan's government. Yet, it offered several channels through which Taiwan's firms could invest indirectly to China.[4] As Taiwan's investment in China grew, the MOEA wanted to ensure that core factories are based in Taiwan and peripheral factories are set up in China.

In contrast with Taiwanese government's limited opening up on outward investment in China, the Chinese government tended to be more ready to embrace investment from Taiwan and Hong Kong as well. In 1980, China set up special economic zones (SEZs) in four cities, namely Shenzhen, Zhuhai and Shantou in Guangdong province (bordering Hong Kong), and Xiamen in Fujian province (across the Taiwan Strait). In 1984, 14 additional coastal cities in China were opened successively to become SEZs. In July 1988, the Chinese government enacted the "Regulations for Encouraging Investment by Taiwan Compatriots". In May 1989, two investment zones for Taiwanese firms in Xiamen and Fuzhou, both in the Fujian province, were established.[5] China's strategy to attract Taiwanese investments by establishing SEZs in coastal cities near Taiwan proved to be a success. In 1991, for example, 74% of Taiwanese investments in China were in Guangdong and Fujian.[6] In March 1994, the Standing Committee of the National People's Congress (NPC) further adopted the "Law on the Protection of Investment by Taiwan Compatriots" which aimed at creating a more favourable investment environment for Taiwanese entrepreneurs.[7] In December 1999, the State Council formulated the "Detailed Rules for the Implementation of the

---

[1] The figures are obtained from the Taiwan Affairs Office of the State Council, People's Republic of China.

[2] Chen X, "Taiwan Investments in China and Southeast Asia: Go West, But Also Go South", *Asian Survey*, vol.36, no.5, May 1996, p. 451.

[3] Lin TC, "Taiwan's Investment Policy in Mainland China: A Domestic Perspective", *Journal of Chinese Political Science*, vol. 3, no.2, Fall 1997, pp. 25–46.

[4] Indirect investment channels include (i) establishing a branch of a Taiwanese company in a third country; (ii) injecting investment in another company located in a third country; (iii) working via a company in a territory outside mainland China; and (iv) making indirect remittance.

[5] Chang MH, "Greater China and the Chinese Global Tribe", *Asian Survey*, vol. 35, no.10, October 1995, pp. 955967.

[6] Statistics of Investment Commission of the Ministry of Economic Affairs, Taiwan.

[7] Chen X, op. cit., pp. 9–10.

Law on the Protection of Investment by Taiwan Compatriots".[8] In addition to the investment privileges, the Taiwanese investors, compared with other Western investors in China, usually had greater access to certain important business information thanks to interpersonal relationship (*guanxi*).[9]

While permitting Taiwan's investment in the mainland under certain conditions, the Taiwanese government had been searching for alternative regions for Taiwanese investors. In 1993, the KMT government began to implement a "Southward policy" to divert part of the mainland investment to other Asian countries.[10] The Southward policy finally proved to be a failure as Taiwan's investment in Southeast Asian countries did not grow as much as expected. On the contrary, Taiwan has injected considerable investment in China since the 1990s. In 1996, former Taiwanese President Lee Teng-hui (1988–2000) announced the "go slow, be patient" policy to prevent Taiwan from being overdependent on China's economy. The policy which was designed to restrict investment in China reflected the deteriorating relationship across the strait and Taipei's escalating vigilance towards Beijing. The Chinese military action against Taiwan between 1995 and 1996 especially caused the island's economy to suffer amid the chaos. Under Lee's policy, investment projects in the mainland that were worth more than US$50 million or related to infrastructure and advanced technology sectors were banned. The policy aimed to not only contain the outflow of massive Taiwanese financial capital to China but also ensure that strategic and technology-oriented sectors are developed on the island. At the same time, between 1997 and 1999, the Southward policy was relaunched with similar dismal results as the first launch as there was no obvious increase in Taiwan's investment in Southeast Asia. As shown in Figure 1, Taiwanese investment in Southeast Asia once accounted for 39% of Taiwan's total outward investment in 1991, but it soon plummeted to 5% in 2000. In comparison, only 10% of Taiwan's total outward investment was in China in 1991, but this ratio increased rapidly to 66% in 1993 and maintained between 28% and 60% from

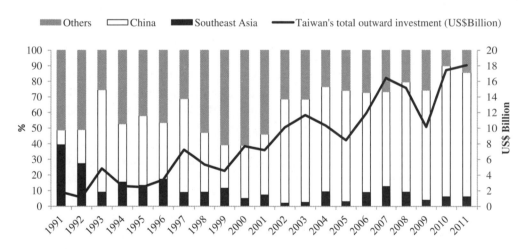

**Figure 1**   Taiwan's Outward Investment by Country/Region, 1991 to 2011

*Note*: Southeast Asia includes Singapore, Malaysia, Thailand, the Philippines, Indonesia and Vietnam.

*Sources*: Monthly Statistics, Investment Commission, MOEA, Taiwan; *Taiwan Statistical Data Book 2011*, Council for Economic Planning and Development, Executive Yuan, Taiwan, p. 278.

---

[8]Taiwan Affairs Office of the State Council, "Actively and Realistically Promote Three Direct Links across the Taiwan Straits by Reliance on the People and in the Interests of the People", 17 December 2003.

[9]Billes, E, "L'ouverture extérieure chinoise: de la Chine à une grande Chine? Une étude du fait sino-transnational" (China's opening up: from China to a greater China? A study on China and overseas Chinese relations), Thèse de Doctorat en Economie Internationale, Université Pierre Mendès France, Grenoble, 1999, pp. 214–216.

[10]The implementation of the Southward policy included the following countries: Malaysia, Singapore, Thailand, Vietnam, Indonesia, the Philippines and Brunei.

1994 to 2000. In fact, after the mid-1990s, more and more Taiwanese enterprises, especially the large ones with advanced technology, have begun to invest massively in China via their holding company in a third region in order to bypass the rules.

Unlike President Lee, former Taiwanese President Chen Shui-bian (2000–2008) realised the difficulty of effectively restricting the outward investment in China and therefore adopted a relatively more open policy. Some analysts believed that Chen's more liberalised policy on outward investment was a result of pressure from Taiwanese entrepreneurs. In comparison with President Lee, the Chen administration was politically weak at the beginning, which explained his susceptibility to domestic business influence.[11] When Chen came to power, Taiwan experienced the most severe economic recession since 1949. Economic growth rate dwindled to −2% in 2002. As the Democratic Progressive Party (DPP) government was short of economic experts in its cabinet, proposals from the business community became imperative for Chen. About a third of Chen's economic council membership was made up of representatives of the business community.[12] Although Chen adopted a more liberalised economic policy towards China, outward investments in high technology sectors in China were still prohibited. The direct transportation, essential for facilitating the trade across the strait, was still banned. Nonetheless, the volume of investment from Taiwan, comprising mostly technology-intensive enterprises continued to increase steadily. Between 2002 and 2011, 64% to 84% of Taiwan's total outward investment, mainly in sectors that manufacture electronic parts, computers and optical products, was in China.

## ECFA as a Milestone of the Cross-Strait Economic Integration

Shortly after KMT regained the presidency in early 2008, cross-strait negotiation, which had halted for nine years, resumed. During the talks between Taiwan-based Straits Exchange Foundation (SEF) and China's Association for Relations across the Taiwan Straits (ARATS), or Chiang-Chen summit,[13] a wide spectrum of agreements had been signed (Table 1). The establishment of cooperative measures across the strait was no surprise as both sides have vigorously sought to improve relations. Contrary to Chen's era — when his strong "Taiwanese consciousness" and pursuit of Taiwan's de facto independence were less favoured by China — President Ma Ying-jeou's greater emphasis on "Chinese ethnicity" and "cross-strait unification" won much China's applause. The re-election of President Ma Ying-jeou in 2012 indicated that the KMT government's economic opening-up policy towards China during the first term of Ma's presidency is supported by the majority of Taiwanese, especially some prominent Taiwanese entrepreneurs, who publicly affirmed that the 1992 consensus is beneficial for Taiwan-China economic cooperation as well as Taiwan's economic development in the future.

At the Fifth Chiang-Chen Summit in June 2010, ECFA and Cross-Strait Agreement on Intellectual Property Right Protection and Cooperation were signed. With the implementation of the early harvest programme under ECFA on 1 January 2011, China began to lower tariffs on 539 Taiwanese goods, ranging from agricultural to manufacturing products such as petrochemicals, machinery, transport equipment and textiles, while Taiwan reduced tariffs on 267 items imported from the mainland. However, Taiwan restricts the import of agricultural goods from China and the

[11]Wong SS, "Economic Statecraft across the Strait: Business Influence in Taiwan's Mainland Policy", *Asian Perspective*, vol. 29, no. 2, 2005, pp. 66–69.

[12]Business leaders were invited to attend formal meetings to review cross-strait investment restrictions and they also met frequently with government officials to offer economic advices. Kastner, SL, "Does Economic Interdependence Constrain, Inform, or Transform? Preliminary Evidence from the Relationship across the Taiwan Strait", *Paper prepared for the International Studies Association annual meeting*, Honolulu, Hawaii, March 2005, p. 12.

[13]Chiang Pin-kung is the chairman of SEF and Chen Yunlin is the chairman of ARATS. The Chiang-Chen Summit followed the previous Cross-Strait talks, or Koo-Wang Summit, which was suspended in 1999.

**Table 1**   Cross-Strait Agreements during Chiang-Chen Summits, 2008 to 2011

| Chiang-Chen Summits | Date | Location | Agreements Signed |
|---|---|---|---|
| First | June 2008 | Beijing | i. SEF-ARATS Minutes of Talks on Cross-Strait Charter Flights<br>ii. Cross-Strait Agreement Concerning Mainland Tourists Travelling to Taiwan |
| Second | November 2008 | Taipei | i. Cross-Strait Postal Service Agreement<br>ii. Cross-Strait Sea Transport Agreement<br>iii. Cross-Strait Air Transport Agreement<br>iv. Cross-Strait Food Safety Agreement |
| Third | April 2009 | Nanjing | i. Joint-Crime Fighting Cooperation<br>ii. Cross-Strait Financial Cooperation Agreement<br>iii. Cross-Strait Air Transport Supplementary Agreement<br>iv. Items of Consensus Reached Concerning Mainland Investment in Taiwan |
| Fourth | December 2009 | Taichung | i. Agreement on Cooperation of Agricultural Product Quarantine and Inspection<br>ii. Agreement on Cooperation in respect of Standards, Metrology, Inspection and Accreditation<br>iii. Cross-Strait Agreement on Cooperation in respect of Fishing Crew Affairs |
| Fifth | June 2010 | Chongqing | i. Economic Cooperation Framework Agreement<br>ii. Intellectual Property Right Protection and Cooperation |
| Sixth | December 2010 | Taipei | i. Cross-Strait Agreement on Medical and Health Cooperation |
| Seventh | October 2011 | Tianjin | i. Nuclear Security Cooperation Agreement |

*Source*: Mainland Affairs Council, Taiwan.

**Table 2**   Planned Tariff Reduction Schedule in the Early Harvest Programme — Trade in Goods

| Mainland's Planned Tariff Reduction Schedule | | | | Taiwan's Planned Tariff Reduction Schedule | | | |
|---|---|---|---|---|---|---|---|
| Original Tariff | First Year (since 01/01/2011) | Second Year (since 01/01/2012) | Third Year (w.e.f. 01/01/2013) | Original Tariff | First Year (since 01/01/2011) | Second Year (since 01/01/2012) | Third Year (w.e.f. 01/01/2013) |
| 0% | 0% | 0% | 0% | 0% | 0% | 0% | 0% |
| 5% | 5% | 0% | 0% | 2.5% | 2.5% | 0% | 0% |
| 15% | 10% | 5% | 0% | 7.5% | 7.5% | 2.5% | 0% |

*Source*: Mainland Affairs Council, at < http://www.mac.gov.tw/ct.asp?xItem=85852&ctNode=6790&mp=204>, (accessed 3 October 2011).

manufacturing items listed in the early harvest programme remain very limited. The tariffs of the aforementioned items will be reduced progressively until the goal of zero tariffs is reached in 2013 (Table 2). In terms of trade in services in the early harvest programme, China opens up 11 service sectors to Taiwanese entrepreneurs for investment, while Taiwan opens nine of its service sectors to the mainland (Table 3).

The Ma administration regarded ECFA as an equivalent to free trade agreement (FTA) and as a means to promote the island's economic growth. Taiwan has been excluded from the growing regional FTAs in recent years. Prior to ECFA, Taiwan had only signed FTAs with a few countries in Central and South America (Panama, Honduras, Guatemala, Nicaragua and El Salvador) which

**Table 3**   Early Harvest Programme — Trade in Services

| | Service Sectors | China Opens to Taiwan | Taiwan Opens to China |
|---|---|---|---|
| Financial Services | Banking | √ | √ |
| | Securities and futures | √ | |
| | Insurance | √ | |
| Business Services | Accounting, auditing | √ | |
| | Computer and related services | √ | |
| | R&D services | √ | √ |
| | Design services | √ | √ |
| | Convention | √ | √ |
| | Exhibition | | √ |
| | Medical — hospital set-up | √ | |
| | Cultural — movie imports | √ | √ |
| | Sporting, recreational services | | √ |
| | Air transport | √ | √ |
| | Distribution — commission agents' services | | √ |

*Source*: MOEA, "Annex IV Sectors and Liberalization Measures", at <http://www.ecfa.org.tw/RelatedDoc.aspx> (accessed 3 April 2011).

accounted for a small proportion of Taiwan's total external trade. This worried the Taiwanese government, especially when the FTA between China and the Association of Southeast Asian Nations (ASEAN) took effect on 1 January 2011. The Taiwanese government feared that ASEAN's further trade negotiations with China, Japan and South Korea to form ASEAN Plus Three would diminish Taiwan's economic significance in the region. The threat of marginalisation pushed the Taiwanese government as well as Taiwanese entrepreneurs to pursue an economic agreement with China. A sustainable economic prosperity subsequent to the deepening of economic relationship with China is also beneficial for the KMT to maintain its political power on the island. The DPP's inability to move the island's economy forward during Chen's presidency, and its failure to provide a credible alternative to the ECFA, has provided the KMT considerable room in promoting economic cooperation with China.

It is believed that the KMT's return to power in 2008 is crucial for Beijing's promotion of unification. China's cooperation with the KMT government in managing cross-strait economic affairs and its offer of orders to Taiwanese manufacturing companies, and the procurement of Taiwan's agricultural products in recent years were considered approaches to boost Taiwanese people's support for the KMT.[14] Apart from the political intention, economically, ECFA also ensures continual flow of Taiwan's investment to the mainland, thus supporting China's export-driven economy as well as facilitating further industrial upgrading. Since its economic opening up in 1979, foreign investments have played a significant role in China's overall external trade. In 2011, for

---

[14] In addition to economic cooperation measures, China has dispatched many business delegations to Taiwan since 2009. For example, in May 2010, Fujian provincial governor Huang Xiaojing led a 3,000-member delegation to Taiwan and claimed that he had made a purchase of NT$24 billion (about US$783 million) from Taiwanese companies. Prior to this, Shanghai mayor Han Zeng also led a delegation that confirmed NT$1.8 billion in business with Taiwan. Su Y, "Hu Frets over Taiwanese Election", *Asia Times*, 4 October 2011, at <http://www.atimes.com/atimes/China/MJ04Ad01.html> (accessed 8 October 2011); "Mainland China's First Procurement Delegation to Taiwan—Special Report ", *People's Daily online*, 3 June 2009, at < http://tw.people.com.cn/BIG5/98292/9401576.html > (accessed 8 October 2011).

example, 52% of China's exports and 50% of its imports were produced by foreign investors.[15] Taiwanese investment is one of the most important foreign investments outside of mainland China. Chinese official figures show that in 2011, Taiwan's investments in China amounted to US$6.7 billion, only behind Hong Kong's at US$77 billion.[16] According to a document "Top 200 Exporting Companies in China" issued by China's Ministry of Commerce in 2009, six of the top 10 exporting companies in China were subsidiaries of Taiwanese enterprises. In particular, Quanta Computer, Foxconn, and Compal — all Taiwanese-owned firms — are leading exporting companies in China.[17] While Taiwanese investments are important for maintaining China's export strength, Taiwan's small market is not so attractive for Chinese companies. Taiwan's small economy and population size of 23 million constitute a limited market size, thus constraining business profitability. As a result, from China's perspective, attracting Taiwan's financial capital into the mainland is far more essential than urging Taiwan to open up its market.

In the long run, institutionalised relations are expected to foster closer trade and investment ties between Taiwan and China. Stronger cross-strait economic relations also mean that the island's economy will be increasingly dependent on the mainland rather than *vice versa*. Due to China's huge economic size, any changes to the Chinese economy will have a powerful impact on Taiwan's small economy. Without signing FTAs with other countries at the same time, Taiwan may lose its leverage in negotiating with China in the future. However, it is unlikely that Taiwan will be able to complete FTA negotiations with its other major trading partners, such as the United States, the EU and Japan, while China has yet to do so.

**Prospects**

In the next four years after Ma Ying-jeou's re-election in January 2012, the development of the cross-strait economic integration is expected to be wider and deeper, covering four areas, namely progress on trade, investment, people and financial services.

First, trade between Taiwan and China is likely to increase further as 90% of the 539 items listed on the early harvest programme have enjoyed zero tariffs since 1 January 2012. Indeed, due to the severe business competition in the Chinese market, the Taiwanese government is very keen on finalising deals on commodity and services trade with China before China makes any further headway in FTA negotiations with South Korea.

Second, in addition to Taiwan's increasing investment in China, Taiwan has lifted the ban on investment from China since 2009. Mainland Chinese citizens can now invest in a variety of sectors, including manufacturing, services and public infrastructure construction, in Taiwan. Due to the financial constraints of the Taiwanese government and economic slowdown in developed countries, it hopes that the opening up of Chinese investment will make up for Taiwan's deficiency in inward foreign investment and further promote Taiwan's economic growth. The current peaceful cross-strait relationship will probably further deregulate Chinese investment in Taiwan.

Third, according to Taiwan Tourism Bureau, foreign visitor arrivals in Taiwan reached a new high in 2011, at about six million people, of which 29% were from mainland China. Figures from Taiwan's Mainland Affairs Council show that tourism revenue from the Chinese tourists was over US$5 billion from 2008 to 2011. Encouraged by booming retail sales in the services sector, the Taiwanese government will continue to open its doors to more individual tourists from various Chinese cities, and the daily quota is also likely to increase.

---

[15] Statistics from the Ministry of Commerce, People's Republic of China, at <http://www.fdi.gov.cn/pub/FDI/wztj/wstztj/wstzjktjjb/t20120119_140565.htm> (accessed 23 February 2012).

[16] Statistics from Ministry of Commerce of PRC, <http://english.mofcom.gov.cn/aarticle/statistic/foreigninvestment/201202/20120207948411.html > (accessed 9 April 2012).

[17] Ministry of Commerce of PRC, "Top 200 Exporting Companies in China", at <http://www.fdi.gov.cn/pub/FDI/qycx/qycx_ch/CNExpTop200_new.jsp> (accessed 8 February 2012).

Fourth, the intensifying cross-strait economic relations have also catalysed the development of financial services sector. In February 2012, Taiwan's Financial Supervisory Commission (FSC) had already approved 11 Taiwanese banks to set up branches in China under ECFA, with six banks already operating their branches in the mainland. Thirteen Taiwanese securities firms and two securities investment and trust companies have established representative offices in China. In addition, Bank of China and Bank of Communications from mainland China had obtained the approval to set up branches in Taiwan at the beginning of 2012. China's promotion of Hong Kong as its offshore *renminbi* settlement centre has attracted the Taiwanese government's attention. More financial-related measures are expected to deregulate in order to actively explore business opportunities in China's financial market.

Even though Taiwan and China will have a deeper economic engagement and integration, the cross-strait economic ties are not decoupled from the global economy. In 2011, weak demand in both Europe and the US are the main reasons behind Taiwan's slower growth. The economic downturn has resulted in a deceleration in Taiwan's exports, particularly its exports to China. The annual growth rate of Taiwan's exports to China was especially weak (9%) in comparison with the annual growth rate of Taiwan's exports to the United States (16%) and to the ASEAN-6 countries (23%) in 2011. As for China, although government spending may be helpful in stimulating economic growth, the country's economic development cannot depend entirely on government's investment for sustainability. In the long run, exports will still be an important driver to generate employment and individual disposable income, which will translate into domestic consumption. In short, the follow-up of ECFA and other economic cooperation measures will provide greater opportunities for both Taiwanese and Chinese entrepreneurs and further connect Taiwan's economy to China. Nonetheless, the global economic situation will continue to play an important role in the cross-strait's long-term economic future.

# 53

# China and the Rise of the BRICS

Anthony P SPANAKOS*

*This chapter discusses how Brazil, Russia, India, China and South Africa have met as a group, what goals the group has and how it has affected global governance.*

The rise of China — its three decades of robust growth in GDP; massive reduction of poverty; expansion of commercial relations with the world over; ascent to the rank of world's most significant exporter and polluter, and its inevitable and increasingly necessary role in global governance — is ubiquitous in the literature on economic development, environmental issues and international affairs, to say nothing of in the news and other media. Although receiving less international attention than the rise of China, recently, and especially since the 2008 global economic crisis, other large developing countries are gaining influence in international affairs of global prominence. Of these, Brazil, Russia and India — countries identified, along with China, by the US investment bank Goldman Sachs as the "BRICs" — have attracted particular attention.

The BRICs held their first summit in June 2009 a few months before the G-20 summit in Pittsburgh. Since then, the four countries met annually, and in 2011, they invited South Africa to join their group, thus becoming "BRICS". Reactions have been mixed. Some argue that the BRICS are replacing the United States and the G-7 as the most important global actors, while others insist that the BRICS are still developing countries with little in common other than their inability and unwillingness to act as global leaders. Between the hype and the critique however is a less controversial but more verifiable conclusion: that the BRICS are cautiously moving towards democratising global governance, giving the developing world a voice on important issues, particularly through the empowerment of the G-20, discussions of reform of the United Nations Security Council and the International Monetary Fund (IMF).

*Anthony P. SPANAKOS is Associate Professor of Political Science and Law and Director of Latin American and Latino Studies at Montclair State University and Adjunct Professor at New York University.

## China's Going Out Strategy and the Birth of the BRICs

The birth of the BRICs could be traced back to China's "going out" strategy. One of the most important changes in reform-era China was the shift from the post-1978 "bringing in" strategy (*yin jinlai*) of attracting foreign direct investment in foreign special economic zones along the coast (and eventually the entire country), to the "going out" strategy (*zou chuqu*) strategy of pursuing new markets and investment opportunities. The primary goal of *zou chuqu* is to usher in a new phase of economic growth in China, one which requires more inputs than the domestic market can provide and aims at diversifying the sources of energy, minerals, food and agricultural products.

Other important aspects of *zou chuqu* include increasing and improving Chinese relations with other countries to get better access to "frontier markets", a diplomacy adopted especially by the Hu-Wen government which aggressively pursued trade agreements, debt forgiveness and infrastructure investments, and built entertainment/convention centres in developing countries. China has also used its newfound commercial status to bolster its "one-China policy", a priority which has lost its urgency with the election of Taiwanese president, Ma Ying-jeou, in 2008.

Finally, the rise of China as a great power has encouraged China to play a more proactive role in international affairs than it had in the past and it has been most ambitious in areas where US presence was weak or non-hegemonic, such as working with ASEAN and establishing the China-Africa summit and the Shanghai Cooperation Organisation. During the global economic recession in 2009, China held strategic talks with the United States on how to address short-term and structural problems in global governance. While some analysts called on China to assume a more assertive form of leadership and to even form a "G-2" with the United States, China refused. Instead, it participated in a summit with Brazil, Russia and India (the first BRICs summit) to lay out its long-term interest in democratising global governance and shifting decision-making away from the G-7 towards the G-20.

## BRICs Rising

The Chinese support for the G-20 and its choice of Brazil, Russia and India for the summit was not accidental. The latter group of countries (as well as some of the developing countries in the G-20) had achieved considerable market growth and maturation, and having overcome some of the challenges to macroeconomic and political stability in the past, were more willing and capable of playing a greater role in regional and global governance. In fact, in 2001, Goldman Sachs' research group identified Brazil, Russia, India and China — emerging markets with large and growing domestic demand — as sources of robust future investment growth. The BRICs were united not by a common political system, similar level of economic development (measured by either GDP per capita or the United Nation's Human Development Index), historic legacy (say, of a common coloniser), linguistic, religious, ethnic, or even geographic components. The countries chosen were all developing countries but even that was not the deciding factor for the grouping (since Goldman Sachs considered adding South Korea).

Rather, Goldman Sachs' justification was based on the size of the countries, their markets and the potential for growth. While the BRICs accounted for 10% of global GDP in 1990, the share increased to 25% in 2010, and is expected to increase to 40% by 2050[1] (Table 1). Considerable scholarly attention has been spent on determining the development stages of the four countries (Brazilian growth was weak between 2001 and 2005; the Russian economy is heavily based on petroleum and natural gas production; development is at too early a stage in India, and the Chinese economy is far larger and more global than the others) and whether other countries (such as South Korea, Vietnam, Indonesia, Mexico and Turkey) should be considered. Critics can claim that China

---

[1] Wilson, D, K Trivedi, S Carlson and J Urúa, "The BRICs 10 Years On: Halfway Through the Great Transformation", *Goldman Sachs Global Economics Paper no. 208*, 7 December 2011, p. 5.

**Table 1**  Global Rank for BRIC Countries in 2011

|  | **Brazil** | **Russia** | **India** | **China** |
|---|---|---|---|---|
| Land area | 5th | 1st | 7th | 2nd |
| Population | 5th | 9th | 2nd | 1st |
| GDP | 8th | 11th | 9th | 2nd |
| Foreign exchange reserves | 7th | 3rd | 6th | 1st |
| No. of mobile phones | 5th | 4th | 2nd | 1st |
| No. of internet users | 5th | 7th | 4th | 1st |
| GDP per capita PPP | 71st | 51st | 127th | 93rd |
| Human Development Index | 73rd | 65th | 119th | 89th |

*Source*: IMF World Economic Database, 2011.

**Table 2**  Global Rank for BRIC Countries in 2050

| **GDP 2050** | **GDP per capita 2050** |
|---|---|
| China (1st ) | Russia (4th ) |
| India (3rd ) | Brazil (11th ) |
| Brazil (4th ) | China (12th ) |
| Russia (5th ) | India (17th ) |

*Source*: Wilson et al., "The BRICs 10 Years On: Halfway Through the Great Transformation", *Goldman Sachs Global Economics Paper no. 208*, 7 December 2011, p. 4.

alone can project influence outside of its region and that none individually, nor the group as a whole, has been willing and capable of proactive leadership in global affairs.

But BRICs are united not by what they are but by the potential to affect a global system of allocation and governance[2] (Table 2). Projections suggest that the BRICs total market size should be almost twice that of the G-7 by 2050. Perhaps more imminently, the BRICs are already contributing to global growth more than the G-7 (not including the United States). In 2009, Brazil and China were the first major economies to emerge from the global recession and a recent International Monetary Fund (IMF) paper found that if growth and productivity increased in Brazil, Russia, India or China by 1%, low-income countries would see increases of 0.7% over three years and 1.2% over five years.[3] That is unlike in previous global recessions when demand in large developing countries led the way out of recession for low-income countries. In fact, a recent Goldman Sachs paper argues that between 2000 and 2010, the BRICs "have contributed to more than half the world's growth…".[4]

This suggests that while the BRICs are best identified by potential to influence global distribution of resources and power, they already have the ability to do so, at least in some select areas. If that is the case now and projections of economic growth are met, the potential of BRICs will be much greater in the future. What then can be expected?

[2]Armijo, LE, "The BRICs Countries (Brazil, Russia, India, and China) as Analytical Category: Mirage or Insight?", *Asian Perspective*, vol. 31, no. 4, 2007 pp. 7–42.

[3]International Monetary Fund, "New Growth Drivers for Low-Income Countries: The Role of BRICs", 12 January 2011, p. 26.

[4]Wilson et al., op. cit., p. 5.

## From BRICs to BRICS

The BRICs first met on 16 June 2009 in Yekaterinburg, Russia. Given the global economic crisis, the vulnerability of the US economy, the sharp criticism of US monetary policy and excessive reliance on the US dollar as a global currency by political leaders and technocrats in Russia and China, the deep stock of US dollar reserves held by the BRICs, and the perception that the BRICs were leading global growth, many commentators expected to see a strong statement from the first BRICs summit. Instead, a mildly worded document emerged in which the countries pledged to improve and democratise global governance.[5] The four countries met again in Brasília in 2010, and during their third summit in Sanya, China, they invited South Africa to join the group. Although investment banks and international financial institutions continue to write about the BRICs, the addition of South Africa gives valuable insight into the values and strategies of Brazil, Russia, India and China.

It is easy to overlook South Africa when considering the BRICs. While the original four countries are among the 11 largest economies in the world, South Africa's is ranked 29th. In terms of GDP per capita it is ranked 104th, ahead of India, but behind China, and it is 123rd in terms of Human Development Index (HDI), behind even India. Recent Goldman Sachs papers on the BRICs focus on other growing emerging markets, the "N-11" countries (Bangladesh, Egypt, Indonesia, Iran, Korea, Mexico, Nigeria, Pakistan, the Philippines, Turkey and Vietnam). South Africa was clearly not the obvious next choice for Goldman Sachs but it was for the BRICs. Goldman Sachs had invented the conceptual category but they decided to *make* BRICs an empirical category. Membership was no longer determined by financial analysts nor was it done on the basis of purely market potential. Now, it is the BRICS which determine who could be in and what it meant to be a BRIC.

Rather than being the countries that drive global growth or comprise some of the largest holders of US foreign currency reserves (as identified by the popular and financial news and media), the BRICS emerge as a different type of potential actor. BRICS now account for some 43% of the world's total population and their claim to represent the world, particularly the developing world, is strengthened by having a member located in Sub-Saharan Africa. This allows the BRICs to gain greater legitimacy for their calls for more democracy in international relations and the development of a more peaceful and harmonious world.

Chinese traditional concerns for "mutual respect", "harmonious development", democratising global governance, giving more voice to poor countries and rejecting hegemony undergird all of the BRICS statements. These values are largely shared by the other BRICS as can be seen in the strong correlation between the votes cast by the PRC (People's Republic of China) and its BRICS partners in the UN General Assembly. Between 1974 and 2008, PRC voting in the UN General Assembly was identical with those of Brazil, India, South Africa and Russia, at 77.83%, 77.3%, 80.30%, and 65.99%, respectively.[6] Yet, when all five countries were serving as members of the UN Security Council in 2011, it was Germany, not South Africa, who joined Brazil, Russia, India and China in abstaining from a vote to authorise the use of force on Libya (the "no fly zone" sought by France, the UK and the United States) on 16 March 2011. At the Sanya Summit, however, South Africa signed a joint statement that condemned the use of force on Libya and queried why humanitarian consequences were not considered.

## Key Issues

The BRICS are too new as an organisation and too different to be able to make any immediate specific policy or personnel proposals (as explained later). Perhaps they will never get to that point

---

[5] Spanakos, AP, "China and Brazil: Potential Allies or Just BRICs in the Wall?", *East Asian Policy*, vol. 2, no. 2, June 2010, pp. 81–89.

[6] Ferdinand, P, "China and the Developing World", in *Charting China's Future: Domestic and International Challenges*, ed. D Shambaugh, Routledge, New York, 2011, pp. 86–94.

since this could be a form of "hegemonism" which the members claim to reject and they have such divergent interests in many areas. Nonetheless, they are capable of presenting a relatively strong and deep commitment to a broad-based agenda, particularly insofar as it leads to democratising global governance and moving towards a more multipolar world.

## *The UN Security Council and the G-20*

The theme of democratising the UN is welcomed by many developing countries, particularly by Africa which has no permanent seat but some 60% of UN Security Council deliberations address African issues and some 70% of peacekeeping take place in Africa.[7] Given BRICS' surging interest in South-South issues and their developing country and emerging status, the BRICS can powerfully argue for a reallocation of seats on the UN Security Council. In 2004, a UN High-Level Panel recommended to expand the UN Security Council from 15 to 24 members, including six new permanent (but non-veto holding) members as well as three additional rotating members. The G-4 (Germany, Japan, Brazil and India) who had been lobbying to become permanent UN Security Council members accepted the idea of being permanent members without veto and South Africa (as a possible choice for an African seat) expressed similar inclination. But by 2005, the prospect of UN Security Council expansion fell apart (partly due to China's unwillingness to have Japan on the UN Security Council). No BRIC or BRICS summit has altered the Chinese position. The joint statement from the Sanya Summit speaks of the need to reform the UN Security Council and to give India, Brazil and South Africa (IBSA) a greater voice, but it stops short of demanding expansion of the Security Council desired by the IBSA countries.

China has tried to de-emphasise the UN Security Council by highlighting the importance of the G-20.[8] Although this does not resolve the issue of democratising global security regimes (the UN Security Council, particularly for Brazil) empowering the G-20 vis-à-vis the G-7 as the primary space for non-security global governance is consistent with the goals of all of the BRICS. Indian diplomats accept a trade-off of the UN Security Council for the G-20 and they have been very skillful at manoeuvring within the G-20. This has been especially the case with Manmohan Singh at the helm, given his expertise in financial and economic matters.[9] South Africa and Brazil also appreciate the opportunity to participate in economic governance and to retain their identities as representatives of their regions and the developing world more broadly.

The road towards an empowered G-20 was paved by agreements between Brazil, India and South Africa, who worked together during the Doha Round of the WTO, and their subsequent activities as the IBSA group and discussion of environmental issues among Brazil, South Africa, India and China. Their work has been aided by some countries in the developed world, which have also pursued the expansion of G-20 authority. The United States encourages the rise of Indian and Brazilian leadership, and sees the G-20 as part of a general strategy of binding China by encouraging its participation in international organisations. Similarly, France and Australia have been very vocal about increasing the voices of leaders from the developing world in discussions of global economic governance.

In 2009, a major breakthrough occurred. The joint statement of Pittsburgh G-20 Summit declared, "Our compact is that: G-20 members will agree on shared policy objectives... G-20 members will set out medium-term policy frameworks... G-20 leaders will consider, based on the results of

---

[7] Adebajo, A, *The Curse of Berlin: Africa After the Cold War,* Hurst & Company, London, 2010, p. 59.

[8] The members include Argentina, Australia, Brazil, Canada, China, France, Germany, India, Indonesia, Italy, Japan, Mexico, Russia, South Africa, Saudi Arabia, South Korea, Turkey, the UK, the United States and the EU. The combined GDP of the G-20 is some 80% of global GDP.

[9] Malone, DM, *Does the Elephant Dance?: Contemporary Indian Foreign Policy*, Oxford University Press, Oxford, 2011, p. 267.

the mutual assessment, and agree with any actions to meet our common objectives".[10] The statement is clear that it is the G-20, not the G-7, or any other group, that is responsible for addressing challenges in global governance. What is more noteworthy is that it has established itself as the chief forum to oversee not only commercial and financial flows, but environmental projects, food production and allocation, and other developmental concerns. It then authorised the IMF and the World Bank to oversee many of the projects and goals that were discussed. This represents a considerable step as all the BRICS not only are present in monitoring global finance and commerce, but have brought in other developing countries and reduced the dominance of the traditional G-7 countries.

### The IMF

Another important area of consensus among the BRICS is the reform of the IMF. Again, as was the case with the G-20, support has come from BRICS and non-BRICS countries. The Chinese (2005) and Australian (2006) presidencies of the G-20 pressured the IMF to agree to a reapportioning of votes, increasing the voting shares of China, South Korea, Mexico and Turkey. These four states contributed an additional US$5.6 billion to justify their new voting rights. In the 2009 G-20 meeting, targets were set for increasing IMF voting for emerging economies by 5%, taken from over-represented countries, with an eye towards reflecting changes in the global economy and assuring the representation of the poorest countries. In these discussions, the BRICS countries have played an important role.

The BRICS have been less effective when they are not working against the United States and/ or the G-7 since much of the consensus that motivates them is linked to resistance to the United States as "unipole". There is considerable ideational diversity among the countries and their interests which complicate fuller integration. This was most visible in the selection of a replacement for Dominique Strauss-Kahn as director of the IMF. A primary concern of the BRICS countries is to increase the voices of the developing world within the IMF and they have insisted that the tradition of selecting a European to head the IMF and an American to head the World Bank should be terminated. For the first time, they found a fairly sympathetic United States which at least appeared willing to consider a non-European to head the IMF. Given the global crisis and the experience of developing world economists in dealing with crises, a very strong case could have been made for a candidate from the developing world. But the BRICS could not agree on whom to select. Moreover, it was not even clear that the individual countries were regional leaders. One of the potential candidates was former Mexican Finance Minister Agustín Carstens, against whom the Brazilians could not mount a plausible challenger and yet whom the Brazilians did not support. The Russians and Indians suggested candidates that were unlikely to receive support from fellow BRICS, and the possible South African candidate was not interested in the position.

The BRICS displayed a more united front in their 29 March 2012 summit in New Delhi, India, where they critiqued the process of leader selection in the IMF and World Bank, precisely at the moment when successors for the directorship of the World Bank appeared. The Obama administration presented Dartmouth College President Jim Yong Kim as its candidate and, for the first time, alternate candidates appeared (actual Nigerian Finance Minister Ngozi Okonjo-Iweala and Columbia economics professor and former Colombian Finance Minister José Antonio Ocampo). The presence of challengers from the developing world was praised in the New Delhi joint statement which also demanded a more fair selection process. Yet as of the Summit's conclusion, neither collectively nor individually did the BRICS support any of the candidates for the position.

---

[10] "G-20 Leaders Statement After Talks in Pittsburgh", Bloomberg News, 24-25 September 2009, at <http://www. bloomberg.com/apps/news?pid=newsarchive&sid=auIe3UTJncpY> (accessed 26 September 2009).

The BRICS did, however, propose the creation of a new development bank whose focus would be emerging markets and would encourage more trade to be conducted in local currency. This proposal, supported by outgoing World Bank President Robert Zoellick, builds on Chinese economic diplomatic efforts to trade in *renminbi* and to reduce the need for some of its commercial partners to use US dollars for trade. Importantly, it does not challenge the Bretton Woods institutions, but neither does it follow a similar logic. It supposes that one of the chief challenges for developing countries is having access to convertible hard currency and it aims to attenuate the need for such currencies by facilitating trade in local currency.

## Potential for What?

If the BRICS are united by their potential, but what is their potential and to do what? Their broad support for democratising global governance — to give stronger voice to developing countries, to reform the UN and Bretton Woods institutions, to shift power in the UN towards the global South — allows them to produce a relatively consistent rhetoric and superficial strategy. This strategy comes at a propitious time when the US government is straining from overstretch and encourages regional leaders to take more responsibility in "regional" issues, and after developed countries see the United States as an opportunistic hegemon (particularly after the George W Bush administration). The confluence of forces has led to an empowered G-20 and a shift to see legitimacy for global institutions needing more participation, leadership and accountability from developing countries. In this, the BRICS have been important agents and have been effective.

The BRICS have been less effective at designing specific policy and personnel proposals. This may change over time, particularly if the BRICS develop as a unit. This is however unlikely given how hard it is for the EU, whose countries have far more common interests and values and whose institutional legacy is longer and deeper, to form a common foreign policy. It is also unlikely because the BRICS not only have divergent interests, but tend to prefer a type of leadership that seeks consensus before taking action (this position is particularly pushed by China). It is not clear that BRICS will be the final form of the group or whether they will invite participation of other countries (Indonesia and/or Turkey). With the participation of more countries, the need for consensus and the inability to take specific action will be more pressing. Finally, GDP growth is expected to decelerate for most of the BRICS within 15 to 25 years, although GDP per capita will still remain small relative to developed countries. Their market size will allow them to be important decision-makers but their influence may peak.

Although it is too soon to make predictions, the BRICS seem to be more concerned with not fundamentally changing global governance, but reforming it so that they and other members of the South have stronger voice and so that one particular voice is not hegemonic. The 2012 BRICS summit which comments on the Arab-Israeli conflict, civil conflict in Syria, possible conflict over Iranian nuclear ambitions, as well as more traditional issues such as making World Bank and IMF governance, global trade, currency, and environmental issues more favourable for developing country interests, is an indication of the BRICS *qua* forum for voice, rather than concrete policy. The new proposed bank suggests that when the BRICS act, they will do so strategically, within the Bretton Woods system, but with the intention of addressing developing country concerns. As Ikenberry wrote recently, "China and other emerging great powers do not want to contest the basic rules and principles of the liberal institutional order; they wish to gain more authority and leadership within it".[11]

---

[11] Ikenberry, GJ, "The Future of the Liberal World Order: Internationalism after America", *Foreign Affairs*, vol. 90, no. 3, 2011, pp. 56–78.

# 54

# China's Soft Power

## Growth and Limits

LAI Hongyi*

*This chapter reviews and assesses China's official programmes and measures for enhancing its international attractiveness. China has achieved modest successes in the recent years, but faces controversies and constraints.*

The concept of soft power was coined by Joseph Nye, a Harvard-based US scholar on international relations. He defined soft power as "the ability to get what you want through attraction rather than coercion or payment".[1] His work was translated into Chinese as early as 2001. Chinese leaders started paying attention to soft power a few years after the concept has attracted attention.[2] China's government has also endeavoured to augment China's soft power in the 2000s.

As a result, international analysts have paid growing attention to China's soft power in the recent decade. For example, a popular book on this topic, *Charm Offensive* in 2007 from Yale University Press, has documented many examples of the growing attractiveness of the Chinese in the developing world.[3] Five years have since passed. Many changes have taken place.

In this chapter, I plan to cover the Chinese official embrace of the concept of soft power, review a range of China's official initiatives for enhancing China's attraction around the world and assess

---

*LAI Hongyi is Associate Professor at the School of Contemporary Chinese Studies, University of Nottingham, United Kingdom.

[1]For a detailed elaboration of the concept, refer to Nye, J, *Soft Power: The Means to Success in World Politics*. New York: Public Affairs, 2004.

[2]For a discussion of China's rationale and efforts to promote soft power through cultural diplomacy in the earlier years, refer to Lai H, "China's Cultural Diplomacy: Going for Soft Power," Singapore: East Asian Institute, NUS, *EAI Background Brief,* no. 308, 26 October 2006.

[3]See Kurlantzick, J, *Charm Offensive: How China's Soft Power Is Transforming the World*, New Haven: Yale University Press, 2007.

the effects of these initiatives. I argue that China has embarked upon programmes and measures for enhancing its soft power, such that it has modestly improved its image in the recent years but that further improvements have been hampered by a range of domestic and external controversies and constraints.

## Wide Acceptance of the Soft Power Concept

Soft power became part of the Chinese official vocabulary as early as 2004. In May 2004, the Politburo of the Chinese Communist Party (CCP) held the 13th group study session regarding the development of social sciences and philosophy (SSP) in China. According to official reports, the Chinese leadership believed that SSP, culture, ideology and the Chinese model would help advance the country's soft power and gain international recognition and respect.

In late 2008, Li Changchun, member of the Standing Committee of the Politburo in charge of cultural affairs and propaganda, called for the utilisation of cultural resources, enhancement of cultural soft power, expansion of the Chinese cultural industry and culture overseas. His calls were incorporated into the Party's proposal for the 12th Five-Year Programme in October 2010.

Since then, China has tried to advance its soft power by carefully designing its foreign policy discourse, conducting public and cultural diplomacy, utilising mega media events, undertaking aid diplomacy and riding on its rapidly ascending global economic status.

## Foreign Policy Discourse

In the recent decade, China has presented several formulations for its foreign policy to serve two purposes. One is to project a peaceful and benign image of a rising China. The other is to provide an appealing Chinese alternative to the US-dominated world order. The latter is often perceived by China and many developing nations as a forceful and indiscriminate imposition of western ideas, institutions and interests.

In 2003, China proclaimed its peaceful rise (*he ping jue qi*), suggesting that China would not pursue the menacing path of rise through force as adopted by Germany and Japan during the first and second world wars.[4] From 2004 to 2005, in order to assuage domestic criticisms and external concerns with a rapidly rising China, the Chinese government modified the formulation to "peaceful development" (*he ping fa zhan*).

From 2005, President Hu Jintao and other Chinese leaders have announced a vision for the world order. In their conceived "harmonious world of lasting peace and common prosperity", different civilisations and political-economic systems can co-exist and achieve harmony amidst diversity (*he yu bu tong*).This formulation implies a rebuttal of the ideal Western world order in which the West tries to impose on the rest of the world.

In addition, in line with its traditional (albeit played-down) call for a multipolar world (versus a unipolar world dominated by the United States), China has also called for multilateralism in world affairs. This is manifested in China's membership in international organisations such as the World Trade Organization, regional organisations such as the Shanghai Cooperation Organisation as well as China's multilateral cooperation and diplomacy.[5]

---

[4]For an in-depth analysis, see Zheng Y and Tok SK, "China's Peaceful Rise (I): Hu-Wen's Core Foreign Policy Strategy," and "China's Peaceful Rise (II): Rhetoric Versus Reality," *EAI Background Brief*, nos. 219 and 220, Singapore: East Asian Institute, National University of Singapore, 9 December 2004.

[5]For a systemic analysis of the Chinese discourse in the 2000s, refer to Scott, D, "Soft Language, Soft Imagery and Soft Power in China's Diplomatic Lexicon," in Lai H and Lu Y (eds.) *China's Soft Power and International Relations*, New York and London: Routledge, April 2012, Ch. 3.

## Public Diplomacy as a New Official Tool

Since 2009, China's leaders have paid close attention to public diplomacy. In April 2009, when China attended the G-20 summit in London, it set up a press centre for its delegation to handle news inquiries and convey its messages. In July 2009, President Hu urged Chinese diplomats to step up public diplomacy (*gong gong wai jiao*) and cultural diplomacy (*ren wen wai jiao*), signalling that the government viewed them as critical diplomatic tools.

Chinese Foreign Minister Yang Jichi, who assumed the post in April 2007, declared in March 2010 at a national legislature press conference that public diplomacy was necessary for a breakthrough in China's diplomacy and that much could be done. He encouraged Chinese diplomats to "reach out to the public, the universities and the media" to introduce China's policies.[6]

In late 2009, the Public Diplomacy Section was upgraded to the Public Diplomacy Office in the Chinese Ministry of Foreign Affairs (MFA), and its staff strength expanded from around 11–12 to 16–17. The office is responsible for guiding public diplomacy of Chinese diplomatic envoys, coordinating public diplomacy within the MFA and managing its 204 websites.

In 2010, the MFA set up a Consultative Committee on Public Diplomacy to give advice and participate in planning, implementation and assessment of public diplomatic efforts. Its members include former high-ranking diplomats such as Zhou Wenzhong, Chen Jian, Wu Jianmin and Liu Guijin.

In the spring of 2010, *Public Diplomacy Quarterly* was launched by the Foreign Affairs Committee of the Chinese People's Political Consultative Conference. Zhao Qizheng, the former director of the Information Office of the State Council, serves as the editor-in-chief. Meanwhile, research and teaching institutes on public diplomacy were set up in Beijing, Qinghua, and Beijing Foreign Language and Yunnan Universities.

In recent years, Chinese diplomats have actively improved and undertaken public diplomacy abroad through public addresses, publishing in mainstream newspapers of the host countries, receiving media interviews, and attending seminars and conferences. Chinese diplomats, whose professionalism has improved significantly, have become more skilful in conducting public diplomacy.

## Cultural Diplomacy: Expanding Initiatives

In contrast with its more recent and formal attention to public diplomacy, the Chinese government's focus on cultural diplomacy began many years ago. The most noticeable efforts are reflected in the rapid expansion of Confucius Institutes (CIs) and Confucius Classrooms. In addition, there have been major initiatives in the recent few years to expand the global influence of China's media, and the implementation of new and bold media initiatives aims to project a positive image.

One of the most watched initiatives of Chinese cultural diplomacy has been the CIs. First launched in 2004 as a platform for Sino-foreign collaboration for the learning of Mandarin and Chinese culture, the number of CIs expanded rapidly to 322 (plus 369 Confucius Classrooms) in 96 countries and regions in October 2010. With a total of 71 CIs, the United States has one of the largest concentrations of CIs.[7]

In addition, China has invested heavily in new major initiatives to expand the global influence of its media. Around 2009–2010, the Chinese government allocated 45 billion *yuan* to three major news outlets, namely, the Chinese Central Television (CCTV), Xinhua News Agency and the *People's Daily*, to expand the international influence of their media programmes. The aim was to eventually build up a Chinese "CNN".

---

[6]"Yang J, "Public Diplomacy Is Now Born Upon Demand and Timely and Much Can Be Done", posted at <http://news.xinhuanet.com/politics/2010-03/07/content_13115553.htm> (accessed 2 July 2012).

[7]Information posted at <http://english.hanban.edu.cn/node_10971.htm> (accessed 2 July 2012).

In recent years, some of the news programmes in China, which targeted the international audience, have become more flexible in their style. *China Daily*, for example, welcomes news commentaries from elite outside China who are moderately critical of issues in China. Hosts of China's international TV channels, like the English channel under CCTV, pose tough questions to invited foreign guests. This style increasingly resembles that of TV hosts in the United States and the UK.

One of the most audacious attempts to use the new media for cultural diplomacy was China's national image video. It aired for 20 hours on the giant TV screen at Times Square in New York during President Hu's visit to the United States in 2009. Featuring some of the best known Chinese celebrities such as NBA basketball star Yao Ming and pianist Lang Lang, the short film presented artistic images of a rapidly transforming China.

In July 2011, the official Xinhua agency booked a premium LED advertisement slot in the northern side of Times Square in New York, a slot previously occupied by Hong Kong and Shanghai Banking Corporation for years. The monthly rental reportedly exceeded US$300,000 and Xinhua was expected to roll out its advertisements for China or Chinese brand names from August 2011.

## Mega Events as Soft Power Showcases

In recent years, China had hosted three events which had attracted a great deal of international and domestic media attention. They included the Beijing Olympic Games in 2008, Shanghai Expo in the summer of 2010 and Guangzhou Asian Games in late 2010. These events provided an unparalleled platform for the Chinese central and local governments to conduct public and cultural diplomacy and to showcase the positive side of China, especially its rapid modernisation and friendly populace.

In particular, the spectacular opening and closing ceremonies of the Beijing Olympic Games helped portray a powerful and peacefully rising China. The generally smooth completion of the Games was regarded as a success for China. The Games attracted an estimated 211 million TV audience in the United States, the most-watched TV event in US history. They also attracted 4.7 billion viewers throughout the world, which was 20% higher than that of the 2004 Olympic Games in Athens.[8]

The Shanghai Expo attracted a record 73 million visitors including probably over four million foreign visitors. Nevertheless, some Chinese tourists were criticised for their undesirable behaviour.

## Aid Diplomacy for Goodwill Harvest

Chinese scholars and officials perceive soft power in broad terms which include friendly assistance that could help establish a good image of China. In recent years, China has provided generous economic assistance to nations (especially Africa and Europe) troubled by rising debts. These goodwill gestures and offers serve to create a bond between China and recipient countries.

At a China-Africa conference in Addis Ababa, Ethiopia in mid-December 2003, Premier Wen Jiabao stated two points: China had fulfilled its commitments of cancelling debts totalling $1.27 billion of 31 African countries, and China would open its markets to exports from the 34 least developed African countries on a preferential, duty-free basis and would train 10,000 African professionals by 2006.[9]

---

[8]See "Olympic Audience Hits 4.7 Billion," posted at <http://www.sportbusiness.com/news/ 167799/olympic-audience-hits-4-7-billion> (accessed 2 July 2012).

[9]"China Cancels Africa's Debt," posted at <http://www.odiousdebts.org/odiousdebts/index.cfm? DSP=content&Content ID=9341> (accessed 2 July 2012).

In November 2009, at a two-day China-Africa summit, Premier Wen announced China's three pledges: (i) extend US$10 billion in concessional loans to help African nations build their financing capacity over the next three years; (ii) write off government debts of some of the poorest of those countries; and (iii) build 100 new clean-energy projects for Africa over the same period to help it cope with climate change.

At the Millennium Development Goals summit in New York in 2010, Premier Wen stated that China's debt cancellation "for the heavily indebted poor countries and the least developed ones" amounted to 25.6 billion *yuan* (or about US$3.83 billion at the prevailing exchange rate).

Economic assistance was also extended to EU member countries in deep financial difficulties. China pledges to keep its EU bond holdings. In July 2010, China bought €400 million of Spanish 10-year government bonds. Reports in mid-2011 suggested that China had spent billions of *euros* on Portuguese and Greek bonds alone.[10] In October 2011, following the EU's 50% debt write-off in exchange for Greece's additional austerity measures, European leaders looked eagerly to China, instead of the United States for rescue. This indicated China's rapidly growing international status.

## Boosts to Soft Power

In recent years several major developments, which constitute critical manifestation of soft power, have boosted China's status and helped it obtain varying degrees of admiration from countries around the world. In 2009, China surpassed Germany to become the largest exporter in the world. In mid-2010, it eclipsed Japan to become the world's second largest economy. These amazing records are testimonial to the success of China's economic reform and opening.

Joseph Nye considered membership and leverage in major international organisations as manifestations of soft power. In this regard, China's influence has been significant. It is one of the five permanent members of the Security Council of the United Nations. Along with Russia, China co-leads the Shanghai Cooperation Organisation, which plays a significant role in the security and economy of Central Asia. China has been a key driver in the Six-Party Talks that aim to find a peaceful resolution to the security concerns in the Korean Peninsula.

In the recent year, China's role in key international economic organisations has also been greatly enhanced. In the wake of the 2008 financial crisis, China has jointly led the call for the reform of global financial governance. It has actively participated in G-20 meetings, which it has been a member since 1999.

More importantly, China's voting right in the International Monetary Fund (IMF) has been increasing over the decades, from 2.58% in 1980 (the ninth largest among single member states) to 2.95% in 2001 and to 3.82% in 2011 (the sixth largest). In 2011, a Chinese was nominated as deputy managing director of the IMF. Back in June 2008, Justin Lin Yifu, a Chinese national, became the World Bank's chief economist.

## Gains and Limits of China's Soft Power

With regards to public opinion, the PEW Research Center, a widely known US-based non-partisan research agency which specialises in tracking and analysing domestic and international public opinion, polled the public opinion of citizens of 13 to 21 countries from North America, Latin America, Western Europe, the Middle East, Africa, South Asia, East Asia, and Southeast Asia between 2005 and 2011.[11] The average percentage of the public with a favourable impression of China went through a roller-coaster ride over the said period.

---

[10]See "Capitalizing on the Euro Crisis," posted at <http://www.spiegel.de/international/world/0,1518, 734323,00.html> (accessed 26 July 2011).

[11]The author is mainly interested in the global opinion on China. In Figure 1 and in the discussion in this section, the 13 to 21 countries mentioned did not include China, though the PEW centre polled the Chinese.

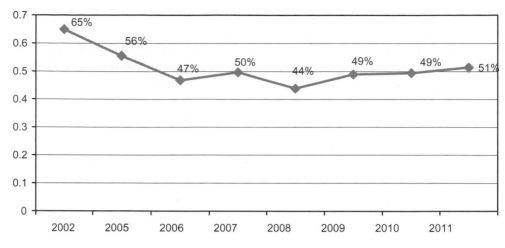

**Figure 1**   World Opinion of China

*Note*: Average percentage of respondents with favourable view among nations surveyed.

*Source*: *PEW Opinion Survey.*

In 2002, in a survey of four nations, the percentage peaked at 65%. In 2005, a poll of 13 countries in a PEW opinion survey showed that the percentage stood at a high of 56%, probably thanks to China's active overtones in projecting its peaceful rise, and to favourable economic deals with and aid to other nations.

This percentage declined over the years to a low of 44% in 2008, probably due to the Tibetan riots, negative western media coverage, as well as the disruption to the torch relay of the Beijing Olympic Games in the West. However, the percentage has been improving consistently since 2008, reaching a decent 51% in 2011 (Figure 1).

In 2011, 15 out of 21 countries viewed China positively. Furthermore, in 15 of the 22 nations polled, the general opinion is that China either will replace or has already replaced the United States as the world's superpower. Among 18 polled nations, 47% held this opinion, up from 40% in 2009.[12]

Nevertheless, as stated earlier, controversies involving China tend to undermine China's image. They include firstly, ethnic riots since 2008 such as the Tibetan riots in the spring of 2008; Urumqi riots in 2009; and protests in Inner Mongolia in May 2011. These riots suggest inter-ethnic tensions and discontent with China's ethnic policies.

China's restrictions on information and its handling of dissidents are another stumbling block to its soft power. In March 2010, Google announced its withdrawal from the Chinese market, citing the pressure from China for self censure, attacks on its website, and the blocking of Facebook, Twitter, YouTube, Google Docs and Blogger in China.

The bad press did not stop there. In the same year Liu Xiaobo, a political dissident in China, was awarded the Nobel Peace Prize "for his long and non-violent struggle for fundamental human rights in China". Between 2007 and June 2011, Hua Jia, a Chinese political and social activist, was sentenced to three and a half years in prison. These incidents gave the global media (especially the western media) opportunities to project China in a negative light to the global public.

China has also been unwilling to take an active and popular stance on movements for democracies or crises with grave implications for human rights. This puts China in an awkward position. China has long been criticised by the West for its passive stance on the Darfur humanitarian crisis. In the spring of 2011, a wave of democracy protests swept through the Middle East. China has largely tried to distance itself from these events in line with its stance of non-interference. At home, it had been on high alert against a similar outbreak. In the Middle East, some protestors

---

[12] For reports and information, refer to <http://pewresearch.org/> (accessed 2 July 2012).

posed banners criticising China. Many people in the region view China negatively for its inability to take a stance and for its association with some of those unpopular regimes.

In the recent years, the economic rise of China has caused anxiety and discomfort in some countries. China's exports compete fiercely with those from a number of European countries, such as Italy and Spain. Along with ethnic riots, they led to negative sentiments against China in Europe in 2008. This has been somewhat moderated by China's support of crisis-hit countries including Spain in the *eurozone*.

External tensions have also played a part in China's image abroad. Tensions between China and several Southeast Asian nations over the South China Sea recently have led to an outbreak of anti-China sentiments, especially in Vietnam and the Philippines and have reversed some of the impressive inroads China has made with the Association of Southeast Asian Nations (ASEAN) in the recent one over decade. The compromise at the 19th ASEAN Summit in Bali in November 2011 had helped to restrain the trend to some extent.

Apart from domestic and external controversies, China's expansion of soft power faces several technical, cultural and political constraints. The first major constraint is the lack of a strong incentive system for promoting good public and cultural diplomacy. In addition, China's attempts to enhance the profile and influence of its media may be obstructed by the deep-rooted distrust in the Chinese media, especially by those outside China. The Chinese media has long been viewed as toeing the official line and failing to cover events independently.

In sum, despite its ardent efforts in the past decade, China has managed to tilt global public opinion only slightly in its favour. In 2011, among the 23 countries surveyed by the PEW Research Center, the United States continued to trump China with a 60% favourable rating against China's 52%. China thus still has a long way to go if it hopes to obtain a favourable global standing.

# 55

# China's Efforts to Enhance its Energy Security

ZHAO Hong*

*China's primary concern is to ensure that it has sufficient energy to support its high economic growth. Domestically, it is diversifying its energy structures and improving energy efficiency. Internationally, it is expanding oil investments overseas to hedge against high oil prices in the long run.*

Over the past decades, China has emerged as an economic giant in the world with real annual GDP growth rate of 10% on average between 1978 and 2010. With the Chinese government being fully committed to the goal of high economic growth and poverty reduction, the current development momentum is expected to continue for decades to come. The uncertain global economic environment may slow this Asian giant in the short run but its remarkable economic transformation is a long-run trend.

China is at a stage in its economic development where its oil consumption has just taken off and will not decelerate in the foreseeable future. According to calculations by the Asian Development Bank (ADB), the income elasticity of oil consumption has historically been about 0.5, so that 1% economic growth translates into 0.5% growth in oil consumption,[1] thus China annual oil consumption growth rate is about 5%. China currently consumes 7.9 million barrels of oil per day (2007), which accounts for 9.3% of the world's total consumption.[2] China's accelerated growth and structural transformation will continuously fuel rapid growth of oil consumption for some time to come.

---

*ZHAO Hong is Visiting Senior Research Fellow at the East Asian Institute, National University of Singapore.
[1]Asian Development Bank, *Asian Development Outlook 2009 Update*, <http://www.adb.org/sites/default/files/pub/2009/ado2009-update.pdf> (accessed 26 June 2012).
[2]US Department of Energy, Energy Information Administration, *International Energy Outlook 2008*, <http://www.eia.gov/forecasts/archive/ieo08/index.html> (accessed 26 June 2012).

It is widely believed that the current deterioration of the global economic outlook will have a negative impact on the world's oil demand in the short term. However, the slow but still healthy growth of developing countries will help prop up demand. In the coming years, global oil demand growth will increasingly come from Asia, in particular China and India. As the world's largest developing economy, the primary concern for China is to ensure that it has sufficient energy to support high economic growth and prevent debilitating energy shortfalls that could trigger social and political turbulence. Domestically, it is taking measures to diversify its energy structures and improve energy efficiency. Internationally, it is expanding oil investments and cooperation overseas, attempting to hedge against high oil prices in the long term.

## China's Energy Security Concerns

### Increasing Reliance on Oil Imports

China's top concern is the increasing imports of oil. With limited reserves and relatively flat domestic production, China currently relies on international markets for over half of the oil it consumes. In comparison with US' decreased oil import dependence from about 70% 10 years ago to below 50% now, China's oil import dependence had increased from 28% in 2001 to 55% in 2011, which is above the warning line based on the international standard,[3] and may increase to 80% as predicted by International Energy Agency (IEA). With its growing dependence on foreign energy, potential disruption in energy supply poses the greatest risk to China's economic security.[4]

Moreover, China is heavily dependent on oil imports from Middle East and Africa, which are geopolitically unstable. In 2010, China imported 190 million tons of oil, about 40% of which were from the Middle East, 24% from Africa, 7% from Russia, and 30% from America and other regions (Figure 1).

China is already second only to the United States as an oil consumer and third in imports, after the United States and Japan. However, US reliance on imported oil has been declining since 2005. Against the backdrop of expanding domestic production of oil and gas, biofuel and shale gas, and improving energy efficiency, US dependence on oil imports is projected to fall to 45% by 2035, from 51% in 2009. Over the past three years, which began the shale gas revolution, the United States had increased more than 100 billion cubic metres of natural gas supply, equivalent

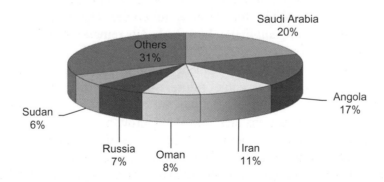

**Figure 1**   China's Crude Oil Imports by Source, 2010

*Source*: *China Customs Statistical Yearbook*, 2010, General Administration of Customs of the PRC.

---

[3]"*Woguo 2020 nian zhanlue shiyou chubei liang jiang da shijie dier*" (China's Strategic Oil Reserves will Reach the Second-Largest in the World in 2020), at <http://www.china5e.com/show.php?contentid=207204> (accessed 26 June 2012).

[4]Ibid.

to 84 million tons of oil.[5] Moreover, the majority of US oil imports come from its own hemisphere, with next-door Canada supplying more than 23%. Only 17% of US oil imports came from the Persian Gulf in 2009, while 22% were from Africa.

What really worries the Chinese leadership, however, is the risk that oil prices will add to the already elevated inflation. Most of China's oil consumption is not used in passenger vehicles but in industry and agriculture, where government price controls are either absent or less effective. Energy accounts for a third of the cost of grain production. Food prices are rising twice as fast as consumer prices overall. The Chinese government remembered clearly that inflationary pressures had helped fuelled the 1989 Tiananmen Square protest, and that the uprisings in the Middle East in the early 2011 were reminiscent of the Tiananmen event, also triggered by high inflation. It is predicted that if oil price rises to US$150 per barrel, China's manufacturing cost will double.[6] This imported inflation may lead to a new round of soaring prices which can seriously affect China's economy which is already on a slowdown.

The aforementioned projections imply that China will have a persistently high level of spending on oil and gas imports. The IEA predicts that China will overtake the US after 2025 to become the world's largest spender on oil and gas imports. In 2011, spending on oil and gas imports had already reached about 4% of China's GDP.

## Sea Lane Security

Most of China's imports and exports, and particularly trade with the EU, the Middle East and Africa, are seaborne, through the Strait of Malacca before entering the South China Sea. Even China's crude imports that are shipped from Venezuela and South American countries have to pass through either the Philippines archipelago or the Luzon Strait between the Philippines and Taiwan, while crude imports from elsewhere are shipped via the Indian Ocean through the Strait of Malacca. By 2010, the Middle East and Africa had already accounted for 40% and 24% of China's total crude oil imports, respectively, and the IEA predicts that the proportion of China's oil imports from the Middle East will rise to at least 70% by 2015.

Given that oil is pivotal to China's economic development and socio-political stability, ensuring navigability of China's sea lanes of communication — the Indian Ocean-Strait of Malacca route through which most of China's crude oil imports from the Middle East and Africa are shipped — is important. In this respect, the Chinese government is exceptionally concerned about physical interruptions of oil supply and price. If supply shocks due to temporary disruption to overseas oil supply or sudden hike in oil prices happen, China could well find itself in the same boat as Japan in the 1973 oil crisis, which put a stop to Japan's high economic growth. Thus in late 2003, Chinese President Hu Jintao expressed grave concern over the strategic vulnerability of the Strait of Malacca, which "certain major powers" were trying to control, and also for the fact that 80% of the country's energy supplies pass through the Strait of Malacca.[7]

China's concerns about its future energy security are rooted in the fears of potential crisis in the Middle East and Africa, and continuing US power and predominance in the Gulf and surrounding regions. Beijing expects the United States to remain powerfully engaged in the Gulf, Central Asia, South Asia, Afghanistan, the Horn of Africa and the Strait of Malacca, all critical areas near major oil suppliers and key transport routes and choke points. Moreover, the United States will remain the most formidable naval power with control over the energy shipping routes

---

[5]*"Zhongguo jianshe shiyou chubei tixi ke bu ronghuan"* China Needs to Establish its Oil Reserve System, 1 February 2012, at < http://www.china5e.com/show.php?contentid=207532> (accessed 25 June 2012).

[6]Fu S, *"shiyou dazhan yichu jifa, dui zhongguo jingji yingxiang jihe?"* (How will the oil war affect China's economy?) At < http://www.china5e.com/show.php?contentid=207683> (accessed 26 June 2012).

[7]Storey, IJ, "China a Major Player in South East Asia Pipeline Politics", *The Straits Times*, 23 October 2009.

of the Gulf, the Indian Ocean and the South China Sea, which are all vital to China's economic and energy security.

## Climate Change

Climate change is likely to be one of the most significant challenges confronting China and other countries as well. China is now one of the world's largest carbon emitters, and hence one of the major contributors to global climate change. Although the per capita emission is still relatively low in China, aggregate carbon dioxide ($CO_2$) emission is expected to increase in the near future. As the world's largest coal producing and consuming country, China surpassed the United States to become the largest carbon emitter in the world in 2006, and will soon overtake the entire European continent around 2013.

China has begun to encounter problems due to climate change. Scientists predict that China will face severe environmental impacts as carbon emission level increases. These include the melting of glaciers, particularly in Tibet and Tianshan; frequent droughts, storms, floods and rising incidence of natural disasters caused by extreme weather; declining agricultural production (an estimated drop of 10% by 2030);[8] rising sea level which could displace 67 million people; and a 40% increase in the population threatened by plague.[9]

While expanding coal production is the cheapest and most secure option, it comes with rising external cost. China's emissions come from numerous sources, the electricity and heat sector being the largest source. Based on a breakdown of China's emissions by the IEA, the power sector, which is mainly fuelled by coal, contributes most of China's $CO_2$ emissions, and its share is projected to rise from 49% in 2005 to 52% in 2015 and 54% in 2030; the transport sector's share is also expected to increase from 6.6% in 2005 to 7.7% in 2015 and 11% in 2030.[10]

Compared with the world average level, China's energy consumption structure shows a higher energy consumption centring on coal and a lower proportion of oil and gas, and this consumption pattern will continue. In 2009, total world primary energy consumption in terms of energy mix ratio corresponding to oil and gas, coal and other resources was 6:3:1, whereas that of China was 2:7:1.[11] China's coal-dominated energy structure is attributed to its rich coal reserves and scarcity in oil and gas resources. In 2009, China's proven coal reserves was reported to be 114.5 billion tons, accounting for 14% of the world's total proven reserves, whereas its confirmed oil reserves were reported to be 2.1 billion tons, accounting for only 1.2% of the world's total proven reserves.[12]

China's pattern of energy consumption structure can be attributed to its industrial development process, as it joined the East Asia's "flying geese model". China embraced the processing industries that were transferred out of Japan and Asian newly industrialised economies (NIEs), and it thereafter developed into the world's factory and subsequently, the world's market. China's economic structure by sector in 2008 was basically industry at 11%, agriculture at 49% and services at 40%, and that gave a comparison to India's economic structure where industry accounted for 18%, agriculture 29% and services 52%. Data has shown that the services sector still accounts for a low percentage in China's GDP. Hence, it is no surprise that China's economic growth requires higher energy consumption. For example, in 2009, China's total GDP was US$9,228.2 billion (in purchasing power parity term), 2.4 times that of India (US$3,832.7 billion), but China's total primary energy consumption was nearly five times that of India. Further, according to a survey

[8]Bustelo, P, "China and Climate Change: Responsible Action?", *Analyses of the Elcano Royal Institute*, no. 68, 2007, p. 1; Kim MJ and RE Jones, "China: Climate Change Superpower and the Clean Technology Revolution", *Natural Resources & Environment*, vol. 22, no. 3, 2008, p. 10.
[9]"Melting Asia", *The Economist*, 5 June 2008.
[10]International Energy Agency, *World Energy Outlook 2007*, OECD Publishing, 2007, p. 314.
[11]BP Global, *BP Statistical Review of World Energy*, June 2010.
[12]Ibid.

conducted by the Chinese Academy of Sciences in 2006, China ranked only 54th among 59 countries in terms of energy efficiency.[13] If China continues on its "business-as-usual" path, the IEA predicts that China's emissions will rise by 3.3% annually over the next 25 years, hitting 11.7 billion tons by 2030, double the United States' estimated emissions level of 5.8 billion tons.[14]

Therefore, China faces increasing pressures from the international society on $CO_2$ emissions and climate issues. Environmental issues, apart from supply security, have become an increasingly important factor influencing China's energy policies. It is imperative for China to adopt a coordinated economic development model by improving energy efficiency, diversifying energy sources and making adjustments to its economic structure.

## Enhancing China's Energy Security

Solving energy security problem has been an ongoing major concern and debate in China. Some advocate securing energy supply primarily by traditional means, while others argue that China should curb demand for energy and focus on conservation. Some also point to China's problematic energy system, suggesting the need to increase energy efficiency and develop local renewable energy sources. There are others who believe that maintaining stable geopolitical relations between countries will safeguard China's energy security and help shape its policy. The public debate had generated a range of possible approaches and the Chinese government has clearly explored, adopted and improvised various measures to formulate and implement its energy policies and strategies.

### *Policies and Legal Framework*

The challenge that China currently faces, as the Chinese government has realised, is to curb carbon emissions without compromising economic growth. It needs to successfully set the right goals and implement the right policies. The National Development and Reform Commission (NDRC) thus sets out policy guidelines and targets every five years in the Five-Year Programme (FYP) submitted to the People's Congress. Climate change issues came into the 10th FYP (2001–2005) for the first time as NDRC set guidelines on energy saving while the greater emphasis was still on economic development. In the 11th FYP (2006–2010), the NDRC set ambitious environmental targets to reduce energy consumption by 20% per unit of GDP. In 2007, the NDRC unveiled its first National Climate Change Strategy, with the primary objective of setting mitigation and green targets.

### *Energy Conservation*

Energy conservation has become an important target for China as demonstrated in its aggressive policy implementation efforts. With technological advances, implementing energy-saving measures is more feasible and effective than pursuing new energy innovations. In 2004, the Chinese government published a medium- and long-term energy conservation plan to emphasise the principles and objectives of energy conservation. In the 11th FYP, the central government targeted a decrease in energy intensity by 20% by 2010 from the 2005 level; the reduction made in 2008 was 10.1%. On 26 November 2009, China further announced that it will lower its carbon emissions relative to the size of its economy by as much as 45% by 2020.[15]

The central government has also launched various programmes specifically aimed at environmental protection. The total output of China's energy-saving and environmental protection

---

[13]Masataka O, "India and China's Strategies in Middle Eastern Oil-Producing Nations", FY2006 20th Research Report and Symposium, the Institute of Energy Economics, Japan, December 2006.

[14]BP Global, *BP Statistical Review of World Energy*, June 2010.

[15]"China Sets Target for Emission Cuts", *The Washington Post*, 27 November 2009.

industries reached 1.7 trillion *yuan* in 2009, accounting for about 5% of China's GDP. The environmental protection industry accounted for 26% of the total output, followed by the energy-saving industry at 14% and the resources recycling industry at 60%.[16] The 12th FYP (2011–2015) had identified and included the new energy industry as the key emerging and strategic area supported by the government, such as information technology, biotechnology, new-energy automobiles, etc.

### Energy Diversification

China is accelerating the diversification of energy resources in order to reduce coal and oil dependence. Wider use of renewables including solar and wind power, nuclear power, and biomass fuels has been increasingly encouraged. In February 2005, the Renewable Energy Law, with the goal of diversifying energy supplies and alleviating both air pollution and greenhouse gas emission, was enforced. The NDRC had launched a programme aimed at increasing the share of renewables in China's primary energy use to more than 18% by 2020 and more than 30% by 2050 through the commercialisation of renewable technologies.[17]

The growing emphasis on energy efficiency, clean coal processes, and carbon capture and storage has resulted in a boost to renewable energy sources in recent years. However, the scale-up will take time, and reliance on fossil fuel will remain considerable for the foreseeable future. Therefore, China will continue to place greater focus on nuclear power and natural gas, which are relatively cleaner and emit less $CO_2$.

Despite its late start in the nuclear field, China has made impressive stride in the construction of nuclear power plants. It was only as recent as in the late 1991 that China's first civilian nuclear power reactor, Qinshan Nuclear Power Plant, went into operation in China's eastern Zhejiang province. In 2012, China has seven power plants with 13 operating nuclear reactors situated in Zhejiang and Guangdong provinces. Altogether, these facilities yield slightly more than 10 gigawatts (GW) of total generating capacity, which contributes to only 2% of China's electricity needs.[18] There is a great potential for nuclear power development in China. The 12th FYP (2011–2015) targets 43 GW of reactor capacity to be in operation by the end of 2015. To achieve this goal, the State Council had authorised the building of 26 nuclear power plants, of which 12 have begun construction, with 53 additional nuclear rectors.[19]

China has abundant natural gas reserves. According to China's Ministry of Land and Resources, China has 31 trillion cubic metres of shale gas reserves, nearly 50% higher than in the United States. If China can successfully develop its shale gas production, the annual production can reach 100 billion cubic metres.[20] Shale gas production has been booming in the United States. Over the past three years, the United States had increased its natural gas supply to more than 100 billion cubic metres, which is equivalent to 84 million tons of oil, thus triggering the shale gas revolution. By tapping the shale gas resources, the United States has thus drastically reduced its oil imports from the Middle East, thus successfully gaining energy independence. China can take a leaf out of the US experience to expand natural gas production and supply through opening up its domestic energy markets and encouraging competition. By increasing natural gas supply, China can replace gasoline consumption with liquefied natural gas, thus reducing dependence on external oil imports and eventually achieving its own energy independence.

[16]"Fast Growth for Environmental Protection Market: Report", *China Daily*, 7 May 2010, <http://www.chinadaily.com.cn/bizchina/2010-05/07/content_9822550.htm> (accessed 25 June 2012).
[17]"*Xin neng yuan gui hua cao an: xin neng yuan bi zhong da zeng*" (New Energy Revitalisation Plan: The Share of New Energy will Greatly Increase), 2010, <http://www.china5e.com/show.php?contentid=118355> (accessed 25 June 2012).
[18]Weitz, R, "Beijing Confronts Japanese Nuclear Meltdown", *China Brief*, vol. xi, no. 6, 8 April 2011.
[19]Ibid.
[20]"*Zhongguo zhunbei xiang kaicai yeyanyou da yuejin*" (China prepares to develop share gas), 15 February 2012, < http://www.china5e.com/show.php?contentid=209974> (accessed 26 June 2012).

## *Overseas Quest for Energy Resources*

When China became a net oil-importing country in 1993, the central government's strategy was to develop China's oil industry by "establishing oil fields abroad", the mission of which was undertaken by two state-owned companies, namely China National Petroleum Corporation (CNPC) and China Petroleum and Chemical Corporation (also known as Sinopec). After a decade of overseas investment, China has made some achievements. For instance, from 1995 to 2006, total Chinese NOC (national oil companies) investment flows abroad had reached US$27.2 billion, covering over 200 oil exploration and development projects in more than 50 countries. In 2006, Chinese NOCs produced 685,000 barrels of equity oil per day overseas, and it is projected that China's equity oil output will reach 1.1 million barrels per day by between 2013 and 2015. China's overseas oil expansion is now concentrated in three strategic areas: Middle East-North Africa (e.g. Iran, Sudan), Russia-Central Asia (e.g. Kazakhstan) and Latin America (e.g. Venezuela).

Compared with the Western countries, China's oil reserve system is still lagging behind. The strategic oil reserve system originated from the 1973 Middle East war. The IEA required its member states to have at least 60 days of oil reserves, which was subsequently increased to 90 days after the second oil crisis in the 1980s. Currently, the strategic oil reserves of the United States, Japan, Germany and France are all above 90 days. The United States boasts the world's largest oil reserve system by volume, with 727 million barrels of oil that can last more than 150 days.

In 2011, China imported 250 million tons of crude oil, an increase of 6% over 2010. China's current oil reserves can last only for 30 days although it has been making progress in this regard. China started building its oil reserve system in 2000 and by January 2010, four oil reserve bases (Zhenhai, Zhoushan, Huangdao and Dalian) have been commissioned for use, holding total oil reserves of about 100 million barrels. When the second construction phase of the oil reserve base completes by the end of 2012, China's oil reserves will reach 274 million barrels. It targets to complete the construction of the entire strategic oil reserve system, which will hold 500 million barrels of oil reserves in total, or roughly equivalent to 90 days of its oil imports by 2020.[21]

## Challenges Ahead

In spite of the impressive endeavors and achievements, China still faces challenges and constraints in implementing its energy plans and policies. Given the systemic reliance on fossil fuels, especially oil and coal, as in the case of developing countries like India, China is essentially "locked in" to its use of such energy sources, making the challenges of adaption and diversification to alternatives like renewable energy problematic. As long as China continues to rely on coal, which accounts for over 70% of its primary energy, it is inevitable that it will continue to bear the disrepute as the world's leading carbon emitter.

That said, China faces many other problems and challenges. Some energy policies and environmental laws cannot be implemented effectively due to certain institutional factors. For example, in China, the local governments lack knowledge and resources to administer environmental laws and energy policies, thus causing delay in implementation of energy projects. Local officials, though aware of the severity of China's environmental problems and the importance of environmental protection, are more concerned about GDP growth, which is an important criterion tied to their political performance and promotion. Hence, environmental protection is a low priority in their official agenda, and surveys had shown that only a minority of local government officials would take regulatory action to ban factories or firms that are heavy polluters.[22] Further, environmental

---

[21]*"Woguo 2020 nian zhanlue shiyou chubei liang jiang da shijie dier"* (China's Strategic Oil Reserves will Reach the Second-Largest in the World), 30 January 2012, < http://www.china5e.com/show.php?contentid=207204> (accessed 25 June 2012).

[22]Tong Y, "Bureaucracy Meets the Environment: Elite Perceptions in Six Cities", *China Quarterly*, vol. 189, 2007.

regulators, including the judiciary and environmental agencies, remain weak and are hampered by various enforcement barriers. Beijing, therefore, must strengthen the environmental regulatory structure before the country can advance further to establish a climate-friendly policy regime and meet its ambitious targets.

Supporters of renewable energy name the diversification of energy sources, reduction in carbon emissions, and the development of green industries and jobs among the multiple benefits of renewable energy. But the potential of renewable energy to offset fossil fuel use is less impressive, especially in rural China. Although there is potential for renewable energy development in many other parts of China, the objective is mainly to make electricity more available to rural areas rather than to secure bulk power supply sources. Renewable energy sources, particularly wind and solar, have yet to gain confidence or acceptance in local counties due to the lack of capital and technologies.

# 56

# The South China Sea Disputes

## Current State of Play and Future Prospects

Katherine TSENG Hui-Yi*

*Frictions in the South China Sea area interrupt regional stability and threaten freedom of navigation. Issues like allowable activities in foreign Exclusive Economic Zones, sovereignty over land features, strategic deployment by claimants and other interested parties are deteriorating the prospects for dispute resolutions.*

Since 2010, competition among countries in East Asia over maritime interests in the South China Sea has heated up, turning the region into, what some had described as, the new central theatre of conflict.[1]

The world kept a close watch on how China — the largest claimant state with seemingly more bargaining power — would react to its neighbouring ASEAN states, and there were critical analyses of China's posture on whether it has become more assertive or even aggressive in staking a claim on nearly the entirety of the South China Sea. The South China Sea had, in recent years, seen cyclic pattern of intermittent flare-ups in the disputed areas — fishery conflict and illegal fishing activities by civilian fishermen, the increased presence of China's national enforcement agencies, and rising nationalism — thereby inciting countries to rise up in arms and issue provocative statements, which was soon followed by some fence-mending from high-level officials making visits to garner support and cooperation.

However, data revealed so far indicate that the prospects of exploiting oil and gas reserves in the South China Sea may not be rewarding, due to the requirement of state-of-art technology yet to be well-developed. Global energy consumption has far outweighed the estimated recoverable amounts of oil and gas, casting great shadows over expectations of claimants. Another concern is Chinese

---

*Katherine TSENG Hui-Yi is Research Associate at the East Asian Institute, National University of Singapore.
[1] Kaplan, R, "The South China Sea is the Future of Conflict", *Foreign Policy*, September/October 2011, at <http://www.foreignpolicy.com/articles/2011/08/15/the_south_china_sea_is_the_future_of_conflict?page=full> (accessed 30 June 2012).

deliberate ambiguity in its South China Sea positions. Despite a mild and cautious step taken by Beijing in distinguishing disputes over sovereignty of islands and interests of oceanic spaces, the nine-dash line map is left unexplained. Claimants, except China, thus rely on regional organisation, the ASEAN, for a binding code that would more efficaciously deter deleterious behaviours. However, whether such a hard law could help generate constructive resolutions remains an open question in view of the complexity of the South China Sea disputes.

### Understanding the Complexity of Claims

The long-standing disputes contain two components: sovereignty claims and those over maritime interests under the structure of the United Nations Convention on the Law of the Sea (UNCLOS).

### *Sovereignty Claims*

The South China Sea is a semi-enclosed sea of approximately 3.5 million square kilometres. Among thousands of islets dispersed in this area, two major island groups — the Spratly and Paracel Islands — are at the centre of disputes. Sovereignty claims over the Paracel Islands are largely bilateral in nature between China and Vietnam, both of which had long developed numerous incongruities.[2] Sovereignty claims surrounding the Spratly Islands, however, are more complicated as multiple claimants assert sovereignty and maritime rights over the islands. Other maritime features that had stirred up troubled waters include the Macclesfield Bank and the Scarborough Shoal.[3] Vietnam, China and Taiwan all claim "indisputable sovereignty" over maritime features of these islands.

Other claimants advance sovereign claims too, as the Philippines claim 53 features, and Malaysia claims 12.[4] In terms of actual control, Vietnam currently occupies 25 features, whereas the Philippines occupies eight, China, 12, Malaysia, five and Taiwan, one.[5] (Figure 1 and Table 1)

### *Maritime Interests — Natural Resources*

A different yet equally important dimension in the South China Sea dispute is the competition over maritime resources. The related maritime rights over these resources are under the claims of Exclusive Economic Zones (EEZs) and continental shelf. However, the EEZ claims of claimants give rise to boundaries that overlap into each other's zone. Yet, all claimant states hold that they have complied with and based their propositions on the UNCLOS. All claimants, except Taiwan, have acceded to the UNCLOS.[6]

---

[2]The disputes between China and Vietnam over the Paracel Islands can be traced back as early as in the 1950s, and gained wide attention again in early 1970s when Hanoi announced its move to negotiate contracts with foreign firms for the exploration of oil in the Gulf of Tonkin, part of the South China Sea. The two had disputed over the Paracel Islands, and other maritime features in the South China Sea ever since.

[3]Macclesfield Bank and Scarborough Shaol are currently claimed and controlled by the Philippines. China claims sovereignty over it, as part of its Paracel, Spratly, and Zhongsha Islands Authority, and Taiwan does the same.

[4]Fravel, MT, "Maritime Security in the South China Sea and the Competition over Maritime Rights", in *Cooperation from Strength: the United States, China and the South China Sea*, eds. P Cronin and W Rogers, Center for New American Security, Washington, DC, January 2012.

[5]Ibid.

[6]All claimants have ratified the UNCLOS: the Philippines on 8 May 1984; Indonesia on 3 February 1986; Vietnam on 25 July 1994; China (PRC) on 7 June 1996; Malaysia on 14 October 1996; Brunei on 5 November 1996; and Thailand on 15 May 2011. See "Chronological Lists of Ratifications of, Accessions and Successions to the Convention and the Related Agreements as at 03 June 2011", at <http://www.un.org/depts/los/reference_files/chronological_lists_of_ratifications.htm> (accessed 30 June 2012).

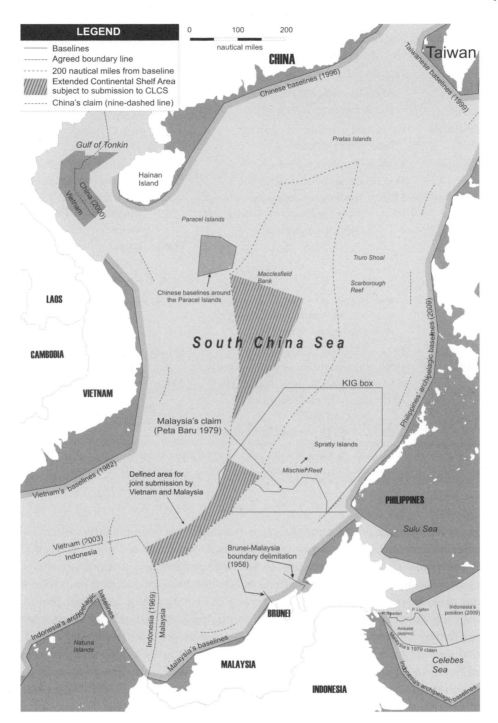

**Figure 1**   Map of South China Sea

*Source*: This map was created by I Made Andi Arsana and Clive Schofield for the National Bureau of Asian Research (NBR) and originally appeared in "Maritime Energy Resources in Asia: Legal Regimes and Cooperation," ed. Clive Schofield, NBR Special Report, February 2012, iv.

The claims over maritime interests lie in jurisdiction, rather than sovereignty, over designated maritime spaces. Unlike sovereignty claims which are based on the proprietorship of land features, jurisdictional rights are a derivative. These jurisdictional rights are exercised with certain limitations. The UNCLOS endows such jurisdictional rights on treaty parties, along with limitations such as giving due regard to other states, obligations to cooperate with regional and global initiatives over the protection of marine environment, and commitments to navigation freedom on the high seas.[7]

---

[7]UNCLOS Part V, Exclusive Economic Zone, Articles 55 to 75.

**Table 1**   Claims over Spratly and Paracel Islands

|  | **Spratly Islands** | **Paracel Islands** |
|---|---|---|
| Claimants | China, Taiwan, Vietnam (complete), Malaysia (part), the Philippines (part) and Brunei (part-fishing zones) | China, Taiwan and Vietnam |
| Geopolitical significance | Oil, natural gas, fisheries, shipping links, Straits of Malacca | Oil, natural gas, fisheries, shipping links, Straits of Malacca |
| Ownership and claims (from 20th century) | **1930s**:  French Occupation<br>**WWII**:  Japanese occupation<br>**1951**:    Japan renounced claims in the San Francisco Treaty; claimed by Vietnam | **1930s**:  French occupation<br>**WWII**:  Japanese occupation<br>**1951**:    Japan renounced claims in the San Francisco Treaty; claimed by Vietnam<br>**1956**:    France withdraws, South Vietnam controlled islands<br>**1958**:    claimed by China |
| Current administration | China, Taiwan, Malaysia, the Philippines and Vietnam. Vietnam controls the most number of islands. | Hainan province, China |
| Notable conflicts and developments | **1974**:  China and Vietnam<br>**1988**:  China and Vietnam (Johnson Reef)<br>**1992**:  China and Vietnam (Da Lac Reef)<br>**1995**:  China and the Philippines (Mischief Reef)<br>**2002**: ASEAN Declaration of Conduct | **1974**:    China and Vietnam (Battles of the Paracel Islands)<br>**2002**:    ASEAN Declaration of Conduct |

*Source*: China's Territorial Disputes in the South China Sea and East China Sea, Zhao, *China Briefing*, 31 May 2011, <http://www.china-briefing.com/news/2011/05/31/chinas-territorial-disputes-in-the-south-china-sea-and-east-china-sea.html> (accessed 30 June 2012).

In this aspect, the Chinese proposition attracts harsh criticism. China claims virtually the entire South China Sea with its nine-dash line map that dates back to as early as 1947.[8] China seems to rely on "historical waters and rights", which has yet to be clearly established, much less well-received by international adjudicating bodies and the international community, to vindicate its position.[9]

Besides the nine-dash line map, controversy also exists regarding maritime features in the southern part of the South China Sea, mainly, the group of Spratly Islands. Debates over whether these maritime features can be classified as "islands" and thus generate derivative claims of EEZs and continental shelves have prevailed for decades. The disharmony is attributable to Article 121 (3) of UNCLOS, in which the definition of an "island" or [a] "rock" remains an open question after UNCLOS came into force in 1994. Hence, even without the nine-dash line map, Chinese EEZ claims over the southern part of the South China Sea are still questionable.[10]

---

[8]The nine-dash line map was first produced by the Nationalist Party government (Kuomintang) in 1947 when it ruled mainland China. The PRC government inherited the map and the claim thereon.

[9]See International Court of Justice judgment, such as The Fisheries Jurisdiction Case (UK versus Iceland), at <http://www.icj-cij.org/docket/index.php?sum=646&code=bi&p1=3&p2=3&case=56&k=f9&p3=5> (accessed 30 June 2012) International arbitration reports by the International Tribunal for the Law of the Sea (ITLOS), such as The Southern Bluefin Tuna Case, have touched on this concept. Boyle, A and MD Evans, "The Southern Bluefin Tuna Arbitration", *The International and Comparative Law Quarterly*, vol. 50, no. 2, April 2001, pp. 447–452.

[10]China has not clarified whether it based the nine-dash line South China Sea map on UNCLOS, or on other legal grounds. Further, China does not specify if it asserts sovereignty, maritime rights like EEZ claims, continental shelf claims, etc. China's claim of "indisputable sovereignty" is obscure and unclear. Consequently, China did not touch on

## *Maritime Interests — Navigation and High Seas Freedom*

The South China Sea is located astride an important transportation route utilised heavily by countries in East Asia for their energy supplies from the Middle East. More than a quarter of the world's trade traverse via the South China Sea, which connects, southwards, to the Straits of Malacca and the Indian Ocean, and to the Bashi Channel that goes north and westwards to the Pacific Ocean.[11] South China Sea is the world's second busiest international sea lane and regarded as a communication hub that accommodates energy transportation vital to East Asian countries. As such, dominance over this area presages the rise of a future naval power, which regional countries in the area are nervously projecting that of their common neighbour, China.

As a result, intermittent flare-ups pose potential threat to regional peace and stability. Confrontation between China and members of ASEAN, particularly the Philippines and Vietnam, brings the issue back to the burner, obliterating the hard-won tranquility achieved by claimants' self-restraint and by regulation under the 2002 Declaration on the Conduct of Parties in the South China Sea.

Chinese perceptions of maritime rights in EEZs differ largely from UNCLOS principles. China maintains that coastal states can impose stricter control over foreign states' activities in the EEZs,[12] in particular military activities. Tensions between Beijing and Washington constantly flare high due to the intermittent hydrographic surveys and reconnaissance activities conducted by the United States in Chinese EEZs. Several incidents that occurred in the past decades, including the loss of life of a Chinese pilot in the 2011 Hainan collision incident and the *USNS Impeccable* incident in May 2009,[13] have led to chokepoints in Sino-American relations.[14]

---

the debate over Article 121 (3). However, China acceded to the UNCLOS in 1992, with no queries raised about the section on EEZ. Nevertheless, Chinese claims in the northern part of the South China Sea are largely uncontested, which are measured and established from the coastline of Guangdong and Hainan provinces.

[11]More than half the world's annual merchant fleet tonnage passes through the South China Sea, and a third of all maritime traffic. The oil transported through from the Indian Ocean, en route to East Asia, is more than six times the amount that passes through the Suez Canal, and 17 times the amount that transits the Panama Canal. See Kaplan, R, "The South China Sea is the Future of Conflict", *Foreign Policy*, September/October 2011, at <http://www.foreignpolicy.com/articles/2011/08/15/the_south_china_sea_is_the_future_of_conflict?page=full> (accessed 30 June 2012). In 2009, among the huge volume of sea transportation, 70% of Japan's energy needs and 65% of China's go through the South China Sea. Beukel, E, "China and the South China Sea: Two Faces of Power in the Rising China's Neighborhood Policy", DIIS Working Paper, July 2010, p. 9.

[12]Kraska, J and B Wilson, "Beijing's Legal and Political 'Warfare' to Deny Littoral Access: Foreign Military Activities in China's EEZ", *Asian Defense Journal*, 24 May 2009, pp. 24–27.

[13]On 1 April 2001, a US-EP3 spy plane collided with a Chinese fighter jet 70 miles off the coast of Hainan Island. The Chinese fighter jet crashed, killing the pilot; the US spy plane made an emergency landing at a Chinese airbase on Hainan Island. China regarded the landing as illegal. This incident was the Bush administration's first real foreign-policy crisis. The United States sought business-like interaction and quick resolution, but China reacted harshly, with a victim mentality, moral indignation and accusation to extract a formal apology. Beijing preferred to sort out the dispute via formal diplomatic channel. US Secretary of State expressed "regret", but not "apology". Confidential information revealed in 2006 shows that Bush secretly engaged Saudi Arabia's Prince Bandar to conduct the delicate negotiations with Beijing over the release of the detained US crew. US did not apologise for conducting reconnaissance activities off the Chinese coast and refused to take responsibility for the collision. It only expressed sincere regrets towards the loss of life of a Chinese pilot.

[14]Fang Y, "Exclusive Economic Zone Regime in East Asian Waters: Military and Intelligence-Gathering Activities, Marine Scientific Research (MSR) and Hydrographic Surveys in an EEZ", Working Paper no. 198, S Rajaratnam School of International Studies, 21 May 2010. See Valencia, M, "The Impeccable Incident: Truth and Consequences", *China Security*, vol. 5, no. 2, Spring 2009, World Security Institute.

## Recent Incidents and Developments in 2011

### *A Turbulent 2011*

The year 2011 saw an increasing number of disturbing incidents that challenged regional stability in the South China Sea. Fresh round of tension erupted in June 2011 when the Philippines and Vietnam were trapped in a series of confrontation with China. The Philippines complained that the Chinese intruded their territorial waters, while Vietnam accused China of blatantly cutting off the seismic exploration cables of its research vessels (Table 2).[15]

## Deciphering the Disputes: Crux and Red Herring

The claimants' energy competition and insatiable thirst for natural resources in the South China Sea region are major reasons for the dispute. Claimants eye living and non-living resources, ranging from the abundant fisheries, deep-sea minerals and various oceanic resources, to the crucial oil factor.[16] Yet, the exploration and exploitation of these resources need to be viewed together with challenges brought about by technology development and advanced management capability.

### *Fishery Resources*

Collective resources management and marine environmental protection are exemplary challenges of unsustainable fishery practices. The UN Global Environmental Facility (GEF) has suggested that the South China Sea alone constitutes as much as one-tenth of global fish catch.[17] Fish resources are a significant primary source of animal protein and major food source in East and Southeast Asia. In 2007, the Food and Agriculture Organization (FAO) of the UN announced that Asia's consumption of fish reached 74.5 million tons, accounting for two-thirds of global fish consumption.[18] In 2008, the supply of fish almost reached a crisis when a total of 85% of marine fish stocks were threatened by unsustainable fishing practices, among which 53% had been over-exploited and 32% were nearly depleted and in need of recovering. However, for long-term sustainability, an integrated and collective effort towards preservation and sustainable resource management are urgently needed to address problems of over-fishing. Alternative regulations, such as seasonal fishing ban, demarcating protected breeding zones and instituting a licence system regarding allowable catch volumes, etc, are of referential values.

### *A Tale of Oil Reserves*

The oil factor is undeniably significant. It is reported that the South China Sea is home to huge untapped oil and gas reserves in its deep seabed, but claims of scale of these reserves vary widely.[19]

[15]Goldstein, L, "The South China Sea's Georgia Scenario", *Foreign Policy*, 11 July 2011, <http://www.foreignpolicy.com/articles/2011/07/11/the_south_china_seas_georgia_scenario> (accessed 30 June 2012).

[16]Scholars have spared no efforts in assessing the potential of natural resources in the South China Sea areas. See Schofield et al., "From Disputed Waters to Seas of Opportunity: Overcoming Barriers to Maritime Cooperation in East and Southeast Asia", NBR *Special Report*, no. 30, July 2011; Schofield, C, "What's at Stake in the South China Sea? — Geographical and Geopolitical Considerations", Conference Paper, Conference on Joint Development and the South China Sea, 16–17 June 2011, Singapore.

[17]Ibid., Schofield's article in NBR Special Report no. 30, at p.9. The UN GEF comprises 10 partnership organisations, including the UN Development Programme, the UN Environment Programme, the World Bank, the UN FAO and the Asian Development Bank.

[18]The State of World Fisheries and Aquaculture 2010, the Food and Agriculture Organization of the United Nations, Rome, 2010, <http://www.fao.org/docrep/013/i1820e/i1820e00.htm> (accessed June 2012).

[19]Schofield's article in NBR Special Report no. 30, op. cit. pp. 11–13.

**Table 2**   Timeline of South China Sea Issues in 2011

| Date | Events |
|---|---|
| 4 March 2011 | Two Chinese patrol boats were alleged to have threatened to ram a Vietnamese survey ship near the Reed Bank. |
| 27 May 2011 | Chinese patrol boats cut the cables of a Vietnamese ship while performing an underwater survey of the South China Sea. |
| 1 June 2011 | Manila reported that Chinese navy boats erected pillars and set unloaded materials near Amy Douglas Bank within the Philippine EEZ |
| 5 June 2011 | The South China Sea dispute dominated discussions at the Shangri-La Dialogue in Singapore. US Defense Secretary Robert Gates warned that "there will be clashes in the Sea unless multilateral mechanisms are strengthened." |
| 9 June 2011 | Vietnam reports that a Chinese fishing boat, supported by Chinese naval patrols, cut a cable being used by a craft operated by state-run company Petro Vietnam. Vietnam said that the ship was operating over its continental shelf and within its exclusive economic zone. |
| 13 June 2011 | Vietnam held live-fire drills in the South China Sea. Anti-China protests break out in Hanoi. Taiwan mulls strengthening its presence in the area by sending missile boats. |
| 26 June 2011 | China and Vietnam agreed to hold talks. China signed pact with Vietnam to resolve the conflict through "negotiations and friendly consultations", though no details were provided on how these negotiations took place. |
| 28 June 2011 | The United States and the Philippines began routine navy drills near the South China Sea. |
| 6 July 2011 | The Philippines' Foreign Secretary Alberto del Rosario visited China to seek diplomatic solution. Although China rejected a proposal to submit the dispute to a UN tribunal, the two nevertheless agreed "not to let the maritime disputes affect the broader picture of friendship and cooperation." |
| 15 July 2011 | Vietnam and the United States launched a series of naval exchanges. The exercises were confined to noncombat training and were stressed by the US to be part of routine exchanges that were planned months in advance. China deemed the timing of the exercises "inappropriate," saying they should have been rescheduled. |
| 19 July 2011 | The South China Sea dispute was a key topic of discussion at the ASEAN Regional Forum in Bali. Indonesian President Susilo Bambang Yudhoyono expressed frustration over the drawn-out nature of the talks and urged foreign ministers to accelerate negotiations and finalise guidelines. |
| 25 July 2011 | Progress was deemed to have been made during the ASEAN Regional Forum. China and ASEAN established a deal to formulate a set of guidelines for future negotiations to establish a "code of conduct" as a "first step" towards a more comprehensive binding code of conduct. |
| 1 September 2011 | Philippine President Benigno Aquino III visited China, with trade and investment at the top of the agenda. The two countries signed a five-year plan to boost trade by six times to reach $60 billion and promote tourism and language training. Aquino also sought to mend fences as tensions had increased over the South China Sea. |
| 11 October 2011 | China and Vietnam held talks about control of disputed islands in potentially oil-rich waters claimed by both nations. Both sides signed an agreement that seeks a peaceful resolution for the dispute by maintaining direct communications between the leaders of both countries. |
| 18 October 2011 | Japanese Foreign Minister Koichiro Gemba proposed a multilateral framework to settle maritime disputes in the South China Sea during a tour of Indonesia and other Southeast Asian countries, with China reiterating its intention to resolve territorial disputes in the South China Sea through talks between nations that are directly involved, rather than involving other countries. |

*(Continued)*

**Table 2**   (*Continued*)

| Date | Events |
|---|---|
| 27 October 2011 | The presidents of the Philippines and Vietnam agreed to strengthen cooperation between their maritime forces in response to incidents in the South China Sea. ExxonMobil discovered oil and gas off Vietnam's central coast in an area which falls within Chinese claims to the South China Sea. |
| 21 November 2011 | During the East Asia conference, the United States and ASEAN countries aligned to effectively pressure China on their claims to hold "indisputable sovereignty" over the South China Seas. In spite of Chinese warnings not to bring up the issue, 16 of the 18 nations spoke out on the question of territorial rights, putting China on the defensive. |

*Source*: Timeline: Disputes in the South China Sea, Yeo M, 1 July 2011, <http://www.siiaonline.org/?q=research/timeline-disputes-south-china-sea> (accessed June 2012).

The vast potential energy reserves prove to be of strategic importance to East Asian countries that depend heavily on oil imports traversing the South China Sea lane. However, unattainable and difficult exploration and exploitation has greatly undermined the value of these resources.

A general industry rule of thumb attainable in oil exploration and exploitation is the 10% recovery rate.[20] However, conventional assessment uses total estimates of oil and gas resources, instead of calculating the recoverable reserves by applying the 10% recovery rate rule. The Chinese estimates of oil and gas resources vary considerably between 105 billion and 213 billion barrels, but estimates of recoverable reserves is in fact between 10.5 billion and 21.3 billion barrels, applying the 10% recovery rate rule. Henceforth, failure to make such a distinction would lead to unrealistic high estimates. Studies conducted by the United States and Russia show a different reality.

The US Geological Survey (USGS) in its "Assessment of Undiscovered Oil and Gas Resources in Southeast Asia, 2010" identified total conventional oil resources in the South China Sea region to be 15.6 billion barrels, or approximately 1.6 billion barrels if the 10% recovery rule is applied.[21] An assessment by Russia's Research Institute of Geology of Foreign Countries approximated recoverable oil resource at 1.8 billion barrels.[22]

Another flashpoint besides crude oil is gas reserves. The Chinese calculation for South China Sea gas reserves is relatively optimistic, but the magnitude of uncertainties of the estimates is analogous to that for oil reserve estimates.[23] Another factor that undermines the credibility of the Chinese estimates is the failure to distinguish between conventional and unconventional gas reserves. Though unconventional gas resources, especially gas hydrates, are deemed an attractive alternative to conventional gas resources, the exploitation, requiring advanced technologies that far outweigh current capabilities, is commercially unviable for sustainable development.

Technological barriers, taken altogether with the aforementioned factors, render the estimates of oil and gas reserves highly doubtful and unreliable. Further, taking into account the 2010 global consumption of conventional oil totalling 26.9 billion barrels according to the US Energy Information Administration (EIA),[24] the oil reserves potential in the South China Sea may not be as significant as alleged. While oil is indeed a significant factor that propels the South China Sea dispute, it is obvious that tales of abundant oil reserves should be taken with a pinch of salt.

---

[20]The industry "rule of thumb" for frontier provinces suggests that only 10% of estimated *in situ* resources can be recovered. It is also argued that this figure may be of the order of 30% in more established provinces due to technological advancement. Supra note 16, in Schofield's conference paper and Schofield's article in NBR Special Report no. 30, p.12.
[21]Schofield's article in NBR Special Report no. 30, op. cit., p. 12.
[22]Schofield's article in NBR Special Report no. 30, op. cit., p. 12.
[23]Yet, gas reserves hold considerable promise, as recovery rate is as high as 75%. However, estimates of the total reserves volume were varied and unreliable, and given the challenging marine and geological conditions, exploitation may not be economically viable.
[24]Schofield's article in NBR Special Report no. 30, op. cit., p. 13.

## Activities in the EEZs

There are competing claims over territorial sovereignty and several claimant countries overlap in their EEZ claims in the South China Sea. Though it remained to be seen whether claimants could reach a consensus over "the disputed areas", records have shown that fewer disputes had taken place in territorial waters. In other words, boundary demarcation of EEZs and the type of activities undertaken within are major causes of tensions among parties.

The nature of permissible activities in EEZs are founded broadly on two principles, namely resource-related activities exclusive to coastal states and non-resource-related activities imposed on all states. Simply put, under the UNCLOS framework, the undertone of allowable activities is resource-linked. Coastal states are granted exclusive rights over natural resources in EEZs and land-locked neighbouring states with no direct access to offshore natural resources shall also be entitled the rights on an equitable basis.[25] Non-resource-related activities are, theoretically, open to all states and subject to the jurisdiction of coastal states.[26] In this regard, UNCLOS does not specify forbidden activities in foreign EEZs.

Controversies arise when military activities such as military manoeuvres, surveys, research and reconnaissance, which are regarded as non-resource-related activities and are not clearly specified in UNCLOS take place in the EEZs. One concern of coastal states is the information thus collected may be applied for military-relevant purposes. This is particularly so as China and the United States, key players in the South China Sea, increase the frequency of their reconnaissance activities in other states' EEZs.

The United States has not ratified the UNCLOS, but is willing to respect and abide by the spirit and regulations within the UNCLOS regime. The UNCLOS does not address the specific issues of military activities in foreign EEZs. But provisions in UNCLOS imply that when controversial activities like military drills or surveys take place in foreign EEZs, due regard must be paid to the interests of coastal states to maintain regional order and stability.

China is siding with the minority group in opposing any military acts to be held in its EEZ without its prior permission.[27] In its interpretation of the UNCLOS, China argues that military vessels navigating in EEZs must follow the conditions of "innocent passage" and must not engage in military activities. The series of incidents over the past decade have shown that incongruent interpretation in the usage of EEZs has adverse impacts on Sino-American relations and regional stability.[28]

Despite objections, various states continue to conduct military-related activities in foreign EEZs. China persists in its pursuit to conduct military surveys and research activities, mainly in the East China Sea region, and fewer activities in the South China Sea. Data has shown that Chinese research vessels were sighted on 16 occasions in 1998, 30 times in 1999 and 24 times in 2000 in areas within Japanese-claimed EEZs,[29] conducting activities which the Japanese authority regarded as for both military and marine research purposes.

The Chinese research vessel incidents continued apace into the mid-2000s,[30] causing further tension to the fragile Sino-Japanese relations. After several rounds of political wrestling and intense negotiations, on 13 February 2001, the two sides agreed on a mutual prior notification

---

[25] United Nations Convention on the Law of the Sea (UNCLOS), Part V, Exclusive Economic Zone, Articles 55 to 75.

[26] Ibid.

[27] Kraska and Wilson, op. cit., p. 25.

[28] While these activities had been conducted in the past, tensions escalated since the beginning of the 21st century, after the April 2001 collision between a US surveillance aircraft and Chinese fighter jet.

[29] The National Institute for Defense Studies, "Japan", *East Asian Strategic Review*, 2000, pp. 104–105; and "Japan", *East Asian Strategic Review*, 2001, pp. 200–203.

[30] "Chinese Research Ship Spotted in Japanese Waters", Kyodo News Service, 1 May 2000; and "Japan Watching Mainland Ship Near Summit Island", *South China Morning Post*, 23 July 2000.

system.[31] The agreement is an innovative instrument aimed at facilitating activities that are deemed to trigger confrontations. The system requires research vessels to give notice, including submission of mandatory information such as purpose of research, type of vessels and equipment used, area to be surveyed, etc., to the other party two months prior to their activities in areas "near and in which both take interests", but avoids specifying any lines or areas beyond which notifications are mandated.[32] Although frictions intermittently interrupt smooth implementation of the agreement, the mutual prior notification system set up under the agreement represents an exemplary approach of how countries with conflicting claims could proceed to mitigate disagreements and ensure regional security.[33]

## Looking Ahead

### *A Step Forward*

After months of flare-ups between China, Vietnam and the Philippines, the annual ASEAN Regional Forum held in July 2011 in Bali, Indonesia, brought good and bad news. ASEAN and China agreed upon a set of guidelines for resolving their disputes.[34] However, reactions from the representatives varied. Both China and Vietnam applauded the deal as a milestone that signifies a good start.[35] The Philippines, on the contrary, highlighted the concern that the deal is not legally binding and urged various parties to take efforts to "add teeth" to the new deal.[36]

The 2011 Bali Guidelines serves two main functions: first, to affirm the commitment to formulate mutually beneficial and peaceful resolution; second, to reassure the benefits of a common security facilitated by a combination of sprouting regional trade exchange and active promulgation of the 2002 DOC. In short, the Guidelines is regarded as a symbolic gesture, rather than a breakthrough to the stalemate. Quoting former ASEAN Secretary-General Rodolf Severino on the 2002 DOC, "[t]he effect is to convey a sense of stability in the region";[37] the words still ring true today after a decade of spats over sovereignty issues.

The Guidelines brought relative calm to the South China Sea issue during the second half of 2011, and the start of 2012 despite initial polarised reactions and comments. The return of peace can be attributed to the 2011 Guidelines, and to the rapprochement achieved among China, Vietnam and the Philippines in the second half of 2011. China and Vietnam entered into an agreement that includes setting up a hotline between the two countries' capitals to resolve crises,[38] and institutionalising half-yearly talks aimed at finding "a mutually acceptable basic and long-term

---

[31]"Japan, China Agreement on Maritime Notice System Detailed", BBC Monitoring Asia Pacific-Political, 13 February 2001.

[32]Valencia, MJ and Y Amae, "East China Sea Regime Building", *Ocean Development and International Law*, no. 34, 2003, pp. 189–208, at p. 198.

[33]There is no similar implementation of prior notification system for parties in the South China Sea disputes. This could be attributed to the more complex dimension of the controversy and China's tough stance to take a bilateral approach in resolving disputes.

[34]Downie, E, "A Step Forward, then a Step Back in the South China Sea Dispute", *Foreign Policy*, 21 July 2011, <http://blog.foreignpolicy.com/posts/2011/07/21/a_step_forward_then_a_step_back_in_south_china_sea_dispute> (accessed 30 June 2012).

[35]Ibid.

[36]Downie, op. cit. The set of guidelines, which merely reiterates the need to conform with the 2002 DOC, is not legally binding and also lacks a deadline for the implementation of a legal accord to resolve the conflict.

[37]Wu, S and Ren H, "More Than a Declaration: A Commentary on the Background and the Significance of the Declaration on the Conduct of the Parties in the South China Sea", *Chinese Journal of International Law*, 2003, pp. 311–319, at p. 318.

[38]Cohen, D, "China, Vietnam Ink Deal", *The Diplomat Blog*, 13 October 2011, at <http://the-diplomat.com/china-power/2011/10/13/china-vietnam-ink-deal/> (accessed 30 June 2012).

approach to solving maritime disputes".[39] Nonetheless, Vietnam wasted no time in reaching out to India to seek alliance and support,[40] which could acquire momentary peace and stability in the South China Sea region for ASEAN claimants as well as China, which currently faces rigorous domestic challenges.

The peace is considered a transitory phase in the protracted South China Sea disputes. What began as friction sparks were often overblown to retaliatory diplomatic admonitions and intense political wrestling, followed by suspension of high-level exchange and official activities in the next stage, and a cooling-off period. However, claimant states today take prompt actions to initiate fence-mending measures by signing friendship agreements or memorandums of understanding. Judging from the strong trade and economic links between China and ASEAN, the cycle of tension and détente will continue to persist. Notwithstanding trade and economic factors, certain dynamics like rising nationalistic sentiment region-wide would cast a dark shadow on the future of the region.

### *Future Direction — Yet to Be Clarified*

In a recent press conference, China appeared to take a step further to clarify its claims over the South China Sea,[41] a long-awaited, albeit small, breakthrough. A closer analysis of the statement shows that the Chinese Ministry of Foreign Affairs made a distinction between the disputes over "territorial sovereignty of the islands and reefs of the Spratly Islands" and the disputes over maritime demarcation. More importantly, the statement expressed clearly that no countries, including China, have sovereignty claims over the entire South China Sea.[42]

The clarifications are major advancements by the Chinese authority in response to the international outcry over the ambiguity of its claims in the South China Sea. The distinction between sovereignty disputes and maritime boundary demarcation reaffirms China's position: to resolve the disputes in accordance with international maritime laws. Hence, arguably, the statement manifested China's determination to pursue peaceful resolution and good-neighbourly policy with claimant states.

Beijing's explicit statement suggested that the nine-dash line map does not represent a claim to maritime rights; neither does it refer to claims of sovereignty over oceanic spaces. The map explicitly refers to only the historical rights that China has long upheld to justify its alleged "indisputable sovereignty". However, the "historical rights" concept has no established grounds to be being widely acknowledged by the international legal community. An educated guess would be that the lines indicate sovereignty claims over the islands, reefs and other land features.

Despite the step forward, there are drawbacks that require attention. Beijing still employs the vague and controversial term "indisputable sovereignty" in its claims over islands, land features and adjacent waters in the South China Sea. The lack of clarity would only lead the international community to attribute the ongoing upheavals to China.

China upholds the principle "non-intervention" in domestic affairs and "mutual reciprocity" in its diplomatic relations with other nations, preferring not to multilateralise issues. The statement that "no countries, including China, could assert sovereignty claims over the entire South China Sea areas" seems to suggest that China would not claim sovereignty over the entire South China Sea if all other claimants abide by the same declaration. On this note, China has also borrowed

---

[39] Ibid.

[40] Wu, S and Ren H, op. cit.

[41] Ministry of Foreign Affairs of the People's Republic of China, Foreign Ministry Spokesperson Hong Lei's Regular Press Conference on 29 February 2012, at <http://www.fmprc.gov.cn/chn/gxh/tyb/fyrbt/t909551.htm> (accessed 30 June 2012).

[42] Ibid.

similar interpretations in the 2002 DOC, which calls for "self-restraint in the conduct of activities that would complicate or escalate disputes" in the handling of disputes with one's neighbours.[43]

Indeed, it takes two to tango. Beijing needs to exercise caution in its assertion and in dealing with its ASEAN neighbours. The onus is on China to integrate itself into the international community dominated by Western values of capitalism, democracy, human rights and rule of law. ASEAN countries may blame China for not doing enough and expect more preferential treatments in their exchanges with China. This may raise expectations even in the negotiation of sensitive issues like territorial sovereignty and border demarcation.

With rights come responsibility, just like greater prowess invites tougher challenges. China's mere presence in the region is enough reason for the dilemma it now faces. It will be a long journey ahead for all claimants to reach a resolution to the South China Sea disputes. It is still too early to judge whether a new direction will emerge in China's approach to the disputes. Yet, the small steps that China has taken would translate to significant progress towards the resolution of the disputes.

---

[43]Fravel, MT, "All Quiet in the South China Sea: Why China is Playing Nice (For Now)", *Foreign Affairs*, 22 March 2012, at <http://www.foreignaffairs.com/articles/137346/m-taylor-fravel/all-quiet-in-the-south-china-sea?page=show> (accessed 30 June 2012).

# 57

# China and Global Governance

PANG Zhongying and LYE Liang Fook*

*Though it is expected to take on more responsibilities globally, China is reluctant to do so due to its pressing domestic agenda and its unwillingness to play a leading role on the world stage.*

The official principle guiding China's foreign policy is to "keep a low profile" (*tao guang yang hui*) and to "get some things done" (*you suo zuo wei*). Chinese paramount leader Deng Xiaoping reportedly said in 1992 that China will become a big political power if it keeps a low profile and work hard for some years; and it will then have more weight in international affairs.[1] Deng also reportedly said that China should never seek hegemony and never seek leadership.

Since Deng's remarks 20 years ago, China has come a long way. Today, China is the world's second largest economy and some say it will catch up with the United States within a decade. It has the world's largest foreign reserves at US\$3.2 trillion as of end-2011. At various international and regional platforms, China is seen as a key player when issues like the state of the world economy, global warming and climate change, aid to developing countries and nuclear non-proliferation are being discussed. Also, with the European Union mired in its debt crisis, China is seen as a possible white knight to restore confidence in the *eurozone*. From being an international "pariah" shunned by others following the 1989 Tiananmen crackdown, China is now being courted like a "bride" by various countries and organisations.

As a beneficiary of the existing world order and given its predominance on the world stage, there are greater calls for China to play a more active role in global governance. Global governance here generally refers to states and other interested actors coming together to jointly address common concerns or challenges that affect more than one state or region. In particular, the United States has

---

*PANG Zhongying is Director, Centre on the New Global Governance, People's University of China. LYE Liang Fook is Assistant Director and Research Fellow at the East Asian Institute of the National University of Singapore. This chapter incorporates points made by Pang Zhongying in an earlier draft but the views expressed here and any inherent mistakes are entirely Liang Fook's own.
[1] Chen D and Wang J, "Lying Low No More? China's New Thinking on the *tao guang yang hui* Strategy", *China: an international journal*, vol. 9, no. 2, September 2011, p. 197.

variously called on China to be a "responsible stakeholder" and a "responsible actor" to "shoulder more international responsibilities" and even to work together to create "international norms that reduce conflict around the world".[2] Inherent in these calls is the rising expectation for China to do more to contribute to regional, if not international, peace, stability and prosperity.

While China is well aware of these expectations, it has so far resisted pressure to do too much on the world stage. This is primarily due to its domestic agenda where many pressing issues such as economic rebalancing, regional disparities, uneven income distribution, employment generation, rampant corruption and serious pollution call out for simultaneous attention. While China's development based on hard indicators in absolute terms may seem stellar, it is still a developing country on a per capita level basis. Hence, the constant refrain by its leaders to the external audience to look at China in a more comprehensive way and at a deeper level. China also indicates that it does not have the intention to play a leadership role or even to be a hegemon on the world stage.

Where it can, China has played a limited role in addressing global common challenges and issues in line with its national interests. These roles serve a number of objectives. For one, China seeks to make adjustments within the existing world order to better reflect the shifting balance of power in China's favour. This is a logical extension of China's desire for a multipolar world order in which the US ability to act unilaterally is constrained. China also wants to ensure the security of vital sea lanes that bring in vital resources (whether in terms of goods, energy or minerals) to sustain its growth and development. Furthermore, China aims to forge and reinforce a positive international image of itself based on the principles of mutual respect and mutual benefit.

In line with these objectives, China has, for instance, sought to work with others to improve the representation of developing countries (China included) in organisations such as the World Bank or the International Monetary Fund (IMF). China has also cast itself as playing a part with other like-minded countries in areas such as fighting global warming and climate change, maritime piracy and nuclear proliferation. China's involvement in these areas can best be described as incremental in nature and is proceeding at a pace that China is comfortable with.

## Global Economic Governance

To many Chinese, including policy makers and individuals alike, the term "global governance" is a relatively new concept introduced by the West to China. To them, many problems of the world today are global in nature and affect all nations. More importantly, there seemed to be a consensus that countries around the world including China ought to play a role in seeking joint solutions to these problems at the global level. Much of the debate has in fact centred on the nature and degree of China's involvement rather than on whether China ought to be involved in the first place.

China appears to have articulated more of its views on global governance since the onset of the world financial crisis in the fall of 2008. In particular, Chinese State Councillor Dai Bingguo's speech delivered on behalf of President Hu Jintao at the G8 plus developing countries dialogue in July 2009 is regarded as China's first official statement on global governance.[3] In his speech, Dai singled out the need to improve and strengthen "global economic governance" to promote the coordinated and sustainable development of the world economy. Although Dai confined his reference to global governance to global economic governance, he identified several features of

---

[2]This call to China and the United States to work together to create international norms to reduce conflict around the world was made by US President Barack Obama when he visited China in November 2009. See "Remarks by President Barack Obama at Town Hall Meeting with Future Chinese Leaders", Office of the Press Secretary of the White House, 16 November 2009.

[3]President Hu Jintao was in Italy to attend the G8 Summit. However, due to the unrest that broke out in Xinjiang in July 2009, Hu had to shorten his trip to return home, leaving State Councillor Dai Bingguo to deliver his speech. Earlier, in preparing this speech, the Chinese Ministry of Foreign Affairs had met with Chinese scholars who were experts in the study of global governance to seek their views. Pang Zhongying was one of the scholars who joined the discussions.

global economic governance which are also applicable to global governance. They included elements such as balanced representation; mutual benefits; win-win outcomes; equal representativeness, voice and decision-making rights, and adherence to the principle of taking on board the interests of all relevant parties. Below is Dai's elaboration of China's views on global economic governance according to its goal, its participants, its method and its mechanism.

1. *Goal of governance*. The fundamental goal of global economic governance is to push forward the development of the global economy in a balanced, universally beneficial and win-win manner. Balance means taking into account the needs and balancing the concerns of both the developed and the developing countries. Universal benefit means maintaining the interests and bringing tangible benefits to all the countries in the world and their people. Win-win means combining the interests and linking the development of one country with all the others.
2. *Participants of governance*. Global economic governance should involve all the countries around the world. Countries, no matter large or small, strong or weak, rich or poor, are all parts of the global economy and should participate in governance equally and enjoy relevant representativeness, voice and decision-making rights. Equal participation is reflected not only in form but more importantly in substantial content and decision-making. Only in this way can we ensure rationality and justice, and guarantee the reputation and effectiveness of global economic governance.
3. *Way of governance*. Global economic governance requires countries to solve the difficulties caused by economic globalisation through consultations and cooperation. It is important to follow the democracy principle, listen to the opinions of all parties concerned, take care of and reflect the interests and demands of all countries, especially the developing ones. We should respect differences, take into consideration the different national conditions of countries and allow different approaches of the developed and the developing countries. We should insist on and advocate cooperation and encourage countries to strengthen communication and coordination and use their advantages respectively to address common challenges.
4. *Mechanisms of governance*. Global economic governance requires appropriate mechanism arrangements. The development of the world economy makes it hard for some mechanisms to fully reflect the demands of the international community. Representativeness needs to be expanded to effectively tackle the global challenges. Governance should be targeted at problems in different areas and at various levels. In terms of governance mechanisms, relevant international standards and rules should be formulated on the basis of equal consultations and consensus reached among all the interested parties. Experience and best practices should be disseminated and countries should intensify exchanges and cooperation to jointly build an effective global economic governance structure.[4]

Following the July 2009 dialogue, the term "global governance" apparently gained greater prominence in Chinese official documents. In China's 12th Five-Year Programme (2011–2015) unveiled in October 2010 and in the Chinese Premier's Central Government's Work Report to the National People's Congress in March 2011, the term "global economic governance" occupied a prominent place. In the latter document, Premier Wen Jiabao stated that China will play an "active part in multilateral diplomacy" and ride on the G20 summit and other diplomatic forums to strengthen the "coordination of macroeconomic policies" and "advance the reform of the international

---

[4] "Dai Bingguo Attends the G8 and Developing Countries Dialogue", Chinese Foreign Ministry's website, 9 July 2009 at <http://www.mfa.gov.cn/eng/zxxx/t572654.htm> (accessed 2 May 2012).

economic and financial system". He further added that China would play a "constructive role" to help resolve "hot issues" and "global problems".[5]

Beyond official pronouncements, China's stellar economic growth amidst the economic doldrums in the United States and the EU since 2008 has positioned it as a key player in restoring market confidence and maintaining the stable growth of the world economy. This was evident at the G20 Pittsburgh Summit in September 2009 where members agreed that the G20 would become the "premier forum" for international economic cooperation, supplanting the Western-dominated G7 and G8 that have been the primary forums for decades. This was a clear acknowledgement that fast growing economies such as China and India now play a much more important part in world growth.

Going even further, China has pushed for an increase in the representation and voice of developing countries (China included) in global financial institutions such as the IMF and World Bank. In turn, these institutions recognise the importance of making the necessary adjustments to strengthen their legitimacy and effectiveness. In April 2010, the World Bank approved an increase in the voting power of Developing and Transition Countries (DTCs) at the International Bank for Reconstruction and Development to 47.19%, marking a 4.59 percentage point shift to DTCs since 2008. It further approved an increase in the voting power of DTCs at the International Financial Corporation to 39.48%, a 6.07 percentage point shift to DTCs. Likewise, the IMF Board of Governors approved in December 2010 a package of reforms on quota and governance in the IMF in favour of emerging market and developing countries. These reforms, when effective, will see China's quota and voting shares in the IMF rise to 6.39% (from the current 4%) and 6.07% (from the current 3.81%) respectively.[6]

### Other Aspects of Global Governance

Apart from its proactive efforts to shape the global financial architecture more to its favour, China is trying to play a more active role in other areas of global governance. These include its role in fighting climate change, nuclear weapons proliferation and piracy attacks, and promoting stability on the Korean Peninsula. However, China's involvement in these areas has received a rather mixed response, including at times criticisms that it is not doing enough. Yet, China does not seem unduly ruffled by these criticisms and has continued to play a role at a pace and level of involvement that it is comfortable with.

On fighting climate change, China subscribes to the principle of "common but differentiated responsibilities". In China's view, the developed countries should shoulder a heavier burden as they have contributed the most to current global emissions of greenhouse gases. Nevertheless, China has indicated on several occasions its readiness to play a part to fight climate change. For instance, just before the Copenhagen Climate Change Conference in December 2009, the Chinese government announced a unilateral commitment to reduce $CO_2$ emissions per unit GDP by 40–45% by the year 2020 based on the 2005 level.[7] Despite this commitment, after the conference, the British Foreign Secretary Ed Miliband reportedly accused China of ganging up with Sudan, Bolivia and other

---

[5]Premier Wen Jiabao *Central Government Work Report*, Beijing, 5 March 2011.

[6]These reforms will come into effect once they have met the necessary legal threshold which in many cases involves securing the necessary parliamentary approval of concerned countries. The process is expected to be completed by the Board of Governors' Annual Meetings in October 2012.

[7]In its 12th Five-Year Programme for National Economic and Social Development (from 2011–2015), the government outlined more specific national targets such as by 2015, to reduce carbon dioxide emission per unit GDP by 17% and energy consumption per unit GDP by 16% as compared with that in 2010; raise non-fossil fuel consumption as a proportion of the total energy consumed to 11.4%; increase the acreage of new forests by 12.5 million ha, with the forest coverage rate raised to 21.66%, and increase the forest growing stock by 600 million cubic metres.

leftwing Latin American countries to "hijack" efforts to prevent a deal from being reached.[8] In spite of these criticisms, China has so far resisted pressure to do more on the climate change front as it regards itself as a developing country grappling with many domestic socio-economic challenges.

On nuclear weapons proliferation, China's public position is that it does not encourage or support nuclear proliferation. Most notably, China appears keen to work with other countries to enhance nuclear security and nuclear safety. This was most evident at the two nuclear security summits held in April 2010 and March 2012. China has also hosted the Six-Party talks to promote stability on the Korean Peninsula and its eventual denuclearisation. Despite its efforts, China has been criticised for failing to take firmer actions against North Korea for its alleged sinking of the *Cheonan* warship and the shelling of *Yeonpyeong* Island in March and November 2010 respectively. Likewise, China, together with Russia, has been criticised for obstructing the United Nations from imposing sanctions against Iran over the latter's alleged nuclear weapons' ambitions. Even worse, China has been accused of supplying nuclear equipment, expertise and technology to Iran.[9]

On fighting piracy, China has since the end of 2008, sent its navy to provide armed escort of vessels in the Gulf of Aden. According to China's Ministry of Defence, up till the end of 2011, its navy had escorted more than 4,300 vessels from China and other countries over the past three years. The Chinese navy also reportedly escorted vessels belonging to the United Nations Food Programme four times, saved 42 ships that were boarded or trailed by pirates and picked up eight ships released by pirates.[10] These statistics were meant to show a China working closely with the international community to keep the major sea lanes of communications open. Conversely, there are others who regard China's anti-piracy efforts as depicting a more aggressive intent — a China that is able to project its naval power well beyond its shores to protect its growing overseas interests.

In an effort to better portray itself as a responsible member of the international community, China's State Council Information Office published the country's first ever white paper on foreign aid in April 2011. The key message of the white paper was to show that China, while grappling with its own development, had been providing aid to other "developing countries with economic difficulties" and "fulfilling its due international obligations". The white paper stated that by end 2009, China had provided a total of RMB256.3 billion in aid (including grants, interest-free loans and concessional loans) to foreign countries. It had also trained 120,000 managerial and technical personnel in other developing countries and sent over 21,000 medical personnel and 10,000 teachers to help these countries.[11] In terms of the sheer volume or quantity of its foreign aid, China easily out ranked other countries. Yet, this fact has not fully assuaged criticisms or concerns surrounding China's global intentions and ambitions.

## Not an Easy Road Ahead

China's efforts to play a role in global governance have not been and will not be easy. A key challenge, as alluded earlier, is the dilemma that China has to grapple with. On the one hand, China wants to be seen as a responsible member of the international community by being involved in addressing global concerns. It wants to play this role despite its many pressing domestic issues that require urgent attention. Yet, it has been criticised by other countries for not doing enough such as

[8]"Ed Miliband: China Tried to Hijack Copenhagen Climate Deal", *The Guardian*, 20 December 2009.
[9]"China's Non-Proliferation Words vs. China's Nuclear Proliferation Deeds", a report by the Nuclear Control Institute in Washington D.C. at <http://www.nci.org/i/ib12997.htm> (accessed 30 March 2012).
[10]"Navy ensures ships can navigate a sea of danger", *China Daily*, 26 December 2011.
[11]"China's Foreign Aid", *Xinhuawang*, 21 April 2011 at <http://news.xinhuanet.com/english2010/china/2011–04/21/c_13839683.htm> (accessed 30 March 2012).

in areas of combating climate change, fighting nuclear weapons proliferation and maintaining stability on the Korean Peninsula.

On the other hand, there have also been concerns expressed about China's ulterior motives or ambitions in some areas that China has been involved in, such as its anti-piracy operations. These have been perceived in some quarters as an attempt by China's navy to project an overseas presence that goes beyond China's conventional coastal defence strategy. It therefore appears that China's actions are often a subject of much contention.

A great deal of these concerns about China's intentions or ambitions can be attributed to the nature of the authoritarian political system in China and the values that underpin such a system which are at odds with the political system and values in mature democracies elsewhere. On top of this key difference, China's heft is being magnified by not only its growing presence on the world stage but also its stellar economic performance at a time when the economies in the United States and the EU are just muddling along. The image of a rising China versus a declining United States or the EU has heightened anxieties about a Chinese behemoth.

Notwithstanding these external perceptions of China, a practical way forward is for Beijing to continue with its efforts in collaborating with other countries to jointly address global concerns. In this endeavour, China would require much perseverance, patience and diplomatic finesse to assuage the concerns of other countries that China does not seek to dominate the world. And the best way to convince its sceptics is through consistent actions rather than words.

# Index